Attacks on the Press in 1998

Cover Photo: Malaysian policeman keeps an eye on foreign journalists during a news conference held by Inspector General of Police Rahim Noor in Kuala Lumpur on September 24, 1998, to discuss the arrest of former Deputy Prime Minister Anwar Ibrahim. (AP Photo/Ed Wray)

330 Seventh Avenue, 12th Floor
New York, New York 10001
Phone: (212) 465-1004 • Fax: (212) 465-9568
E-Mail: info@cpj.org • website: http://www.cpj.org

Begun in 1981, the Committee to Protect Journalists responds to attacks on the press everywhere in the world. CPJ investigates more than 2,000 cases every year and takes action on behalf of journalists and their news organizations without regard to political ideology. Join CPJ and help promote press freedom by defending the people who report the news. To maintain its independence, CPJ accepts no government funding. We depend entirely on your support.

Agence France-Presse, The Associated Press, IDT, LEXIS•NEXIS, and Reuters provided electronic news and Internet services that were used to conduct research for this report.

The Committee to Protect Journalists is most grateful to the following foundations and corporations, whose long-term commitments to the cause of global press freedom constitute the core operating and project support for our organization's programs:

A. H. Belo Corporation Foundation
The Ford Foundation
The Freedom Forum
John S. and James L. Knight Foundation
Robert R. McCormick Tribune Foundation
Joyce Mertz-Gilmore Foundation
Samuel I. Newhouse Foundation Inc.
Open Society Institute
St. Petersburg Times
The Tinker Foundation

Editor: Alice Chasan
Associate Editor: Jesse T. Stone

Copyright © 1999, Committee to Protect Journalists, New York.
All rights reserved.
Printed in the United States of America.

Attacks on the Press in 1998: A Worldwide Survey by the Committee to Protect Journalists
ISSN: 1078-3334
ISBN: 0-944823-18-1

Board of Directors
of the Committee to Protect Journalists

Honorary Chairman
Walter Cronkite
CBS News

Chairman
Gene Roberts

Vice Chairman
Terry Anderson

Directors

Franz Allina
Capital Defender Office

Peter Arnett
CNN

Tom Brokaw
NBC News

Josh Friedman
Newsday

James C. Goodale
Debevoise & Plimpton

Cheryl Gould
NBC News

Katharine Graham
The Washington Post Company

Karen Elliot House
Dow Jones & Co.

Charlayne Hunter-Gault
National Public Radio

Alberto Ibargüen
The Miami Herald

Walter Isaacson
Time Magazine

Bill Kovach
The Nieman Foundation

Jane Kramer
The New Yorker

David Laventhol
Times Mirror

Anthony Lewis
The New York Times

John R. MacArthur
Harper's Magazine

David Marash
ABC News

Kati Marton

Michael Massing

Judith Moses
The Mosaic Group

Victor Navasky
The Nation

Frank del Olmo
The Los Angeles Times

Burl Osborne
The Dallas Morning News

Erwin Potts
McClatchy Newspapers

Dan Rather
CBS News

John Seigenthaler
The Freedom Forum
First Amendment Center

Bernard Shaw
CNN

Paul C. Tash
St. Petersburg Times

Thomas Winship
International Center for Journalists

Executive Director
Ann K. Cooper

Attacks on the Press in 1998

Preface
by Sylvia Poggioli

In Belgrade, on the morning of October 14, 1998, a group of journalists gathered on the street outside their office building. I watched as plainclothes policemen standing guard barred them from entering.

The night before, their independent newspaper, *Danas*, had been shut down by police on the charge that the paper had "spread fear, panic, and defeatism." The *Danas* shutdown—and that of another independent paper, *Dnevni Telegraf*—came hours after Yugoslav president Slobodan Milosevic had struck a deal with the U.S. special envoy Richard Holbrooke which averted NATO airstrikes against Serbia in retaliation for months of assaults by its security forces against the majority ethnic Albanian population of Kosovo. A week earlier, two independent radio stations had been silenced.

The journalists outside the *Danas* building—several of whom had risked their lives to report truthfully about the nationalist hysteria that destroyed their country and claimed so many lives—had seen all this before: The Belgrade regime had ordered a similar crackdown against the independent media in 1995, shortly after Milosevic had signed the Dayton peace accord that put an end to the war in Bosnia.

But this time, the circumstances were more ominous. Two weeks earlier, Deputy Prime Minister Vojislav Seselj, leader of the ultra-nationalist Radical Party, had said in parliament, "We may not be able to shoot down every NATO plane, but we'll grab those within our reach," and the various "foreign agents" he listed as potential targets included Serbian independent journalists, several of whom he mentioned by name. And on October 1, Seselj had menacing words for journalists working "in the service of foreign propaganda" in Serbian-language broadcasts on the Voice of America, Deutsche Welle, Radio Free Europe, Radio France International, and the BBC. "If we find them in the moment of aggression, they shouldn't expect anything good," he warned.

Following these threats, some Serbian journalists who had been singled out by Seselj left the country. A few days later, the Serbian parliament passed a draconian new media law. In violation of both the Serbian and Yugoslav constitutions, it established a system of prior censorship of press statements critical of the Serbian government and exorbitant fines for those who dared to flout the law by publishing such statements.

Sylvia Poggioli, *National Public Radio's senior European correspondent, has covered the Balkans since 1988—from Slobodan Milosevic's rise to power through the disintegration of Yugoslavia and its aftermath. She has also covered Eastern and Central Europe before and after the collapse of Communism.*

When I heard Seselj's threats against journalists, I could not help but think about the incredibly high price the press has paid in the bloody breakup of Yugoslavia. At least 45 journalists were killed during the fighting between 1992 and 1995. And from the war's outset, journalists were perceived by the regimes in power as either agents of the state or as its enemies. Through massive purges of journalists who would not toe the government line, manipulation, and outright lies, the state-run media fomented the ethnic hatred that led to the Croatian and Bosnian wars. That pattern was repeated this year as the long-festering crisis in Kosovo exploded.

Kosovo's ethnic Albanian combatants, too, posed dangers for journalists covering the fighting. As a foreign reporter, I often witnessed armed Kosovo Liberation Army (KLA) rebels harassing and even menacing my Albanian interpreter because he was not with them in the trenches. The Kosovars showed even less tolerance for Serbian journalists working for independent or foreign media outlets in KLA-controlled areas, trying to provide fair and balanced coverage.

Harassment of the media is not exclusive to the Balkans; *Attacks on the Press in 1998* contains much crueler examples of repression by authoritarian regimes elsewhere in the world. But what makes ill-treatment of the media in the former Yugoslavia particularly disturbing is that this region has been the object of intense diplomatic involvement and scrutiny by the international community over the past several years. Yet Western diplomacy has focused mainly on regional stability at the expense of freedom of information and free speech.

Not only in the Balkans, but throughout Eastern and Central Europe, regimes frequently pay lip service to democratic principles, including support for independent media. The constitutions of most of these countries embrace the right of press freedom, but post-communist governments—including those formed by dissidents who came to power after 1989—have been reluctant to relinquish control of the media. Communist-era media legislation remains on the books in many parts of the region and, throughout the area, state-run television and radio stations still hold virtual monopolies over most broadcast frequencies and thus effectively control the flow of information.

I dwell on these examples not only because these countries are part of my beat, but primarily because many of them aspire to become full-fledged members of the Western community of nations. Several are poised to become NATO members, and their democratization efforts are under close Western scrutiny. Yet too often their most zealous monitors have been free-market missionaries whose democracy-building yardstick is limited to privatization of

Attacks on the Press in 1998

industry and the creation of a consumer society. In assisting post-communist countries in their transition to democracy, Western governments have shown little interest in encouraging the creation of open and free media in these formerly closed societies.

This year, the Committee to Protect Journalists chose a journalist from this part of the world—Pavel Sheremet of Belarus—to receive a 1998 International Press Freedom Award. (See page 66 for Sheremet's story.) His example and that of many other courageous journalists in the post-communist world illustrate that a free press is the measure of how fully democratic an emerging democracy is willing to be.

Attacks on the Press in 1998

Table of Contents

v	**Preface** by Sylvia Poggioli
1	**Introduction** by Ann K. Cooper
5	**Journalists Murdered in 1998** 24 Journalists Who Died in the Line of Duty
21	**Journalists in Prison in 1998** 118 Cases of Journalists Imprisoned Around the World
62	**Enemies of the Press: The 10 Worst Offenders of 1998**
66	**1998 International Press Freedom Awards**
72	**How CPJ Investigates and Classifies Attacks on the Press**
73	**AFRICA**
137	**Special Report: Nigeria** Outliving Abacha: Six Journalists' Prison Stories Introduction by Kakuna Kerina
159	**THE AMERICAS**
199	**Special Report: Latin America** Banding Together by Joel Simon
209	**ASIA**
263	**Special Report: Southeast Asia** Freedom Takes Hold: ASEAN Journalism in Transition by A. Lin Neumann
275	**CENTRAL EUROPE AND THE REPUBLICS OF THE FORMER SOVIET UNION**

311	**THE MIDDLE EAST AND NORTH AFRICA**
352	**Special Report: Algeria** Siege Mentality: Press Freedom and the Algerian Conflict by Joel Campagna
371	**CPJ at a Glance: Facts About the Organization and its Activities**
373	**CPJ Publications**
375	**How to Report an Attack on the Press**
376	**Ways to Participate in CPJ**
379	**Becoming a Member of CPJ**
381	**John S. and James L. Knight Foundation Challenge Grant Contributors**
382	**CPJ Emergency Response Fund**
383	**Contributors**
387	**Staff**
388	**Book Order Form**
389	**Index of Countries**

Attacks on the Press in 1998

Introduction
by Ann K. Cooper

Last summer, when I told people I was joining the Committee to Protect Journalists, I often got a cynical response. "Shouldn't that be 'the Committee to Protect People from Journalists?'" many deadpanned. Such was the view of our profession in the United States, as the Starr investigation into the Clinton-Lewinsky matter moved toward its congressional denouement at the end of 1998.

In this book, our annual accounting of press freedom around the world, we take you beyond that U.S. perspective, to countries where a journalist can land in jail for publishing something truthful, but unflattering, about the president.

We introduce you to some genuine heroes who make journalism a highly respected profession. In many countries of Latin America, for instance, public opinion polls rank the press as the second most admired institution after the Catholic Church. And we document the imprisonment, the torture, even the assassination, of journalists determined to expose crime or government corruption. Even a random look through these pages yields stories of high drama:

- Larisa Yudina, a newspaper editor murdered for her outspoken opposition to the dictatorial ruler of Kalmykia; her killing silenced the only public voice to challenge what amounts to a political fiefdom that operates largely beyond Moscow's control in southern Russia;
- Nizar Nayyouf, now in his seventh year in a Syrian prison, denied medical treatment for Hodgkins disease until he renounces his critical coverage of Syria's human rights record;
- Pradeep Kumara Dharmaratne, a Sri Lankan newspaper correspondent hospitalized after police tortured him for exposing their role in selling bootleg liquor; later, Dharmaratne's house was burned to the ground.

You will also meet Nosa Igiebor, a Nigerian editor whose three-year-old daughter had a gun held to her head when security agents came to arrest her dad; Anna Zarkova, a crime reporter in Bulgaria who was blinded in her left eye after an assailant doused her face with acid; and Grémah Boucar, a radio broadcaster from Niger who received one of CPJ's 1998 International Press Freedom Awards.

Ann K. Cooper *is the executive director of the Committee to Protect Journalists. Before joining CPJ in 1998, she was a foreign correspondent for National Public Radio for nine years, serving as bureau chief in Moscow and Johannesburg. She is co-editor of* Russia at the Barricades, *a collection of eyewitness accounts of the August 1991 coup in the Soviet Union. In 1995-96, she was the Edward R. Murrow fellow at the Council on Foreign Relations. She has also worked as a reporter for* The Sun *in Baltimore and* National Journal *magazine, among other publications.*

We knew Boucar had suffered harassment, that his offices had been looted, in a country where the military government was determined to silence his radio talk shows because they are the only outlet for opposition voices. What we did not know, until he arrived in New York to receive his award last November, was the harrowing tale of the night Boucar spent stuffed inside a sack, from which he could hear police officers debating how to kill him. His life was saved, he said, only when one policeman pointed out that since Boucar's family had witnessed his arrest they would be able to identify the killers. The story came up during a casual conversation, and Boucar's account was so straightforward, so matter-of-fact, that he might have been describing some minor change in his radio station's program lineup. In other words, a story that made us gasp was an event treated as almost normal by this journalist, who somehow manages to keep operating his independent radio station, newspaper, and magazine, under the nose of military thugs.

As I do so often in this work, I wondered what I would do in Boucar's place. You are likely to confront the same question as you read some of the hundreds of stories of attacks on the press during the year in 118 countries.

Verifying individual attacks on journalists and the newspapers, magazines, radio and television stations they work for is the bedrock of our work. It is on the basis of this meticulous reporting, carried out according to the highest journalistic standards, that CPJ is able to advocate on behalf of our colleagues around the world. And that advocacy is effective because we do it in the way that journalists know best: getting the story out clearly and forcefully in media campaigns and appeals to governments.

Equally important is the moral support that CPJ offers to besieged colleagues who are determined to fight for their right to freedom of expression. I hope you will read this book for the very human stories that it tells, about people taking risks, sticking by principles, and confronting decisions that rarely face journalists working in the comparative safety of industrial democracies such as the United States, France, or Japan. They are the stories of journalists who think and act independently, who do vital work in countries ruled by dictators, or lacking in strong press freedom safeguards. Their stories are not just a record of the state of press freedom, but also a tribute to colleagues who share our profession, but not our protections.

Of course, these stories also make up a kind of report card for the year: Just how dangerous was it for journalists, and where were there gains or losses for press freedom?

Among the gains: Dictators who had waged ruthless campaigns of suppression against the press fell in Indonesia and Nigeria, allowing journalists in both countries to breath freer than they had for years. Indonesia's new government lifted most

Attacks on the Press in 1998

press restrictions, and the military men in charge of Nigeria released all but one of the 17 journalists who had been imprisoned at the beginning of 1998. But in both countries, journalists cautioned that true reform was far from guaranteed.

Some of the setbacks: Onerous new press laws in several countries, including Jordan and the Federal Republic of Yugoslavia, slapped fresh restrictions on the media. The end of the year brought an explosion of violence against journalists in Sierra Leone and the Democratic Republic of Congo, countries riven by civil war. And the lawlessness that chronically plagues Colombia made it the deadliest country for journalists. Four were assassinated by gunmen on the street, sending chillingly public messages to colleagues who dare investigate Colombia's organized crime, government corruption, or drug trafficking.

Worldwide, 24 journalists were murdered because of their work, two fewer than in 1996 and 1997. These numbers are down significantly from the early 1990s, when the annual death toll was two or three times greater, in large part because of the targeting of journalists by factions at war in Algeria and Tajikistan.

At year's end, we recorded 118 journalists in prison for their work—a small but significant decline from the 129 imprisoned a year earlier. That's progress, but not nearly enough. With more countries wielding insult laws and criminal libel statutes to muzzle expression, more journalists than ever face a stark choice: Exercise self-censorship or risk going to jail for hard-hitting reporting.

As the name of our book signals, its subjects include repression and violence. But it also contains stories of some encouraging new trends emerging in the global fight for greater press freedom. Journalists throughout the world, recognizing the strength that comes from solidarity, are organizing press freedom advocacy groups. And CPJ has been the model and mentor for these new organizations. With our help, Mexican journalists launched their own press freedom monitoring organization, joining similar groups in Peru and Argentina. In November, CPJ lent support and expertise to the founding conference of the Southeast Asian Press Alliance, whose mission is to promote press freedom throughout Southeast Asia.

Such transnational contacts are compelling for today's journalists, who recognize that the permeability of borders in the electronic age allows democratic inclinations into places long hermetically sealed against ideas of freedom. For example, when Nigerian journalists gathered in Ghana last summer under CPJ's auspices to take stock of their past under the late dictator Gen. Sani Abacha and contemplate their uncertain future, they listened to the Argentine editor Horacio Verbitsky tell of how his country's journalists have weathered the transition from military dictatorship to democracy.

The multiplier effect of local journalists actively defending press freedom has already had reverberations throughout the world. It has brought members of our profession together across time zones and national boundaries to share strategies for countering the forces of repression. We believe these local and regional press monitors will be vital in further illuminating news of attacks on the media. The brighter the spotlight we shine on abuses, the greater our chances of ending them.

24 Journalists Murdered in 1998

Throughout the year, CPJ carefully tracks the cases of journalists who are killed because of their profession—murdered in revenge for revealing unwelcome truths, assassinated in callous disregard of the universal right to free expression, killed as a consequence of political or military upheaval. In 1998, CPJ confirmed the killings of 24 journalists in 17 countries. All died on assignment or as a direct result of their professional work. As the stories that follow reveal, most were cold-blooded assassinations, carried out by gunmen who mowed down journalists on the street, broke into their homes, or even, in a case in the Philippines, burst into the broadcast booth to silence a hard-hitting radio journalist while he was on the air.

These journalists were reporting on local events and local problems, yet the themes they dealt with are familiar to most of us: government corruption, drug trafficking, environmental scandal. These are universal issues, reported on by journalists in the north and south, rich countries and poor, industrial societies as well as agrarian states. The reporters who paid with their lives were exposing the problems, in the journalistic hope that by shedding light on them, they might one day be solved. Their deaths are the most dramatic example of another universal problem: Despite Article 19 of the Universal Declaration of Human Rights, which guarantees freedom of expression to all, press freedom violations occur every day, and they occur in all regions of the world. Like our colleagues who lost their lives, we at CPJ also hope that by exposing the problem we can move toward solving it.

The death toll that CPJ compiles each year is one of the most widely cited measures of the state of press freedom in the world. The 24 confirmed murders in 1998 was slightly below the 26 killings recorded in both 1997 and 1996. But CPJ lists another 12 killings as unconfirmed. In each of these cases, CPJ so far has been unable to confirm whether the journalists were killed because of their work.

Our research identified Colombia as the most deadly country for journalists in 1998; at least four were killed for their work, assassinated in the streets in revenge or as a grisly warning to others who would expose the country's widespread corruption and drug trafficking. These deaths bring the number of journalists murdered in Colombia since 1986 to 50.

CPJ documents murders of journalists not to prove that reporting is hazardous, but to help illuminate the dire threats that face press freedom, which is essential to the formation and functioning of a free and open society. When word reaches CPJ that a journalist has been killed, the program coordinator for the region immediately begins the careful and time-consuming process of determining whether the journalist was killed because of his or her profession—whether as an act of retribution, as a casualty of war, or in some other circumstances connected to journalistic duties. Our criteria define journalists as people who cover news or comment on public affairs, in print, in photographs, on radio, television or on-line; reporters, writers, editors, publishers, or directors of news organizations are all included. A case is not categorized as confirmed until we are sure that the death was related to the victim's journalistic work.

In the following list are brief accounts of the murders of journalists killed in 1998 that CPJ has been able to document. (Information on each of these murders, sometimes in greater detail, is found among the case histories appended to the essay on the country where the murder occurred.)

Attacks on the Press in 1998

24 Journalists Murdered in 1998

Research by CPJ indicates that the following individuals were murdered in 1998 because of their work as journalists. They either died in the line of duty on assignment, or were deliberately targeted for assassination because of their reporting or their affiliation with a news organization.

Listed by name, affiliation, date of death, and place of attack.

Afghanistan: 1

Mahoud Saremi, IRNA (Iranian News Agency), August 8, Mazar-i-Sharif

Saremi was Afghanistan bureau chief for the official Iranian news agency, IRNA. He disappeared, along with a group of Iranian diplomats, on August 8, when Taliban fighters seized the northern city of Mazar-i-Sharif and captured the Iranian consulate. On September 10, a Taliban spokesman admitted that Saremi and eight other Iranians had been found murdered near Mazar-i-Sharif. On August 10, CPJ urged the Taliban leader, Mullah Mohammad Omar, to investigate Saremi's disappearance; after learning of the assassination, CPJ called on him to launch an investigation into the killing.

Angola: 1

Simao Roberto, *Jornal de Angola*, June 5, Luanda

Roberto was a reporter for the government-owned *Jornal de Angola*. He was gunned down in his car outside the newspaper's offices in Luanda as he returned from the presidential palace, where he had covered a meeting of the Council of Ministers. Roberto was known as a critic of government. His colleagues believe he was killed because of his work as a journalist. Police subsequently presented three suspects they said carried out the attack, but a few days later one of the suspects denied involvement and said he had been forced to admit to the crime to get a lesser charge on another offense. No one to date has been charged with Roberto's murder. CPJ condemned the murder in a letter to President Jose Eduardo dos Santos and urged him to ensure a thorough investigation and prosecution of the killers.

Bangladesh: 1

Saiful Alam Mukul, *Daily Runner*, August 30, Jessore

Mukul was editor of the *Daily Runner*, a Bengali-language newspaper. He was returning to his home in Jessore when he was killed by what police say may have been a small homemade bomb. He was pronounced dead on arrival at Jessore General Hospital. The *Daily Runner* was known for its exposés of gang activity, political corruption, and human rights abuses, and had published stories critical of guerrilla activity around Jessore. Mukul halted production of the newspaper in June because of financial difficulties. Mukul wrote a poem for the paper's final issue expressing his frustration with a society grown complacent toward the problems of crime and corruption. After announcing on August 15 that the *Daily Runner* would resume publication September 1, Mukul repeatedly told friends, family and even police that he feared an attack on him was imminent. Journalists around the country were outraged at his murder. CPJ called for a full investigation and urged Prime Minister Sheikh Hasina Wajed to address the problem of escalating violence against journalists.

Brazil: 2

Manoel Leal de Oliveira,
***A Região*, January 14,**
Itabuna, Bahia

Leal was publisher and editor of *A Região*, the largest weekly in southern Bahia State. He was shot dead by assailants who had followed him as he was driving home. Leal was known for his critical reporting on local authorities, in which he frequently denounced the mayor of Itabuna and a civil police marshal in the Bahia capital of Salvador for corruption. Although two witnesses identified one of the assailants, police never questioned him, and the investigation has been closed. CPJ urged President Fernando Henrique Cardoso to launch an investigation by federal police, since local journalists fear Leal may have been targeted by local authorities.

José Carlos Mesquita,
TV Ouro Verde, March 10,
Ouro Preto do Oeste, Rondônia

Mesquita was host of a news program on TV Ouro Verde. He was murdered in Ouro Preto do Oeste in Rondônia State by three unidentified gunmen. He had just finished recording "Espaço Aberto," a program that featured politically sensitive topics, such as the safety of public transportation. Local journalists are convinced he was killed in retaliation for his work. CPJ urged President Fernando Henrique Cardoso to undertake a thorough investigation of the murder.

Burkina Faso: 1

Norbert Zongo, *L'independant*,
December 13, Ouagadougou

Zongo was editor in chief of the weekly newspaper *L'independant*. He was found dead in his car, along with his brother, his chauffeur, and a fourth, unidentified person. The inside of the vehicle was burnt and the bodies were charred, although the exterior of the car was not burnt. A rear door was riddled with what appeared to be bullet holes. The private newsweekly had recently published articles accusing

Attacks on the Press in 1998

President Blaise Compaore's brother of complicity in the death of his chauffeur. CPJ wrote to President Compaore asking that he launch a thorough and impartial investigation into Zongo's death and bring the perpetrators to justice.

Canada: 1

Tara Singh Hayer, *Indo-Canadian Times,* November 18, Vancouver

Hayer was the publisher of *Indo-Canadian Times*, Canada's largest and oldest Punjabi weekly. He was shot dead in the garage of his home in Vancouver, British Columbia. An outspoken critic of Sikh fundamentalist violence both in Canada and India, Hayer had been partially paralyzed and confined to a wheelchair after an assassination attempt in 1988. Police have linked the man convicted in that attack to the International Sikh Youth Federation and Babbar Khalsa, two militant international organizations working for an independent Sikh homeland in India. CPJ urged Canadian Prime Minister Jean Chrétien to ensure that Hayer's murder is aggressively investigated, and wrote to Indian Prime Minister Atal Bihari Vajpayee asking him to cooperate fully with the investigation.

Colombia: 4

Oscar García Calderón *El Espectador,* February 22, Bogotá

García, a bullfighting reporter for the Bogotá daily *El Espectador,* was forced into a taxi by unidentified assailants as he was leaving the newspaper's offices. He was shot three times, and his body was dumped near the attorney general's office. In the year before his murder, according to colleagues at the paper, García had uncovered links between drug traffickers and bullfighting and had proposed writing a book on the subject. García had asked a colleague to arrange a secret meeting with the attorney general to explain how traffickers used bullfighting and cattle ranching to launder money. CPJ sent a letter of inquiry to Attorney General Alfonso Gómez Méndez on February 24, and raised this case in a letter to President Ernesto Samper on March 20, the first anniversary of the murder of Gerardo Bedoya Borrero, the opinion editor of the Cali daily newspaper *El Pais* who was an outspoken critic of drug trafficking.

Nelson Carvajal Carvajal, Radio Sur, April 16, Pitalito

Carvajal, a highly regarded radio journalist in the town of Pitalito in Huila Department, was shot 10 times outside the elementary school where he taught. The gunman and an accomplice escaped by motorcycle, according to the testimony of several eyewitnesses. Carvajal was the producer of five community programs on Radio Sur, a local affiliate of Radio

Cadena Nacional (RCN). In addition to programming on topics ranging from health services to rural development, Carvajal provided investigative reporting about alleged government corruption. In one case, Carvajal reported that the former mayor of Pitalito had misappropriated public funds. On January 5, 1999, police arrested the former mayor and two other local politicians, all owners of a local construction company. Authorities are still looking for the two hired assassins. CPJ wrote a letter on April 27 to President Ernesto Samper urging him to ensure a vigorous investigation of the crime.

Bernabé Cortés Valderrama, Noticias CVN, May 19, Cali

Cortés was a reporter for the nightly news program "Noticas CVN." A gunman shot him as he was emerging from a taxi outside his aunt's home in Cali. The taxi driver was also killed. The gunman fled in a car driven by an accomplice. In his 18 years as a journalist in Cali, Cortés had covered everything from drug trafficking to government corruption. In 1992, he was briefly detained by guerrillas from the National Liberation Army (ELN). Colombian authorities believe that Cortés was killed in retaliation for a story aired on July 11, 1997, about a military operation to destroy a large cocaine laboratory near the town of Corinto, an area controlled by the Revolutionary Armed Forces of Colombia (FARC), a second guerrilla group. Cortés' report featured dramatic footage of rebels firing on the soldiers who had destroyed the cocaine lab. In November, Colombian police charged Julio César Ospina Chavarro with the murder. Police searched his home and found the gun used in the murder and the license plate from the stolen car used by the assailants. An informant told the prosecutor's office that Ospina Chavarro said drug traffickers from Corinto hired him to kill Cortés. Cortés' funeral in Cali drew several thousand people who were outraged by the crime. CPJ wrote a letter to President Ernesto Samper on the day of the murder expressing profound indignation.

Amparo Leonor Jiménez Pallares, "QAP" and "En Vivo" August 11, Valledupar

Jiménez was a television reporter until just months before her murder. She was dropping off her son at school when a gunman shot her three times in the head and then fled on a motorcycle driven by an accomplice. According to the attorney general's office, she was killed by members of a paramilitary death squad in retaliation for a story she broadcast in 1996. Her report concerned the estate of a former government official, Carlos Arturo Marulanda, where paramilitary forces were terrorizing peasants. While she was returning from reporting the story, a group of armed men confiscated her tapes, and upon her return home she began to receive frequent death

Attacks on the Press in 1998

threats. When, in early 1998, the government did not renew the broadcast license of "QAP," the news program where Jiménez worked, she reported for "En Vivo," broadcast in Valledupar on Canal A. Later in the year, she began full-time work for a government program to reintegrate former guerrillas into Colombian society. She also participated in Redepaz, a national peace advocacy group. In August, Colombian authorities detained Libardo Humberto Prada and charged him with her murder. An arrest warrant has been issued for Marulanda in connection with the murder of several peasants who were living on his property. Marulanda's brother, Francisco Alberto, was arrested on the same charges in May. On August 12, CPJ wrote a letter to President Andrés Pastrana urging an investigation into the murder.

Congo: 1

Fabien Fortuné Bitoumbo, Radio Liberté, August 29, Mindouli

Bitoumbo was a journalist with the station Radio Liberté and the former editor in chief of the privately owned newspaper *La Rue Meurt*. He was gunned down at point-blank range by an armed group known as the Ninja militia, which was loyal to former Prime Minister Bernard Koleas. Bitoumbo was on assignment, accompanying Minister of Mining and Industry Michel Mampouya on a trip to Mindouli, west of Brazzaville, when the group was taken hostage by the militia. Bitoumbo was reportedly the only hostage killed.

Ethiopia: 1

Abay Hailu, *Agiere*, February 9, Addis Ababa

Abay was a reporter for the weekly *Agiere* and editor in chief of the now-defunct *Welafen*. He died on February 9 after nearly a year's imprisonment. He was arrested on February 22, 1997, after publishing a report about the threat of Islamic fundamentalism in Ethiopia. He remained in jail because he was unable to meet bail, and was sentenced in November to a year in prison. Initially refused treatment for a deteriorating medical condition, he was eventually hospitalized, but died five days later.

Georgia: 1

Georgy Chanya, *Rezonants*, May 26, Gali, Abkhazia

Chanya was a correspondent for the independent Georgian daily newspaper *Rezonants*. He was killed while reporting on fighting between Abkhaz rebels and Georgian guerrillas near Gali in the separatist region of Abkhazia. He was following a band of guerrillas and was killed during a raid on their camp.

His mutilated body, found on May 26, had to be identified by personal documents he had been carrying. CPJ called on leaders from both sides in the conflict to protect journalists working in conditions of armed conflict and guarantee their right to practice their profession.

Mexico: 2

Luis Mario García Rodríguez, *La Tarde*, **February 12, Mexico City**

García was a reporter for the Mexico City daily newspaper *La Tarde*. He was murdered in the Colonia Guerrero neighborhood by several assailants who ambushed him and shot him in the head five times. García had reported extensively on corruption in the national attorney general's office and among the Federal Judicial Police. In a series of articles published in late 1997, García reported that members of the Federal Judicial Police were collaborating with the Arellano Félix brothers, who run the Tijuana drug cartel. A few days before the murder, a Federal Judicial Police officer and an army captain interrogated García about his sources, according to an editor at *La Tarde*. In an incident last year, both García and his young son were shot and injured when García's car was raked with gunfire. Because of widespread suspicion that the Federal Judicial Police may have been involved in the crime, CPJ wrote to President Ernesto Zedillo, urging the appointment of a special prosecutor to insure that the killers are brought to justice.

Philip True, *San Antonio Express-News*, **December 15, Jalisco**

True, a U.S. citizen based in Mexico City, was a correspondent for the Texas newspaper *San Antonio Express-News*. He left home November 28 for a 10-day assignment in the Sierra Madre Occidental of Nayarit and Jalisco states to report on the local Huichol Indians. He was last seen alive in the village of Chalmotitia on December 4. His body was found at the bottom of a ravine on December 15, after an intensive search by the Mexican military. The medical examiner's report disclosed that True had been strangled and sustained a head injury that was not attributable to a fall. Evidence also showed that he had been sexually assaulted. His body had been partially covered with rocks in an apparent attempt to conceal it. Neither his wedding ring nor his watch was taken, indicating that robbery was not a motive. Mexican police arrested two Huichol Indians, who confessed to the killing and are being held pending trial. CPJ urged President Ernesto Zedillo to mount a military search for the missing journalist when True failed to contact his wife after 10 days. After True's body was found, CPJ wrote to Zedillo again, urging a full investigation into True's death.

Attacks on the Press in 1998

Nigeria: 2

Tunde Oladepo, *The Guardian*, February 26, Abeokuta, Ogun

Oladepo was a senior correspondent with *The Guardian* newspaper of Lagos. He was murdered by five masked gunmen, who entered his home early in the morning and shot him to death in front of his wife and children. Nothing was removed from Oladepo's residence, ruling out robbery as a motive. Oladepo was until recently bureau chief of *The Guardian's* state office in Ogun and was covering political affairs. Co-workers believe he was murdered because of his work as a journalist.

Okezie Amaruben, *Newsservice*, September 2, Enugu

Amaruben was publisher of *Newsservice* magazine. He was shot and killed by an Enugu State police officer. Amaruben was checking on a printing job being done for him in a shop when he was accosted by police officers who verbally and physically attacked him. One placed a pistol to his forehead and hit him with the gun after he had identified himself as a journalist. People at the scene told the police officers that Amaruben was not the person they were looking for. He was being forced into a police vehicle when the officer fired his gun and the bullet pierced Amaruben's skull. Authorities confirmed that the officer who shot Amaruben was arrested shortly after the murder. CPJ strongly condemned the killing in a letter to Gen. Abdulsalami Abubakar and requested an immediate and impartial investigation.

Philippines: 1

Rey Bancayrin, Radio DXLL, March 30, Zamboanga City

Bancayrin was a well-known broadcaster for radio station DXLL in the southern region of Mindanao. He was shot to death March 30 while on the air. Two unidentified gunmen entered the broadcast booth while he was talking to a listener and shot him three times at point-blank range. The killers calmly left the station and escaped. Bancayrin was known for his outspoken attacks on local corruption, illegal logging, and drug smugglers. The Zamboanga Press Club called his death "a blow to press freedom." In a letter to President Fidel V. Ramos, CPJ pointed out that Bancayrin was the 33rd journalist killed in the line of duty in the Philippines since the overthrow of Ferdinand Marcos in 1986 and called for an immediate investigation into his murder.

Russia: 2

Larisa Yudina,

Yudina was editor of the only alternative news outlet in the

Sovietskaya Kalmykia Segodnya,
June 8, Elista, Kalmykia

Russian autonomous republic of Kalmykia. She was found dead of multiple stab wounds and a fractured skull on the outskirts of the capital, Elista. Yudina, a political activist, was frequently harassed and threatened for her exposés of local corruption and hard-line rule by the republic's president, Kirsan Ilyumzhinov. On the day of her disappearance, June 7, she went to meet a source who was to provide evidence of financial improprieties by local firms. Yudina's troubles with Kalmyk authorities as a journalist and local leader of the liberal opposition Yabloko party had been documented by foreign and Russian press freedom groups. The public outcry over her death caused the federal prosecutor to take over the case, and three suspects have been arrested. CPJ called on President Boris Yeltsin to publicize the progress of the investigation and prosecute those responsible for the murder.

Anatoly Levin-Utkin,
Yuridichesky Petersburg Segodnya
August 24, St. Petersburg

Levin-Utkin was deputy editor of the weekly newspaper *Yuridichesky Peterburg Segodnya*. He was beaten unconscious on August 21 in the doorway of his apartment and robbed of his briefcase, which contained information for the next installment in an investigative series on rivalries between local financial and political figures. Cash and personal valuables were also taken. He suffered severe brain trauma and died on August 24 without regaining consciousness. The newspaper's editor said in an August 25 news conference that he believed the murder was connected to the series of articles on the customs and secret services published in the first two issues of the three-week-old newspaper, for which Levin-Utkin had done research and reporting. The editor said he had received phone calls demanding the names of those who worked on the series, but had refused to divulge the information. Levin-Utkin had just finished collecting documents and photos for the third installment on the day he was attacked. In a letter to President Boris Yeltsin, CPJ condemned the fatal beating and decried the intimidation of journalists and the climate of fear in Russia that stifles media freedom.

Rwanda: 1

Wilson Ndayambadje, National Rwanda Radio and TV,
January 28, Gisenyi

Ndayambadje, a radio and television reporter in Gisenyi, was beaten to death by Emmanuel Rutayisire, a national army soldier. Rutayisire was charged with the murder, convicted, and sentenced to death by a military tribunal on January 29. He was executed the same day.

Attacks on the Press in 1998

Sierra Leone: 1

Edward Smith, British Broadcasting Corporation (BBC) April 13, Banbanduhun

Smith, a Sierra Leonean citizen, was a reporter for the BBC who had covered the northeastern region (Makeni and Kono districts) of Sierra Leone since the Armed Forces Ruling Council took power in May 1997. He was killed while traveling with West African peacekeeping soldiers when Rebel United Front forces ambushed their vehicles. He had previously worked as a reporter for the independent newspaper *Vision* and as editor of *The Storm* newspaper.

Thailand: 1

Sayomchai Vijitwittayapong, *Matichon*, January 10, Phichit

Sayomchai was an investigative reporter for Bangkok's third-largest daily newspaper, *Matichon*. He was found dead of a gunshot wound in his car on January 10 in the city of Phichit in central Thailand. He was last seen leaving his Bangkok home on January 9 with a tape recorder and camera, on his way to meet a village headman. Colleagues believe he was killed because of his reporting on corruption in the construction industry. He had received death threats and reportedly had refused a bribe to drop his investigation.

12 Journalists Killed: Motive Unconfirmed

When the motive for a journalist's murder is unclear, but there is reason to suspect that it was related to the journalist's profession, CPJ classifies that death as "unconfirmed." CPJ continues its research to identify the reasons for the crime and its efforts to persuade authorities to investigate the killings and apprehend and punish the culprits.

Colombia: 5

Didier Aristizábal Galeano, Santiago de Cali University, March 2, Cali

Aristizábal was shot to death in Cali after leaving the Santiago de Cali University. Local journalists report that Aristizábal was followed by two men riding a Yamaha motorcycle. They shot him nine times when he stopped for a traffic light and then fled the scene.

Aristizábal worked as a political reporter for radio station Todelar in Cali until 1994, when he joined the faculty of Santiago de Cali University as a professor of journalism. In 1996, he took a position as chief press officer for the Cali Fair, a bullfighting tournament. At the end of 1997, he helped the National Police in Cali set up a radio news station.

CPJ, which has not been able to confirm that Aristizábal was killed for his journalistic work, sent a letter of inquiry about the murder to Attorney General Alfonso Gómez Méndez on March 5, and mentioned the killing of Aristizábal in a letter to President Ernesto Samper on March 20, the first anniversary of editor and columnist Gerardo Bedoya Borrero's murder.

José Abel Salazar Serna, Todelar, March 14, Manizales

Salazar, host of the radio program "Juventud en Acción" (Youth in Action) on the Todelar station in the central Colombian town of Manizales, was found dead in his apartment in Manizales. He had been stabbed 15 times. Salazar had broadcast appeals for peace and coexistence.

Gustavo Adolfo Montes Castaño, a minor, was detained and charged by the attorney general's office with murdering Salazar during a quarrel.

CPJ mentioned Salazar's murder in a letter to President Ernesto Samper on March 20, the first anniversary of the murder of editor and columnist Gerardo Bedoya Borrero, citing the killing as one of eight recent murders of journalists and calling for a full and swift investigation.

Néstor Villar Jiménez, September 11, Villavicencio

Villar, a prominent journalist and former congressman, was killed by gunmen in Villavicencio, capital of Meta Department. Villar had attended a meeting of mayors and had gone to a bar. There, an unidentified individual shot him in

Attacks on the Press in 1998

the head three times. The assailant fled on a motorcycle driven by an accomplice.

Villar's journalistic career started with the local radio station Macarena. He then worked as an economic reporter for the newspapers *La República* and *El Siglo*, as well as for the magazine *Síntesis*, all of which are Bogotá-based. He started his political career around 1995. He had been a representative in the lower house of Congress from the conflict-ridden Vaupés Department. At the time of his death, he was contractor for the municipality of Mitú, the Vaupés Department capital.

Although Villar was not working as a journalist at the time of his death, local journalists believe that he may have been targeted because of his stance against drug trafficking during his career as a journalist.

José Hernan Henao Ortiz, in police custody on other unrelated charges, is the leading suspect in the case, according to the attorney general's office, which has not been able to establish a motive for the crime. Authorities are investigating whether the assassination might have been related to the murder of Nestor's brother Orlando, a journalist and aide to former President Ernesto Samper. Orlando was killed in Bogotá on October 8, 1994.

Saúl Alcaraz, October 14
Medellín

Alcaraz, the spokesperson for Instituto Mi Río, an environmental group in Medellín, was shot dead at his home while watching a soccer game. According to local journalists, several men claiming to be police came to Alcaraz's home and shot him six times when he resisted being forced into a car. Alcaraz, 29, was a former correspondent for the regional broadcast network Teleantioquia.

José Arturo Guapacha,
***El Panorama*, October 15**
Cartago

A gunman shot Guapacha, editor of *El Panorama*, inside an auto repair shop in the town of Cartago, in the Western Valle del Cauca Department, a region dominated by drug traffickers. Local journalists say Guapacha had written stories criticizing the drug trade and had published the names of people who owed back taxes to the municipal government. He may also have been killed because of his efforts to organize local journalists to fight for better working conditions.

Guapacha, 39, had worked as a journalist for 18 years. He started his career at radio stations Radio Cadena Nacional (RCN) and Todelar. At the time of his death, he was editor of *El Panorama*, a local magazine he founded in 1988.

CPJ wrote to Attorney General Alfonso Gómez Méndez on October 29, urging a complete and impartial investigation.

Democratic Republic of Congo: 1

Belmondo Magloire Missinhoun, *La Pointe Congo*, September 3, Kinshasa

Missinhoun was owner of the financial newspaper *La Pointe Congo*. He was a citizen of Benin but had lived in Kinshasa for 30 years. He was last seen on September 3 when he was arrested following a traffic accident with a military vehicle in Kinshasa and taken to an unknown location. Police investigatons into the journalist's disappearance have yielded no results. Missinhoun had close ties to former dictator Mobutu Sese Seko. His newspaper has not published since the end of the Mobutu regime.

Ethiopia: 1

Tesfaye Tadesse, *Mestawet* and *Lubar*, June 7, Addis Ababa

Tesfaye was the owner and editor of the now-defunct publications *Mestawet* magazine and *Lubar*, a newspaper. He was stabbed and hacked to death in front of his home on June 7 by two unidentified assailants, who fled by car. Tesfaye, a lawyer by training, was an activist and member of the Ethiopian Human Rights Council. He was previously jailed by Prime Minister Meles Zenawi's Ethiopian Peoples Revolutionary Democratic Front in 1993. CPJ urged Meles to ensure a thorough investigation of the murder and the prosecution of those responsible for the crime.

Iran: 1

Majid Sharif, *Iran-e-Farda*, November 24, Tehran

Sharif was a writer and political commentator who had contributed to the monthly magazine *Iran-e-Farda*. His body was found in a Tehran morgue on November 24; he had been missing since November 20. Sharif reportedly died of a heart attack, but the circumstances of his death remain unclear. His death coincided with the disappearance and death of four other Iranian writers and critics in November and December. In January, Iran's Intelligence Ministry, in a shocking admission, announced that several rogue agents were behind "the hateful murders which took place recently." It did not specify whether Sharif was one of those murdered by intelligence agents.

Peru: 2

Isabel Chumpitaz Panta and José Amaya Jacinto, Radio Satélite, April 6, La Unión

Chumpitaz was a well-known journalist who produced a daily show called "The People's Voice" for Radio Satélite, which advocated peasants' rights. Her husband, Amaya, was a regu-

Attacks on the Press in 1998

lar contributor to "The People's Voice." She and her husband were murdered on the night of April 6, when a group of men armed with pistols and automatic weapons entered their family home in La Unión. Chumpitaz's brother, Walter, who produces a daily program on Radio Satélite that also advocates for peasants' rights, was stabbed in the chest and severely wounded. The assailants beat her mother and attempted to rape her sister. The public prosecutor in Piura has requested life sentences for 11 people detained and charged with the murders. Relatives of Chumpitaz believe she was killed because of her reporting about the illegal collection of money from local farmers by the company Emoycsa, and they claim there were irregularities in the police investigation. Local authorities maintain robbery was the motive for the attack. CPJ urged President Alberto K. Fujimori to devote the full resources of his office to ensuring that those responsible for the crime are brought to justice.

Philippines: 1

Nelson Catipay, DXMY Radio, April 16, Cotabato City

Catipay was a correspondent for radio station DXMY in Cotabato City in Mindanao. He was killed April 16 while traveling in a minivan to a news conference in the town of Sultan Kudarat. Two unidentified men, also passengers in the van, shot him nine times, according to police reports. His killers fled the scene. Before joining DXMY in February, Catipay was a commentator at another radio station, where he denounced abuses and corruption in government. Police suspect his death may be related to a land dispute in the area. CPJ wrote to President Fidel V. Ramos to urge an immediate investigation into the murder.

Russia: 1

Ivan Fedyunin, *Bryanskie Izvestia*, March 31, Bryansk

Fedyunin was a political reporter with the local *Bryanskie Izvestia* newspaper who covered the Duma and regional and national political events. He was stabbed to death in his apartment on March 31. Police and colleagues discovered his body April 2. Co-workers at the newspaper say he had recently published articles about alleged criminal activities of local companies involved in renovating apartments and believe his death was related to his professional work. Others speculate the death was related to his personal life. Police reportedly arrested a suspect, but he has not been identified.

JOURNALISTS KILLED IN 1998

CPJ Confirms 472 Journalists Killed* in Past 10 Years

From 1989 through 1998, the most dangerous countries for journalists were: Algeria, Colombia, Russia, Tajikistan, Croatia, India, Bosnia and Herzegovina, Turkey, Rwanda, Peru, and the Philippines.

117 in the AMERICAS
Colombia: 43
Peru: 17
Brazil: 10
El Salvador: 10
Mexico: 10
United States: 7
Guatemala: 4
Haiti: 4
Argentina: 2
Canada: 2
Venezuela: 2
Chile: 1
Dominican Republic: 1
Ecuador: 1
Honduras: 1
Panama: 1
Paraguay: 1

131 in EUROPE & THE REPUBLICS OF THE FORMER SOVIET UNION
Russia: 31**
Tajikistan: 29
Croatia: 26
Bosnia and Herzegovina: 21
Soviet Union: 8**
Georgia: 4
Ukraine: 3
Azerbaijan: 2
Romania: 2
Slovenia: 2
Belgium: 1
Ireland: 1
Lithuania: 1

94 in the MIDDLE EAST & NORTH AFRICA
Algeria: 59
Turkey: 20
Lebanon: 6
Iraq: 5
Egypt: 2
Cyprus: 1
Iran: 1

78 in ASIA
India: 22
Philippines: 16
Pakistan: 8
Cambodia: 6
Sri Lanka: 5
Indonesia: 4
Bangladesh: 3
Afghanistan: 2
Thailand: 2
China: 1
Papua New Guinea: 1

60 in AFRICA
Rwanda: 17
Somalia: 9
Angola: 7
Chad: 4
South Africa: 4
Burundi: 3
Ethiopia: 3
Liberia: 2
Nigeria: 2
Sierra Leone: 2
Zaire: 2
Burkina Faso: 1
Congo: 1
Sudan: 1
Uganda: 1
Zambia: 1

*All figures above reflect the number of journalists killed in the line of duty.
**Between 1989 and 1991, eight journalists were killed in what was then the Soviet Union: three in Azerbaijan, three in Russia, and two in Latvia.

Attacks on the Press in 1998

118 Journalists in Prison As of December 31, 1998

At the end of each year, CPJ attempts to document every case of everyone held in prison anywhere in the world on charges related to journalistic work. This includes newsgathering, writing, editing, publishing, broadcasting, and photojournalism. It applies to opinion, analysis, and commentary, as well as to factual reportage. We undoubtedly miss some cases. Information about these journalists and their convictions is often extremely difficult to obtain and verify. There are many reported instances of journalists' jailings that we do not consider confirmed because we cannot verify the information or because we cannot demonstrate a direct relationship between the imprisonment and the journalist's work. Based on all information available to us, we have verified 118 journalists in prison for their work as of December 31, 1998. The largest number, 27, were held in **Turkey**, while **China** and **Ethiopia** each held a dozen journalists prisoner. **Sierra Leone**, which last year had no journalists in prison, held 11 journalists at year's end—all of them caught up in the civil strife that has prevailed in the country since President Ahmed Tejan Kabbah returned to fight the rebels who had ousted him from elected office in 1997.

Information about all the imprisoned journalists, held in 25 countries from **Algeria** to **Vietnam**, is presented here chronologically.

The total is down from 129 confirmed cases of journalists in prison one year earlier. The most significant reduction was in **Nigeria**, where the June death of military dictator Sani Abacha—named one of CPJ's 10 Worst Enemies of the Press (see page 62) just a month earlier—led to the release of all but one of 17 imprisoned reporters and editors. Among those freed was *Sunday Magazine* editor Chris Anyanwu, a recipient in absentia of CPJ's 1997 International Press Freedom Award. In November, Anyanwu received her award, belatedly but in person, at CPJ's annual awards ceremony in New York City. She was followed at the podium by Doan Viet Hoat, a journalist from **Vietnam** who was in a Vietnamese prison when he was named an awardee in 1993. Hoat was freed in 1998 after eight years in prison.

At the end of 1998, officials in **Eritrea** freed Ruth Simon, the local correspondent for Agence France-Presse, who had been held for 20 months. Simon's release came one month after CPJ had honored her in absentia at the November benefit with an International Press Freedom Award.

The freeing of Anyanwu, Hoat, and Simon demonstrates that governments do respond to pressure; as Press Freedom Award recipients, each of these three journalists was the focus of intense efforts by CPJ to gain their release. But campaigns to free dozens of other imprisoned journalists continue, and 1998 saw scant progress in the three countries with the worst records.

Turkey's total has changed little from the 29 held a year earlier. Five of the 27 were newly imprisoned in 1998; all five are affiliated with pro-Kurdish publications. These numbers illuminate Turkey's long-standing pattern of outlawing reporting on the ongoing civil war with Kurdish insurgents in the southeastern part of the country. And the fact that 25 journalists imprisoned before 1998 remain behind bars is evidence of the Turkish government's failure to make good on its promises to CPJ in July 1997 to push for the release of all imprisoned journalists and the reform of the statutes used to criminalize journalism.

Ethiopia persisted in its practice of flouting the rule of law by intimidating outspoken journalists with frequent jailings without charge. Most of China's imprisoned journalists have been held since the early 1990s for publishing alleged "state secrets" or writing and distributing political leaflets critical of Communist Party rule. But in a disturbing milestone, the Chinese government in 1998 prosecuted an Internet entrepreneur for sharing e-mail addresses with a dissident website—an ominous sign that Beijing intends to squelch yet another medium of free expression.

Every name on this list represents someone who we, as fellow journalists, believe was unjustly imprisoned because of his or her work. Not everyone on this list is a career journalist, however. We include political analysts, human rights activists, and others who have been prosecuted because of opinion pieces or news features they have written or broadcast. All working journalists in these countries are directly threatened by such prosecutions, and thus we have an obligation to defend such imprisoned writers as colleagues.

In totalitarian societies where independent journalism is forbidden, CPJ often defends prosecuted writers who would be defined by their governments as political dissidents rather than journalists. This category would embrace the *samizdat* publishers of the former Soviet Union, the wall-poster essayists of the pre-Tiananmen period in China, and the underground pamphleteers of today's Burma. CPJ also classifies as an imprisoned journalist anyone with a news media background in an authoritarian or totalitarian state who is prosecuted for campaigning for free expression. We believe that working in the defense of press freedom is as legitimate an activity for a journalist as reporting or editing.
In addition to the 118 confirmed cases reported here, we have listed another 4 "unconfirmed" cases of imprisoned journalists, in Sudan and Turkey (see page 61). In these cases, we could not verify that the journalists were in prison at year's end, and we are seeking additional information from local sources and clarification from the governments in question.

Attacks on the Press in 1998

118 Imprisoned Journalists

The following is a list of journalists imprisoned around the world. Cases appear chronologically, and are grouped according to the countries in which the journalists are held.

Algeria (2)

Please send appeals to:
His Excellency Liamine Zeroual
President of the High Council of State
The Presidential Palace
El Mouradia
Algiers, Algeria
Fax: +213-260-9618

Djamel Eddine Fahassi, Alger Chaîne III
Detained: May 7, 1995

Men presumed to be state security officials detained Fahassi, a reporter for the government-run French-language radio station Alger Chaîne III and formerly a contributor to *Al-Forqane*, a weekly organ of the Islamic Salvation Front (FIS) that was banned in March 1992. Officials have refused to acknowledge his arrest.

Aziz Bouabdallah, *Al-Alam al-Siyassi*
Detained: April 12, 1997

Bouabdallah, a reporter for the Arabic-language daily *Al-Alam al-Siyassi*, was abducted by three armed men from his home in Algiers. The men, believed to be Algerian security agents, forced Bouabdallah into a waiting car. CPJ later received information that Algerian authorities were holding Bouabdallah in an Algiers detention center. He was reported to have been tortured repeatedly. Authorities have denied any knowledge of his detention.

Benin (2)

Please send appeals to:
Predident Mathieu Kerekou
c/o Embassy of the Republic of Benin
2737 Cathedral Avenue, NW
Washington, D.C. 20008
Fax: +202-265-1996

Maurice Chabi, *Les Echos du Jour*
Pascal Zantou, *Les Echos du Jour*
Imprisoned: December 15, 1998

Chabi and Zantou, respectively chief editor and reporter for the independent daily *Les Echos du Jour*, each received a six-month prison sentence for libel. Education Minister Léonard Padonou Jijoho filed the complaint against the journalists in response to the publication of an article in the newspaper's August 26 edition which reported he had misappropriated public funds.

Burma (8)

Please send appeals to:
His Excellency Gen. Than Shwe
Prime Minister and Minister of Defense
Chairman of the State Peace and Development Council
Ministry of Defense
Signal Pagoda Road
Rangoon, Burma

U Win Tin
Imprisoned: July 4, 1989

U Win Tin, a former editor of two daily newspapers and vice chair of Burma's Writers Association, was arrested and sentenced to three years' hard labor. The sentence was subsequently extended by 10 years in 1992. His arrest is believed to have been for his opposition activities. U Win Tin was active in establishing independent publications during the 1988 student democracy movement, and he also worked closely with National League for Democracy leader Daw Aung San Suu Kyi and was reportedly one of her closest advisers. Prison authorities again extended U Win Tin's sentence on March 28, 1996, by seven years, after they convicted him of smuggling letters describing conditions at Rangoon's Insein Prison to Yozo Yokota, the U.N. special rapporteur for human rights in Burma. He is reported to be in very poor health, and was transferred to Rangoon General Hospital in 1997.

U Maung Maung Lay Ngwe,
Pe-Tin-Tan
Imprisoned: September 1990

U Maung Maung Lay Ngwe was arrested and charged with writing and distributing publications that "make people lose respect for the government." The publications were titled, collectively, *Pe-Tin-Tan*. In 1998, CPJ was unable to obtain new information on his status.

U Myo Myint Nyein, U Sein Hlaing, *What's Happening*
Imprisoned: September 1990

U Myo Myint Nyein and U Sein Hlaing were arrested for contributing to the preparation, planning, and publication of the satirical news magazine *What's Happening*, which the Burmese government claims is anti-government propaganda. They were sentenced to seven years in prison. On March 28, 1996, they were among 21 prisoners tried inside Insein Prison and given an additional seven-year sentence under the Emergency Provisions Act for smuggling letters describing prison conditions to Yozo Yokota, the U.N. special rapporteur for human rights in Burma. In 1998, CPJ was unable to obtain new information about their status.

Daw San San Nwe
U Sein Hla Oo
Imprisoned: August 5, 1994

Dissident writer San San Nwe and journalist Sein Hla Oo were arrested on charges of spreading information damaging to the state and contacting anti-government groups. They were sentenced on October 6, 1994, to 10 years and seven years in prison, respectively. Three other dissidents, including a former UNICEF worker, were sentenced to between seven and 15 years in prison on similar charges. Officials said the five had "fabricated and sent anti-government reports" to diplomats in foreign embassies, foreign radio stations, and foreign journalists. San San Nwe allegedly met two French reporters visiting Burma in April 1993 and appeared in a video they produced to spread propaganda about the government. Both U Sein Hla Oo and Daw San San Nwe were previously imprisoned for their involvement in the National League for Democracy, Burma's main pro-democracy party. As of December 1994, all five were being held at the Insein Prison in Rangoon. In 1998, CPJ was unable to obtain new information about their status.

Ma Myat Mo Mo Tun
Imprisoned: 1994

Ma Myat Mo Mo Tun, the daughter of imprisoned writer Daw San San Nwe, was arrested in 1994 and sentenced to seven years in prison for spreading information injurious to the state. She is alleged to have recorded "defamatory letters and documents," made contact with "illegal" groups, and sent anti-government articles to a journal published by an expatriate group. In 1998, CPJ was unable to obtain new information about her status.

Ye Htut
Imprisoned: September 27, 1995

Ye Htut was arrested on charges of sending fabricated news abroad to Burmese dissidents and opposition media, and sentenced to seven years in prison. Among the organizations to which Ye Htut allegedly confessed sending reports was the Thailand-based Burma Information Group (BIG), which publishes the human rights newsletter *The Irrawaddy*. Burma's official media claimed that BIG had presented a false picture of the country to foreign governments and human rights organizations. In 1998, CPJ was unable to obtain new information on his status.

Cameroon (1)

Please send appeals to:
His Excellency Paul Biya
President of the Republic of Cameroon
Presidential Palace, Yaoundé, Cameroon
Fax: 237-221-699

Michel Michaut Moussala
Aurore Plus
Imprisoned: September 3, 1998

Moussala, editor of *Aurore Plus*, was convicted of defaming Jean Tchoussa Moussa Mbatkam, director general of the National Ports Department of Cameroon (ONPC) and a deputy of the ruling Rassemblement Democratique du Peuple Camerounais

(RDPC) party. He was sentenced to six months in prison and fined one million CFA (US$1,783). In addition, the newspaper was ordered to suspend publication for six months.

The suit cited a December 16, 1997, *Aurore Plus* article titled "ONPC, Tome II, Tchoussa Moussa at the Centre of a Failed Coup," which reported that Moussa had taken advantage of his position as director of the ONPC to stage a coup d'état. Moussala was arrested on September 3, 1998, by police officers who presented a warrant that had been issued shortly after his January conviction.

China (12)

Please send appeals to:
Jiang Zemin
President, State Council
Beijing 100032
People's Republic of China
Fax: 86-10-6512-5810

Hu Liping, *The Beijing Daily*
Imprisoned: April 7, 1990

Hu, a staff member of *The Beijing Daily* newspaper, was arrested on April 7, 1990, and charged with "counterrevolutionary incitement and propaganda" and "trafficking in state secrets," according to a rare release of information on his case from the Chinese Ministry of Justice in 1998. He was sentenced by the Beijing Intermediate People's Court to a term of 10 years in prison on August 15, 1990, and he is being held in the Beijing Municipal Prison.

Zhang Yafei, *Tielu*
Imprisoned: September 1990

Zhang, a former student at Beifang Communications University, was arrested and charged with dissemination of counterrevolutionary propaganda and incitement. In March 1991, he was sentenced to 11 years in prison and two years without political rights after his release. Zhang edited *Tielu* (Iron Currents), an unofficial magazine about the 1989 crackdown at Tiananmen Square.

Chen Yanbin, *Tielu*
Imprisoned: Late 1990

Chen, a former university student, was arrested in late 1990 and sentenced to 15 years in prison and four years without political rights after his release. Together with Zhang Yafei, he had produced *Tielu* (Iron Currents), an unofficial magazine about the 1989 crackdown at Tiananmen Square. Several hundred mimeographed copies of the magazine were distributed. The government termed the publication "reactionary" and charged Chen with disseminating counter-revolutionary propaganda and incitement.

Liu Jingsheng, *Tansuo*

Liu, a former writer and co-editor of the pro-democracy jour-

Attacks on the Press in 1998

Imprisoned: May 1992

nal *Tansuo*, was sentenced to 15 years in prison for "counter-revolutionary" activities after being tried secretly in July 1994. Liu was arrested in May 1992 and charged with being a member of labor and pro-democracy groups, including the Liberal Democratic Party of China, Free Labor Union of China, and the Chinese Progressive Alliance. Court documents stated Liu was involved in organizing and leading anti-government and pro-democracy activities. Prosecutors also accused him and other dissidents who were tried on similar charges of writing and printing political leaflets that were distributed in June 1992, during the third anniversary of the Tiananmen Square demonstrations.

Wu Shishen, Xinhua News Agency
Imprisoned: October or November 1992

Arrested in the fall of 1992, Wu, a Xinhua News Agency reporter, received a life sentence in August 1993 for allegedly providing a Hong Kong journalist with a "state-classified" advance copy of President Jiang Zemin's 14th Party Congress address.

Bai Weiji
Imprisoned: April 1993

Bai, who once worked for the Chinese Foreign Ministry monitoring foreign news and writing news summaries, was sentenced in May 1993 to 10 years in prison for passing information and leaking national secrets to Lena Sun, a correspondent for the *Washington Post*. His appeal was rejected in July 1993. His wife, Zhao Lei, also arrested for the same offense, was released in 1996.

Ma Tao, *China Health Education News*
Sentenced: August 1993

Ma, editor of *China Health Education News*, received a six-year prison term for allegedly helping Xinhua News Agency reporter Wu Shishen provide a Hong Kong journalist with President Jiang Zemin's "state-classified" 14th Party Congress address. According to the Associated Press, Ma is believed to be Wu's wife.

Gao Yu, free-lancer
Imprisoned: October 2, 1993

Gao was detained two days before she was to depart for the United States to start a one-year research fellowship at Columbia University's Graduate School of Journalism. On November 10, 1994, she was tried without counsel and sentenced to six years in prison for "leaking state secrets" about China's structural reforms in articles for the pro-Beijing Hong Kong magazine *Mirror Monthly*. Gao had previously been jailed for 14 months following the June 1989 Tiananmen Square demonstrations and released in August 1990 after showing symptoms of a heart condition. In January 1997, Chinese authorities rejected an appeal for bail on medical grounds. Several international organizations, including

CPJ, renewed the call for her release in 1998 when her family reported that her physical condition had seriously deteriorated, but the Chinese authorities again rejected the appeal.

Khang Yuchun, *Freedom Forum*
Sentenced: December 1994

Khang was tried with 16 others on charges of being members of counter-revolutionary organizations, most notably the Chinese Progressive Alliance, the Liberal Democratic Party of China, and the Free Labor Union of China. Among the accusations against him was that he commissioned people to write articles and set up *Freedom Forum*, the magazine of the Chinese Progressive Alliance. He was sentenced in December 1994 to 12 years in prison for "organizing and leading a counter-revolutionary group" and an additional seven-year imprisonment for "counter-revolutionary propaganda."

Wang Ming
Imprisoned: November 1996

Wang was sentenced to three years' re-education through labor for writing "Declarations on Citizens' Freedom of Speech," an open letter which called on the government to release dissidents Wei Jingsheng and Wang Dan. He is being held in Xishanping Reeducation Brigade in Sichuan Province.

Lin Hai, software entrepreneur
Imprisoned: March 25, 1998

Lin, a software entrepreneur and computer engineer, was arrested and charged with "inciting the overthrow of state power" for giving e-mail addresses of 30,000 Chinese residents to *VIP Reference*, an on-line magazine published in the United States which supports democratic reform in China. Lin was tried by the Shanghai Number One Intermediate People's Court on December 4. The four-hour trial was closed to the public. He told the court that he was innocent, and that he provided the addresses to *VIP Reference* in the hope that he could eventually exchange e-mail addresses with the magazine to build up his Internet business, according to the Hong Kong-based Information Center of Human Rights and Democratic Movement in China. *VIP Reference* used the addresses to expand its distribution of articles on human rights and democracy within mainland China. On January 20, 1999, the court announced that it had found Lin guilty and sentenced him to two years in prison.

Shi Binhai
China Economic Times
Imprisoned: September 5, 1998

Shi, an editor with the Beijing-based *China Economic Times* newspaper in Beijing, was taken from his home by National Security Ministry personnel on September 5. The Security Ministry did not give an explanation for the arrest, nor did it inform Shi's family where he was being held. A leading voice in Beijing journalism, Shi is also the editor of the best-selling book *Political China: Facing the Era of Choosing a New Structure*,

… a groundbreaking collection of 39 essays by journalists, academics, and former government officials calling for political reform. Sources in China fear that Shi was arrested as a result of his work on the book. A Shanghai native, he was imprisoned in 1989 for his role in the Tiananmen Square democracy movement. He was released in 1991. As of December 31, no charges had been announced against Shi, and he had not been tried or convicted of any crime.

Cuba (4)

Please send appeals to:
His Excellency Fidel Castro
President of Cuba
c/o Permanent Mission of Cuba to the United Nations
315 Lexington Avenue New York, NY 10016 United States
Fax: 1-212-689-9073

Lorenzo Páez Núñez, Buró de Prensa Independiente de Cuba
Imprisoned: July 10, 1997
Released: January 4, 1999

Páez Núñez, then a correspondent with the independent news agency Buró de Prensa Independiente de Cuba (BPIC), was detained on July 10, 1997, because of a report he published on the Internet about a police officer who allegedly killed a young man during harvest celebrations in Pinar del Río. Páez Núñez was convicted after a one-day trial, for which he was not permitted to have a lawyer. He was sentenced to 18 months in prison for defaming the national police. On December 19, 1997, CPJ sent a letter to the Cuban authorities, asking for information on Páez Núñez's legal status. On January 20, 1998, CPJ sent a letter asking that Páez Núñez be released. He was released on January 4, 1999.

Bernardo Rogelio Arévalo Padrón, Línea Sur Press
Imprisoned: November 18, 1997

State Security officers in Aguada de Pasajeros detained and jailed Arévalo Padrón, a correspondent with the Línea Sur Press news agency in Cienfuegos Province. He had been sentenced to six years in prison on October 31, 1997, by the Provincial Chamber of the Court of Aguada de Pasajeros, after being convicted of a "lack of respect" for President Fidel Castro and Carlos Lage, a member of the Cuban State Council. The conviction stems from a story Arévalo Padrón published on the Internet, reporting that a helicopter transported meat from a farm in Aguada de Pasajeros to Havana for Cuba's political elite, despite the fact that the people of Aguada de Pasajeros did not have enough to eat.

Arévalo Padrón is serving his sentence in Ariza Prison in Cienfuegos, where he shares a filthy cell with common criminals. On November 28, 1997, an Aguada de Pasajeros court rejected Arévalo Padrón's petition to review the conviction. On December 19, 1997, CPJ wrote to Cuban authorities inquiring about Arévalo Padrón's legal status. On January 20, 1998, CPJ again wrote to Cuban authorities, asking for Arévalo Padrón's release.

On December 19, 1998, Arévalo Padrón wrote a letter to President Castro, saying that the Spanish government had granted him a visa, and asking that he be allowed to leave Cuba.

Juan Carlos Recio Martínez, CubaPress
Imprisoned: June 15, 1998

Authorities detained Recio Martínez, correspondent for the independent news agency CubaPress in the province of Villa Clara, and interrogated him for six days. The inquiry stemmed from an incident in the fall of 1997, when Cecilio Monteagudo Sánchez, a member of the dissident Democratic Solidarity Party (PSD), asked Recio Martínez to type a leaflet calling on Cubans to abstain from voting in the local October elections. Recio Martínez refused Monteagudo's request, but did not report the incident to authorities.

Recio Martínez was questioned again on November 3, 1997. He was charged with "acts against state security," but was released pending his trial, which was set for November 25, 1997. That court date was postponed. He was tried and convicted by the People's Provincial Tribunal of Villa Clara on February 6, 1998, and sentenced to a year of correctional labor.

Recio Martínez began serving his sentence on June 15, 1998, in the Abel Santamaría agricultural cooperative in Villa Clara Province. On June 18, CPJ sent a letter to President Fidel Castro saying that even though Recio Martínez is permitted to leave the cooperative after his work is completed each day, CPJ views mandatory forced labor as a form of confinement and therefore considers Recio Martínez to be a prisoner.

Manuel Antonio González Castellanos, CubaPress
Imprisoned: October 1, 1998

State Security agents arrested González Castellanos, a correspondent for the independent news service CubaPress, on charges of "sedition" (desacato) in San Germán, Holguín Province.

According to his colleagues and relatives, González Castellanos was arrested after making critical statements about President Castro to State Security agents who had stopped him and insulted him as he was returning from a friend's house.

When family members learned of González Castellanos' detention and tried to contact him at the local police station the following morning, they were met by a group of protesters who insulted them. Relatives of the journalist were so indignant that they

Attacks on the Press in 1998

painted "Abajo Fidel" (Down with Fidel) on the walls of their house. Later that day, an estimated 2,000 people gathered outside González Castellanos' home and screamed insults. State Security agents broke into his home, and beat and arrested two of González Castellanos' relatives along with a political dissident who was also present. One of the relatives was released after a few days, but was told she could be imprisoned. According to local sources, many of the protesters who gathered in front of González Castellanos' home were farm workers who had been told they would be docked a day's pay if they did not participate in the demonstration. After the protest rally, the family's phone was cut off for nearly a week.

While the sedition charges against González Castellanos stem from an interaction that is unrelated to his journalistic work, local journalists suspect that González Castellanos was deliberately provoked by State Security agents in retaliation for news reports filed from Holguín about the activities of political dissidents. CPJ wrote a letter to President Castro on October 16, condemning the imprisonment of González Castellanos.

In July, González Castellanos was contacted by a man claiming to have information for him from a Cuban exile in Miami. When they met, the source questioned González Castellanos about his journalistic work and told him that a Cuban exile group wanted to recruit him for subversive activities. González Castellanos declined the offer and later determined that the man with whom he had met had never been in touch with the exiles in Miami he claimed to represent. González Castellanos believed the man was a State Security agent attempting to entrap him.

González Castellanos has been harassed by guards, who have confiscated a book, *Academic Journalism*, and letters. As of December, González Castellanos had not been brought before a judge.

Democratic Republic of Congo (2)

Please send appeals to:
Laurent-Désiré Kabila
President of the Republic
Ngaliema, Kinshasa
Democratic Republic of Congo
Fax: 011-243-88-02120 / 1-202-234-2609

Albert Bonsange Yema,
L'Alarme, L'Essor Africain
Imprisoned: February 7, 1998

Yema, editor of the opposition newspapers *L'Alarme* and *L'Essor Africain*, was arrested in connection with a February 7 article, published in both newspapers, calling for the release of jailed opposition leader Joseph Olengankoy.

On June 1, the State Security Court convicted Yema of "threatening state security" and sentenced him to one year in prison. He is serving his sentence in Makala Central Prison. Yema is a diabetic, and is now receiving treatment at the general hospital in Kinshasa. Yema's conviction contravenes the country's press law, which only allows for civil penalties in this case because Yema is not the author of the article in contention.

Mbakulu Pambu Diambu,
Radio-télévision Matadi (RTM)
Imprisoned: November, 1998

Diambu, president of the local chapter of the Congolese Press Union (UPC) and a broadcaster with the private station Radio-télévision Matadi (RTM), was arrested in late November and detained at the Matadi National Information Agency (ANR) offices. Diambu appeared before the Kinshasa Military Court and was charged with breaching state security for hosting an RTM television program on which he allegedly interviewed representatives of the Congolese Rally for Democracy rebel forces.

Ethiopia (12)

Please send appeals to:
His Excellency Prime Minister Meles Zenawi
Office of the Prime Minister
c/o Ministry of Foreign Affairs
Addis Ababa, Ethiopia Fax: 251-1-552-030

Sisay Negussie, *Agere*
Imprisoned: March 1997

Sisay appeared before a court on April 7, 1997, and was detained at Kerchele Prison for failing to present a bail guarantee of approximately US$600. At press time, CPJ had no further information about his status.

Samson Seyoum, *Tequami* and *Agere*
Imprisoned: April 18, 1997

Samson, former editor in chief of *Agere* and *Tequami*, was sentenced to an undisclosed prison term for "inciting war and spreading Islamic Fundamentalism," in articles he had published in *Agere*. Detained before the sentencing and unable to produce the bail of approximately US$730, Samson had just completed an 18-month prison sentence which he had begun

Attacks on the Press in 1998

in December 1995 after his conviction on charges of libel for an article in *Tequami*.

Sisay Agena, *Ethiop*
Imprisoned: September 8, 1997

Sisay, publisher of *Ethiop*, was arrested on September 8 on unknown charges, and detained. He was released on bail on September 10, but on September 16 he was taken back into custody and moved from the Region 14 Criminal Investigation Office to the Central Criminal Investigation Office Prison.

Tamrat Gemeda, *Seife Nebelbal*
Imprisoned: October 1997

Tamrat, former editor in chief of *Seife Nebelbal*, was arrested on charges of involvement with the guerrilla organization, the Oromo Liberation Front (OLF).

Tamrat Serbessa, *Wenchif*
Imprisoned: October 14, 1997

Tamrat, editor in chief of *Wenchif*, was detained at the Central Criminal Investigation Office Prison. The journalist was charged on five counts, including libel against President Negasso Gidada. This charge stemmed from a report in *Wenchif* that claimed the president was drunk at a gathering.

Tesfaye Deressa, *Urjii*
Solomon Nemera, *Urjii*
Imprisoned: October 16, 1997

Tesfaye, editor in chief of the newspaper *Urjii*, and Solomon, the paper's deputy editor, were abducted from a tea room near *Urjii*'s offices. The journalists were first detained at the Central Criminal Investigation Office Prison and were later taken to a district police prison. The two were held on charges related to a report in *Urjii* about the recent killing of alleged Oromo Liberation Front (OLF) members in the Mekanissa area. The article contradicted the government media's version of the same story.

Tesfaye and Solomon appeared three times before a district court, but the proceedings were postponed each time because of requests by police for more time to continue their investigation. After the journalists' court appearance on December 12, 1997, police said they had concluded their investigation but were awaiting the prosecutor's decision about bail. No decision had been made when Tesfaye and Solomon appeared again in court on December 19, 1997. They were scheduled for another court appearance on January 9, 1998. At press time, CPJ had no new information on their status.

Garoma Bekele, *Urjii*
Imprisoned: October 27, 1997

Garoma, publisher of the newspaper *Urjii*, was detained on suspicion of being a member of the outlawed Oromo Liberation Front (OLF). Garoma is being held at the Central Investigation Office Prison along with others who have been

IMPRISONED JOURNALISTS

detained for their alleged connection to a series of OLF bombings in Addis Ababa, Dire Dawa, and Harar. On October 31, 1997, Garoma appeared in court and made an appeal for release on bail, but was denied by the prosecutor. He was given a new court appointment for January 13, 1998. At press time, CPJ had no new information on his status.

Fisseha Alemu, *Tarik*
Imprisoned: March 24, 1998

Police arrested Fisseha, editor in chief of the Amharic-language independent weekly newspaper *Tarik*, and held him at the Ma'ekelawi Central Criminal Investigation Office.

Authorities would not provide an explanation for Fisseha's arrest, but local journalists believe it was in connection with an article published in *Tarik* on January 31 which reported that Ethiopian orthodox monks from the Tigray region were engaged in cannabis production. Fisseha was later transported to the Addis Ababa Central Prison, where he is currently being held.

Wondwossen Asfaw, *Atkurot*
Imprisoned: April 1998

Wondwossen, editor in chief of the privately owned newspaper *Atkurot*, was detained on unspecified charges at the Addis Ababa Central Prison. He remains in prison, because he was unable to post bail of 10,000 birr ($US1,500).

Tesfa Tegegn, *Beza*
Imprisoned: June 19, 1998

Tesfa, the former editor in chief of the privately owned newspaper *Beza*, was detained and held at Addis Ababa Central Prison on unspecified charges. This was Tesfa's second incarceration during 1998. He had been detained in March and was released on June 10 on bail of 2,000 birr (US$286).

Tilahun Bekele, *Fetash*
Imprisoned: September 1998

Tilahun, editor in chief of *Fetash*, was detained during the last week of September at the Ma'ekelawi Central Criminal Investigation Prison Office on charges of libel against the Crown Mineral Water Company.

Gabon (3)

Please send appeals to:
His Excellency Omar Bongo
President of the Republic of Gabon
Presidential Palace
Libreville, Gabon
Fax: 233 21 664 089

Michel Ongoundou-Loundah, *La Griffe*
Raphael Ntoutoume Nkoghe, *La Griffe*
Pulcherie Beaumel, *La Griffe*
Imprisoned: August 12, 1998

Publication director Ongoundou-Loundah, editor in chief Nkoghe, and reporter Beaumel of the private weekly *La Griffe*, were each sentenced to eight months in prison and fined 3,000,000 CFA (US$5,000) in damages and interest payable to Air Gabon Director General René Morvan. The case was in connection with an article published in a June

Attacks on the Press in 1998

issue of *La Griffe* reporting that Morvan was involved in ivory trafficking.

Iraq (1)

Please send appeals to:
President Saddam Hussein
c/o Iraqi Mission to the United Nations
14 East 79th Street
New York, NY 10021 United States

Aziz al-Syed Jasim, *Al-Ghad*
Imprisoned: April 18, 1991

Jasim, editor of *Al-Ghad* magazine and former editor of the official daily *Al-Thawra*, was taken into custody at a secret police station in Baghdad and has not been heard from since. Reports suggest that his refusal to write a book about Iraqi President Saddam Hussein precipitated his arrest. Government officials deny that he is in prison.

Kuwait (5)

Please send appeals to:
His Highness Sheikh Sa'ad al-Abdallah al-Sabah,
Crown Prince and Prime Minister
Al-Diwan al-Amiri
Al-Safat
Kuwait City, Kuwait
Telegrams to:
His Highness Sheikh Sa'ad al-Abdallah al-Sabah
Kuwait City, Kuwait Fax: +965-243-0121

Ibtisam Berto Sulaiman al-Dakhil, *Al-Nida*
Fawwaz Muhammad al-Awadi Bessisso, *Al-Nida*
Usamah Suhail Abdallah Hussein, *Al-Nida*
Abd al-Rahman Muhammad Asad al-Husseini, *Al-Nida*
Ahmad Abd Mustafa, *Al-Nida*
Sentenced: June 1991

The five journalists were given life sentences for working for the Iraqi occupation newspaper *Al-Nida*. They were taken into custody after Kuwait's liberation and charged with collaboration. The trials, which began on May 19, 1991, in martial-law courts, failed to comply with international standards of justice. The defendants were reportedly tortured during their interrogations. Their defense—that they were coerced to work for the Iraqi newspaper—was not rebutted by prosecutors. On June 16, 1991, the journalists were sentenced to death. Ten days later, following international protests, all martial-law death sentences were commuted to life terms.

Libya (1)

Please send appeals to:
Revolutionary Leader
Col. Muammar al-Qadhafi
c/o Libyan Mission to the United Nations
309-315 E. 48th St.
New York, NY 10017 United States

IMPRISONED JOURNALISTS

Abdallah Ali al-Sanussi al-Darrat
Arrested: 1974 or 1975

Al-Darrat, a journalist and writer from Benghazi, was arrested without trial. Since the time of his arrest, there has been no new information about his case.

Madagascar (2)

Please send appeals to:
President Didier Ratsirka
c/o Embassy of the Republic of Madagascar
2374 Massachusetts Avenue N.W.
Washington, D.C. 20008 United States

Harry Rahajason, *L'Express de Madagascar*
Christian Chatefaux, *L'Express de Madagascar*
Sentenced: December 28, 1998

The Magistrate Court sentenced Chatefaux and Rahajason, editor in chief and reporter, respectively, for the newspaper *L'Express de Madagascar*, to three-month prison terms for contempt of court. The contempt citation stemmed from a case filed by the public prosecutor of the Antsirabe Republic, who had sued the newspaper for allegedly insulting a magistrate in a June 1997 article. Chatefaux was sentenced for delaying the publication of the plaintiff's response to the article.

Nigeria (1)

Please send appeals to:
His Excellency General Abdulsalami Abubakar
Chairman of the Provisional Ruling Council
  and Commander in Chief of the Armed Forces
State House, Abuja
Federal Capital Territory, Nigeria
Fax: 011-234-95232

Niran Malaolu, *The Diet*
Imprisoned: December 27, 1997

A special military tribunal (SMT) in Jos arraigned Malaolu, editor of the daily newspaper *The Diet*, for alleged involvement in a coup plot. He had been arrested without charge at the paper's offices. On April 28, 1998, Malaou was tried and convicted by the tribunal for "information gathering" and "implication in the alleged coup plot of December 1997," and sentenced to life imprisonment with no right of appeal. On July 10, Malaolu's sentence was reduced to 15 years. He is currently in jail in Katsina Prison, where he is reportedly critically ill and denied medical treatment.

Peru (5)

Please send appeals to:
His Excellency Alberto K. Fujimori
President of the Republic of Peru
Palacio de Gobierno
Lima 1, Peru
Fax: 51-1-426-6770

Attacks on the Press in 1998

Javier Tuanama Valera, *Hechos*
Imprisoned: October 16, 1990

Tuanama, editor in chief of the magazine *Hechos*, was sentenced in 1992 to 15 years in prison by a "faceless" judge from the Superior Court of Lambayeque. (In Peru, "faceless" judges hide their identities to prevent reprisals by guerrilla groups.) He was first detained on October 16, 1990, and charged with having links to the rebel group Túpac Amaru Revolutionary Movement (MRTA).

Tuanama was acquitted twice of the charges in 1994. He was released, but was soon arrested again when a former member of the MRTA—acting under the Repentance Law, which allows terrorists to surrender and inform on former comrades—confessed that Tuanama had recruited him into the group. The same individual later recanted, but Tuanama remained in Picsi Prison in the northern city of Chiclayo. After a second trial, he was sentenced to 10 years in prison.

CPJ protested Tuanama's conviction in a trial that fell far below international standards of due process. In June 1995, one of Tuanama's sisters complained that his medical condition was deteriorating because he had no access to medical care for his acute arthritis. In April 1996, he was transferred to the Huacaris Prison in Cajamarca.

CPJ inquired about Tuanama's legal status in a December 22, 1997, letter to which Peruvian authorities did not reply. His case remains under review by the ad hoc commission that was established by President Alberto K. Fujimori in 1996 to examine the files of those convicted under Peru's anti-terrorism laws.

Hermes Rivera Guerrero, Radio Oriental
Imprisoned: May 8, 1992

Rivera, a reporter for Radio Oriental in Jaén Province, Cajamarca Department, was sentenced to 20 years in prison for alleged terrorist activity. Rivera reported that Idelfonso Ugarte, a policeman, originally arrested him without charge on May 8, 1992, and later brought the charges against him. Rivera's wife, Dilsia Miranda, accused the officer of demanding US$500 for the release of her husband and making uninvited sexual advances toward her. When she refused him, Miranda said, Ugarte apparently falsified evidence to show Rivera's participation in terrorist attacks.

On January 26, 1995, Rivera, who was being held at Picsi Prison in Chiclayo, sewed his mouth closed and began a three-week hunger strike to protest his sentence. On March 7, 1995, his defense lawyer appealed for a review of Rivera's case by the Supreme Court of Peru. The court overturned the 20-year sentence on September 5, 1995, and ordered a retrial.

CPJ sent a letter of inquiry on December 22, 1997, but Peruvian authorities did not provide any information on Rivera's legal status. In December 1998, his case was still under review by the ad hoc commission that was established by President Alberto K. Fujimori in 1996 to examine the files of those convicted under Peru's anti-terrorism laws.

Pedro Carranza Ugaz, Radio Oriental
Imprisoned: November 29, 1993

Carranza, a correspondent with Radio Oriental in Jaén Province, Cajamarca Department, was detained on November 29, 1993, and sentenced on November 7, 1994, to 20 years in prison for being a member of the Túpac Amaru Revolutionary Movement (MRTA). He is currently being held in Huacaris Prison in Cajamarca. In December 1998, his case remained under review by the ad hoc commission that was established by President Alberto K. Fujimori in 1996 to examine the files of those convicted under Peru's anti-terrorism laws.

Augusto Ernesto Llosa Giraldo,
***El Casmeno*, Radio Casma**
Imprisoned: February 14, 1995

Llosa, editor in chief of the newspaper *El Casmeno* and a reporter with Radio Casma, was arrested in the northern city of Casma and charged with involvement in a 1986 terrorist incident in Cuzco, where he was staying in a hotel at the time. Police raided his home and confiscated several documents, including National Association of Journalists (ANP) posters urging the release of several detained journalists, and an issue of ANP's newsletter.

A secret tribunal of the Fifth Criminal Chamber of the Superior Court of Cuzco convicted Llosa, and he was sentenced to six years in prison on August 1, 1995. Three weeks after the verdict, he was unexpectedly transferred to the maximum security Yanamayo Prison. Llosa petitioned the Supreme Court for the nullification of his sentence and was granted a retrial. On June 30, 1997, he was convicted again and sentenced to five years in prison. Llosa again requested the sentence be nullified.

CPJ sent a letter inquiring about Llosa's legal status on December 22, 1997, but received no response. In December 1998, his case was still under review by the ad hoc commission that was established by President Alberto K. Fujimori in 1996 to examine the files of those convicted under Peru's anti-terrorism laws.

Johny Eduardo Pezo Tello,
Doble A
Imprisoned: November 20, 1998

Pezo Tello, a news program host on radio station Doble A in Yurimaguas, Alto Amazonas Province, Loreto Department, was jailed on charges of terrorism for reading a letter sent by the Túpac Amaru Revolutionary Movement (MRTA) on the air on November 17.

Pezo Tello, host of several news programs and a music show, received a phone call during his music show on November 17 from a man identifying himself as Comrade

Attacks on the Press in 1998

Rolando of the MRTA. The caller ordered Pezo Tello to read a letter that the MRTA had sent to the radio station, and threatened to harm Pezo Tello and his family if he refused.

Pezo Tello left the radio station, intending to report the threats to the police, but two men who were waiting outside the station cautioned him to heed the caller's demand. After apologizing to the audience and declaring his opposition to MRTA's principles, Pezo Tello read the press release on the air.

On November 19, officers from the National Anti-Terrorism Agency (DINCOTE) arrived at the radio station and took him to the Yurimaguas police station, where they interrogated him. Pezo Tello was summoned to the police station to present a more detailed statement the next day, which he did. On the basis of his testimony, the DINCOTE officers issued a formal statement on November 21, accusing him of supporting terrorism.

On November 21, Pezo Tello was taken before Provincial Attorney Marco Tulio Correa Sánchez, who confirmed the DINCOTE accusation and charged him with having made a statement supporting terrorism. The same day, Yurimaguas Provincial Judge Hugo Zela Campos found there was sufficient evidence to initiate proceedings against Pezo Tello and ordered his arrest. Pezo Tello was transferred from the police station, where he had spent the night of November 20, to the Yurimaguas prison.

CPJ wrote to President Alberto K. Fujimori on December 16, urging Pezo Tello's release.

On December 23, Judge Zela ruled that the charge against Pezo Tello was unwarranted. Because the charge involved terrorism, however, the case was transferred to the Superior Court of Lambayeque for adjudication. The court dismissed the charges and Pezo Tello was released on January 18, 1999.

Russia (2)

Please send appeals to:
President Boris Yeltsin
The Kremlin
Moscow, Russian Federation
Fax: 011-7-095-206-5173; 206-6277

Grigory Pasko, *Boyevaya Vakhta*
Imprisoned: November 20, 1997

Pasko, a military officer of the Russian Pacific Fleet and a correspondent for *Boyevaya Vakhta*, was arrested on November 20, 1997, and jailed in Vladivostok for allegedly passing classified information to foreign agents. The charges stemmed from a series of articles and reports by Pasko in the military newspaper *Boyevaya Vakhta*, in Japan's *Asahi* daily, and on the NHK television company of Tokyo that discussed the environmental hazards caused by Russia's decaying nuclear submarine fleet. Pasko was arrested at Vladivostok airport after returning from Japan. Federal Security Bureau (FSB) agents searched his apartment and confiscated documents he had gathered for his investigation, as well as cassettes, books, and his computer.

Although offficials admit that none of the confiscated documents were classified, they claim the series of reports as a whole, published and aired over a three-year period, posed a threat to Russia's national security. The FSB classified the case as a state secret, making it difficult for Pasko's attorneys to mount a proper defense.

On October 14, 1998, a Pacific Fleet naval court in Vladivostok began a closed trial against Pasko, on charges of high treason and revealing state secrets. Pasko's lawyers moved that he be released from custody during the trial. The three presiding judges immediately postponed the proceedings and sent the motion to the Military Board of the Supreme Court in Moscow for review. That court rejected the motion on November 26, and Pasko thus remains in custody. He faces up to 20 years in prison if convicted.

Altaf Galeyev, Radio Titan
Imprisoned: May 27, 1998

On May 27, 1998, Bashkir police raided the Ufa offices of Radio Titan, the sole independent radio station in the Republic of Bashkortostan, beating and arresting staff members and supporters. Police seized the radio equipment and detained the entire staff, including Galeyev, the manager and news director, and Lilia Ismagilova, the station's executive director. These official reprisals came shortly after Radio Titan aired interviews with three opposition candidates who were barred from the June 14 presidential elections.

Ismagilova and the other staff members were released the next day, but Galeyev was held for firing several shots in the air when police stormed the station's office. On June 4, he was formally charged with "hooliganism" and the illegal use of firearms under Article 213(3) of the Bashkir penal code. Following his arrest, Galeyev was placed in a pre-trial detention center in Ufa. If found guilty, he faces a possible prison sentence of four to seven years. Galeyev, who is in poor health, was allowed to see a lawyer, but no court hearing was held.

Attacks on the Press in 1998

On January 5, 1999, a hearing took place to determine whether Galeyev would be released until his trial began. The judge ruled that he must remain in detention. His trial was scheduled to begin on January 21, 1999, but was postponed at the request of Galeyev's lawyer. A new date has yet to be set.

Sierra Leone (11)

Please send appeals to:
President Ahmed Tejan Kabbah
State House
Freetown, Sierra Leone
Fax: 232-22-225-615

Dennis Smith, Sierra Leone Broadcasting Service (SLBS)
Gipu Felix George, SLBS
Olivia Mensah, SLBS
Maada Maka Swaray, SLBS
William Smith, *We Yone*
Hilton File, WBIG-FM103
Ibrahim B. Kargbo, *Citizen*
Imprisoned: February 1998

Sierra Leone Broadcasting Service (SLBS) broadcaster Dennis Smith; SLBS director George; SLBS newscaster Mensah; SLBS newscaster Swaray; and *We Yone* reporter William Smith, appeared in Magistrate Court Number One, presided over by Judge Claudia Taylor. The case was postponed until April 6 because all the defendants were not in court. On April 14, Kargbo, managing editor of the newspaper *Citizen*, and File, owner and managing director of WBIG-FM103 and a former British Broadcasting Corporation Network Africa correspondent, were charged with treason in the Magistrate's Court.

On August 23, File, George, Dennis Smith, Mensah, and Kargbo, along with 11 other Sierra Leonean citizens, were found guilty of treason for collaborating with the ousted Armed Forces Ruling Council (AFRC) junta. On August 24, after a four-month trial, Justice Redmond Cowan sentenced the five journalists to death by hanging. The journalists have appealed the sentences. At year's end, Swaray and William Smith were still awaiting sentencing.

Mildred Hancile, Sierra Leone Broadcasting Service (SLBS)
Conrad Roy, *Expo Times*
Mano Mbompa Turay, *Eagle*
Amadu Jalloh, *Liberty Voice*
Imprisoned: February 1998

Hancile, a reporter and production assistant with SLBS; Roy, an editor with the newspaper *Expo Times;* Turay, editor of the now-defunct newspaper *Eagle*; and Jalloh, a senior journalist with the newspaper *Liberty Voice*, appeared in Magistrate's Court to face charges ranging from treason and aiding and abetting the enemy, to conspiring to overthrow a legally constituted government.

Somalia (1)

Please send appeals to:
Mohamed Ibrahim Egal
President of the Republic of Somaliland
State House of Somaliland
Fax: 252-213-3414

Hassan Said Yusuf, *Jamhurya*
Imprisoned: May 25, 1998

Police arrested Yusuf, chief editor of the independent daily newspaper *Jamhurya*, for "insulting important personalities, circulating false information and criticizing the leaders of the republic."

Yusuf was arrested in connection with several articles published in June, July, and September 1997, and on February 2, March 1, and March 31, 1998. Included were articles about a dispute between the army and the government; about the outbreak of a Rift Valley disease that was later denied; about 33 punitive amputations ordered by an Islamic court in the town of Buro; and about remarks concerning the prosecutor general and officials of the justice system.

South Korea (2)

Please send appeals to:
President Kim Dae Jung
The Blue House
#1 Sejong-no,
Chongno-gu
Seoul, Republic of Korea
Fax: 822-770-0253

Ham Yun Shik, *One Way*
Imprisoned: February 28, 1998

Ham, publisher of *One Way* magazine, was charged with criminal defamation by President Kim Dae Jung's political party, the National Congress for New Politics (NCNP), as a result of highly critical articles regarding Kim's background and political ideology published in the magazine in 1997 during the presidential campaign. On July 2, a Seoul court sentenced Ham to one year in prison for criminal defamation.

Son Chung Mu, *Inside the World*
Imprisoned: June 1, 1998

Son, the publisher of *Inside the World* magazine, was arrested on June 1. Prosecutors charged Son with criminal defamation and accepting a bribe from former Agency for National Security Planning (NSP) chief Kwon Young Hae to slander then-presidential candidate Kim Dae Jung during the 1997 campaign. Son had also been charged with related "crimes against reputation" in February by the public prosecutor's office but was not arrested at the time. The charges were brought by the National Congress for New Politics (NCNP), President Kim Dae Jung's political party, in the aftermath of his victory in the December 1997 elections. The party took exception to articles published in Son's magazine in 1997 as well as a book he wrote during the 1997 election campaign, *Kim Dae Jung: X-File*, all of which were highly critical of Kim. On September 23, Son was found guilty of criminal libel and sentenced to

Attacks on the Press in 1998

two years in prison. The charge that he accepted a bribe to slander Kim and thereby thwart his election was dropped.

Syria (8)

Please send appeals to:
His Excellency Hafez al-Assad
President
c/o His Excellency Ambassador Walid Al-Moualem
Embassy of the Syrian Arab Republic
2215 Wyoming Avenue, N.W.
Washington, D.C. 20008 United States
Fax: 202-234-9548

Qaiss Darwish, *Al Ka'ayda*
Imprisoned: August 1984

Darwish, a journalist with the magazine *Al Ka'ayda*, was arrested by military security agents in August 1984 and later sentenced to 15 years in prison for alleged membership in the Party for Communist Action. He is in Sednaya Prison.

Faisal Allush
Imprisoned: 1985

Allush, a journalist and political writer who has been in jail since 1985, was sentenced in June 1993 to 15 years' imprisonment for membership in the banned Party for Communist Action. He is reportedly being held in Sednaya Prison.

Anwar Bader, Syrian Radio and Television
Imprisoned: December 1986

Bader, a reporter for Syrian Radio and Television, who has been in jail since his arrest by the Military Interrogation Branch in December 1986, was convicted in March 1994 of being a member in the Party for Communist Action. He was sentenced to 12 years in prison.

Samir al-Hassan, *Fatah al-Intifada*
Imprisoned: April 1986

Al-Hassan, Palestinian editor of *Fatah al-Intifada*, who has been in jail since his arrest in April 1986, was convicted in June 1994 of being a member of the Party for Communist Action. He was sentenced to 15 years in prison.

Marwan Mohammed, *Al-Baath*
Imprisoned: October 18, 1987

Mohammed, a technician and journalist with the official *Al-Baath*, was arrested by military security agents on October 18, 1987. He was convicted and sentenced in 1993 to 10 years in prison for alleged membership in the Party for Communist Action. He is currently in Sednaya Prison.

Nou'man Abdo, *Al-Tariq*
Imprisoned: 1992

Abdo, a journalist working with the magazine *Al-Tariq* (organ of the Lebanese Communist Party), was arrested sometime in 1992 and later convicted and sentenced in 1993 to 15 years in prison for alleged membership in the Party for Communist Action (PAC). He is currently in Tadmour Prison.

Nizar Nayyouf, *Sawt al-Democratiyya*
Imprisoned: January 1992

Nayyouf, a former free-lance journalist, leading member of the independent Committees for the Defense of Democratic Freedoms and Human Rights in Syria (CDF) and editor in chief of its monthly *Sawt al-Democratiyya*, was arrested in January 1992 and later convicted by the Supreme State Security Court of membership in an unauthorized organization and of disseminating false information. He was tortured during his interrogation.

CPJ learned in September 1998 that Nayyouf, who is serving a 10-year sentence in solitary confinement in Mezze military prison, was gravely ill and faced death unless he received immediate treatment for Hodgkins disease. Syrian authorities have refused him treatment unless he pledges to refrain from political activity and renounces alleged "false statements" he made about the human rights situation in Syria.

Salama George Kila
Imprisoned: March 1992

Kila, a Palestinian writer and journalist, was arrested in March 1992 by Political Security in Damascus. His trial began in the summer of 1993. According to the London-based International PEN, Kila had "reportedly written an article on censorship in Syria for a Jordanian daily paper." The court ruled that he was guilty of a misdemeanor rather than a felony. Since the maximum sentence for a misdemeanor is three years, his release was expected in March 1995. But he remains in prison.

Togo (2)

Please send appeals to:
His Excellency President Gnassingbe Eyadéma
Office of the President
Lomé, Togo
Fax: 011-228-21-20-40

Elias Hounkali, *Le Nouveau Combat*
August 6, 1998

National police arrested and detained Augustin Asionbo and Pamphile Gnimassou, editors in chief of the privately owned *Tingo Tingo* and *Abito*, respectively, and Hounkali, a reporter with the privately owned weekly *Le Nouveau Combat*, for "attacking the honour" of the president and his wife.

The arrests follow the publication in the August 6 edition of *Le Nouveau Combat*, of articles titled "The Widow Mrs. Bobi Mobutu Demands Mrs. Badagnaki Eyadéma Return Her 17 Trunks of Jewelry Missing in Lomé," and "Eyadéma Fishes For a Letter of Congratulations from Chirac." Assionbo was exonerated and released on August 8. Gnimassou was released on an unspecified date. Hounkali remains in prison.

Attacks on the Press in 1998

Edoh Amewouho, *Le Nouveau Combat*
November 10, 1998

Amewouho, a reporter with the privately owned weekly newspaper *Le Nouveau Combat*, was arrested and taken to the Lomé National Police Station. The following day, he was transferred to Lomé Prison. The arrest was in connection with the publication of two articles in the August 6-13 edition of the newspaper titled, "The Widow Mrs. Bobi Mobutu Demands Mrs. Badagnaki Eyadéma Return Her 17 Trunks of Jewelery Missing in Lomé," and "Eyadéma Fishes For A Letter of Congratulations from Chirac."

Tunisia (2)

Please send appeals to:
M. Zine El Abidine Ben Ali
President of the Republic of Tunisia
Presidential Palace
Tunis, Tunisia
Fax: 216-1-744-721

Hamadi Jebali, *Al-Fajr*
Imprisoned: January 1991

Jebali, editor of *Al-Fajr*, the weekly newspaper of the banned Islamist Al-Nahda party, was sentenced to 16 years in prison by the military court in Bouchoucha on August 28, 1992. He was tried along with 279 others accused of belonging to Al-Nahda. Jebali was convicted of "aggression with the intention of changing the nature of the state" and "membership in an illegal organization." During his testimony, Jebali denied the charges against him and displayed evidence that he had been tortured while in custody. Jebali has been in jail since January 1991, when he was sentenced to one year in prison after *Al-Fajr* published an article calling for the abolition of military courts in Tunisia. International human rights groups monitoring the mass trial concluded that it fell far below international standards of justice.

Abdellah Zouari, *Al-Fajr*
Imprisoned: February 1991

Zouari, a contributor to *Al-Fajr*, the weekly newspaper of the banned Islamist Al-Nahda party, was sentenced to 11 years in prison by the military court in Bouchoucha on August 28, 1992. He was tried along with 279 others accused of belonging to Al-Nahda. He has been in jail since February 1991, when he was charged with "association with an unrecognized organization." International human rights groups monitoring the trial concluded that it fell far short of international standards of justice.

Turkey (27)

Please send appeals to:
His Excellency Bulent Ecevit, Prime Minister
The Republic of Turkey, Basbakanlik
06573 Ankara, Turkey

IMPRISONED JOURNALISTS

Sinan Yavuz, *Yoksul Halkin Gücü*
Imprisoned: August 9, 1993

Yavuz, editor of the left-wing weekly *Yoksul Halkin Gücü*, was arrested during a police raid on an Istanbul fabric shop. Police reportedly had been told that the shop served as a front and arms-trafficking station for Devrimci Sol (Dev Sol), an outlawed leftist organization responsible for numerous armed terrorist operations in Turkey. The charges under which Yavuz was prosecuted show that he was alleged to be a member of Dev Sol, apparently on the basis of his affiliation with *Yoksul Halkin Gücü*, which the state asserts is Dev Sol's publishing arm. The evidence against Yavuz consisted of unspecified "documents" relating to Dev Sol and two copies of the magazine *Kurtulus* (a legal, far-left publication), which had allegedly been discovered during a search of the fabric shop. Yavuz was alleged to have resisted arrest after attempting to flee during the raid. He had been detained on previous occasions but released for lack of evidence.

Yavuz confessed to nothing in police custody, but the prosecution said that other members of Dev Sol who were detained in the same roundup stated that Yavuz was a member of the group. According to court documents, Yavuz waved a Dev Sol banner in the courtroom during his trial. He was convicted, sentenced on December 29, 1994, to 12 years and six months in jail, and sent to Canakkale Prison.

Hüseyin Solak, *Mücadele*
Imprisoned: October 27, 1993

Solak, the Gaziantep bureau chief of the socialist magazine *Mücadele*, was arrested and charged under Article 168/2 of the Penal Code with membership in Dev Sol, an outlawed underground leftist organization responsible for numerous terrorist operations in Turkey. He was convicted on the strength of statements from a witness who said he had seen Solak distributing *Mücadele*.

Transcripts of Solak's trial indicate the prosecution witness also testified that Solak had hung unspecified banners in public, and had served as a lookout while members of Dev Sol threw a Molotov cocktail at a bank in Gaziantep. The prosecution also cited "illegal" documents found after searches of Solak's home and office. Solak confessed to the charges while in police custody, but recanted in court.

Solak was convicted of violating Article 168/2 of the Penal Code and sentenced on November 24, 1994, to 12 years and six months in prison. He is in Cankiri Prison.

Ismail Besikçi
Imprisoned: November 13, 1993

Besikçi, a prominent scholar and author of numerous books and articles on the Kurds in Turkey, was arrested and charged on November 13, 1993, with violating the Anti-Terror Law for an article he wrote in the now-defunct daily *Yeni Ülke*. He was tried, convicted, and sentenced to one year in prison. Since this initial conviction, Besikçi has been prosecuted and convicted in other cases for articles he published on the Kurdish question in the now-defunct pro-Kurdish daily *Özgür Gündem*, and for books he has written on the subject. By the end of 1997, he had been sentenced to more than 100 years in prison. He is in Bursa Prison, with additional charges pending against him.

Hasan Özgün, *Özgür Gündem*
Imprisoned: December 9, 1993

Özgün, a Diyarbakir correspondent for the now-defunct pro-Kurdish daily *Özgür Gündem*, was arrested during a police raid on the paper's Diyarbakir bureau on December 9, 1993, and charged under Article 168 of the Penal Code with being a member of the outlawed Kurdistan Workers' Party (PKK).

Transcripts of Özgün's trial show that the prosecution based its case on what it described as *Özgür Gündem*'s pro-PKK slant and followed a pattern of state harassment of journalists affiliated with the publication. The prosecution also used as evidence copies of the banned PKK publications *Serkhabun* and *Berxehun* found in Özgün's possession, as well as photographs and biographical sketches of PKK members found in the newspaper's archive. The state also cited Özgün's possession of an unauthorized handgun as evidence of his membership in the PKK.

In his defense, Özgün maintained that the PKK publications were used as sources of information for newspaper articles, and that the photos of PKK members found in the archive were related to interviews the newspaper had conducted. Özgün admitted to purchasing the gun on the black market, but denied all other charges.

The Ministry of Justice replied to CPJ's request for information on Özgün's case saying that, "In fact, Mr. Özgün had extensive ties to the PKK terrorist organization. Accordingly, he was convicted of the following charges: being an active member of the PKK terrorist organization; being a courier for the PKK's mountain team; inciting the public to participate in propaganda activities organized by the PKK; informing the PKK of rich locals who could be targeted for extortion and ransom schemes organized by the organization; supplying food and medicine for the members of the PKK terrorist organization; carrying a gun without a license; providing arms for PKK mountain teams; distributing separatist propaganda material on behalf of the PKK terrorist organization." Özgün is currently in Aydin Prison.

Serdar Gelir, *Mücadele*

Gelir, Ankara bureau chief for the weekly socialist magazine

Imprisoned: April 25, 1994

Mücadele, was detained on April 16, 1994, and arrested and imprisoned 10 days later, charged with being a member of an illegal organization.

During his trial, the prosecution introduced into evidence a handwritten note—written on a copy of the weekly socialist magazine *Kurtulus*—found in Gelir's possession, which discussed local elections. Excerpts from the note said that "the state has held elections in Kurdistan by force, with the force of 150,000 soldiers. The state has shown that it can hold elections in this region by blood. By disqualifying the representatives of the Kurdish people, by massacring the Kurdish people, that [sic] the state can get the results it wants from the elections."

The prosecution also claimed that Gelir had handwritten a four-page document that discussed revolution, colonialism, and armed struggle. Prosecutors further alleged that Gelir had attended an illegal demonstration and distributed copies of the magazine. This was cited as proof of his membership in Dev Yol, an outlawed organization. They said that Gelir had confessed to the accusations in police custody but later recanted.

In his defense, Gelir said that he was covering the demonstration for *Mücadele*, and his lawyer added that Gelir had filed a story on the event. Gelir said that he had been detained on April 6 and held for 16 days, but was released due to lack of evidence. On April 25, he was arrested again and then charged. Gelir cited the Turkish government's hostility toward the press.

The Ministry of Justice told CPJ that Gelir was charged and convicted under Article 168/2 of the Penal Code and Article 5 of the Anti-Terror Law 3713 and sentenced to 15 years imprisonment by the Ankara State Security Court for being a member of an armed, illegal leftist organization (Revolutionary Left/Dev Sol). Court records, however, indicate that he was sentenced to 12 years and six months and confined in Ankara Closed Prison. According to Gelir's lawyer, the Court of Cassation had quashed the verdict against him due to procedural errors. He is set to be re-retried under the same article. He is currently in Bartin Prison.

Utku Deniz Sirkeci, *Tavir*
Imprisoned: August 6, 1994

Sirkeci, the Ankara bureau chief of the leftist cultural magazine *Tavir*, was arrested and charged under Article 168/2 of the Penal Code with membership in the outlawed organization Dev Sol.

Court records from his trial show that the state accused Sirkeci of throwing a Molotov cocktail at a bank in Ankara, but the documents do not stipulate what evidence was intro-

Attacks on the Press in 1998

duced to support the allegation. Prosecutors also cited Sirkeci's attendance at the funeral of a Dev Sol activist to support the charge that he was a member of the organization.

In his defense, Sirkeci said he attended the funeral in his capacity as a journalist. He provided detailed testimony of his torture at the hands of police, who he alleged coerced him to confess. He was convicted and sentenced to 12 years and six months in prison and confined to Ankara Closed Prison.

Aysel Bölücek, *Mücadele*
Imprisoned: October 11, 1994

Bölücek, a correspondent in Ankara for the weekly socialist magazine *Mücadele*, was arrested at her home and charged under Article 168/2 of the Penal Code, based on information the police had obtained and on a handwritten document allegedly linking her to the outlawed organization Dev Sol. She has been in prison since her arrest.

Court documents from her trial show the state also used as evidence the October 8, 1994, issue of *Mücadele* to support its argument that the weekly was the publication of Dev Sol. The prosecutor said that the October 8 issue insulted security forces and state officials, and praised Dev Sol guerrillas who had been killed in clashes with security forces.

The defense argued that it was illegal for the defendant to be tried twice for the same crime. (Earlier in 1994, Bölücek had been acquitted of a charge of membership in Dev Sol for which the primary evidence had been the same handwritten document.) The defense accepted the claim that Bölücek had written the document, but said that she was forced under torture to write it while in police custody. The defense also said that a legal publication could not be used as evidence, and that the individuals who made incriminating statements about Bölücek to the police had done so under torture and subsequently recanted. Bölücek was convicted of membership in an outlawed organization and sentenced to 12 years and six months in prison on December 23, 1994. She is being held in Canakkale Prison.

Özlem Türk, *Mücadele*
Imprisoned: January 17, 1995

Türk, a reporter in Samsun for the weekly socialist magazine *Mücadele*, was arrested at a relative's home and charged with violating Article 169 of the Penal Code for alleged membership in the outlawed Revolutionary People's Liberation Party-Front.

Court documents from her trial state that the prosecution's evidence included the fact that Türk collected money for *Mücadele*, as well as a handwritten autobiography allegedly found in the home of a member of the Revolutionary People's Liberation Party-Front. Two people testified that she was a member of the group.

Türk maintained that the money she had collected came from sales of copies of *Mücadele*. Türk said she was forced to confess to the charges under torture. The only material evidence presented at the trial were copies of legal publications—*Mücadele*, *Tavir*, and *Devrimci Genclik*—found at her home, and copies of her alleged autobiography. Police provided expert testimony to authenticate the incriminating document.

According to court documents, Türk was convicted under Article 168/2 of the Penal Code and sentenced to 15 years in prison. She is in Canakkale Prison.

Baris Yildirim, *Tavir*
Imprisoned: March 21, 1995

Yildirim, a columnist for the leftist cultural magazine *Tavir*, was arrested, charged, and subsequently tried and convicted under Article 168 of the Penal Code for membership in the outlawed organization Dev Sol, but interviews with his colleagues in 1996 indicated that his conviction was based largely on the fact that he worked for *Tavir*.

At his trial in the State Security Court, the prosecution introduced statements of informants who said that Yildirim was a spokesman for the organization, and that he had taken part in throwing Molotov cocktails and hanging banners around Izmir on orders from the organization. The prosecution alleged that Yildirim had participated in the break-in at the center-right True Path Party's Izmir offices.

Yildirim was convicted on December 17, 1996, and sentenced to 12 years and six months in prison. He is being held in Buca Prison in Izmir.

Burhan Gardas, *Mücadele*
Imprisoned: March 23, 1995

Gardas, the Ankara bureau chief for the weekly socialist magazine *Mücadele*, has been the target of several prosecutions since 1994 relating to his work as a journalist. Court records state that Gardas was arrested on January 12, 1994, at his office and charged with violating Article 168/2 of the Penal Code. During a search of the premises, the police reportedly found four copies of "news bulletins" of the outlawed organization Dev Sol. The prosecution also said that police found banners with left-wing slogans and photographs of Dev Sol militants who had been killed in clashes with security forces. The prosecution said that when Gardas was taken into custody he shouted anti-state slogans and that he was using *Mücadele*'s office for Dev Sol activities.

Gardas denied all charges. His attorney argued that the confiscated illegal publications were part of the magazine's archive, and that Gardas had been tortured while in detention. His lawyer presented a medical report to document the torture. Gardas was released on May 14, 1994, pending the outcome of his trial.

While awaiting the verdict in the 1994 prosecution, Gardas was arrested on March 23, 1995, when police raided the office of the weekly socialist magazine *Kurtulus*, the successor to *Mücadele*, where he was the Ankara bureau chief. The new charge was violating Article 168/2 of the Penal Code. During the raid, police seized three copies of *Kurtulus* "news bulletins" and six articles from *Kurtulus* discussing illegal rallies.

Court documents from his second trial, which was held at the Number 2 State Security Court of Ankara, reveal that the prosecution's evidence against Gardas consisted of his refusal to talk during a police interrogation—allegedly a Dev Sol policy—and his possession of publications which the prosecution contended were the mouthpieces of outlawed organizations, including *Mücadele* and *Kurtulus*. The state also introduced the statements of Ali Han, who worked at *Kurtulus*' Ankara bureau, saying that Gardas was a Dev Sol member. Gardas denied the claim, and his lawyer argued that his silence during police interrogation was a constitutional right and proved nothing.

On July 4, 1995, the Number 1 State Security Court of Ankara sentenced Gardas to 15 years in prison on the 1994 charge. In 1996, he was convicted and sentenced to an additional 15 years on the second set of charges. He has thus been convicted twice of membership in Dev Sol, each time based on his work as a journalist. Gardas is reportedly serving successive sentences at Aydin Prison.

Necla Can, *Kurtulus*
Imprisoned: April 9, 1995

Can, a reporter for the leftist weekly *Kurtulus*, was arrested and imprisoned after she attended a political dissident's funeral in her capacity as a journalist.

Can was tried along with 19 other alleged members of the outlawed Revolutionary People's Liberation Party-Front (DHKP-C)—formerly known as Dev Sol—for violating Article 168/2 of the Penal Code. Trial documents obtained in December 1997 state that Can was apprehended by police at her home on April 9, 1995, after two people told authorities that Can was a member of DHKP-C. The two informants later recanted.

Can's lawyer told CPJ that the basis for the charge against her had been her attendance at the funeral of a DHKP-C member. In Can's defense, her lawyer said that she had been there as a journalist. The lawyer also said that Can had testified in court to being beaten while in custody.

Can was convicted on December 21, 1997, and sentenced to 12 years and six months in prison. She is in Istanbul's Umraniye Prison.

Özgür Güdenoglu, *Mücadele*
Imprisoned: May 24, 1995

Güdenoglu, Konya bureau chief of the socialist weekly magazine *Mücadele*, was arrested, charged, tried, and convicted under Article 168 of the Penal Code. He was sentenced to 12 years and six months in prison for alleged membership in the outlawed organization Dev Sol. His prosecution is part of the state's long-standing pattern of harassment of *Mücadele*. He is in Nigde Prison.

Bülent Öner, *Atilim*
Imprisoned: June 15, 1995

Öner, a reporter for the now-defunct weekly socialist newspaper *Atilim*, was taken into custody during a police raid on the newspaper's Mersin bureau on June 15, 1995, and, according to court documents, formally charged with membership in the outlawed Marxist-Leninist Communist Party (MLKP) on June 24 under Article 168 of the Penal Code.
Investigators reportedly found numerous unspecified "documents" linking Öner to the MLKP. At his trial, two witnesses testified for the state, which asserted that *Atilim* was the publication of the MLKP and further accused Öner of writing and distributing unspecified declarations of the group. According to court documents, the prosecutor stated that banners depicting a "disappeared" political activist were found in Öner's office. Öner was convicted and sentenced to 12 years and six months in jail and sent to Erzurum Prison. He is currently in Gaziantep Prison.

Fatma Harman, *Atilim*
Imprisoned: June 15, 1995

Harman, a reporter for the now-defunct weekly socialist newspaper *Atilim*, was taken into custody during a police raid on the newspaper's Mersin bureau in June 15, 1995, along with Bülent Öner, also a reporter for *Atilim*.

Harman was formally arrested on June 24, 1995, and charged with violating Article 168 of the Penal Code for alleged membership in the outlawed Marxist-Leninist Communist Party (MLKP). *Atilim*'s lawyer reports that the prosecution based its case on the argument that *Atilim* was the publication of that group. The prosecution introduced copies of *Atilim* found in Harman's possession as evidence of her affiliation with the MLKP, and said that several unspecified banners were found in the *Atilim* office. The prosecution also alleged that Harman and Öner both lived in a house belonging to the MLKP. She was convicted and sentenced on January 26, 1996, to 12 years and six months in prison, and confined to Adana Prison.

Attacks on the Press in 1998

Erdal Dogan, *Alinteri*
Imprisoned: July 10, 1995

Dogan, an Ankara reporter for the now-defunct socialist weekly *Alinteri*, was detained by police on July 10, 1995. He was charged with violating Article 168/2 of the Penal Code, for alleged membership in the outlawed Turkish Revolutionary Communist Union (TIKB).

Court papers from his trial indicate that the prosecution argued that *Alinteri* was the publication of the TIKB. The case against Dogan was based on the following evidence: 1) a photograph of Dogan, taken at a 1992 May Day parade, allegedly showing him standing underneath a United Revolutionary Trade Union banner; 2) a photograph of Dogan taken on the anniversary of a TIKB militant's death; 3) a photograph alleged to show Dogan attending an illegal demonstration in Ankara; 4) a statement of an alleged member of the TIKB, who said Dogan belonged to the organization. The defense claimed that the incriminating statement was extracted under torture. Dogan's lawyer told CPJ that the photograph from the militant's memorial was blurry, and Dogan testified in court that he had attended the May Day parade as a journalist. He was convicted and sentenced to 12 years and six months in prison, and was initially confined to Bursa Prison. He is currently in Sakarya Prison.

Sadik Çelik, *Kurtulus*
Imprisoned: December 23, 1995

Although Çelik, Zonguldak bureau chief for the leftist weekly *Kurtulus*, was detained and charged with violating Article 168/2 of the Penal Code for alleged membership in the outlawed Revolutionary People's Liberation Party-Front (DHKP-C), the state's case rested almost exclusively on his activities as a reporter and Zonguldak bureau chief for *Kurtulus*.

Court documents from his trial state that Çelik was detained on December 23, 1995. The prosecution said that *Kurtulus* was the publication of the DHKP-C, and that Çelik's position with the magazine proved he was a member of the group. Çelik was accused of conducting "seminars" for the DHKP-C at the magazine's office, propagandizing for the organization, transporting copies of the magazine from Istanbul to Zonguldak by bus, and organizing the magazine's distribution in Zonguldak. The prosecution said that Çelik's name appeared in a document written by a leader of the DHKP-C (it is not clear whether the document was introduced as material evidence). The prosecution also said Çelik's refusal to testify in police custody proved his guilt.

The defense argued that the prosecution could not substantiate any of its claims. Çelik acknowledged distributing the magazine in his capacity as *Kurtulus*' bureau chief. He said that he held meetings in the office to discuss matters pertaining to the magazine. The defense presented the statements of two *Kurtulus* reporters, corroborating Çelik's statements.

Çelik was convicted and sentenced on October 17, 1996, to 12 years and six months in prison. Court documents indicate that he was sent to Ankara Closed Prison.

Erhan Il, *Devrimci Emek*
Imprisoned: February 16, 1996

Il was a reporter for the now-defunct far-left magazine *Devrimci Emek*, and had previously been its editor in chief from 1993 to 1994. Court documents state that Il was arrested and charged under Article 168/2 of the Penal Code for alleged membership in the Turkish Communist Leninist Labor Party's (TKEP-L) youth organization. The prosecution also alleged that he rented a house in December 1994 for the TKEP-L, stored weapons for the organization, and possessed a counterfeit I.D.

Il's colleagues at *Devrimci Emek* told CPJ that he was prosecuted on the basis of articles published in the magazine during his tenure as editor. In response to an inquiry from CPJ, the Ministry of Justice stated that Il was convicted "according to amended Article 8/1 of the Anti-Terror Law [disseminating separatist propaganda], and not according to Article 168 of the Penal Code[.]" He is in Byrampasa Prison.

Ibrahim Çiçek, *Atilim*
Imprisoned: March 15, 1996

Çiçek, former editor in chief of the leftist weekly *Atilim*, testified at his trial that he was detained on March 15, 1996, on his way to his father's home, and his wife was detained the following day at their home. Çiçek was charged under Article 168 of the Penal Code with alleged membership in an illegal organization, but his lawyer said that the only evidence against Çiçek was his affiliation with *Atilim*, which the state asserted was the mouthpiece of the Marxist-Leninist Communist Party (MLKP).

According to the Ministry of Justice, Çiçek "was taken into custody in relation to the armed attack carried out by the MLKP illegal leftist organization against government office buildings in the Sultanbeyli district of Istanbul as well as the offices of the MHP political party in the same district around 1 a.m. on March 14, 1996. The incident prompted the decision of the Istanbul State Security Court to detain Çiçek with his collaborators on March 29, 1996. Currently, he is in Bayrampasa Prison in Istanbul."

Court documents show that Çiçek was charged with being a leader of the MLKP (Article 168/1 of the Penal Code)—specifically, of ordering an armed assault on the offices of an ultra-right-wing party in Istanbul—and of running *Atilim*. The prosecutor introduced as evidence a story

Attacks on the Press in 1998

from *Atilim*'s March 23, 1996, issue about the assault on the ultra-right-wing party. Two people gave statements to authorities implicating Çiçek. According to the defense, Çiçe said that he was tortured by police, but made no confession. He was convicted and sentenced to a minimum of 15 years in prison.

Yazgül Güder Öztürk, *Kurtulus*
Imprisoned: March 31, 1996

According to court documents from her trial, Öztürk, a reporter for the weekly socialist magazine *Kurtulus*, was detained and imprisoned on March 31, 1996, charged with violating Article 168/2 of the Penal Code for alleged membership in the outlawed Revolutionary People's Liberation Party-Front (DHKP-C). The prosecution accused her of gathering information for DHKP-C in Gaziantep, near the Syrian border, and Konya, in central Turkey. She was also accused of attending unspecified illegal demonstrations in Istanbul and the funeral in Adana of two DHKP-C members killed during a robbery in Ankara.

According to Öztürk's lawyer, the prosecution said that she had coordinated the DHKP-C's propaganda activities. In her defense, Öztürk cited her work as a journalist and denied all charges. She was convicted and sentenced to 12 years and six months in prison. She is in Bayrampasa Prison.

Serpil Günes, *Alinteri*
Imprisoned: September 7, 1996

Günes, an editor and owner of the now-defunct socialist weekly *Alinteri*, was arrested in Izmir in a police raid on a vacation apartment where she and several of her *Alinteri* colleagues were staying. Günes was charged under Article 168 of the Penal Code for her alleged membership in the outlawed Turkish Revolutionary Communist Union (TIKB).

During her trial, the prosecution stated that police found a counterfeit I.D. card in Günes' possession, and seized unspecified illegal publications and handwritten documents which purportedly linked her and her colleagues to the TIKB. The prosecution produced witnesses who testified that she was a member of the group. Günes denied all the accusations.

Günes' lawyer characterized her conviction in this case as a "political decision" and said that she received the maximum 15-year sentence because the state considers *Alinteri* the mouthpiece of the TIKB.

Günes' lawyer told CPJ that about 20 cases against her stemming from articles published in the paper during her tenure were suspended following the August 14, 1997, amnesty for editors. Her lawyer said Günes has been fined nearly one billion Turkish lira in her capacity as owner of *Alinteri*. CPJ sees in these previous convictions a pattern

IMPRISONED JOURNALISTS

of state harassment of *Alinteri* for publishing news and dissenting opinion.

Former *Alinteri* staffers said Günes was charged with and convicted of violating Article 7 of the Anti-Terror Law (propagandizing on behalf of an outlawed organization) and Article 312 of the Penal Code (inciting racial hatred) for articles published in the newspaper during her tenure.

On December 2, 1998, the Court of Cassation overturned the verdict and ordered a retrial for Günes under Article 168 of the Penal Code. She is in Usak Prison.

Nabi Kimran, *Iscinin Yolu*
Imprisoned: September 9, 1996

Kimran was editor of the leftist weekly *Iscinin Yolu*, which was subject to repeated government harassment during his tenure.

According to court documents, police apprehended Kimran on a bus during a police operation in advance of the anniversary of the outlawed Marxist-Leninist Communist Party (MLKP). He was charged under Article 168 of the Penal Code for his alleged membership in the MLKP. During his trial, the prosecution alleged that Kimran was a leader of the organization. The charge was based on a statement of an alleged MLKP sympathizer, who said that Kimran had given instructions to bomb a city bus. Kimran was also caught with a counterfeit I.D., which he admitted having because of his fear of being detained in the course of his journalistic work. The prosecution stated that police searching Kimran's apartment found documents in his handwriting that demonstrated his affiliation with the MLKP.

Kimran is currently being held in Sakarya Prison. His lawyer told CPJ that Kimran had also faced charges under Articles 7 (engaging in propaganda for an outlawed organization) and 8 (disseminating separatist propaganda) of the Anti-Terror Law. Staffers from the socialist weekly *Atilim* said these charges arose from news articles that appeared in *Iscinin Yolu* during Kimran's tenure. The Penal Code violation case was prosecuted, but the Anti-Terror Law cases were eventually suspended following the government's August 14, 1997, amnesty for jailed editors.

Ayten Öztürk, *Kurtulus*
Imprisoned: October 13, 1997

On September 19, 1997, an arrest warrant was issued for Öztürk, editor of the leftist weekly *Kurtulus*, for violating Article 168/1 of the Penal Code.

Öztürk surrendered to the court on October 13, and thereupon was charged with leading the outlawed Revolutionary People's Liberation Party-Front (DHKP-C). The main evidence cited at her trial was her publication and distribution of an unspecified "special edition" of *Kurtulus*.

Attacks on the Press in 1998

The prosecution also said she had met with two alleged members of the DHKP-C. She was convicted on December 24 and sentenced to 12 years and six months in prison. She is in Ankara Closed Prison.

In September 1997, Öztürk had faced charges under Article 7 of the Anti-Terror Law for allegedly spreading propaganda in the press on behalf of an outlawed organization. Those charges were voided on September 4 by an Istanbul State Security Court in accordance with the government's August 14, 1997, amnesty for editors.

Ragip Duran, *Özgür Gündem*
Imprisoned: June 16, 1998

Duran, Istanbul correspondent for the French-language daily *Liberation* and a veteran reporter who has worked for the Agence France-Presse news agency, the British Broadcasting Corporation, the now-defunct pro-Kurdish daily *Özgür Gündem*, and other Turkish daily newspapers, began serving a 10-month jail term in Saray Prison for violating provisions of Turkey's Anti-Terror Law.

Duran was tried and convicted in December 1994 of propagandizing on behalf of an outlawed organization under Article 7 of the Anti-Terror Law, and his sentence was ratified by the Court of Cassation in October 1997. The charge stemmed from an article he wrote about his interview with Abdullah Ocalan, leader of the outlawed Kurdistan Workers' Party (PKK), which appeared in *Özgür Gündem* on April 12, 1994.

Dogan Guzel, *Özgür Gündem*
Imprisoned: July 31, 1998

Guzel, a cartoonist for the now-defunct pro-Kurdish daily *Özgür Gündem*, was arrested and charged under Article 159 of the Turkish Penal Code with insulting the state and armed forces. The charge stemmed from four cartoons published in *Özgür Gündem* between May 1993 and October 1993.

During his trial, the prosecution introduced as evidence his use of the phrase "Khape TC" when referring to the Turkish Republic in each of the cartoons. "Khape TC" has a negative connotation, meaning "weak," "prostitute," or " bastard." Guzel was convicted on four separate counts of violating Article 159 and sentenced to 40 months in prison.

Eylem Kaplan, *Ülkede Gündem*
Ayse Oyman, *Ülkede Gündem*
Imprisoned: November 18, 1998

Kaplan and Oyman, reporters for the pro-Kurdish daily *Ülkede Gündem* in Malatya, were arrested in a nationwide police roundup of journalists working with the publication. They are charged with violating Article 169 of the Penal Code (aiding an outlawed organization).

According to the indictment, the prosecution accused the two journalists of collecting political and military information in Elazig, Bingöl, and Tunceli "under the cover of news." The prosecution accused the journalists of interviewing relatives of Kurdistan Workers' Party (PKK) members who had been killed, and accused Eylem of traveling to PKK military camps and taking photographs of guerrillas. Police state that they discovered film containing these photos in the newspaper office. According to the prosecution, "they brought to the newspaper bureau interviews that praised the members of the PKK in the name of news." The prosecutions's evidence consisted of "nine cassettes of interviews conducted by the accused that were seized in the newspaper office, which were propagating on behalf of the PKK and were derogatory against the state."

The trial of Kaplan and Oyman is underway in the Malatya State Security Court, and they are in Malatya Prison.

Ali Kemal Sel, *Ülkede Gündem*
Imprisoned: November 19, 1998

Sel, the Malatya bureau chief for the pro-Kurdish daily *Ülkede Gündem* since December 1996, was arrested in a nationwide police roundup of journalists working for the publication. He was charged with aiding an outlawed organization under Article 169 of the Penal Code.

According to official court documents from his indictment, Sel was accused of using two reporters from the paper to collect political and military information "in the name of news" in the towns of in Elazig, Tunceli, and Bingöl and passing it on to the outlawed Kurdistan Workers' Party (PKK). The state's accusation read: "In the so-called newspaper, he used Eylem Kaplan and Ayse Onan to collect political and military information" such as "the starting hours of the soldiers and their routes; the lists of the material the soldiers were going to pass from the check-points; the pressure put on the people of the region; information about village evacuations. This information, which was against the state and in accordance with PKK's views was sent to the so-called newspaper [*Ülkede Gündem*] in the name of news."

Prosecutors state that during a search of Sel's office and home they found "documents that were pro-PKK." His trial in the Malatya State Security Court is currently underway. He is in Malatya Prison.

Uzbekistan (1)

Please send appeals to:
His Excellency Islam Karimov
President of the Republic of Uzbekistan
Tashkent, Uzbekistan
Fax: 011-371-395-525

On June 11, 1998, the Syrdariya regional court sentenced

Attacks on the Press in 1998

Shadi Mardiev, Samarkand Regional Radio
Imprisoned: November 15, 1997

Shadi Mardiev, a 62-year-old reporter with the state-run Samarkand regional radio station, to 11 years in prison for defamation and extortion.

The case against Mardiev stemmed from a June 19, 1997, broadcast he which satirized the corrupt practices of deputy prosecutor Talat Abdulkhalikzada. Abdulkhalikzada accused Mardiev of defamation, and further alleged that the reporter had used the threat of the impending broadcast to attempt to extort money from him, according to Mardiev's lawyer.

On November 15, 1997, Mardiev was arrested on charges of defamation and extortion under four articles of the Uzbek penal code. Mardiev, known for his critical stance toward corrupt officials and for his writings in the satirical journal *Mushtum*, was held in pretrial detention at a jail in Samarkand until June 11, when his case was brought before the Syrdariya regional court.

Mardiev's health has reportedly deteriorated during his imprisonment in Qizil-Tepa, in the Navoi region of Uzbekistan. On August 3, 1998, the Supreme Court rejected the appeal filed by Mardiev's lawyer, upholding the sentence.

Vietnam (1)

Please send appeals to:
His Excellency Le Kha Phieu
General Secretary of the Central Committee
Communist Party of Vietnam
1 Hoang Van Thu
Hanoi, Socialist Republic of Vietnam

Bui Minh Quoc, *Lang Biang*
Imprisoned: September 1997

Quoc, a poet, journalist and correspondent for North Vietnamese radio during the Vietnam War, was placed under administrative detention by authorities in the southern resort town of Dalat. He is subject to constant surveillance and frequent interrogation. He is not allowed to leave the vicinity of his house, is prevented from having contact with family members without the presence of an armed guard and has been told by authorities not to have contact with foreigners or Vietnamese living abroad.

He was the president of the Dalat Writer's Association and the editor of the literary and cultural magazine *Lang Biang* before his pro-democracy ideas attracted the attention of authorities in 1990. Since that time, the magazine has been closed down and he has been expelled from the Communist Party because of his views. The order of administrative detention issued against Quoc came after he was accused of circulating pro-democracy letters calling for open trials of dissidents and other legal reforms.

With the passage of a decree allowing for virtually unlimited use of administrative detention in April 1997, Vietnamese authorities have used the tactic to silence dissidents. Administrative detentions are seldom reported in the press and are not subject to formal charges and public trials.

Attacks on the Press in 1998

Four Unconfirmed Cases of Imprisoned Journalists

CPJ could not confirm that the journalists below remained in prison as of December 31, 1998. We are continuing to investigate these cases and welcome any information.

Sudan (2)

Osama Ghandi, Sudanese Television
Hassan Saleh, Sudanese Television
Imprisoned: February 1996

Television cameraman Osama Ghandi and technician Hassan Saleh of the state-owned Sudanese Television were arrested and accused of being involved in an alleged coup attempt. They were among 10 civilians who went on trial in late August 1996 in an in camera military court trial, in which most of the defendants were military officers. Ghandi told the court on Sept. 18 that military intelligence agents had coerced his confession by torturing him. CPJ received reports in 1997 that the military court had reached a verdict, although it was not clear whether the two journalists were convicted or if they remained in prison. At press time, CPJ had received no new information on their status.

Turkey (2)

Kamber Inan, *Kurtulus*
Imprisoned: July 11, 1995
Released: 1998?

Inan, a reporter for the far-left weekly magazine *Kurtulus*, was arrested in his home in Istanbul and charged under Article 168/2 of the Penal Code for his alleged membership in the Revolutionary People's Liberation Party-Front (DHKP-C). Court documents from his trial obtained from Inan's lawyer said that Inan had refused to answer questions during his detention. He was convicted and sentenced to 15 years in prison and confined to Bayrampasa Prison. According to Inan's lawyer, Inan is believed to have been released. CPJ is continuing its investigation to confirm the journalist's release.

Asaf Sah, *Kurtulus*
Imprisoned: January 4, 1996
Released: 1998 ?

Sah, an Antakya reporter for the far-left weekly magazine *Kurtulus*, was arrested and imprisoned as part of the state's campaign of harassment against the magazine. Sah was tried under Article 169 of the Penal Code for allegedly aiding an outlawed organization. He was convicted and sentenced on April 16, 1996, to three years and nine months in prison and confined to Nevsehir Prison. CPJ is continuing its investigation to verify reports that Sah has been released from prison.

Enemies of the Press: The 10 Worst Offenders of 1998

On May 3, in conjunction with World Press Freedom Day, CPJ announced its annual list of the top 10 enemies of the press worldwide. Those who made the list this year, as in the past, earned the dubious distinction by exhibiting particular zeal for the ruthless suppression of journalists. Nigeria's Gen. Sani Abacha and Burma's Senior Gen. Than Shwe headed a roster that includes a number of repeat offenders and a troubling cast of newcomers.

Gen. Sani Abacha, Nigeria

Five years into his dictatorship, Abacha escalated his outrageous assault on the country's once-thriving independent press and reneged on his promise to return the country to democracy. His brutal tactics kept 21 Nigerian journalists behind bars. In May, Nigeria held more journalists in prison than any other African nation. The February murder of *Guardian* editor Tunde Oladepo, in front of his wife and children, and the April life sentence meted out to *Diet* editor Niran Malaolu, were warnings to journalists not to criticize Abacha's stage-managed referendum to secure his succession unopposed.

Senior Gen. Than Shwe, Burma

Than Shwe presides over the cosmetically renamed State Peace and Development Council, but a junta is still a junta, and this stifling regime has changed little since the military seized power in 1988. Burma is a nightmare for free expression. Fax machines, photocopies, and computer modems are illegal. There are no independent newspapers. Foreign broadcasts are frequently jammed. In this climate of oppression, the Burmese people are kept in the dark about even the nature of their own government.

President Alexander Lukashenko, Belarus

Ignoring international protests of repeated press freedom violations, Lukashenko wages an ongoing, Soviet-style campaign against independent and foreign media in Belarus. His March directive "On Enhancing Counter-Propaganda Activities Towards Opposition Press" forbids state officials to make any documents available to independent media and bans government advertising in all but state-run venues. Lukashenko's routine suppression of the press is typified by the censorship and shutdown of the independent newspaper *Svaboda* (Freedom). A staged trial of ORT (Russian television) personnel in Minsk sentenced them to silence—or two years in prison.

President Fidel Castro, Cuba
Despite implicit promises to Pope John Paul II that there would be greater room for freedom of expression, Castro continues his control over all media outlets and his harsh treatment of independent journalists, who are routinely detained, arrested and beaten, or forced into exile, especially before major political events. In a new effort to staunch the flow of information from the island, Castro created a special task force within the State Security Agency to muzzle the independent press. Journalists try to file stories by phone with colleagues abroad in order to communicate with the outside world, but the Castro regime routinely monitors their calls and interrupts telephone service.

President Suharto, Indonesia
With Indonesia's economy in free fall, Suharto continued to run roughshod over the media to prevent open, independent coverage of business and politics. Under Suharto, journalists were arrested, harassed, threatened by the military, and driven into hiding. Despite this persecution, Indonesian journalists still attempted to provide broad coverage of the rising opposition to Suharto. But publications that once dared to report on the Suharto clan's financial dealings remained closed by state order. Meanwhile, cronyism endured, exacerbating the economic crisis, and reporters were fearful that digging too deeply into the country's financial troubles could cost them their jobs—or their lives.

President Saparmurat Niyazov, Turkmenistan
The self-proclaimed "father of all Turkmen" rules his country like the old-style totalitarian, cult-of-personality Soviet dictator he is—

making Turkmenistan the most repressive of the former Soviet states. A pervasive culture of fear stifles all dissent. Reporters for Radio Liberty (RL), the only alternative non-state source of information in the Turkmen language, are routinely harassed, beaten, and forced into exile. And in recent months, several have been imprisoned by Niyazov's state security forces. Despite his record, Niyazov has been feted by President Clinton, Vice President Gore and others seeking access to Turkmenistan's vast natural gas and oil reserves.

Prime Minister Meles Zenawi, Ethiopia

Lauded by U.S. policy makers as one of the new generation of African leaders for his ostensive contributions to the democratization of Africa, Meles is in fact an autocrat who attempts to suppress all press criticism of his regime. His deliberate campaign of detention and harassment of Ethiopia's independent press has spurred scores of journalists to flee the country. In 1997 he imprisoned 16 journalists, many of whom are being held without charge. Journalists continue to be targeted by police and threatened with prosecution by a partisan judiciary.

President Zine Abdine Ben Ali, Tunisia

Ben Ali's decade of rule has reduced the Tunisian press to one of the most restricted in the Arab world. Journalists face swift reprisal for even the most benign independent reporting of political affairs in the Tunisian police state. They are dismissed from their jobs, denied accreditation, and barred from leaving the country for anything that is perceived as critical coverage. As a result, self-censorship has become virtually institutionalized. The foreign press is also targeted: Ben Ali has expelled four correspondents since 1991, and foreign news entering Tunisia is sytematically censored.

President Jiang Zemin, China

Jiang's one-party state continues to control all forms of media, effectively making independent reporting impossible. Press that fail to toe the Communist Party line remain subject to harsh censure. All Internet communications by local and foreign news media are monitored and subject to state censorship. The release of two famous dissidents after intense international pressure suggests a mild thaw in the climate for free expression, but it is far too early to celebrate a Beijing Spring. For reform to be meaningful, the 10 journalists still in prison in China must be freed.

Prime Minister Abd al-Salam al-Majali, Jordan
In little more than a year in office, al-Majali has mounted a harsh offensive against Jordan's outspoken independent press, known for its aggressive coverage of the Israel-Jordan peace treaty, the economy, alleged government corruption, and human rights abuses. Last year, al-Majali's cabinet enacted draconian amendments to the press law, decimating the independent weekly press just before parliamentary elections. This brazen manipulator muzzles the media through intimidation, by arresting and prosecuting outspoken journalists, and by censorship.

HONORED FOR THEIR EXTRAORDINARY COURAGE

The 1998 International Press Freedom Awards

The International Press Freedom Awards are given annually by CPJ to journalists around the world who have courageously provided independent news coverage and viewpoints under difficult and often dangerous conditions. To defend press freedom, award winners have risked arrest, imprisonment, violence against themselves and their families, and even death.

The following five journalists received awards on November 24 in New York City at the Eighth Annual International Press Freedom Awards ceremony:

Besieged broadcaster **Grémah Boucar**, director of one of Niger's only private radio stations, exemplifies the experiences of Africa's few truly independent radio broadcasters. Since early 1997, he and his staff have been repeatedly arrested, harassed, and threatened. At risk of being shut down at a moment's notice, he has not compromised the content of Radio Anfani's hard-hitting journalism, and has attracted support from fellow citizens, diplomatic representatives of many Western nations, and international organizations such as CPJ.

Boucar, who also publishes *Anfani* newspaper and magazine, launched Radio Anfani (FM 100MHZ) in 1994, during the administration of Niger's first democratically elected president, Mahamane Ousmane. Radio Anfani journalists have been attacked for their coverage of Col. Ibrahim Baré Maïnassara's military dictatorship and its actions to eliminate any viable political opposition. Articles in the *Anfani* newspaper criticized certain government officials, and broadcasts on Radio Anfani generated international criticism of Maïnassara's subsequent electoral victories, widely believed to have been fraudulent. Many of Boucar's colleagues believe that it is just a matter of time before President Maïnassara's irritation with Anfani's objective reporting and popularity among the citizenry prompts him to permanently shut down the station.

The plight of Boucar, 39, typifies that of all journalists working under military dictatorships in the West Africa sub-region, where CPJ documents the greatest number of press freedom abuses in sub-Saharan Africa.

No one exemplifies the remarkable transformation of Latin American journalism better than **Gustavo Gorriti**. During the 1980s, Gorriti made his name as a war correspondent, hiking along jungle trails to report on the brutal conflict in his native Peru. He survived abduction by armed commandos in Peru before leaving the country in 1992. After four years in the United States, Gorriti joined the staff of the Panama City daily *La Prensa*, one of Latin America's leading newspapers.

In 1996, Gorriti wrote a series of articles documenting how Colombian drug traffickers with close ties to the Panamanian government were using banks to launder money. He also found that a major trafficker with close ties to the Cali drug cartel had made a US$51,000 contribution to President Ernesto Pérez Balladares' campaign fund. Angered by Gorriti's reports, the government announced on August 5, 1997, that it would not renew his work visa and ordered him to leave Panama by August 28.

Gorriti responded with a full-scale legal and communications onslaught: He contested the expulsion and asked for the intervention of the Inter American Human Rights Commission of the Organization of American States. He wrote op-eds for *The New York Times* and *Newsweek*. He was profiled in *The Wall Street Journal*, *The Washington Post*, and on National Public Radio. Facing international condemnation, the Panamanian government was forced to back down. On October 14, 1997, Gorriti's work visa was extended for another year.

Throughout his long and varied career, Gorriti, 50, has distinguished himself not only as one of Latin America's top investigative reporters, but also as an uncompromising advocate for press freedom.

Goenawan Mohamad has been a crusader for press freedom since his university days. In 1967, he set up the short-lived independent student newspaper *Harian Kami*. Now, after sparring for decades with President Suharto's authoritarian government, it is Goenawan who remains on the public stage while his nemesis has been forced to resign.

In 1971, Goenawan founded *Tempo*, an independent weekly magazine patterned after Western magazines such as *Time* and *Newsweek*. *Tempo* became the most respected and highest-circulation news magazine in Indonesia and served as a training ground for a generation of journalists. It sought to keep the Suharto government accountable to the public, and set new journalistic standards for the country with a mix of political commentary and investigative reporting on human rights and official corruption.

Tempo was banned for a short time in 1982 when it reported on violence instigated by the government-backed Golkar Party at an opposition campaign rally. In 1994, the magazine went too far for the regime when a cover story criticizing Indonesia's purchase of 39 used navy ships from the former East Germany drew attention to a dispute between B. J. Habibie, the author of the deal and then a powerful cabinet minister, and a number of senior generals. *Tempo* was banned and its publication license revoked in June 1994.

After the 1994 ban, Goenawan led an effort by some 150 former *Tempo* staffers to challenge the dominance of the official Indonesian Reporters Association (PWI), by forming the Alliance of Independent Journalists (AJI), Indonesia's only independent reporters association. He used his international contacts to set up the Institute for Studies in the Free Flow of Information (ISAI), which monitors attacks on the press in Indonesia.

With the Indonesian political and economic crisis far from resolved, Goenawan, 57, is now poised to play a role in what may be the greatest drama of his turbulent career—bringing a genuinely free press to his country. Suharto is gone, but his successor, Habibie, who played a central role in the banning of *Tempo*, is now cast in the role of a reform-minded transitional president. Goenawan and a group of former *Tempo* staffers reopened the magazine on October 6. Speaking at the time of the relaunch, he said, "We have to make the government commit itself to press freedom."

Pavel Sheremet has endured every conceivable type of official harassment for his coverage of Belarus' slide toward authoritarianism. Minsk bureau chief for the Russian public television company ORT since 1995 and editor in chief of the newspaper *Belorusskaya Delovaya Gazeta* since 1995, Sheremet—a Belarussian citizen—has been imprisoned, stripped of his credentials, and barred from traveling to the West or working as a journalist until January 1999. At the same time, the 27-year-old Minsk-born journalist has become a popular public figure for standing up to President Aleksander Lukashenko's campaign to silence critics and control independent and opposition news media.

Sheremet, who in 1995 won the Belarus PEN Center's Adamovich Prize as best television reporter, has earned the regime's anger by covering opposition rallies and exposing Lukashenko's Soviet-style political tactics. In an incident that strained relations with Russia, Sheremet, his cameraman, and their driver—all Belarusian citizens—were arrested and charged with illegally crossing the border on July 22, 1997, while filming a report on smuggling and border security at Belarus' frontier with Lithuania. Belarus pressed charges against Sheremet and one crew member. In January 1998 they were found guilty of crossing the border, "exceeding their professional rights as journalists," and participating in a conspiracy. Sheremet received a two-year suspended sentence and was barred from traveling abroad for one year.

The Belarus government denied CPJ's request to temporarily waive the travel restrictions so that he could accept the 1998 International Press Freedom Award in person in New York. Authorities finally lifted the ban on November 26—two days too late.

Ruth Simon, 36, a correspondent for the news agency Agence France-Presse (AFP), was held without formal charges from April 25, 1997, until December 29, 1998. An Eritrean citizen, she was arrested after reporting that President Isaias Afwerki told participants at a seminar that Eritrean soldiers were fighting alongside rebels in neighboring Sudan.

Simon is married and the mother of two children, the youngest of whom was six months old when Simon was arrested. She was responsible for the clandestine publications of the Eritrean People's Liberation Front during the war for independence from Ethiopia, and was the editor in chief of BANA, the publication of the Association for the Reintegration of Eritrean Women Guerrilla Fighters. She was the first journalist to be arrested in Eritrea since it became a state in 1993. President Afewerki personally ordered Simon's imprisonment for "publishing false information."

In reply to CPJ's letter demanding Simon's release, the Eritrean foreign ministry said Simon's actions violated the national press law, which states that "any journalist who misinforms the public or any institution is liable to the damage he/she may cause as a result." Refusing to elaborate further on the charges against Simon, the letter also stated that, "[Simon's arrest] is, therefore, [a] purely legal issue which does not require or allow any kind of intervention from any comer."

More than 300 prominent journalists, media executives, human rights activists, and others at CPJ's annual awards dinner at the Waldorf-Astoria signed an appeal to President Afwerki urging Simon's immediate and unconditional release.

Brian Lamb was the 1998 recipient of CPJ's **Burton Benjamin Memorial Award,** for distinguished achievement in the cause of press freedom. The award honors the late CBS News senior producer and former CPJ chairman, who died in 1988. Lamb's breakthrough achievement in conceiving, defining, and establishing a public affairs television network that would give voice to all the people added a new dimension to the nation's and world's understanding of press freedom. With the creation nearly 20 years ago of C-SPAN—the Cable-Satellite Public Affairs Network, a nonprofit network subsidized by the cable industry—the medium of television made a leap toward more fully realizing its potential to inform and illuminate. C-SPAN has demystified the workings of government for tens of millions. It now reaches 73 million households on its primary channel and more than 50 million on C-SPAN2, with its gavel-to-gavel coverage of sessions and hearings of the U.S. Congress. Not only has it helped create a more informed electorate, it has become a vehicle for viewers to participate in the democratic process in new ways.

Lamb, the visionary behind this accomplishment, is unstinting in his efforts to make information widely available to the public, whatever its source—government, private or nonprofit sectors, meetings open to the few or many, or the written word. It is a goal that complements the press freedom standard of the Committee to Protect Journalists: Democracy can flourish only when citizens have the right and the ability to freely express and have access to information, opinions, and views.

For more information about the International Press Freedom Awards, visit CPJ's website at <www.cpj.org>.

Attacks on the Press in 1998

International Press Freedom Award Winners 1991-1997

1991
Pius Njawe, *Le Messager*, Cameroon
Wang Juntao and Chen Ziming,
  Economics Weekly, China
Bill Foley and Cary Vaughan, United States
Tatyana Mitkova, TSN,
  former Soviet Union
Byron Barrera, *La Epoca*, Guatemala

1992
David Kaplan, ABC News, United States
Muhammad Al-Saqr, *Al-Qabas*, Kuwait
Sony Esteus, Radio Tropic FM, Haiti
Gwendolyn Lister, *The Namibian*, Namibia
Thepchai Yong, *The Nation*, Thailand

1993
Omar Belhouchet, *El Watan*, Algeria
Doan Viet Hoat, *Freedom Forum*, Vietnam
Nosa Igiebor, *Tell* magazine, Nigeria
Veran Matic, Radio B92, Yugoslavia
Ricardo Uceda, *Si*, Peru

1994
Iqbal Athas, *The Sunday Leader*, Sri Lanka
Aziz Nesin, Turkey
Yndamiro Restano, Cuba
Daisy Li Yuet-Wah, Hong Kong
  Journalists Association, Hong Kong
In memory of staff journalists, *Navidi
  Vakhsh*, Tajikistan

1995
Yevgeny Kiselyov, NTV, Russia
José Rubén Zamora Marroquín,
  Siglo Veintiuno, Guatemala
Fred M'membe, *The Post*, Zambia
Ahmad Taufik, Alliance of Independent
  Journalists (AJI), Indonesia
Veronica Guerin, *Sunday Independent*, Ireland

1996
Yusuf Jameel, *Asian Age*, India
J. Jesús Blancornelas, *Zeta*, Mexico
Daoud Kuttab, Internews Middle East,
  Palestinian National Authority
Oscak Isik Yurtçu, *Özgür Gündem*, Turkey

1997
Christine Anyanwu, *The Sunday Magazine*,
  Nigeria
Ying Chan, *Yazhou Zhoukan*, United States
Shieh Chung-liang, *Yazhou Zhoukan*,
  Taiwan
Victor Ivancic, *Feral Tribune*, Croatia
Freedom Neruda, *La Voie*, Ivory Coast
Yelena Masyuk, NTV, Russia

Burton Benjamin Memorial Award

1991
Walter Cronkite
CBS News

1992
Katharine Graham
The Washington Post Company

1993
R.E. Turner
Turner Broadcasting System Inc.

1994
George Soros
The Soros Foundations

1995
Benjamin C. Bradlee
The Washington Post

1996
Arthur Ochs Sulzberger
The New York Times

1997
Ted Koppel
ABC News

How CPJ Investigates and Classifies Attacks on the Press

CPJ's research staff investigated and verified the cases of press freedom violations described in this volume. Each account was corroborated by more than one source for factual accuracy, confirmation that the victims were journalists or news organizations, and verification that intimidation was the probable motive. CPJ defines journalists as people who cover news or write commentary. For additional information on individual cases, contact CPJ at (212) 465-1004. CPJ classifies the cases in this report according to the following categories:

Attacked
In the case of journalists, wounded or assaulted. In the case of news facilities, damaged, raided, or searched; non-journalist employees attacked because of news coverage or commentary.

Censored
Officially suppressed or banned; editions confiscated; news outlet closed.

Expelled
Forced to leave a country because of news coverage or commentary.

Harassed
Access denied or limited; materials confiscated or damaged; entry or exit denied; family members attacked or threatened; dismissed or demoted (when it is clearly the result of political or outside pressure); freedom of movement impeded.

Imprisoned
Arrested or held against one's will; held for no less than 48 hours.

Killed
Murdered, or missing and presumed dead, with evidence that the motive was retribution for news coverage or commentary. Includes accidental deaths of journalists in the line of duty.

Legal Action
Credentials denied or suspended; fined; sentenced to prison; visas denied or canceled; passage of a restrictive law; libel suit intended to inhibit coverage.

Missing
No group or government agency takes responsibility for the journalist's disappearance; in some instances, feared dead.

Threatened
Menaced with physical harm or some other type of retribution.

OVERVIEW OF
Africa
by Kakuna Kerina

Civil war and political upheaval had a devastating impact on journalists throughout the region this year. Journalists in the Democratic Republic of Congo (DRC), Liberia, Angola, the Republic of Congo, and Sierra Leone were not only the targets of governments desperately clinging to power, but they were simultaneously targeted by rebel armies and militia factions attempting to overthrow those governments. And their colleagues working in countries the West views as the "new African democracies"—including Uganda, Ghana, and Namibia—have learned from bitter experience that they must still contend with governments that use military and presidential decrees, colonial-era sedition and criminal libel laws, and the threat of detention without charge to control the press.

One of Africa's most vile dictators died this year, leaving the valiant journalists of his country in less immediate peril but facing an uncertain future. Gen. Sani Abacha, Nigeria's military ruler, had conducted a reign of terror against the country's press, threatening and imprisoning scores of journalists since he seized power in 1993. His successor, Gen. Abdulsalami Abubakar, came into power pledging democratic reforms, including a transition to elective government. Within a few months, he released 16 of the 17 journalists whose incarceration had boosted Nigeria to first place as the worst jailer of journalists in Africa in 1997. Those who came out brought harrowing stories of their treatment at the hands of Abacha's minions, and deep skepticism about Abubakar's promises for

---

Kakuna Kerina *has been program coordinator for Africa since September 1995. An award-winning documentary filmmaker, and author, she has studied, worked in, and traveled throughout Africa for more than 35 years.*
Research assistant **Matthew Leone** *contributed significantly to this section, researched the majority of the cases, and wrote many of the country summaries.*
Former research assistant **Selam Demeke** *also researched casework included in this section.*
   The CPJ Africa program wishes to thank Reporters Respond and the Hellman/Hammett Fund of Human Rights Watch for its support of journalists in emergency circumstances in the region.
   CPJ is grateful for the cooperation of a number of press freedom and human rights groups, and individuals throught the region. These include: the West African Journalists Association; the Media Institute of South Africa; Médias Pour La Paix; the Media Institute of Kenya; Burkinabe Movement of Human Rights and Peoples; and the International Journalism Center/Lagos.
   The Freedom Forum supported CPJ's work in Africa with a grant that funded the CPJ/West African Journalists Association's "State of the Media in Nigeria" conference held in Accra in August 1998. Efforts in the region were also supported by the Institute of International Education, and by Gene Roberts, chairman of CPJ's board of directors.

democratization in Nigeria. (See "Outliving Abacha: Six Journalists' Prison Stories," page 137.)

In August, CPJ held a conference in Ghana that provided leading Nigerian journalists their first opportunity to meet without the threat of security raids or detention. They joined colleagues from Ghana, Zambia, and Argentina—another country with a dark past under military dictatorship—to discuss their experiences under Abacha and beyond. Most participants stressed that without long-term reforms such as the abrogation of Abacha-era decrees used to crack down on the press and the expunging of journalists' criminal records, any celebration of a new era of press freedom in Nigeria was decidedly premature.

For many journalists, the wave of democratization that swept across the region earlier this decade is a distant memory. During that period, the press's exposure of corrupt autocratic and dictatorial regimes, combined with the popular demand for more representative governments, enlivened the democracy movement in the region. While some of the military dictators and one-party rulers of previous decades have reinvented themselves as democrats, far too many have done so through manipulated elections, and persist in their intolerance of critical reporting. And the same journalists who midwifed the transition to democracy in those countries found themselves in detention cells or courtrooms facing reprisals for continuing to call for the transparency in government that was promised in previous election campaigns.

Radio remains the most effective means to communicate with the majority of the population throughout the region, and it is not a coincidence that Africa's broadcasters are now being targeted by governments who wish to keep their constituencies in the dark about their corruption and gross abuses of power. Radio broadcasters like Mustapha Thiombiano of Burkina Faso, and CPJ 1998 International Press Freedom Award recipient Grémah Boucar of Niger, who were licensed during the wave of democracy earlier in the decade, are now struggling to hold on to those licenses. (See page 66 for more on the International Press Freedom Awards and Grémah Boucar.) Licenses are even more difficult to obtain for independent journalists who wish to operate television stations. Governments that used to engage broadcasters in protracted legal battles on trumped-up charges have now lost patience and are resorting to cruder strong-arm tactics to force independent journalists off the air. Throughout the year, they sent soldiers to destroy broadcast studios, vandalize or confiscate transmitters, and detain staff.

Observers will be watching the Nation Group in Kenya to see just how far the region's rulers can be expected to tolerate press freedom. This year, the Nation Group finally received broadcast licenses and frequencies for both radio and television, seven years after it submitted its applications.

The impact of war on the region's journalists cannot be overstated. Six neighboring countries have sent troops into the Democratic Republic of Congo (DRC) to support either Laurent Kabila or the rebel insurgents. Journalists in all of these countries—Namibia, Angola, Rwanda, Uganda, Zimbabwe, and the DRC—have risked harassment, imprisonment, and physical harm in their attempts to cover the conflict and expose government officials' private war-related business enterprises. Foreign correspondents became targets of soldiers, state security agents, and police in a number of countries, and sometimes even by citizens who believed the jingoistic propaganda disseminated by their governments. In the DRC, for example, reporting became so dangerous by August that foreign correspondents left the country en masse. In countries where the war has drained scarce resources and taken many lives, independent publications have reported these stories, fueling public outcry.

At year's end, Ethiopia held more journalists in prison than any other African country—an ignominious record that the country has held for all but one of the past five years. But for most of the year, the DRC rivaled Ethiopia; since Laurent Kabila ousted Mobutu Sese Seko in May 1997, his regime has imprisoned more than 70 journalists, some repeatedly.

Unresconstructed military dictators still rule by decree in Niger and Nigeria; and former-military-dictators-turned-presidents in countries like The Gambia and Burkina Faso are no more tolerant of diverse views and critical opinion than their military brethren. What is encouraging, however, is that the citizens of these countries have begun to challenge the leaders' failure to live up to their promises of democratic institution-building, and have vigorously supported their independent media. In Niger, thousands marched in the streets to protest the military assault on Radio Anfani when soldiers vandalized the station and arrested the staff. When Norbert Zongo, editor in chief of the leading opposition newspaper in Burkina Faso, *L'Independant*, died in a suspicious car crash in December, more than 10,000 people attended his funeral. The government was forced to create a board of inquiry after calls for an impartial investigation into Zongo's death spilled over into widespread demonstrations.

Journalists associations in the region such as the West African Journalists Association have become much stronger forces in the area of advocacy. CPJ has worked closely with these groups to create intraregional networks for collaboration and communication, and to advocate more effectively on behalf of journalists in danger.

This year, the number of African newspapers and magazines available on the Internet skyrocketed. Radio stations like Joy-FM of Ghana, and Sud-FM of

Senegal are also broadcasting live on the Internet. Many journalists are now online, bringing a world of research and information to their fingertips, as well as providing a global audience for their work. Although cost continued to limit private Internet access to a privileged few in the region, public Internet kiosks—roadside stands where anyone can access the Internet for a fee, or check their free e-mail on services such as Hotmail and Juno—are springing up throughout the region.

Many observers offer a pessimistic prognosis for press freedom in Africa, predicting a continuation of the downward spiral that began at mid-decade. While it is undeniable that press freedom has lost ground in many countries of the region, it is also true—and perhaps more important—to note that the courage of the region's journalists in the face of often incomprehensible repression and brutality has prevented the complete reversal of the press freedom gains of the early 1990s. Now, they must exceed those efforts of previous years to keep the few functioning democratic institutions alive as numerous heads of state backslide into despotism to stay in power.

Angola

Against the backdrop of an endless war that has killed more than half a million Angolans and devastated the economy, the country's journalists are under constant threat of death as they attempt to strengthen their profession and provide uncensored information in a treacherous environment. Since 1994, five journalists have been murdered in Angola—all of them known for their critical reporting on President Jose Eduardo dos Santos' Popular Movement for the Liberation of Angola (MPLA) government.

The most recent victim, Simao Roberto, a reporter with the state-owned newspaper *Jornal de Angola*, was gunned down in broad daylight on June 5. To date, none of perpetrators of these crimes has been brought to justice, confirming the country's reputation as one of the most dangerous for journalists, and one where those who use violence to silence the press do so with impunity.

The 1994 Lusaka Accords, designed to end nearly three decades of civil war between the MPLA and the rebel National Union for Total Independence of Angola (UNITA), led by Jonas Savimbi, are effectively dead. The two groups' 1997 power-sharing agreement, known as the Government of National Unity, has collapsed. Elections are scheduled for 2000, but it appears unlikely that the electoral process will function properly as long as the war between the government and UNITA rages on.

Although Angola's constitution guarantees freedom of expression and of the press, the government chooses to ignore violations of these rights, and continues to censor the media. Anonymous death threats and the specter of government bans shadow independent journalists who probe state affairs. And the few independent privately run publications have been targets of violent reprisal. For example, in February, arsonists set fire to the Luanda-based independent weekly *Agora*.

The practice of self-censorship is common at the state-owned Radio Nacional, Televisao Publica de Angola, *Jornal de Angola*, and the news agency Angop. All government journalists are on notice from Minister of Mass Communication Hendrick Vall Neto: If they publish or broadcast any reports that are considered critical of the state, they face certain detention on criminal libel charges.

While two privately owned radio stations have been operating in Luanda, and one each in Benguela, Cabinda, and Huila, only Radio 2000 and Radio Ecclesia, a Catholic station, are considered truly independent. The 1997 ban on Radio 2000's broadcast of the Voice of America's Portugal-to-Africa program, "Linha Directa, Linha Aberta" (Direct Line, Open Line), remains in effect.

April 3
Victoria Ferreira, *Folha 8* IMPRISONED
Felisberto Neto, *Folha 8* IMPRISONED

Ferreira and Neto, reporters for the independent newspaper *Folha 8*, were arrested at the Setima Esquadra police station in Luanda, where they had gone to cover a report that a murder had allegedly taken place in the police station.

Both journalists were repeatedly interrogated for several hours about whether they were spies for the rebel group UNITA, and about an anonymous letter, containing political commentary, that had been published in the newspaper.

They were released without charge on April 9 following intervention by the Luanda provincial police commander, who said the arrest was a misunderstanding.

June 5
Simao Roberto, *Jornal de Angola* KILLED

Roberto was a reporter for the government-owned *Jornal de Angola*. He was gunned down at 1 p.m. outside the newspaper's offices in Luanda as he returned from the Futungo de Belas, the presidential palace, where he had covered a meeting of the Council of Ministers. Roberto was known as a critic of the government. His colleagues believe he was killed because of his work as a journalist. Police subsequently presented three suspects they said carried out the attack, but a few days later one of the suspects denied involvement and said he had been forced to admit to the crime in exchange for a lesser charge in another matter. No one to date has been charged with Roberto's murder. CPJ condemned the murder in a letter to President Jose Eduardo dos Santos and urged him to ensure a thorough investigation and prosecution of the killers.

Burkina Faso

The December 13 death of Norbert Zongo, publisher of the independent weekly newspaper *L'Independant* and the president of the Society of Private Press Editors, raised the hostilities brewing among Burkina Faso's opposition politicians, independent media, and President Blaise Compaore's ruling Congress for Democracy and Progress (CDP) to the level of direct confrontation.

Initial official reports that Zongo had died in a car accident were challenged by the public and the press, who immediately called for an impartial commission to investigate the circumstances of his death. Although Zongo's body and those of his three companions were found charred beyond recognition inside a car whose interior was completely burnt, the outside of the vehicle was untouched by the fire. The vehicle was riddled with what appeared to be bullet holes. The combined pressure of widespread demonstrations, the presence of more than 50,000 mourners at Zongo's funeral, and an international outcry forced the government to name an investigative commission. But at year's end, local human rights groups challenged the independence of the appointees.

Reports that Zongo was preparing to publish articles implicating the president's brother in his chauffeur's murder have fanned the flames of distrust of the government, which is widely regarded as pursuing its own financial interests at the expense of its impoverished citizens.

Few critics expected Compaore to evolve from the leader of one of Africa's bloodiest coup d'états in 1987 into a genuine supporter of multiparty democracy. And many believe recent events are proof that the CDP intends to stall the implementation of democratic reforms mandated by the country's 1991 constitution. In November, Compaore won a second seven-year term in elections that the opposition declared were fraught with irregularities, and influenced by CDP patronage and manipulation of the state media. The independent media—comprised of a dozen private radio stations, one television station, and a number of newspapers and magazines—have been outspoken in their criticism of the CDP government, decrying the fact that former military junta officers dominate the party leadership.

December 13
Norbert Zongo, *L'Independant* KILLED

Zongo, publisher of the leading opposition weekly newspaper *L'Independant* and president of the Society of Private Press Editors, was found dead in his car on the road between Sapouy and Ouagadougou. Also found dead inside the vehicle were Zongo's brother, the chauffeur, and a fourth unidentified person. The inside of the car was burnt and the bodies were charred, although the car's exterior was not burnt. A rear door was riddled with what appeared to be bullet holes. The private newsweekly had recently published articles accusing President Blaise Compaore's brother of complicity in the death of his chauffeur. CPJ wrote to President Compaore asking him to launch a thorough and impartial investigation of the deaths and bring the perpetrators to justice.

Burundi

Almost a quarter of a million people have been casualties of Burundi's war, ongoing since 1993. It has become an almost insurmountable challenge to report on such issues as the massacres committed by both Hutu rebels and Tutsi-dominated government troops, or the flow of arms into the country that helps to sustain the fighting.

Fear of reprisals from all sides has forced many journalists to practice self-censorship, and security risks inhibit reporting from conflict areas. Reporting on press freedom violations can provoke swift reprisals. When the news service Net-Press reported that state intelligence service agents had seized copies of the pro-opposition newspaper, *L'Aube de la Démocratie*, the same agents then forcibly shut down the news agency and detained its director. Privately owned newspapers rarely publish on a regular schedule, and the few that are sold are regarded by local citizens as mere propaganda sheets for political extremists.

Military dictator Maj. Pierre Buyoya's regime has waged a full-scale attack on the country's journalists, using the intelligence service as its weapon. Local journalists are outraged at Buyoya's decommissioning of the National Communication Council, a media regulatory body that is currently con-

Attacks on the Press in 1998

trolled by the special services branch of the president's office. In May, more than 50 journalists from both state and privately owned media signed a petition urging Buyoya to end his regime's escalating assaults on the press.

Radio remains the most effective means of reaching the population, especially in the countryside, and the two major stations are state-run. The European Union and the United States have funded local radio programming with the hope of discouraging the type of hate radio that promoted the genocide of earlier years.

March 25
L'Aube de la Démocratie CENSORED

Intelligence service agents seized copies of the pro-opposition newspaper, *L'Aube de la Démocratie* (The Dawn of Democracy), published by the predominantly Hutu Frodebu political party. No official reason was given for the seizure.

The arrest was believed to be in connection with an article published in the newspaper, reporting that Minister of Defense Alfred Nkurunziza had been arrested by security agents in Nigeria while he was escorting arms that were destined for Burundi.

March 27
Net-Press CENSORED
Jean Claude Kavumbagu, Net-Press
HARASSED

Intelligence service agents closed the office of the Bujumbura-based Net-Press news agency and detained Kavumbagu, Net-Press's director, for questioning. He was released the same day, and the office was re-opened without explanation for the arrest, which is believed to be in connection with the agency's March 25 publication of an article about the government's seizure of copies of *L'Aube de la Démocratie*.

Cameroon

Local journalists and international observers reported extensively on the irregularities and fraud that marred the October 1997 elections, in which President Paul Biya consolidated power for the ruling Cameroon Democratic Movement (CPDM) and extended his 15-year tenure by another seven years. Not surprisingly, these elections failed to bring about greater freedom of expression, and journalists faced a variety of state reprisals for their critical coverage, including arbitrary detention on criminal defamation charges. In December, political satirist Nyemb Ntoogue, who said he had been given the choice in numerous death threats from anonymous individuals of "abandoning his career as journalist and death by machete," fled into exile.

Pius Njawe—editor of the weekly *Le Messager* and a 1991 recipient of CPJ's International Press Freedom Award—is the country's most beleaguered journalist. Since 1993, Njawe's publications, *Le Messager* and the satirical weekly *Le Messager Popoli*, have been banned and seized more than 13 times. Njawe has been arrested repeatedly, and he has faced legal action on charges ranging from defamation of the head of state to publishing unsourced information. In January, Njawe was sentenced to a two-year prison term for violation of the 1962 subversion law, despite pressure from local and international press freedom groups. The charges against Njawe stemmed from an article he had published in late 1997 reporting that Biya had suffered a heart attack while attending a soccer match.

Reporting on official corruption is a risk few journalists appear willing to take, and those who have dared to scrutinize the government have become targets for reprisal. In July, judicial police arrested the publication director of the privately owned magazine *Le Jeune Detective* in connection with an article that questioned the involvement of the Minister of Economy and Finance in the embezzlement of public funds.

While Cameroon is actively privatizing other state holdings, it has kept a virtual monopoly over broadcasting—the most effective means of reaching a largely illiterate population. A few community radio stations launched operations in remote rural areas, taking advantage of the Law on Mass Communications, which allows for the creation of private broadcast media. But the dozen radio stations reaching the majority of the population remain under state control, as is the Cameroon Radio and Television (CRTV) station. Both state-owned and independent newspapers are available on the Internet.

January 13
Michel Michaut Moussala, *Aurore Plus*
IMPRISONED, CENSORED
Aurore Plus LEGAL ACTION

Moussala, editor of *Aurore Plus*, was convicted of defaming Jean Tchoussa Moussa Mbatkam, director general of the National Ports Department of Cameroon (ONPC) and a deputy of the ruling Rassemblement Democratique du Peuple Camerounais (RDPC) party. He was sentenced to six months in prison and fined one million CFA (US$1,783). In addition, the newspaper was ordered to suspend publication for six months.

The suit cited a December 16, 1997, *Aurore Plus* article titled "ONPC, Tome II, Tchoussa Moussa at the Centre of a Failed Coup," which reported that Mbatkam had taken advantage of his position as director of the ONPC to stage a coup d'état. Moussala was arrested on September 3, by police officers who presented a warrant that had been issued shortly after his January conviction.

Attacks on the Press in 1998

January 13
Pius Njawe, *Le Messager* IMPRISONED, THREATENED

Njawe, editor of the independent weekly *Le Messager*, was sentenced to a two-year prison term and fined 500,000 CFA (US$1,000) for "disseminating unsourced news with the intention of affecting the head of state" and "undermining national security." Njawe was detained in Douala's Central Prison.

On April 14, Njawe's sentence was reduced on appeal to one year in prison. On April 16, the Supreme Court of Cameroon rejected his appeal and on August 20, the Supreme Court rejected his request for conditional release following his sentencing on January 13. On October 10, Njawe, a 1991 recipient of CPJ's International Press Freedom Award, was pardoned by presidential decree. He was released on October 12.

January 16
Samuel Eleme, *La Detente* LEGAL ACTION

Eleme, publication director of the independent magazine *La Detente*, was convicted of defamation and sentenced to three years in prison and a fine of 1,000,000 CFA (US$1,700). The charges were in connection with a series of articles published in October 1997 reporting that John Mandengue Epee, director of a Cameroonian insurance company, had committed a number of thefts in Nigeria before settling in Cameroon.

March 28
Aime Mathurin Moussi, *La Plume du Jour* HARASSED

Three plainclothes police officers arrested Moussi, publication editor for the private weekly *La Plume du Jour*, at his residence in Yaoundé and took him to an unknown location. Moussi was subsequently released on an unspecified date.

July 2
Patrick Tchouwa, *Le Jeune Detective* LEGAL ACTION

Judicial police agents arrested Tchouwa, director of publication for the privately owned magazine *Le Jeune Detective*, at a hotel in Yaoundé. Tchouwa was detained at the Elig-Essono judicial police station. His arrest is in connection with the June 25 publication of an article which reported on the involvement of the Minister of Economy and Finance in a case of embezzlement of public funds.

On October 20, a Yaoundé court handed Tchouwa a three-month suspended sentence and a fine of 500,000 CFA (US$875).

November 12
Christopher Ezieh, *The Herald* IMPRISONED

Police arrested Ezieh, a reporter with the thrice-weekly, English-language independent newspaper *The Herald*, in Yaoundé and detained him at the Kumba police station. The arrest was in connection with an article published in the November 11 edition of the newspaper reporting that Peter Acham, governor of South-West Province, had ordered a 60-percent salary reduction for Kumba City Hall employees. Ezieh was released on November 16.

December 14
Nyemb Ntoogue, *Le Messager-Popoli* THREATENED

Ntoogue, also known as Nyemb Popoli, chief editor of the biweekly *Le Messager-Popoli*, fled the country after unknown assailants appeared at his home and terrorized his family. He had previously received numerous death threats, including a "choice" between "abandoning his career as a journalist and death by machete."

Cape Verde

On February 18, government authorities suspended the operations of the private radio station Radio Comercial, partly owned by a member of the political opposition, reversing press freedom gains in a country that has made a strong transition to multi-party democracy. Authorities said the frequency given to the station in 1997 was only provisional. But no similar action was taken against other broadcasters with provisional frequencies, suggesting strongly that the suspension was political. Self-censorship persists among state journalists, who fear demotion or outright dismissal for any perceived critical coverage of President Antonio Mascarenhas Monteiro and his Movement for Democracy party.

February 18
Radio Comercial CENSORED

Government authorities suspended the operations of the private radio station Radio Comercial on the grounds that the frequency given to the station in 1997 was "provisional." No similar action was taken against other radio stations with provisional frequencies. The station resumed broadcasting on November 7.

Chad

President Idriss Déby's transformation from a military dictator with strong ties to Libya and Sudan to a democratically elected president in 1996 was accompanied by increasing intolerance for the private press. Despite last year's multiparty elections for a National Legislative Assembly, and the hope for more freedoms under a constitution adopted by referendum in 1996, the government has reverted to intimidating the press in subtle and not so subtle ways.

In most cases, defamation suits have replaced his previous regime's overt acts of violence against the media. Yet the March flogging of a journalist by a soldier demonstrates that the independent press still has reason to be afraid—and that the country is a long way from true freedom of the press, an essential component of the democratic reforms that Déby claims to champion.

A number of journalists squared off against the state in court this year. In 1997, Déby filed a defamation case against *N'Djamena-Hebdo* after the independent weekly newspaper referred to him as a "partisan president." The judiciary, whose lack of independence has been widely condemned, ruled in the government's favor after a 15-day trial.

Despite the government's pattern of harassment, the privately owned press continues to report opposing views on such issues as the country's oil reserves, the environment, forced migration, and the means through which the government will distribute future oil revenues. As a result, authorities have accused journalists of being the "grave-diggers" of lucrative oil deals with foreign investors. This kind of pressure has led many journalists in both state-run and privately owned media to self-censorship.

Information reported by the state-owned media is strictly monitored and manipulated. When 100 Chadian soldiers supporting Laurent Kabila in the conflict in the Democratic Republic of Congo were reportedly killed in an ambush in October, officials stated that only two had died. And when government troops reportedly committed atrocities in the ongoing conflict between the north and south of the country, authorities invoked security concerns when barring independent journalists from reporting from the affected regions.

Prohibitively high government licensing

fees have stunted the growth of privately owned radio. In a country where illiteracy is high, this translates into lack of access to information. La Voix du Payson (The Voice of the Peasant), based in Deba and operated by an international Catholic organization, is currently the only private radio station in operation.

February 12
Yaldet Begoto Oulatar, *N'Djamena Hebdo*
LEGAL ACTION
Dieudonne Djonabaye, *N'Djamena Hebdo*
LEGAL ACTION

A correctional tribunal sentenced Oulatar and Djonabaye, director and chief editor, respectively, of the newspaper *N'Djamena Hebdo*, to two-year suspended prison sentences, fines of 100,000 CFA (US$180), and a symbolic sum of 1 CFA as compensation for defaming President Idriss Déby. Their sentences were in connection with the article "Déby, Un President Partisan," published in the paper's December 11, 1997, issue.

The two journalists appealed the judgment on February 13. At year's end, however, their case had not yet been forwarded to the Court of Appeal.

March 29
Dieudonne Djonabaye, *N'Djamena Hebdo*,
Radio France International ATTACKED

Soldiers arrested Djonabaye, editor in chief of the independent weekly *N'Djamena Hebdo* and a correspondent with Radio France International, at the main entrance of the Eperview military camp, where he had an appointment to interview a French officer. He was taken to the army's command center in N'Djamena, where he was interrogated and flogged with an electric cable. He was released by the director of the gendarmerie that day without any explanation for the attack.

June 3
Sy Koumbo Singa Gali, *L'Observateur*
IMPRISONED, LEGAL ACTION
Polycarpe Togomissi, *L'Observateur*
IMPRISONED, LEGAL ACTION

Gali and Togomissi, director of publication and reporter for the independent bimonthly *L'Observateur* respectively, were detained by court order at N'Djamena Prison, where they were held until their release on bail on June 12. Wada Abdelkader Kamougué, the president of the National Assembly, had filed a lawsuit against the journalists for defamation in connection with an article, written by Togomissi, titled "Le Dossier Pétrole Est Une Vaste Fumisterie Selon Yorongar N'Garléji" (The Oil Issue is a Big Joke According to Yorongar N'Garléji). The article was published in the July 9, 1997, edition.

On July 20, 1998, the High Court sentenced Gali and Togomissi to two-year suspended sentences and fined them 1 million CFA (US$1,680) each, although the maximum fine allowed by law for this charge is 500,000 CFA (US$890). The journalists appealed the ruling.

On December 29, the Court of Appeal sentenced Gali and Togomissi to one-year suspended sentences and fines of 500,000 CFA (US$890). The rulings contradict Article 44 (3) of Law N.29 concerning the press, which states that reporting only what someone has said does not incur liability for defamation.

Congo

Ongoing fighting between numerous ethnic-based militias such as the Cobras, which support head of state Denis Sassou-Nguesso, and the Zoulous, loyal to ousted President Pascal Lissouba, has terrorized civilians and claimed thousands of lives. Among the casualties this year was Fabien Fortune Bitoumbo, a correspondent for the

state-owned Radio Liberté. Bitoumbo was accompanying the minister of mining and industry on a trip to an area controlled by the Ninja militia group, which is loyal to Bernard Kolelas, a former prime minister and sometime Lissouba ally, when the entourage was taken hostage. On August 29, Ninja members executed Bitoumbo, solely because he was a journalist, shooting him at point-blank range.

The media are required to "show loyalty to the government" by order of a 1995 statute, which allows the seizure of printing presses during political emergencies. A 1996 press law requires the independent press to obtain commercial licenses and imposes exorbitant penalties for slander and defamation. The state retains control of electronic media with the exception of one radio station operated by Sasssou-Nguesso's political allies.

Journalists practice self-censorship in this treacherous environment, knowing they are potential targets all of the warring militia factions. In September, uniformed men raided the offices of the independent magazine *La Rue Meurt* and seized its computers. At year's end, as gun battles flared between the Ninja and Cobra militias in Brazzaville, many independent newspapers permanently ceased publishing.

August 29
Fabien Fortune Bitoumbo, Radio Liberte, *La Rue Meurt* KILLED

Bitoumbo, a broadcaster with the privately owned radio station Radio Liberté and the former editor in chief of the privately owned magazine *La Rue Meurt*, was gunned down at point-blank range by the Ninja militia, loyal to former Prime Minister Bernard Kolelas. Bitoumbo was on assignment, accompanying Minister of Mining and Industry Michel Mampouya on a trip to Mindouli (150 kilometers west of Brazzaville) when the group was taken hostage by the Ninja militia. Bitoumbo was reportedly the only hostage killed.

September 5
La Rue Meurt HARASSED

A group of armed uniformed men entered the editorial offices of the privately owned weekly magazine *La Rue Meurt* at 4 a.m., after sealing off the surrounding area of the neighborhood, and removed the magazine's computer equipment. Authorities offered no explanation for the raid and seizures.

Democratic Republic of Congo

Despite widespread optimism that Laurent-Désiré Kabila and his Alliance of Democratic Forces for the Liberation of the Congo (ADFL), who toppled the 32-year dictatorship of Mobutu Sese Seko, would bring greater freedom to the people of the country he renamed the Democratic Republic of Congo, he has sadly replaced one despot with another. The country's press has faced accusations of subversion and espionage ever since Kabila seized power—more than 71 journalists were detained without charge, attacked, or harassed since he took control in Kinshasa—and this year saw a record-breaking number of incidents of press freedom violations, with no end to the crisis in sight.

Journalists who have written about crackdowns against citizens espousing pro-democracy views under Kabila have themselves been imprisoned. No journalist has been immune from Kabila's intolerance for opposing views. When images of human rights violations by ADFL forces appeared on state-owned Radio Television National du Congo (RTNC), security agents quickly rounded up journalists working for the television station.

In August, the Congolese Rally for Democracy, a rebel movement, took up arms against Kabila; by late August, the rebels were on the outskirts of Kinshasa. Kabila labeled the rebellion a foreign invasion by Rwanda and Uganda, former allies who had helped bring him to power, and whose involvement was later revealed primarily by Ugandan independent journalists.

State media emphasized U.S. ties to the governments of Uganda and Rwanda, and Communications Adviser Dominique Sakombi accused foreign correspondents and employees of the international media of being "auxiliaries of the aggressors." Amid this increasingly antagonistic climate, foreign correspondents encountered hostile crowds, and soldiers who accused them of being spies and who arbitrarily detained them, even as journalists portrayed the humanitarian crisis in Kinshasa caused by rebels who cut the city's power supply and disrupted the distribution of drinking water. When one photographer took pictures of a woman carrying water on her head, Information Minister Didier Mumenge personally confiscated the film. Officials lectured journalists on ethics, while the state media broadcast hate messages against Tutsis, who were collectively accused of supporting the rebellion.

On August 25, the government confined the movement of foreign correspondents to organized pools. Many journalists were perplexed by the arbitrariness of the restrictions: Those in the pools were allowed to witness and report on Kabila's troops shooting captured rebels and throwing them from bridges to their death, while colleagues who ventured out on their own had been arrested—and in the case of a Reuters television crew, beaten in custody—for filming Kinshasa street scenes.

In late August, after troops from Angola, Namibia, Zimbabwe, and Chad poured into the country to support Kabila's efforts to repel the rebels from the capital, most of the international media headed home. Congolese journalists were left to report the news, without support or protection. State security agents raided the daily *Le Soft*, arresting staff and confiscating computer equipment after the newspaper published an article about a deal involving the government and a major diamond and mineral mining company whose chairman is Zimbabwean by birth. Authorities perceived the article as suggesting they were selling off the country's vast riches in return for Zimbabwe's military assistance.

In late November, CPJ wrote to Pope John Paul II shortly before he was to meet with Kabila at the Vatican, urging him to raise the press freedom crisis in the DRC and to use the moral authority of his office to seek the amelioration of conditions for journalists. At year's end, local journalists expressed little hope for an improvement of the press freedom climate. Instead, they anticipated an escalation of harassment and intimidation, citing the country's ongoing war and the Kabila government's penchant for blaming its military failures on the independent press.

February 7
Albert Bonsange Yema, *L'Alarme*, *L'Essor Africain* IMPRISONED

Yema, editor of the opposition newspapers *L'Alarme* and *L'Essor Africain*, was arrested in connection with a February 7 article, published in both newspapers, calling for the release of jailed opposition leader Joseph Olengankoy.

On June 1, the State Security Court convicted Yema of "threatening state security" and sentenced him to one year in prison. He is serving his sentence in Makala Central Prison. Yema is a diabetic, and is now receiving treatment at the general hospital in Kinshasa. Yema's conviction contravenes the country's press law, which only allows for civil penalties in this case because Yema is not the author of the article in contention.

February 20
Le Soft International CENSORED

Authorities seized and burned copies of *Le Soft International*, the Belgian edition of the independent Kinshasa newspaper *Le Soft*, which had arrived at the Kinshasa airport for sale in the Democratic Republic of Congo.

The confiscated edition carried the front-page headline, "Tshisekedi, Eternally Persecuted," accompanied by a 1997 photo of opposition leader Etienne Tshisekedi surrounded by a crowd that included an army officer who supported then-President Mobutu Sese Seko.

February 25
Modeste Mutinga, *Le Potentiel* IMPRISONED

Mutinga, editor and managing director of *Le Potentiel*, was arrested and detained at the headquarters of the National Security Council (CNS) in connection with an article published in the February 19 edition of the independent newspaper titled "Kabila's Kassai Sulk." The article reported on the forcible return of opposition leader and former prime minister Etienne Tshisekedi to his home town in the Kassai Province.

April 1
Radio Amani CENSORED

In late April, the government banned the Kisangani-based Catholic Archdiocese radio station Radio Amani for challenging a ban on political commentaries and press reviews by private broadcasters, and for "complicity with the British Broadcasting Corporation."

April 11
Michel Luya, *Le Palmares* IMPRISONED

Luya, editor of the independent Kinshasa daily newspaper *Le Palmares*, was arrested without charge in connection with the April 4 publication of a statement by opposition leader Etienne Tshisekedi titled "Message to the People." He was released on April 14.

April 12
Peter Boehm, *Die Tageszeitung* IMPRISONED, LEGAL ACTION, EXPELLED

Boehm, a correspondent for the German newspaper *Die Tageszeitung*, was arrested on April 12 while photographing a volcano in Goma. He was detained in the Kinshasa civil prison and charged with espionage. Boehm was deported to Germany on May 15. The charges against Boehm were still pending at year's end.

April 18
Andre Ipakala, *La Reference Plus* IMPRISONED

Military security agents arrested Ipakala, editor of the independent daily newspaper *La Reference Plus*. The action is believed to be in connection with an article published on April 15 reporting that members of President Kabila's entourage maintained "private jails" in their residences. Ipakala was released on April 20 after being extensively interrogated about his sources for the article.

May 15
Jose Kajangwa, Radio et Télévision National du Congo IMPRISONED

Kajangwa, the director general of Radio et Télévision National du Congo, was arrested with a team of broadcasters, reporters, and commentators in connection with the television broadcast of "Never Again," a program pro-

Attacks on the Press in 1998

duced by a United Nations agency in Kinshasa. The program contained images of the killings of Hutu refugees in the eastern region of the country during 1997. President Kabila had previously blocked a U.N. investigation into similar massacres, that were allegedly committed by the Kabila-led Alliance of Democratic Forces for the Liberation of the Congo. Kajangwa and the other journalists detained at the National Information Agency, were released over a period of 30 days.

May 21
Thierry Kyalumba, *Vision* IMPRISONED
Kingongo Saleh, *Vision* HARASSED
Bonane Ya Nzanzi, *Vision* HARASSED

Kyalumba, publication director of *Vision*, was arrested following the independent biweekly's publication of a series of articles he wrote reporting that Minister of Finance Tala Ngai had committed embezzlement. Ngai ordered Kyalumba's arrest without prior judicial permission.

Kyalumba was detained for 30 days at Makala Central Prison, during which time Saleh, *Vision*'s editor, was sought by intelligence agents for arrest in connection with the publication of a series of articles he wrote criticizing financial misappropriation by Contributions Director Batumona. *Vision* editorial director Nzanzi was also sought by intelligence agents for reporting on the nomination of Leta Mangassa as the head of the National Information Agency. Neither Saleh nor Nzanzi, who were both in hiding, was caught.

May 25
Kidimbu Mpese, *Le Soft* IMPRISONED
Awazi Kharomon, *Le Soft* IMPRISONED
Military intelligence service agents arrested *Le Soft* production editor Mpese and assistant editor in chief Kharomon for "publishing articles which undermine government actions." The articles, which were published in the May 21 edition of the independent newspaper, reported on the transfer of funds from the central bank to an armed forces account. The journalists were released on June 8.

June 3
Nlanda Ibanda, *Le Soft* THREATENED

An army major general summoned Ibanda, director of information for *Le Soft*, in connection with an article he wrote that was published in the independent daily on May 28 titled, "Juan Kabara is in a Delicate Situation." Once in custody, troops threatened to whip the journalist until a superior officer intervened. Ibanda was released later that day.

June 15
Achille Ekele Ngolmya, *Pot Pourri* IMPRISONED
Guy Kassongo Kilmbwe, *Pot Pourri* IMPRISONED

Security agents arrested Ngolmya and Kilumbwe, director and editor of the independent newspaper *Pot Pourri*, respectively, in connection with the publication of an article which reported that the minister of public works misappropriated a tractor and other agricultural equipment. The journalists were taken to the National Security Council, where they were detained for nine days before being freed on the order of President Laurent Kabila.

July 11
Modeste Mutinga, *Le Potentiel* HARASSED

Security service agents prevented Mutinga, editor and managing director of the independent newspaper *Le Potentiel*, from boarding a plane for New York at Kinshasa Airport. He was detained for four and a half hours, and security service agents conducted a search of his luggage before seizing his passport, airline tickets, and copies of that day's issue of *Le Potentiel*. Mutinga's passport was returned later that week and he was allowed to leave the country.

August 1
Freddy Loseke Lisoumbou, *La Libre Afrique* IMPRISONED

Military security forces arrested Lisoumbou, editor in chief of the three-times independent weekly *La Libre Afrique*, and held him at the National Security Council (CNS) headquarters. The arrest was in connection with an article published in the newspaper reporting on the "flight" from the country of Special Counsel to the Chief of State and Chief of the CNS, Mr. Kazadi. Loseke was released after several weeks.

August 19
David Guttenfelder, The Associated Press THREATENED

Soldiers detained Guttenfelder, a photographer for the Associated Press, as he sat in a car at a gas station in Kinshasa. They took him to a remote location, where they threatened his life. After several hours, the journalist persuaded the soldiers to take him to their commanding officer, who ordered his release.

August 20
Hugh Neville, Agence France-Presse (AFP) IMPRISONED
Lara Santoro, *Newsweek* IMPRISONED

Neville, special correspondent for AFP, and Santoro, an Italian journalist with the United States-based *Newsweek* magazine, were detained for questioning at the Kasumbalesa border station as they were speaking by satellite telephone with the secretary of Katanga Province. The journalists, who were accused by police of engaging in espionage, were detained at the Lubumbashi Secret Police headquarters until August 22, when they were forcibly taken to the border and expelled into Zambia.

August 23
Michael Huggins, Worldwide Television News (WTN) IMPRISONED
Michael Pohl, Worldwide Television News (WTN) IMPRISONED
Jonathan Colignon, Worldwide Television News (WTN) IMPRISONED

Three journalists from WTN—Huggins, a producer who holds both Australian and British citizenship; Pohl, a cameraman from Germany; and Colignon, an assistant who is a citizen of both the Democratic Republic of Congo and Belgium—were detained for questioning while filming in Kinshasa. The three carried accreditation from the Ministry of Information, which they displayed to the authorities. The television crew was first taken to the Ministry of Information, and then to the headquarters of the state security forces, where they were held incommunicado until August 25. During their detention, they were brought before Information Minister Didier Mumenge, who informed them that if their tape had fallen into the wrong hands, the rebels would have known what was happening in Kinshasa.

August 24
Foreign correspondents THREATENED

Dominique Sakombi, spokesman and spiritual adviser for President Laurent Kabila, issued a statement accusing foreign journalists of being agents of the country's aggressors. Sakombi stated that, "Some Western journalists operating in this country could easily be confused with trouble-making monsters. By their venomous, sinful writing and the poison of their reporting, they are responsible for an enormous sin against our people...The international media have shamefully set themselves on the side of the aggressors... God will quickly send the angel of death, finally dispersing them like dust."

August 24
Sipho Maseko, Reuters Television ATTACKED
Roger Koy, Reuters Television ATTACKED

Reuters cameraman Maseko, and Koy, a stringer, were detained for "filming a strategic installation" while shooting street scenes in Kinshasa. While in custody at the Ministry of Information, the journalists were assaulted by soldiers, who punched Maseko and Koy, hit them with rifle butts, and whipped them across the buttocks with belts. Koy, who is Congolese, was accused of being a traitor for working with foreign journalists. The journalists were released the same day.

August 29
Stephen Smith, *Libération* HARASSED

Security agents arrested Smith, a reporter for the Paris-based newspaper *Libération*, at his hotel on charges of "seditious writing" and "insulting the president." He was transported to the headquarters of the National Information Agency (ANR). The arrest is believed to be in connection with an article he wrote reporting that the country has historically relied on others to do its fighting. Smith was released later that day.

September 1
Modeste Mutinga, *Le Potentiel* HARASSED

Twenty members of the police special services arrested Mutinga, editor and managing director of the Kinshasa newspaper *Le Potentiel*, detained him for six hours, and then released him. Mutinga was questioned about an article published in the August 17 edition of *Le Potentiel*, reporting that a US$1,000,000 grant which President Laurent Kabila had reportedly given to the Congolese press was being distributed only to pro-government newspapers.

September 9
Semy Dieye, Voix du Peuple IMPRISONED
Lokota Itoko, Voix du Peuple IMPRISONED
Kuku Mamenga, Voix du Peuple IMPRISONED
Ntole Demazu, Voix du Peuple IMPRISONED

Imbanda Lokenga, Voix du Peuple IMPRISONED
Pronto, Voix du Peuple IMPRISONED

Military intelligence agents arrested Dieye, Itoko, Mamenga, Demazu, Lokenga, and Pronto, broadcasters with the national radio station Voix du Peuple, and accused them of "complicity with the rebels." The journalists were detained at the Kokolo 50th Brigade Military Camp until their release on September 16. They were re-arrested on September 18 and detained at the Military Detection of Anti-Patriotic Activities headquarters until their release on September 28. Upon release they were banned from future broadcasting work.

September 28
Albert Ntumba, *L'Alerte* IMPRISONED
Deby Bonsange, *L'Alerte* IMPRISONED

Ntumba and Bonsange, editor and editor in chief for *L'Alerte*, respectively, were arrested following the publication in the independent newspaper of an article reporting that Minister of State for the Interior Gaetan Kakudji had departed for Belgium during wartime. Bonsange was released from detention on October 20, and Ntumba was released at the end of October.

October 3
Belmonde Magloire Missinhoun, *La Pointe Congo* MISSING

Missinhoun, a citizen of Benin and owner of the Kinshasa-based independent financial newspaper *La Pointe Congo*, was last seen when he was arrested shortly after a traffic accident with a military vehicle in Kinshasa and transported to an unknown location. Police investigations into the journalist's disappearance have yielded no results to date. Missinhoun has lived in Kinshasa for approximately 30 years. *La Pointe Congo* has not published since the end of the Mobutu regime. It is feared that the journalist, who had close ties to the Mobutu regime, has been killed.

October 16
Paulin Tusumba Nkazi A Kanda, *Le Peuple* IMPRISONED

Kanda, editor of the independent newspaper *Le Peuple*, was arrested at his home for publishing a list of 29 people who allegedly financed the current rebellion in the country. Kanda was detained for four days at the Kinshasa police station before his release on October 20.

October 21
Clovis Mwamba Kayembe, *L'Alarme* IMPRISONED

Kayembe, a reporter for the opposition newspaper *L'Alarme*, was arrested in connection with an article he wrote about the departure for Belgium of Minister of State for the Interior Gaetan Kakudji, during wartime. Kayembe appeared before the appeals court subsequent to his arrest, and was detained at the Penitential and Reeducation Center of Kinshasa (CPRK). He was released on an unspecified date.

October 29
Bayard Kabango Mbaya, *La Flamme du Congo* IMPRISONED

A squad of heavily armed men in civilian clothes arrested Mbaya, a reporter with the independent newspaper *La Flamme du Congo*, at the newspaper's offices. He was taken into custody following an unsuccessful search for Gustave Kalenga, the paper's editor, whom the armed men had come to arrest. The search was in connection with an article published in the paper's October 20 edition, criticizing Abdoulaye Yerodia, the cabinet director of the chief of state. Mbaya was eventually transported to Kin Prison in Maziere, where he was held until his release on November 3.

November 1
Mbakulu Pambu Diambu, Radio-Télévision Matadi (RTM) IMPRISONED

Diambu, president of the local chapter of the Congolese Press Union and a broadcaster with the private station Radio-Télévision Matadi (RTM), was arrested in late November and detained at the Matadi National Information Agency offices. Diambu appeared before the Kinshasa Military Court and was charged with breaching state security for hosting an RTM television program on which he allegedly interviewed representatives of the Congolese Rally for Democracy rebel forces.

November 3
Gustave Kalenga, *La Flamme du Congo* IMPRISONED

Security agents of the National Information Agency (ANR) arrested Kalenga, editor of independent *La Flamme du Congo*, at the newspaper's offices. The arrest was in connection with an article published in the October 20 edition of the newspaper criticizing the Cabinet Director of the Chief of State, Abdoulaye Yerodia. *La Flamme du Congo* ceased publishing on the same date, and soldiers and security agents were posted in front of its offices to arrest Kalenga, who had gone into hiding when he received information about the pending arrest.

Kalenga was arrested when he returned to the newspaper's offices. He was released from headquarters of the National Security Counsel on November 10.

November 5
Awazi Kharomon, *Le Soft* IMPRISONED
Lubamba Lutoko, *Le Soft* IMPRISONED
Bébé Ediya, *Le Soft* IMPRISONED

Officers of the Rapid Intervention Police (PIR) arrested Kharomon, Lutoko, and Ediya, assistant editor in chief, commercial director and journalist, and intern, respectively, for the Kinshasa daily *Le Soft*, and detained them at the premises of the National Security Counsel along with newspaper employees Ricky Milunda, Buka, and Freddy, and a visitor, Kenda Waling. Kileba Pok-a-Mes, editor in chief of *Le Soft*, went into hiding. Police confiscated the *Le Soft*'s computers, printers, and other equipment, effectively closing the newspaper. The arrests are believed to be in connection with an article published in the November 3 edition of *Le Soft*, reporting on a joint venture between Gécamines, the major diamond and mineral mining company in the country, Ridgepoint, a private mineral marketing firm, and the government of the Democratic Republic of Congo.

November 19
Franck Baku, *La Reference Plus* LEGAL ACTION
Kitungano Milenge, *La Reference Plus* LEGAL ACTION

Baku and Milenge, reporters for the independent daily *La Reference Plus*, appeared before a Gombé court after being summoned by judicial police on an unspecified charge. The summons is believed to be in connection with a series of articles published in *La Reference Plus* reporting on the dismissal of 315 government officials.

November 21
Michel Museme Diawe, Radio et Télévision National du Congo (RTNC) IMPRISONED

Diawe, a senior reporter for RTNC, was arrested and detained at the Kokolo Military Camp after being accused by soldiers of "deserting" his position at the state television station. Diawe was released on November 29.

December 19
Yvette Idi Lupantsha, Radio et Télévision National du Congo IMPRISONED
Risasi Gisonga, IMPRISONED

Congolese National Police officers arrested Idi and Risasi, respectively news presenter and editor for the state-owned Radio et Télévision National du Congo, without charge at the station's Lingwala branch offices. The journalists were transported to the former headquarters of the military district of Kinshasa. Idi and Risasi were accused of being "traitors to the republic" and of having acted as spies for the United States for giving copies of a video cassette of a press conference held by President Laurent Kabila to U.S. Ambassador William Swing. They were released on December 22.

December 26
Freddy Loseke Lisoumbou, *La Libre Afrique* ATTACKED

Agents of the Special Group of the Presidential Security Service (GSSP) arrested Lisoumbou, editor in chief of the thrice-weekly *La Libre Afrique*, and whipped him more than 100 times during his detention. Lisoumbou was first taken to the offices of the Congolese National Police, then transferred to the Gombé offices of the GSSP, where he was assaulted. Lisoumbou was questioned about his sources for an article published in the December 22 edition of the newspaper titled "Un Gros Poisson a la Presidence de la Republique qui Veut a Destabiliser Kabila" (A Big Joke to Presidency of the Republic Who Wants to Destabilize Kabila), reporting that President Laurent Kabila's cabinet chief had misappropriated public funds. Lisoumbou was released later that day after being threatened with rearrest for any similar future reporting.

December 26
Robert Ndaye Tshisense, KHRT HARASSED

Tshisense, director of KHRT, an East Kasai-based private television station, was arrested on the order of the local head of the ruling political party, the Alliance of Democratic Forces for the Liberation of Congo (AFDL), for failing to broadcast political programs favorable to President Laurent Kabila. He was released the same day.

December 27
Mwin Murub Fel, RTKM
HARASSED

National Information Agency agents arrested Fel, a broadcaster with the private television station RTKM. The agents threatened Fel for allowing the broadcast of an interview with Cleophas Kamitatu Massamba, an official of the former Mobutu regime who was imprisoned for eight months by the government of President Laurent Kabila. Fel was released the same day.

Djibouti

Hassan Gouled Aptidon, who has run the country since Djibouti's independence from France in 1977, was elected president in 1993 in the country's first elections. His term will expire in May 1999 and his nephew and cabinet chief, Ismail Omar Gelleh, is his designated successor as well as the de facto leader of the country.

Government representation is among the issues dividing the population along ethnic lines between the Issa (Somali) majority and the Afar minority, as is a looming Afar-led insurgency reportedly gathering strength in the north of the country. In 1998, a reported 3,500 French troops remained in Djibouti to respond to any outbreak of unrest in this strategically located country at the tip of the Red Sea.

In the past few years, the independent print media have been allowed to function freely. However, against the backdrop of heightened ethnic tension, the government has begun exerting increasing pressure on the private press. Criminal Affairs Squad agents arrested Omar Ahmed Vincent and Aboubaker Ahmed Aouled, director of publication and editor in chief, respectively, of the weekly *Le Populaire*, on charges of "incitement to ethnic hatred" after the April 26 edition of the newspaper reported that Finance Minister Yacin Elmi Bouh was involved in an embezzlement scheme. Each was sentenced to two months in prison, and *Le Populaire* was suspended for six months. The government controls all radio broadcasting, which is the main source of information for the mostly rural population.

February 17
Ahmed Abdi Farah, *Al Wahda* IMPRISONED
Kamil Hassan Ali, *Al Wahda* IMPRISONED

Farah, the publishing director for the bimonthly Djibouti Opposition Front newspaper *Al Wahda*, and Ali, a correspondent for *Al Wahda*, were arrested and detained in Gabode prison. The action was in connection with several articles published in the February 5, 1997, edition of the newspaper that were critical of the government's policies. Both journalists were released on February 26. Their equipment, confiscated upon their arrest, was not returned.

May 5
Omar Ahmed Vincent, *Le Populaire*
IMPRISONED, HARASSED
Aboubaker Ahmed Aouled, *Le Populaire*
IMPRISONED, HARASSED
Le Populaire CENSORED

Officers of the Criminal Affairs Squad arrested Vincent, director of publication of the weekly *Le Populaire*, and Aouled, the paper's editor in chief, at the newspaper's editorial offices. They also confiscated the paper's computer equipment.

The arrests were in connection with an article published in the April 26 edition of *Le Populaire* reporting that Finance Minister Yacin Elmi Bouh was involved in an embezzlement scheme. Vincent and Aouled were held overnight at the Criminal Affairs Squad and transferred to Gabode Central Prison on May 6.

On May 7, *Le Populaire* was suspended for 6 months. On May 24, Vincent and Aouled were sentenced to two months in prison for "incitment to ethnic hate." The journalists were released on July 8.

Equatorial Guinea

Teodoro Obiang Nguema M'basogo came to power in a 1979 coup and immediately executed his uncle, the authoritarian ruler he deposed. M'basogo's dictatorial style of governance hasn't changed appreciably since then. This year, M'basogo allowed foreign journalists to cover a trial that offered a rare and uncomfortable window into the country's history of rule by iron fist. He may have believed this openness could help restore the international credibility and foreign aid the country lost in 1993 after he brutally cracked down on his political opposition.

The result was apparently not what authorities had expected. On May 31, eight foreign correspondents covering the trial of 117 citizens from the Bubi ethnic group were expelled from the country because authorities viewed their reports of irregularities in the proceedings and signs that the defendants had been tortured as "tendentious." The Bubi defendants are accused of secession for attacking government forces in January on Bioka, the oil-rich but impoverished island that they inhabit. For the foreseeable future, local journalists will continue to practice self-censorship in an environment rigidly intolerant of critical viewpoints, where the media are tightly controlled by the state.

Attacks on the Press in 1998

May 31
El Pais EXPELLED
La Vanguardia EXPELLED
El Heraldo de Aragon EXPELLED
EFE EXPELLED
TVE EXPELLED

The government ordered the expulsion from the country of eight correspondents for the Spanish newspapers *El Pais*, *La Vanguardia*, *El Heraldo de Aragon*, the Spanish news agency EFE, and the Spanish state television channel TVE. Since May 25, the journalists had been covering the trial of 113 opposition activists. On May 30, the government "invited" the journalists, whose reporting they claimed was "tendentious," to leave the country.

Eritrea

At the end of the year, Eritrea and Ethiopia were on the verge of full-scale war over a small area on their common border. Attempts at mediation, brokered by a host of African and Western governments, have failed because of the sheer determination of both President Isaias Afwerki and Ethiopia's Prime Minister Meles Zenawi to wage a war that the two poverty-stricken countries can ill afford. The fact that Afwerki and Meles were comrades in arms and victors in a protracted war against Ethiopia's former Marxist military dictator Mengistu Haile Mariam is just one of a number of ironic factors contributing to the personal nature of this conflict.

Any reporter who doubted that the regime would punish independent reporting had only to take note of the 20-month detention without charge of Agence France-Presse (AFP) correspondent Ruth Simon. In this hostile environment, local journalists stuck to strictly pro-government reporting and carefully confined the topics they covered to those that reinforced the regime's nationalistic fervor, such as Ethiopia's forced deportation of Ethiopian citizens of Eritrean discent. In contrast, there was little critical coverage when the Eritrean government began its expulsion of Eritrean citizens of Ethiopian origin.

When the conflict began in May, privately owned magazines and newspapers were being published, and were being sold and read freely. Their content, however, is regulated by a 1997 press law mandating that both news and opinion conform to the official interpretation of "the objective reality of Eritrea." The broadcast media, consisting of one television and one radio station, remain under government control, and there are no provisions in effect allowing for private ownership of broadcast media. Although private ownership of the print media is allowed, newspapers and magazines must obtain licenses from the Ministry of Information, and all reporters must be registered with the ministry.

In November, CPJ presented an International Press Freedom Award to Ruth Simon in absentia—part of a campaign to bring world attention to her plight and to secure her release. At that time, Simon was the only female journalist in detention in the region, and she had been imprisoned without charge since April 1997—longer than any other journalist in the region. She was released in December, but at press time, the Eritrean government had not clarified the terms of her release. (See page 66 for more on Ruth Simon and the International Press Freedom Awards.)

May 11
Ruth Simon, Agence France-Presse
THREATENED

President Isaias Afwerki announced that Simon, a correspondent for the Agence France-Presse (AFP) news agency, who had been imprisoned since April 25, 1997, would face trial for violating the national press law and that the state intended to sue AFP for using a "so-called agent" to disseminate false information.

In response to CPJ's June 25, 1997 letter to Afwerki demanding Simon's release, the Eritrean Ministry of Foreign Affairs said that Simon was arrested for violating the national press law.

In November, Simon received CPJ's 1998 International Press Freedom Award and her plight was raised in meetings with White House and U.S. State Department officials.

On December 29, an Eritrean Information Ministry spokesman said that Simon had been released and CPJ confirmed that Simon had been freed.

Ethiopia

Incarceration has long been Prime Minister Meles Zenawi's punishment of choice for journalists, so it was not surprising that Ethiopia once again led Africa in the number of journalists in prison at the end of the year—or that Meles again earned a place among CPJ's 10 worst Enemies of the Press (see page 62). Repeated crackdowns on the independent media throughout the year testified to a repressive environment that is expected to deteriorate even more as Ethiopia and Eritrea spar on the brink of a full-scale war.

Although Meles has argued that press freedom threatens democracy because the media could incite ethnic hatred, his treatment of the press reveals his own antidemocratic impulses. For example, on July 13, Shimelis Kemal, Berhanu Negash, and Teferi Mekonnen, editors of the independent newspaper *Nishan*, were arrested in Addis Ababa after the publication of an article warning against ethnic intolerance toward Eritreans. They were released the next day, but were arrested again on July 15 and remained in detention for more

Attacks on the Press in 1998

than three months after they issued a statement criticizing their initial arrest.

Numerous statutes severely restrict reporting and grant the state broad powers to silence journalists. Press Proclamation 34, issued in 1992, bans dissemination of information that the government deems dangerous to the society. Article 8 of the law leaves the definition of "secret information" open to broad interpretation and does not offer specific guidelines on what constitutes a "criminal offense against the safety of the state, the administration, or national defence." Zealous prosecutors and a compliant judiciary perpetuate a system that cycles journalists through the country's prisons on ad hoc charges or often no charges at all. Because the bail and fines imposed on journalists are prohibitive, they often languish behind bars.

Newspapers and magazines must register with the Ministry of Information in order to be granted a publishing license, and reporters must also register with the ministry. The state continues to control all broadcast media.

Ethiopia's dubious distinction of imprisoning the greatest number of journalists in sub-Saharan Africa for all but one of the past five years has had a severe impact on the country's journalists, causing many to leave the profession. For those who remain and persevere in their profession, imprisonment has sometimes proven fatal: In February, Abay Hailu, editor of *Wolafen*, died after prison authorities denied him medical treatment for a serious ailment.

January 2
Dawit Kebede, *Fiameta* IMPRISONED

Dawit, manager and editor in chief of the independent Amharic-language weekly *Fiameta*, was arrested in connection with three published articles reporting that police of the Wereda 24 Police Station Prison detained citizens without court orders, kept them in dark cells, and tortured them. The newspaper published the names of the tortured prisoners and reported that one prisoner was killed and secretly buried while in custody. Police demanded that Dawit reveal his sources, which he refused to do. He was released on January 12 on an unspecified amount of bail.

January 12
Mukemil Shehibo, *Beza* IMPRISONED

Mukemil, editor in chief of the independent Amharic-language weekly *Beza*, was detained at the Region 14 Police Commission on charges of publishing false information. The charges were in connection with an article which appeared in *Beza* about the dismissal of a district policeman. The same information was orginally published in the biweekly *Addis Lesan*, which reported on corruption within Addis Ababa's regional police force. Mukemil was released on an unspecified date.

January 16
Birru Tsegaye, *Tobia* HARASSED
Goshu Moges, *Tobia* HARASSED
Taye Belachew, *Tobia* HARASSED
Anteneh Merid, *Tobia* HARASSED
Tobia ATTACKED, HARASSED, CENSORED

Addis Ababa police arrested editor in chief Birru, acting manager Goshu, editor Taye, and deputy editor Anteneh of the independent newspaper *Tobia* without charge. Five hours after the arrests, *Tobia*'s editorial offices were destroyed by a fire of undetermined origin.

The arrests are believed to be in connection with the publication of a circular from a local United Nations agency, in the previous week's issue of *Tobia*, urging foreign workers to stockpile food, cash, and oil supplies in anticipation of a possible humanitarian crisis in Ethiopia.

Goshu and Anteneh were released on July 29, although the Federal First Instance Court had ordered their release earlier in the month. Birru and Taye were later released on unspecified dates on bail of 10,000 birr (US$1,500) each.

January 22
Berhanu Leyewe, *Keyete*, *Taime Fiqir*
IMPRISONED

Berhanu, managing editor of the privately owned weekly newspapers *Keyete* and *Taime Fiqir*, was arrested without charge and detained at an unknown location. Berhanu was released on an unspecified date.

January 22
Lulu Kebede, *Neka* IMPRISONED, HARASSED

Police arrested Lulu, former editor in chief of the now-defunct independent Amharic-language weekly *Neka*, on libel charges in connection with an article that appeared in *Neka* in 1995. The article reported that most members of the then-newly elected Ethiopian Parliament were rubber-stamping the decisions of a few influential members of parliament. Lulu, who was unable to make the 2,000 birr (US$300) bail, was detained in Addis Ababa Central Prison. He fled to Kenya after his release on an unspecified date.

On August 22, Kenyan security agents arrested Lulu and several other refugees in connection with the bombing of the U.S. embassy in Nairobi. The arrest occurred even though Lulu, as a refugee, was under the protection of the United Nations High Commissioner for Refugees. On August 27, Lulu was unconditionally released by Kenyan authorities.

January 31
Iyob Demeke, *Tarik* HARASSED

Police detained Iyob, publisher of *Tarik*, and questioned him about an article published on January 31 reporting that Ethiopian orthodox monks from the Tigray region were engaged in cannabis production. Iyob was released the same day on bail of 5,000 birr (US$750).

The week prior to its publication in *Tarik*, the same information had been broadcast on a weekly police program on state-owned Ethiopia Television without repercussion.

February 10
Kifle Mulat, *Ethio-Time*, Ethiopian Free Press Journalists Association (EFPJA)
IMPRISONED

Security police summoned Kifle, editor in chief of *Ethio-Time* and chairman of the coordinating committee of the EFPJA, to the Ma'ekelawi Central Criminal Investigation Office in connection with an EFPJA statement listing the names of detained journalists. The officers ordered Kifle to issue another statement describing detained editors of the newspaper *Urjii* as terrorists rather than journalists. The next day, Kifle returned to the Ma'ekelawi Central Criminal Investigation Office, as instructed, and informed the authorities that EFPJA would not make such a statement. He was subsequently detained at Addis Ababa Central Prison, where he was held until his release on an unspecified date.

February 13
Abay Hailu, *Wolafen* KILLED

Abay, editor of the Amharic-language weekly newspaper *Wolafen*, died of lung failure at Menilik Hospital. He had been serving a one-year prison sentence, handed down on November 25, 1997, in connection with articles he published about the threat of Islamic fundamentalism in Ethiopia.

Abay was detained on February 27, 1997, and kept in jail because he was unable to present bail of 5,000 birr (approximately US$715). He had a lung ailment and was moved to the prison hospital. After two months, although he had not yet recovered, Abay was released from the prison hospital. He was admitted to Menilik Hospital a few weeks later, where he died after a five-day stay.

Attacks on the Press in 1998

March 24
Fisseha Alemu, *Tarik* IMPRISONED

Police arrested Fisseha, editor in chief of the Amharic-language independent weekly newspaper *Tarik*, and held him at the Ma'ekelawi Central Criminal Investigation Office.

Authorities would not provide an explanation for Fisseha's arrest, but local journalists beleive it is in connection with an article published in *Tarik* on January 31 which reported that Ethiopian orthodox monks from the Tigray region were engaged in cannabis production.

Fisseha was detained at the Ma'ekelawi Central Criminal Investigation Office Prison, and later transported to the Addis Ababa Central Prison where he is currently being held.

April 1
Wondwossen Asfaw, *Atkurot* IMPRISONED

Wondwossen, editor in chief of the privately owned newspaper *Atkurot*, was detained on unspecified charges at the Addis Ababa Central Prison. He remains in prison, because he was unable to post bail of 10,000 birr ($US1,500).

April 4
Dawit Kebede, *Fiyameta* IMPRISONED

Plainclothes security agents arrested Dawit, publisher and editor in chief of the Amharic-language independent weekly *Fiyameta*, at his home. The agents transported him to Ma'ekelawi Central Criminal Investigation Office Prison, and then to Awassa (430 kilometers south of Addis Ababa), but did not provide any explanation for the arrest.

The arrest was in connection with a story published in the March 25 issue of *Fiyameta* reporting that a 17-year-old girl had been abducted by the president of the South Nations Regional State with the complicity of state police.

May 4
Tsegaye Ayelew, *Genanaw* IMPRISONED

Tsegaye, editor of the privately owned weekly newspaper *Genanaw*, was detained at the Ma'ekelawi Central Criminal Investigation Office Prison in Addis Ababa. His arrest was in connection with an article published in a November 1997 issue of the newspaper reporting about new Ethiopian bank notes. He was released on September 9 on bail of 12,000 birr (US$1,700).

May 9
Alemayehu Kifle, *Zegabi, Genanaw* IMPRISONED

Alemayehu, editor of the privately owned newspaper *Zegabi*, was arrested in connection with an article he wrote for the independent newspaper *Genanaw* in 1996, in which he described the conditions of detention in Ethiopian jails. Unable to meet his 4,000-birr (US$600) bail, Alemayehu remained in prison until his release on May 20. He immediately went into hiding.

May 12
Alemayehu Sherew, *Tarik* IMPRISONED

Alemayehu, deputy editor of the privately owned newspaper *Tarik*, was arrested for publishing an article about cannabis production in monasteries in the Tigre region. Alemayehu, who is being detained at the Ma'ekelawi Central Criminal Investigation Office Prison in Addis Ababa, was reportedly ill with tuberculosis and had not received any medical care during his detention. He was released on an unspecified date.

May 12
Dawit Taye, *Aemro* IMPRISONED

Dawit, a journalist with the weekly *Aemro*, was arrested in connection with an editorial he wrote about security issues published shortly after a 1995 assassination attempt on Egyptian President Hosni Mubarak in Addis Ababa. Dawit could not pay his 3,500-birr (US$530) bail and was immediately detained. He was released on an unspecified date.

May 15
Mekonnen Worku, *Maebel* IMPRISONED

Mekonnen, deputy editor in chief of the privately owned newspaper *Maebel*, was detained for an unspecified charge at the Ma'ekelawi Central Criminal Investigation Office Prison. He was released on September 8.

June 19
Tesfa Tegegn, *Beza* IMPRISONED

Tesfa, the former editor in chief of the privately owned newspaper *Beza*, was detained and held at Addis Ababa Central Prison on unspecified charges. Tesfa had been released on June 10, on bail of 2,000 birr (US$286) after his detention in March at the Addis Ababa Central Prison.

July 1
Zegeye Haile, *Genanaw* IMPRISONED, LEGAL ACTION

Zegeye, publisher and editor of *Genanaw*, an independent weekly newspaper, was arrested and detained without charge. On July 8, Zegeye was fined 10,000 birr (US$1,430) and sentenced to a two-year suspended sentence for publishing articles deemed libelous. The decision says the suspended sentence will be enforced if Zegeye publishes any story deemed offensive by the authorities during the next four years.

July 11
Bizunesh Debebe, *Zegabi* IMPRISONED

Bizunesh, publisher and deputy editor of the Amharic-language weekly *Zegabi*, was detained after her bail guarantor for a previous charge withdrew his collateral for the bail. She was held at Ma'ekelawi Central Criminal Investigation Office Prison and released 13 days later, after meeting bail of 10,000 birr (US$1,500).

July 13
Shimelis Kemal, *Nishan* IMPRISONED
Berhanu Negash, *Nishan* IMPRISONED
Teferi Mekonnen, *Nishan* IMPRISONED

Shimelis, Berhanu, and Teferi, editors of *Nishan*, were arrested in Addis Ababa in connection with an article published in the independent newspaper's first edition. The article criticized the government for detaining and deporting Eritreans, and it warned against ethnic animosity. The editors were released on July 14, but then rearrested the next day after they issued a statement criticizing the initial arrests.

Shimelis, Berhanu, and Teferi, who did not appear in court despite a law requiring such an appearance within 48 hours of an arrest, were released during the last week of September.

September 28
Tilahun Bekele, *Fetash* IMPRISONED

Tilahun, editor in chief of *Fetash*, was detained during the last week of September at the Ma'ekelawi Central Criminal Investigation Office Prison on charges of libel against the Crown Mineral Water Company.

October 5
Samson Seyoum, *Goh* IMPRISONED

Samson, editor in chief of the privately owned newspaper *Goh*, was detained without charge at the Ma'ekelawi Central Criminal Investigation Office Prison. He was released during December.

Gabon

President Omar Albert-Bernard Bongo,

Attacks on the Press in 1998

sub-Saharan Africa's second-longest-ruling leader and one of France's staunchest allies in the region, was declared the winner of the December 1997 elections, further consolidating his Democratic Party of Gabon's grip on power. The polls, which virtually eliminated all opposition parties from participation in government, were marred by serious irregularities, the manipulation of state broadcast media, and crackdowns on the independent media for publishing opposition party platforms.

Although there are a number of privately owned newspapers and radio stations, the government continues to control all television broadcasting in the country. Authorities relentlessly clamped down on the private media this year, through bans on both the broadcast and print media and jail terms for journalists. And the private radio stations currently in operation face closure at a moment's notice.

On February 20, the National Communication Council, a body composed of presidential appointees, banned the private radio station Radio Soleil for five weeks. The station, which has close ties to the opposition National Union of Timberworkers, was prevented from broadcasting an editorial criticizing President Bongo. On August 12, Michel Ongoundou-Loundah, Raphael Ntoutoume Nkoghe, and Pulchérie Beaumel, respectively publication director, editor in chief, and reporter for the private weekly newspaper *La Griffe*, were each sentenced to an eight-month prison term and fined CFA 3,000,000 (US$5,000) in damages payable to René Morvan, director general of the state-owned Air Gabon. In June, the newspaper had reported that Morvan was involved in ivory smuggling. On August 13, state security agents raided the offices of *La Griffe*, detained employees, seized their identity cards, and returned later that evening to confiscate 12,000 copies of the newspaper.

In December, when listeners called in to Radio Soleil's program, "Feed-Back," to discuss fraudulent government activities during the December 1997 elections, authorities jammed the station's signal. Reporting on allegations of torture in Gabon's prisons and financial impropriety by government officials has also brought swift reprisals.

February 20
Radio Soleil CENSORED

The National Communication Council banned the independent station Radio Soleil from broadcasting in connection with an editorial broadcast that week which satirized Gabon's President Omar Bongo. The radio station has close ties to the National Union of Timberworkers opposition party. The station has since resumed broadcasting.

August 12
Michel Ongoundou-Loundah, *La Griffe* IMPRISONED, LEGAL ACTION
Raphael Ntoutoume Nkoghe, *La Griffe* IMPRISONED, LEGAL ACTION
Pulcherie Beaumel, *La Griffe* IMPRISONED, LEGAL ACTION
La Griffe CENSORED

Publication director Ongoundou-Loundah, editor in chief Nkoghe, and reporter Beaumel for the private weekly *La Griffe*, were each sentenced to eight months in prison and fined 3,000,000 CFA (US$5,000) in damages and interest payable to Air Gabon Director General René Morvan. The case was in connection with an article published in a June issue of *La Griffe* reporting that Morvan was involved in ivory smuggling.

On August 13, state security agents entered the editorial offices of *La Griffe*, detained employees for three hours and seized their identity cards. Later that same evening, security agents seized 12,000 copies of *La Griffe* along with computer disks. The seizure was carried out under orders of the attorney general to destroy the newspaper's edition. The seizure of the computer disks prevented the newspaper from publishing the following day.

December 7
Radio Soleil CENSORED

Authorities jammed broadcasts by the privately owned radio station Radio Soleil were jammed and turned off the station's telephone lines. That same day, the Conseil National de la Communication (National Communication Council) issued a press release criticizing Radio Soleil for a lack of "journalistic ethics" during "Feed-Back," a listener call-in program. Recent broadcasts of the program aired listeners' calls denouncing what they perceived as fraudulent activities during the December 6 presidential elections. The CNC also warned Radio Soleil that the station would be permanently suspended for any subsequent offenses.

The Gambia

Yahya A. J. J. Jammeh seized power in 1994 as a 29-year-old army lieutenant, and was elected president in the September 1996 elections that were fraught with irregularities. Jammeh's efforts to shed his image as a military strongman and remake himself into a civilian leader have brought him some international credibility and the return of foreign aid that had been cut off during the earlier years of his dictatorship. The independent media, however, have yet to receive any benefits from the president's makeover; press freedom violations that began after the 1994 coup have escalated rather than declined.

The 1996 Newspaper Decrees #70 and #71 enacted exorbitant fines for any contravention of the 1994 Newspaper Act, which criminalizes the failure of independent publications to register annually with the government, and increased the registration bond for existing newspapers by 100 percent. State-owned publications are not subject to these decrees, whose clear intent is to financially cripple the independent press and thereby eliminate the competition. The state-run radio station, Radio Gambia, broadcasts censored news, and the country's only television station is firmly under state control. "Political literature" is also barred by decree.

On February 5, agents of the National Intelligence Agency (NIA), which has far-reaching powers of arrest, exercised that power on the owner and news editor of Citizen FM radio after the station reported that the director of the NIA was involved in a counterfeiting scandal. The following day, NIA agents returned and sealed the radio station's offices, which it shared with the independent newspaper *New Citizen*, forcing the station to go off the air and the newspaper to stop publishing. On August 28, a Banjul court fined the journalists, and confiscated their equipment.

In this hostile climate, many journalists who have been targeted with reprisals for their critical coverage of the state and its policies increasingly face bankruptcy as a result of the state's unrelenting assault.

February 5
Boubacar Gaye, Citizen FM radio
IMPRISONED
Ebrima Sillah, Citizen FM radio
IMPRISONED
Citizen FM radio CENSORED
New Citizen CENSORED

National Intelligence Agency (NIA) agents arrested Gaye and Sillah, the proprietor and news editor, respectively, of Citizen FM radio, and transported them to NIA headquarters for questioning about a report on Citizen FM concerning the firing of NIA's director of operations for his involvement in a counterfeiting scandal. The Ministry of Information and Justice charged that the report was "irresponsible and deceptive," and violated national security. Authorities cited Citizen FM's failure to pay a 1,000 dalasis (US$100) licensing fee.

On February 6, NIA officials and more than a dozen armed soldiers sealed off the Citizen FM offices, which are shared by the *New Citizen* newspaper, and ordered all staff members to leave the premises, forcing the station off the air and *New Citizen* to stop publishing.

Gaye was released on bail on February 9 and ordered to report daily to the NIA, where he was rearrested the following day. On February 12, Gaye pleaded innocent to charges of operating an unlicensed radio station.

On March 5, Gaye was charged in a Banjul court with operating a radio station without a license under the 1913 Telegraph Station Act. Gaye pleaded innocent to the charge. On August 28, Gaye was found guilty of the charges and the Magistrate imposed a fine of 300 dalasis (US$30) and ordered the transfer of all of Citizen FM's broadcast equipment to the state.

August 30
Theophilus George, *Daily Observer*
HARASSED
Baba Galeh Jallow, *Daily Observer*
HARASSED
Demba Jawa, *Daily Observer* HARASSED
Managing director George, editor in chief Jallow, and news editor Jawa of the independent newspaper *Daily Observer*, were arrested and detained at an unknown location. The arrest was in connection with an article published in the *Daily Observer* about the discovery of armored cars and an armory behind a collapsed wall of the State House. The journalists were released on September 1.

Ghana

As Ghanaians look optimistically toward the presidential elections scheduled for 2000—hoping to avoid the devastating political crises and civil wars plaguing the West Africa sub-region—President Jerry Rawlings has endorsed Vice President John Atta Mills for the candidacy of the ruling National Democratic Congress (NDC). The NDC has the advantage of campaigning with the full support of state media, which rarely air or publish opposition viewpoints or critical reporting on the government, and reach far more of the population than the country's independent radio stations. Nevertheless, Ghana's vibrant private press is expected to continue to cover the full range of issues and views in the run-up to the election.

Although the December 1996 vote was considered free and fair by international observers, the cornerstones of an open society remain shaky. Government harassment in the form of arrests and protracted legal battles continue to frustrate the independent press's efforts to report on such subjects as corruption and economic issues including the privatization of public industries and international investment in the country. Political prisoners languish behind bars, and the judiciary is less than independent, especially in media-related cases. Although the constitution guarantees free expression, the courts continue to enforce criminal defamation laws—some dating back to the colonial era—that punish reporting deemed likely "to injure the reputation of Ghana."

On July 23, the Court of Appeal sentenced two newspaper editors—Haruna Atta of *The Weekend Statesman*, and Kweku Baako, Jr., of *The Guide*—to one-month prison terms for contempt of court, and the journalists' publishers were fined US$3,000 each, in a lawsuit brought by First Lady Nana Konadu Agyemang Rawlings in 1997. She had sued the two journalists and their publications for stories about her sister joining the opposition New Patriotic Party.

January 19
Kweku Baako, Jr., *The Guide* HARASSED

The Ministry of Communications summoned Baako, editor of the independent weekly newspaper *The Guide*, to the Police Criminal Investigation Division Flying Squad headquarters. He was questioned in connection with a letter printed in the November 13-19, 1997, issue of the newspaper titled "Is Warrant Officer Salifu Amankwa Heading a Task Force or a Para-military Unit?" Baako was released the same day after writing a statement explaining the circumstances surrounding the publication of the letter.

May 29
Bunmi Aborisade, *The Independent* HARASSED
Lewis Asubiojo, *The Independent* HARASSED

Immigration Department agents arrested Aborisade and Asubiojo, columnist and reporter respectively with *The Independent* who were in exile in Ghana in connection with their critical reporting on the Abacha regime in Nigeria. The officials demanded the journalists' passports and transported them to the offices of the Immigration Department where they were threatened with deportation.

Aborisade and Asubiojo were released after posting bail bonds of 1.5 million cedis (US$645.00) each with surety, and immigration authorities ordered them to cease their critical coverage of Nigerian politics in the Ghanaian press.

July 23
Haruna Atta, *The Weekend Statesman* IMPRISONED, LEGAL ACTION
Kweku Baako, Jr., *The Guide* IMPRISONED, LEGAL ACTION
Kinesic Publications LEGAL ACTION
Western Publications LEGAL ACTION

The Court of Appeal found Atta, editor of *The Weekend Statesman*, and Baako, editor of *The Guide*, guilty of contempt of court charges. The editors were sentenced to one month's imprisonment. Their publishers, Kinesic Publications and Western Publications respectively, were fined 10 million cedis (US$3,000) each.

The contempt conviction was the result of a lawsuit charging that the journalists had published libelous information about First Lady Nana Konadu Agyemang Rawlings. An earlier court order had restrained them from publishing anything about the Mrs. Rawlings pending the outcome of the lawsuit.

Lawyers for the two journalists filed a notice of appeal and a stay of execution of the court's order pending the hearing of the application.

Atta and Baako remained in custody without bail as the Supreme Court recessed for the summer holiday beginning July 24. By late July, the journalists were moved from Nsawam Medium Prison to notoriously worse prisons: Baako to Winneba Prison in the central region, and Atta to Akuse Prison in the eastern region.

On July 31, the Court of Appeal dismissed an application for bail filed by the jailed editors pending the determination of an appeal of their conviction. The court ruled that the application was without merit. Atta and Baako were released from prison on August 22.

July 27
Ebenezer Ato Sam, *Free Press* IMPRISONED, LEGAL ACTION
Tommy Thompson Publications Ltd. LEGAL ACTION

Sam, the suspended editor of the *Free Press*, was found guilty of contempt of court and sentenced to a 21-day jail term in default of a 5 million cedis (US$2,000) fine. The sentence was handed down in an Accra High Court presided over by Justice Owusu Sekyere.

Two million cedis (about US$870) were also awarded to the plaintiff, Minister of Local Government and Rural Development Kwamena Ahwoi, against Tommy Thompson Publications Limited, publishers of the *Free Press*.

The contempt of court conviction arose from a libel suit brought earlier by Ahwoi against the *Free Press*. The suit challenged a *Free Press* article reporting that Ahwoi had embezzled funds from the district common fund to finance his brother's cocoa purchasing business. The *Free Press* had settled the case out of court with Ahwoi for 7.5 million cedis (US$3,000). Sam was released from prison on August 22.

Guinea

Lansana Conte, who seized power in a 1984 military coup d'état and assumed the presidency in the 1993 elections that were widely condemned for their vote-counting irregularities, was re-elected to a second term in December. Less than 24 hours after the elections, Alpha Conde, leader of the opposition Guinean People's Rally (RPG), was arrested. Conde was subsequently charged with plotting to overthrow the government—an allegation that has been denounced by both citizens and international observers.

Government-owned broadcast media and the country's only daily newspaper, which rarely publishes opposition viewpoints or critiques of the government, provided one-sided coverage of the elections. Journalists who tried to provide balanced coverage ran afoul of the authorities. On December 24, the National Council on Communications (CNC) revoked the accreditation of Mouctar Bah, Conakry correspondent for Agence France-Presse (AFP) and Radio France Internationale (RFI), for the "malicious character" of his election coverage.

Although several independent weeklies scrutinize the government, these newspapers operate under the constant threat of seditious libel charges for any coverage

Attacks on the Press in 1998

deemed insulting to the president. The constitution provides for some freedom of expression, but defamation and slander are criminal offenses.

Foreign journalists were expelled this year for their coverage of socio-economic problems arising from the increasing number of refugees streaming into Guinea to escape conflicts in neighboring countries.

January 7
Foday Fofana, *L'Independent*, British Broadcasting Corporation (BBC) EXPELLED

Fofana, a Sierra Leonean reporter with *L'Independent* and correspondent for the BBC, was expelled from Guinea to Sierra Leone. The expulsion occurred immediately after his release from a three-month detention at the Conakry Central Detention Centre for having reported on the alleged assault of a civilian by an assistant commander at the Alpha Yaya Refugee Camp in Conakry.

Fofana was accused of "attacking state security," "lies and the use of lies," "attempting to usurp title and function," and "violation of judicial measures concerning foreign visits to Guinea."

March 8
Aboubacar Conde, *L'Independent* HARASSED

Mafanco police arrested Conde, editor in chief of *L'Independent*, and detained him at a police station in Conakry. He had been interrogated on March 6 in connection with an article, published the same week, reporting on negative public opinion of the government's December 26, 1997, closure of the private newspapers *L'Independent* and *Le Lynx*. Conde was released on March 9.

March 16
Saliou Samb, *L'Independent* EXPELLED

The Territorial Control Office (Direction de la Surveillance du Territoire [DST]) expelled

Samb, a Senegalese national who is assistant editor in chief of *L'Independent*. He was accused of "forgery" and "the use of forgery" regarding his identification documents. DST agents took Samb into custody at the newspaper's editorial offices in Conakry and forced him to board an airplane en route to Dakar.

March 17
Abdoulaye Sankara, *L'Independent*
HARASSED

Agents of the Territorial Control Office arrested Sankara, a Burkina Faso national and a reporter with *L'Independent* newspaper without charge. He was released the same day and voluntarily returned to Burkina Faso.

Kenya

Independent news coverage could have served a crucial role as the parliament passed a constitution review bill at year's end that reportedly could curb the power of the presidency, and which may have far-reaching effects long after President Daniel arap Moi's current term expires in 2003. But instead, the independent print media were hobbled by limitations on press freedom long familiar to Kenya's journalists. Bans and arbitrary detentions continued throughout the year, and a compromised judiciary routinely handed down defamation convictions and restraining orders in response to broadcasts and articles the courts deemed to be defamatory.

Local journalists said that restrictions on the press allowed corrupt practices by government officials to go unreported and therefore unchecked. In July, when Patrick Mayoyo, a reporter for the leading daily newspaper *Nation*, broke a story on kickbacks in the customs department that led to the arrests of high-ranking officials, he received threats and was followed. On November 10, Bernard Liru, a correspondent with the privately owned *East African Standard*, died from injuries sustained in a suspicious automobile crash after he had published a story reporting on government administrators' graft and malfeasance involving the Mumias Sugar Company. The circumstances of the crash led local journalists to call for an official investigation into Liru's death.

In December, the government allocated radio and television frequencies to the Nation Media Group, ending a seven-year ordeal for the country's leading private media company, which had been kept out of broadcasting by the government monopoly. The government began selectively distributing private broadcasting licenses in 1996 to applicants linked to the ruling Kenya Africa National Union and to stations without news programming.

March 31
Target LEGAL ACTION

The High Court awarded former State House Comptroller Abraham Kipsang Kiptanui damages of approximately US$250,000 in his libel suit against the independent magazine *Target*. The suit was in connection with an article published in the January 16-31, 1996, issue of Target titled "3 Billion Shilling Deal Off." Presiding Justice J. C. Juma ruled that the apology offered by *Target* was tantamount to an admission of guilt for defamation.

March 31
The Star HARASSED

Six plainclothes police officers went to offices of the independent newspaper *The Star* to search the premises. Employees barred the officers from entering, and then locked themselves in their offices, because the police did not present a search warrant.

Attacks on the Press in 1998

The attempted search is suspected to be in connection with an article printed in the March 27-30 issue of the newspaper titled "How 'Coup' Was To Be Executed," reporting that top government leaders were planning a coup for March 21. According to the article, the leaders planned to blame the coup on key opposition figures.

April 17
Finance LEGAL ACTION, CENSORED
Njehu Gatabaki, *Finance* LEGAL ACTION
Finance Journal LEGAL ACTION, CENSORED
Finance Institute Limited LEGAL ACTION, CENSORED

The Nairobi High Court issued an order restraining the owners of *Finance* magazine from publishing articles about businessman Samuel Kamau Macharia or his family.

Macharia had filed a civil suit earlier that week against *Finance* in connection with an article published in the August 5 issue of the magazine. The court, which ruled that the article contained "injurious falsehoods," placed the same restraint on *Finance* editor in chief and member of parliament Gatabaki, and on Finance Institute Limited and *Finance Journal*, which he owns.

April 17
The Dispatch LEGAL ACTION, CENSORED

Judge Mbogholi Msagha issued a temporary restraining order against the publishers and editors of the independent Nairobi weekly journal *The Dispatch*, barring them from publishing any defamatory material against government ministers Musalia Mudavadi and Chrisanthus Okemo.

The judge's order followed two separate lawsuits filed by Mudavadi and Okemo that week, alleging that they were defamed in articles that appeared in *The Dispatch*. They have sued for damages and legal expenses.

June 29
Magayu Magayu, *The Star* LEGAL ACTION
Francis Mathenge Wanderi, Star Publishers Ltd. LEGAL ACTION

Magayu, editor of the biweekly independent newspaper *The Star*, and Wanderi, managing director of Star Publishers Ltd. were charged with publishing an "alarming" publication in connection with an article titled "How the Coup Was to be Executed." The editors also face two other charges for printing and publishing between September 30, 1997, and June 19, without securing the necessary printer's bond. They were released after posting bail of 200,000 shillings (US$3,400).

July 1
Francis Wanderi, *The Star* LEGAL ACTION
Magayu Magayu, *The Star* LEGAL ACTION
Kamau Ngotho, *The Star* LEGAL ACTION
The Star LEGAL ACTION

Deputy State House Comptroller John Lokorio filed a libel suit against *The Star* newspaper, Wanderi, its managing director, Magayu, its editor in chief, and Ngotho, its news editor. The lawsuit stemmed from an article published in the June 23-25 issue of the newspaper titled "Moi Loses Grip on State House—Kipsigis Flushed Out as V-P Race Heats Up," and an article titled "State House Bosses Defy Nyachae Order," published in the June 30-July 2 edition of the paper.

July 8
Tony Gachoka, *Post on Sunday* HARASSED

Gachoka, editor of the Nairobi-based independent weekly magazine *Post on Sunday*, locked himself in his office to avoid being arrested by 10 plainclothes policemen. The police had no arrest warrant but said that Henry Nyaosi, head of the Criminal Investigations Division, wanted Gachoka to report to him for "a chat."

July 10
Imanene Imathiu, *Nation* ATTACKED

Administration Police (AP) officers beat Imathiu, a Meru-based correspondent for the *Nation*, Kenya's leading independent English-language daily, as he photographed an alleged victim of an extortion syndicate. AP officers accosted and assaulted Imathiu, dragging him toward a cell as he shouted, "Kill me, but you cannot take my camera." Imathiu, who was investigating allegations of corruption at the AP camp, was treated at a local district hospital for injuries sustained during the assault.

July 16
Finance CENSORED
Njehu Gatabaki, *Finance* CENSORED
Finance Institute Limited CENSORED

The Kakamega High Court ordered the police commissioner to impound the June 28 edition of the independent magazine *Finance*, and any future publications mentioning Joshua Kulei, a businessman and former aide to President Daniel arap Moi.

Finance Institute Limited, the magazine's publisher and member of parliament Njehu Gatabaki, and *Finance*'s editors are also barred from publishing statements about Kulei which may be construed as prejudicial, defamatory, or libelous.

October 2
Blamuel Njururi, *Kenya Confidential* HARASSED

Njururi, editor of the independent Nairobi weekly *Kenya Confidential*, was interrogated by police about an article published in a late September issue of *Kenya Confidential* titled "The Kenya Police: A Monstrous Disaster." Njururi was released later the same day.

Lesotho

On September 22, armed forces from South Africa and Botswana, acting under the mandate of the 14-country Southern African Development Community (SADC), entered Lesotho to protect Prime Minister Pakalitha Mosisili's ruling Lesotho Congress for Democracy government from a threatened coup. The turmoil followed months of widespread demonstrations by opposition groups who claimed fraud in the May elections, in which the LCD won 60 percent of the vote, and 79 of the 80 National Assembly seats.

Foreign troops and government soldiers committed numerous press freedom violations during the crisis. Most of the independent media's editorial offices were plundered in the looting that followed the SADC military action. The Media Institute of Lesotho has launched an appeal for international aid to help the press rebuild. In September, Greg Marinovich, a Pulitzer Prize-winning free-lance photojournalist, and Sam Kiley, a correspondent with *The Times* of London, were wounded by gunfire. On November 3, South African troops forcibly entered the home of Naleli Ntlama, a columnist for the independent newspaper *Public Eye*, after he described the South African National Defense Force's action in Lesotho as an invasion of the country. Ntlama evaded the soldiers as they searched the city for him. On October 7, Minister of Communications 'Nyane Mphafi instructed state-employed journalists who were covering opposition demonstrations to resign or face dismissal.

The government strictly monopolizes the airwaves, but extensive radio and television broadcasts from surrounding South Africa reduce its influence. During the crisis, hostile crowds harassed and threatened South African journalists in retaliation for the abusive behavior of their country's soldiers.

Liberia

Charles Taylor, the National Patriotic Front of Liberia (NPFL) faction leader, who was elected Liberia's president in 1997 after a bloody six-year civil war, once promised to "to destroy the country." His campaign promise to rebuild it may prove more difficult to fulfill. The country's infrastructure has been decimated, half the population was displaced in the conflict, and psychological trauma afflicts many Liberians, including the child-soldiers exploited in the war. The Taylor government's refusal to allow the press to function freely is a clear sign that Liberia remains a nation in need of extensive nation-building.

Despite the fact that scores of journalists have fled into exile during the country's protracted civil war, Liberia's independent media have managed to survive years of harassment and attacks. Many independent newspapers and radio stations trying to rebuild must cope with ruined editorial offices, printing press equipment, and radio transmitters. Taylor owns KISS-FM, the only radio station currently broadcasting nationwide. There are two private radio broadcasters: a station owned by the Catholic Church, and the Swiss-based Fondation Hirondelle's news station, Star Radio, which is also funded by the United States Agency for International Development (USAID). State-owned television broadcasts sporadically.

On January 7, the state launched a sustained campaign against Star Radio, using crushing fines and other methods to influence the station's news programming and extract more revenue from the station's management.

On October 14, the Ministry of Information ordered local media to immediately cease posting information on the Internet—a directive aimed at Star Radio

Attacks on the Press in 1998

which the Ministry of Justice reportedly called illegal. On October 23, the Ministry of Posts and Telecommunications revoked the short-wave frequencies assigned to the station, and on October 28, the Ministry of Labor fined Star Radio US$1,000 for the "illegal employment" of its news director and administrator, who were foreign nationals. On October 29, the station paid a US$2,000 broadcast registration fee and resumed its Internet postings. Star Radio's short-wave operations, however, remain suspended—preventing the station from reaching much of the rural population for an upcoming polio eradication campaign—until work permits for its foreign employees are granted by the Labor Ministry.

State security agents and police continue to violate journalists' rights with impunity. In January, police barred the only operating printing facility in Monrovia, Sabannoh Press, from publishing the independent newspaper *Heritage*, which one week earlier had printed an article critical of the Taylor government. When a group of former militia members stormed Sabannoh and attacked journalists, government security guards at the site did not intervene. Instead of preventing the crimes in progress, police who were called to the scene when security guards refused to assist the journalists detained the author of the offending article.

There have been numerous reports in the international press of Liberian soldiers fighting with Revolutionary United Front (RUF) rebels in neighboring Sierra Leone and engaged in arms trafficking. But the Liberian press has been treading softly around this explosive story of their government's involvement in the face of Taylor's vehement denials. Reporting on the controversy would result in severe reprisals—a risk that no Liberian journalist has so far been willing to take.

AFRICA

January 6
Heritage CENSORED

Liberian authorities barred the only operating printing press in Monrovia from publishing the newspaper *Heritage*. Local journalists believe that the ban stemmed from an article published one week earlier, which criticized President Charles Taylor's government for its strained relations with the West African Peacekeeping Forces.

January 7
Star Radio CENSORED

The Liberian Ministry of Mail and Telecommunications closed Star Radio, a news and information station run by the Swiss-based nongovernmental organization Fondation Hirondelle. Star Radio was accused of illegally using two frequencies, although the ministries of planning, foreign affairs, and information approved the radio station's operations, which started on July 15, 1997. Star Radio resumed broadcasting on February 6.

November 23
J. Kpanquor Jallah, Jr., *Heritage* HARASSED
Mr. Nagbe, *The News* ATTACKED
Sabannoh Printing Press ATTACKED
Inquirer CENSORED
The News CENSORED

A group of former combatants from an unnamed militia faction stormed the Sabannoh Printing Press, attacked journalists and Sabannoh employees, destroyed copies of the independent *Inquirer* and *The News* newspapers, and vandalized printing machinery.

The attack was in response to a November 21 front-page story published in the *Heritage* newspaper, titled "Ex-Fighters Plan Mass Demonstration," reporting that former combatants planned a demonstration to demand that the government pay them benefits.

Jallah, the *Heritage* reporter who wrote the story, was briefly detained at the scene by police. He was released after colleagues demanded that the police produce a warrant for his arrest, which they did not possess. Nagbe, a reporter with *The News*, received a deep laceration on his back during the attack. A security guard assigned to protect the printing press reportedly pointed him out as a journalist to the attackers. Neither government security guards, posted at the printing press since the commencement of the September 18 fighting in Monrovia, nor the armed police officers who arrived on the scene, intervened to stop the vandalism or assaults on journalists and employees.

Madagascar

The Association for the Renewal of Madagascar party of President Didier Ratsiraka—the former military ruler who was returned to power through 1996 elections that observers declared were free and fair—gained a slight majority in the May parliamentary elections that led to the appointment of Prime Minister Tantely Andrianarivo.

Journalists are accustomed to working in a relatively free environment, and routinely report critically on government policies and sensitive issues such as conditions in the nation's prisons, where torture is allegedly routine. But the December 28 sentencing of Christian Chatefaux, editor in chief of *L'Express de Madagascar*, and Harry Rahajason, a reporter with the newspaper, to three-month prison terms for contempt of court has stirred fears that the days of autocracy could return.

December 28
Christian Chatefaux, *L'Express de Madagascar*
IMPRISONED
Harry Rahajason, *L'Express de Madagascar*
IMPRISONED

The Magistrate Court sentenced Chatefaux and Rahajason, editor in chief and reporter, respectively, for the newspaper *L'Express de Madagascar*, to three-month prison terms for contempt of court. The contempt citation stemmed from a case filed by the public prosecutor of the Antsirabe Republic, who had sued the newspaper for allegedly insulting a magistrate in a June 1997 article. Chatefaux was sentenced for delaying the publication of the plaintiff's response to the article.

Malawi

Four years after President Bakili Muluzi's jubilant defeat of "President-for-Life" Hastings Kamuzu Banda, Malawi's fledgling democracy has yet to offer any guarantees of press freedom—despite Muluzi's pledge to "make sure that journalists are free to criticize the government."

The official ban on state advertising in opposition newspapers set the stage for a year of confrontation between the state and the privately owned media. Because the government is the largest advertiser, the ban—ordered after the independent *Daily Times*'s and *Malawi News*'s critical coverage of government mismanagement and corruption—is a significant economic setback for the two publications.

Parliament has yet to act on pending legislation that would liberalize ownership of broadcast media and permit political opponents access to the airwaves. Press freedom organizations object to a provision of the bill that would create a communications regulatory body under the authority of the Minister of Information because it would be susceptible to political influences. The legislation would also reserve all AM frequencies for state use for seven years.

The Malawi Broadcasting Corporation Act, which created the state-owned Malawi Broadcasting Corporation (MBC), bars opposition parties from airing dissenting opinions on official channels. Currently, there are four operating FM frequency radio stations: state-run MBC 11, the nominally independent commercial FM 101, a community radio station using pilot broadcasting, and a religious station. There are no local independent broadcasters.

Print media reach a much smaller audience than the state-controlled broadcast media, and journalists at privately owned publications face constant harassment from the state. On January 15, soldiers raided the offices of the independent *Daily Times* and demanded copies of the July 5, 1997, edition of the newspaper, which reported that the HIV infection rate among soldiers was higher than in Malawi's general population. Because soldiers have assaulted journalists who criticize the ruling United Democratic Front party, many journalists use pseudonyms as protection from arrest.

The United Nations Development Program and other foreign donors have linked future aid to growth of a free press in the country. A Japanese aid pledge of US$765 million was accompanied by a warning from Japan's ambassador to Malawi that "reports of authorities exercising control over the freedom of the press ... is a matter of concern."

January 5
Daily Times LEGAL ACTION

A Malawi high court judge ordered the *Daily Times* newspaper to pay a fine of K90,000 (US$3,000) for defamation to Malawi's ambassador to France and former cabinet minister Ziliro Chibambo. Chibambo had sued the *Daily Times* following the newspaper's December 11, 1995, publication of an article reporting that he was in a dispute with a Blantyre businessman over debts.

January 15
Daily Times ATTACKED

Soldiers stormed the offices of the *Daily Times* threatening to kill journalists "who play games with the army." They also demanded copies of the July 5, 1997, issue of the newspaper, which ran a story reporting that the rate of HIV was higher in the army than in the general population. On January 16, 10 soldiers wearing military fatigues and face masks and driving an official army vehicle stormed the offices, damaging a computer, a mounted security camera, and demanding the original transcript of the article.

March 1
Hamilton Vokhiwa, *Weekly News*
CENSORED

Information Minister Sam Mpasu ordered the dismissal of Vokhiwa, editor of the state-owned newspaper *Weekly News*. The action followed the publication of a reader's letter which criticized the education system introduced by the United Democratic Front government in 1994 as more expensive than the previous system under the Malawi Congress Party.

September 18
The National Agenda CENSORED

The Registrar-General of Malawi issued a ban on the newspaper *The National Agenda*, stating that the directors of Chikonzero Publications, the paper's parent company, registered false names when they were obtaining their business license. A High Court injunction reversed the ban the following day.

Namibia

Parliamentary representatives of the ruling South West Africa People's Organization (SWAPO) pushed through a constitutional amendment allowing President Sam Nujoma to seek a third five-year term in December 1999. As Nujoma refuses to cede power, tensions between the government and the media, which have been escalating over several years, have risen to a new high.

On December 14, Defense Minister Erikki Nghimtina ordered ministry officials to withhold all news and information about the conflict in the Democratic Republic of Congo from the independent daily *Namibian*; at year's end he subsequently extended the news blackout to all print media, but did not elaborate on the reasons for the blackout. The minister cited "distortions" in *Namibian*'s coverage of the conflict, which was available to Congolese Rally for Democracy rebels on the Internet.

The government's treatment of the press during wartime is only the latest in a string of official actions and statements during the year that has raised concern among international and regional press freedom organizations. Proposed laws, such as the Powers, Privileges and Immunities Act of 1996, would require journalists and others to reveal their sources. On February 13, Judge Nic Hanna subpoenaed Hannes Smith, editor of the *Windhoek Observer*, to surrender documents in connection with an article published in the January 27, 1996, edition of the independent newspaper. The article stated that an employee of the *Windhoek Observer* had met with one of the people involved in the September 1989 killing of Anton Lubowski, a lawyer and SWAPO political activist. When Smith failed to produce the documents, he was sentenced to four months in prison for contempt of court.

Private radio stations operate relatively freely, and even state-controlled broadcast outlets, which far outnumber the privately owned stations, have, on occasion, presented reporting that scrutinized the government. However, on June 25, a reporter for the Namibian News Agency was reminded by

Minister of Information Ben Amathila that the agency was funded by the government, and should therefore be sensitive to reportage about the government.

On August 7, President Nujoma ordered a summons for defamation to be served on *Windhoek Observer* editor Smith, as well as the paper's publisher and printing company. The charges arose from articles and editorials published in the newspaper that, according to the president, "injured his good name and reputation and his feelings and dignity."

February 9
Hannes Smith, *Windhoek Observer*
IMPRISONED, LEGAL ACTION

Judge Nic Hanna subpoenaed Smith, editor of the independent newspaper *Windhoek Observer*, to surrender documents quoted in an article published on January 27, 1996. The article stated that an employee of the newspaper had met with one of the people involved in the September 1989 killing of Anton Lubowski, a lawyer and political activist for the South West African People's Organization.

Smith appeared in court on February 10 and 12. He initially refused to surrender the documents or reveal his sources, but subsequently said that the documents were either lost or stolen. On February 13, Smith was sentenced to four months in prison for contempt of court. He was held in detention for seven days and then released on US$220 bail pending the outcome of his appeal.

August 7
Hannes Smith, *Windhoek Observer*
LEGAL ACTION
Ester Smith, *Windhoek Observer*
LEGAL ACTION

President Sam Nujoma ordered a summons to be served on *Windhoek Observer* editor Hannes Smith, demanding 1,015,000 Namibian dollars (US$168,032) for defamation. The summons also cited *Windhoek Observer* publisher Ester Smith, and John Meinert, owner of a printing company.

The summons was in connection with articles and editorials that appeared in the June 20 and July 18 editions of the *Windhoek Observer* that President Nujoma claimed "injured his good name and reputation and his feelings and dignity."

On the same day, Home Affairs Minister J. Ekandjo also served a summons for defamation on the same defendants, demanding 200,000 Namibian dollars (US$33,110) in damages in connection with an article titled, "Attorney General Resigns His Post." Minister Ekandjo claimed that the article implied that he abused his position, subverting the rule of law and administration of justice.

October 7
Fred Simasiku, *New Era* HARASSED

James Sankwasa, acting permanent secretary of information and broadcasting, who is also managing director of the state-owned newspaper *New Era*, suspended Simasiku, a reporter with *New Era*. The action stemmed from an article Simasiku wrote for the paper's August 24 edition titled "Demonstrators Insult Muyongo." The article quoted Victor Muituti, an official of the opposition Democratic Turnhalle Alliance Party, who said that Sankwasa was aware of a secession plot.

Sankwasa had initially sued the newspaper for 500,000 Namibian dollars (US$89,103) for defamation, but later dropped the charges.

December 14
Namibian HARASSED

Minister of Defense Erikki Nghimtina instructed the ministry to withhold any news and information about the conflict in the Democratic Republic of Congo (DRC) from the independent daily newspaper *Namibian*.

The ministry claimed the order was in

response to "distortions" the newspaper had published about the conflict. The ministry also claimed that because the *Namibian* is published on the Internet, rebels in the DRC can access the allegedly distorted reports.

Niger

In 1996, Col. Ibrahim Baré Maïnassara dragged Niger back to authoritarian rule when he overthrew the country's first democratically elected government. Now Niger's repressive climate threatens free expression as well. A wave of retribution has fallen on the independent press as journalists try to report on pro-democracy demonstrations and strikes by unpaid civil servants.

In April, as opposition parties' supporters demonstrated in the streets of Niamey, the government barred private radio stations from broadcasting "news and statements" likely to "increase political tension" in the country—an effective ban on opposition statements and coverage of their activities. In May, after Moussa Tchangari, editor in chief of the independent weekly *Alternative*, read a statement on the air signed by local journalists and foreign correspondents protesting the ban on Radio Anfani, presidential guards arrested him as he walked out of the station's offices. Security forces routinely violate constitutionally—and internationally—recognized free expression standards with impunity, including attacking journalists covering demonstrations. And when the minister of the interior personally horsewhipped a journalist in his office with no official repercussions, journalists understood that the government was setting the stage for even worse punishment if they continued to defy the state's dictates.

Niger's citizens have vigorously supported the country's independent media. In fact, their vocal support may have very well saved the life of Grémah Boucar, the director of Radio Anfani and a 1998 recipient of CPJ's International Press Freedom Award, who has repeatedly been arrested, harassed, and threatened for his journalistic work in both print and broadcast media. In April, security agents and police abducted Boucar from his home, tied him up, and threw him into a sack, where he listened as his captors discussed how they would dispose of his body. His life was saved, he said, only when one policeman pointed out that since Boucar's family had witnessed his arrest, they would be able to identify the killers. (For more on Grémah Boucar and the International Press Freedom Awards, see page 66.)

In July, following protests by local and international journalists and human rights organizations, the government repealed a provision of a restrictive 1997 press law that established mandatory sentences for crimes such as "insulting the president." The repeal allows courts to impose suspended sentences or consider mitigating circumstances in sentencing journalists.

In October 1997, the president of the High Council for Communication (CSC) announced that all newspapers that do not have a professionally licensed chief editor would be suspended from publishing. The CSC also ordered private radio stations to stop broadcasting live international news programs such as those of the British Broadcasting Corporation and the Voice of America—closing the country to outside information. Independent radio station managers were required to sign a contract accepting liability for any future charges that might result from such broadcasts.

April 15
Nouvelle Impremerie de Niger ATTACKED

Several unidentified armed men surrounded and set fire to the premises of the Nouvelle

Impremerie de Niger, a privately owned printing house. The fire department put out the blaze, which damaged the printing house.

April 18
Saadou Assane, *Le Republicaine*
ATTACKED

Police violently assaulted Assane, a photojournalist with the independent daily *Le Republicaine*, while he was covering opposition demonstrations in Maradi. His photography and audio recording equipment was confiscated.

The demonstrators were calling for President Ibrahim Baré Maïnassara's resignation and protesting a concurrent rally organized by the ruling Rassemblement pour la Democracie et le Progress party.

May 4
Moussa Tchangari, *Alternative*
IMPRISONED

Presidential guards arrested Tchangari, editor in chief of the independent weekly *Alternative*, shortly after he read a statement on Radio Anfani condemning President Ibrahim Baré Maïnassara efforts to intimidate and censor the press. On April 30, President Ibrahim Baré Maïnassara ordered journalists not to broadcast news related to opposition activity because "it might increase political tension."

Tchangari's statement was a joint declaration issued by local independent journalists and foreign correspondents. After being arrested, Tchangari was transported to the presidential camp. He was released without charge on May 7.

May 4
Keita Souleymane, British Broadcasting Corporation (BBC) IMPRISONED

Police arrested Souleymane, a BBC correspondent in Zinder, in connection with his coverage of an pro-democracy rally on May 2 held in Damagaram. Souleymane, who was reportedly questioned for "spreading false information," was released without charge on May 11.

May 7
Mamane Abou, *Le Republicain* IMPRISONED

Police detained Abou, owner of Niger's largest printing company and editor of the independent newspaper *Le Republicain*, on suspicion of arson and insurance fraud. The arrest is believed to be in connection with the attempted arson of Abou's printing house that was reportedly committed by 16 military officers on April 15. Abou was detained at the Niamey Civil Prison and released on May 26.

May 13
Le Democrate CENSORED
Haske CENSORED
La Tribune du Peuple CENSORED
Le Citoyen CENSORED
Alternative CENSORED
L'Anfani CENSORED
Le Flic CENSORED
L'Enquete CENSORED
Paon Africain CENSORED
Le Soleil CENSORED
Le Republicain CENSORED

The government ordered 11 private newspapers to cease operations for nonpayment of taxes. The newspapers affected by the order were: *L'Anfani*, *Alternative*, *Le Citoyen*, *Le Flic*, *L'Enquete*, *Paon Africain*, *Le Democrate*, *Haske*, *Le Republicain*, *Le Soleil*, and *La Tribune du Peuple*. *Le Republicain* was closed down despite the fact that the paper had previously paid its outstanding taxes.

The office of the president subsequently offered to broker a deal between the newspapers and the national lottery agency to allow the lottery agency to pay the collective taxes and fees for the affected newspapers in exchange for advertising space. The newspapers subsequently resumed publishing without agreeing to the deal.

October 27
Ibrahim Hanidou, *La Tribune du Peuple*
LEGAL ACTION
Abdul Mounime Ousseyni, *Citoyen*
LEGAL ACTION
La Tribune du Peuple LEGAL ACTION
Citoyen LEGAL ACTION

The Niamey Court of First Instance sentenced Hanidou, chief editor of the weekly *La Tribune du Peuple*, and Ousseyni, chief editor of the weekly *Citoyen*, to six-month suspended sentences for defamation. The consul of Niger in Jedda, Saudi Arabia, had filed a complaint against the journalists in response to *La Tribune du Peuple*'s and *Citoyen*'s reports that the diplomat was "persona non grata" in Saudi territory and that he was implicated in a "passport trafficking affair." The two newspapers were also ordered to pay damages of 3 million CFA (US$5,400) to the diplomat and 100,000 CFA (US$180) in fines.

Nigeria

For Nigeria's besieged independent journalists, the death of military dictator Gen. Sani Abacha on June 8 saved some lives among their ranks. However, the July 7 death in prison of Moshood Abiola, the putative winner of the 1993 democratic elections, dashed their hopes for true democracy and press freedom in the near future.

Gen. Abdulsalami Abubakar, a senior career soldier who was virtually unknown outside of military circles, emerged as Abacha's successor. The country's watchdog press dug in their heels to face off with yet another dictator, and immediately exposed Abubakar's relationship with his mentor, close friend, and neighbor, Gen. Ibrahim Babangida. The former military ruler, who has remained a potent behind-the-scenes force within the military since he ceded power to Abacha in a 1993 coup d'état, has now assumed a public role in Abubakar's regime. Ironically, he has begun courting the same press that he targeted earlier in the 1990s.

Abacha's death did nothing to expunge one of his despotic legacies—a wide selection of onerous decrees which the Abubakar government could use to punish journalists who continue to criticize official actions: The Detention of Persons Decree No. 2, allowing indefinite, incommunicado detention of citizens; the Offensive Publications Decree No. 35 of 1993, which allows the government to seize any publication deemed likely to "disturb the peace and public order of Nigeria"; and the Treason and Treasonable Offenses Decree No. 29 of 1993, which was used in 1995 by a special military tribunal to convict Kunle Ajibade, Chris Anyanwu, George M'bah, and Ben Charles-Obi as "accessories after the fact to treason" for reporting on an alleged coup plot, continue to threaten journalists. The four journalists, who were released by Abubakar in June, would certainly still be serving their 15-year prison terms if Abacha had lived. (See page 137 for "Outliving Abacha: Six Journalists' Prison Stories," a special report on Nigeria.)

The Mass Media Commission, a proposed regulatory body that would be granted wide powers to restrict journalists' ability to practice their profession, and grants the state authority to silence the press in the name of national security, remains on the regime's agenda. In the meantime, the independent media are watching the new regime carefully, judging Abubakar on his actions rather than his promises.

At year's end, Niran Malaolu, editor of the privately owned newspaper *The Diet*, remained in prison. Malaolu, who was arrested in December 1997, was convicted

Attacks on the Press in 1998

on April 28 by a Special Military Tribunal for involvement in an alleged coup plot against Abacha. On July 10, Malaolu's sentence was reduced to 15 years—still a horrifying prospect given the deplorable conditions he must endure in Katsina Prison, where he is reportedly critically ill and denied medical treatment. Although the scores of journalists released this year may begin to rebuild their lives, Malaolu's imprisonment serves as a reminder that egregious press freedom abuses could begin again at any time unless the country undertakes long-term reforms and true democratization.

January 5
Obi Chukwumba, *African Concord* IMPRISONED

State Security Service (SSS) operatives arrested Chukwumba, the deputy editor of *African Concord* magazine, at the magazine's editorial offices in Ikeja, Lagos. He was detained at the Ikoyi, Lagos, SSS detention facilities. Chukwumba has since been released. The government did not issue a statement explaining the reason for his arrest.

January 9
Omega Weekly HARASSED

State Security Service (SSS) operatives raided the editorial offices of the Ibadan-based magazine *Omega Weekly*, demanding to see the publication's managing director and its editors. The publication's editors immediately went underground. Reasons for the raid were unknown.

February 14
Niran Malaolu, *The Diet* IMPRISONED, LEGAL ACTION

A Special Military Tribunal (SMT) in Jos arraigned Malaolu, editor of the daily newspaper *The Diet*, for alleged involvement in a coup plot. He had been arrested without charge at the paper's offices on December 28, 1997.

On April 28, Malaolu was convicted by the SMT for "information gathering" and "implication in the alleged coup plot of December 1997," and sentenced to life imprisonment with no right of appeal.

On July 10, Malaolu's sentence was reduced to 15 years. He is currently in jail in Katsina Prison, where he is reportedly critically ill and denied medical treatment.

February 22
Lanre Arogundade, Nigerian Union of Journalists (NUJ) HARASSED
Lanre Ogundipe, Nigerian Union of Journalists (NUJ) HARASSED

Security officers harassed Arogundade, Lagos State chairman of the Nigerian Union of Journalists (NUJ), and Ogundipe, NUJ national president, at Murtala Mohammed International Airport in Lagos. They confiscated the journalists' passports and other documents.

Arogundade and Ogundipe were en route to Dakar to attend the annual conference of the West African Journalists Association (WAJA). Their passports were returned only after each journalist completed a special security form which required the names of three persons in Nigeria and Dakar who would be accountable for them.

February 27
Tunde Oladepo, *The Guardian* KILLED

Oladepo was a senior correspondent with *The Guardian* newspaper of Lagos. He was murdered by five masked gunmen, who entered his home early in the morning and shot him to death in front of his wife and children. Nothing of value was removed from Oladepo's residence, ruling out robbery as a motive. Oladepo was until recently bureau chief of *The Guardian*'s Ogun State office.

AFRICA

March 3
Yusuph Olaniyonu, *This Day*
ATTACKED, HARASSED
Sunday Ode, *New Nigerian*
ATTACKED, HARASSED
Emmanuel Ogunyale, *Nigerian Tribune*
ATTACKED, HARASSED
Yewande Oluchi, African Independent TV
ATTACKED, HARASSED
Kola Oshiyemi, News Agency of Nigeria
ATTACKED, HARASSED
Chukudi Nwabuko, *This Day*
ATTACKED, HARASSED
Robert Kajo, *This Day*
ATTACKED, HARASSED
Bassey Udo, *Post Express*
ATTACKED, HARASSED
Monday Emoni, *TheNEWS*, and *TEMPO*
ATTACKED, THREATENED
Mustapha Isa, African Independent TV
ATTACKED, HARASSED

Police arrested and assaulted reporters Olaniyonu, Ode, Ogunyale, Oluchi, Oshiyemi, Nwabuko, Kajo, Udo, and Isa, who were covering a pro-democracy rally in Lagos. They assaulted Emoni, a photo editor for the independent weeklies *TheNEWS* and *TEMPO* and destroyed his camera. The nine detained journalists were released later that day.

March 9
Joshua Ogbonna, *Rising Sun* IMPRISONED

Police from the Criminal Investigation Department (CID) in Ikoyi, Lagos, arrested Ogbonna, publisher of the newspaper *Rising Sun*, at his editorial offices. The arrest is believed to be in connection with a series of articles published in February which were critical of an Abuja hotelier with close ties to Gen. Sani Abacha's campaign to succeed himself as president. Ogbonna was released on an unspecified date.

March 10
Abdul Rahma Maliki, Kwara State Television
ATTACKED

Police beat Maliki, a reporter with Kwara State Television, in Ilorin. He was covering a march by students of the Kwara State Polytechnic School who were protesting the scarcity of fuel in the state. The police were attempting to prevent both the demonstration and media coverage of the students' activities.

March 12
Joe Ajaero, *Vanguard* IMPRISONED

State Security Service (SSS) agents arrested Ajaero, labor correspondent for the independent *Vanguard* newspaper, and media attorney Femi Falana at a seminar on labor law at the Satellite Hotel in Ilorin.

Ajaero and Falana were held at the Kwara State SSS office until March 18, when they appeared before the Ilorin Magistrate Court and were unconditionally released.

March 22
John Edward, *Prime Sunset* IMPRISONED
Ganiyu Adeoye, *Prime Sunset* IMPRISONED

State Security Service (SSS) agents arrested Edward, publisher of the newspaper *Prime Sunset*, and Adeoye, the assistant editor, at the offices of Satellite Press in Ogba, Lagos. They were released on March 27.

March 24
Chidi Nkwopara, *National Concord*
IMPRISONED
Donatus Njoku, *The Statesman*
IMPRISONED

Nkwopara, Imo State correspondent for the newspaper *National Concord*, and Njoku, a reporter with *The Statesman* newspaper, were arrested while investigating an oil blowout at the Akri Oil Flow station in Oguta, Imo State.

Attacks on the Press in 1998

Nkwopara and Njoku were accused of espionage by the Agip Oil Company and detained for more than five hours before being moved to the Oguta police station. They were released on an unspecified date.

March 26
NULGE News, CENSORED
The True NULGE News CENSORED

Osun State Military Administrator Lt. Col. Anthony Obi ordered *NULGE News* and *The True NULGE News*, newsletters of the Osun State chapter of the National Union of Local Government Employees (NULGE), to immediately cease publication. Authorities stated that the existence of the two publications threatened effective government administration in the state.

March 27
Danlami Nmodu, *Tell* IMPRISONED

Seven State Security Service (SSS) agents raided the home of Nmodu, Kaduna bureau chief of *Tell* magazine, at 5:30 a.m. They arrested him and took him to the *Tell* editorial offices.

The SSS agents searched the offices and removed copies of back issues. The agents then took Nmodu to the SSS Kaduna headquarters, where he was held incommunicado for several days and warned to cease writing articles deemed inflammatory by the SSS.

Nmodu was released during the week of April 6.

April 2
Sam Akpe, *Pioneer* HARASSED
Roland Esin, State Broadcasting Station HARASSED

Akpe, a reporter with the state-owned newspaper *Pioneer*, and Esin, a reporter with the State Broadcasting Station, were suspended without pay in connection with their reporting on government activities. Akpe was suspended for his analysis of an oil company crisis, and Esin for broadcasting a critique of the efficacy of the government's computerization plans.

April 6
Morgan Omodu, Radio Rivers HARASSED

Omodu, general manager of the state-owned Radio Rivers, was fired on the orders of the state military administrator, Col. Musa Shehu, after Radio Rivers broadcast a report that the United Nigeria Congress Party (UNCP) senatorial primaries had been canceled and one of the aspirants, Dr. Ombo Isokariari, was disqualified.

April 6
Isaac Agbo, *The Diet* ATTACKED

Special Military Tribunal (SMT) security officers in Jos severely assaulted Agbo, Plateau State correspondent of *The Diet* newspaper. According to the officers, Agbo, who was covering the SMT trial of 26 coup plot suspects, was beaten for driving on the same road used by official vehicles conveying the suspects to court.

April 15
Ademola Adeyemo, *This Day* ATTACKED
Dan Ukana, *This Day* ATTACKED
Wale Ogundoyin, *Omega* ATTACKED
Sanya Adejokun, *Nigerian Tribune* ATTACKED

Anti-riot police severely beat reporters Adeyemo and Ukana of the newspaper *This Day*, Ogundoyin of *Omega* magazine, and Adejokun of the newspaper *Nigerian Tribune* while they were covering a pro-Abacha political rally in Ibadan. A shot fired by one of the policemen narrowly missed Adeyemo.

April 20
Independent Communications Network Limited (ICNL) HARASSED, CENSORED
Austin Uganwa, ICNL IMPRISONED
B. Osoba, ICNL IMPRISONED

Forty-six armed State Security Service (SSS) agents raided the Lagos offices of the Independent Communications Network Limited (ICNL), publishers of the weekly magazines *The News* and *TEMPO*, and the daily newspaper *P.M. News*. They arrested Uganwa, a senior writer, and Osoba, senior project writer. Six employees of the Printing Press Limited, the company's printer, were also arrested, halting production of that day's edition of *P.M. News*.

The SSS agents had a list of senior editorial staff members marked for arrest, but none of the editors were on the premises of either location.

The detained employees of ICNL filed an 80 million naira (US$950,000) lawsuit against the government in the Lagos Federal High Court, challenging their illegal detention.

At midnight on the morning of April 22, seven SSS agents raided the premises of the Printing Press Limited (PPL), where they arrested Finance and Administrative Manager Samson Adeyemi, Press Manager W. Odofin, and security officer Hassan Turaki, whom they transported to the SSS criminal investigation offices at Alagbon Close in Ikoyi, Lagos. Later that morning SSS agents completely sealed the ICNL offices. The SSS operatives returned that afternoon and confiscated 12 computers, two laser printers and a scanner, valued at 1,000,000 naira (US$10,582).

Despite this crackdown, 50,000 copies of *P.M. News* were on sale that day, and 60,000 copies of *TEMPO* were on sale throughout Lagos on April 23.

On April 23, Nigerian authorities shut down and occupied the editorial offices of the ICNL and PPL. Journalists and other workers were ordered to leave both premises. The police officers and State Security Service (SSS) operatives who carried out the raid and the occupation gave no reason for these actions.

April 21
Kayode Adedire, Osun State Broadcasting Corporation CENSORED
Femi Adefila, Osun State Broadcasting Corporation CENSORED

Adedire, director of news and current affairs, and Adefila, a reporter with the state-owned Osun State Broadcasting Corporation (OSBC) in Osogbo, were suspended indefinitely for a television report on an ultimatum issued by the Nigerian Labor Congress (NLC) to the state government in connection with the ongoing fuel scarcity crisis. The OSBC management deemed the report offensive and embarrassing to the state government.

April 29
Rotimi Obamuwagun, Ondo State Television Corporation HARASSED
Seinde Adeniyi, Ondo State Television Corporation HARASSED
Ola Bamidele, Ondo State Television Corporation HARASSED

Journalists Obamuwagun, Adeniyi and Bamidele of the Ondo State Television Corporation (ODTV), were fired for "subversive activities" when they aired a press release issued by the Ondo State Council of the Nigerian Union of Journalists (NUJ) describing the February 1997 attack on ODTV's general manager Dunni Fagbayibo by unknown soldiers.

During the July 25-26 weekend, the Ondo State Executive Council reinstated the three journalists.

May 6
Femi Adeoti, *Sunday Tribune*
IMPRISONED, LEGAL ACTION

State Security Service (SSS) agents arrested and detained Adeoti, editor of the *Sunday Tribune*, in Ibadan after summoning him to their headquarters. His arrest was in connection with the lead story of the May 3 edition of the paper, titled "Genesis of Ibadan Bloodbath."

Attacks on the Press in 1998

Adeoti was arraigned before the Ibadan chief magistrate court on May 18 on charges of rioting, arson, and sedition. He was granted bail on June 4 by the Oyo State High Court and released.

May 8
Biodun Ogunleye, *Vanguard* ATTACKED

State Security Service agents assaulted Ogunleye, a photojournalist for the independent newspaper *Vanguard*, at the Lagos State military administrator's residence in Marina, Lagos Island.

At the time of the assault, Ogunleye was on assignment to photograph a government building. The agents seized him and drove him to the administrator's residence, where they beat him severely.

August 18
Independent Communications Network Limited (ICNL) THREATENED

At a press conference in Alagbon, Assistant Commissioner of the Police and Head of the Task Force on Terrorist Activities Alhaji Zakari Biu alleged that the management of the Independent Communications Network Limited (ICNL), publishers of *TheNEWS* and *TEMPO* magazines, was connected with a 1986 bombing at the Durbar Hotel in Kaduna. Biu claimed that James Bagauda Kaltho, senior correspondent for *TheNEWS* and *TEMPO*, was the bomber and had been killed in the blast.

According to Kaltho's colleagues, the journalist, who has been missing since March 1996, died in 1998 while in detention at the Kaduna State Security Services headquarters.

August 18
TheNEWS/TEMPO/PM News Group THREATENED, HARASSED

At a press conference on August 18, Alhaji Zakari Biu, assistant commissioner of police and head of the Task Force on Terrorist Activities, alleged that James Bagauda Kaltho, the Kaduna-based senior correspondent for *TheNEWS* magazine, was the bomber responsible for the January 18, 1996, bombing of the Durbar Hotel in Kauduna, and that he had died in the attack. He further alleged that the publishers of *TheNEWS* and *TEMPO* were involved in the bombing.

On September 9, during a visit to *TheNEWS* and *TEMPO* magazine editorial offices, Minister of Information and Culture John Nwodo, Jr., promised the magazine's management that the government would investigate Kaltho's death, based on Kaltho's employers' claim that he was arrested by security agents before the bomb blast. Nwodo said copies of the management's official statement on Kaltho's disappearance would be sent to the Inspector General of Police and the National Security adviser "to find out the veracity of the claims." Nwodo also said "Clearly, you have made the speech based on information that you have been given. The reliability of the information will be subjected to rigorous test, and if your lead is anything to go by, the government will re-open that lead and get whatever information required."

August 28
Okezie Amaruben, *Newsservice* KILLED

Amaruben, publisher of the Enugu-based quarterly magazine *Newsservice*, was shot in the head by an Enugu State police officer. Amaruben had gone to check on a printing job at a shop on College Road where he was accosted by police officers who verbally and physically attacked him. One of the officers placed a pistol on Amaruben's forehead and struck him on the mouth with the gun after he identified himself as a journalist. Amaruben was being forced into a police vehicle when the officer fired; the bullet pierced Amaruben's skull. A police spokesman confirmed the arrest of the policeman who shot Amaruben.

Rwanda

The fighting between the Tutsi-dominated government of the Rwanda Patriotic Army (RPA) and Hutu insurgents continued. Casualty figures are clouded by misinformation, censorship, and security risks in the combat areas that restrict journalists' ability to report on the crisis. The state controls the broadcast media, justifying its actions on national security grounds based on the previous government's use of radio to incite ethnic hatred in 1994. So it is not surprising that information on controversial government activities, such as the forced relocation of citizens in the northwest region into refugee camps, is rarely broadcast by the state. Independent newspapers circulate in Kigali, but they are not distributed in the rural areas where the majority of the population lives.

As more than 100,000 suspects sit in overcrowded jails, a number of whom will face trial before the Tanzania-based International Criminal Tribunal for Rwanda (ICTR) for involvement in the 1994 massacres of ethnic Tutsis and moderate Hutus, media coverage of the ICTR trials could bolster a sense among the surviving population that justice has been served. Independent observers have described the ICTR trials as hasty, and journalists' coverage of the judicial process has not necessarily led to improvements in how the trials are being conducted. Foundation Hirondelle, a Swiss-based NGO, financially supports Radio Agatashya, which covers news of the region and reports daily on the ICTR trials. The British Broadcasting Corporation and the Voice of America's Rwandan-language services, Agence France-Presse, the United Nations' Integrated Regional Information Network, and Rwandan newspapers generally only cover the more high-profile cases.

The dangers to local journalists remain great as they struggle to practice their profession in an extremely hostile environment. On January 28, Wilson Ndayambadje, a reporter for the Rwandan National Radio and Television in Gisenyi, was beaten to death by a government soldier. On May 2, Emmanuel Munyemanzi, the head of production services at Rwandan National Television, disappeared on his way home from work and has not been seen since. Two months before Munyemanzi's disappearance, the director of the Rwandan Information Office had accused him of sabotage for a production mistake that occurred during a political debate.

January 28
Wilson Ndayambadje, Rwandan National Radio and Television KILLED

Emmanuel Rutayisire, a Rwandan soldier, killed Ndayambadje, a reporter with the Rwandan National Radio and Television in Gisenyi, by beating him to death. Rutayisire was convicted of murder, sentenced to death by a military tribunal and executed on January 29.

May 2
Emmanuel Munyemanzi, Rwandan National Television MISSING

Munyemanzi, head of production services at Rwandan National Television, disappeared while returning to his home from work. Two months before his disappearance, he had been accused of sabotage by the director of the Rwanda Information Office (Orinfor), following a technical problem that occurred during the taping of a political debate. Munyemanzi was suspended and transferred to Orinfor's Studies and Programmes Bureau.

Sierra Leone

The notion that the state is justified in censoring journalists during wartime to protect troops and maintain national security has been shot full of holes in Sierra Leone. The official strategy of attempting to control unfavorable coverage of the ongoing conflict between the government of President Ahmed Tejan Kabbah and the combined forces of the Armed Forces Revolutionary Council (AFRC) and the Revolutionary United Front (RUF) rebels backfired as the RUF advanced on Freetown at the end of the year. The population of the city, the government, and the Nigerian-led West African Peacekeeping Forces (ECOMOG) were apparently all caught unawares. As the RUF increasingly threatened Freetown, the government continued to maintain that "everything was under control." Freetown residents' only warning was the approaching sound of gunfire and artillery.

Local journalists firmly believe that if they had been allowed to report freely, civilians alerted to the impending violence could have been prepared with food and supplies to hole up in their homes during the siege, or could have escaped to safer areas of the city. Instead, the RUF rebels entered Freetown in a ferocious assault, resorting to terror tactics including hacking off people's limbs with machetes to punish perceived nonsupporters and send a message to the government.

While reporting of ECOMOG positions and troop strengths could possibly put soldiers at risk, local journalists' reports on ECOMOG performance caused more of a political than a security liability. And the government's desire to win the battle of perception by censoring unfavorable war reports may have hurt it militarily. Local journalists, discouraged from reporting any weakness, were thereby restrained from informing an international audience of the inadequate financial and logistical support for ECOMOG.

The government's adversarial relationship with some journalists began soon after ECOMOG troops, acting under the banner of the Economic Community of West African States (ECOWAS), intervened in Sierra Leone and on March 10 reinstated Kabbah, who had been ousted in a May 1997 coup by the AFRC along with help from the RUF guerrillas. The Kabbah government began identifying those who had supported the coup, and commenced sedition prosecutions. On August 23, five journalists were convicted of treason and sentenced to death. (See the synopsis of the legal action against them below.)

Throughout the year, the government continued to react harshly to war coverage and to equate reporting on the conflict from the field with sedition. On December 8, British Broadcasting Corporation (BBC) correspondent Winston Ojukutu-Macauley reported that 8,000 refugees, fleeing heavy fighting, were headed toward Freetown on the highway from the northern part of the interior, and BBC correspondent Sylvester Rogers reported that rebels outside Makeni had killed an ECOMOG soldier. Sierra Leone Criminal Investigation Department (CID) officers subsequently arrested the journalists on the order of Information Minister Julius Spencer. Ojukutu-Macauley, Rogers, and BBC correspondent and *Concord Times* reporter Sulaiman Momodu, who was also arrested by CID officers, were all charged with "false reporting" and "reporting news on the war without clearing their stories in advance with ECOMOG." This action effectively banned war reporting, as military officials were often unavailable to clear stories. On December 9, an official statement on state radio described the journalists' reporting as "unpatriotic behavior and a criminal act which is tantamount to acting as a propagandist for the rebels."

It was clear to many journalists that the government would not tolerate stories that portrayed anything other than government fortitude, and that their fellow citizens were beginning to believe and support the government's hostile position toward the private press. On December 22, a crowd set upon Kabba Kargbo, a free-lance reporter who was working for the independent newspaper *Pathfinder*, calling him an "alarmist," after his interview on the BBC "Focus on Africa" program. During the interview, Kargbo stated that he had witnessed the December 20 attack by rebels on Waterloo, and that the rebels appeared militarily superior to ECOMOG. CID agents took Kargbo into custody, stating it was "for his own protection."

The RUF has said it will "deal with" certain journalists if they are caught, leaving independent journalists at risk from both President Kabbah's government and the RUF rebel forces. On December 31, Sylvester Rogers was threatened by a rebel commander for his "biased" reporting. Rogers' arrest by the government for similar reasons apparently did not help him in the ongoing propaganda war in a country that now threatens to become the site of some of the worst atrocities since the 1994 Rwandan genocide.

January 10
Sylvanus Kanyako, *Herald Guardian*
IMPRISONED

Authorities arrested Kanyako, a journalist with the independent newspaper *Herald Guardian*, in connection with an article published on January 9, which urged parents not to send their children to school because of the insecurity in the country. Kanyako was taken to an unnamed official's house and tortured. He was then transferred to police custody and detained without charge.

January 10
Mohamed Kallon, *Herald Guardian*
IMPRISONED
David Koroma, *Herald Guardian*
IMPRISONED

Koroma and Kallon, reporters for the *Herald Guardian*, were arrested by National Intelligence Agency agents at the newspaper's editorial offices for writing articles critical of a senior government official. The journalists were transported to the official's residence, where they were tortured before being detained at the Slatter Terrace Police Headquarters in Freetown. Koroma was admitted to the Kingsley Barracks Police Hospital for treatment of injuries sustained during the torture. Kallon was released without charge on January 12 and Koroma was released later the same month.

January 14
Desmond Conteh, *We Yone* IMPRISONED, HARASSED
Michael Danielson, *Independent Observer* IMPRISONED, HARASSED

Conteh, senior writer for the newspaper *We Yone*, and Danielson, a journalist with the *Independent Observer*, were arrested for allegedly passing information to a clandestine pro-democracy radio station. Both journalists were released on January 21.

January 14
Anthony Swaray, free-lancer IMPRISONED

Swaray, a free-lance journalist, was arrested for allegedly supplying information to a clandestine pro-democracy radio station. He was released without charge on January 21.

Attacks on the Press in 1998

January 16
Standard Times CENSORED

The ruling junta banned the *Standard Times* newspaper for an indefinite period of time in connection with the publication of an article which quoted the deposed President Ahmed Tejan Kabbah criticizing France and China for supporting the junta.

January 30
Sorie Sudan Sesay, *Independent Observer* HARASSED, LEGAL ACTION

Sesay, a senior writer for the *Independent Observer*, went into hiding following the issue of a warrant for his arrest in connection with an article reporting that Iranian soldiers were due to arrive in Sierra Leone to aid the Revolutionary United Front (RUF) rebels.

February 13
Teun Voeten, *Vrij Nederland, De Morgen* MISSING

Voeten, a free-lance reporter with the Dutch magazine *Vrij Nederland* and the Belgian newspaper *De Morgen*, went into hiding after his life was threatened by Revolutionary United Front (RUF) rebels. Voeten went into hiding near Makeni and was able to avoid kidnapping and execution with the help of a soldier from the Armed Forces Ruling Council (AFRC) and a local clergyman. Voeten arrived safely in Belgium on March 8.

March 25
Print media CENSORED

The government banned 22 newspapers, including *Express, New Pioneer, Rolyc, Independent Observer, New Times, Morning Post, Watch, Triumph, Financial Times, Reporter,* and *New Nation*, on the grounds that they were not legally registered. Because no newspapers had been required to register prior to the ban, the ruling appears to be discriminatory, and based upon the editorial content of the affected papers.

March 26
Sorie Fofana, *Vision* IMPRISONED

Police arrested Fofana, editor of the newspaper *Vision*, and held him at the Criminal Investigation Department in Freetown. The arrest was in connection with a story reporting that President Kabbah's military adviser, Sheka Mansaray, refused to allow police to search his car at the Freetown checkpoint. Fofana was released the following day on the orders of Attorney General Solomon Berewa.

March 31
Dennis Smith, SLBS IMPRISONED, LEGAL ACTION
Gipu Felix George, SLBS IMPRISONED, LEGAL ACTION
Olivia Mensah, SLBS IMPRISONED, LEGAL ACTION
Maada Maka Swaray, SLBS IMPRISONED, LEGAL ACTION
William Smith, *We Yone* IMPRISONED, LEGAL ACTION
Hilton Fyle, WBIG-FM103 IMPRISONED, LEGAL ACTION
Ibrahim B. Kargbo, *Citizen* IMPRISONED, LEGAL ACTION

Sierra Leone Broadcasting Service (SLBS) broadcaster Dennis Smith, SLBS director George, SLBS newscaster Mensah, SLBS newscaster Swaray, and *We Yone* reporter William Smith, appeared in Magistrate Court Number One, presided over by Judge Claudia Taylor. The case was postponed until April 6 because all the defendants were not in court. On April 14, Kargbo, managing editor of the *Citizen* newspaper, and Fyle, owner and managing director of WBIG-FM103 and a former BBC Network Africa correspondent, were charged with treason in the Magistrate's Court.

On August 23, Fyle, George, Dennis Smith, Mensah, and Kargbo, along with 11 other Sierra Leonean citizens, were found guilty of treason for collaborating with the ousted Armed Forces Ruling Council (AFRC) junta. On August 24, after a four-month trial, Justice Redmond Cowan sentenced the five journalists to death by hanging. The journalists have appealed the sentences.

April 13
Edward Smith, British Broadcasting Corporation (BBC) KILLED

Smith, a Sierra Leonean national and a correspondent with the BBC covering the northeastern Makeni and Kono districts, was killed when a West African Peacekeeping Forces (ECOMOG) convoy he was traveling with was ambushed by Rebel United Front (RUF) forces. Smith previously worked as a reporter for the independent newspaper *Vision*, and as editor of the newspaper *Storm*.

April 30
Punch HARASSED

Minister of Information Julius Spencer, speaking on state-run Sierra Leone Broadcasting Service, publicly accused journalists from the independent newspaper *Punch* of collaborating with the ousted Armed Forces Ruling Council (AFRC) junta.

The accusation was made in connection with an article that ran in the April 29 issue of *Punch* titled, "Guinea Refused to Hand Over [AFRC Chairman] A.K. Sesay on Orders." The same story was carried by the newspaper *Vision* on April 25 and *Standard Times* newspaper on May 1, but neither newspaper nor their staff have faced similar accusations by government officials.

June 3
Print media HARASSED

The Income Tax Department announced a prohibitive 383-percent tax assessment increase for newspaper publishers. The tax assessments were determined arbitrarily without the requisite financial audits.

Notice of objections to the taxation procedure could only be registered after half of the assessed tax was paid. The Sierra Leone Association of Journalists registered a complaint with the Ministry of Finance, but it was not acknowledged by the authorities. On June 24, Minister of Information Julius Spencer announced that all editors must pay any outstanding tax in full within two weeks or risk closure of their newspapers.

July 2
Joseph Mboka, *Democrat* IMPRISONED
Jonathan Leigh, *Independent Observer* IMPRISONED
Ahmed Kanneh, *Newstorm* IMPRISONED

Mboka, editor of *Democrat*, Leigh, managing editor of the *Independent Observer*, and Kanneh, managing director of *Newstorm*, were arrested for violating Proclamation 1, an emergency regulation banning the publication of information about the war with Revolutionary United Front (RUF) rebel forces.

Mboka's arrest was in connection with an article, published in the June 30 edition of the *Independent Observer*, titled "Danger, Sankoh To Return," about the arrest in Nigeria of RUF leader Foday Sankoh. Mboka was released later the same day without charge. Leigh and Kanneh were subsequently released on an unspecified date.

Leigh's arrest was in connection with an article, published in the June 30 issue of the *Independent Observer*, about the Sierra Leonean army's recruitment of 3,000 former Armed Forces Revolutionary Council junta soldiers. Kanneh's arrest was in connection with an article, published in the June 30 issue of *Newstorm*, about the murder of an employee of the national power company by an West African Peacekeeping Forces soldier and his death sentence.

Attacks on the Press in 1998

July 14
Foday Fofana, *Star* LEGAL ACTION
Alusine Fofana, *Star* LEGAL ACTION

Foday Fofana and Alusine Fofana, reporters with the independent *Star* newspaper, were summoned to the Magistrate's Court in Freetown and charged with publishing defamatory, libelous, and false reports likely to disturb the public.

The charges stem from a lawsuit filed by Frank Kposowa, president of the Sierra Leone Association of Journalists, in connection with an article published in the June 22 edition of the *Star* which alleged that Kposowa was a supporter of the Revolutionary United Front (RUF) rebel group, and that he had received one million leones (US$600) from Armed Forces Revolutionary Council junta spokesman Allieu Kamara to publish articles favorable to the junta.

No plea was taken from the journalists, but they were forced to pay bail in the amount of two million leones (US$1,200) each. The case was adjourned until August 5, and at press time had not come to trial.

July 15
Umaru David, *Champion* LEGAL ACTION
David Konteh, *Champion* LEGAL ACTION

David and Konteh, reporters with the independent *Champion* newspaper, appeared in the Freetown Magistrate's Court where they were charged with publishing defamatory, libelous, and false reports likely to disturb the public.

The charges stem from a lawsuit filed by Frank Kposowa, president of the Sierra Leone Association of Journalists (SLAJ), in connection with an article published in the June 22 edition of the *Star* newspaper, which alleged that Kposowa was a supporter of the Revolutionary United Front (RUF) rebel group, and that he had received one million leones (US$600) from Armed Forces Revolutionary Council (AFRC) junta spokesman Allieu Kamara to publish articles in favor of the AFRC junta.

No plea was taken from the journalists, but they were forced to pay bail of two million leones each (US$1,200). The case was adjourned until August 5, but at year's end it had not yet come to trial.

December 8
Winston Ojukutu-Macauley, British Broadcasting Corporation (BBC) IMPRISONED, LEGAL ACTION
Sylvester Rogers, BBC IMPRISONED, LEGAL ACTION
Sulaiman Momodu, BBC, *Concord Times* HARASSED

At 5:00 p.m., two plainclothes Criminal Investigations Department (CID) officers arrested Ojukutu-Macauley, Freetown correspondent for the BBC, at the Sierra Leone Telecommunications Center. Ojukutu-Macauley was taken to CID headquarters, where he was held in a cell with criminal detainees.

Information Minister Julius Spencer ordered the arrest following Ojukutu-Macauley's December 8 BBC broadcast reporting that 8,000 refugees, fleeing heavy fighting in the northern part of the country, were headed toward Freetown on the highway. President Ahmed Tejan Kabbah, while on a visit to The Gambia, ordered Spencer to make the arrest.

On the same day, Rogers, the Makeni correspondent for the BBC, was arrested by police following the journalist's December 8 report that an West African Peacekeeping Forces (ECOMOG) soldier had been killed by Revolutionary United Front (RUF) rebels. Rogers was being held in Makeni because fighting between ECOMOG and rebel forces had cut off road access to Freetown.

At approximately 6:00 p.m. the same day, Momodu, a reporter with the independent newspaper *Concord Times* and a stringer for the BBC, was arrested by plainclothes detectives at his residence in Freetown and transported to

CID headquarters. Shortly after his arrest, Momodu escaped from CID custody and was being sought by police for arrest.

At a December 9 press briefing held at the Wilberforce Barracks, Information Minister Spencer announced that Momodu, Ojukutu-Macauley and Rogers were arrested on charges of "false reporting" and "reporting news on the war without clearing their stories in advance with ECOMOG."

On December 10, 1998, Ojukutu-Macauley appeared before Magistrate Naomi Tunis in Magistrate's Court #1A, who charged him with "false publication contrary to Article 98 of the Penal Code of 1998." Ojukutu-Macauley pleaded not guilty and was released on a six million leones (US$ 3,500) bail.

Rogers was later released by police and admitted to the Makeni government hospital for treatment for malaria.

On December 11, CPJ wrote to the government of Sierra Leone condemning the arrests, and received a written reply on December 20 from John Leigh, Sierra Leone's ambassador to the United States, accusing the journalists of being "terrorist propaganda agents in the pay of the AFRC/RUF junta."

December 11
Mildred Hancile, Sierra Leone Broadcasting Service (SLBS) IMPRISONED
Conrad Roy, *Expo Times* IMPRISONED
Mano Mbompa Turay, *Eagle* IMPRISONED
Amadu Jalloh, *Liberty Voice* IMPRISONED

Hancile, a reporter and production assistant with SLBS; Roy, an editor with the newspaper *Expo Times*; Turay, editor of the now-defunct newspaper *Eagle*; and Jalloh, a senior journalist with the newspaper *Liberty Voice*, appeared in Magistrate's Court to face charges ranging from treason and aiding and abetting the enemy, to conspiring to overthrow a legally constituted government.

December 22
Kabba Kargbo, free-lancer HARASSED

Freetown Criminal Investigation Department (CID) police arrested Kargbo, a free-lance reporter working for the independent newspaper *Pathfinder*, and took him to the CID headquarters, telling him it was for his own protection. They detained Kargbo as a crowd of people was about to attack him for being an "alarmist" for remarks he made during an interview on the British Broadcasting Corporation (BBC) program "Focus on Africa." In the interview, Kargbo said that he had witnessed the December 20 rebel attack on Waterloo (32 kilometers east of Freetown), and that the rebels appeared militarily superior to the West African Peacekeeping Forces.

Somalia

Since the last United Nations peacekeeping forces withdrew from Somalia in March 1995, the country has continued its descent into clan warfare. At year's end, international correspondents visited Mogadishu at great risk. But the risk is even greater for local journalists who struggle in a deadly environment to publish small newsletters. Various armed factions operate radio stations to air hard-line propaganda.

The breakaway Somaliland Republic, headed by President Mohammed Ibrahim Egal, has declared its independence, although it is not officially recognized by any governments or international bodies. But recent reprisals against the press sent a troubling message about Egal's respect for freedom of the press. In March, police arrested Hassan Saed Yusuf, editor of the independent Somali-language daily newspaper *Jamhurya*, and its English-language sister publication, *The Republican*, on the order of Prosecutor General Hassan Hersi

Ali in connection with a *Jamhurya* editorial reporting that Ali was curtailing press freedom to prevent a debate over leadership in Somaliland.

Yusuf was arrested earlier in the year for "insulting important personalities, circulating false information, and criticizing the leaders of the Republic." At press time, Yusuf—who was interrogated 14 times throughout the year in connection with the *Jamhurya* editorial—remained in prison. Increasing intolerance toward critical reporting has resulted in more cases being brought against the private press by government officials angered by reporting about state corruption.

March 4
Yassin Mohamed Ismail, *Republican* HARASSED
Republican CENSORED

Police arrested Ismail, editor of the independent English-language weekly newspaper *Republican*, at the order of Prosecutor General Hassan Hersi Ali.

According to the National Printing & Publishing Company, the parent company of *Republican*, the arrest and ban is part of an effort by authorities to prevent critical coverage of the government.

Ismail, who was not charged, fled the country shortly after the arrest. *Republican* is reportedly no longer publishing.

March 4
Hassan Saed Yusuf, *Jamhurya* IMPRISONED
Jamhurya CENSORED

Police arrested Yusuf, editor of the independent Somali-language daily newspaper *Jamhurya*, at the order of Prosecutor General Hassan Hersi Ali.

Yusuf was charged with defamation in connection with an editorial published in *Jamhurya* reporting that Ali was curtailing press freedom to prevent a debate over leadership in Somaliland.

Ali also warned the National Printing Press, the parent company of *Jamhurya*, to close its operations or face unspecified legal actions.

May 25
Hassan Saed Yusuf, *Jamhurya* IMPRISONED

Police arrested Yusuf, chief editor of the independent daily Somali-language newspaper *Jamhurya*, for "insulting important personalities, circulation of false information, and criticizing the leaders of the republic." Yusuf was detained at Hargeisa Central Prison. The arrest is believed to be in connection with several articles published in the June, July, and September 1997, and February 2, March 1, and March 31, 1998, issues of *Jamhurya*. The articles in question reported on discord between army brigades and the government, and punitive amputations performed on 33 people on the orders of an Islamic court in Buro.

South Africa

When Nelson Mandela retires as president after national elections that will take place sometime between May and July 1999, South Africa's democratic order will be firmly in place. Yet Deputy President Thabo Mbeki, Mandela's anticipated successor, will inherit a raft of problems: political violence in the countryside, rampant crime in urban centers, and government corruption. The independent media, which have made significant press freedom gains in South Africa's strongly independent courts, look to assist the nation in tackling these pressing issues, while vigorously scrutinizing an often highly sensitive government.

On September 29, the Supreme Court of Appeal ruled in *National Media v. Bogoshi* that journalists are not liable in defamation suits, even if offending reports turn out to be untrue, as long as media professionals can show that they were reasonable or careful in their work. The groundbreaking decision reversed a lower court judgment against National Media, the owner of the weekly newspaper *City Press*. Presiding Judge Joos Hefer wrote, "If we recognize, as we must, the democratic imperative that the common good is best served by the free flow of information and task of the media in the process, it must be clear that strict liability cannot be defended."

In November, the independent, though government-funded, Human Rights Commission (HRC) announced it would cancel an investigation into suspected racism at two leading newspapers, *Mail & Guardian* and *Sunday Times*. But the commission said it would pursue a broader examination of racial prejudice throughout the media.

On August 18, an inquest court subpoenaed several editors of leading news organizations, demanding photographs, video footage, or transcripts pertaining to public demonstrations related to the vigilante killing of a gang leader. Reuters, one of the subpoenaed news organizations, said that it would not break its policy of protecting confidential sources and refusing to divulge information obtained by journalists. In a separate case, reports on gang activities by the *Hangklip Herald*, *Hermanus Herald*, and *Gansbaai Herald* contributed to the arrest of Rooi Darkies gang members, but on May 11, the offices of those newspapers were set ablaze in an apparent reprisal.

In a number of instances this year, the government reversed itself on harsh actions against journalists. Authorities relented in their plan to deport Zimbabwe-born Newton Kanhema, an investigative reporter with *The Sunday Independent*, and a recipient of a Cable News Network (CNN) African Journalist of the Year award, who had angered Deputy President Mbeki by exposing a US$1.5 billion arms deal between South Africa and Saudi Arabia. Officials also apologized for the June 27 beating of Thabo Mabaso, a reporter for the independent newspaper *Cape Argus*, who has lost sight in his left eye as a result of the attack, and suspended the police officers accused of assaulting Mabaso.

This year, the country's first private television station, E.TV—a joint venture of local companies and the U.S.-based Time Warner Corporation—was launched, only to face a possible shutdown by the Independent Broadcasting Authority (IBA) for violations of its broadcast license. The IBA grants licenses based upon the broadcasters' production of local programming.

A more subtle but significant press freedom issue involves media ownership by conglomerates whose business interests may impede critical reporting. Observers are closely watching local media outlets that have received substantial foreign investment or have been bought outright by foreign investors, to ascertain whether editorial coverage is being influenced by the interests of their new partners.

May 11
Hangklip Herald ATTACKED
Hermanus Herald ATTACKED
Gansbaai Herald ATTACKED

The southern Cape editorial offices of the *Hangklip Herald*, *Hermanus Herald*, and *Gansbaai Herald* were set on fire in what was believed to be a revenge attack for the newspapers' reporting on regional criminal gangs. A gasoline can was found on the premises after the fire, which caused about R300,000 (US$58,600) worth of damage. Police have launched an investigation into the arson.

June 27
Thabo Mabaso, *Cape Argus* ATTACKED

Ten policemen assaulted Mabaso, a reporter with the independent newspaper *Cape Argus*, at the Gugulethu police station after he had reported a traffic accident. He was detained overnight and released the following day. Mabaso, who lost sight in his left eye as a result of the assault, was treated at a local hospital and discharged on June 29. Cape Town police issued an official apology and launched an internal investigation into the attack. On July 20, nine Cape Town policemen were suspended from duty for involvement in the assault.

Sudan

Since the June 1989 military coup that brought the Islamist-led regime of Lt. Gen. Omar Hassan al-Bashir to power, the state has kept a tight rein on Sudan's press. Although some privately owned newspapers exist, they function under severe constraints, engaging in self-censorship on sensitive topics such as the country's ongoing civil war, government corruption, domestic unrest, or criticism of the Islamic law under which the country is governed. Frequent state reprisals in recent years—ranging from the suspension or permanent closure of outspoken newspapers to long-term detention and torture of offending journalists—have taught journalists that critical reporting is a risky business.

In July, the army warned local and foreign journalists against writing about national security and military operations without official consent. Authorities also doled out sanctions against private newspapers through suspension and censorship. In May, the pro-government Press and Publications Council imposed a three-day closure on the privately owned *Al-Sharia al-Siyasi* and *Al-Rai al-Akher*—the former for reporting that the turnout for a constitutional referendum was low, and the latter for inciting "religious groups against each other." Two months later, one edition of each of the two papers was confiscated without explanation, reportedly for their criticism of the new country's constitution.

Sudanese Foreign Minister Mustafa Uthman Ismail denied any government interference in the closures during a May interview with the London-based daily *Al Sharq al Awsat*: "We have a Press and Publications Council that deals with any instances of violation of the law by the press. The government has no authority over the press, and it has no power to suspend any newspaper or punish any journalist …. The climate of freedom and democracy in Sudan speaks for itself, and I invite you to verify things for yourself."

Tanzania

In September, the Tanzanian chapter of the Media Institute of Southern Africa petitioned the High Court to declare provisions of Broadcasting Services Act No. 6 of 1993 unconstitutional because it restricts private broadcasters to a maximum range of five of the country's more than 20 administrative regions.

The case is a direct challenge to state-owned radio, the only media that broadcast throughout the entire country. State broadcasters gave President Benjamin Mkapa and his ruling Chama Cha Mapinduzi (CCM) party a powerful advantage in the nation's first multiparty elections in 1995. The CCM also returned to power on the semi-autonomous island of Zanzibar, where journalists face reprisals for reporting on differences between the island's majority Muslim population and the Christian majority in the rest of the country. Presidential and legislative elections are set for 2000, but as long as access to information is limited, the country appears poised to continue its 35-year history of de facto one-party rule.

On December 8, Tanzanian police barred Ali Sultan, a free-lance reporter for the *Daily Mail* newspaper, from entering the Vuga Magistrate Court in Zanzibar, where 18 members of the opposition Civic United Front (CUF) were on trial for high treason. In July, police interrogated Betty Masanja, a reporter for the privately owned Dar es Salaam Television (DTV), and threatened to charge her with treason if she did not provide them with a written statement disclosing information she had obtained during an interview with the CUF vice chairman, who is one of the defendants. The state could use Masanja's statement as evidence in the trial, effectively making her a witness for the prosecution.

Most private radio stations do not produce their own news programs because of meager budgets and the prohibitive costs of production. While stations carry foreign news programs, only a small percentage of the broadcasts report local news.

Independent newspapers—some of which were banned this year for "unethical articles"—publish critical reports about the government and its policies, but they are read by a small segment of the population because of low literacy rates and the prohibitive cost for the majority of citizens.

January 4
Mwinyi Sadala, *Nipashe* HARASSED
Khalfan Said, *Guardian* HARASSED
Pascal Mayalla, Dar es Salaam Television (DTV) HARASSED

Sadala and Said, photojournalists for the *Nipashe* and *Guardian* newspapers, respectively, were accused of obstructing the police and detained at the Madema police station. The arrest was in connection with the journalists' efforts to interview detained opposition leaders. Mayalla, a DTV photojournalist, was arrested at an unspecified location and questioned by police for filming demonstrations in Zanzibar. The three journalists were released the same day without charge.

January 4
Ally Saleh, British Broadcasting Corporation (BBC) HARASSED

Police went to the home of Saleh, a BBC correspondent, to arrest him for "inciting the public" in his reports on demonstrations in support of opposition leaders who were being held on charges of treason. Saleh, who had gone into hiding after being warned of the impending arrest, eluded the officers.

April 11
Balinagwe Mwambungu, *Mfanyakazi* HARASSED

Police arrested Mwambungu, managing editor of *Mfanyakazi* newspaper, at his home in Upanga, Dar es Salaam. The arrest was in connection with a front-page article published on April 11 which reported that the ruling party, Chama Cha Mapinduzi (CCM), was "wayward" in addressing Muslim fundamentalist riots at the Mwembechai mosque.

Mwambungu was interrogated and released from police custody without charge on a surety bond the same day.

April 15
Peter Saramba, *Majira* HARASSED

Tanzanian police detained Saramba, a reporter for the newspaper *Majira*, for five hours and interrogated him before releasing him without charge. His detention was in connection with an article which was published in the April 14 issue of *Majira*, reporting that police forced civilians to join them in a search for the bodies of miners killed in a mining accident.

Attacks on the Press in 1998

April 16
Kiondo Mshana, *Taifa Letu* HARASSED

Police detained Mshana, editor of *Taifa Letu*, after he voluntarily reported to a police station at their request. The police demanded that he reveal the identity of the author of an article, published in the April 8-14 edition of *Taifa Letu*, which quoted an imprisoned Islamic leader. Mshana was released on police bond and ordered to report regularly to the police for further interrogation.

June 3
Ally Mwankufi, *Mtanzania* ATTACKED, HARASSED

Mwankufi, a photojournalist with the privately owned Kiswahili newspaper *Mtanzania*, was beaten and detained by police in Dar es Salaam while photographing police arresting murder suspects in the Kinondoni district. Police confiscated his press card and camera and took him to Oysterbay police station along with the murder suspects. He was interrogated and released without charge. Mwankufi's camera and press card were returned.

June 8
Arusha Leo CENSORED
Msonda CENSORED
Kasheshe CENSORED

Information Minister Mwiru announced the banning of the independent newspapers *Arusha Leo*, *Msonda*, and *Kasheshe* under Section 25(1) of the Newspaper Act, No. 3 of 1976, because of "persistent featuring of pornographic cartoons and unethical articles." The editors of the publications met with Mwiru on June 11 to request that he overturn the ban.

July 30
Betty Masanja, Dar es Salaam Television (DTV) THREATENED, HARASSED

Police interrogated Masanja, a journalist with the privately owned DTV, and forced her to write a statement about a television interview she conducted with the Civic United Front (CUF) Party vice chairman, which was aired in 1995. Police reportedly threatened to charge her with treason, along with 18 CUF activists who were already in court.

August 19
Mtanzania CENSORED

Zanzibar Minister of Information, Youth, Tourism and Culture Issa Mohammed Issa banned the privately owned Kiswahili newspaper *Mtanzania* after it failed to apologize for publishing an article in the August 16 issue about the ruling Chama Cha Mapinduzi party's internal disagreements. Local journalists consider the ban illegal, stating that, according to the Zanzibar Newspaper Act, only the president has the authority to ban publications.

Togo

The government of Togo made little effort to portray the flawed June elections as legitimate. President Gnassingbé Eyadéma, who has ruled the country since seizing power in a 1967 coup d'état, simply declared himself the winner. And by deftly exploiting the country's deep ethnic divisions and ruthlessly disposing of his opponents, Eyadéma has extended his reign as Africa's longest-sitting head of state. The state media offered little coverage of the main opposition candidate, Gilchrest Olympio, son of Togo's first post-independence leader, Sylvanus Olympio, who was reportedly killed by Eyadéma during a 1963 coup.

Togo's independent press has a formidable foe in Eyadéma, who has steadfastly pursued his goal of silencing them through draconian laws providing criminal penalties for defamation, and specific proscriptions against defaming government officials and the head of state.

Among the major Western powers, only France continues to grant Eyadéma high-level diplomatic support. It was thus not surprising that an article titled "Eyadéma Fishes For a Letter of Congratulations from the Great Chirac," published in the August 6 edition of Le Nouveau Combat, touched a nerve: Edoh Amewouho and Elias Hounkali, the reporters who wrote the offending article, remain imprisoned at press time. A compromised judiciary has aided in institutionalizing the state's frequent arrests of journalists who are deemed pro-opposition. The government continues to pressure advertisers to withhold advertising from publications expressing critical views to force the independent press into bankruptcy.

Private ownership of radio and television is permitted, but the range of the stations is limited. State-run broadcast media reach the entire population.

Eyadéma's manipulation of the electoral process and his systematic suppression of a viable opposition has managed to escape international scrutiny because the country is a small impoverished one with few natural resources. It remains the responsibility of the private press to publicize the magnitude of Eyadéma's abuse of power for over three decades.

August 6
Augustin Asionbo, *Tingo Tingo*
IMPRISONED
Pamphile Gnimassou, *Abito* IMPRISONED
Elias Hounkali, *Le Nouveau Combat*
IMPRISONED
Pamphile Gnimassou, *Abito* IMPRISONED
Elias Hounkali, *Le Nouveau Combat*
IMPRISONED

National police arrested and detained Asionbo and Gnimassou, editors in chief of the privately owned *Tingo Tingo* and *Abito*, respectively, and Hounkali, a reporter with the privately owned weekly *Le Nouveau Combat*, for "attacking the honour" of the president and his wife.

The arrests follow the publication in the August 6 edition of *Le Nouveau Combat*, of articles titled "The Widow Mrs. Bobi Mobutu Demands Mrs. Badagnaki Eyadéma Return Her 17 Trunks of Jewelry Missing in Lomé," and "Eyadéma Fishes for a Letter of Congratulations from the Great Chirac." Asionbo was exonerated and released on August 8. Gnimassou was released on an unspecified date. Hounkali remains in prison.

November 10
Edoh Amewouho, *Le Nouveau Combat*
IMPRISONED

Amewouho, a reporter with the privately owned weekly newspaper *Le Nouveau Combat*, was arrested and taken to the Lomé National Police Station. The following day, he was transferred to Lomé Prison. The arrest was in connection with the publication of two articles in the August 6-13 edition of *Le Nouveau Combat* titled, "The Widow Mrs. Bobi Mobutu Demands Mrs. Badagnaki Eyadéma Return Her 17 Trunks of Jewelry Missing in Lomé," and "Eyadéma Fishes for a Letter of Congratulations from the Great Chirac."

Uganda

Uganda's dynamic independent press has remained critical and outspoken even as the country's political system remains closed to political parties, making the media the primary forum for political debate. The 1995 constitution restricts freedom of association and assembly, and while political parties are allowed to exist in name, they may not engage in any organizing of constituencies or campaigning.

The independent press—the bulwark of pluralism and civil society—remains vulner-

Attacks on the Press in 1998

able to draconian statutes, such as sedition laws, modeled after the colonial-era laws that were used to control dissent. And the restrictions on political parties are now being enforced against the private press. On December 17, police arrested George Lugalambi, editor of the triweekly independent newspaper *The Crusader,* and charged him with "promoting sectarianism." The charge stemmed from an article in the newspaper that quoted the opposition National Democrats Forum chairman, Chapaa Karuhanga—who was also arrested the same day—as saying that President Museveni is a dictator and a thief, unlike his predecessors Milton Obote and Idi Amin, who were merely dictators.

Regional and international media have come to rely on Uganda's journalists in their coverage of the war and related official corruption. In fact, it was the country's independent investigative journalists who exposed Uganda's and Rwanda's involvement in the rebellion to oust Democratic Republic of Congo President Laurent Kabila. But those who scrutinize the powerful risk a brutal response. After *The Monitor* published a story in its October 29 edition that exposed the practice of torture by government and military intelligence officers, Ogen Kevin Aliro, the paper's chief sub-editor and the author of the article, was assaulted by six unidentified men. The government has yet to release the results of its investigation into the incident.

October 29
Ogen Kevin Aliro, *The Monitor* ATTACKED

At approximately midnight, six unidentified men attacked Aliro, chief sub-editor of the Kampala independent daily *The Monitor*, near his residence in Ntindi, Kampala. He was hospitalized and, on November 12, underwent surgery for injuries sustained during the attack, including a compound collarbone fracture and a fractured shoulder blade.

As Aliro attempted to telephone for assistance, one of the attackers said, "You are looking for your cell phone to call your friend Kazini for assistance?" James Kazini, the chief of staff of the Ugandan Army, and Aliro are acquaintances.

The attack is believed to be in retaliation for Aliro's investigative report, titled "Safe Houses: A Return to the Shadows?", published in the October 27 edition of *The Monitor*, reporting that torture is being practiced at "safe houses" run by the Internal Security Organization (ISO) and the Department of Military Intelligence (DMI).

Zambia

In the wake of a 1997 coup attempt, President Frederick Chiluba's ruling Movement for Multiparty Democracy (MMD) party arrested and prosecuted opposition politicians for allegedly conspiring to overthrow the government. Journalists who sought to cover the coup attempt and the trials have risked assault, detention, censorship, and legal action.

Although Chiluba has lifted the state of emergency he imposed after the coup attempt, his government has continued to crack down on the independent press. Zambia, in fact, holds the record for more pending criminal defamation cases and other legal actions against journalists than any other country in Africa.

Nevertheless, the independent press has remained resilient and undaunted. The independent daily newspaper *The Post* has been a watchdog over the Chiluba government from its inception, and authorities have responded with a torrent of lawsuits over the years. On January 20, as part of their ongoing attempts to permanently silence *The Post*, MMD members of parliament called for the arrest of Fred M'membe, editor in chief of the paper, for contempt of parliament in connection with an editorial published in the January 16 edition. M'membe, a 1995 recipient of CPJ's International Press Freedom Award, and his colleagues at *The Post*, have been the target of numerous lawsuits within the last two years.

As the government sought to limit coverage of the alleged coup plotters' trials, journalists and media outlets reporting on the proceedings found themselves in harm's way. On February 1, police assaulted Amy Merz, a cameraperson for the Cable News Network (CNN), when she attempted to film Kenneth Kaunda, the former president and leader of the opposition United National Independence Party, outside the courthouse where he was facing charges of alleged involvement in the attempted coup. On April 7, police detained Dickson Jere, a reporter for *The Post*, in connection with an interview he conducted with Kaunda. And on May 19, state authorities obtained an ex-parte injunction from the Ndola High Court barring *The Post* from publishing statements made by witnesses in the treason trials of the alleged conspirators. Journalists for the state-owned daily newspaper *Zambia Daily Mail* faced disciplinary action for publicly protesting the newspapers' limited and biased coverage of the trials.

Although the country has privatized several industries, Chiluba has reneged on pledges to liberalize the state-dominated broadcasting sector by granting licenses to independent journalists. The few privately owned radio stations offer little news on local political events, nor do they carry international news. The most popular privately owned station, Radio Phoenix, is an affiliate of both the Voice of America and the British Broadcasting Corporation. Since 1997, however, it has been barred from carrying foreign broadcasts. Local television programming is limited to the government-owned Zambia National Broadcasting Corporation (ZNBC). Although the opposition has some access to the ZNBC, the majority of programming is slanted toward the government. Trinity Broadcasting, a 24-hour evangelical station whose programming originates in the United States, is the only other television outlet in the country.

The Post and the two government dailies, the *Zambia Daily Mail* and the *Times of Zambia*, are available to an international audience on the World Wide Web, but because of the high cost of computer equipment and service provider fees, Internet access is beyond the reach of most of Zambia's citizens.

January 8
Graham Robertson, South African Broadcasting Corporation CENSORED
Eddie Taderera, South African Broadcasting Corporation CENSORED

Police barred South African Broadcasting Corporation journalists Robertson and Taderera, and an unnamed Zambia Information Services cameraman from filming outside the Lusaka High Court during a habeas corpus hearing for former president, Kenneth Kaunda. Robertson and Taderera were warned that they "risked arrest" if they ignored the order. Zambian laws prohibit the use of tape recorders or cameras inside courtrooms, but this restriction does not extend to conducting interviews with the defendant and his lawyer, or other activities outside the courthouse.

January 13
Fred M'membe, *The Post* LEGAL ACTION
Reuben Phiri, *The Post* LEGAL ACTION
Lucy Sichone, *The Post* LEGAL ACTION

The Zambian High Court summoned M'membe, editor in chief of *The Post* and a 1995 recipient of CPJ's International Press

Freedom Award (see page 66); Phiri, a senior reporter with the newspaper; Sichone, a columnist for *The Post* and chairperson of the Zambia Civic Education Association; and Zulu, president of the Zambia Independent Monitoring Team, to answer contempt of court charges.

The order to appear followed a complaint filed by Attorney General Bonaventure Mutale, stating that Sichone and Zulu had made derogatory remarks in an article about the detention of former President Kenneth Kaunda. Mutale said that *The Post* violated his January 10 directive against commenting about the ongoing habeas corpus case against Kaunda.

On January 19, M'membe and Phiri appeared before High Court Judge James Mutale, who said that he would refer the matter to the director of public prosecutions to determine whether it merited prosecution.

January 20
Fred M'membe, *The Post* HARASSED

Ruling Movement for Multiparty Democracy members of parliament ordered the arrest of M'membe, editor in chief of *The Post* and a 1995 recipient of CPJ's International Press Freedom Award (see page 66), in connection with an editorial titled "Useless House" that was published in the January 16 issue. The editorial stated that the Zambian parliament had rendered itself "useless" by the "spineless" conduct of some of its members.

On January 28, National Assembly Deputy Speaker Simon Mwila ruled that the editorial was a "prima facie case of contempt of Parliament," adding that whatever decision was reached could not be challenged by any other body because "the House is a final authority on matters pertaining to preserving its powers, rights and privileges."

On February 17, M'membe demanded that parliament refer the contempt case against him to the Director of Public Prosecutions (DPP). The DPP would decide whether he should be prosecuted before a court of law in accordance with Section 27 of the National Assembly (Powers and Privileges) Act.

February 1
Amy Merz, Cable News Network (CNN) ATTACKED

Zambian police assaulted Merz, a CNN cameraperson, and attempted to seize her broadcast camera equipment. The police roughed her up and caused US $500 worth of damage to her camera equipment.

The police were attempting to stop the filming of opposition United National Independence Party leader Kenneth Kaunda at a court appearance in Lusaka. Police also suspected Merz of having previously interviewed Kaunda, who is barred from talking to the press.

April 7
Masautso Phiri, *The Post* LEGAL ACTION

The Kabwe Magistrate Court charged Phiri, former special projects editor for *The Post*, with "conduct likely to cause a breach of the peace" in a case originally filed in September 1997. The case was in connection with Phiri's August 23, 1997, arrest, when he was detained for two days before being released on a police bond for photographing a violent police dispersal of an August 1997 opposition rally in Kabwe.

April 8
Dickson Jere, *The Post* HARASSED

Police detained Jere, a reporter for *The Post*, and took him to the Lusaka Police Headquarters for questioning in connection with an interview with former President Kenneth Kaunda, published in the October 27, 1997, issue of the newspaper. He was released without charge the same day.

May 19
The Post CENSORED

The Zambian government obtained an ex-parte injunction from the Ndola High Court, barring the newspaper *The Post* from publishing statements made by state witnesses scheduled to testify in the trial of those allegedly involved in an October 1997 coup attempt

The state's action is believed to be in connection with an article published in the May 18 edition of *The Post*, titled "163 to Testify in Coup Trial," and an article published in the May 19 issue titled "State has Evidence Problems."

June 25
Steward Mwila, *Crime News, Confidential*
IMPRISONED

Police and immigration officers detained and searched Mwila, editor of the defunct *Crime News* and *Confidential* newspapers, as he was preparing to travel to South Africa. The immigration officers had a search warrant stating that they were looking for "subversive materials."

The detention is in connection with Mwila's statements to *The Post* newspaper earlier in the year that he had participated in a government-sponsored plot to discredit Chief Justice Matthew Ngulube with a bogus rape story published in *Confidential* in 1996. The government denied playing any part in the alleged plot.

Zimbabwe

Since Zimbabwe's independence in 1980, President Robert Mugabe has maintained a de facto one-party state under the Zimbabwe African National Union-Patriotic Front (ZANU-PF), whose electoral victories have been bolstered by self-serving campaign laws, crackdowns on the opposition, and state-run media that overshadow the independent press. The government directly controls all broadcasting and a number of daily newspapers, and influences state-owned publications by reviewing editorial policies and appointments.

The constitution contains no explicit protections for freedom of the press. And journalists are keenly aware that the colonial-era Official Secrets Act, which criminalizes receiving official information from unauthorized government officials, and the Parliamentary Privileges and Immunities Act, which has been used to coerce reporters into revealing sources, are weapons at the disposal of the state. The government tightly controls the flow of information, especially about the military.

Only a relatively independent judiciary, strong trade unions, and a small but persistent privately owned independent press keep Mugabe from imposing total autocracy.

In November, there were nationwide strikes staged by the Zimbabwe Congress of Trade Unions (ZCTU). The ZCTU protested a 67 percent fuel price hike, claiming that if the government is able to send troops to support President Laurent Kabila in the Congo, it should also provide gasoline subsidies for Zimbabwe's population. Mugabe responded by invoking the Presidential Temporary Measures Act to ban national strikes for six months. On November 18, local journalists and human rights activists protested a news blackout on the state-owned Zimbabwe Broadcasting Corporation's coverage of the strikes.

At the close of the year, parliament had not passed legislation to liberalize the Zimbabwe Broadcasting Corporation and the other state-controlled broadcast media, in defiance of a 1995 Supreme Court ruling ordering the government to end its monopoly on broadcasting.

Outliving Abacha:
Six Journalists' Prison Stories

Introduction
by Kakuna Kerina

For Nigeria's besieged independent press, the time that elapsed between the sudden death of reviled strongman Gen. Sani Abacha on June 8 and Chief Moshood Abiola's fatal heart attack on July 7 proved to be the cruelest month ever for the profession. Abiola, owner of the nation's largest independent media house, the Concord Group, and widely believed to have won the presidency in 1993's democratic elections, was imprisoned by Abacha in 1994. He became Nigerian journalists' weapon-of-choice in their battle against the military regime which responded with a calculated, and almost successful, campaign to decimate the independent press. With Abiola's death in detention, the euphoria the press enjoyed upon Abacha's demise dissipated as quickly as it had erupted.

Amidst this maelstrom, Gen. Abdulsalami Abubakar, a senior career soldier who was virtually unknown outside of military circles, emerged as Abacha's successor. The watchdog private press immediately exposed Abubakar's relationship to his mentor, close friend, and neighbor, former military dictator Gen. Ibrahim Babangida, who has remained a potent force within the military since he ceded power to Abacha in a 1993 palace coup d'état. Babangida has now assumed a public role in the current regime's desperate attempt to placate military fatigue-weary citizens' demands for an immediate transition to democratic rule, courting the same press that was targeted during his regime.

The 139-year-old Nigerian press is the continent's most prolific and vociferous, setting the standards for media practitioners throughout the region. This decade they met their match in the Abacha regime, which set new standards of abusive treatment of the press with tactics such as indefinite detentions without charge, secret trials by military tribunals, torture by police and state security agents, disappearances, office bombings, and bans and seizures of publications.

The regional impact of the regime's decimation of the private press was exemplified by the unprecedented deterioration of press freedom in the West Africa sub-region. Gambian ruler Yahya Jammeh's importation and enactment of restrictive Nigerian decrees, many aimed at silencing the press, has paralyzed the country's legal system. At the time of Abacha's death, exiled Nigerian journalists based in Ghana were being threatened with deportation to Nigeria for critical commentary published in and aired on Ghanaian media. Nigerian security agents faced no impediments in February 1997 when they kidnapped *Razor* publisher Moshood Fayemiwo in broad daylight in neighboring Benin and transported him to Nigeria, where he was detained incommunicado, chained to a pipe, and tortured until his release in September.

The Committee to Protect Journalists held a conference in Ghana in August, providing leading Nigerian journalists the first opportunity in years to meet without the threat of security raids or detention. As they discussed political events in their country with colleagues from Ghana, Zambia, and Argentina, many expressed the view that Abubakar's recent release of detained journalists was not an indication of lasting change, nor did it constitute a "honeymoon" as expressed by Western observers. The resounding opinion of the conference participants was that the Nigerian press had a long way to go before they could freely practice their profession.

A host of decrees remain available to the regime, should it grow weary of what it regards as "ungrateful" journalists who repeatedly criticize the actions of its officials: The Detention of Persons Decree No. 2 allowing indefinite, incommunicado detention of citizens; the Offensive Publications Decree No. 35 of 1993, which allows the government to seize any publication deemed likely to "disturb the peace and public order of Nigeria"; and the Treason and Treasonable Offenses Decree No. 29 of 1993, which was used in 1995 by a special military tribunal to convict Kunle Ajibade, Chris Anyanwu, George M'bah, and Ben Charles-Obi as "accessories after the fact to treason" for reporting on an alleged coup plot, continue to threaten journalists. The four journalists, who were released by Abubakar last summer and whose stories appear below, would likely still be serving their 15-year prison terms if Abacha were still in power.

Abubakar's tacit endorsement of the controversial 1995 draft constitution is also widely regarded by the media as an indication of the regime's refusal to enact systemic change that would reverse the damage inflicted on the media and civil society as a whole. The draft constitution ensures the creation of a Mass Media Commission that would be granted sweeping powers to restrict journalists' ability to practice their profession, and grants rulers the authority to silence the press in the name of national security.

Abubakar's quiet demeanor and his public pronouncements of a commitment to press freedom were put to the test during the late 1998 escalating unrest in the oil-rich Niger Delta region. Government harassment of journalists covering the crisis, specifically the arrest and subsequent banning of *The Punch* correspondent Ofonime Umannah from the area, could signify the return to Abacha-era tactics at a critical time preceding the February 1999 presidential elections and May 1999 scheduled hand-over to civilian rule.

Yesterday's cynics, who claimed the country would disintegrate without Abacha's totalitarian rule, are today's skeptics, questioning whether democracy can flourish without the military. Critics point to the regime's promotion of former military ruler and recently released detainee, Gen. Olusegun Obasanjo, as an example of Abubakar's contradictory message on democracy.

Although the release of 16 of 17 jailed journalists in June and July brought relief to their families and colleagues, the ordeal has not ended. These journalists may now begin to rebuild their lives, but the continued imprisonment of Niran Maloulu, editor of *The Diet* newspaper, serves as a warning to journalists that while Abacha, the tyrant who put them behind bars, is gone, his successor Abubakar could take away their freedom on a whim.

Nigeria's independent journalists are hailed by their fellow citizens as the true heroes and heroines in the pro-democracy struggle to rid the country of successive military regimes. They have fought for every citizen's right for free expression at great risk to themselves and their families. Their courage in the face of often incomprehensible brutality is an example to us all, and most certainly the pride of their colleagues and profession worldwide. The extraordinary resilience of these journalists is captured in the six personal accounts that follow.

The Pen is Still Mightier

by Kunle Ajibade

The news of my release did not come as a surprise. There had been two batches of releases before ours, and after the death of Abacha, I knew something would happen.

There is nothing you can compare to freedom. In prison, I learned that people could be so cruel. There is no reformation going on in our prisons.

I was taken to Makurdi on October 18, 1995. I was not allowed the use of a mosquito net, and that place is mosquito-infested because it is a stone's throw from the Senue River. They only allowed the net in September 1997. I received chloroquine injections at the end of every month. To this day, I don't really know what effect the monthly dose will have on my health.

The meals we received were very poor. We were fed gabsar (corn meal). In the morning it was kunnu (a non-alcoholic beverage made from corn), in the afternoon another corn-based meal. The same thing was repeated in the evening. People were dying because of the poor facilities and the feeding. And when people around me were dying just like that, I felt dehumanized and unsafe. There was no medical care until December 18, 1997, after the death of Maj. Gen. Yar'Adua. Then the government sent two doctors regularly to give me checkups.

To survive the solitude of confinement, I read extensively. After screening, and a lot of hassles, some of my books were sent to me.

My happiest day in prison was when they brought my second son to me. My wife was carrying his pregnancy when I was arrested. He was born January 16, 1996, and he was brought to Makurdi Prisons in April 1996. I had sent his name, Folarinwa, from prison. He was four months old when I saw him for the first time. My incarceration caused my wife a lot of problems. That she delivered safely was a great relief. My son is now two-and-a-half years old.

To be frank, Abacha's death was a relief because I knew that freedom was near for me. And it would afford us the opportunity to address the problems of this country. This is what Nigerians expect of the current regime, to address the problems critically.

While I was in prison, I asked myself about the kind of country we are in. Not only because of my situation, but also because of the prison system itself. The warders are poverty-stricken; their salary is poor and always late. Criminals keep coming and going. The system is simply incapable of reforming anybody.

I was arrested by the State Security Service (SSS) on May 23, 1995. They interrogated me about a story we did on the coup, then they told me to go home. But I later learned that it was the Directorate of Military Intelligence (DMI) which asked the SSS to arrest me because of the stir George M'bah's arrest had caused.

I was allowed to go home on May 23 and they told me to report to them on May 24. The next day, as a law-abiding citizen, I reported back to the SSS. They just asked me to board a station wagon and drove me to the DMI offices at Apapa.

On getting there, I was interrogated by three lieutenant colonels. They wanted me to divulge the source of our story. I told them that it was never done. Interestingly, they had demanded my source previously at DMI, at the Special Investigation Panel, and later at the tribunal. When it was clear that I was not going to say what they wanted, they told me I was not helping myself. They all walked out and asked a soldier to take me to one of their cells. It was a very terrible cell. I was there for one week.

I subsequently wrote a story, which was intercepted. As punishment, they transferred me to a worse cell. Before this, I had complained to some soldiers about the state of my first cell. They said I should consider myself lucky, because George M'bah, that man from *Tell*, was in a terrible place. So, when I got to the cell, I met M'bah there and a few hours later, they brought Ben Charles-Obi. It was a damp place without light. We were sleeping on the bare floor, but our spirits were high.

They gave us Swan (mineral water) containers to urinate in and to pour the urine through the window. That was how we were living before I collapsed and I was taken to the military hospital on Awolowo Road in Ikoyi. It was from there that I was taken before the military tribunal.

The entire trial was done hastily and the judgment was done summarily. It was a charade, an unfortunate one. I think it is the nature of a military tribunal to be so lackadaisical about the rights of the accused. In our own case, I think Brig. Gen. and Chairman of the Treason Tribunal Patrick Aziza just followed a written script. Jail this person. Jail that. So, everything was geared toward that objective. They gave me a lawyer who was more with them than with me. It took about one-and-a-half hours.

Then the second time was my judgment day. It was also the day they brought in Dr. Beko Ransome-Kuti, a leading human rights activist and chairman of the Campaign for Democracy. To buttress the comedy, let me tell you what happened on that day. They brought Dr. Beko to the lobby. I told him that they would soon deliver judgment on my case, and I was likely to bag life imprisonment. Dr. Beko said, "Was it that bad?" He then said if they gave me life, he was sure he would bag the death penalty.

And when Aziza gave me life in jail, let me tell you, and M'bah will also confirm this, I just smiled and laughed. I never knew that any person in his right senses would jail a person for life on account of a story he published. I told myself it would not last long. When the Provincial Ruling Council commuted my term to 15 years, we felt they must be crazy. We just thanked God that nobody was shot, especially the military officers.

Looking back on those three years, I have no regrets at all. It is actually professionally fulfilling. I got to know through the experience that the pen is mightier than the sword. The soldiers were afraid of the power of the pen. The recruit mentality still haunts the soldiers and no soldier likes to be frightened. Which is what they feel the critical press has been doing to them. That is why they have been so ferocious. They destroy. We expose destruction and build. I can never leave journalism because of what has happened.

My message to my colleagues is that truth will always prevail. The energy they put into the struggle should constantly be renewed. Journalists are in constant touch with the aspiration of the people. And the people will always win.

This narrative was originally published in TheNEWS *shortly after Kunle Ajibade's release from a three-year incarceration. Ajibade recounted his experiences in an interview with* TheNEWS *assistant editor Adeghenro Adebanjo.*

Rats on Two Legs

by Chris Anyanwu

It was a journey that spanned 1,251 days. I moved 10 times through the nation's most notorious detention centers, through spooky, forsaken prisons. It was a tour of a world which, even in my worst nightmares, I could never have imagined. I had a taste of life at its most raw, perhaps its lowest and, in the process, got a fuller appreciation of human nature and our creator.

Kirikiri Women's Prison was the first prison I had seen in my life. I was led through the gate by 20 armed men in three trucks and two jeeps. The first whiff of air hit my nose, my stomach wrenched, and I bent over and threw up in the reception hall. The thought of prison was abhorrent to every nerve in my body. It was mortifying enough to be tossed around in the Black Maria military vehicle, but to be caged like an animal was devastating. By the time I got to the cell, all I wanted was to close my eyes. I wished the night would draw on and on. For eight days I lived on bottled water. I had nightmares every night. Within eight days, my hair went grey.

Flip the scene. State Security Service (SSS) detention center, Ikoyi. I am marooned in a huge building. Locked in all day, drapes drawn, the room dark, dank, airless. My only neighbors are monstrous rats that not only hop, but actually walk on two legs. Now I hear the pounding in the wide, echo-filled hall as the heels of military shoes hit the cement floor with force. Minutes later, I am in handcuffs and leg-chains.

Imagine a woman in a long tight skirt, arms cuffed, legs chained, attempting to climb a narrow, shaky ladder four feet high into an airless police truck. She is propped up by two soldiers while another 38 armed men surround the scene. Imagine, in the dark container, the vehicle speeding at 120 mph, five other trucks blaring their sirens, the heavy Black Maria creaking thunderously with every bump, bounce, or jerk. A sudden stop at a street light and the bench slides in the opposite direction. I hit the floor, slide, and ram my head into the metal frame. We return after a 45-minute jolly ride round town. It is part of the breaking-down process.

The tribunal. Fifteen stiff men in uniforms sat on cushioned chairs on a raised platform. Ten uniformed men stood at strategic corners of the hall, automatic weapons in their arms. I sat on a bench facing the high table. Leg irons removed, I could at least cross my legs. In 30 minutes flat, Patrick Aziza, chairman of the tribunal, said he was giving me life imprisonment for being an "accessory after the fact of treason." It was the first time I had ever heard of such a crime. How did I become an accessory to a treasonable crime after it was committed? By publishing news of a coup in my weekly, *The Sunday Magazine* (*TSM*).

Before and during this sham, I was denied contact with the outside and not permitted to meet with my lawyer. A military man just out of law school was imposed on me. He was not permitted to contact my staff, relatives, or anyone who could help my case. No witnesses were allowed. He was not permitted to visit me. We met at the tribunal. In the first few minutes of his presentation, the judge advocate threatened him with a court-martial. He crawled into his shell and let his superior officers have their way.

In March 1995, there was widespread speculation of an imminent coup d'état. Coups are big news in Nigeria because, in 38 years of independence, it has been the traditional mode of power succession. Coups jolt society. They reorder the affairs of the nation and the individual. There is no greater, more compelling "new and urgent matter of public debate" than a coup. In the 1995 coup scare, the weight of the story was elevated more by the status of the individuals arrested. It was, therefore, a matter of compelling duty to the public to publish.

As we began to investigate the story, I received a telephone call from an official ordering me not to publish "if you love your children." But there was a compelling need to inform the public of what was happening. In a news-breaking situation such as this, every journalist calls up his or her contacts. Contacts are assets in journalism, not a crime. *TSM*, like other publications, employed all legal avenues to get to the heart of the story, and this included talking to military men, government people, civilians, and relatives of suspects.

It was, therefore, rather amazing when the Aziza military tribunal claimed that I was "instructed" to publish the stories by one of our sources who happened to be a distant relative of one of the accused. Nothing could persuade them that a news source does not dictate the story. Put simply, I went to prison for 1,251 days for interviewing a stark, illiterate man, barely able to communicate, since he spoke only his native language. This is an effort to give our readers a true and accurate picture.

To muddy the waters, they fabricated a story suggesting that one of the accused plotters had a financial interest in our company and we, therefore, wrote about the coup to help him escape justice. The accusation was baseless since neither the man, nor anyone remotely connected with him, even held shares. But in any case, no law stops any Nigerian citizens from investing in private-sector enterprises and, if he had been an investor, nothing stopped the magazine from covering news of such overwhelming public concern. No one imprisoned the editors of the Concord Group for covering the ordeal of its proprietor, the late Abiola.

I was faced with a situation in which military men wanted to redefine journalism, dictate to me how I was to gather my information and how I was to write my story. I would not stand for that. What was clear was that Abacha and his team saw women as the weakest link in the chain of humanity and, therefore, put the squeeze on me to break the media chain. The cheap blackmail they fabricated was meant to pull the wool over the eyes of the fickle-minded who would believe any story. They could not find a convenient blackmail against my male colleagues: Kunle Ajibade, Ben Charles-Obi, and George M'bah. But they imprisoned them just the same, using my case as a benchmark for the trial of all journalists.

TSM was not the only publication to run stories of the coup-scare. All other magazines and newspapers, except those with links with the regime, published. No other editor is known to have been overtly threatened in the manner I was. It was a sexist act of intimidation, another in a series of measures, including the forgery and printing of fake editions of *TSM* by Abacha's agents, aimed at scaring me off mainstream journalism. What was at issue was the right of the individual to hold a nonviolent thought, express a nonviolent opinion. Abacha's position was that no one had the right to call his acts into question, and he demonstrated it amply throughout his administration. The landscape is littered with his victims who suffered solely for exercising their freedom of thought, freedom of speech, or freedom of choice.

I was merely one of the earlier victims. I held dissenting views. That was a crime in his eyes. The coup was a convenient "package" for silencing foes and dissenters. I was programmed into it. Without doubt, I suffered unwarranted punishment and a terrible insult. I am not bitter. I only hope that future generations of journalists are spared the same fate. Although the Abubakar regime has shown good sense in releasing journalists and other political prisoners, fear of media repression is far from gone. One significant way of putting this fear to rest would be to expunge the stain of the convictions from the records of innocent journalists. Journalists do not plan coups, they do not carry them out. They write about them.

There is a world of difference—and 1,251 days—between an observer and an actor.

Anyanwu, editor in chief and publisher of the weekly The Sunday Magazine, *had served three years of her 15-year jail sentence when she was released in June 1998 by Gen. Abdulsalami Abubakar. She originally wrote this article for* Index on Censorship. *Anyanwu is a recipient of CPJ's 1997 International Press Freedom Award.*

My Trial Was a Charade

by Ben Charles-Obi

The journey to the zoo started that memorable afternoon in May 1995. I had been underground in hiding following incessant security surveillance of *Classique* and some of the staff, when the *Classique* advertising manager informed me that the publisher wanted to see me in the office.

On arrival, the publisher said I was wanted at the Directorate of Military Intelligence (DMI). I asked her what was the reason for the invitation but she couldn't give me any additional information, so we both left for the DMI.

We got there at about 4:30 p.m. and we were ushered into the office of the second in command, Capt. Bashir Manuai. As soon as we entered, he yelled at me and tried to disarm me psychologically.

He held out the then-current edition of *Classique*, captioned,

"Colonel Shauib: Man Who Betrayed Coup Suspects." Then he shook his head stating that the story had caused some security problems and discredited the government's coup allegation, prompting people to demand the release of the arrested suspects. Finally, he concluded by saying he had been mandated to extract the source of the story at all costs.

I responded by dwelling on the ethics of the journalism profession that forbid a journalist from disclosing his source. But he insisted, and began screaming when I said it was not possible.

A Capt. Mumuni joined us with other security operatives and it became a shouting session. As the interrogation continued, the commanding officer, Lt. Col. Kolawole John-Olu, came in. John-Olu would have been an asset to this country if he had not joined the wrong profession. He was very brilliant, but unfortunately, he used his intelligence in a negative way. Unlike Capt. Mumuni, who was shouting, John-Olu tried to cajole me. He praised the new look of *Classique*, and said the magazine had become authoritative like *Tell*, *TheNEWS*, and *TEMPO*.

Then he brought out the current edition of *Classique* and said the story had embarrassed then-head of state Gen. Sani Abacha. He demanded that I disclose the source for the story. As the interrogation continued, he received a phone call which he claimed came from Maj. Hamza El-Mustapha, Abacha's chief security officer He said it was Mustapha who ordered my arrest. I said John-Olu was pretending friendliness. During the lengthy interrogation session with Capt. Mumuni and other security agents participating, they threatened to take me to the Special Investigative Panel (SIP) and the Special Military Tribunal (SMT) where they were certain that I would be convicted, condemned, and shot. That was when my journey to the gulag began.

I was dumped in a room where I sat and slept on a bare floor for about five days. From there, at Park Lane, Apapa, I was moved to DMI headquarters, where I shared a cell with Kunle Ajibade of *TheNEWS*. The mosquito bites were terrible and the premises were hellish. It was my first encounter with Ajibade. However, I had met Mrs. Chris Anyanwu of *The Sunday Magazine* at Park Lane where she was detained in a cell next to mine. Initially, they tried to stop us from interacting, but later we had useful discussions where we shared our experiences, and our spirits were lifted.

From DMI, Ajibade and I were moved to a dungeon in Apapa. There, we met George M'bah of *Tell* magazine. That was where we had our worst experiences in a four-by-four room that was completely dark and without ventilation. We were not allowed to see sunlight. We were held in solitary confinement for about two months and devoured by voracious malarial mosquitoes. We were each fed with 20 Naira (US$ 0.25) per day. We narrowly missed death in that place. In fact, Ajibade almost died at one point when he fell into a coma. M'bah and I started shouting and banging on the door until somebody came in and saw him collapsed on the floor. The prison guard insisted that he needed permission to take him to the hospital, but eventually, they rushed Ajibade to a military hospital at Apapa from where he was taken to the SIP and the SMT.

My interrogation at the SIP was patently ceremonious and gang-like. An officer just walked into my cell early in the morning and ordered me to get dressed. When I came outside, I beheld a gang of warlike soldiers dressed in war fatigues and in a shooting stance. I was chained like an armed robber, thrown into an army truck, and driven to the SIP at Ikoyi where the so-called interrogation did not last more than 10 minutes.

As soon as I entered the SIP, the panel's chairman, Brig. Gen. Felix Mujakperuo, shouted at me, saying, "We will finish you," and punching the table like Mike Tyson. He brought out the edition of *Classique* on Col. Shuaib and demanded the source of the story. I refused and he cut me short, saying that if I didn't cooperate, I would be taken to the tribunal, condemned, and executed. He then switched to pidgin English: "My friend, if you like your life make you talk better. Make you cooperate or we will kill you. We no bring you here for grammar."

I stood my ground and said they should go to court if they felt offended by the story. The man said I should be carried out of the room, threatening that I would see fire. I was then taken back to my cell.

The so-called trial lasted no more than 15 minutes. It was a farce and a charade. A young officer came to me and asked, "Are you Mr. Ben Charles-Obi?" I said yes. He gave me a piece of paper stating I was charged with treason. I asked him, "Treason?" He replied, "Yes," and left. Later he returned to retrieve the paper, and then another young officer handed another piece of paper to me. This time, I was charged with being an "accessory after the fact of treason." I thought they were really confused.

The new officer introduced himself as my lawyer. I replied, "I don't know you from Adam, how can you be my lawyer?" I wondered how the government could be the defense in their own case, because as I saw it, the government was now the prosecutor, the defense lawyer, the judge, and the appellate authority. It was more than an Alawada (traditional traveling circus) show.

I asked the lawyer if there were any documents linking me with the coup, or anything showing that I attended a clandestine meeting. He replied that there wasn't. I then asked him to explain "accessory after the fact of treason." He said, "My brother, I do not know." I decided that I was not going to dignify the kangaroo tribunal with a formal defense.

I was eventually brought before the tribunal. The prosecutor, a colonel, read out the charge against me and the copy of the *Classique* edition on Col. Shuaib. They brought two witnesses to testify against me. Capt. Mumuni was the first; he said that he was the one who had interrogated me and that the story was highly sensitive. The second witness was a Lt. Bature, attached to the SIP. He also testified that the *Classique* story disturbed the SIP the day it was published. Ironically, the two witnesses confirmed the authenticity of our story.

After they testified, my statement (of innocence as my defense) was read publicly. SMT Chairman Brig. Gen. Patrick Aziza shook his head as my statement was read. Aziza then announced that he agreed with the prosecution that I was the editor of *Classique* who authorized the publication of the story which debunked the coup allegation and then pronounced, "You are hereby sentenced to life imprisonment." I could do nothing but weep that such a thing could still be happening in 20th-century Nigeria.

I was taken to the Inter-center [State Security Service Interrogation Center], which is located in the Ikoyi Cemetery. For some time, we were practically living with ghosts. It was like we were abandoned for death. There, I met Col. Lawan Gwadabe and all the originally condemned officers of the so-called coup plot that we had reported was a fraud.

My arrival enlivened the place, because the coup plot detainees had heard of the journalists' travails resulting from our attempts to sensitize the world to their plight. At Inter-center, my cell was next to Col. Bello-Fadile's. He told me, in one of our many discussions, that he was sorry for giving false testimony against Gen. Obasanjo, Maj. Gen. Yar'Adua, and Col. Gwadabe. He said he was tortured until he "confessed" that he had been to Gen. Obasanjo's residence. He said that contrary to his testimony, he had never met Yar'Adua.

Later, Gen. Obasanjo was brought to Inter-center and placed in a cell opposite mine. Obasanjo looked confused. But he eventually became a father figure to us, leading prayer sessions.

From Inter-center, we were all taken to Kirikiri Prisons. As we arrived, Fadile began weeping and begging Obasanjo and Yar'Adua for forgiveness, saying that he had almost shed innocent blood. He prostrated himself before Obasanjo and Yar'Adua who said they had forgiven him. Later he wrote confession letters to Obasanjo, Yar'Adua, and Gwadabe about his false testimony.

Although I was not allowed access to radio and newspapers, I still had a way of getting information. When Abacha died, the warders were excited and talked about it with detainees. Initially, I didn't believe it was true. And I collapsed when I heard that Chief Moshood Abiola had died in detention. In fact, I warned my informants to stop joking. But when it was confirmed, I was devastated.

Initially, members of my family were not allowed to see me at Agodi Prisons in Ibadan, but later, the rule was relaxed. I had access to two people once in a month—my mother, Mrs. Julliet Obi, and my elder sister, Mrs. Ayo Obiageli Sangobiyi. My colleagues and human rights activists in Oyo State were also wonderful. Specifically, Olalere Fagbola, *Punch* bureau chief in Ibadan, really helped me.

I saw that the Nigerian military has completely lost touch with reality. It has deviated from the civilized standards of military institutions worldwide and degenerated into a gestapo institution. It is not only an army of occupation but a terrorist institution that has become a killer, a torturer, and a maimer of the people they are paid to protect.

I call on Gen. Abubakar to restructure the military. The military has no business in government. Abubakar was used by Abacha to announce the phantom coup. Later, when he got to know, he spoke against the execution of the condemned people. Abubakar was not part of the original clique that framed innocent people. That clique comprised Abacha, Ismaila Gwarzo, Hamza El-Mustapha, Col. Abibu Idris Shuaibu, and Gen. Abdulahi.

I'm not exonerating Abubakar. I feel that he should have resigned if he didn't like the system. I'm not grateful to him for releasing us, I'm grateful to God, my colleagues, the international community, and human rights groups. I thank Nosa Igiebor, Bayo Onanuga, Wole Soyinka, Olisa Agbakoba, Anthony Enahoro, Gani Fawehinmi, Femi Falana, and so many other people. They are the people who released political detainees, not Abubakar.

There is nothing to be equated with freedom. Honey is sweet, but freedom is sweeter than honey. My imprisonment affected my earlier plans but I have no regrets at all.

This narrative by Ben Charles-Obi, editor of the now-defunct Classique *magazine, was originally published in* Tell *magazine as an interview with Yemi Olowolabi.*

I Knew I Would Outlive Abacha

by George M'bah

My release came as a surprise because in Biu Prison we had what I call "Philistinic restrictions," and I was kept in a total news blackout. The first inclination I had about my release was on Monday evening [July 20, 1998] when the chief superintendent of the prison called me into his office. He told me that the government had been releasing people. Then he said, "If we have offended you in any way, please forgive us, we all make our mistakes."

The following evening, the man called me again and said that the head of state made a broadcast on Monday and that I had been released. I then signed all necessary papers and he gave me Naira

500 (US$6) for transportation. I left the prison and checked into a hotel for the night before continuing on to Lagos.

Throughout my years of incarceration, I had no access to books. When I arrived at Biu Prison in 1995, they said I could only read the Bible and confiscated all the books I had in my possession. After some time, I was tired of reading the Bible, so I asked the warden for a copy of the Koran. I was given an English translation copy. I think one of the guards saw me reading it and reported me. So, the next day, all hell broke loose. They said I wanted to cause a religious riot and they confiscated the Koran. For the following eight months, I wasn't given anything to read. They would bring books from the library for other detainees, but they wouldn't give me any. They said I had not come there to read.

Throughout 1996, I never received any medical care, despite the fact that I was ill. They would give me tablets. I don't know whether it was the correct dose because they called it "half treatment." Yet every two or three weeks, I continued to become ill.

I couldn't eat the prison food because they only served tuwo (corn porridge). They said I could buy something else for myself, so I started giving them money to buy bread and other little things. I paid for it with part of the money Gen. Obasanjo and Chris Anyanwu gave me, which was only N1,200 (US$14).

By November 1996, I was already out of money and my drugs had finished. My case was reported to the comptroller at Maiduguri. He came and I complained about the food and the fact that my drugs were finished. He said he would go and see the chairman of the Biu Local Government to give me N1,000 (US$12) to buy the medicine, but I never heard anything from him again.

Biu Prison is a 1912 Native Authority Prison constructed during the colonial era by the British. My cell was a big room. I was held in solitary confinement and given a bug-infested mattress without a bed or a blanket. The prison authorities said that they didn't want me to break my back and that was why they didn't give me a bed for the three years since my arrest on May 5, 1995.

I was arrested by Maj. George Ukachi. Originally he had asked for Adegbenro, the writer of the story. My only contribution to the story was my interview with Col. Godwin Ugbo, acting director, Defense Information. So, when I got to the restaurant, he said, "Your magazine has been worrying the government. And the government is planning to appoint Nosa Igiebor (the editor in chief) as the Minister of Information, and appoint you to a position. Just give me your bank account. Government can put money in it for you and show me land that you want. They will build you a house, and give you a car, and you will be comfortable."

I told him I was not interested because I was not that kind of journalist, and that he would not find those kinds of journalists at *Tell*, because we are serious-minded people. Then, I asked him what was going on with this coup business. He said there was no problem, that we could meet the following day at the officer's mess in Marina, Lagos. He said I should give him my name for him to leave at the reception so that they could allow me to see him at 3:30 p.m. for a talk. So, I said let me go, it was getting to 6:00 p.m. He said, "Relax, you are going to see our Oga." Then he brought out his gun. I didn't know that officers had surrounded the restaurant. They said I should enter their vehicle. I said, "Okay, let us go and see your Oga." That was how I was arrested.

They interrogated me about 10 times. I met the Group B investigation Panel in July 1995 where you go before all these big generals. They put me at the center, and asked me how we got the story. I told them I did not know anything about the story, that I only contributed to it. Then they asked me why did *Tell* establish *Dateline* (a weekly tabloid newspaper)? I told them it was just part of being competitive. But they said we established *Dateline* because the government might close down *Tell*.

Then, they kept asking how we got the story on the death of Maj. Oni. I told them that my only contribution was the interview with Col. Ugbo. They brought Col. Ugbo to confirm. He started shouting: "I told him not to publish it. I told him not to publish it." I said even if he said I should not publish it, the editors do not take instruction from anybody.

At the trial, they said I was trying to cause civil war with that report. They also said I was trying to save coup plotters. So, I was charged with "accessory after the fact of treason." The first military lawyer who defended me was one Ahmed, who left because of a death in his family. He was replaced with an Igbo lawyer named Maduko, who said if I had not done the interview with Ugbo that I would not have been part of it, so, they should let me go because I was innocent. Special Military Tribunal

Chairman Brig. Gen. Patrick Aziza and the others left. Later Aziza said, "We like making scapegoats to deter others from the irresponsibilities of Nigerian journalism that make black white and white black."

Aziza sentenced me to life imprisonment in a trial that did not last 30 minutes. At first, I broke down because I couldn't understand what was going on. I was also surprised that from the day I was sentenced, I was kept in chains. Just my hands were chained, but when I was going out they would put on the leg irons. One thing I was sure of was that in the civilized world, this could not last. Abacha could not last forever. That was my only hope.

So, I relaxed, because detention has always been part of the hazards of the job. I have no regrets. Journalists have gone through a lot of things in this society, because we only work in the public interest.

This narrative by George M'bah, Tell's senior assistant editor, was originally published in the magazine as an interview with Adebola Adewole, Wola Adeyemo, and Mikali Mumuni.

God and Mandela Inspired Me to Survive Abacha's Gulag

by Onome Osifo-Whiskey

I was on my way to church with my four children, between three and nine years of age, when, just half a kilometer from home, some vehicles obstructed mine and forced me to a halt. Some men jumped out with guns and demanded that I get out of my car. At first, I thought they were hired assassins, because we had recently received death threats at *Tell*. I was relieved to learn that they were State Security Service (SSS) agents when they told me to follow them to their office. I asked about my children, and they said I should abandon them in the street. I refused to do so, stating that even if I committed all the offenses in the world, my children cannot be said to have committed them. We argued over this and eventually they said they would take them to my house. I said that if they knew the location of my residence, why didn't they arrest me there so that the children could be spared this experience.

After a flurry of radio activity with their headquarters, we drove back to my home. When we arrived, men with guns surrounded my car, shouting, and then they quickly overpowered me and threw me into their car and drove off. It was the most humiliating, traumatic experience children of that age could have.

When I look back at my experiences in prison, I experienced both physical and psychological pain during my two detentions. Here is a situation where you are detained, and only those who captured you know why they took you. They even make it appear as if you are responsible for your detention. The pain is a grievous one. Grievous in terms of the expectation of a country that was the hope of democracy for Africa by 1960, but that has now gone overboard into the land of state harassment of its own individuals.

But we are still being arrested and harassed for offenses that are either ill-defined or not defined at all. Even laws enacted by the state are simply thrown aside by the people who operate the detention system. It is tragic that after so much progress, with the kind of intellectual attainment of this country that has even won a Nobel Prize, we still cannot run a civil society.

And it is the more painful not so much because it is you, but because you appreciate the fact that at the end of the 20th century we are worse off than we were in colonial times. Our experiences have been an abortion of great expectations, ideals, and desires that Nigeria should have showcased to the rest of the world.

During my detention, I was never physically tortured. For the 173 days that I was imprisoned by the SSS, I did not have the privilege of due process of law. So, my accusers were also the inflicters of my punishment. When you are in SSS detention you are quarantined as if you were somebody suffering from smallpox. Nobody speaks to you. You are held incommunicado and you are not even allowed to speak with your jailers. You are not allowed access to any information of any kind. You may not even know where you are in the first place. I believe prison incarceration is better because you will rub shoulders with other inmates.

I was held on the grounds that I was a threat to state security because I worked for a media house that is considered to be "unfriendly." And because I have a certain level of responsibility, I must be equally guilty.

I was asked about things as varied as the illness of Gen. Sani Abacha and our sources for our knowledge. And this becomes rather pathetic considering the fact that the illness of a person like Gen. Abacha is of fundamental importance to the public in view of his position as head of state. And in any other society, it is reported with much interest. In Russia, which is just emerging into an open society, still with rigorous restriction here and there regarding press freedom, the heart operation of President Yeltsin was not a hidden affair. It was reported by the Russian press. But here it becomes a very serious state offense, capable, in the eyes of those who are knowledgeable about state security, of abolishing the Nigerian state—with one stroke of the pen.

They were also demanding to know who our supporters are. And *Tell* is a company that has existed for seven years. Any business anywhere in the world is supported by the market system. The dictatorship of the market is, in fact, more severe than the dictatorship of military juntas. But they don't realize this. So if you can survive the harsh economic environment under which the press operates today, you must be financed by foreign embassies. If they know that we collect money from foreign organizations, they should come forward and show the evidence.

My freedom came as a total surprise because in detention, one learns not to rely on such information. But when the prison authorities sent for me, what came to my mind was that I was in for another round of interrogation. They said they had revoked the order under which I was being kept, but they didn't say I was being given my freedom. So they told me to go and pack, and I was given only 30 minutes to comply.

When I arrived at the director's office, he greeted me and said I was free to go. I thought this was a joke. When I was being taken from SSS headquarters in Abuja to prison in February, I was initially told that I had been released. I later learned the opposite from the same director.

Ironically, I had just finished reading Mandela's biography a few weeks before I was arrested. He was a monumental inspiration to me, and when you realize that the man went through this thing for 27 years, you are encouraged. For the first 36 days, I wore the same clothes. I had to beg and plead until they bought me some second-hand shorts and T-shirts, which I could change into and wash my original clothes. I had also lost 10 kilograms in weight.

I learned that if you are in the lion's den and you see how the lion roars, you get used to it. Detention and the fear of detention will become demystified. Detention itself is a demystification of detention. It is a demystification of the power of captivity that they exercise over you. The positive aspect is that you will become stronger in your resistance to the pain and agony of detention. If they realize that you do not break down easily, that is a plus for you.

This narrative by Tell *managing editor Onome Osifo-Whiskey was originally published as an interview with Shola Oshunkeye.*

They Wanted My Magazines to Die

by Babafemi Ojudu

I think the authorities had me under surveillance before I traveled to Kenya. I have been a wanted person probably over the stories we (*TheNEWS*) did on the failing health of the then-head of state Gen. Abacha, and the one on Abacha's business link with a private businessman by the name of Chaugory. When they arrested me, they were particularly interested in the source of those stories. They threatened and tortured me, but I refused to budge. They also wanted to know my mission in Kenya, and the U.S.A., and other places I had been to earlier in the year. I told them, but they seemed unimpressed. They alleged that my publishers, the Independent Communications Network Limited (ICNL), were being sponsored by the U.S. and British governments. I told them it was not true. They also alleged that I was a friend of Walter Carrington, the former American ambassador to Nigeria, and Nene, the South African envoy to Nigeria. In fact, I told them that these are the people I would want to be close with, but in actual fact we were not friends.

I ought to have been released since April, but the individuals involved thought that I was too stubborn, and they decided to punish me. Further, the intention was to cripple my organization. They reasoned that since I am with them and Bayo (Bayo Onanuga, the editor in chief of *TheNEWS*) had gone into exile, the magazines would die. But to their surprise, the magazines were still coming out regularly. So, they wanted to know who was behind the operations.

I was afflicted with typhoid and jaundice and I never received any medical treatment. I thought I would die the next day, that was why I wrote my will. I was tortured throughout. I was kept in solitary confinement. I was not allowed to go out of my cell. I slept, shat, urinated, ate, and did everything in the confined room. The experience was so terrible.

I was never spoken to for more than five minutes everyday. In the morning, they would say, "Wetin you go chop?" (What will you eat?) They came back in the evening to ask the same question. That is all, no further conversation. I sat in that place for a whole nine months. It was a mental torture. At one time, I asked for the Bible or Koran; they refused. No books, nothing.

Zakari Biu, assistant police commissioner and head of the task force on terrorist activities, came to visit me once. He just abused me. He told me that I was a quack journalist. That I did not go to a school of journalism. To him, you can have a Ph.D., but if you did not go to a school of journalism, you are not a journalist. He further boasted that he would deal with me. He wanted to impress Abacha that he was working hard. He thought he was doing what he did to us in the interest of Abacha.

Help me convey my unreserved appreciation for those who worked for my freedom—the Nigerian press, international organizations and others. I say thank you and God bless. Please, keep the flag flying.

In November 1997, Babafemi Ojudu, managing editor of TheNEWS and TEMPO newsmagazines, was arrested without charge by authorities while attempting to return to Nigeria after attending a conference in Kenya. He was released in July 1998.

Attacks on the Press in 1998

OVERVIEW OF
The Americas

by Joel Simon

Over the past decade, journalists have played a vital role in the democratic development of Latin America. Through probing, critical, and aggressive reporting, they have brought a measure of political accountability to a region long known for its autocratic regimes. But they have also paid a terrible price: Their independent reporting has engendered a violent backlash costing the lives of 117 journalists since 1989. In the last few years, journalists have fought back by publicizing attacks against their colleagues and forming national press freedom organizations. In the process, they have not only made it safer to practice their profession, but also have made press freedom in Latin America an issue of international concern and a yardstick by which other basic freedoms are measured. (See special report, page 199.)

The growing public support for journalists has not stopped the violence, but it has substantially changed it. During 1998, eight journalists in Latin America were killed in the line of duty. (A Canadian newspaper publisher, Tara Singh Hayer, was murdered in Vancouver in November by radical Sikh separatists angered by his reporting on local issues.) CPJ continues to investigate the murders of another seven journalists. While the numbers have not declined significantly from the previous year, when CPJ documented ten murders in the region, what has changed is the murdered journalists' prominence.

The 1997 murders of such well-known journalists as José Luis Cabezas in Argentina and Gerardo Bedoya Borrero in Colombia fueled widespread public protest; the 1998 murders of Manoel Leal de Oliveira in rural Brazil and Luis

---

Joel Simon *worked as a Mexico-based associate editor for* Pacific News Service *before joining CPJ in 1997. He is the author of* Endangered Mexico: An Environment on the Edge *(Sierra Club Books, 1997), and is a frequent contributor to the* Columbia Journalism Review.
Research assistant **Marylene Smeets**, *who contributed much of the documentation for this section and wrote several country descriptions, worked with the U. N. Mission for the Verification of Human Rights in Guatemala (MINUGUA) from 1994 to 1997. She is a graduate of the University of Amsterdam and the Paul H. Nitze School of Advanced International Relations at The Johns Hopkins University.*
The Robert R. McCormick Tribune Foundation provided substantial support toward CPJ's work in the Americas in 1998. A two-year grant from the Tinker Foundation is supporting CPJ's campaign to eliminate criminal defamation from the Americas.
Research for the report on press freedom groups in Latin America was made possible by support from the Freedom Forum.

Mario García Rodríguez from a small-circulation newspaper in Mexico City went largely unnoticed. With the notable exception of Philip True, the Mexico correspondent for the *San Antonio Express-News* who was murdered by local Indians while on a reporting and hiking trip in the Sierra Madre Mountains, most of the journalists killed in 1998 were small-town or rural-based reporters who appear to have been targeted by corrupt local officials.

The public outcry over the murder of prominent journalists has made it safer for those working for major publications. But substantial risks remain for reporters who work for less visible outlets. The reasons are complex, stemming from the economic gulf that separates thriving cities from impoverished small towns in most of the region. And the disparity is growing as Latin America's large urban centers become integrated into the global economy, while many rural areas are left behind. Nowhere is this trend more pronounced than Brazil, where reporters for major media outlets in Rio de Janeiro and São Paulo have resources and power that rival their counterparts in Washington and New York. Meanwhile, in impoverished areas such as Mato Grosso do Sul, journalists struggle to do their job largely unsupported by their colleagues.

Other obstacles persist. Politicians use promises of government concessions and personal friendships with media owners to try to influence coverage. More significant, journalists who push the limits of press freedom know that they risk prosecution under anachronistic press laws. For example, judicial police in Panama tried to arrest journalist Herasto Reyes in December on criminal defamation charges stemming from an August 27 article in which he linked President Ernesto Pérez Balladares to a financial scandal. Reyes' colleagues from the daily *La Prensa* surrounded Reyes and physically blocked the police from carrying out the arrest.

In September, two Chilean journalists were briefly arrested under the country's Pinochet-era State Security Law. In other countries, politicians accused of corruption and malfeasance, alleged drug traffickers, and military officials accused of human rights violations have used criminal defamation laws to stifle investigative reporting or punish journalists who have exposed wrongdoing.

Such laws pose a threat not only to journalists, but also to the development of strong democratic institutions. In nearly every country in the Americas, defamation laws, often promulgated by military dictators or dating from the turn of the century, define libel as a criminal offense punishable by prison terms. Under most of these statutes, truth is not a defense, reporting on criminal investigations is not privileged, and journalists can be compelled to reveal their sources. In the case of an error made during a good-faith effort to report an issue of public interest, a printed correction does not offer protection from prosecution. Many countries also have laws that equate questioning the honor of a public official to an attack on the state. Mexico's defamation law, written in 1917 just after the revolution, is typical of these statutes. It defines defamation as "hurtful communication made against a person, whether true or false, determined or undetermined, that can cause that person dishonor, discredit, prejudice, or expose them to the ridicule of another person." Those judged guilty of such an offense can be sentenced to up to two years in prison.

These laws criminalize behavior that is at the very heart of the journalistic profession: Because a functioning democracy depends on the free exchange of ideas, journalists should never face criminal prosecution because of material they publish. In instances where a plaintiff can demonstrate malice—in other words, that the journalist knew or should have known that the facts in a story were wrong at the time of publication—civil litigation should provide adequate redress for the aggrieved party.

With support from the Tinker Foundation, CPJ has launched a campaign to eliminate criminal defamation laws from the Americas. As part of our documentation for this project, we have included a short section on criminal defamation laws in the descriptions of countries where such statutes have been actively used to stifle independent reporting.

An important development for press freedom in the Americas during 1998 was the creation in April of the Special Rapporteur for Freedom of Expression of the Inter-American Commission on Human Rights of the Organization of American States (OAS). CPJ supported the initiative, which was unanimously ratified by the heads of state attending the Summit of the Americas meeting in Santiago, Chile. In November, Santiago Canton, an Argentine lawyer, was selected to fill the post. He will be responsible for monitoring press freedom throughout the Americas, and alerting the commission to violations of the provisions of inter-American law that guarantee freedom of expression.

The overall situation for the press in Latin America continues to improve. With the exception of Cuba, the Latin American press operates more freely and with fewer restraints than at any time in its history.

Antigua and Barbuda

With elections in this tiny Caribbean island nation scheduled to be called in March 1999, tensions have been rising between the press and Prime Minister Lester B. Bird. Arsonists burned the offices of *The Outlet* on November 19 after the newspaper published a story on a large quantity of arms purchased by the government. Publisher L. Tim Hector, who is also deputy leader of the opposition United Progressive Party, called the fire "an act of state terrorism."

While it is clear that the fire was deliberately set—diesel fuel was poured throughout the building—some journalists said it was political dispute rather than an attack on press freedom. The day after the fire, the Ministry of Information building was torched in what some describe as political retribution by United Progressive Party supporters. Prime Minister Bird pledged to seek the assistance of Scotland Yard in investigating both blazes.

Journalists agree, however, that the powerful Bird family, which controls the ruling Antigua Labor Party, has long used its political influence to quash negative coverage. Of the three local radio stations, one is government-run and the other two are controlled by members of the Bird family. The sole television station is also state-run, while a brother of the prime minister owns the country's only cable company. In September 1996, the government shut down a radio station started by Winston Derrick and Samuel Derrick, editor and publisher, respectively, of the *Daily Observer* newspaper, alleging it was operating without a license. The appeal was expected to be heard in 1998, but has been postponed until February 1999.

Argentina

There has been a notable decline in violent attacks against the Argentine press, attributable to the changes wrought by public furor over the murder of photojournalist José Luis Cabezas in January 1997. Nevertheless, threats, harassment, and an explosion in punitive lawsuits continued to pose challenges for journalists, particularly those in the provinces.

In Argentina, as elsewhere in Latin America, the press has gained widespread public support for its role in exposing the military regime's murderous record and investigating corruption in the current government. But pursuing such stories has also created dangers for journalists: Those subjected to new levels of scrutiny have frequently lashed out.

For example, during an explosive interview in January with Gabriela Cerruti, editor of the newsmagazine *trespuntos,* Navy Capt. Alfredo Astiz was not only unrepentant about his role as a member of the notorious death squads in the 1970s, but warned Cerruti that he was "technically the best-trained man in this country to kill a politician or a journalist." The ensuing outcry over the published report forced Adm. Carlos Marrón to sentence Astiz to 60 days' confinement. He was released from custody after 12 days, but stripped of rank, uniform, and his pension. The same day that Astiz was released, Cerruti received two threatening phone calls.

While the widespread revulsion over the Cabezas murder seemed to create an atmosphere of greater security for journalists in the capital, Buenos Aires, reporters working for provincial news outlets have been threatened and harassed by local authorities. The Association for the Defense of Independent Journalists (Periodistas), the Argentine press group founded in 1996 by 24 leading Argentine journalists, documented more than 100 such cases in 1998.

A flurry of lawsuits filed mostly by public officials has made life difficult for many of the country's top reporters. In March, President Carlos Saúl Menem, Latin America's most litigious leader, won a US$150,000 judgment against the weekly magazine *Noticias*. The National Court of Appeals ruled that the magazine and its editors Jorge Fontevecchia and Héctor D'Amico, had violated the president's privacy when it published an article describing the flight of Menem's illegitimate son and the boy's mother to Paraguay because of fears for their safety. The president never disputed the accuracy of the report. While *Noticias* has appealed the decision to the Supreme Court, there is little hope for an impartial hearing since six of the nine justices were appointed by Menem after he expanded the number of presiding judges in a blatant effort to gain political control of the court.

After protracted and costly litigation, journalists have been hit with enormous damage awards in defamation cases. In March, a judge ordered television news reporter Bernardo Neustadt to pay US$80,000 to another judge who claimed that she was defamed by a guest on his television show in 1993. In August, a former civil servant won a US$50,000 judgment against Eduardo Aliverti, a radio news reporter and columnist for the Buenos Aires daily *Página/12*, stemming from a story Aliverti broadcast in 1991. Both cases are on appeal.

In another troubling decision in April, *Página/12* was ordered to publish a statement from a presidential aid who was angered that the paper reported that he had been recruiting Argentine mercenaries to fight in Croatia. While Argentine law does not specifically recognize the "Right to Reply," justices have the authority to compel news outlets to publish statements from individuals who feel they have been maligned, even in instances where the accuracy of the news reports has not been called into question (as was the case with *Página/12*).

Argentine journalists also expressed concern that the government is using legislation to control the press; pending bills would raise sales taxes on newspapers and make the use of hidden cameras illegal (Argentine investigative television programs have used hidden cameras to expose police corruption). There was also a widespread public debate—in forums, on radio talk shows, and in the press itself—about the fact that media ownership is becoming increasingly concentrated in the hands of large conglomerates with no public accountability. Journalists who have criticized the government have seen their radio and television shows canceled. Periodistas alleged that government pressure led to the firing of Olga Wormat, host of a popular radio show on FM Horizonte. Wormat was dismissed after she aired a controversial interview with Labor Minister Ermán González. In another incident, television journalist Joaquín Morales Solá accused Constancio Vigil, a major shareholder in Channel 9 and a close friend of Menem, of forcing the cancellation of his news talk show in September.

January 26
Esteban Mac Allister, free-lance photographer
THREATENED

Mac Allister, a free-lance photographer who is vice president of the Asociación de Reporteros Gráficos, received a death threat on his office answering machine the day after he spoke at a ceremony commemorating the murder of photographer José Luis Cabezas. Until April 1997, Mac Allister worked for *Noticias*, the magazine Cabezas worked for at the time of his death. The message—"You're dead, you're dead"—was left in a voice that had been electronically distorted to prevent identification.

January 27
Gabriela Cerruti, *trespuntos* THREATENED

An unidentified man threatened Cerruti after she published an interview with Capt. Alfredo Astiz in the January 14 issue of the Buenos Aires weekly *trespuntos*.

Astiz, who worked for the infamous Navy School for Mechanics (ESMA) that was responsible for the torture and disappearance of thousands of Argentinians during the country's dirty war, told Cerruti he did not regret any of the kidnappings and murders he had carried out. Astiz also claimed to be the best-trained man in Argentina to kill journalists and politicians.

A January 27 presidential decree sanctioned Astiz for giving an interview without permission from his superiors. Astiz was also stripped of his rank and pension.

That same day, an unidentified man called the editorial offices of *trespuntos* twice and warned Cerruti to be careful.

February 1
David Leiva, Nueva Argentina, *La Opinión* HARASSED

Three unidentified individuals fired shots at the house of Leiva, director of the radio station Nueva Argentina and editor in chief of the bimonthly *La Opinión* of Orán, in the northern department of Salta.

According to the Argentine press freedom organization Periodistas, Leiva was harassed because of an article published in early January in *La Opinión* on local politician Eduardo Augusto, who had been arrested on December 2, 1997, for drug possession. After the article appeared, government advertising in the magazine was canceled. On January 15, Leiva received the first of several death threats, conveyed in writing and by telephone.

March 9
Manuel Romani, Canal 4 Video Sur ATTACKED

A public works foreman attacked Romani, host of the news program on Canal 4 Video Sur, the local television station in San Carlos Centro in Santa Fe Province, as he was filming a municipal truck that had fallen into a ditch. According to Periodistas, an Argentine press freedom organization, Adrián Caballero, the foreman, tried to stop Romani from filming and then attacked him with a machete. The reporter suffered cuts and gashes that required surgery.

March 11
Héctor D'Amico, *Noticias* LEGAL ACTION
Jorge Fontevecchia, *Noticias* LEGAL ACTION
Noticias LEGAL ACTION

In a split decision, the National Court of Appeals ruled that Fontevecchia, D'Amico, and the newsweekly *Noticias* had violated President Carlos Saúl Menem's "right to privacy" when the magazine printed a story about the president's illegitimate son. The court ordered Fontevecchia and D'Amico, director and editor, respectively, of *Noticias*, to pay US$150,000 in damages. They appealed the decision to the Supreme Court.

The appeals court ruled in the president's favor despite the fact that the article was based largely on public court documents and reported on areas of clear public interest, including death threats made against the president's son, and expensive jewels given by Menem to the boy's mother.

April 18
Andrés Klipphan, *Página/12* THREATENED

Anonymous death threats were made against Klipphan, a reporter for the daily *Página/12*, in connection with his investigation of police corruption in Buenos Aires Province.

Klipphan informed CPJ that a man phoned his home and said: "If you keep on being a nuisance, we are going to kill you." On April 21, Klipphan returned home to find that part of the conversation that he had had during lunch had been left on his answering machine.

On April 22, a threatening letter assembled from cut-up newsprint was sent to *Página/12*'s offices. It read, "Do not forget Cabezas," a reference to the photographer who was murdered on January 25, 1997. The letter was accompanied by a photo of a cadaver and signed "The Big Family of Buenos Aires," which is how the Buenos Aires Province police department identifies itself.

As a result of the threats, *Página/12* took Klipphan off the police corruption story.

November 23
Clarín THREATENED

The offices of the daily newspaper *Clarín* were evacuated after a caller threatened to blow up the building. Authorities cordoned off the street and searched *Clarín*'s offices, but did not find a bomb.

December 29
Alberto Carlos Vila Ortiz, *Rosario/12*
ATTACKED

Two unidentified individuals assaulted Vila Ortiz, columnist for the daily *Rosario/12*, a supplement of the national daily *Página/12*, in the doorway of his home in the city of Rosario, Santa Fe Province.

According to information provided by the Argentine press freedom organization Periodistas, the attack occurred just after midnight. Vila Ortiz heard knocks on his window and went outside, where two men jumped him. One of the assailants grabbed Ortiz's arms and held them behind his back, while the other pulled down his swim trunks and inserted a screw into his scrotum. When a neighborhood security guard blew his whistle and ran toward Vila Ortiz's house, the attackers fled. Vila Ortiz required surgery for his injuries.

Because of his muckraking political reporting, Vila Ortiz has been receiving threats for the last six years. In 1995, he was attacked by three assailants, who stabbed him 12 times in the stomach. In 1994, he was forced to resign from his job as editor in chief of *La Capital*, the largest daily in Rosario, after he and his family were threatened.

Bolivia

The Bolivian press is vibrant and independent, despite the country's poverty and low literacy rate. After a long battle, journalists succeeded in July in killing amendments to the press law which would have allowed judges to compel journalists to reveal their sources. While the 1925 press law defines defamation as a criminal offense punishable by up to two years in prison (the sentence can be doubled if the official in question is the president, vice president, or a minister), there were no prosecutions in 1998. Journalists say the criminal defamation statutes are not a hindrance to their work because the special tribunals established under the press law to try journalists for offenses related to their profession generally rule in favor of the journalists. CPJ, however, opposes all such special tribunals for journalists because they can be—and generally are—used to persecute rather than protect the press.

Although the Asociación de Periodistas de La Paz has petitioned the government to enforce a law limiting the practice of journalism to those who have university degrees, the Inter-American Court of Human Rights in Costa Rica ruled in 1985 that laws requiring the mandatory licensing of journalists violate the American Convention on Human Rights.

While physical attacks against the press are rare, journalists were roughed up in two separate incidents in the city of Santa Cruz. After protests by local press groups, the police commander in Santa Cruz was dismissed and President Hugo Banzer publicly apologized.

Brazil

Amidst a deep economic crisis, Brazilians re-elected President Fernando Henrique Cardoso on October 4. Several regional newspapers were fined in October under an electoral law that prohibits the publication of political opinion or electoral propaganda immediately before an election.

The murders of two journalists highlight the dangers facing reporters working in the country's hinterlands, where political bosses and the military continue to exert de facto control. Manoel Leal de Oliveira was killed in March after he criticized local officials in the town of Itabuna; later that month, television news host José Carlos Mesquita was killed after he criticized local authorities in Ouro Preto do Oeste.

Most regional media outlets are dominated by powerful families who regard them as vehicles to advance their political ambitions. The prime example is the Collor de Mello family, which used its media empire in impoverished Alagoas State as a springboard to local politics and, eventually, the presidency. Reporters who criticize regional civilian and military authorities face constant threats and occasional violence.

Ironically, while Brazil's rural journalists face some of the worst conditions in Latin America, those working in major media markets such as Rio de Janeiro and São Paulo enjoy some of the best. With a reputation for investigative reporting and the resources of huge media conglomerates behind them, Brazilian journalists have earned widespread public support and growing political power. Since 1992, when aggressive reporting on corruption forced the resignation of President Fernando Collor de Mello, investigative journalism has become a staple of the Brazilian media (in fact, some journalists now worry that coverage has become too scandal-driven).

Journalists throughout Brazil share a concern that the country's outdated print law, drafted under the military dictatorship, is being used to limit press freedom. Lawsuits remain common. Although there were no new convictions resulting in a prison sentence, the risk continues to hang over all Brazilian journalists. One clause of the 1967 law punishes journalists who publish false or "truncated" news that "causes the loss of confidence in the banking system" with up to six months imprisonment; a journalist who offends "public morals and good customs" can be jailed for up to a year.

Efforts to reform the law and to ensure that any new legislation affirms and strengthens the freedom of expression guarantees granted in the 1988 constitution have been hampered by members of Congress, who have proposed that journalists be subject to fines of up to US$100,000 for defamation with no limit on the damages that can be imposed on media owners. The proposed bill would also make it easier for politicians to invoke the "Right to Reply," under which media outlets are required to give aggrieved parties space or time to respond to allegations made in the press. The current bill is stalled in the Congress, and a vote is not expected until a new legislature is chosen in January 1999.

Other legislation limits the practice of journalism to those with a university degree and prohibits journalists from printing the name of a minor accused of a crime. A bill before the Senate would prohibit journalists from publishing the names of crime victims.

January 14
Manoel Leal de Oliveira, *A Região* KILLED

Two unidentified men fatally shot Leal, the

Attacks on the Press in 1998

publisher and editor of *A Região*, the largest weekly in southern Bahia State. At 7:50 p.m., three men in a white van began following Leal's car as he was driving to his home in the town of Itabuna. When Leal got out of his car, two men stepped out of the van and shot him six times. The driver turned the van around, picked up the gunmen, and sped off, according to members of Leal's family.

Leal was known for his critical reporting on local authorities. In his coverage, he frequently denounced Fernando Gomes, the mayor of Itabuna, and Gilson Prata, a Civil Police marshal in the Bahia State capital of Salvador.

CPJ sent a letter to President Fernando Henrique Cardoso on March 31, urging a complete and impartial investigation. CPJ further urged that the investigation be conducted by the federal police, since many local journalists with whom CPJ has consulted fear that Leal may have been targeted by local authorities.

According to Leal's son, the investigation was closed on November 18. The police did not interrogate Marcone Sarmento, the man who was identified by two eyewitnesses as one of the assailants, nor did they question the people who had been the subjects of Leal's investigative reporting.

March 10
José Carlos Mesquita, TV Ouro Verde
KILLED

Three unidentified individuals shot and killed Mesquita, host of a news program with the station TV Ouro Verde in the town of Ouro Preto do Oeste in Rondônia State. Mesquita had just finished recording "Espaço Aberto," a program that featured politically sensitive topics, such as the safety of public transportation. Local journalists are convinced he was killed in retaliation for his work.

CPJ sent a protest letter on March 31 to President Fernando Henrique Cardoso urging a complete and impartial investigation.

Chile

Legal restrictions continue to hamper the press, despite Chile's robust economy and developing democratic institutions. A panoply of onerous laws—many of them promulgated in the 1970s and early 1980s under the dictatorship of Gen. Augusto Pinochet—criminalize criticism of public officials, control television broadcast licenses, and allow military tribunals to try journalists accused of sedition.

While prosecutions are rare, the threat of legal action hangs over the media. In January, Rafael Gumucio, host of the news show "Plan Zeta" on Canal 2, and Paula Coddou, a reporter for *Cosas* magazine, were jailed overnight after Gumucio criticized Supreme Court Justice Servando Jordán in an interview with Coddou. Under provisions of the State Security Law which criminalize criticism of public officials, Jordán initiated legal proceedings against José Ale and Fernando Paulsen. The two were formally indicted during the first week of January 1999.

While journalists acknowledge that the threat of legal action undermines their ability to work freely, attempts to reform the press law have been stalled in Congress for nearly five years. A report released in November by Human Rights Watch entitled *The Limits of Tolerance: Freedom of Expression and the Public Debate in Chile* noted that, "at present freedom of expression and information is restricted in Chile to an extent unmatched by any other democratic society in the Western hemisphere."

Legal reform is only the first step in creating a more professional and pluralistic press. Self-censorship and a concentration of media ownership also limit the diversity of viewpoints available to Chileans. Two media companies—both of which have ties to conservative politics—control nearly all

THE AMERICAS

newspapers in the country (two independent papers, *La Epoca* and *Hoy*, closed in 1998). While the Chilean press gave extensive coverage to Pinochet's detention in England in November and December, editorials and opinion pieces reflected the conservative perspectives of the media owners rather than diverse views about Pinochet suggested by public opinion polls.

The good news is that Chilean journalists have begun to discuss the challenges facing the press at public forums hosted by universities and public institutions. During the Summit of the Americas, held in Santiago in March, CPJ co-hosted a panel discussion titled "Press Freedom and the Consolidation of Democracy in Latin America." Commenting on a recent study that determined that 85 percent of television news stories in Chile were based on government sources, television reporter Alejandro Guillier noted, "I think we [journalists] remain trapped in a society that is profoundly authoritarian ... and encourages hypocrisy as a mechanism of survival."

January 13
Fernando Paulsen, *La Tercera*
LEGAL ACTION
José Ale, *La Tercera* LEGAL ACTION

Supreme Court Justice Servando Jordán prosecuted Paulsen and Ale, reporter and editor, respectively, of the Santiago daily *La Tercera*, under the State Security Law which criminalizes criticism of government officials.

The charges stem from a story by Ale that ran on January 7, analyzing Jordán's two-year tenure as chief justice of Chile's Supreme Court. Ale wrote that during that period, "the prestige of Chile's judiciary fell to one of its lowest levels ever." Jordán, currently a justice of the Supreme Court, filed a suit invoking Article 6b of the State Security Law, which holds that it is a crime against public order to insult, among others, "members of the Superior Tribunals of Justice."

Paulsen was prosecuted and tried in the same proceeding because of *La Tercera*'s publication of two letters criticizing Jordán's tenure.

After a lower court judge ruled that there were no grounds for prosecution, Jordán appealed the decision. A three-judge panel from the Santiago Court of Appeals upheld the lower court's ruling on March 11, but a second panel of judges who reviewed the matter reinstated the case. On September 16, the journalists were arrested at the newspaper's office and jailed overnight. On September 17, they were released on bail. The judge in the case closed the investigation in January 1999, and indicted the journalists for the original charges.

Colombia

Four journalists were murdered in Colombia during the year in reprisal for their work—more than in any other country—earning it the dubious distinction of being the world's most lethal place for the press. The four assassinated journalists were: Oscar García Calderón, a reporter for the Bogotá daily *El Espectador*; Nelson Carvajal Carvajal, a producer for Radio Sur; Bernabé Cortés Valderrama, a reporter for the nightly newsprogram "Noticias CVN"; and Amparo Leonor Jiménez Pallares, a former television news reporter. CPJ continues to investigate the deaths of five other journalists killed during 1998 to determine the motive.

Escalating civil war and pervasive criminal violence create a deadly climate for the press. All parties in Colombia's brutal conflict, from paramilitary death squads to guerrillas and local politicians, target journalists. But the leading threat continues to be violence associated with the drug trade. While the two powerful cartels that dominated drug trafficking in the 1980s have been largely dismantled, the smaller and more decentralized drug trafficking organizations that have emerged recently have also been linked to many attacks against the press.

Profits from the drug trade also subsidize the political violence. Right-wing paramilitary groups with ties to the military and the large landowners now control and are financed by coca production and processing throughout the country. In August, members of a paramilitary unit murdered Amparo Leonor Jiménez Pallares in retaliation for a report she produced in 1996 on an enormous estate in Cesar Department owned by a former government official.

While the two country's leftist guerrilla groups say that their involvement in the drug trade is limited to protecting small coca farmers, the circumstances surrounding the murder of Bernabé Cortés Valderrama suggest a more direct role. In May, local drug traffickers in Cali, angered over a television report in which Cortés showed that guerrillas were protecting a large cocaine laboratory, ordered his murder, according to the preliminary findings of the attorney general's office.

Guerrillas often kidnap journalists and release them only after they agree to disseminate the rebels' propaganda. In April, a group of reporters was detained and held for three days by left-wing guerrillas from the National Liberation Army (ELN). Three journalists who went out to look for their colleagues were detained two days later by members of a paramilitary group.

The history of violence against the Colombian press—second only to Algeria in the number of journalists killed in the last decade—is a sad testament to the integrity of journalism in a country where other institutions have been badly compromised by corruption. Against daunting odds, Colombia's press remains vital and aggressive, but recent developments have raised concerns about what one journalist described as a "crack" in the press's reputation. Several sports reporters have been accused of accepting money from the Cali drug cartel, and two journalists were charged with "illicit enrichment" in October (one was later acquitted).

Local journalists also allege that then-President Ernesto Samper, angered over aggressive reporting on contributions made by members of the Cali cartel to his presidential campaign in 1994, continued to use the power of his office to undermine the independent press. Under Samper—who was replaced by newly elected President Andrés Pastrana in August—the government denied broadcast licenses to critical television news programs while distributing concessions for radio frequencies to the president's friends and supporters. The concentration of media ownership also accelerated under Samper. Some journalists fear that the press's independence will be compromised by the commercial and political interests of the new owners. Several editorial staffers, including columnist and investigative reporter Fabio Castillo, were forced to leave the Bogotá daily *El Espectador* in March after it was purchased by a financial group with close ties to Samper's Liberal Party in December 1997.

Pastrana, a former television reporter, has promised to "recover the press freedom" lost under Samper. Prior to the peace talks which Pastrana initiated with members of Colombia's largest guerrilla force in January 1999, journalists played an active role in the peace process by reporting extensively on the different factions, including the paramilitary units, and by offering analysis and context. Journalists can also find some solace in the fact that what could have been the year's most deadly attack was aborted when policed deactivated a powerful bomb placed in front of the Medellín offices of the Bogotá daily *El Tiempo*.

February 22
Oscar García Calderón, *El Espectador*
KILLED

García, a bullfighting reporter for the Bogotá daily *El Espectador*, was forced into a taxi by unidentified assailants as he was leaving the newspaper's offices. He was shot three times, twice in the head and once in the neck. His body was found dumped near the office of Attorney General Alfonso Gómez Méndez.

During the year before his murder, according to colleagues at the paper, García had uncovered links between drug traffickers and bullfighting and had proposed writing a book on the subject. García had asked a colleague to arrange a secret meeting with the attorney general to explain how traffickers used bullfighting and cattle ranching to launder money.

CPJ sent a letter of inquiry to Attorney General Alfonso Gómez Méndez on February 24, and raised this case in a letter to President Ernesto Samper on March 20, the first anniversary of the murder of editor and columnist Gerardo Bedoya Borrero.

April 16
Nelson Carvajal Carvajal, Radio Sur KILLED

Carvajal, a highly regarded radio journalist in the town of Pitalito in Huila Department, was shot 10 times outside the elementary school where he taught. The gunman and an accomplice escaped by motorcycle, according to the testimony of several eyewitnesses.

Carvajal was the producer of five community programs on Radio Sur, a local affiliate of Radio Cadena Nacional (RCN). In addition to programming on topics ranging from health services to rural development, Carvajal provided investigative reporting about alleged government corruption. In one case, Carvajal alleged that former Pitalito Mayor Ramiro Falla Cuenca had misappropriated public funds. Falla was subsequently investigated on the basis of information aired on Carvajal's program.

On January 5, 1999, police arrested the former mayor and two other local politicians, Fernando Bermúdez Ardila and Marco Fidel Collazos. All three are owners of a local construction company. Authorities are still looking for the two assassins hired to carry out the crime.

CPJ wrote a letter on April 27 to President Ernesto Samper, expressing CPJ's deep alarm about the murder and urging him to ensure a vigorous investigation of the crime.

May 19
Bernabé Cortés Valderrama, Noticias CVN
KILLED

A gunman hired by drug traffickers shot Cortés at 11:30 a.m. as he was emerging from a taxi outside his aunt's home, according to government sources. The taxi driver was also shot and killed in the attack. The gunman fled the scene in a Mazda automobile driven by an accomplice.

Cortés was a reporter for the nightly news program "Noticas CVN" on the Telepacifico network at the time of his death. In his 18 years as a journalist in the violent city of Cali, Cortés had covered everything from drug trafficking to government corruption. In 1992, he was briefly detained by guerrillas from the National Liberation Army (ELN). Colombian authorities suspect that Cortés was killed in retaliation for a story aired on July 11, 1997, about a military operation to destroy a large cocaine laboratory near the town of Corinto, an area controlled by the Revolutionary Armed Forces of Colombia (FARC), another guerrilla group. Cortés' report featured dramatic footage of rebels firing on the soldiers who had destroyed the cocaine lab.

In November, Colombian police detained Julio César Ospina Chavarro and charged him with the murder. A gun found in his home tested positive as the murder weapon, and police also found the license plate from the stolen Mazda used by the assailants. A confidential informant told the prosecutor's office that drug traffickers in Corinto angered by the report on the destruction of the cocaine laboratory had hired Ospina Chavarro to kill Cortés.

CPJ wrote a letter to President Ernesto Samper on the day of the murder and urged him to use the resources of his office to bring those responsible to justice. Cortés' funeral in Cali drew several thousand people who were outraged by the crime.

August 6
Radio Caracol LEGAL ACTION

The Ministry of Communications imposed administrative sanctions on Radio Caracol requiring a three-day shutdown of the station and the suspension of its nationally and internationally syndicated programs. Application of the sanctions has been delayed pending the outcome of the station's appeal.

The sanctions stem from a June 18 incident in which sports commentator Edgar Perea urged listeners to vote for Liberal Party presidential candidate Horacio Serpa. During the World Cup soccer match between Denmark and South Africa, Perea said, "Edgar Perea and the people of the group are drinking Aguila beer, which is the only thing Horacio Serpa will drink ... vote for Horacio Serpa!"

According to local journalists, Perea, who had been elected to the senate in March as a representative of the Liberal Party, routinely made statements supporting Serpa during his coverage of the World Cup soccer matches in June.

CPJ wrote to President Andrés Pastrana on October 28, urging his government to abandon efforts to close Radio Caracol, and to work toward the repeal of any legislation that can be used to restrict media.

August 11
Amparo Leonor Jiménez Pallares, "QAP" KILLED

Jiménez was killed by members of a paramilitary death squad in retaliation for a story she broadcast in 1996 about a large estate belonging to Carlos Arturo Marulanda, a former government official, according to local journalists and government sources. A gunman shot her three times in the head after she had dropped her son off at school. He then fled on a motorcycle driven by an accomplice.

In August 1996, when she was a reporter for the nightly news program "QAP," armed men stopped Jiménez and demanded her tapes as she was returning from reporting a story on paramilitary forces who were terrorizing peasants on Marulanda's estate. Further along the same road, a second group of armed men confiscated her tapes. At the time Jiménez was preparing the report, Marulanda was serving as Colombia's ambassador to the European Community.

After returning to city of Valledupar, Jiménez began to receive frequent death threats. At the beginning of 1998, "QAP" lost its broadcast license. In January, she began working for "En Vivo" (Live), broadcast in Valledupar on Canal A. Later in the year, she gave up reporting to work full time for the Presidential Program for Reinsertion, which helps former guerrillas reintegrate into Colombian society. She also volunteered for Redepaz, a national peace advocacy group.

In August, Colombian authorities detained Libardo Humberto Prada and charged him with the murder. An arrest warrant has been issued against Marulanda in connection with the murder in 1994 of several peasants who were living on his property. Marulanda's brother, Francisco Alberto, was arrested on the same charges in May.

On August 12, CPJ wrote a letter to President Andrés Pastrana urging an investigation into the murder.

Costa Rica

Costa Rica's strong democratic institutions have nurtured a vibrant press, and President Miguel Angel Rodríguez has generally sup-

ported the media. Yet punitive press laws have sometimes inhibited the full exercise of press freedom.

Costa Rica took a major step toward the elimination of the most onerous statues in 1998, when President Rodríguez proposed in an October speech that libel legislation be modified to conform to international standards. If the proposed changes are approved by the Costa Rican legislature, reporters could only be prosecuted for libel if they acted with malice by publishing statements that they knew, or should have known, were false (this is the malice standard first articulated in the U.S. Supreme Court in *The New York Times Co. v. Sullivan*). Under current standards, the burden of proof is on the reporter to demonstrate that published information is true.

Rodríguez, who took office in May, has also proposed abolishing a law holding newspaper editors legally responsible for all defamatory articles. Congress is expected to pass the new legislation in early 1999.

In other positive developments, the Constitutional Court overturned legislation that prohibited the media from publishing poll results on the day of an election; the court also sent another proposed law, which would make it more difficult for reporters to gain access to financial data, back to the legislature because of procedural errors in the way the law was drafted.

Despite the advances, serious problems remain. Defamation is a criminal rather than a civil offense in Costa Rica. In addition, under the "Right to Reply," individuals who feel they have been treated unfairly can legally compel a media outlet to grant them equal space or time for rebuttal. Finally, legislators can force journalists to testify about articles, as occurred in June when the Legislative Assembly ordered editors from the daily *La Nación* to appear to answer questions about a story linking Colombia's Cali drug cartel to Costa Rican business and politicians. One of the legislators who participated in the questioning was mentioned in the story.

Cuba

Nearly 3,000 foreign journalists traveled to Cuba in January to cover the visit of Pope John Paul II. Yet in a clear demonstration that Cuba uses a policy of selectively granting visas in order to influence coverage, the government denied visas to a handful of foreign journalists who had written stories critical of President Fidel Castro. CPJ protested this policy, as well as a crackdown on independent Cuban journalists that earned Castro a place on CPJ's list of the 10 worst Enemies of the Press. (See page 62 for more on the Enemies of the Press.)

While reporters covering the pope's visit were allowed to work unimpeded, Cuban journalists reported that State Security agents kept them under constant surveillance.

Although Cuba's communist government controls all media outlets, independent journalists have evaded the restrictions by dictating stories over the telephone to colleagues outside the country. The stories—which range from political commentaries to reports on human rights abuses—are circulated on the Internet, published in newspapers in Miami and in Europe, and broadcast into Cuba by Radio Martí, the U.S. government's office of Cuba Broadcasting. Some Cuban journalists describe themselves as disaffected with the Castro regime, but others say their sole interest in joining the independent press is to provide accurate information.

Since the first independent press agency was founded in 1994, many journalists have gone into exile, been jailed, or forced to leave the profession due to constant harassment. In October, Ana Luisa López Baeza, one of Cuba's top journalists, defected and moved to Miami; reporter Jorge Luis Arce Cabrera left for France that same month.

But there are always new journalists to replace those who leave or can no longer work. Currently, there are about 40 independent journalists divided among eight agencies. The newest agency, Cuba Verdad, was founded in January, just prior to the pope's visit.

Working conditions are extraordinarily difficult. Cubans are prohibited from owning a fax machine or a computer, and even typewriters have been confiscated. Journalists' phones are constantly monitored, and lines are often cut off during sensitive conversations. Many journalists allege that they are conspicuously followed at close range, a form of psychological pressure known as the "Japanese check." Journalists have been harassed and shouted down by organized mobs; they are frequently detained and questioned by State Security agents.

The government has an array of repressive laws at its disposal to stifle the independent press. The penalty for publishing "anti-government propaganda" is a year in prison; those criticizing Castro can be penalized with up to three years imprisonment; "aiding the enemy" can be punished with up to 14 years in prison. Three journalists were in prison at the end of 1998; a fourth has been sentenced to a year of forced labor. (See page 21 for information on the imprisoned journalists.) Conditions for political prisoners are especially difficult. Journalist Bernardo Arévalo Padrón, who is serving a six-year sentence for showing a "lack of respect," was beaten in April by State Security officials, who accused him of writing anti-government posters in prison.

Although the anticipated opening of Cuban society in the aftermath of the pope's visit did not materialize, there was a six-month lull in the systematic repression of independent journalists. It ended in August, when the conviction of dissident Reynaldo Alfaro García for providing false information provoked a vigorous protest. In an effort to quell possible protest, dissidents—including some journalists—were detained on the eve of a September 8 religious procession in honor of Cuba's patron saint.

Prior to a December 10 opposition rally on the 50th anniversary of the Universal Declaration of Human Rights, State Security officers went to journalists' homes and physically prevented them from covering the event. They used the same tactic to keep journalists from covering the December 16 trial of a dissident who was arrested at the December 10 rally.

Despite these strictures, spaces have been opening in Cuba for both local and foreign journalists. Although Castro had asserted to a visiting delegation from the American Society of Newspapers Editors (ASNE) in June that he would not allow any new U.S. news bureaus in Cuba, he announced in November that he had given permission for the Associated Press (AP) to open a bureau in Havana. AP, which was expelled from Cuba in 1969, joins CNN, which is the only U.S. media organization with a permanent presence in the country.

Cuban journalists say the foreign journalists serve as a strong deterrent against public abuses. For example, the presence of a CNN camera crew outside the courthouse where journalist Mario J. Viera was to be tried for slander on November 27 apparently forced the authorities to show restraint when a protest erupted. After three protesters were arrested, the trial was postponed indefinitely.

Writing on May 3, International Press Freedom Day, Raúl Rivero, a poet and Cuba's leading journalist, noted, "Independent journalism without faxes, without computers, with constant telephone interruptions, under harassment and threats ... will serve as a base for a return to a free press, followed by the growth of a democratic society with powerful civil institutions."

January 21
Miami Herald LEGAL ACTION

Miami Herald reporters were uniformly denied visas to cover the visit of Pope John Paul II to Cuba, which took place from January 21 through January 25.

In private conversations with the paper's editors, Cuban authorities said that the paper's chances of receiving visas were remote because of "longstanding criticism of the *Herald*'s and *El Nuevo Herald*'s coverage of Cuba."

CPJ wrote to President Fidel Castro on January 20, protesting the fact that many foreign journalists were denied visas for the pope's visit.

January 21
Matilde Sánchez, *Clarín* LEGAL ACTION
Rodolfo Pouzá, América TV
LEGAL ACTION
Mario Pérez Colman, *La Nación*
LEGAL ACTION

Sánchez, a reporter for the Argentine daily *Clarín*, Pouzá, a reporter for América TV, and Pérez, a reporter for the daily *La Nación*, were denied visas to cover the visit of Pope John Paul II to Cuba.

Concepción Muñoz, a spokeperson for the Cuban Embassy in Buenos Aires, was quoted in the local press saying the decision was based on the reporters' critical coverage of Che Guevara's burial in October.

CPJ wrote to President Fidel Castro on January 20, protesting the fact that many foreign journalists were denied visas to report on the pope's visit.

January 21
Telemundo LEGAL ACTION

Reporters from the Miami-based Telemundo television network were uniformly denied visas to cover the visit of Pope John Paul II to Cuba, which took place from January 21 until January 25.

CPJ wrote to President Fidel Castro on January 20, protesting the fact that many foreign journalists were denied visas to report on the pope's visit.

January 21
Peter Katel, *Newsweek* HARASSED

Katel, a former *Newsweek* correspondent, was denied a visa to cover the January visit of Pope John Paul II to Cuba.

Officials in the Cuban Interest Section in Washington, D.C., told Katel they did not know why he had not received a visa. Katel suspects it was in reprisal for a story he had written about exiled Cuban writer Eliseo Alberto, which appeared in the international edition of *Newsweek* on September 1, 1997. The article described Alberto's controversial memoir about his disaffection with the Castro regime's policy of coddling intellectuals who are loyal to the government.

CPJ wrote to President Fidel Castro on January 20, protesting the fact that many foreign journalists were denied visas to report on the pope's visit.

January 30
Jorge Luis Arce Cabrera, Buró de Prensa Independiente de Cuba THREATENED
Jesús Egozcue Castellanos, Línea Sur Press THREATENED

Arce, Cienfuegos correspondent for Buró de Prensa Independiente de Cuba, and Egozcue, Aguada de Pasajeros correspondent for Línea Sur Press, were threatened with imprisonment by a State Security official, Lt. Orebis Montes de Oca, who visited Arce's home in Cienfuegos on January 30.

Montes told the journalists they could soon be arrested or imprisoned if they wrote stories that "tarnished Cuba's image." Montes warned Arce that he would be watched closely because he had disseminated "false information" in previous reports.

Authorities were incensed that Arce had attended Pope John Paul II's mass in Havana during the pontiff's recent visit, because Arce had only had permission to travel to Havana to arrange for a visa to leave the country. Arce left for France on October 23.

February 27
David Adams, *St. Petersburg Times*
HARASSED, EXPELLED

Adams, Latin America correspondent for the *St. Petersburg Times* who was denied a visa to cover the January visit of Pope John Paul II to Cuba, was granted a visa to report from the island in February. He traveled there on February 26, but was forcibly ejected the next day.

Upon arrival in Havana on the 26th, Adams checked in at the Hotel Nacional. At 1:30 a.m. on February 27, he was awakened by three officers from the Interior Ministry, who escorted him to the airport and detained him there until 7:30 a.m., when he was put on a plane to Cancún, Mexico. When Adams asked for an explanation for his expulsion, he was told, "you should know (usted debe saber)."

After returning to the United States, Adams was told by officials at the Cuban Interest Section in Washington, D.C., that his expulsion was the result of a bureaucratic error and that he would soon be granted another visa.

When Adams had not received a visa by May 6, his editor, Paul C. Tash, sent a letter to the Cuban Interest Section asking for an explanation.

On May 26, CPJ sent a private communication to the Cuban Interest Section requesting that Adams be granted a visa. A few days later Adams received a call from the Interest Section saying that it would soon issue the visa.

Adams was granted a three-month unrestricted visa to travel to Cuba on June 17. He left the following day, and was able to report in Cuba for more than two weeks without interference.

While in Havana, Adams met with officials in the Foreign Ministry, who told him that they had not granted him a visa previously because they were generally unhappy with Adams' reporting on Cuba.

May 7
Luis López Prendes, Buró de Prensa Independiente de Cuba (BPIC)
THREATENED

Three men forced López's mother into a van, and began asking her where they could find her son, the correspondent for Buró de Prensa Independiente de Cuba (BPIC). López had been reporting on corruption, drug trafficking, and prostitution in the beach resort of Playas de Este.

July 21
All foreign journalists HARASSED

President Fidel Castro told all foreign journalists to leave a session of the National Assembly. He criticized the foreign press for its negative coverage of Cuba, and suggested that the deputies would not be able to discuss matters freely as long foreign journalists were present.

While Castro has previously barred foreign reporters from National Assembly debates, this was the first time he explained why. "We want to be alone to discuss with greater freedom. This does not mean it will be a secret," Castro said. "There is no secret among 601 delegates or among journalists, members of the national media. Let's make a distinction, and let's respectfully distinguish between the national media and the multinational media."

Castro reportedly was incensed about a story in the July 19 *Miami Herald* reporting that he had been treated in October for a potentially fatal brain ailment. The story later proved to be false.

September 10
Juan Antonio Sánchez Rodríguez, CubaPress
IMPRISONED, THREATENED

State Security officials detained Sánchez Rodríguez at noon as he walking through Havana. He was taken to the town of Pinar del Río, west of Havana, where he works as a CubaPress correspondent, and was confined in the town's State Security headquarters. One of the agents who detained Sánchez Rodríguez gave his name as "Isidro."

Local sources informed CPJ that Isidro had followed Sánchez Rodríguez during festivities honoring Cuba's patron saint on September 8. Sanchez Rodríguez's colleagues suspect that the journalist was detained because he had argued with Isidro and insulted President Fidel Castro.

Sánchez was freed on September 16 without charges or explanation. He was warned that he was being classified as "dangerous." Local journalists say such warnings can result in legal prosecution and up to four years in prison.

September 15
Mario Julio Viera González, Cuba Verdad
LEGAL ACTION

José Peraza Chapeau, head of the legal affairs division of the Foreign Ministry, sued Viera, founder of the news agency Cuba Verdad, for slander. Viera had written an article calling Peraza a hypocrite for delivering a speech advocating the independence of the International Criminal Court while turning a blind eye to the lack of independence of the Cuban judiciary.

Viera's article, "Naked Morals" (Moral en Calzoncillos), was posted on the website of the Miami-based agency, CubaNet, on June 24. The Provincial Tribunal in Havana set his trial for November 27, but a noisy protest in support of Viera outside the tribunal forced a postponement. If convicted, Viera could be sentenced to a year in prison, plus an additional six months if he refuses to retract his statement.

September 16
Jesús Labrador Arias, CubaPress
HARASSED

Five State Security agents interrogated Labrador Arias, the CubaPress correspondent in Manzanillo, Granma Province, for two hours in the Manzanillo State Security headquarters. The agents threatened to charge Labrador Arias with "illegally exercising his profession" since Labrador Arias has not formally studied journalism. They also threatened to charge him with spreading false information. While they acknowledged that Labrador Arias' reporting was accurate, the agents argued that it wasn't "the entire truth"

Throughout the year, Labrador Arias has suffered constant harassment, fines, detentions, and interrogations, according to his colleagues. He was twice the target of a stone-throwing attack, and once of an "act of repudiation" by a vigilante group tied to the Communist Party, intended to ostracize opponents of the Castro regime. State Security officials have Labrador Arias under constant surveillance, and have instructed his friends not to lend him their telephones for reporting purposes (Labrador Arias does not have a phone).

October 1
Manuel Antonio González Castellanos, CubaPress IMPRISONED

State Security agents arrested González Castellanos, a correspondent for the independent news service CubaPress, on charges of "sedition" (desacato) on the evening of October 1 in San Germán, Holguín Province.

According to colleagues and relatives of the journalist, González Castellanos was arrested after he made critical statements about President Fidel Castro to State Security agents who had stopped him and insulted him as he was returning from a friend's house.

When family members learned of González

Castellanos' detention and tried to contact him at the local police station the following morning, they were met by a group of protesters who insulted them. González Castellanos' relatives were so indignant that they painted "Down with Fidel (Abajo Fidel)" on the walls of their house. Later that day, an estimated 2,000 people gathered outside González Castellanos' home and screamed insults. State Security agents broke in and beat and arrested two relatives along with a political dissident who was also present. One of the relatives was released after four days, but was told she could face imprisonment. According to local sources, many of the protesters who gathered in front of González Castellanos' house were farm workers who had been told they would be docked a day's pay if they did not participate in the demonstration. After the protest rally, the González Castellanos family's phone was cut off for nearly a week.

While the sedition charges against González Castellanos stem from an interaction that is unrelated to his journalistic work, local journalists suspect that González Castellanos was deliberately provoked by State Security agents in retaliation for news reports filed from Holguín about the activities of political dissidents.

In July, González Castellanos had been contacted by a man claiming to have information for him from a Cuban exile in Miami. When they met, the source questioned González Castellanos about his journalistic work and told him that a Cuban exile group wanted to recruit him for subversive activities. González Castellanos declined the offer and later determined that the man with whom he had met had never been in touch with the exiles in Miami he claimed to represent. González Castellanos believed the man was a State Security agent attempting to entrap him.

While in prison, González Castellanos has been harassed by guards, who have confiscated a book, *Academic Journalism*, and letters. As of December, González Castellanos had not been brought before a judge.

October 23
Edel José García Díaz, Centro Norte del País (CNP) HARASSED

A State Security officer interrogated García Díaz, a reporter with the independent news agency Centro Norte del País (CNP) based in Caibarién, Villa Clara Province. He questioned García Díaz for an hour and a half, and warned him he could soon be tried for spreading "false information."

García Díaz had been summoned to State Security headquarters in Santa Clara, the provincial capital, in relation to an article he wrote in January on foreigners paying in dollars for health care in Cuba.

The director of CNP, Gustavo Rafael Rodríguez, informed CPJ that the reporters in Villa Clara Province were repeatedly summoned to appear at the local State Security offices during the months of August, September, and October.

December 10
Omar Rodríguez Saludes, Agencia Nueva Prensa (ANP) HARASSED
Jorge Olivera, Habana Press HARASSED

Early in the morning, a State Security officer known as Isidro took Rodríguez Saludes, a reporter for the independent news agency Agencia Nueva Prensa, into custody at his Havana home and brought him to the Department of Technical Investigations of the Interior Ministry. He was held for the day, but was not interrogated, according to his colleagues.

Rodríguez Saludes was apparently detained solely to prevent him from reporting on an opposition rally in support of human rights that was being held in Butari Park in connection with the 50th anniversary of the Universal Declaration of Human Rights.

During the days leading up to the anniversary celebration, State Security officers visited several other journalists to try to persuade them not to report on the rally. On the day of the rally, almost all journalists were monitored by State Security personnel and members of the Vigilance and Protection System (SUPV), a vigilante group tied to the Communist Party. Three State Security officials stopped Habana Press director Jorge Olivera as he was walking to the rally in Butari Park. They told Olivera that he could not proceed, and they forcibly removed him from the vicinity of the rally, dragging him for two blocks.

December 15
Jesús Zúñiga, Cooperativa de Periodistas Independientes HARASSED
Marvin Hernández Monzón, CubaPress HARASSED
Orlando Bordón Gálvez, CubaPress HARASSED
Lázaro González Valdés, Cuba Verdad HARASSED

State Security officials detained Cooperativa de Periodistas Independientes correspondent Zúñiga; CubaPress correspondents Martínez Pulgarón, Hernández Monzón, and Bordón Gálvez; and Cuba Verdad correspondent González Valdés, to prevent them from covering the December 16 trial of dissident Lázaro Constantín Durán. Constantín, a political dissident, was tried in the Municipal Court of Old Havana for "dangerousness."

State Security officials detained Zúñiga in his home and brought him to the Second Unit of the Revolutionary National Police (PNR) on December 15; Martínez Pulgarón was detained at 6:20 a.m. on December 16 and brought to the same police station. Hernández Monzón, Bordón Gálvez, and González Valdés were detained on the 16th in the vicinity of the Municipal Court and taken to the same police station.

Other independent journalists were either warned not to cover the trial, or put under intensive surveillance by State Security agents.

December 29
Jesús Labrador Arias, CubaPress HARASSED

Officers of the Revolutionary National Police (PNR) arrested Labrador Arias, CubaPress correspondent in Manzanillo, Granma Province. He was detained for 21 hours at the local police headquarters, and released without charge. The police confiscated Labrador Arias' identification card, which Cubans are required to carry with them at all times.

Dominican Republic

Press freedom is generally respected in the Dominican Republic, and journalists reported few problems covering the year's major news stories—from the devastation wrought by Hurricane Georges to the strikes and protests that followed the municipal elections in August. The only violent incident occurred during the visit of Cuban President Fidel Castro in August, when television commentator Rafael Bonilla Ayber was injured in a clash between pro- and anti-Castro demonstrators.

In December, U.S. federal authorities, acting at the request of Dominican authorities, arrested Mariano Cabrera Durán, a liquor store owner in the Bronx, New York, and charged him with participating in the 1975 murder of reporter Luis Orlando Martínez. Cabrera is expected to go on trial in Santo Domingo in January 1999. Martínez, who worked for the magazine *Ahora*, was killed after he published articles critical of President Joaquín Belaguer.

Ecuador

With El Niño-induced flooding, plunging oil prices, a currency devaluation, riots, and a lively political campaign in which former Quito Mayor Jamil Mahuad defeated banana mogul Alvaro Noboa for the presidency, there has been no shortage of news. And for the most part, journalists say they were able to report it without hindrance.

The most serious incident occurred in February after the Quito daily *Hoy* published a story alleging that an advisor to interim President Fabián Alarcón had diverted aid donated to flood victims. Pedro Castro, a local politician in the port city of Guayaquil, led a rock-throwing mob in an attack on the newspaper's local bureau. Alarcón, who took over as president in February 1997 after Congress removed President Abdalá Bucaram for "mental incompetence," was replaced by Mahuad in August.

After taking office, Mahuad immediately negotiated an end to Ecuador's long-standing border dispute with Peru. Journalists from *Hoy*, which supported the peace initiative, say they received a series of threatening phone calls and letters from readers angered by their coverage.

While defamation is a criminal offense in Ecuador punishable by up to three years in prison, no journalists were prosecuted during 1998. Efforts to reform the press law have been hampered by divisions within the press corps between those favoring mandatory licensing of journalists and those who oppose it.

February 6
José Solís, *Hoy* ATTACKED
Gustavo Cortés, *Hoy* ATTACKED

Approximately 60 government employees assaulted Solís and Cortés, reporters in the Guayaquil bureau of the Quito daily *Hoy*, during an attack on *Hoy*'s offices in anger over the paper's coverage of a corruption scandal. The rock-throwing mob was led by Pedro Castro, secretary of the local election board.

In January, *Hoy* ran several articles reporting that presidential adviser Eduardo Sierra had used presidential stationery to solicit donations to buy clothing for Ecuadorians left homeless by El Niño-related flooding. The clothing, shipped from South Florida, instead ended up in stores in the port city of Guayaquil.

June 2
José Barrón Jara Velarde, *El Sol* HARASSED
León Esteban Félix Lafaro, *El Sol* HARASSED

Members of the Ecuadoran army harassed Jara, editor of the Peruvian daily *El Sol*, and Félix, a photographer for the paper, during a press conference held by Ecuador's President Fabián Alarcón at Sucre, an air force base in Quito.

Jara and Félix were in Ecuador to cover the presidential elections. On June 2, they attended a press conference, which President Alarcón held after returning from meeting with Peru's President Alberto K. Fujimori in Brazil. A soldier in civilian clothes stopped the journalists and questioned them about their nationality. The journalists were detained briefly, until Alarcón's press attaché intervened.

After the press conference, the officer again stopped Jara as he was leaving the base with Javier Pérez, a reporter from the Ecuadoran daily *Hoy*. The officer, aided by a member of President Alarcón's security detail, dragged Jara into a bathroom. There they were joined by an armed soldier in uniform. The three men frisked Jara and confiscated two rolls of film. Jara and Pérez were then escorted off the base.

Félix was dragged into the bathroom and subjected to similar treatment by the same individuals when he tried to leave the base. Félix's film and his civilian identification papers were confiscated.

None of the film was returned, according to the journalists.

In a memorandum sent to the Peruvian Embassy in Quito on July 14, the Ecuadoran

Ministry of Foreign Affairs claimed that Jara and Félix were detained because they had failed to properly identify themselves as journalists upon entering the military base. The memo also alleged that the journalists had taken photographs of the runway at the base. Jara and Félix deny both accusations.

The Ecuadorian officials stated that the journalists were not ill-treated during their detention, but acknowledged that the authorities had kept the confiscated film because it contained "classified information."

El Salvador

There have been few violent attacks against the press since the end of the Salvadoran civil war in 1993, but legal impediments, a lack of resources and training, and a series of minor incidents impeded Salvadoran journalists' work.

Although defamation is a criminal offense punishable by up to four years in prison, the most serious legal issue threatening the Salvadoran press is the implementation of Article 272 of the penal code, which grants judges the authority to bar coverage of trials where the moral order, the public interest, or national security could be affected. In at least three instances since the law went into effect in April, Salvadoran judges banned coverage of sensitive trials, including the trial of the men accused of the August 1997 murder of radio newscaster Lorena Saravia.

In February, Salvadoran police announced with great fanfare that they had arrested 13 people, among them several former police officers, for the murder of Saravia, who they alleged had been killed on the orders of a jilted lover. Five men were immediately released because of lack of evidence. Seven months later, the remaining eight were set free by a judge who ruled that they had been framed in an internecine police department dispute. While the motive for Saravia's murder remains unclear, the handling of the investigation has raised concerns about a possible cover-up.

Although a new generation of young reporters has improved the quality of journalism, an emphasis on covering breaking news and press releases means there is little investigative or probing reporting. Because of the possibility of violent reprisal, certain topics remain off limits, particularly the growing power of violent drug traffickers. "No one is looking into this," noted one veteran journalist. "It's just too dangerous."

Guatemala

Considering that CPJ has documented 29 journalists killed in the line of duty in Guatemala since 1981, the virtual halt of violence against journalists this year suggests how dramatically conditions have improved for the Guatemalan press. In the one incident documented this year by CPJ, a police officer who threatened a reporter was suspended from his duties.

While violence has subsided, tensions between the press and the government of President Alvaro Arzú Irigoyen have mounted. Early in the year, Arzú lashed out at the press for reporting on violent crime, arguing that such reports scare away tourists.

Arzú's regime has sought to control the press by depriving critical publications of government advertising—a strategy which forced the sale of the highly acclaimed weekly *Crónica* in December. The magazine's new owners appointed as editor a conservative journalist who is close to the Arzú government. Most of *Crónica's*

Attacks on the Press in 1998

reporters quit in protest. "Guatemala Flash," a radio program which has been on the air for more than 50 years, was also sold to a pro-government investor after what some local journalists described as a government-directed financial boycott.

Although some financial harassment was directed at the daily *elPeriódico*, it has fared well in 1998. Acquired in 1997 by a publishing house that owns *Prensa Libre*, Guatemala's largest newspaper, *elPeriódico* has been able to maintain its independence while developing its investigative reporting.

Despite government harassment, the Guatemalan press continued its drive toward greater independence and professionalization with the support of the country's increasingly assertive civil society. The Asociación de Periodistas de Guatemala (APG), the country's largest press freedom organization, became a member of the International Freedom of Expression Exchange Clearing House (IFEX), and organized journalism workshops in collaboration with San Carlos University.

"The government doesn't realize that political space and freedom of expression aren't gracious concessions of the government but hard-fought gains," noted columnist and APG president Eduardo Villatoro.

January 1
Crónica HARASSED
elPeriódico HARASSED

The weekly *Crónica* and the daily *elPeriódico* have faced financial loss because of a government campaign to deprive them of advertising. The action was taken because of their critical coverage, according to local journalists.

According to an internal government memorandum obtained by CPJ, dated January 21, state agencies were prohibited from advertising in either publication. Presidential spokesman Ricardo de la Torre repeatedly used his weekly meetings with government officials to urge them not to cooperate with *Crónica* or *elPeriódico*, according to a source present at the meetings.

Crónica reported an 80-percent decrease in private-sector advertising since President Alvaro Arzú Irigoyen took office in 1996.

CPJ wrote a letter to President Arzú on April 6 expressing its concern about the harassment, and asking that the government purchase advertising space in an equitable fashion.

On December 1, *Crónica* was sold to Juan Waelti and Jorge Rodas, who appointed Mario David García as editor. García is said by local journalists to be close to the government of President Arzú.

November 20
Hermán René Betancourth Castillo, Emisoras Unidas THREATENED

Ovidio Díaz Gramajo, a police officer, threatened the life of Betancourth, a correspondent for Emisoras Unidas (United Radio Stations) in the municipality of El Tumbador, San Marcos Department, after Betancourth reported on the air that Díaz extorted street vendors.

According to information provided by the Asociación de Periodistas de Guatemala (APG), Díaz and some other police officers confiscated Betancourth's APG credentials during the same incident. After APG sent written protests to the general director of the Civil National Police, the governor of San Marcos, and the mayor of El Tumbador, Díaz was temporarily suspended.

Haiti

While there has been no evidence of direct government persecution of the press since the democratically elected government of President René Préval took power in 1996, an upsurge in drug-related violence and corruption has posed new challenges for journalists. While paramilitary groups such

journalists. While paramilitary groups such as the *tontons macoutes* have disbanded, journalists are still at risk from rogue police commanders and private security forces. In one incident, reporters covering the parliament were roughed up by security guards; in another, private security guards beat up a television reporter on the grounds of the Haiti State University Hospital.

Haiti's high illiteracy rate means that radio is the principal news medium. The number of privately run local stations has doubled in the last few years. Call-in programs give voice to a wide variety of perspectives.

Years of covering political turmoil have made local journalists extremely proficient at reporting breaking news. Investigative and analytical journalism remain rare, however, which journalists attribute to a lack of money and personnel. The Haitian press has stayed away from at least one important but potentially dangerous story—the upsurge in drug trafficking and corruption as the island has become a favored transshipment route of Colombian drug cartels. Because some political disputes are still settled by violence in this fledgling democracy, the press continues to exercise a degree of self-censorship.

April 7
Marc Esnan Fleurissaint, Télévision Nationale d'Haiti (TNH) ATTACKED
Dominique Beauplan, Radio Ginen ATTACKED
Yvlaine Paul, Radio Lumière ATTACKED
Yves Lormé, free-lancer ATTACKED
Henri Israel, Signal FM ATTACKED
Abel Descolines, Radio Galaxie ATTACKED

Security officers beat Fleurissaint, a cameraman with Télévision Nationale d'Haiti (TNH); Beauplan, a reporter with Radio Ginen; Paul, a reporter with Radio Lumière; Israel, a reporter with Signal FM radio; Abel Descolines, a reporter with Radio Galaxie; and Lormé, a free-lance correspondent, during a session of the Haitian parliament.

Jean Bellegarde, chief of security services for the parliament, ordered Fleurissaint to stop filming a heated discussion in the parliament. When Fleurissaint refused, Bellegarde began beating him. Bellegarde had entered the session without having been invited by the parliament's speaker, in violation of house rules.

Israel, Beauplan, Paul, Descolines, and Lormé descended from the press balcony to the floor and confronted Bellegarde. The security chief began fighting with the reporters and was joined by a dozen other security officers. Paul and Lormé lost their tape recorders in the skirmish.

Honduras

Close personal relationships between media owners and President Carlos Flores, along with the corruption of individual journalists, combined to undermine public confidence in the Honduran press.

Flores, who took office in 1997, is the owner of the Tegucigalpa daily *La Tribuna*, whose coverage has been uniformly favorable to his administration. Critics allege that Flores has received generally good press by personally pressuring media owners who criticize him, and rewarding those who support his polices. In his first year in office, Flores named at least 20 former journalists to diplomatic posts, according to local press reports. Francisco Morales, former editor in chief of the Tegucigalpa daily *El Heraldo*, was named ambassador to Spain.

Corruption also takes cruder forms. Many reporters accept bribes from government officials in exchange for positive coverage. As an example, journalists point out that local reporting on the government's response to Hurricane Mitch was highly favorable, while the foreign press raised questions about the efficacy of the relief effort and official inflation of the casualty count.

The government impedes the work of the press through control of the Colegio de Periodistas (College of Journalists), which licenses journalists before they are allowed to work. When Elan Reyes, the spokesperson for Honduran first lady Mary Flake de Flores, became president of the Colegio in November, several dozen journalists walked out in protest.

Jamaica

Except for a few minor incidents in which reporters covering political rallies were verbally harassed, Jamaica's diverse and independent media were able to work unhindered.

The Gleaner Company Limited, owner of *The Daily Gleaner*, continued to appeal a US$2.5 million libel verdict stemming from an Associated Press story that ran in 1987. The story contained allegations that former Tourism Minister Eric Anthony Abrahams had accepted bribes.

Mexico

Compared to his predecessors, President Ernesto Zedillo has demonstrated a strong commitment to press freedom and tolerance for criticism, and journalists have made marked strides toward independence and enterprise during his tenure. But violence still plagues journalists working in the country: Luis Mario García Rodríguez, a reporter covering the drug trade, was murdered in February, and U.S. foreign correspondent Philip True was killed in December.

At year's end, CPJ was continuing to monitor the investigation into the murder of True, the Mexico correspondent for the *San Antonio Express-News*, who was strangled while reporting on the Huichol Indians in northwestern Mexico. In response to CPJ's request, President Zedillo committed the Mexican army to search for True when he was reported missing, and ordered federal authorities to provide logistical support for the murder investigation.

In late December, Mexican authorities arrested two Indians whom they claimed had confessed to murdering True because he had taken photographs without their permission. When the two men were brought into court, however, they acknowledged killing True but said they had acted in self-defense. They also said they had been tortured by Mexican authorities.

García, a police reporter who worked for the Mexico City daily *La Tarde*, was shot dead on a downtown street corner in apparent retaliation for his reporting on corruption.

More than a year after the assassination attempt on Jesús Blancornelas in Tijuana, which left the editor of the weekly *Zeta* gravely wounded and his bodyguard dead, there have been no significant advances in the investigation, despite the fact that a gunman killed at the scene was identified as a member of the Tijuana drug cartel. Blancornelas, who made a full recovery from his injuries, has published detailed descriptions and photos of those believed responsible for the attacks.

Drug trafficking, police corruption, and civil conflict in southern Mexico continue to be the most dangerous assignments for reporters. Journalists, particularly foreign journalists, working in the states of Chiapas and Guerrero have to contend with delays, interrogation, and occasional detentions at government roadblocks. Local consulates also discourage U.S. journalists with lengthy waiting periods for contacts. The Mexican federal government has repeatedly assured CPJ that the visa delays and requests for sources' names are unauthorized.

An attempt to reform and update Mexico's press law—which defines defamation as a criminal offense punishable by up to 18 months in prison—was scuttled in October by media owners, who objected to provisions calling for a government commission to oversee media concessions. But many Mexican journalists say that media owners blocked the legislation because it would have required them to publicize the amount of government advertising they receive. Mexican newspapers often publish government advertising disguised as news reports.

Mexican journalists have made significant strides in self-defense. The Sociedad de Periodistas, a press freedom group formed in late 1997, and incorporated in 1998, has already made an impact. The group was active in demanding security for poet and newspaper columnist Homero Aridjis, who received repeated death threats after he spoke out about the lack of press freedom in Mexico. The group has also pressured the Mexican government to continue the investigation into the attack on Blancornelas, and has petitioned the government for a complete investigation into True's murder.

February 11
Héctor Gutiérrez, *Crónica* THREATENED

An anonymous letter containing a death threat was slipped under the door at the home of Gutiérrez, a reporter for the Mexico City daily *Crónica*, after he published a story on the Cobra Group, which breaks up student demonstrations at the Autonomous National University of Mexico (UNAM). Gutiérrez had written that the Cobra Group was composed of former judicial and riot police officers, as well as former madrinas (paid police enforcers).

February 12
Luis Mario García Rodríguez, *La Tarde* KILLED

García, a reporter for the Mexico City daily *La Tarde*, was murdered at 11:15 p.m. on the corner of Lerdo and Moctezuma streets in the Colonia Guerrero neighborhood. He was ambushed by several assailants, who shot him five times in the head.

During the year and a half García worked for *La Tarde*, he reported extensively on corruption in the national attorney general's office and the Federal Judicial Police (PJF). In a series of articles published in late 1997, García reported that members of the PJF were collaborating with the Arellano Félix brothers, who run the Tijuana drug cartel. Only a few days before the murder, García was interrogated by a federal police officer and an army captain about his sources within the PJF, according to an editor at *La Tarde*.

In 1997, both García and his young son were shot and injured when his car was raked with gunfire.

CPJ wrote a letter on February 19, stating that if the Mexico City district attorney's office determines that García was murdered in reprisal for his work, the federal attorney general's office should assume responsibility for the case. However, because of the suspicion that federal police officers may have been responsible for the crime, CPJ urged the appointment of a special prosecutor.

March 4
Janet Schwartz, *Novedades, Tabasco Hoy* HARASSED
Julia Preston, *The New York Times* HARASSED

Schwartz, a correspondent for the dailies *Novedades* and *Tabasco Hoy*, and Preston, a corre-

Attacks on the Press in 1998

were confined for three hours by hostile villagers in a schoolhouse in San Jerónimo Tulija, Chiapas.

The journalists had gone to San Jerónimo Tulija in response to a communiqué in which the local faction of the Zapatista National Liberation Army (EZLN) invited the press to a meeting. Looking for the press conference, Schwartz and Preston walked into what turned out to be a gathering of followers of the governing Institutional Revolutionary Party (PRI). Approximately 200 villagers trapped them in the schoolhouse where the meeting was being held. They detained the journalists for three hours and confiscated their press credentials, as well as the copy of the EZLN communiqué in the journalists' possession. Schwartz and Preston were released only after the journalists convinced local authorities that they were not Zapatista supporters, but were interested in both sides of the story.

CPJ mentioned this incident in a July 13 letter to President Ernesto Zedillo expressing concern for the safety of journalists covering areas of conflict in Mexico.

March 22
Leoncio Aguilar Márquez, *El Sudcaliforniano*
HARASSED, LEGAL ACTION
Mario Alberto García, *El Sudcaliforniano*
HARASSED, LEGAL ACTION
Luis Miguel Salazar, *El Sudcaliforniano*
HARASSED, LEGAL ACTION

Aguilar Márquez, editor of daily *El Sudcaliforniano*; García, the managing editor; and Salazar, a reporter, were detained in a La Paz police station by agents from the attorney general's office. They were charged with violating a law prohibiting the publication of polls less than a week before an election. In July 1997, *El Sudcaliforniano* published an article by Salazar, in which he predicted the winners of the local congressional election in La Paz, Baja California Sur, based on previous showings.

Aguilar Márquez was briefly handcuffed in the newsroom and an agent drew a gun and threatened a photographer who tried to take pictures of the scene. Aguilar Márquez was held overnight and interrogated in the police station.

García and Salazar, who were wanted for questioning, turned themselves in on March 23, the day after Aguilar Márquez's arrest, and were also held overnight in the police station.

A federal judge declared Aguilar Márquez innocent in April. In a separate decision, García and Salazar were likewise found innocent in August.

April 12
Oriana Elicabe, Agence France-Presse
ATTACKED
Pascual Gorriz, Associated Press
ATTACKED

Police officers at the Tuxtla Gutiérrez airport beat Gorriz, a photographer for Associated Press, and Elicabe, a photographer for Agence France-Presse, and tried to confiscate their film. The photographers were covering the expulsion of a group of foreign human rights observers from Mexico.

CPJ referred to this incident in a July 13 letter to Mexican President Ernesto Zedillo expressing concern for the safety of journalists covering areas of conflict in Mexico.

May 29
Reyes Héctor Suárez Olvera, Televisa
ATTACKED

Suárez Olvera, Huatulco correspondent for the Televisa network, was beaten by several men as he was leaving a Huatulco bar in the early morning hours of May 29. Suárez Olvera suffered a black eye, a broken nose, a large gash above his eye, and a cut on his mouth that required surgery.

While the men who attacked Suárez Olvera ostensibly began beating him after a dispute over a taxi, Suárez Olvera believes he was deliberately targeted because of his work as a erately targeted because of his work as a journalist. His reports for Televisa on the damage done to Huatulco by Hurricane Pauline angered local business leaders, who accused him of damaging the tourist industry. One hotel executive sent a letter to Televisa asking that Suárez Olvera be fired; another suggested that Suárez Olvera had exaggerated his reporting and that the "whole town wants to kick him out."

Suárez Olvera filed a criminal complaint with the Public Ministry on the day of the attack. On June 9, one of the men who attacked him visited his home. After breaking several windows with a rock, the man threatened to kill Suárez Olvera's children if he continued with his complaint. After Televisa aired reports about the incident on June 10, and again on June 11 and 12, the state governor ordered police protection for Suárez Olvera.

June 5
Pascual Gorriz, Associated Press HARASSED

Gorriz, an Associated Press photographer, was confronted by a state police commander in the town of Nicolás Ruiz in Chiapas state while on assignment. The commander ordered police officers to "take away his camera (quitarle la cámara)." When the officers did not comply, the commander began chanting "foreigner, foreigner (extranjero, extranjero)," in a clear attempt to incite the crowd to take action.

On July 13, CPJ wrote a letter to President Ernesto Zedillo expressing concern for the safety of journalists covering conflict areas in Mexico.

July 13
Héctor Gutiérrez, *Crónica* THREATENED
Antonio Carrillo Luna, deputy director of investigations of the Federal District Attorney General's office, threatened to kill Gutiérrez, a reporter for the Mexico City daily *Crónica*, in connection with a story about the official's alleged criminal record.

Gutiérrez informed CPJ that he had been working for four months on an investigation into Carrillo Luna's alleged conviction in 1989 for kidnapping. The story was published in two parts, on July 14 and 15. On the eve of the publication of the first article, Carillo Luna called Gutiérrez and offered him money in exchange for not publishing the story. Carrillo Luna also warned that the journalist would be killed if he refused to accept the bribe. After the story was published, Carrillo Luna resigned.

August 17
Homero Aridjis, *Reforma* THREATENED

Aridjis, a noted author and poet, president of PEN International, president of the environmental organization Group of 100, and a columnist for the daily *Reforma*, received a series of death threats as a result of his defense of press freedom.

Aridjis received a threatening call on August 17—a few weeks after speaking about the lack of respect for freedom of expression in Mexico during a conference in Ottawa, Canada, on "The Artist and Human Rights." After he returned to Mexico, a woman left a threatening message on Aridjis' answering machine, saying: "You'll be sorry, you son of a bitch. Your daughters are whores ... You're going to die very soon."

Aridjis first received threats in November 1997, after speaking at a dinner in Mexico City hosted by CPJ and attended by many of Mexico's leading journalists. At the November 7 gathering, Aridjis discussed attacks on Mexican journalists and criticized the government for its failure to investigate them. "Many of you know that in the last five months five reporters who cover police matters were attacked and one of them was killed," Aridjis noted at the time. "If aggression is tolerated it can become indiscriminate."

One threat occurred the day after he gave a telephone interview to Molly Moore, Mexico City bureau chief for *The Washington Post*. Speaking with Moore by phone on November 26 from New York City, Aridjis discussed the crime wave in Mexico City, including the band of kidnappers who had cut off the ears of their victims. On November 27, the following message was left on his answering machine in Mexico City: "I'm looking for you, dog. Soon you will die like dogs. I have both of you in my sights. I'm going to cut your ears off." Two days later Aridjis' housekeeper spotted two men loitering outside his house.

CPJ wrote to President Ernesto Zedillo on August 28, expressing concern about the threats.

December 4
Philip True, *San Antonio Express-News*
KILLED

True was a Mexico City correspondent for the Texas newspaper, the *San Antonio Express-News*. He left home November 28 for a 10-day trip through the Sierra Madre Occidental of Nayarit and Jalisco states to report on the Huichol Indians.

True was last seen alive in the village of Chalmotitia on December 4. His body was located at the bottom of a ravine on December 15, after an intensive search by the Mexican military. The Jalisco State medical examiner's report disclosed that True had been strangled, and had sustained a head injury that was not attributable to a fall. His body had been partially covered with rocks in an attempt to conceal it. Neither his wedding ring nor his watch were taken, suggesting that robbery was not a motive.

On December 17, CPJ sent a letter to President Ernesto Zedillo, urging that federal authorities conduct the investigation into True's murder.

According to authorities, on December 26 Miguel Hernández and Juan Chivarra, both Huichol Indians, were arrested for the murder and confessed. (The suspects said they were arrested on December 24 and tortured.) They initially said that they had killed True because he had taken pictures without permission. In a December 28 court appearance, however, they changed their testimony, saying they killed him in self-defense. The two were formally charged with homicide and robbery, and are being held pending trial. A second autopsy carried out immediately after the first concluded that True had died from blows to his head and body.

Attacks on the Press in 1998

Nicaragua

The government of President Arnoldo Alemán selectively doled out official information and state advertising in an effort to reward media outlets that supported him and punish those that were critical. Despite these collusive practices, the majority of the Nicaraguan press reported aggressively on political scandals, the allocation of international aid in the aftermath of Hurricane Mitch, and alleged government corruption.

In July, the Mexican multi-national energy company Zeta Gas (which has a Nicaraguan subsidiary) sued television station Telenica 8, which had re-broadcast a segment of the U.S. television newsmagazine "60 Minutes" linking the company to the international drug trade. Defamation is both a civil and a criminal offense in Nicaragua, although the penalty for criminal defamation is exclusively monetary.

July 14
Miguel Mora, Telenica 8 LEGAL ACTION
Telenica 8 LEGAL ACTION

The Nicaraguan subsidiary of Zeta Gas, a Mexican multinational energy corporation, filed a civil suit seeking US$1.25 million in damages from the television station Telenica 8. The complaint was in response to the re-broadcast in April of a segment of the U.S. television newsmagazine "60 Minutes," which linked Zeta Gas to drug trafficking. The company also filed a criminal libel suit against Mora, the station's director. The station's assets were frozen by the judge pending the outcome of the trial.

Zeta Gas is suing Telenica 8 despite the fact

that Zeta Gas company officials responded on the air to the accusations contained in the "60 Minutes" story at the time it was re-broadcast. Zeta Gas CEO Miguel Zaragoza Fuentes, who lives in Mexico, has refused to respond to a petition to appear before the court in Nicaragua.

Panama

Although President Ernesto Pérez Balladares promised in 1997 to repeal "gag laws" on the books since the military government of Omar Torrijos in the late 1970s, authorities continue to use them to muzzle journalists who report on corruption and the growing influence of drug traffickers.

In one dramatic incident in December, police officers tried to arrest journalist Herasto Reyes on charges that an article he published in August defamed President Pérez Balladares. The arrest was thwarted when Reyes' colleagues from the Panama City daily *La Prensa* surrounded the journalist. Meanwhile, two other reporters from *La Prensa*, associate editor Gustavo Gorriti and investigative reporter Rolando Rodríguez, have been battling a lawsuit filed by Attorney General José Antonio Sossa. The charges stem from a 1996 article the two journalists wrote linking Sossa to a drug trafficker. In 1997, authorities tried to expel Gorriti, who is originally from Peru, because of his investigative stories exposing corruption in the Pérez Balladares administration. For his defense of press freedom in Panama and in his native Peru, Gorriti received CPJ's 1998 International Press Freedom Award in November. (For more on Gorriti, see page 66.)

Under the gag laws, criticism of the president or other high officials can result in a prison sentence of up to 10 months; libel is punishable by up to two years in prison. The laws stipulate that all top newspaper editors must be Panamanians, and grant broad censorship authority to the Interior Ministry. A censorship board, which reports to the president, has the authority to confiscate newspapers, shut down radio stations, or fine reporters. The government has little to worry about from television stations: Most of them are owned by relatives and associates of the president.

Rather than repealing the laws, the Panamanian Congress is considering legislation that could further hinder journalists' work. Under the proposed law, local or foreign reporters could be jailed for writing stories that affect global shipping or international trade.

Despite the clear risk, Panamanian journalists have continued to aggressively cover major news stories. In November, Gorriti and Rodríguez published a three-part series in *La Prensa* on José Castrillón Henao, a notorious Colombian drug trafficker who nearly succeeded in bribing his way out of a Panamanian jail.

January 21
Rolando Rodríguez, *La Prensa*
LEGAL ACTION
Gustavo Gorriti, *La Prensa* LEGAL ACTION

Attorney General José Antonio Sossa initiated criminal proceedings against Gorriti and Rodríguez, associate editor and reporter of the daily *La Prensa*, for falsification of documents, refusal to disclose the source of a story, and libel.

The complaints stem from an article published in *La Prensa* in July 1996, which reported that a company that had been accused of being a front for drug traffickers in Panama had made a US$5,000 contribution to Sossa's re-election campaign for the legislature.

After receiving a copy of the check, but before publishing their story, Gorriti and Rodríguez attempted to verify the authenticity of the document by interviewing Sossa. According to the journalists, Sossa spoke with them and promised to search his campaign records.

During the course of the proceedings against them, Gorriti and Rodríguez were barred from leaving Panama and ordered to report before a judge once a month. The journalists appealed the preventive measure, and in October they were granted permission to travel.

December 28
Herasto Reyes, *La Prensa* LEGAL ACTION

Three officers from the Technical Judicial Police (PTJ), raided *La Prensa*'s offices and attempted to arrest Reyes, an investigative reporter, on charges of defaming President Ernesto Pérez Balladares. Reyes' colleagues and other people who had gone to the newspapers' offices to support Reyes blocked the officers from delivering the warrant by physically surrounding the journalist. After a tense confrontation, the police departed, leaving the warrant behind.

The police action stems from an article, published in *La Prensa* on August 27, in which Reyes interviewed José Renán Esquivel, the former director of the Social Security Fund (CSS). Reyes quoted Renán Esquivel as saying that President Pérez Balladares was involved in a financial scandal relating to a CSS housing program in 1982, when he was serving as Minister of Finance.

On August 28, the president filed criminal defamation charges against Renán Esquivel and "any other person who might turn out to have been involved." Prosecutor Javier Chérigo of the First Circuit twice summoned Reyes to give information about Renán Esquivel. Based on the charges filed by the president, the attorney general's office also opened an investigation of Reyes. On December 28, Chérigo issued a warrant for Reyes' arrest, leading to the raid on *La Prensa*'s offices. CPJ distributed a press release the same day decrying the raid and the threat posed by criminal libel to press freedom in Panama.

Attacks on the Press in 1998

After the botched raid on *La Prensa*'s offices, Attorney General José Antonio Sossa ordered Chérigo to block Reyes from leaving Panama to cover the peace process in Colombia. Chérigo refused to carry out the order and resigned on January 5, 1999.

Paraguay

A new penal code that took effect at the end of November could pose major obstacles to the functioning of a free press. The government now has the right to confiscate "written publications" that are being investigated for unspecified "illegal" activities. Another provision of the code prohibits filming, photographing, or recording the voice of any person—including politicians—without his or her consent. The Sindicato de Periodistas del Paraguay (SPP) has denounced the new laws and questioned their constitutionality.

The SPP also publicly protested when President Raúl Cubas Grau, who took office in August, restricted access for journalists assigned to cover the presidential palace. While Cubas said the action was taken for security reasons, he later reversed the policy after journalists described the move as a deliberate attempt to impede their work.

Comments made by former coup leader Gen. Lino Oviedo in December, in which he accused media owners of being "corrupt" and "not paying taxes," have raised concerns about the military's tolerance for free expression. Oviedo, who was sentenced to a 10-year jail term for his role in an aborted 1996 coup against then-President Carlos Wasmosy, was pardoned by Cubas in August. Cubas and Oviedo are political allies in the ruling Colorado Party. Oviedo made the critical remarks about the press in December, soon after the Paraguayan Supreme Court ruled that he return to jail.

Oviedo has refused to comply with the Supreme Court order, raising the specter of a constitutional crisis.

February 2
Radio Uno LEGAL ACTION

Paraguay's National Telecommunication Commission (CONATEL) closed the news station Radio Uno for broadcasting a mock report about a military coup. CONATEL, the state agency that regulates radio and television licenses, accused Radio Uno of disseminating false information.

President Juan Carlos Wasmosy suspended the measure later the same day. On February 3, CONATEL reversed its earlier ruling and began an investigation into Juan Pastoriza, the announcer of the program that broadcast the mock coup.

The Sindicato de Periodistas del Paraguay (SPP) protested the investigation in a letter to CONATEL, arguing that Radio Uno's entire editorial staff should not be punished because of the actions of a single individual. According to SPP, CONATEL has authority only over technical matters. Any legal violation regarding content is properly the responsibility of the judiciary.

Peru

Concerned about evidence of a systematic state-run campaign to discredit Peru's independent press, CPJ staff members traveled to Lima in June as part of an international delegation of press freedom organizations. Attacks on the press declined in the immediate aftermath of the visit—which included interviews with President Alberto K. Fujimori and other high officials—but increased again at year's end, as a series of scandals continued to damage the government's popularity.

Criminal gangs are responsible for a growing share of violence against journalists in Latin America, but in Peru there is clear evidence of government involvement in a campaign against the press that has included jailings, detentions, threats, and constant surveillance. In March, several tabloid newspapers in Lima began publishing pieces attacking prominent investigative journalists, accusing them of being communists, traitors, and "prophets of the devil." The articles stopped appearing after the press freedom delegation met with Fujimori, but resurfaced again in August on a website which journalists say was created by the intelligence services to discredit government opponents.

Independent journalists also experience cruder forms of intimidation. They allege that they are often followed, and that their phones are tapped. Government pressure has forced two television programs off the air—one temporarily and one permanently. There has also been sporadic violence. In August, the house of Hugo Guerra, an editor with the Lima daily *El Comercio*, was hit by gunfire.

Peru and Cuba are the only countries in the Americas where journalists are serving jail sentences for crimes relating to their work. Four journalists remain in jail on terrorism charges after being sentenced by hooded military judges in 1994 and 1996. A fifth was jailed in November after he read a communiqué from the Túpac Amaru Revolutionary Movement (MRTA) on the air.

The fact that journalists can work at all under such difficult conditions owes a great deal to the efforts of the Instituto de Prensa y Sociedad (IPYS), a Lima-based press organization founded in 1993 that has systematically monitored abuses and pressured the authorities to respond. While most of the attention has been paid to journalists in Lima, in November IPYS established a 24-hour toll-free telephone could report press freedom violations. IPYS was immediately deluged with dozens of complaints from provincial journalists about criminal defamation prosecutions, threats, and detentions.

January 1
Angel Páez Salcedo, *La República*
THREATENED

Beginning in January, Páez, chief of the investigative unit of the daily *La República*, started receiving a barrage of telephone death threats, sometimes as many as three a day.

The telephone calls grew more frequent in March and continued through April, May, and June. The calls were made to his office and to his cellular phone; sometimes military music was played in the background.

Eight years ago, Páez created *La República*'s investigative unit. He has reported extensively on corruption in the military and in the government. Since 1996, Páez has written on irregularities in the government's acquisition of airplanes, missiles, and helicopters. Páez has also covered the scandal involving the Army Intelligence Service (SIE), which allegedly engaged in a systematic campaign of telephone espionage of opposition members and independent journalists. Páez's reports were also published in the Argentine daily *Clarín*, where Páez has been a correspondent since 1997.

Throughout the years he worked for *La República*, Páez has been followed, filmed, and threatened; his telephone is tapped. Sources within the military have warned Páez that a file is being kept on him and that he could be indicted in military court for "treason" and "threatening national security."

CPJ sent a letter to President Alberto K. Fujimori on June 8, expressing concern over threats directed against journalists reporting on SIE, the National Intelligence Service (SIN), and SIN adviser Vladimiro Montesinos.
March 3

José Arrieta Matos, Frecuencia Latina/Canal 2 LEGAL ACTION

District Attorney Alejandro Espino Méndez of the 44th Provincial Criminal District Attorney's office filed charges against Arrieta, a reporter who headed the investigative unit at the television station Frecuencia Latina/Canal 2, for "crimes against the administration of justice." Espino charged that Arrieta had bribed José Luis Bazán Adrianzén, a former member of the Army Intelligence Service (SIE), to admit the involvement of the paramilitary group Colina in a 1990 dynamite attack on the home of Congressman Javier Díez Canseco.

On March 19, the Second Criminal Court of Lima threw out the accusation against Arrieta and shifted the focus of its investigation to Bazán, stating that Arrieta was now a witness in the case.

On May 28, Miguel Miranda Nole, an employee of the National Division of Tax Administration (SUNAT), visited Arrieta's Lima home, and demanded that Arrieta's wife provide bookkeeping records from a company that Miranda alleged was owned by the journalist. Miranda said he was investigating whether Arrieta had misappropriated funds. The SUNAT employee left quickly when reporters arrived to cover the visit. Speaking from Miami on June 26, Arrieta denied ever owning a company.

On September 28, Arrieta was granted political asylum by the U.S. Department of Justice.

April 29
El Comercio THREATENED

The daily *El Comercio* received threatening phone calls before and after publishing an interview with a former police captain who revealed a secret government investigation.

On April 29, an editor of the newspaper's supplement *El Dominical* contacted Julio Salas Caceres, a former police captain who resides in Miami, to arrange for a telephone interview later that day. Shortly afterward, the editor later that day. Shortly afterward, the editor began receiving phone calls warning him not to carry out the interview. In the days after the interview took place, the newspaper received a series of threatening calls with warnings not to publish the interview.

In the story, published in the May 3 edition of *El Dominical*, Salas, who used to work for the Customs Duties Fraud Division of the National Police of Peru (PNP), denounced what he termed "Plan Tsunami 97," a secret operation which used customs police to investigate Baruch Ivcher, the former owner of television station Frecuencia Latina/Canal 2. The plan was put into operation in July 1997, around the same time that the Israeli-born Ivcher was stripped of his Peruvian citizenship in reprisal for a series of investigative stories aired on the station. Under Peruvian law, non-Peruvians cannot own media outlets.

The threatening phone calls continued for several days after the publication of the story. The caller warned that the team of *El Dominical* reporters would be killed, along with Salas and his wife. CPJ sent a letter to President Alberto K. Fujimori on June 8, expressing concern over threats directed against journalists reporting on the Army Intelligence Service (SIE), the National Intelligence Service (SIN), and SIN adviser Vladimiro Montesinos.

May 22
César Hildebrandt, Canal 13
THREATENED
Luis Iberico, Canal 9
THREATENED
Gonzalo Quijandria, Canal 9
THREATENED
Cecilia Valenzuela, Canal 9
THREATENED
Fernando Rospigliosi, *La República*
THREATENED
Gustavo Mohme Llona, *La República*
THREATENED

On May 22, both Canal 9 and Canal 13 received a letter warning of attacks on journalists that would be carried out to appear as common crimes. The journalists threatened in the letter were Hildebrandt of Canal 13; Iberico, Quijandria, and Valenzuela of Canal 9; and Rospigliosi of the daily *La República*; and Mohme, *La República*'s owner.

Around the same date, Valenzuela received two phone calls on her cellular phone from a man who threatened to kill her.

In April, Valenzuela reported on corruption in the Armed Forces, specifically the diversion of funds intended for victims of El Niño-induced floods. Valenzuela had also criticized a decree giving military courts jurisdiction over cases involving aggravated terrorism.

CPJ sent a letter to President Alberto K. Fujimori on June 8, expressing concern over threats directed against journalists reporting on the Army Intelligence Service (SIE), the National Intelligence Service (SIN), and SIN adviser Vladimiro Montesinos.

May 26
Cecilia Valenzuela, Canal 9 THREATENED

Valenzuela, director of the television program "Aquí y Ahora" on Canal 9, received a call on her cellular phone from a man who insulted her and threatened to kill her. Valenzuela had been investigating allegations that the Peruvian military had overpaid for weapons purchased through international arms dealers.

June 18
César Hildebrandt, Canal 13 THREATENED

Hildebrandt, host of "En Persona," Peru's most popular nightly news show, received a four-page fax containing death threats. The fax called him a traitor, and warned that he was being watched closely because of his reporting on the National Intelligence Service (SIN) and on SIN adviser Vladimiro Montesinos.

Journalists at Canal 13 informed CPJ that they could not link the threats to any specific investigation underway at the time the fax was received.

August 2
Hugo Guerra Arteaga, *El Comercio*
HARASSED

Unknown assailants fired shots at the home of Guerra, editorial page editor of the Lima daily *El Comercio*, while he and his family were away. One bullet shattered a window. Guerra suspects the attack was a response to the paper's critical stance on President Alberto K. Fujimori's possible re-election bid.

August 4
Jhonny Navarro, *La República* HARASSED
Reneyro Guerra, *La República* HARASSED

Soldiers harassed Navarro, an investigative reporter for the Lima daily *La República* in the northern city of Piura, and Guerra, a photographer for the same newspaper, while they were photographing people painting over political graffiti.

Navarro and Guerra were following up on a tip that the military was destroying signs endorsing an opposition candidate in the October municipal elections. At the scene, they found three heavily armed navy officers supervising approximately five people who were covering a mural with white paint.

Guerra started taking pictures, but was told by one of the officers that photos were prohibited. As the journalists left the scene, they were stopped by the officers. When Guerra and Navarro identified themselves as journalists, one officer said, "That doesn't matter to me. Hand the camera over to me, or I'll shoot you." When Guerra refused to surrender his camera, the officer grabbed him, threw him to the ground, pointed his gun at the photographer, and said, "I'll kill you right here." The journalists were then forced into a pick-up truck and taken to the Piura navy base. After being held for 30 minutes, their camera was returned and the pair were released.

Guerra and Navarro subsequently learned that the pick-up truck belonged to Francisco Hilbck Eguiguren, the ruling Vamos Vecino (Let's Go Neighbor) party's candidate in the municipal elections.

The graffiti being painted over endorsed José Aguilar, the candidate of the independent movement known as Obras Más Obras (Works Plus Works).

August 18
Isaac García Villanueva, Radio Siglo XXI
THREATENED, HARASSED

García, a reporter with Radio Siglo XXI, was harassed and threatened immediately after broadcasting a speech in which Presidential Minister José Tomás Gonzales Reategui illegally endorsed a local candidate in the October 11 municipal elections. Under Peruvian law, it is illegal for government officials to endorse candidates.

On August 18, García recorded a speech given by Gonzales in the Amazonian city of Taraboto, in which the minister urged the audience at a political rally to vote for his nephew Rolando Reategui, a municipal candidate with the pro-government Vamos Vecino (Let's Go Neighbor).

After the rally, Gonzales and his bodyguards instructed García to turn over the tape. García pretended to erase the cassette, but managed to keep the recording of Gonzales' statements by switching tapes.

On September 25, a congressional commission summoned Gonzales to question him about the use of public funds to support Vamos Vecino candidates. That same day, García played his tape on the air during a popular news show. Reategui lost the election and Gonzales was forced to resign.

August 21
César Hildebrandt, Canal 13 LEGAL ACTION

Public prosecutor José Ochoa Lamas began a criminal investigation of Hildebrandt for espionage and treason. The investigation stemmed from a story broadcast on Hildebrandt's popular nightly news show, "Enlace Global con Hildebrandt," which discussed peace treaty negotiations with Ecuador.

On November 9, CPJ wrote a letter to President Alberto K. Fujimori, saying that "the lawsuit has had a chilling effect on Peru's journalists, whose professional obligation demands that they publish or broadcast information of legitimate public interest."

After his news program was taken off the air on three occasions, Hildebrandt terminated his contract with Canal 13 on December 3. He subsequently negotiated a reinstatement with the station management, and his program is expected back on the air in early 1999.

October 26
Cecilia Valenzuela THREATENED

A letter threatening Valenzuela with death was dropped off at her apartment building in an envelope bearing the seal of the Peruvian Congress. The letter read, "you're going to die, bitch (vas a morir, perra)" and was composed of pieces of text clipped from newspapers.

Valenzuela, an investigative journalist whose television program, "Sin Censura," was canceled two weeks earlier, had reported on the Peruvian government's secret peace negotiations with Ecuador in their long-standing border dispute. The owners of Canal 9, which broadcast Valenzuela's program, claimed the show was canceled because of a lack of advertising, but local journalists allege that it was taken off the air because of government pressure.

CPJ wrote a letter to President Alberto K. Fujimori on November 9, expressing concern about this and other threats to press freedom in Peru.

November 2
La República THREATENED
Gustavo Mohme Llona, *La República* THREATENED

Two phone calls were made threatening *La República*.

The first call was placed to the cellular phone of Gustavo Mohme Llona, publisher of the Lima-based daily. The caller said he was speaking on behalf of the "Fifth of April Command (Comando Cinco de Abril)," which refers to the day in 1992 when President Alberto K. Fujimori carried out a self-coup, suspending the constitution. Mohme was warned that he would be killed if he covered the visit of members of the Inter-American Commission on Human Rights, which arrived in Peru on November 8.

The second call was made to *La República*'s offices by a man who identified himself as "Commander Truck (Comandante Camión)," a reference to Alvaro Artaza Adrianzén, a navy officer who was charged in connection with a massacre of Indian peasants that took place in Ayacucho in 1984. The second caller also alluded to the commission's visit, saying "We the patriots aren't going to allow that they intervene in our affairs."

On November 9, CPJ wrote a letter to President Fujimori, expressing its concern about these and other threats to press freedom in Peru.

November 20
Johny Eduardo Pezo Tello, Doble A IMPRISONED

Pezo Tello, a news program host on radio station Doble A in Yurimaguas, Loreto Department, was jailed on charges of terrorism for reading a letter sent by the Túpac Amaru Revolutionary Movement (MRTA) on the air on November 17.

Pezo Tello, host of several news programs and a music show, received a phone call during his music show on November 17 from a man identifying himself as Comrade Rolando of the MRTA. The caller ordered Pezo Tello to read a letter that the MRTA had sent to the radio station, and threatened to harm Pezo Tello and his family if he refused.

Pezo Tello left the radio station, intending to report the threats to the police, but two men who were waiting outside the station cautioned him to heed the caller's demand. After apologizing to the audience and declaring his opposition to MRTA's principles, Pezo Tello read the press release on the air.

On November 19, officers from the National Anti-Terrorism Agency (DINCOTE) arrived at the radio station and took Pezo Tello to the Yurimaguas police station, where they interrogated him. In response to a summons, Pezo Tello went to the police station on November 20 to present a more detailed statement. On the basis of his testimony, the DINCOTE officers issued a formal statement on November 21, accusing him of supporting terrorism.

On November 21, Pezo Tello was taken before Provincial Attorney Marco Tulio Correa Sánchez, who confirmed the DINCOTE accusation and charged him with having made a statement supporting terrorism ("apología al terrorismo"). The same day, Yurimaguas Provincial Judge Hugo Zela Campos found there was sufficient evidence to initiate proceedings against Pezo Tello and ordered his arrest. Pezo Tello was transferred from the police station, where he had spent the night of November 20, to the Yurimaguas prison.

CPJ wrote a letter to President Alberto K. Fujimori on December 16, condemning Pezo Tello's arrest in the strongest possible terms.

On December 23, Zela ruled that the charge against Pezo Tello was unwarranted because the charge involved terrorism, however, the case was transferred to the Superior Court of Lambayeque for adjudication. The court dismissed the charges and Pezo Tello was released on January 18, 1999.

Attacks on the Press in 1998

Suriname

The antagonism between the press and the government that marked the end of 1997, when Desi Bouterse, the Adviser of State, publicly insulted journalists, diminished after journalists denounced the conflict in both domestic and international forums. The press has been able to cover widespread protests and strikes which started in June after Suriname's currency was devalued and its economy stalled. Yet intimidation, lack of information, and the absence of a tradition of investigative journalism contribute overall to a certain degree of self-censorship.

Bouterse, a former army commander who is leader of the ruling National Democratic Party (NDP), repeatedly called reporters "villains and scoundrels" during NDP meetings at the beginning of the year. These insults ceased after reporters notified local authorities and the Caribbean Association of Media Workers. Nevertheless, journalists who write stories critical of the government continue to receive threatening phone calls. And Dutch journalists working in Suriname say they are also the target of intimidation.

Suriname has two daily newspapers and 19 radio stations. The three privately owned television stations broadcast only entertainment programming and international news; the two state-owned television stations feature the government's viewpoint. According to local reporters, government officials only provide information to the privately owned media during periodic press conferences.

June 23
Armand Snijders, United Dutch Publishers (VNU) Newspaper Unit ATTACKED

Three unidentified men in a car accosted

Snijders, a correspondent with United Dutch Publishers (VNU) Newspaper Unit, while he was walking on a dimly lit street in the city of Paramaribo. They dragged him into the car and told him at gunpoint that his articles contained lies; that he was a spy for The Netherlands; and that he should leave Suriname. They drove him around for 10 minutes and then threw him out of the car. Snijders informed CPJ that he was beaten, but not injured.

Trinidad and Tobago

Tensions between Prime Minister Basdeo Panday and the media reached new heights after Julian Rogers, a popular television journalist from Barbados, was denied a work visa and forced to leave the country in May. Hundreds of demonstrators chanted "Panday must go" and "Rogers must stay" as Rogers boarded a plane out of Trinidad. At a November 8 political rally, Panday urged his supporters to "treat [the media] as political opponents who are out to destroy us." Several of Panday's followers took the pronouncement literally and roughed up reporters covering the event.

Panday's three-year war with the media is largely a reflection of the country's complex racial politics. The population is equally divided between those of African and those of Indian descent, but blacks have long held the lion's share of political power. Panday, the first prime minister of Indian descent, has described the press as racist. In 1997, the Media Association of Trinidad and Tobago (MATT) defeated a proposed press law backed by Panday that would have required journalists to report with "due accuracy and impartiality."

There were widespread protests in April, after the government refused to renew a visa for Rogers, who had worked in Trinidad and Tobago for five years. His early morning talk show, "Morning Edition," often featured guests who were critical of Panday and the ruling United National Congress (UNC). At one point, Panday accused Rogers of deliberately screening callers to exclude UNC supporters. MATT described the expulsion of Rogers as a violation of an international agreement which permits Caribbean journalists to work in any country in the region without applying for a visa. In rejecting Rogers' work extension, the government argued that Rogers had been granted annual visas to work in Trinidad and Tobago legally since 1993 on the condition that he train a local journalist to "assume his duties."

United States

Since its founding in 1981, the Committee to Protect Journalists has, as a matter of strategy and policy, concentrated on press freedom violations and attacks on journalists outside the United States. We do not systematically monitor problems facing journalists in any of the developed industrial democracies. We devote most of our efforts to countries where journalists are in the greatest need of international support and protection.

While CPJ recognizes that press freedom requires constant vigilance and aggressive defense everywhere, we are able to rely within the United States on the thorough, professional efforts of organizations with a primarily domestic focus, such as the American Society of Newspaper Editors, the Society of Professional Journalists, the Reporters Committee for Freedom of the Press, the Electronic Frontier Foundation, the American Civil Liberties Union, and the National Association of Broadcasters, among others. We recommend to journalists and

Attacks on the Press in 1998

other researchers the work of these and similar organizations, as well as the ongoing coverage of First Amendment issues provided by the *American Journalism Review*, the *Columbia Journalism Review, Editor & Publisher*, and other specialized publications. On U.S. policy issues directly affecting the ability of U.S. reporters to work safely and legally abroad, CPJ works with U.S. journalism organizations for constructive change.

CPJ's overriding concern in the United States continues to be the safety of immigrant journalists and cases of journalists who are murdered for reasons directly related to their profession. As a U.S. organization that forcefully urges governments to investigate and prosecute the assassinations of local journalists, we believe that it is essential to hold our own government equally accountable when similar crimes are committed at home. Since the widely publicized 1976 murder of *Arizona Republic* reporter Don Bolles, at least 11 other journalists have been murdered in the United States because of their work. In all but one case, the victims were immigrant journalists working in languages other than English. Seven of those 11 homicides remain unsolved. Most received little or no national media attention. In December 1993, CPJ released a report on these murders titled *Silenced: The Unsolved Murders of Immigrant Journalists in the United States*.

As part of its campaign to eliminate criminal defamation laws from the Americas, CPJ has expressed concern to U.S. officials about the fact that at least 19 states and the District of Columbia have laws on the books that classify libel as a criminal offense. Such statues are clearly unconstitutional, and would be overturned by the Supreme Court if any attempt were made to prosecute a journalist under these laws. Because criminal defamation laws have no place in a democratic society, CPJ believes that state legislatures should expunge all criminal defamation statutes in order to set an example for countries throughout the world where journalists are routinely jailed because of what they write.

Uruguay

Uruguayan journalists report no major impediments to their work, but express concern about a punitive press law that punishes defamation with up to three years in prison. In May, Carlos Ardaix, host of a local radio news talk show in Tabere de Salto, was given a five-month suspended sentence after he read a letter on the air from a listener who accused a local obstetrician of malpractice. The case was dismissed in August.

Press groups have also raised objections to several new laws pending before Congress, including one that would require media outlets to publish articles about a defendant who is declared innocent with the same size headline used in the article that announced the arrest.

In a case that deeply divided journalists in Uruguay, Manuel and Felipe Flores Silva and Eduardo Alonso, editors at the weekly magazine *Posdata*, were arrested in April and held for nearly a month on charges of fraud and passing bad checks. The editors allege that their arrest was in reprisal for the magazine's aggressive reporting on police corruption, but prominent local journalists regard that explanation as an attempt to divert public attention from financial malfeasance.

Venezuela

A group of media owners has petitioned the Supreme Court to overturn the 1994 Law for the Practice of Journalism, which mandates that journalists must have both a university degree and a license. The court is expected to rule on the law's constitutionality in early 1999.

Just prior to the December presidential election, there were reports in the press that Hugo Chávez, a former colonel and the leading presidential candidate, had plotted to shoot journalists and opposition leaders if the vote did not go in his favor. Chávez vigorously denied the reports, describing them as an attempt by his opponents to discredit him. He won the election handily, and will take office in February 1999.

Defamation is a criminal offense in Venezuela punishable by up to 18 months in prison. While journalists say that legal action is rare, William Ojeda was convicted in 1996 of defaming two judges in a book he wrote on corruption in the judiciary and served five months in prison in 1997.

Banding Together

by Joel Simon

After he broke a series of stories in March about corruption in the Peruvian military, Angel Páez was in the news every day. His notoriety stemmed not from his bylines, which ran in *La República*, the Lima-based daily where Páez works as an investigative reporter, but from the headlines that ran in Lima's sensationalist tabloids, calling Páez a traitor, a terrorist, and a secret agent of the Ecuadoran army.

"I felt terrified," said Páez, who feared the tabloid attacks were a prelude to a possible arrest or assassination attempt. "I changed my address. I stopped writing stories for a time." He believed the articles were part of a government-orchestrated campaign coordinated by Peru's shadowy National Intelligence Service (SIN) and carried out in reprisal for his reporting. Páez had recently broken a major story on a military deserter, Luisa Zanatta, who had overseen the systematic phone-tapping of journalists and government opponents for the Army intelligence service, a division of the SIN. What infuriated the government was that Páez's stories were published not only in Peru, but the Argentine daily *Clarín*, for which Páez was a correspondent. *Clarín* is the world's largest-circulation Spanish-language daily, and Páez's stories took a heavy toll on Peru's international image.

Initially, Páez considered suing the tabloids for libel, but soon realized that this approach might backfire. Libel is a criminal offense in Peru; if Páez had won the case and the tabloid editors went to jail, Peruvian journalists would have little moral authority the next time the government threw an investigative journalist in jail for breaking a corruption story. After discussing the situation with Ricardo Uceda, a member of the board of a Peruvian press freedom group called the Instituto de Prensa y Sociedad (Institute of Press and Society, or IPYS), Páez decided to fight back using his formidable skills as a journalist: He would investigate the source of the tabloid articles, while Uceda would organize a delegation of international press organizations to Peru to ratchet up the pressure on President Alberto K. Fujimori.

Since taking office in 1990, Fujimori has used a massive spy network to consolidate his hold on power. Journalists have undergone special scrutiny: Their phones have been tapped, their movements followed. Reporters have been detained and questioned on trumped-up terrorism and tax charges; they have been kidnapped and threatened by members of the SIN. For most of that time, the Peruvian press has been too divided and besieged to effectively fight back. But the campaign against Páez seemed to galvanize the press into action.

From the outset, evidence of government involvement in the tabloid campaign was overwhelming. One of the papers, *El Tío*, hit the stands only two weeks before the attacks began and seemed to have been created to smear Páez and the handful of independent journalists in Peru. All four tabloids conducting the smear campaign sold for pennies and were loaded with government advertising. Often, all four published the identical story with the same headline on the same day. In May, Páez unearthed a document that proved to be a smoking gun: a copy of a fax sent to *El Tío* by Augusto Bresani, a political consultant working for the army high command. The fax contained a defamatory text attacking Páez. It was published verbatim as a news story in *El Tío* the following day.

As Páez was collecting evidence, IPYS was organizing the international delegation. "We decided we needed to find a way to show the government that there was a tangible international concern for press freedom in Peru," notes Jorge Salazar, the executive director of IPYS. "In other words, that we are not alone."

From June 22 to 26, IPYS hosted representatives of international press freedom organizations including CPJ, Reporters Sans Frontières, Periodistas (an Argentine press group), and the Freedom Forum. They met with editors, members of Congress, the Attorney General, and the head of the government human rights office. In an hour-and-a-half meeting with Fujimori, members of the delegation questioned the president on a wide variety of press freedom issues. The visit received extensive coverage in Peru. The attacks against Páez and other Peruvian journalists were widely reported internationally, including in *The New York Times*.

Fujimori got the message. Almost immediately after the group's visit, the tabloid campaign against Páez ceased. In subsequent months, conditions for Peruvian journalists improved markedly.

The IPYS-led campaign in Peru was a clear demonstration that when journalists are united in protesting abuses against the press—and willing to cover attacks against their colleagues even when they come from rival publications—leaders are forced to heed. Increasingly, this strategy is being employed throughout the hemisphere. National press freedom groups now exist in Peru, Argentina, Colombia, Brazil, Guatemala, and Mexico, while journalists unions in Paraguay and Ecuador have taken an active role in documenting and protesting abuses.

The rise of press freedom organizations in Latin America owes much to the growing power of the media throughout the hemisphere. Journalists, long tamed by systematic government persecution under the dictatorships, now routinely report on corruption, malfeasance, and human rights abuses. By doing so, the press has helped to create an incipient culture of accountability and gained widespread public trust.

But while overt censorship has disappeared from every country in Latin America but Cuba, the new style of aggressive reporting has all too frequently evoked a violent response from those who are the subjects of scrutiny. 117 journalists have been murdered in Latin America in the last decade. Generally, the murders take place in countries where judicial institutions remain weak or corrupt; nearly all crimes go unpunished. In this environment, the only way to achieve justice is to use the press to bring political pressure on the government to take action. By covering attacks against their colleagues, journalists have made press freedom an issue of public concern. Nowhere has this strategy been more effective than in Argentina, where the press united to protest the brutal murder of photojournalist José Luis Cabezas.

In the early morning of January 25, 1997, a fisherman in the resort town of Pinamar found Cabezas' body in a burnt-out car on the side of a dirt road. Journalist Horacio Verbitsky was at home in Buenos Aires when he got the news later that morning. Even though Verbitsky had never met Cabezas, he grasped immediately that what was in the balance was the country's resolve to end the silence that had fueled the earlier brutality, and to defend a basic principle that had been at the core of the military's repressive campaign: the right to speak, to listen, and to know.

In the year before Cabezas' murder, Verbitsky, one of the country's top investigative reporters, had helped to coalesce a group of journalists in Argentina committed to defending press freedom. In 1996, after Argentine president Carlos Saúl Menem had tried to force a series of restrictive press laws through Congress, Verbitsky called his colleagues and urged them to mount a unified front. The idea was to bring together a small but diverse group of prominent and respected journalists who could speak out with moral authority on the issue of press freedom. The new organization was dubbed simply "Periodistas" (Journalists); Verbitsky's goal in assembling the board was to break the ideological polarization that had characterized every aspect of Argentine life for half a century. Verbitsky—who had participated in the urban guerrilla movement against the dictatorship until 1976—joined forces with television reporter and talk show host Mariano Grondona, who had supported the junta, and Rosendo Fraga, who had worked in the military government of General Roberto Eduardo Viola.

Within a few hours of the Cabezas murder, Periodistas had sent out a press release condemning the killing and demanding an investigation. "Our press release established in the initial moments of confusion that this was an extremely serious case and shaped the coverage in the first days after the attack," said Verbitsky.

Along with Argentina's powerful and well-organized journalists unions, members of Periodistas participated over the next weeks in street protests in Buenos Aires that drew thousands of people, both journalists and non-journalists. Posters of Cabezas, with the slogan "We will not forget!" began to appear all over the city. There were low-speed caravans from Buenos Aires to the site of the murder in Pinamar; eerie moments of silence before soccer matches; and massive coverage of the murder in the newspapers, on the afternoon radio talk shows, and on the nightly news.

"For years, under the dictatorship, it was impossible to react when this kind of thing occurred," Verbitsky noted. "And after the dictatorship ended, there were years of calm, where there weren't any murders, a time when the social wounds could be healed and people learned once again to live in peace. The murder of Cabezas brutally shattered this perspective, and showed that the risk is still under the surface. At the same time, people were reacting to the growing series of attacks on the press—the restrictive laws, the threats, and the previous physical attacks. It's the combination of both these factors that produced such a powerful reaction."

In Mexico, as well, where a new press freedom group, the Sociedad de Periodistas (the Society of Journalists) was formed in 1998, it was a single violent attack that drove home the need for organization. In November 1997, editor Jesús Blancornelas, of the Tijuana weekly *Zeta*, was ambushed and nearly killed by gunmen from the Tijuana drug cartel (Blancornelas' bodyguard was killed in the attack).

Just a few weeks prior to the assassination attempt, Blancornelas had attended a workshop in Mexico City sponsored by CPJ. He spoke about the threats made against his life since he had begun publishing stories about the Arellano Félix brothers, who control the drug trade in Tijuana. At the Mexico City meeting, Blancornelas was elected to an eight-person commission charged with evaluating the risks facing the press and developing a self-defense strategy. The near-fatal attack against him delayed the project, but also infused it with greater urgency. In February, the Mexican commission met in Tijuana to affirm its support for Blancornelas and proceed with the new group, which was legally registered in the summer of 1998.

While press freedom groups have become powerful advocates for beleaguered journalists in their respective countries, their effectiveness is often enhanced by the fact that they share information with international groups through an Internet-based network known as the International Freedom of Expression Exchange, or IFEX. Administered by Canadian Journalists for Free Expression in Toronto, the IFEX network includes more than three dozen press groups, including five from Latin America. A local group can post an alert about a press freedom violation on the IFEX network, thereby generating an instant letter-writing campaign from press groups around the world. Such coordinated responses have forced recalcitrant governments to take quick action. Along with CPJ, the Miami-based Inter American Press

Association and the Paris-based Reporters Sans Frontières are the most active groups in Latin America.

This sharing of information and coordinated advocacy has helped put press freedom on the international agenda throughout the region. When President Clinton visited Argentina in October 1997, the national and international outcry over the Cabezas murder had become so great that Clinton felt compelled to express his concern to President Menem in both public statements and private discussions.

Buoyed by the strong public reaction to his statements in Argentina, Clinton also proposed that the Organization of American States (OAS) take a more active role in protecting press freedom in Latin America. After discussions with press groups in the United States and Latin America, the Inter-American Commission on Human Rights of the OAS created the post of Special Rapporteur for Freedom of Expression, responsible for ensuring that provisions of inter-American law protecting freedom of expression are respected by member states. The creation of the new position was unanimously endorsed by the heads of state attending April's Summit of the Americas in Santiago, Chile. In November, Santiago Canton was named Special Rapporteur. He immediately began a fact-finding tour of Latin America.

Despite the considerable success of the new Latin American press groups, many difficulties remain. In Mexico, the Society of Journalists has been struggling to secure funding and establish an official presence. In Colombia, the Foundation for a Free Press, a group formed in February 1996, has had some success in developing a network for alerting the press about attacks against journalists. But foundation director Ignacio Gómez notes that the public has become so desensitized to violence in Colombia that it is difficult to elicit any public response to violent attacks against the press. "People in Colombia see it as entirely normal when a journalist is killed," says Gómez. Four journalists were killed in Colombia in 1998, more than in any other country. This brings the 10-year toll of murdered journalists to 43—second only to Algeria.

In Argentina, Periodistas appears to be of a victim of its own success. The group's ability to thoroughly document and generate coverage for every attack or threat against the press seems to have substantially reduced the physical risk for journalists. In a country where few criminal investigations result in prosecutions, public pressure to solve Cabezas' murder compelled authorities to pursue the case. In May, Alfredo Yabrán, the reclusive businessman accused of ordering the murder after the photographer published his photo, committed suicide as the police closed in. "Anyone who thought they could silence the press by killing a journalist is going to think twice," noted Verbitsky.

But as the physical risk for journalists has diminished in Argentina, there have been discussions within Periodistas about the group's mandate. Many journalists now feel that the greatest threat to press freedom is not violence, but the concentration of media ownership and the subtle government pressure against media owners. The question the group must answer, according to Verbitsky, is whether to maintain its original, narrower mandate as a press freedom organization that seeks to protect the physical integrity of journalists, or to broaden its focus and become a "media watchdog group" concerned with issues of fairness and accuracy.

Even in Peru, where IPYS has solidified its base of support by hosting the press freedom delegation in June, serious obstacles remain. As in the rest of Latin America, there are deep divisions within the press—some ideological, and some based on the inevitable competition in a country with only a handful of well-paying journalism jobs.

But the work of press freedom groups remains crucial, precisely because of the dearth of other strong institutions in the region's emerging democracies. While enormous financial investments and strong political will are needed to create an independent judiciary or truly competitive political parties, a free press requires no financial investment or direct government support. All that is needed is for the government to allow journalists to work without fear of reprisal.

In Peru, for example, the press is the only independent institution. Fujimori has packed the supreme court with supporters and used espionage as much as overt political repression to gain the upper hand on his political opponents. For example, Javier Pérez de Cuéllar, who ran against Fujimori for president in 1995, often wondered how Fujimori seemed to know exactly what he was going to say and where he was going to campaign. Two years later, a Lima television station reported that Peruvian intelligence agents had been listening in on every phone call that Pérez de Cuéllar made. "What is painful is that they invaded not only my political life, but my private life," complained the former U.N. Secretary General. "It's as if a thief entered our house and stole our sensibilities."

Journalists, meanwhile, have uncovered compelling evidence of a systematic campaign orchestrated by the SIN to intimidate and control the independent press. In 1997, Baruch Ivcher, the majority shareholder of TV station Frecuencia Latina, was stripped of his Peruvian citizenship and forced to return to his native Israel after the station broke stories about military corruption, wire-tapping campaigns, and the personal financial dealing of SIN adviser Vladimiro Montesinos. When Ivcher tried to mount a legal defense, he was hit was tax-evasion charges, his wife and daughter faced legal harassment, and Peru requested that an international arrest warrant be issued through Interpol. Investigative reporter José Arrieta, who broke many of the stories at Frecuencia Latina, was forced into exile in January 1998 and granted political asylum in the United States in July. César Hildebrandt, Peru's leading television journalist, was accused of treason after reporting on negotiations toward an eventual peace treaty with neighboring Ecuador; Cecilia Valenzuela, another top television reporter, had her critical program canceled. And while the attacks against Angel Páez subsided in the wake of the June visit by the press freedom delegation, they heated up again in September after Páez began reporting on the delicate peace negotiations with Ecuador.

This time, Páez says, the Peruvian government went high tech. In the last year, Páez, along with other journalists inside and outside Peru, had developed an electronic network using e-mail to share information and coordinate investigations. By the summer, the journalists were hit with computer virus attacks and forged e-mail messages designed to create confusion and sow discord. In November, Páez discovered a website created by the so-called Association in Defense of Truth (www.aprodev.org). Dressed up as a civic organization, the website's primary intention seemed to be to post defamatory and false information about journalists and government opponents (all the articles about Páez that ran in *El Tío* were on the site).

Spearheaded by Fernando Yovera, a Peruvian reporter who works for the Telemundo television network in Miami, the group of journalists launched a joint investigation of the site. They soon found that it was registered to in the name of Blanca Rivera with an address in Miami. A reverse telephone search of the address, however, showed that the telephone was registered to someone named Guadelupe Wong. Among Peruvian soldiers trained at the School of the Americas in Georgia was an officer named Carlos Rivera Wong. Wong's father's surname was Guadelupe; his mother's was Blanca Rivera. Could Blanca Rivera really be Carlos Rivera Wong? "He worked in military intelligence," Páez points out.

"With the destruction of the civil and judicial institutions, and the virtual disappearance of political parties, the independent press has acquired a primary role in defense of democracy," notes Salazar of IPYS. "It is the press that denounces abuses and keeps the public informed, not the politicians or the judicial institutions which are subordinated to politics."

In other words, if journalists in Latin America want to achieve justice for their colleagues who have been attacked or killed, journalism is their primary weapon. It is only by overcoming traditional rivalries, and organizing to investigate and denounce attacks, that the press can create an environment in which it is able to carry out its work. But as the Peru example also shows, it is not just journalists but all of society which benefits from press freedom. This is because throughout Latin America the development of democratic institutions has been slow and uneven. In most countries, the press remains the only institution widely available to the public, and broadly responsive to its concerns.

OVERVIEW OF
Asia

by A. Lin Neumann

For the second year, the Asian economic free fall determined the climate for the press in Southeast Asia. The flow of information became a crucial variable as governments responded to the social and political dislocations of the economic crisis; some leaders lifted virtually all restrictions on freedom of expression, while others tightened their hold on what was reported and how it was presented.

Economic turmoil boiled over into the political arena for two of Southeast Asia's longest-standing leaders, with starkly contrasting results for the press. The resignation of Indonesia's President Suharto in May paved the way for a flowering of press activity after most restrictions on the media were lifted by the transitional government of President B. J. Habibie. The exhilaration of freedom, however, was tempered by caution over continued social unrest and uncertainty over the eventual scope of promised legal reforms to protect Indonesia's fledgling democracy.

Mahathir Mohamad, Malaysia's prime minister, strengthened his hold over the already tightly controlled Malaysian mainstream press before he proceeded to remove his reform-minded deputy prime minister, Anwar Ibrahim, as a political rival by firing him and then arresting him for corruption and sodomy in September. His plans apparently backfired: Malaysians, weary of whitewashed news and a pro-Mahathir slant on the Anwar crisis, set up web-

---

A. Lin Neumann *is CPJ's program coordinator for Asia.*
Kavita Menon, *research assistant for the Asia program, provided invaluable assistance in compiling the documentation for this section and wrote several of the country summaries.*
Shumona Goel *was the research assistant for Asia until June and also provided excellent research and documentation for this section.*
The World Press Freedom Committee provided both funding and co-sponsorship of CPJ's initiative to convene the founding conference of the Southeast Asian Press Alliance in November. The Freedom Forum and the Institute for International Education provided additional funding for the conference.
CPJ wishes to thank the following organizations for their assistance throughout the year in monitoring press conditions in the region: Institute for Studies in the Free Flow of Information; Alliance of Independent Journalists; Center for Media Freedom and Responsibility; Philippine Center for Investigative Journalism; Reporters' Association of Thailand; Commonwealth Press Union; Bangladesh Centre for Development, Journalism and Communication; Pakistan Press Foundation; Free Media Movement; Pacific Islands News Association; Hong Kong Journalists Association; The Nation *of Bangkok; the* Cambodia Daily; *the* Phnom Penh Post; *and our many other colleagues in Asia.*

sites to share information on the fate of Anwar, who became a focal point for public protest.

Spurred on by the changes in Indonesia and an aggressively free press in Thailand, journalists from these two countries and the Philippines, the third "free press" country in Southeast Asia, announced the formation of the Southeast Asian Press Alliance (SEAPA) at a November conference in Bangkok co-sponsored by CPJ. SEAPA is the first effort to form a multilateral organization in Southeast Asia to promote press freedom and defend journalists.

The alliance will have plenty to do, judging by the strictures on the press in other countries in Southeast Asia. For example, journalists in Cambodia came under the sway of Prime Minister Hun Sen's political party as he consolidated the power he had seized in a 1997 coup. And Vietnam's communist rulers pushed renewed ideological orthodoxy on the state-controlled media.

The Chinese government sent mixed signals about press freedom throughout the year. In the summer and early autumn, Beijing softened its stance on the press by allowing expanded discussion of political topics in some publications in anticipation of state visits by U.S. President Bill Clinton and British Prime Minister Tony Blair. The promise of liberalization intensified when China signed the U. N. Covenant on Civil and Political Rights in October. But the end of the year saw an abrupt reversal of this trend with the reemergence of hard-line attitudes toward the press.

The 50th anniversary of the founding of the People's Republic and the 10th anniversary of the Tiananmen Square democracy movement coincide in 1999, and this potent symbolic juncture has already prompted authorities to take preemptive measures against those who might use the occasion to challenge one-party rule. Some newspapers and publishing houses have been shut down, and both local and foreign journalists with contacts among China's pro-democracy movement have came under increasing pressure. The prosecution of a computer entrepreneur for providing e-mail addresses to a dissident on-line magazine sent ominous signals for the future of Internet freedom in China.

Fortunately, China seemed to be keeping to its bargain in Hong Kong, where the press remained lively and free under the principle of "One Country, Two Systems" which now governs the territory. Nevertheless, Hong Kong journalists remained alert to any sign of retreat from the territory's proud tradition of media independence.

South Asia's political, ethnic, and religious crosscurrents threatened the press in several places, even as journalists organizations consistently took governments to task for attacks on the media. On May 29, the day after Pakistan detonated its first nuclear bomb, Prime Minister Mohammad Nawaz Sharif declared a state of emergency with the potential to undermine press freedom by suspending constitutional protections. He justified the action by raising the possibility that international sanctions in the wake of the blast could lead to public unrest.

In Sri Lanka, the government imposed military censorship on war reporting in June after a series of embarrassing battlefield losses to separatist Tamil rebels in the ongoing civil war.

India's Northeast remained a dangerous place for journalists—especially in Assam—where they frequently find themselves caught between separatist Assamese rebels and Indian Army forces. Although many journalists feared a contraction of civil liberties following the victory of the socially conservative Hindu nationalist Bharatiya Janata Party in national elections, it never materialized.

Afghanistan

In this country decimated by 20 years of civil war, few freedoms of any kind are tolerated and there is no independent local press. In the two years since the ultraconservative Islamist Taliban militia took control of Kabul, the nation's capital, the regime has consolidated its hold over most of the country. The Taliban's rule has been marked by the stringent application of its version of Islamic law: Women are confined to their homes, unless they can be escorted by a close male relative, and enshrouded from head-to-toe in a *burqa* gown. Public executions are held on Fridays in a sports stadium before an audience of thousands. Kabul's streets are vigorously patrolled by squads deployed by the Ministry for the Enforcement of Virtue and the Suppression of Vice, ensuring that citizens adhere to the myriad rules prohibiting everything from watching television to kite-flying.

The Taliban runs the Radio Voice of Shari'ah, which broadcasts propaganda, recitations of Koranic verses, and poems in praise of Allah's law. At least one radio station, Takhar Radio, is run by an anti-Taliban faction headed by Gen. Ahmed Shah Massoud from his stronghold in the northeastern city of Taloquan, but its broadcasting range is limited.

Foreign correspondents allowed into the country by the Taliban must be accompanied by a government minder, and are forbidden to photograph people or to speak to women. Journalists say that, in fact, the rules are haphazardly enforced. Many journalists have attempted to skirt the Taliban's restrictions by disguising their reason for visiting the country. But this became more difficult after foreign aid workers were expelled from Afghanistan at the end of September, raising the visibility of any outsider.

Although there have been sporadic attacks against foreign journalists—including beatings, detentions, and expulsions—victims are loath to report attacks and thereby jeopardize their relationship with the Taliban. The murder of Iranian journalist Mahmoud Saremi, however, gained international attention. Stationed in Mazar-i-Sharif as the Afghanistan bureau chief for Iran's official news agency, IRNA, Saremi was killed along with a group of Iranian diplomats when the Taliban took over the city in early August. Human rights observers believe his assassination was an attempt to block news of the subsequent massacres there.

Some veteran journalists feel that, Saremi's murder notwithstanding, they are in less physical danger now than they were during the years of widespread civil war, when attacks could come from any one of numerous militias.

August 8
Mahmoud Saremi, IRNA KILLED

Saremi, Afghanistan bureau chief for IRNA, the official Iranian news agency, was reported missing on August 8, along with 10 Iranian diplomats, when Taliban fighters secured the northern city of Mazar-i-Sharif. For over a month, Taliban officials repeatedly denied any knowledge of the condition of the Iranians, and refused to take responsibility for their safety. Finally, on September 10, Taliban spokesman Wakil Ahmed Mutawakil admitted that nine of the Iranians had been found dead near Mazar-i-Sharif, at a location under Taliban control. IRNA reported the next day that Saremi's body was among those recovered.

Saremi was the sole foreign journalist in Mazar-i-Sharif when the Taliban militia entered the city, and his death was tantamount to a total news blackout in northern Afghanistan.

Although there have been reports that the Taliban leadership ordered the capture of the consulate where Saremi and his compatriots were based, Taliban officials insist that the assassinations were carried out by "renegades" acting without orders.

CPJ first sent a letter on August 10 to Mullah Mohammad Omar, the head of the Taliban, urging an investigation into Saremi's disappearance, and sent a second letter on September 14, requesting an inquiry into his murder.

Bangladesh

Although the constitution guarantees press freedom, Bangladeshi journalists face considerable risk in practicing their profession. Violent attacks have become disturbingly common, and death threats almost routine. Meanwhile, the government did little to ensure that those responsible for crimes against journalists were punished for their actions.

Many attacks were led by activists from the country's major political parties. Members of the student wing of the ruling Awami League, headed by Prime Minister Sheikh Hasina Wajed, have repeatedly harassed and threatened correspondents who expose their often coercive political tactics at Dhaka University.

Because of authorities' failure to pursue investigations into such attacks, it is difficult to establish the motive for every incident. When Saiful Alam Mukul, editor of the Bengali-language *Daily Runner* newspaper, was murdered in August, it was unclear whether he was killed for publishing reports exposing local gang activity, political corruption, or the movements of guerrillas operating in the district. Financial difficulties—stemming from the government's decision to stop advertising in the paper in February—had forced the *Runner* to cease publication on June 16. Mukul was killed just two weeks after his August 15 announcement that he would relaunch the paper. His murder outraged the nation's journalistic community, and its timing sent a chilling message to those who would dare publish controversial reports of any kind.

Journalists who tackled religious issues also came under fire. In May, local officials in Jessore nearly shut down two newspapers for publishing articles that had apparently offended the Hindu and Muslim communities. And when the writer Taslima Nasreen returned to Bangladesh in September after years of living in exile, she was greeted by large-scale demonstrations staged by conservative Muslims, calling for her execution. She also faced charges for the "deliberate outrage of religious feelings."

Criminal defamation laws remain on the books, and are often used to harass journalists who write about politically sensitive topics. Although government officials have discussed replacing the arrest warrant with a court summons, most journalists are forced to endure arrest and post bail before their case, which then tends to languish interminably in the judicial system.

The existence of more than 500 newspapers and magazines is, however, evidence of a vibrant journalistic community. Local journalists vigorously protest attacks directed against the media, and there are a number of independent publications that continue to air sensitive topics. But in a country where three-quarters of the population are illiterate, electronic media remain most effective in reaching a broad audience. Radio and television are both still controlled by the government, and have been criticized for giving almost no news coverage to the political opposition.

February 5
A.K.M. Bahauddin, *Inqilab*
LEGAL ACTION
A.K.M. Mohiuddin, *Inqilab*
LEGAL ACTION
A.S.M. Baki Billah, *Inqilab*
LEGAL ACTION

The Court of the Chief Metropolitan Magistrate in Dhaka charged three journalists of the pro-Islamic Bengali-language opposition newspaper *Inqilab* with treason, claiming that a report in the January 12 edition of the paper was "false" and "fabricated." The charges carry a penalty of up to 12 years in prison. Editor Bahauddin, chief editor Mohiuddin, and publisher Billah appeared before the court on March 8 and were granted bail. If convicted, they face a maximum sentence of seven years' imprisonment and fines.

According to reports from Bangladesh, the Defense Ministry complained that the daily's article, "Decision to Reduce Number of Unit Level Defense Personnel Bid to Make Bangladesh Defense System Complementary to India's," was published to tarnish the image of the army internationally and to divide the nation.

March 18
Alam Raihan, *Sugandha Kagoj*
IMPRISONED, ATTACKED

Plainclothes detectives from the Dhaka Metropolitan Police arrested Raihan, chief editor of the weekly magazine *Sugandha Kagoj*, at his office. They took him to their headquarters, where he was reportedly tortured.

Raihan appeared before the metropolitan court on March 19, where he was summarily refused bail and ordered to be held in the Dhaka Central Jail. He was charged with publishing "indecent and defamatory news items that confused and tarnished the image of the present government." Bail petitions brought by his family were rejected on three separate occasions by a lower court. Police told reporters in Dhaka that the arrest was made upon "the instruction of higher authorities."

Raihan's colleagues at the magazine suspect that he was arrested because of critical reports exposing the corrupt practices of public officials recently published by *Sugandha Kagoj*. Raihan was ultimately released on bail on the order of the High Court.

March 18
Mozammel Hoq, Media Syndicate
THREATENED, HARASSED
Shaukat Mahmood, Media Syndicate
THREATENED, HARASSED

Officials of the Anti-Corruption Bureau summoned Hoq and Mahmood, the advisory editor and editor, respectively, of the news agency Media Syndicate, and interrogated them for four hours about the activities of their news agency, its sources of information, and its assets. The officials warned the journalists that the government was not happy with their reporting, and threatened to file a case against them, according to Mahmood.

These actions came in apparent response to Media Syndicate's criticism of the government's lack of transparency, of restrictions on press freedom, and of the administration's defensive response to a negative report by the U. S. State Department on human rights conditions in Bangladesh.

The Bangladesh Federal Union of Journalists and the Dhaka Union of Journalists issued a joint statement on March 21, expressing their concern over the harassment of Hoq and Mahmood and the growing incidence of government intimidation against journalists.

CPJ amplified these concerns in a March 30 letter to Prime Minister Sheikh Hasina Wajed, urging her to take a leading role in safeguarding Hoq and Mahmood's right to operate as journalists in an atmosphere free of harassment and intimidation.

Attacks on the Press in 1998

March 18
Jamal Hossain, *Benapole Barta*
LEGAL ACTION
Bokul Mahbub, *Benapole Barta*
LEGAL ACTION
Mohammad Ali, *Benapole Barta*
LEGAL ACTION

Police in Dhaka arrested Hossain, editor and publisher of the Bengali-language weekly *Benapole Barta*; Mahbub, the paper's executive director; and Ali, a reporter for the paper, on charges of defaming Nazma Akhter, an employee of the state-run Rural Electrification Association. Akhter had originally filed criminal defamation charges against the paper on August 29, 1993, after *Benapole Barta* published a story characterizing her as "an influential lady who hobnobs with customs authorities and vigilance agencies and works for large importers of goods from India."

The magistrate's court in Dhaka convicted the three on March 19 of this year. They were sentenced to one year in prison. On March 23, after spending four days in jail, they were released on bail pending an appeal of their conviction to the Jessore Sessions Court.

March 30
Hafizur Rahman Minto, *Inqilab* ATTACKED

An armed gang beat Minto, a local correspondent for the pro-Islamic Bengali-language opposition newspaper *Inqilab*, in the town of Narayanganj. Local journalists and political leaders condemned the assault.

Journalists from Narayanganj believe the action was related to a series of investigative articles Minto wrote on the abuse of women and children sold into slavery for sex and labor.

April 15
BTV cameraman, ATTACKED

During an angry display in the national assembly, agitated members of parliament from the main opposition Bangladesh Nationalist Party (BNP) of former Prime Minister Begum Khaleda Zia damaged a camera of the state-run BTV station that was recording the parliamentary proceedings before they staged a walkout from the house. They also accused Speaker Humayun Rasheed Choudhury of partisanship in barring them from the floor, hurled papers and books at his rostrum, and assaulted parliament officials.

BNP party members were refused the floor after the previous day's general strike during which several people, including opposition activists, were killed. Prime Minister Sheikh Hasina Wajed condemned the unruly behavior of the BNP members.

April 20
Absar Uddin Chowdhury, *Dainik Karnaphuli*
IMPRISONED
Mamunur Rashid, *Dainik Karnaphuli*
IMPRISONED
Mofizur Rahman, *Dainik Comilla Barta*
IMPRISONED
Iqbal Ahmed, *Dainik Muktakantha*
IMPRISONED
Yasin Hira, *Dainik Muktakantha*
IMPRISONED
Dainik Karnaphuli
THREATENED

Plainclothes policemen raided the office of *Dainik Karnaphuli*, a Chittagong-based pro-Islamist daily newspaper, and arrested Chowdhury and Rashid, the publisher and and joint news editor, respectively, in connection with the publication of a leaked copy of questions used in a nationwide high school examination. On the same day, police also arrested Rahman, editor and publisher of the Comilla-based *Dainik Comilla Barta*; Ahmed, publisher of the Bengali-language newspaper *Dainik Muktakantha*; and Hira, a correspondent for *Dainik Karnaphuli*, for publishing the questions.

All five journalists were charged under the

Official Secrecy Act of 1980, and released on bail pending trial. They face stiff fines and imprisonment of up to four years each if found guilty. On April 21, the Chittagong district government issued a statement warning *Dainik Karnaphuli* that its publishing license could be revoked for violating the Press and Publication Ordinance of 1974 and the Official Secrecy Act.

Colleagues believe the journalists were targeted by the government in retaliation for their investigation of corruption among government officials, who routinely sell questions on crucial examinations. The journalists published the exam questions as examples of the material being sold.

The Bangladesh Federal Union of Journalists, the Dhaka Union of Journalists, and the council of editors and publishers of newspapers, the Bangladesh Sangbadpatra Parishad, condemned the government's draconian measures against their colleagues.

CPJ sent a letter to Prime Minister Sheikh Hasina Wajed on April 22 expressing concern about a pattern of attacks against independent journalists that may threaten press freedom in Bangladesh. CPJ asked her to demonstrate her commitment to democracy by using the influence of her office to immediately drop all charges against Chowdhury, Rashid, Rahman, Ahmed, and Hira.

May 10
Dainik Lokesamaj
LEGAL ACTION

The Deputy Commissioner of Jessore District issued a show-cause notice to the Bengali-language newspaper *Dainik Lokesamaj*, stating that the newspaper's license to publish would be canceled unless it could prove such action unwarranted. The notice was issued against the paper for publishing material that offended both the Hindu and Muslim communities.

District officials delivered a show-cause notice to another local vernacular daily just three days later for the same offense. The Jessore government took action in these cases even though both newspapers had publicly apologized for the articles, and succeeded in appeasing the religious groups that had initially protested the papers' insensitivity.

Following demonstrations by the Jessore Union of Journalists and threats by local journalist leaders that they would launch a hunger strike to protest the government's actions, the district administration halted its moves to shut down the papers. CPJ included this case in a letter sent to Prime Minister Sheikh Hasina Wajed on June 24, urging her to use the power of her office to investigate attacks on the press and curb abuses of power directed against journalists in Bangladesh.

May 13
Dainik Purabi LEGAL ACTION

The Deputy Commissioner of Jessore District issued a show-cause notice to the Bengali-language newspaper *Dainik Purabi*, threatening to cancel the paper's license to publish unless it could prove that such action was unwarranted. This notice was essentially identical to one issued three days earlier to another local vernacular daily, in response to articles both papers had published that had apparently offended the district's Hindu and Muslim communities.

Journalists groups were angered by the local government's actions, taken despite the fact that both newspapers had apologized for the articles and succeeded in appeasing the religious groups that had initially protested them. Many in Bangladesh feel that the Press and Publication Ordinance of 1974 gives district administrators over-broad discretionary powers, allowing them to cancel publishing licenses without sufficient basis.

Although the government did not take further action against the papers—perhaps moved by the Jessore Union of Journalists' demonstrations and threats of continued agitation—CPJ cited these threats in a letter sent to Prime Minister Sheikh Hasina Wajed on June 24, urging her to repeal statutes, such as the 1974 ordinance, which leave journalists vulnerable to political pressure.

May 26
Manav Zamin ATTACKED, THREATENED, HARASSED

A gang of about 30 young men invaded the daily *Manav Zamin*'s offices in Dhaka. Two employees of the tabloid newspaper—from the finance and circulation departments—were injured by the gang, believed by witnesses to be members of the youth wing of the Jatiya Party (JP).

Witnesses say some of the attackers carried guns while others used sticks as they shattered windows, broke telephones, and toppled furniture. Back issues of the paper were also burned during the raid. Police registered cases of arson, terrorism, and vandalism, and posted guards outside *Manav Zamin*'s office for a few days after the incident. But an editor from the paper said that little else was done to investigate the matter and identify the attackers.

The chairman of the JP is Gen. Hussain Muhammad Ershad, who was the president of Bangladesh from 1982 to 1990. The JP was apparently angered by the newspaper's report that Gen. Ershad had purchased the anti-impotence drug Viagra on a recent visit to London. The gang threatened to kill the paper's editor, Matiur Rahman Chowdhury, and burn down *Manav Zamin*'s office if the paper continued to run such unflattering stories.

On June 12, *Dainik Ittefaq*, Bangladesh's largest-circulation daily paper, ran a rare front-page commentary mentioning the attack on *Manav Zamin* as one of many incidents in which those who attack the press are not brought to justice. In a June 24 letter to Prime Minister Sheikh Hasina Wajed, CPJ cited this editorial as an expression of the journalistic community's growing dismay with a system that does not protect them, and urged the prime minister to make good on her home secretary's June 17 pledge to more aggressively investigate such crimes and punish those responsible.

June 9
Masud Ahmed, *Manav Zamin* ATTACKED
Abdul Aziz, *Banglabazar* ATTACKED
Faruq Ahmed Bakht, *Dainik Dinkal* ATTACKED
Nijamul Huq, *Bhorer Kagoj* ATTACKED
Mostfa Ahmed Chowdhury, *Manuebarta* ATTACKED

A group of unidentified men assaulted five newspaper correspondents outside the Rajnagar police station in the northeastern town of Mulvibazar. The journalists were reporting on the kidnapping of seven people who were abducted in connection with a water dispute between two parties in the villages of Ghargaon and Raktagram. The assailants beat the journalists and warned them to stop covering the story.

According to the Bangladesh Centre for Development, Journalism and Communication (BCDJC), the correspondents attacked were Ahmed of *Manav Zamin*; Aziz of *Banglabazar*; Bakht of *Dinkal*; Huq of *Bhorer Kagoj*; and Chowdhury of *Manuebarta*.

CPJ mentioned this incident in a letter sent to Prime Minister Sheikh Hasina Wajed on June 24, alerting her government to the fact that violent crimes against journalists appear to be on the rise in Bangladesh, while perpetrators typically go unpunished.

June 18
Abdullah Farooq, *Sangbad* HARASSED
Dainik Muktakantha ATTACKED
Manav Zamin ATTACKED
Bhorer Kagoj ATTACKED
Daily Star ATTACKED
Ajker Kagoj ATTACKED
Banglabazar Patrika ATTACKED

Political activists assaulted several journalists and damaged at least nine press vehicles during a nationwide general strike called by the opposition Bangladesh Nationalist Party (BNP). Although the BNP had announced that vehicles marked "press" would be free to move during the strike, there were several violent incidents directed against the media.

According to CPJ's sources, Farooq, a reporter for the daily Bengali-language newspaper *Sangbad*, was harassed and robbed. An autorickshaw owned by the vernacular newspaper *Dainik Muktakantha* was set on fire, and one used by the Bengali-language tabloid daily *Manav Zamin* was hit with a home-made grenade. In similar incidents around the city, vehicles belonging to the vernacular dailies *Bhorer Kagoj, Ajker Kagoj*, and *Banglabazar*, and the English-language newspaper *Daily Star* were damaged.

CPJ included these incidents among the concerns expressed in a letter sent on June 24 to Prime Minister Sheikh Hasina Wajed, decrying the government's failure to protect the press from partisan violence.

July 26
Delwar Hossain, *Dainik Dinkal*
THREATENED

An armed gang entered the Gazipur Press Club, threatening journalists there with murder if they continued to pursue certain news stories.

The gang allegedly went to the press club looking for *Dainik Dinkal* correspondent Delwar Hossain. His paper is one of several vernacular dailies—including *Dainik Inqilab, Ajker Kagoj, Dainik Muktakantha, Banglabazar Patrika, Manav Zamin*, and *Dainik Sangram*— that published articles about attacks on landless peasants at the Dewaliabari Landless Shelter in Gazipur, and possible improprieties in the office of Gazipur's Additional District Magistrate.

The gang allegedly insulted Hossain and demanded to know the names of other reporters who had covered these stories. The Bangladesh Centre for Development, Journalism, and Communication reported that the gang threatened to "kill the persons responsible for the reports."

CPJ sent a letter of inquiry to the Information Minister on August 3, requesting an investigation, and noting that such threats are made in Bangladesh with alarming regularity.

August 30
Saiful Alam Mukul, *Daily Runner* KILLED

A group of unidentified assailants killed Mukul, editor of the Bengali-language newspaper *Daily Runner*, at around 9:30 p.m. as he was returning to his home in the Bejpara district of Jessore. Mukul was rushed to Jessore General Hospital, but was pronounced dead on arrival. There were conflicting reports about whether Mukul had been shot or hit by a small, hand-thrown bomb, or both.

While police have not conclusively established a motive for the crime, the *Daily Runner* had a reputation for exposing gang activity, political corruption, and human rights abuses, and had published several stories critical of guerrilla activity in the area around Jessore.

The paper had been out of print since June 16, when management halted production in part because of financial difficulties, but also to protest the growing complacency toward crime and corruption in Bangladesh; it was scheduled to resume publication on September 1. In the weeks after his August 15 announcement that the paper would be relaunched, Mukul had repeatedly expressed fears to friends, family, and even to police that an attack on his life was imminent.

Journalists around the country expressed their outrage over the murder, suspecting that the attack was designed to silence Mukul and crush the *Daily Runner*. CPJ sent a letter to Prime Minister Sheikh Hasina Wajed on September 1, condemning Mukul's assassination and urging the government to address the problem of escalating violence against journalists.

September 25
Taslima Nasreen, free-lancer
THREATENED, LEGAL ACTION

Nasreen, a prominent writer and feminist activist, returned to Bangladesh after years in exile, only to face renewed calls for her execution by religious extremists and a warrant for her arrest on charges that her newspaper columns had offended religious sensibilities. Nasreen returned to Dhaka in order to spend time with her mother, who is seriously ill, but has attempted to keep her whereabouts secret.

On September 25, the same day that about 2,000 conservative Muslims marched through the streets of the capital to demand that Nasreen be publicly hanged, police searched for her to serve her with an arrest warrant issued by a Dhaka criminal court judge. The court ordered the confiscation of Nasreen's property if she did not appear to face the legal proceedings against her.

The warrant stemmed from a complaint originally brought in 1994, in which a Dhaka resident complained that a book of Nasreen's newspaper columns, *Nirbachito Columns*, had offended his religious sensibilities. On November 3, a Dhaka lower court rejected the petition for bail that Nasreen had submitted through her lawyer, on the grounds that the court is unable to grant bail in absentia. Nasreen emerged from hiding on November 22 to appear before the High Court, which did grant her request for bail.

Nasreen still faces a second charge of breaching Section 295A of Bangladesh's penal code, which punishes those who engage in "deliberate and malicious acts intended to outrage the religious feelings of any class of citizens by insulting its religion or religious beliefs." Those charges were brought by the government in June 1994 after fundamentalist clerics raised a furor over comments Nasreen allegedly made in an interview with the Calcutta-based Indian daily *The Statesman*, advocating the revision of the Koran. Nasreen has since repeatedly denied these charges, claiming that she was misinterpreted.

Nasreen was granted asylum in Sweden, after fleeing Bangladesh in August 1994, when Muslim clerics issued a fatwa, or religious decree, sentencing her to death. The cash reward for her murder reportedly stands at 200,000 takas (US$5,000).

CPJ wrote to Prime Minister Sheikh Hasina Wajed on October 2, asking that Taslima Nasreen be protected from the various threats to her security, and that the charges against her be dropped. CPJ further urged the government to consider amending Section 295A of the penal code, so that it cannot be used to punish those exercising their right to free speech.

November 9
Shafiuddin Bitu, *Inqilab* ATTACKED
Emran Hossain, *Daily Star* ATTACKED
Khaled Mahmud, *Dainik Dinkal* ATTACKED
Farhad Hossain, *New Nation* ATTACKED
Tarif Rahman, *The Independent* ATTACKED
Anisur Rahman, *Daily Star* ATTACKED
Shamim Noor, *Ajker Kagoj* ATTACKED
Nurun Nabi Robi, *Dainik Janakantha* ATTACKED
Sanjeev Basak, *Dainik Muktakantha* ATTACKED

Political activists assaulted nine newspaper photographers who were covering a three-day general strike called by the opposition Bangladesh Nationalist Party (BNP). Such strikes virtually shut down the country, with sometimes violent repercussions for those who attempt to work, or even travel by vehicle. Although the press is supposedly exempt from these restrictions—along with police, ambulance crews, and fire fighters—they are often attacked.

Bitu, of the newspaper *Inqilab*, was hit by shrapnel on November 9 when pro-strike activists threw a homemade bomb at him; Emran Hossain, of the newspaper *Daily Star*, and Mahmud, of the newspaper *Dainik Dinkal*, were beaten by BNP activists armed with clubs; Farhad Hossain, of the newspaper *New Nation*, sustained head injuries when he was caught in a bomb blast.

On November 10, the second day of the protest, Tarif Rahman of the daily *Independent*; Anisur Rahman of the *Daily Star*; Noor of *Ajker Kagoj*; Robi of *Dainik Janakantha*; and Basak of *Dainik Muktakantha* were assaulted by police who joined forces with an anti-strike mob.

The political activists apparently assaulted the photographers because they did not want their activities documented, and because the journalists' equipment made them easily identifiable. Several press vehicles were also badly damaged during the strike, presumably because they, too, were obvious targets.

November 18
Mufti Abdul Hye, *Jago Mujahid*
IMPRISONED
Manzur Ahmed, *Jago Mujahid* IMPRISONED

Plainclothes police officers raided the editorial office of the magazine *Jago Mujahid* in Dhaka, seizing the August, September, and October 1998 issues, as well as photographs and wall calendars depicting Taliban guerrillas and other Islamic militants. The police arrested Hye, the paper's publisher and editor, and Ahmed, the executive editor, under the broad provisions of Bangladesh's Special Powers Act (SPA), which allows for the arbitrary arrest and detention of any citizen suspected of engaging in activities that threaten national security. *Jago Mujahid* had published articles encouraging Bangladeshi Muslims to launch an armed revolution modeled after the Taliban movement in Afghanistan.

Under the SPA, detainees can be held for up to three months without a court hearing, and police are not required to file formal charges against them. Police said they intended to keep Ahmed and Hye in detention for 30 days.

On November 19, CPJ wrote a letter to Prime Minister Sheikh Hasina Wajed protesting the use of the SPA to circumvent basic legal protections. CPJ stressed that if Ahmed and Hye are suspected of engaging in criminal activity, authorities should make the charges a matter of public record, and present the evidence for such claims before an open court. CPJ's sources report that Ahmed and Hye were eventually released on bail.

Burma

Burma remains one of the world's most closed regimes, with no independent local media and little opportunity for foreign reporters to penetrate the veil of repression. Senior Gen. Than Shwe, head of the ruling military junta, earned a place among CPJ's annual 10 worst Enemies of the Press. (See page 62 for more information on CPJ's Enemies of the Press.)

The ruling State Peace and Development Council (SPDC) and its intelligence chief Lt. Gen. Khin Nyunt, marked the 10th anniversary of its brutal 1988 coup by stifling dissent, arresting opponents, and further isolating the country. There are no independent, privately held newspapers or broadcast outlets. Fax machines, computer modems, satellite dishes, and videotape recorders are strictly licensed; unlicensed owners risk heavy fines and prison sentences. A handful of journalists who began their careers in the 1950s when journalism could still be practiced in the country now work for foreign news agencies. But they practice self-censorship for fear they'll be arrested if they report stories that anger the junta.

Local reporters and most foreign media continue to be barred from interviewing the country's opposition leader, 1991 Nobel Peace Prize laureate Daw Aung San Suu Kyi. Many foreign correspondents find it impossible to obtain required work visas, and those who enter on tourist visas are deported if they are caught working as journalists. Even those with official accreditation report being followed by government agents and having great difficulty meeting with opposition leaders, whose movements are closely monitored by the military. According to an exile magazine, the *Irawaddy News*, Daw San San, a senior member of Suu Kyi's opposition National League for Democracy (NLD) party, was sentenced to 20 years in prison because she spoke on the telephone to a reporter for the British Broadcasting Corporation.

Given the absence of local independent media, the public remains heavily dependent on short-wave radio broadcasts from the BBC, VOA, Radio Free Asia, and the Norway-based Democratic Voice of Burma for reliable news of their country.

Stung by worldwide censure for its information policies and dismal human rights record, the junta has lashed out at critics, accusing Western media of attempting to subvert the country. "The West Bloc and their media are trying to disturb stability, disrupt (the) economy and unity, and incite unrest in countries which do not accept their influence," said Minister of Information Maj. Gen. Kyi Aung in July in the state-run newspaper *New Light of Myanmar*.

Cambodia

Hotly contested elections in July, marred by charges of fraud, led to months of political stalemate. But in November, Prime Minister Hun Sen formed a coalition government that allowed him to consolidate the power he seized in a 1997 coup. And Hun Sen's Cambodian People's Party (CPP) has come to dominate the Khmer-language media. All six national television stations are controlled by the CPP, and 11 pro-Hun Sen radio stations are closely regulated. The sole independent radio station, Sambok Khmum, was closed by the government in September after it broadcast coverage of opposition rallies protesting election irregularities. In January, already tough press regulations were stiffened by a decree allowing the government to indefinitely suspend publications on a variety of national security grounds.

The climate for the media in Phnom Penh has worsened; many journalists believe that government surveillance of the press, including wiretapping, is now routine. In October, the pro-Hun Sen Khmer-language newspaper *Rasmei Kampuchea* (Light of Cambodia) cited government spokesman Khieu Kanharith saying that the government planned to shut down Cambodia's two de facto newspapers of record—*The Cambodia Daily* and weekly *Phnom Penh Post*—for "serious professional mistakes" in their coverage. These rival English-language papers, owned by U.S. investors, were established in the early 1990s when the United Nations was overseeing attempts to normalize and democratize Cambodia. The threat was publicly rescinded following strong protests by CPJ and the American embassy in Phnom Penh.

January 8
Kumnit Koan Khmer LEGAL ACTION, CENSORED
Andarakum LEGAL ACTION, CENSORED
Neak Torsou LEGAL ACTION, CENSORED
Kolbot Angkor LEGAL ACTION, CENSORED
Samleng Samapheap LEGAL ACTION, CENSORED
Proyuth LEGAL ACTION, CENSORED

The Information Ministry suspended six opposition newspapers—*Kumnit Koan Khmer*

(Thought of Khmer Children), *Neak Torsou* (Combatant), *Andarakum* (Intervention), *Kolbot Angkor* (People of Angkor), *Samleng Samapheap* (Voice of Equality), and *Proyuth* (The Fighter)—charging them with a variety of offenses including defamation and adversely affecting the morale of soldiers. Secretary of State for Information Khieu Kanharith defended the decision, saying the papers had violated the country's press law by threatening national security, political stability, and defaming Cambodia's political leaders and its national institutions.

One paper described Second Prime Minister Hun Sen as a dog, and another reported that the country's parliament has a "Vietnamese head and a Khmer body." A third paper reported that Hun Sen would kill the deposed co-Premier Prince Norodom Ranariddh should he return to Cambodia.

On December 23, 1997, the ministry issued a new decree requiring journalists to use two official sources when reporting about the fighting or any event that could affect the political and security atmosphere. It is not clear whether the newspapers were accused of breaching this directive.

The papers were to have been shut down for 30 days and faced court proceedings, but on January 15 Hun Sen lifted the ban.

January 9
All media, THREATENED, LEGAL ACTION, CENSORED

Secretary of State for Information Khieu Kanharith presented the Information Ministry's revisions to the country's controversial three-year-old press law, detailing new restrictions on what can be published on security and political issues.

According to the new law, journalists can be subjected to criminal prosecution for publishing information considered "secret by state institutions, that can damage state sovereignty, and damage the stability of the Kingdom of Cambodia." This includes revealing information about military or police actions that could "lead to the failure of operations or bring danger to the Royal Cambodian Armed Forces and police." The regulations further restrict information intended to incite or support secessionist movements, carrying arms against the government, damaging the monarchy, supporting the Khmer Rouge, or affecting the value of the national currency. Journalists face criminal charges, including jail terms and heavy fines, for violating the press law.

January 11
Nou Kim Y, *Nokor Khmer* ATTACKED

Unidentified gunmen fired at opposition journalist Nou Kim Y, editor in chief of the Khmer-language newspaper *Nokor Khmer*, causing no injury but damaging his car. Nou Kim Y, whose newspaper supports the royalist FUNCINPEC party of deposed co-Premier Prince Norodom Ranariddh, told officials that he had received death threats last year, but there was no immediate connection between the two incidents.
Nou Kim Y fled Cambodia shortly after Prince Ranariddh was ousted in July 1997, but had recently returned and resumed publication of his newspaper.

June 8
Thong Uy Pang, *Koh Santepheap* (Island of Peace) ATTACKED

Thong Uy Pang, editor in chief and publisher of the popular *Koh Santepheap* (Island of Peace) daily newspaper, was shot twice in the shoulder at close range at a temple near Phnom Penh on June 8 as he was preparing to pray at the grave of his parents, according to news reports. He survived the attack and was hospitalized. His attacker fled.

While the gunman's motive is not known, *Koh Santepheap* ran a front-page story on June 10 accusing "powerful politicians in the present

Attacks on the Press in 1998

government" of being behind the attack. No details were given. It was the third attack on *Koh Santepheap* staff in recent years. In October 1997, two grenades were thrown at Thong Uy Pang's home and office but he escaped injury.

CPJ wrote a letter to Second Prime Minister Hun Sen urging his government to devote maximum effort to investigating the attack on Thong Uy Pang and bringing those responsible to justice in a court of law.

October 4
Cambodia Daily THREATENED
Phnom Penh Post THREATENED
Joe Cochrane, Deutsche Presse-Agentur THREATENED

The October 4 edition of the pro-government, Khmer-language daily newspaper *Rasmei Kampuchea* (Light of Cambodia), quoted government spokesperson and Secretary of State for Information Khieu Khanarith saying that the government of Cambodia plans to shut down two independent English-language newspapers in Phnom Penh, *The Cambodia Daily* and the biweekly *Phnom Penh Post*. The story also said that British and U.S. journalists would be temporarily expelled from the country. The front-page article in *Rasmei Kampuchea* said that Joe Cochrane, a correspondent for the German news agency Deutsche Presse-Agentur who is a former reporter for *The Cambodia Daily*, was "anti-government." It accused *The Cambodia Daily* of biased coverage of an alleged assassination attempt against Cambodia's Prime Minister Hun Sen. It also said that the *Phnom Penh Post* is "a publication that has always been against the Royal Government."

In the article, Khanarith was quoted as saying, "The masses are angry at British and American journalists, and they will have to leave the country because we cannot protect them." The Information Ministry has confirmed that Khanarith made the statements contained in the article.

Journalists in Phnom Penh have taken the threats seriously and say that Khanarith's remarks reflect growing tension between the press and government in the aftermath of national elections in July, which press accounts reported to have been flawed.

Following the threat, U.S. Ambassador Kenneth Quinn issued a sharply worded letter warning Hun Sen not to move against the press. CPJ protested the threat and called on Hun Sen's government to rescind the statements.

Later, journalists in Phnom Penh reported that the government has backed away from the threat in the face of international pressure.

China

Speculation that President Jiang Zemin's appointment of economic reformer Zhu Rongji as premier in March would quickly lead to political reform was sadly mistaken. The much-discussed thaw in the chilly climate for free expression in China that was apparent last year was reversed with a vengeance this year, especially after U.S. President Bill Clinton's visit in June. And the decision to sign the U.N. International Covenant on Civil and Political Rights in October did little to change the climate of free expression in the country. Activists associated with attempts to form an opposition political party advocating a free press and other reforms were detained and imprisoned late in the year. In December, the Department of Propaganda of the Communist Party's Central Committee began a series of reprisals against independent-minded newspapers and publishing houses. *Cultural Times*, **an influential newspaper in Guangzhou, near Hong Kong, was shut down, and senior editorial staff members of another Guangzhou newspaper,** *The Hong Kong-Guangzhou Information Daily*, **were dismissed. Both foreign and local jour-**

nalists faced harassment, censorship, persecution, and expulsion.

China's constitution has long guaranteed freedoms of association and expression which, in practice, have been over-ridden by other clauses relating to national security and the primacy of the Communist Party. Journalists report that while they can cover local corruption and grievances against such low-level functionaries as police, they receive little support from editors and publishers of the state-run newspapers when they do so. According to some reporters, threats from powerful private business interests against journalists who cover their activities are also growing. Such threats may have given partial impetus to the creation in August of the Committee for Safeguarding Legal Rights of Journalists, under the auspices of the state-sanctioned All-China Journalists Association (ACJA). Official news accounts claimed that the committee would "protect the rights of the nation's 500,000 journalists." But the lack of an independent press makes it difficult to believe that such a committee would do anything to represent the interests of journalists who run afoul of powerful officials.

In a speech to law enforcement officials in late December, Jiang said the crackdown was likely to last for at least a year. "Any factors that could jeopardize our stability must be annihilated in the early stages," Jiang said, demonstrating the repressive approach to the press that earned him a place on CPJ's annual list of the 10 worst Enemies of the Press. (See page 62 for more information on the Enemies of the Press.)

In a rare interview, Li Peng, the chairman of the National People's Congress (NPC), ruled out democratic reforms in China. Addressing the issue of the press during the interview with the German newspaper *Handlesblatt*, Li, second in the Communist Party hierarchy, said: "The principle of freedom of the press should be followed, but no individual's freedom should hinder the freedom of others." Voicing the standard party line, Li warned that "press freedom should be conducive to national development and social stability."

In practice, this policy means that journalists have little or no freedom to discuss political questions that might challenge the national leadership. In September, for example, Shi Binhai, an editor with the newspaper *China Economic Times*, was detained without charges, leading to speculation that he was punished for co-editing the book *Political China: Facing the Era of Choosing a New Structure*, a compilation of articles by intellectuals and former government officials on the need for political reform. The publication in August was initially taken by many as a sign that the range of ideas allowed to be discussed was broadening, but in November the book was banned. In early January 1999, authorities suspended the operations of China Today Publishers, the publishing house that issued *Political China*, and ordered two of its top editors to write "self-criticisms"—the standard ideological punishment in China.

Coverage of dissidents repeatedly sparked the authorities' ire. Two foreign correspondents—one Japanese and one German—were summarily expelled at different times from the country. Both had had contacts with dissidents. In September, Natalie Liu, a free-lance CBS News producer working in Beijing, was arrested at home by police. Liu, a legal resident of the United States who holds a Chinese passport, was released three days later and allowed to leave the country. She had helped arrange an interview with former political prisoner Bao Tong, which aired on CBS the day President Clinton arrived in China.

At least 12 journalists remain imprisoned in China, including Gao Yu, a reporter serving a six-year sentence for "leaking state secrets" in articles she wrote for *Mirror*

Attacks on the Press in 1998

Monthly, a Hong Kong magazine. Although she is seriously ill and has been honored by numerous international groups, Beijing has refused to heed calls for her release. (See page 27 for more information on Gao Yu.) Wang Dan, a leader of the 1989 Tiananmen Square protest movement, was released from prison and sent into exile in the United States in April, continuing a pattern of deporting democracy movement leaders. Late in the year, an article in *The People's Daily*, the official newspaper of the Communist Party, reported that 190 people had received prison terms for distributing or storing illegal political publications, but it was not possible to independently verify that report.

March 25
Lin Hai, software entrepreneur
IMPRISONED, LEGAL ACTION

Shanghai police arrested Lin, a software entrepreneur and computer engineer, and charged him with "inciting the overthrow of state power" for giving e-mail addresses of 30,000 Chinese residents to *VIP Reference*, an on-line magazine published in the United States which supports democratic reform in China. He faces life in prison if convicted. He is currently being held in Shanghai's public security detention center.

Lin was tried by the Shanghai Number One Intermediate People's Court on December 4. The four-hour trial was closed to the public and conducted in secret. He told the court that he was innocent, and that he provided the addresses to *VIP Reference* in the hope that he could eventually exchange e-mail addresses with the magazine to build up his own Internet business, according to the Hong Kong-based Information Center of Human Rights and Democratic Movement in China. *VIP Reference* used the addresses to expand its distribution of articles on human rights and democracy within mainland China.

Lin's wife, Xu Hong, told reporters that police seized her from a restaurant and detained her at a local police station near the courthouse for six hours on the day of the trial to prevent her from attending the court session or discussing it with foreign journalists.

In a December 9 letter to President Jiang Zemin, CPJ said that Lin's prosecution goes to the heart of journalistic freedom in China. CPJ urged Jiang to use his influence to dismiss the charges against Lin Hai and ensure free access to the Internet.

April 19
Wang Dan EXPELLED

Wang, a leader of the 1989 Tiananmen Square democracy movement and one of China's leading dissidents, was released from prison, ostensibly for medical reasons, and immediately expelled from China and sent into exile in the United States.

Upon his arrival in the United States, he entered Henry Ford Hospital in Detroit for a brief medical evaluation. His release had been widely expected as a goodwill gesture linked to President Clinton's June visit to China.

Wang had been serving an 11-year prison term on a 1996 conviction of plotting to overthrow the government. He had been detained since May 1995 but was not convicted until 1996. Following the violent crushing of the Tiananmen Square revolt, the charismatic student leader was imprisoned for four years. Upon his release he continued to speak and was a frequent contributor to foreign magazines and newspapers.

Wang was expelled from China under similar circumstances to Wei Jingsheng, who was forced into exile in November last year shortly after a Sino-U.S. summit in Washington.

The release into exile of prominent dissidents is seen by many observers as a strategy by the Chinese to mute the voices of prominent dissident figures who are denied access to the press in China.

Wang's offenses consisted of publishing articles in the overseas press which were deemed objectionable by Beijing, and of receiving donations from overseas human rights groups.

June 20
Arin Basu, Radio Free Asia CENSORED
Patricia Hindman, Radio Free Asia CENSORED
Feng Xiaoming, Radio Free Asia CENSORED
Apple Daily CENSORED
Next Magazine CENSORED

China withdrew the visas of Basu, Hindman, and Feng—Washington-based correspondents for the U.S. government-run Radio Free Asia—just before they were to cover President Bill Clinton's state visit to China. Visas to cover the visit were also denied to two Hong Kong-based publications, *Next Magazine* and the newspaper *Apple Daily*, whose owner, Jimmy Lai, has long been a target of harassment by Beijing.

Basu, Hindman, and Feng were initially granted visas by the Chinese Embassy in Washington on Friday, June 19, as part of the large press contingent traveling to Beijing to cover President Clinton's nine-day visit to China, which began June 24. Embassy officials withdrew the visas the day after they were issued and the three were unable to leave with other journalists to cover the visit. President Clinton called the action "highly objectionable."

In a letter to President Jiang Zemin, CPJ called on China to allow the three journalists, together with *Apple Daily* and *Next Magazine*, to cover the Clinton visit. CPJ noted that the visa action is emblematic of China's culture of secrecy and tight controls on the press.

September 2
Natalie Liu, CBS News IMPRISONED, HARASSED

Fourteen officers from the Beijing Municipal Security Bureau arrived at the residence of Liu, a free-lance associate producer working with CBS News, around 10 a.m. and took her into custody. Liu's mother and two small children witnessed the event. Sources close to the family said that the uniformed officers videotaped and photographed the apartment's interior before handcuffing Liu and taking her away. The officers refused Liu's repeated requests to be informed of the grounds for her detention. Agents also seized the journalist's notebooks, address book, videotapes, and photographs.

Liu was held in a windowless cell for two and a half days without charge and interrogated repeatedly. Officers demanded that she write a confession to unspecified crimes, but she refused to do so.

Liu, who is a legal permanent resident of the United States, holds a Chinese passport under the name Liu Qingyan. She began working for CBS News in Beijing in 1997, and was due to return to the United States on Monday, September 7, accompanied by her children. She had applied to the Chinese government for official accreditation as a foreign correspodent, but it had not been granted at the time of her arrest.

Liu was unconditionally released on September 5, following vigorous protests by CPJ to the Chinese government about the manner of her arrest and treatment. She left Beijing for her home in the United States on September 7.

September 5
Shi Binhai, *China Economic Times* IMPRISONED

Shi, an editor with the *China Economic Times* in Beijing, was taken from his home in Beijing by National Security Ministry personnel, who also searched his house. The Security Ministry did not give an explanation for the arrest, nor did it inform Shi's family where he was being held.

Shi, a leading voice in Beijing journalism, is also the editor of the best-selling book *Political China: Facing the Era of Choosing a New Structure*, a groundbreaking collection of 39 essays by journalists, academics, and former government officials calling for political reform. Sources in China expressed fears that Shi was arrested as a result of his work on the book.

A Shanghai native, Shi was imprisoned in 1989 for his role in the Tienanmen Square democracy movement. He was released in 1991.

The most recent arrest came just three days after Beijing authorities detained Natalie Liu, a free-lance Chinese television producer with CBS News in Beijing, and held her for two days without charge, during which time they questioned her about her journalistic work.

In a letter to President Jiang Zemin, CPJ called for Shi's immediate and unconditional release.

October 4
Yukihisa Nakatsu, *Yomiuri Shimbun*
EXPELLED

Nakatsu, a reporter for the Japanese daily newspaper *Yomiuri Shimbun*, was ordered to leave China after his third interrogation by security officials since September 27, when he returned to Beijing from a trip to Tibet. Nakatsu had gone to Tibet with about 20 other Japanese reporters. When he returned, security agents searched both his home and his paper's Beijing office, seizing Nakatsu's notes and certain documents.

A spokesman for China's foreign ministry said that Nakatsu had "obtained state secrets ... breaking the law on national security of the People's Republic of China." Foreign Ministry officials in China maintain that Nakatsu "confessed his crimes" before leaving, but a spokesman for *Yomiuri Shimbun* in Tokyo said that Nakatsu was expelled from China because he refused to disclose his sources or explain how he came across sensitive documents.

Colleagues of Nakatsu in Beijing told reporters that they believe his deportation had very little to do with his visit to Tibet, and was instead prompted by his connections to Chinese journalist Shi Binhai, an editor with the *China*

Economic Times, who was arrested on September 5 by officials of China's National Security Ministry. Shi is the co-editor of the pro-reform book *Political China: Facing the Era of Choosing a New Structure*. No reason was given for his arrest.

On October 5, China's ambassador to the United Nations, Qin Huasun, signed the International Covenant on Civil and Political Rights (ICCPR) and said that China "respects and protects civil and political rights and opposes any acts that violate a citizen's legitimate rights."

In an October 7 letter to President Jiang Zemin, CPJ protested the expulsion and called on China to grant journalists the universally recognized right to practice their profession without interference.

November 17
Juergen Kremb, *Der Spiegel* EXPELLED

Agents from the Ministry of State Security entered the office of Kremb, a reporter for *Der Spiegel* in Beijing, searched the premises, pushed him against a wall, and accused him of illegally obtaining state secrets. The agents asked him to sign a confession stating he had violated Chinese law, which he refused to do. The next day, he was ordered to leave the country within 48 hours and told that he would not be allowed back in China for five years.

Kremb, who lived in China for eight and a half years before moving to Singapore in July, told reporters that he may have been targeted because of his reporting on Chinese dissidents. In 1997, he published a book on Wei Jingshen, the dissident writer who was expelled from China. Kremb was in China to work on several stories and had obtained the required visa and accreditation. It was his fourth trip to the country since July.

Kremb is the second reporter to be expelled from China since October. In a similar incident, Yukihisa Nakatsu, a Beijing correspondent for Japan's *Yomiuri Shimbun* newspaper, was ordered to leave on October 4 after being accused of violating state security.

In a November 18 letter, CPJ urged President Jiang Zemin to lift the explusion order against Kremb and allow him to continue his work freely. CPJ noted that although China signed the International Covenant on Civil and Political Rights on October 5, and thus explicitly guaranteed freedom of expression, the Beijing government continues to use harsh secrecy laws and state-sponsored attacks against journalists to control the flow of information and stifle the press.

Fiji

Fiji took a dramatic step toward greater openness this year with the enactment of a new constitution containing broad protections for the press. Drawing from language contained in Article 19 of the Universal Declaration of Human Rights, Section 30 of the constitution, which went into effect in July, states: "Every person has the right to freedom of expression, including: freedom to seek, receive and impart information and ideas; through freedom of the press and other media."

In January, the government initiated a thorough reexamination and reform of the country's repressive media laws, many of which have their origins in harsh legislation passed by fiat during the British colonial period. Despite calls from conservative politicians to follow the example of such repressive states as Malaysia and Singapore, the government chose to follow an open model, rejecting press licensing and a proposal for a government-sanctioned council to oversee the media. The existing industry-sponsored Fiji News Council will continue to mediate disputes among the government, the public, and the press. An Official Information Act, which would allow greater public access to government records, is to replace the current restrictive Official Secrets Act and is expected to be approved by parliament in early 1999.

Despite the reform climate, the government of Prime Minister Sitiveni Rabuka rejected appeals from CPJ and Fijian press organizations and passed the Emergency Powers Act of 1998 in July. The measure gives the government the power to impose direct censorship on the media should a national state of emergency be declared.

Substantial tension persists between the country's largest daily newspaper, the Rupert Murdoch-owned *Fiji Times*, and the national parliament. The *Fiji Times*' aggressive reporting and critical commentary on parliamentary proceedings have angered the legislative leadership in recent years, leading to the filing of criminal charges against the paper under the tough Parliamentary Privilege and Powers Act. No new charges, which carry potential jail terms, were filed this year, but the paper was threatened several times by politicians on the floor of the parliament.

July 16
All journalists THREATENED

Fiji's Senate and House of Representatives passed the Emergency Powers Act 1998, permitting government "censorship and the control of and suppression of publications, writings, maps, plans, photographs, communications, and means of communications," according to information released by the Pacific Islands News Association.

Special sessions of both the House and Senate were convened for the purpose of considering the Act, which was expedited so that the government would retain emergency powers under Fiji's revised constitution.

CPJ wrote a letter to Prime Minister Sitiveni Rabuka protesting the legislation on July 8, when the bill was still being debated.

## Attacks on the Press in 1998

Hong Kong

An uneasy status quo prevailed during the first full year of Chinese sovereignty after the handover of the former colony by Britain in 1997. Hong Kong journalists are finding a relative lack of openness in the administration of Tung Chee-hwa, the chief executive, but they still enjoy one of the freest presses in Asia.

In the grips of its worst economic downturn in a generation and with China cracking down on free expression in the mainland, Hong Kong remains both the international center for independent Chinese-language journalism and the headquarters for most of the regional media.

Fear of political pressure and signs of an uncharacteristic reticence to ruffle feathers continue to surface, however. In July, television reporter Christopher Leung angrily denounced the failure of China Television Network (CTN) to air a documentary he had produced on ethnic unrest in the Western province of Xinjiang. The documentary, "Crying Wolf," offered a rare glimpse into a little-known Muslim separatist movement in one of China's most remote and forbidden areas. Leung said the piece was killed because CTN, a satellite network owned by Taiwanese and broadcast in Mandarin to Chinese audiences worldwide, caved in to political pressure from Beijing, a charge the network denied. As a result of the controversy, Leung quit his job and returned to the United States, his adopted home.

Local reporters and editors say that self-censorship of issues that might be sensitive to Beijing remains a problem, as it has been for several years, even before the handover. Other concerns are on the horizon. A provision in Hong Kong's Basic Law, which governs the territory as a Special Autonomous Region of China, mandates the eventual drafting of a law punishing "sedition." Journalists and civil libertarians worry that the definition of sedition could make it a crime to publish material related to independence for Tibet or Taiwan—topics that are extremely sensitive to Beijing. Others complain that the government is less accessible than it was during the last years of British rule.

August 19
Albert Cheng, Commercial Radio Station
ATTACKED

Two unidentified men slashed Cheng, the outspoken host of a popular and influential radio program, "Teacup in a Storm," with a meat cleaver at about 6:30 a.m. in the parking lot of Commercial Radio. Cheng was admitted to Queen Elizabeth Hospital with at least six deep cuts on his back, legs, and one hand. He spent about six hours in surgery as doctors reconnected muscle, bone, and nerve tissue.

There is widespread suspicion among the press in Hong Kong that Cheng was targeted for his journalistic work. The *Hong Kong Standard* newspaper declared that if "this dastardly attack was a warning to him to desist from critical remarks or to be more circumspect in what he says on the radio, then all those who respect media freedom will condemn it and rise to the defense of journalistic freedom."

One week after the attack, on August 26, Cheng said in an interview with government radio that he also believed the attack was in retaliation for his work, but he did not specify any suspect.

In an August 20 letter to Hong Kong Chief Executive Tung Chee-hwa, CPJ condemned the attack and urged the Hong Kong government to act swiftly to guarantee a thorough investigation into the crime.

On October 9, Cheng, who was still recovering from his injuries, returned to his radio show in the protection of a police security guard.

Police have detained 17 suspects in the case, many of them gang figures, but Cheng has yet to be able to make any positive identifications during police line-ups. None of the suspects has been charged in the case.

India

When the Hindu nationalist Bharatiya Janata Party (BJP) won control of the government in February, observers worried that an erosion of civil liberties would soon follow if the party imposed its brand of religious conservatism on traditionally secular India. Despite these fears, the government placed no new restrictions on the country's lively and generally free press.

Nevertheless, India's complex political, ethnic, and religious conflicts make the country a dangerous place to report the news. Journalists covering secessionist conflicts in India's northeastern states continue to be vulnerable to attack from both armed rebels and state security forces. On January 13, Ankur Barbora, a special correspondent for the newspaper *Asian Age*, disappeared from Calcutta under mysterious circumstances. Though police claimed they had conducted investigations in West Bengal, Assam, and Nagaland, they were unable to discover what had happened to Barbora. The journalist's colleagues at the *Asian Age*, however, believe he was abducted—and possibly killed—because of his reporting in the Northeast.

Authorities continue to use laws punishing speech that might provoke ethnic or religious tensions against the press. In January, for example, four employees of India's official television network, Doordarshan, were arrested and detained on charges that their report on a recent massacre in Assam was divisive, and dangerously exploited the conflict between Assamese Hindus and the indigenous Bodo community.

The escalating conflict between Indian and Pakistani troops in the northwestern state of Jammu and Kashmir did not take the toll on the media it had in the past. Although the local press still receives threats and ultimata from armed Hindu and Muslim militants seeking to influence coverage, CPJ documented no physical assaults against journalists this year. Some in the media say that Kashmiri journalists, fearful of attack, practiced a degree of self-censorship. Eight journalists have been murdered in Kashmir since 1989, when the secessionist movement became an all-out war.

Political violence remains a threat to the press. In March, about 50 armed men who were allegedly members of the state's ruling Dravida Munnetra Kazhagam (DMK) Party attacked the office of the newspaper *Dinamalar* in the southern state of Tamil Nadu. The group assaulted the guard on duty and destroyed a substantial amount of property. *Dinamalar* had recently been critical of the DMK during parliamentary elections. In June, in the neighboring state of Kerala, a crowd of activists associated with the ruling Communist Party-Marxist (CPM) severely beat two reporters and two photographers for their coverage of a double-murder case in which CPM members had been implicated. Such attacks often occur with the tacit approval of state authorities, and so are rarely investigated.

January 11
Avirook Sen, *India Today* ATTACKED
Suparna Sharma, *Indian Express* ATTACKED

Around midnight, Sen, a correspondent for the news magazine *India Today*, and his wife, Sharma, a reporter for the English-language daily newspaper *The Indian Express*, were beaten by policemen in Guwahati, Assam.

Sen and Sharma were on their way home

Attacks on the Press in 1998

from a friend's house. Just as they were about to take an autorickshaw, a police patrol jeep blocked their way. Two policemen got out of the jeep and charged to either side of their rickshaw. The policemen refused to recognize their press identification cards, dragged Sen out of the rickshaw by the collar and interrogated him while beating him up. When Sharma begged them to stop, the police responded by beating her severely. The police took the two journalists to the Chandmari police station. They were not allowed to make a phone call. They were taken to a nearby hospital and treated.

Sen and Sharma filed a case with a local police station. Local journalists condemned the attack, which they believed to be related to Sen's work as a journalist.

CPJ included the attack on Sen and Sharma in a February 25 letter to the Indian government, protesting the various abuses against journalists working in Assam.

January 15
Hitesh Medhi, Doordarshan LEGAL ACTION
Pratap Bordoloi, Doordarshan LEGAL ACTION
Ramani Malakar, Doordarshan LEGAL ACTION
Deben Tamuly, Doordarshan LEGAL ACTION

Police arrested four senior officials of the News Division of the Guwahati, Assam, bureau of the official Indian television network, Doordarshan, and charged them under Section 153A(1) of the Indian Penal Code with promoting disharmony between Assamese Hindus and the indigenous Bodo community.

The arrests were made on orders from Prafulla Mahanta, Assam's Chief Minister. Medhi, Doordarshan's joint director; Malakar, the news editor; Bordoloi, the assistant news editor; and Tamuly, the network's news producer, were taken from their respective homes late in the evening and held in the Geeta Nagar Police Station. They were released the next day on bail of R10,000 (nearly US$300) apiece pending trial, but face stiff fines and imprisonment of up to five years each if convicted.

A press release issued by the state government said that Doordarshan's January 14 broadcast, about a January 13 attack by Bodo militants that left at least 18 dead, contained "highly inflammatory words and visual representations."

On February 25, CPJ wrote to India's Prime Minister Inder Kumar Gujral, expressing concern over the government's actions against Doordarshan and detailing several attacks against the press in Assam.

February 26
The Kashmir Times CENSORED

State security officers intercepted distribution of Srinagar's leading English-language daily early in the morning when senior officers seized three bundles of *The Kashmir Times* at the airport in Srinagar.

The officers refused to give any explanation to the driver who had brought the papers to the airport. The driver reported the incident to the paper's editor in chief, Ved Bhasin. The Jammu and Kashmir state government has denied involvement in the incident and claims that it occurred without the government's consent.

March 1
Dinamalar ATTACKED

According to reports from the *Hindu* and *The Statesman* newspapers, 50 armed men attacked the Madurai office of the Tamil-language daily newspaper *Dinamalar* in the early morning. Wielding clubs and knives, the gang members assaulted the office watchman, hurled four Molotov cocktails, and destroyed property—including press equipment, windows, electrical fixtures, furniture, and automobiles. This action came during the country's parliamentary elections and followed the newspaper's recent

ASIA

critical coverage of Tamil Nadu's ruling Dravida Munnetra Kazhagam (DMK) party.

Local journalists' organizations and leaders of various political parties within the state have condemned the incident.

Although Chief Minister M. Karunanidhi ordered an investigation into the attack, when no action had been taken in over a month, the paper filed a formal complaint with the Press Council of India in New Delhi. *Dinamalar*'s letter to the Press Council, dated April 18, accuses M.K. Alagiri, the DMK party boss and son of Chief Minister Karunanidhi, of organizing the raid.

As of June 8, officials had not moved to punish those responsible.

June 16
Tony Dominic, *Malayala Manorama* ATTACKED
Josey George, *Deepika* ATTACKED
Chandra Bose, *Mathrubhumi* ATTACKED
P. Manoj, *Mathrubhumi* ATTACKED

Four journalists in Kollam, Kerala, were violently assaulted outside the District Court in Kollam, while covering a double-murder case in which members of the ruling Communist Party-Marxist (CPM) were charged with murdering two political opponents, according to the International Press Institute (IPI).

The journalists—Tony Dominic of *Malayala Manorama*, Josey George of *Deepika*, and Chandra Bose and P. Manoj of *Mathrubhumi*—were set upon by a crowd of CPM activists when the two photographers among them tried taking pictures of the accused entering the court. According to IPI, the mob destroyed the photographers' cameras, then beat the photographers and their colleagues, who had attempted to intervene. The report also indicated that police stayed away from the court premises until the violence had subsided, taking no steps to protect the journalists or control the crowd.

All four journalists were briefly hospitalized following the attack. CPJ sent a letter of inquiry on June 19 to the chief minister of Kerala, E.K. Nayanar, urging him to investigate the incident and bring the attackers to justice. According to *The Week* magazine, on June 27 the Kerala Regional Committee of the Indian Newspaper Society also submitted a memorandum to the chief minister "to ensure that the culprits did not go free because of their political connections."

July 18
Ajit Kumar Bhuyan, *Natoon Samoy* ATTACKED, THREATENED

Bhuyan, editor of the Assamese-language weekly newspaper *Natoon Samoy*, was at home with his family in Guwahati on Saturday at around 8:45 p.m., when a group of about 20 armed men in civilian clothes surrounded his house. They shouted at the family in Hindi to come outside and threatened to open fire if the order was not obeyed.

Once the occupants came out with their hands raised, the armed men forced Bhuyan to accompany them back inside the house. They searched and ransacked the three-story building, which also houses the offices of Bhuyan's newspaper. According to Bhuyan, nothing was taken from the residence or the office.

Bhuyan later told reporters that he felt his life was in danger and that he was being targeted because of his newspaper's criticism of the Indian Army in Assam.

After the raid, military authorities in Assam faxed a letter to local newspapers denying responsibility for the incident. Bhuyan was informed privately by local police officials that they had no prior knowledge of or involvement in the raid, despite laws that require army units to be accompanied by local police or magistrates on investigative raids.

Bhuyan believes that the attackers were soldiers, because they spoke Hindi, which is not the local language, and because he recognized one of the men as an army captain. Other than the brief denial sent to the newspapers, no official statements explaining the incident were made by police, military, or governmental authorities.

A well-known journalist in Assam, Bhuyan's stinging attacks on the Indian army and local corruption have frequently brought him into conflict with the government. He was arrested four times in 1997 under various national security laws, and was also arrested that year for complicity in the kidnapping and murder of social activist Sanjay Ghosh. In each instance, he was released and neither tried nor convicted of any crime.

The most recent attack on Bhuyan has a chilling similarity to events preceding the 1996 murder of Assamese editor Parag Kumar Das, with whom Bhuyan worked closely. Before he was killed, Das had been repeatedly charged with crimes for which he was never tried, and his home was raided by military authorities. His murder remains unsolved.

In a letter to Prime Minister Atal Behari Vajpayee of India on July 21, CPJ condemned the attack and raised the fear that Bhuyan might be killed unless national authorities immediately intervened. CPJ called on the prime minister to launch an immediate investigation into the raid on Bhuyan's home and office, and to make the findings of that investigation public.

Indonesia

After 32 years of autocratic rule, President Suharto, a perennial among CPJ's annual 10 worst Enemies of the Press (see page 62), resigned on May 21, driven from power by an economic meltdown, enraged students, and widespread rioting. Suharto's sudden departure triggered a wave of cries for "reformasi," or political reform, that swept aside most restrictions on the press and led to a sudden blossoming of the media in a country that has rarely experienced unbridled free expression.

Within days of Suharto's exit, new publications were springing to life and journalists were free to say virtually anything without fear of official harassment. Despite the ongoing economic crisis, news vendors clogged streets, feeding a public clamor for information and opinion about the unfolding political drama that had overtaken the country.

But the Suharto system has not yet changed. His resignation left in place not only Suharto's hand-picked deputy and best friend, Bacharuddin Jusuf (B. J.) Habibie, to lead the nation, but also virtually the entire governmental superstructure of privilege, control, and cronyism that had kept Suharto in power.

Although the media have been operating freely, restrictive Suharto-era statutes remain on the books. Still, Habibie amnestied most political prisoners, including Andi Syahputra, a member of the Alliance of Independent Journalists who was imprisoned in 1996 for insulting Suharto in print.

The clearest sign of the new freedom came in October when the government allowed *Tempo*, once Indonesia's premier weekly magazine, to reopen. The Suharto regime had closed *Tempo* in 1994. Goenawan Mohamad, *Tempo*'s founder and chief editor, reassembled a staff of veteran reporters, found the financing, and took the plunge after deciding that Habibie's government was serious about political reform. Sales have exceeded expectations and the *Tempo* group may soon expand into other media. Goenawan, a recipient of CPJ's 1998 International Press Freedom Award, said shortly before the relaunch of the magazine, "The best thing the press can contribute is to develop a culture of transparency and accountability in the government. We hope *Tempo* will become a place that will help defend and expand our freedoms." (See page 66 for information on the International Press Freedom Awards, and page 263 for more information about Goenawan Mohamad and the press in Indonesia.)

Lt. Gen. Mohamad Yunus, appointed by Habibie as Information Minister, has spearheaded press freedom reforms. He has eliminated the requirement that radio and television outlets broadcast hourly government-prepared news bulletins, lifted censorship of foreign publications sold in Indonesia, and ended mandatory membership in the state-sanctioned journalists union. In August, Yunus told a CPJ representative during a meeting in his Jakarta office, "This is my basic point: The people should be the ones to decide. They need information. The more, the better." Despite his reformist agenda, Yunus has also had to spend his time in office denying Australian newspaper reports alleging that he was in command of troops who murdered five Australia-based reporters in the East Timor town of Balibo in 1975.

The sporadic fits of rioting and violent unrest that continued to sweep the country after Suharto's resignation left journalists vulnerable to physical danger. In November, three journalists were badly beaten in Jakarta during student demonstrations, leading to calls for the military to respect the rights of the working press.

March 6
Margiono, *D&R Magazine* THREATENED, LEGAL ACTION
D&R Magazine THREATENED

The government-backed Indonesian Journalists Association (PWI) suspended Margiono, editor in chief of the Jakarta-based *D&R Magazine*, from the association for two years. The decision was made during an emergency meeting ordered by Minister of Information Gen. R. Hartono. PWI claimed that the magazine's March 7 cover photograph satirizing President Suharto violated the Indonesian Journalistic Code of Ethics. The suspension prohibits Margiono from working as a journalist until PWI restores his membership.

Minister Hartono issued a statement saying that Margiono and his magazine will be tried under the Indonesian criminal code for defaming the president. According to news reports, authorities are investigating the allegation and have questioned Margiono and Bambang Bujono, *D&R Magazine*'s managing editor. If convicted of criminal defamation, Margiono and Bujono could each be sentenced to up to seven years in prison. Minister Hartono also threatened to revoke *D&R Magazine*'s publishing license.

CPJ sent a letter to President Suharto on March 12, condemning the suspension of Margiono and expressing concern about the government's reported plans to charge Margiono and *D&R Magazine* with defamation. CPJ decried the use of criminal defamation statutes by government officials to shield themselves from public scrutiny, and urged Suharto to use the influence of his office to reverse the suspension of Margiono and ensure his ability to work as a journalist without fear of reprisal.

With the resignation of President Suharto on May 21, the new Indonesian government of B. J. Habibie eased most restrictions on the press. Margiono did not lose his membership in the PWI, the case against *D&R Magazine* was dropped, and the magazine has continued to publish without further harassment.

March 6
Stephanie Vaesson, NOS LEGAL ACTION, EXPELLED
William Cooper, WTN HARASSED
Gaap Leemeier, NOS HARASSED
Indonesian media worker, HARASSED
Indonesian media worker, HARASSED

Police detained Vaesson, a correspondent for the Dutch radio and television station NOS;

Ibrahim Saleh, a former member of parliament from the armed forces; Vaesson's Indonesian assistant; Leemeier, a Netherlands-based NOS reporter; Cooper, a Jakarta-based World Television News cameraman; and Cooper's Indonesian soundman at the parliament compound for 11 hours on March 6. They were released before midnight.

Vaesson reportedly had led a camera crew—including Cooper and Saleh—planning to film a story with Saleh in the chambers where, 10 years earlier, he had interrupted an assembly plenary session to protest the nomination of Sudharmono to the post of vice president.

The next day, March 7, Akmadsyah Naina, the director of journalistic affairs at the Indonesian Ministry of Information, revoked Vaesson's press credentials and ordered her to leave the country within a week, citing her interference in the People's Consultative Assembly. No sanctions were imposed on the other journalists.

March 10
Ging Ginanjar, SBS Radio IMPRISONED
Adi Hermawan, *Merdeka* IMPRISONED

Ging Ginanjar, a stringer for the Melbourne-based SBS radio station, and Adi Hermawan, a correspondent for the daily *Merdeka*, were arrested at a meeting of a pro-democracy group, the Indonesian People's Congress, that had convened in a Jakarta restaurant to discuss plans to challenge President Suharto's reelection.

Police arrested eight others, including film star Ratna Sarumpaet, and charged the activists with sowing hatred against the government under the subversion law, for which the maximum penalty is death. When Sarumpaet asked to see a warrant for their arrest, the police refused.

Roy Pakpahan, a reporter for *Suara Pembaruan*, witnessed the arrest and detailed the incident in a pretrial hearing.

Although Hermawan was reportedly released from custody after several days, Ginanjar remained in the Jakarta police detention center. At the end of March, Ginanjar tried to file a lawsuit against the police who carried out the arrest but, according to a March 31 report from Indonesia, the court refused to admit any wrongdoing by the police.

On May 21, a North Jakarta District Court found Ginanjar and Sarumpaet guilty of ignoring a police order and sentenced the pair to two months and 10 days in prison, the exact amount of time they had already been detained. Following the sentencing, they were released. The more serious charge of "spreading hatred" was dismissed.

March 18
Allan Nairn, free-lancer EXPELLED

The Indonesian government ordered Nairn, a U.S. journalist and human rights activist, to leave the country. The expulsion followed a news conference at which Nairn reported that the U. S. military was supporting Indonesian repression by training Indonesian troops in violation of a six-year-old congressional ban.

Nairn produced what he claimed was a Pentagon list of dozens of training operations conducted in Indonesia over the past six years. U.S. officials have denied illegal practices in Indonesia, claiming that the training is not covered by the congressional resolution that excludes Indonesian troops from taking part in a U.S. training program for foreign soldiers known as International Military Education and Training or IMET. Nairn also referred to the program in an article he wrote for the March 30 edition of *The Nation*, a New York City-based magazine.

Nairn had long been on the Indonesian government's journalists blacklist for allegedly interfering in internal affairs, especially in relation to East Timor. Akhmadsyah Naina, director of journalism at the Information Ministry, told reporters that Nairn was being deported for entering the country without a journalists visa.

April 17
All Journalists THREATENED, HARASSED, CENSORED

Under the guise of a continuing investigation into a bombing incident that occurred on January 18, military authorities have visited and questioned reporters, editors, and publishers. At least five journalists subsequently went into hiding following visits to their offices by military authorities. Others have been fired or taken off sensitive assignments, while still others have been told by their editors to be careful about the kind of stories they should write.

The January 18 bombing in Tanah Tinggi, Central Jakarta, severely damaged an apartment; the military blamed the incident on the banned Democratic People's Party (PRD). Military authorities claim to have found a list of 28 journalists and news organizations who have been in contact with the PRD on a computer file in the damaged apartment, which was said to have been occupied by the PRD. Surya Paloh, the general manager of the newspaper *Media Indonesia*, was summoned by the military in late January to answer questions about his alleged ties to the PRD. One reporter, Meilani Dhamayanti, was fired by *Media Indonesia* following a January 20 report she wrote on the bombing incident that quoted jailed PRD activist Budiman Soejatmiko disclaiming responsibility for the bombing.

Discussing the allegations against the journalists, the Greater Jakarta military chief, Maj. Gen. Syafrie Syamsuddin, was quoted in an article in *Media Indonesia* in February saying that some independent journalists are a threat to national stability because they "claim to be promoting human rights. But in fact they are violating human rights, because the effect of their activities harms the wider population."

Calls and visits from military investigators have continued at many news outlets. Included on the list of targeted news organizations are the leading newspapers *Bernas*, *Media Indonesia*, *Suara Pembaruan* and *Kompas*. Staffers at the magazines *D&R*, *Panji Masyarakat*, and *Forum Keadilan* have also been questioned.

May 9
Paul Watson, *Toronto Star* EXPELLED

In the course of covering rioting in the city of Medan, Watson, the Asia bureau chief of the *Toronto Star* newspaper, was detained by security personnel on May 6, interrogated for nine hours, and deported to Kuala Lumpur on May 9. Two rolls of film Watson shot of the rioting in Medan were taken from him before he was deported. In his published account of the incident in the *Toronto Star*, Watson said that police officers checked his passport and detained him when they found that he was in Indonesia on a business visa instead of a journalist's visa.

Watson, who is based in Hong Kong, noted that he had visited Indonesia on a similar visa twice in the last four months. He said that he identified himself as a writer at the airport upon his arrival in Indonesia and that immigration authorities had stamped the business visa into his passport. When he was first detained, he gave the police officers his business card.

Watson also said that at least three other journalists had been detained briefly in Medan in the course of covering the rioting. The Cable News Network (CNN) also reported from Medan that soldiers attempted to prevent one of its crews from filming the riots.

May 14
All television stations and journalists CENSORED

Information Minister Alwi Dahlan sent a letter to the country's five private television stations and the state television channel TVRI stating that, in consultation with the commander in chief of the armed forces, Gen. Wiranto, a ban was being placed on all news of riots in the interest of national stability. The letter urged television stations to give priority to news with a "calming" influence. The minister's action followed several days of student demonstrations, during which the killing of six protesters was given widespread coverage in the electronic media.

The new censorship rules required private television stations to filter all coverage of events through the state television channel, TVRI. Beginning on May 16, each station sent a crew to TVRI headquarters in the morning to receive reporting assignments. Each station then edited its segments, and sent them back to TVRI for clearance. The results went into a "TV pool," to be distributed to all stations for morning and afternoon broadcasts.

The system of censorship put a temporary end to critical television news coverage that began around the time of President Suharto's re-election in mid-March. The censorship system was lifted on May 22, the day after Suharto's resignation.

May 16
Sayuti, *Media Indonesia* ATTACKED
Tutang Muchtar, *Sinar* ATTACKED
Riyanto Oemar, *Republika* ATTACKED
Ika Rais, *Pikiran Rakyat* ATTACKED
A.R. Rochim, *Aksi* ATTACKED
Hermansyah Pani, *Surya* THREATENED, HARASSED
Munawar Mandailing, Antara ATTACKED
Hindayoen Nts, *Kompas* ATTACKED
Edi Romadhon, *Kedaulatan Rakyat* ATTACKED
Yuyung Abdi, *Jawa Pos* ATTACKED

In the weeks leading up to the resignation of President Suharto on May 21, attacks against journalists escalated along with the pace and intensity of public protests against the government.

Journalists who were injured in these attacks include:

Sayuti, a photographer for the Jakarta newspaper *Media Indonesia*, was shot in the chest while photographing security forces firing on a crowd in Tanah Abang, Central Jakarta. He was hospitalized.

Muchtar, a photographer for the Jakarta news weekly *Sinar*, was beaten by eight members of the security apparatus while covering a student demonstration at the Rawamangun Teacher Training Institute in Jakarta. Although he showed his attackers his journalist identification card, they beat him and seized his camera.

Oemar, a reporter for the Jakarta newspaper *Republika*, suffered serious injuries when anti-riot police beat him while he was covering a demonstration in Bandung.

Rais, a reporter with the Bandung newspaper *Pikiran Rakyat*, suffered bruises on his arm after security personnel beat and temporarily detained him.

Rochim, a reporter for the weekly Jakarta paper *Aksi*, was threatened with a pistol, and suffered serious injuries when security forces beat him.

Pani, a journalist for the Surabaya newspaper *Surya*, was threatened by anti-riot police while covering a student demonstration in Mataram, Lombok.

Mandailing, a senior reporter at the Medan, Sumatra, bureau of Antara, the official national news agency, was assaulted by security forces outside the entrance to the University of North Sumatra campus. When he showed his journalist identification card, security guards seized it and ripped it up. He was subsequently detained at a police center in Medan and had to be hospitalized for several days for his injuries.

Nts, a photographer for the Jakarta newspaper *Kompas*, and Romadhon, a photographer for the Yogyakarta newspaper *Kedaulatan Rakyat*, were beaten by security forces while taking photographs at a student demonstration at General Soedirman University in Purwokerto, Java.

Abdi, a photographer at the Surabaya newspaper *Jawa Pos*, was kicked by motorcycle troops while photographing a protest in front of the local parliament building in Surabaya.

September 30
Rudy Goenawan, *Jakarta-Jakarta*
LEGAL ACTION

Goenawan, a reporter with *Jakarta-Jarkata* magazine, was summoned to appear at police headquarters in connection with a criminal investigation into a story he wrote in issue Number 609 of *Jakarta-Jakarta*, published in July. His story cited an allegation that a Chinese woman, known only as Vivian, was raped by a group of men who told her, "You must be raped because you are Chinese." According to the story, the quote originated in Internet reports on the May riots. The same statement was printed in a June 10 story in *The New York Times* and was circulated in other media in Jakarta.

On August 12, a group of 22 Muslim organizations, reportedly led by the influential Indonesian Committee for World Muslim Solidarity (KISDI), complained to Jakarta police chief Maj. Gen. Noegroho Djajoesman, that the story insulted the Moslem people of Indonesia. The group urged criminal action against Goenawan and *Jakarta-Jakarta* under Article 156 of the penal code, which prohibits defaming a religious group. This colonial era law carries a maximum penalty of five years in prison and was used frequently during the Suharto era to prosecute journalists. By issuing a summons for Goenawan, the police took the first step toward prosecuting the reporter.

The Alliance of Independent Journalists in Jakarta called on the police not to prosecute the case.

CPJ wrote to President B. J. Habibie to raise the concern that the use of such laws can have a chilling effect on freedom of expression. CPJ noted Indonesia's impressive strides toward a free press since the May resignation of President Suharto, but noted that laws remain on the books which can be used to prosecute journalists for libel- and defamation-related offenses that most democratic states would handle in civil, rather than criminal, court.

CPJ further urged Habibie to use his influence to stop the prosecution of Goenawan and to ask the parties to this dispute to settle their difference in civil court.

November 10
John Stackhouse, *Toronto Globe and Mail*
EXPELLED

On November 10, Stackhouse, a correspondent with the *Toronto Globe and Mail* newspaper based in New Delhi, was deported from Jakarta's Sukarno Hatta Airport shortly after his arrival. He was told by a customs and immigration official that his name was on a blacklist of journalists compiled by the Indonesian armed forces. The Canadian embassy was subsequently told that Stackhouse had been blacklisted because of articles he had written about East Timor in 1997 and that he would not be permitted to enter Indonesia at least until the end of 1998. At the time of the incident, Stackhouse held a valid journalist's visa issued by the Indonesian embassy in New Delhi.

The scrutiny of journalists' work, the compiling of blacklists by the armed forces, and the requirement that journalists obtain special visas are reminiscent of the restrictive and repressive policies carried out by the Suharto government. It was a common practice under Suharto to deport foreign journalists who displeased the regime and to use visa requirements to prevent some reporters from covering events in Indonesia.

The requirement that journalists carry a special visa is inconsistent with democratic practices. Currently, most visitors, be they tourists or businesspeople, are granted visas automatically upon arrival in Indonesia. In other democratic countries in Southeast Asia, such as the Philippines and Thailand, no special visa is required for visiting journalists, and harassment of foreign correspondents is rare.

CPJ wrote to President B. J. Habibie, urging him to lift the expulsion order on John Stackhouse immediately and allow him to report from Indonesia. CPJ also asked that Indonesia review its visa policies for journalists and bring them in line with the democratic practices of neighboring countries.

November 11
Saptono, Antara News Agency ATTACKED
Eddi Hasby, *Kompas* ATTACKED
Tatan Agus, *Gatra Magazine* ATTACKED
Bambang Wisudo, *Kompas* ATTACKED

Saptono, a photographer with the official Antara News Agency, was attacked while documenting an incident in which a student drove into a group of soldiers near the parliament building during a large protest demonstration. Although Saptono identified himself as a journalist, security forces seized his camera and dragged him along the street. He suffered a broken leg and other injuries, and was hospitalized in serious condition. "I saw one female student trampled on the head by a soldier. Then suddenly they beat me, though I told them I was a newsman," said Saptono after the attack.

Two other photographers working at the scene, Hasby of the daily newspaper *Kompas* and Agus of *Gatra Magazine*, attempted to assist Saptono but were also beaten, though not as severely. Wisudo, a reporter for *Kompas*, was beaten by soldiers and fled the scene.

In the aftermath of the attacks, more than 200 journalists representing most major Indonesian news organizations gathered at the parliament building to protest the treatment of their colleagues and demand an apology from the government. The Alliance of Independent Journalists (AJI) in Jakarta issued a statement protesting the attack and calling on police and soldiers to respect the rights of the working press. "The violent treatment of journalists is clearly a criminal act and a blatant violation of the security forces' duty to protect society," the AJI statement said. "The security forces should also protect journalists engaged in their profession."

CPJ called on President B. J. Habibie to investigate the attack and to hold the perpetrators accountable for their actions. CPJ also urged Habibie to issue immediate instructions to police and soldiers responsible for maintaining order during demonstrations to respect the right of journalists to do their job without interference.

Macau

When Macau reverts to Chinese rule in December 1999 after 400 years as a Portuguese colony, it will become the latest experiment in the policy of "One Country, Two Systems" under which Hong Kong is now governed and which China hopes to impose on Taiwan.

A gambling enclave at the mouth of China's Pearl River with a population of 450,000, Macau is tiny, but it has lucrative casinos and large foreign currency reserves that have helped fuel a crime wave in recent years. Macau's essentially free media have frequently probed allegations that its loosely regulated financial sector has been a haven for money-laundering activities by corrupt Chinese gangsters, shady Portuguese officials, and mainland business executives.

As gambling revenue has decreased during the Asian economic crisis and uncertainty about the future under Beijing has grown, the organized crime syndicates known as "triads"—notorious for their historic role in the many vices of Macau—have escalated their violent competition. There were 24 triad-related killings in Macau during the year, and numerous bombings and arson attacks.

The violence has also affected journalists. A bomb planted in a motorcycle in September injured 10 journalists and four policemen who had been lured to the site by another blast just minutes earlier. Police said the attack may have been an attempt to frighten the press away from aggressive coverage of the gangs.

The criminal terror and relatively permissive legal climate under Portugal has led many observers to believe that Macau will lose much of its separate identity when China takes over. Residents may simply be relieved to have a strong power replace the weak and often corrupt Portuguese administration. A "basic law," similar to the one that governs Hong Kong, is set to provide the legal foundation for the transition, but it is unclear whether it will guarantee Macau's relative autonomy after China takes over.

September 8
Maria Cheang Ut-ming, TVB ATTACKED
Leung Wing-kuen, *Oriental Daily News* ATTACKED
Eight journalists ATTACKED

A bomb placed inside a motorcycle exploded in Macau early in the morning, injuring 10 journalists and four policemen who had been drawn to the site to investigate an earlier blast. Police sources were quoted in news reports saying that the second bomb may have been triggered by remote control.

The incident followed a string of bombings in Macau, but was the first that may have specifically targeted journalists. The 10 injured journalists all worked for television stations and newspapers in Hong Kong or Macau. Police described the attack as a "two-pronged act of organized crime intimidation against police and journalists." None of the journalists' injuries was reported to be life-threatening.

In recent years, violence has escalated in Macau, apparently as a result of so-called "triad" crime syndicates competing over gambling revenues. Macau Judiciary Police spokesman Man Hao blamed the syndicates for the incident, telling reporters, "They were trying to hit two targets. One was the police and the other the press. The police because of the work we have been doing and the files we have lodged in court against them. The press because it is their responsibility to report the truth which can damage the [triad] societies."

The Macau Journalists' Union denounced the violence and urged the police and government authorities to investigate the incident quickly and thoroughly. In a letter to Gov. Gen. Vasco Rocha Vieira, CPJ called on the Macau government to do everything within its power to see that the perpetrators of the crime are brought to justice as soon as possible.

In response, the governor general's office wrote to CPJ on September 9 with assurances that an investigation was underway.

Malaysia

With all major media outlets owned or controlled by Prime Minister Mahathir Mohamad's ruling coalition, it was relatively easy for him to manage the flow of mainstream domestic news coverage when he launched a campaign in September to oust his deputy prime minister turned political reformer and rival, Anwar Ibrahim. The forced resignations in July of three pro-Anwar editors—two from major national newspapers and one from a television station—signaled the beginning of the process leading to Anwar's arrest and trial on sexual misconduct charges.

But Mahathir had not reckoned with the depth of public sentiment against his regime and in favor of "reformasi," the catch-all slogan for political change that started in neighboring Indonesia and soon spread to Malaysia. Almost overnight, Internet sites sprouted to variously spread news and information about the Anwar case and coordinate the largest anti-government demonstrations in 30 years.

In Kuala Lumpur, many journalists walked off the job at mainstream newspapers rather than face the kind of mandatory self-censorship that prevailed after Anwar's arrest. Sales of major newspapers reportedly declined following the arrest, and there were informal reader boycotts to protest perceived pro-government coverage of the case, especially in English and Malay-language papers. In one particularly telling anecdote, a senior editor at the *New Straits Times*, the leading English-language daily newspaper, told CPJ that even her family was bitterly divided by the press coverage of Anwar. "My own father won't read my paper," she said, "because he is angry about our [pro-Mahathir] coverage."

As a result of the pro-government bias in the mainstream press, the readership of opposition newspapers skyrocketed. The circulation of *Harakah*, the official publication of a small opposition Islamic political party, grew from 60,000 before Anwar's arrest to almost 300,000 in just weeks when the paper's editors began devoting major coverage to Anwar and the reform movement. As a result, Malaysia's ubiquitous Special Branch intelligence police summoned the editor for questioning and tried to force the paper to sell copies only to party members.

In Malaysia's cautious multiracial political environment, one of the government's chief preoccupations is controlling the reading and viewing habits of the ethnic Malay majority, while leaving the minority Chinese and Indian populations comparatively less constrained. Thus Chinese-language newspapers are freer to report on anti-government viewpoints, and those papers also saw their circulation climb during the crisis.

In a country long hostile to the foreign news media, there were a number of troubling incidents. British television news crews were blocked for several hours from transmitting footage of pro-Anwar demonstrations by satellite in September, and the government threatened to censor Australian television news reports from the annual meeting of the Asia Pacific Economic Cooperation forum held in Kuala Lumpur this year.

July 14
Johan Jaafar, *Utusan Malaysia* HARASSED

Jaafar, who oversees the leading Malay-language daily newspaper *Utusan Malaysia*, was pressured to resign his post by the ruling United Malays National Organization (UMNO), according to news reports and CPJ sources. He submitted his resignation on July 14.

Malaysian journalists say that recent reports in *Utusan Malaysia* and other media have proven embarrassing to some UMNO party leaders. For example, prominent coverage was given to severe operational problems at Malaysia's new airport. And the newspaper is perceived to have sided with Deputy Prime Minister Anwar Ibrahim in its coverage of intraparty struggles over political and economic reform, especially charges of cronyism and nepotism which surfaced in advance of last month's UMNO party congress.

The newspaper is part of the Utusan Melayu (Malaysia) Bhd. group, whose stock is largely owned by UMNO. Anwar made Jaafar editor in chief of the group in 1992.

Following Jaafar's resignation, CPJ wrote a letter to Prime Minister Mahathir Mohamad, expressing alarm over the resignation and its portent of an impending crackdown on the local press.

July 19
Ahmad Nazri Abdullah, *Berita Harian* HARASSED

Nazri, the chief editor of the Malay-language *Berita Harian*, Malaysia's largest newspaper, resigned his post, apparently over conflicts with the government. The resignation took effect immediately.

Berita Harian is owned by New Straits Times Press. That company is controlled by the ruling United Malays National Organization (UMNO), which is headed by Prime Minister Mahathir Mohamad. Nazri is an ally of Deputy Prime Minister Anwar Ibrahim, who is locked in a political battle with Mahathir.

Four days earlier, on July 15, Johan Jaafar, editor in chief of the daily *Utusan Malaysia*, also resigned. Both newspapers had been backing a bid by Anwar to raise questions of corruption and nepotism within UMNO.

Malaysian journalists have said they feared that a broader crackdown on the press could follow these resignations.

July 22
All journalists THREATENED

In the aftermath of the resignations of two top editors from leading daily newspapers, Malaysian officials demanded loyalty from journalists.

"It is important that the stewardship of the national economy of the honorable prime minister be accepted without any further speculation," said Daim Zainuddin, minister of special functions and a leading adviser to Prime Minister Mahathir Mohamad, on July 22.

One day earlier, the information ministry advocated self-censorship during the economic crisis and avoiding "derogatory stories" by the foreign press.

"The Malaysian media should not collaborate with foreign reporters by exchanging information," Shafie Apdal, a top Information Ministry official, was quoted as saying by the domestic news agency, Bernama.

On July 14, Johan Jaafar, who oversees the leading Malay-language daily newspaper *Utusan Malaysia*, was pressured to resign his post by the ruling United Malays National Organization (UMNO), according to news reports and CPJ sources. Five days later, Ahmad Nazri Abdullah, the editor of the country's other leading Malay-language daily, *Berita Harian*, was also pressured to resign.

Both editors were allies of Deputy Prime Minister Anwar Ibrahim, who had been calling for an end to corruption and nepotism inside the ruling party.

Journalists in Malaysia have expressed fears that the recent statements and resignations could herald a crackdown on the press. The press in Malaysia is strictly licensed by the government, and most major news outlets are controlled by the ruling UMNO party, of which Mahathir is president.

August 9
All journalists THREATENED

Information Minister Mohamed Rahmat announced plans to impose new rules and restrictions that will allow the government to more closely monitor the movements of foreign journalists in the country.

Foreign journalists working in Malaysia are already required to register with the Home Ministry in order to obtain a work permit. They also must provide the information ministry with details about their personal and professional background, as well as information about their employer, before obtaining a press pass. While Rahmat did not reveal the specifics of his proposal, he did threaten that "If there is negative and bad news, we will then know who is responsible…so that we can resolve any problems that arise."

CPJ wrote to Prime Minister Mahathir Mohamad, protesting the Information Minister's statements. The letter also noted the recent resignations of two top editors, both under pressure from the country's political leadership, and pointed to threats by the deputy information minister to "come down hard" on journalists who "threaten political stability or national unity" as evidence of the increasingly hostile relationship between the government and the press.

October 5
All journalists THREATENED

The New Straits Times, Malaysia's most influential English-language newspaper, ran a signed editorial urging the government to crack down on foreign reporters and publications. The editorial suggested that foreign reporters were pursuing a political agenda designed to harm Malaysia.

The paper, which is controlled by the ruling United Malays National Organization, ran two editorials on October 5 and 6 recommending that government authorities follow the lead of Singapore and get tough on foreign journalists.

"It is time Malaysia adopts a hard stand on irresponsible foreign media, especially those that insist on peddling mass disinformation and sensationalism instead of reporting accurately and in an impartial manner," wrote Abdullah Tan on the daily's editorial page on October 5.

Both editorials accused foreign reporters of siding with former deputy prime minister Anwar Ibrahim, whose dismissal and subsequent arrest on September 2 under the repressive Internal Security Act (ISA) sparked widespread protests in Malaysia and condemnation abroad.

"We would urge the Malaysian government to adopt Singapore-style 'hardball' tactics with the press where errant media companies and their reporters will be sued, have their circulation banned or restricted and errant reporters detained under the ISA," wrote Tan on October 6.

The October 5 commentary singled out the *Asian Wall Street Journal*, *Time Magazine*, the *Far Eastern Economic Review*, and the cable television channel CNBC for specific criticism. Media observers are taking the threats seriously, especially in light of Prime Minister Mahathir Mohamad's recent crackdown on his political opponents.

The editorial is widely believed to represent official sentiment, because "Abdullah Tan" is almost certainly a pen name, according to Malaysian journalists, and has never been seen in print before.

In a letter to the paper, Urban C. Lehner, the publisher and executive editor of *The Asian Wall Street Journal*, denied that his paper was pursuing any political agenda in Malaysia.

Nepal

Prime Minister Girija Prasad Koirala, who by year's end held a tenuous grip on power, had a mixed record in his dealings with the media. Koirala has repeatedly voiced his support for a free press, and even emphasized the role of journalists as educators central to the democratic project. Nevertheless, his administration has shown little tolerance for the open exchange of news and opinion on the Maoist insurgency that continues to threaten Nepal's stability.

When Koirala took office in April, he pledged to restore "law and order." The government's crackdown on Maoist rebels includes censorship and harassment of the press. Although the Home Minister has denied any knowledge of a campaign to censor news of the conflict, police in several cities prevented the distribution of newspapers containing details of fighting between government and rebel forces.

Despite constitutional guarantees of press freedom, the 1989 Anti-State Crimes and Penalties Act criminalizes dissemination of information deemed harmful to state interests. Some journalists complain that reporting on guerrilla activities leaves one vulnerable to harassment and violent intimidation by both government forces and Maoist insurgents.

Nepal is one of the poorest countries in the world, and nearly 80 percent of its population lives in the countryside. The print media thus face the daunting challenges of distributing papers across extraordinarily rough terrain and of building circulation among a cash-strapped and largely illiterate public. In this environment, radio remains the most effective medium.

The government has begun to grant licenses to a handful of private FM radio stations. Although most stations broadcast music and entertainment, one station, Radio Sagarmatha, has emerged as a model for news and public affairs broadcasting in South Asia. Radio Sagarmatha, a community station, receives funding from international organizations, and works cooperatively with local groups such as the Nepal Forum for Environmental Journalists, the Nepal Press Institute, and Worldview Nepal. It has managed to skirt a ban on broadcasting independent news with a news analysis program that reviews newspaper stories.

June 9
Ajko Samacharpatra CENSORED
Jana Ekta CENSORED
Jadanesh CENSORED
Janahwan CENSORED
Yojana CENSORED
Jana Bhawana CENSORED

Since June 9, local police in districts where there has been some support for the Maoist movement have been confiscating newspapers to block the distribution of any information about rebel activities. The daily *Ajko Samacharpatra* and weeklies *Jadanesh*, *Janahwan*, *Yojana*, *Jana Ekta*, and *Jana Bhawana*—all published in Kathmandu—were seized by police in Sindhulimadhi. Similar seizures were reported in Gorkha, Sindhuli, Rukum, Salyan, Tanahun, Dhading, and Jajarkot.

On July 2, police in Kathmandu instructed transport firms not to deliver newspapers containing articles on the government's operations against Maoist rebels, and burned those copies of the offending papers that had already been loaded onto trucks and buses.

There is widespread suspicion in Nepal that, far from being isolated incidents, these actions were directed by the Home Ministry as part of a strategy to contain the rebel movement. *The People's Review*, a political and business weekly published in Kathmandu, reported that journalists in Nepal are currently facing harassment and violent intimidation by both government forces and Maoist insurgents.

CPJ sent a letter to the Nepalese government on July 6, expressing deep concern that the government's recent crackdown on Maoist rebels had apparently expanded to include censorship and harassment of the local press.

August 17
K.P. Gautam, *Gorkhapatra* LEGAL ACTION
Uddhav Upadhyay, *Gorkhapatra* LEGAL ACTION
Shiva Adhikari, *Gorkhapatra* LEGAL ACTION

A district court judge held the Nepali-language daily *Gorkhapatra* in contempt of court. A lawyer employed by the district court brought charges against the paper for publishing a June 18 article Gautam had written about judicial corruption.

Gautam, a correspondent for the paper, was given the option of apologizing for the article or spending five days in jail. The judge also fined Upadhyay, *Gorkhapatra*'s chief editor, and Adhikari, the paper's executive chairman when the article was published, 500 Nepalese rupees (US$8) each.

The story was titled "Judges Absorb the Salaries of Their Lowest Staff." Gautam had based the article on a report issued by the Auditor General, which had been discussed at a meeting held by the Public Accounts Committee of the House of Representatives. Ishwar Prasad Khatiwada, the judge who ruled against Gautam in the contempt case, was one of those accused in the report of drawing excess wages.

The *Gorkhapatra* management appealed the

case, which was heard on December 23. As we went to press, the judge had not yet delivered a verdict.

North Korea

On the 50th anniversary of its founding in September, North Korea officially declared Marshal Kim Jong Il as its "Great Leader," symbolically lifting him to the position held by his father, Kim Il Sung, the founder of North Korea, who died in 1994. Little is likely to change as a result, however, as the younger Kim had already been running the country since the death of the patriarch. Kim the Elder is revered as a deity, a fact symbolized by a constitutional amendment passed this year proclaiming him to be the nation's "Eternal President."

Kim Jong Il presides over a nation with no independent press and a population kept in isolation from news of the outside world. Information about North Korea is extremely difficult to obtain. The handful of foreign journalists allowed to visit are kept on a very tight leash by government minders, and the few North Korean websites offer a highly filtered view of the country, mostly proclaiming the triumphs of socialism and the evils of capitalist South Korea, with whom the North is in a perpetual state of war.

Occasionally, the tightly controlled press provides a note of inadvertent comic relief. The official Korean Central News Agency informed its readers in June that Korean military leaders invented a flying car 400 years ago and used it to combat enemies. According to Master O Myong Ho, a researcher at the History Institute of the Academy of Social Sciences, the flying car, equipped with "flexible wings" and "jet propulsion," repelled Japanese aggressors in 1592.

Attacks on the Press in 1998

Pakistan

As he faced the various crises besetting his administration, Prime Minister Mohammad Nawaz Sharif displayed a distinct tendency toward authoritarianism. The government's extreme sensitivity to criticism had troubling implications for the press, which was also vulnerable to attacks from militant groups.

When Pakistan responded to neighboring India's nuclear tests with its own series of blasts at the end of May, the economic fallout was devastating. International sanctions imposed against the country for daring to push its way into the nuclear club led to a $32 billion debt burden, a radically devalued currency, and steep price hikes on most basic commodities. In an effort to minimize social disorder, Sharif declared a national state of emergency on the day after the tests were launched and suspended constitutionally established rights—including the freedoms of expression and association—along with guarantees regarding arbitrary arrest and detention. In June, a joint session of parliament approved the declaration and provided for its enforcement for up to six months. Although Pakistan's Supreme Court restored civil liberties in July, it upheld the emergency decree.

In November, in response to factional violence that claimed the lives of more than 1,000 people in Karachi, the capital of Sindh Province and the commercial heart of Pakistan, the prime minister announced a state of emergency in Sindh. Sectarian violence in Sindh Province posed dangers for the press, with an especially ominous bombing in July directed against the Karachi newspaper *Dawn*, the country's most widely circulated English-language daily.

During the year, the government embarked on a systematic campaign of harassment to punish news organizations that challenged the administration. Among the hardest hit was the Jang Group of Newspapers, Pakistan's largest newspaper publishing company.

Also disturbing was the prime minister's push for a 15th amendment to the Constitution—the so-called Shariat Bill—which would give the federal government greater power to establish Islamic law in Pakistan. Journalists and human rights activists pointed out that Pakistan is already an Islamic state, and saw the amendment as an attempt by the administration to establish a dictatorship under the cloak of religion. Although the bill was languishing in the senate at year's end, some in Pakistan worried that Sharif's moves gave confidence to religious extremists, some of whom have threatened journalists for what they regard as anti-Islamic writings.

July 1
Jang Group of Newspapers HARASSED
Maleeha Lodhi, *The News* THREATENED
Kamran Khan, *The News* THREATENED
Kamila Hyat, *The News* THREATENED
Marianna Babar, *The News* THREATENED
Kaleem Omar, *The News* THREATENED
Beena Sarwar, *The News on Sunday* THREATENED
Irshad Ahmed Haqqani, *Jang* THREATENED
Mahmood Sham, *Jang* THREATENED
Sohail Wariach, *Jang* THREATENED
Nasir Beg Chughtai, *Jang* THREATENED
Mudassir Mirza, *Jang* THREATENED
Khawar Naeem Hashmi, *Jang* THREATENED
Sohaib Marghob, *Jang Sunday Magazine* THREATENED
Abid Tahimi, *Jang Sunday Magazine* THREATENED
Sajjad Anwar, *Jang Sunday Magazine* THREATENED
Mir Shakil-ur-Rahman, Jang Group of Newspapers HARASSED, LEGAL ACTION

In July, Sen. Saifur Rahman, an adviser to Prime Minister Mohammad Nawaz Sharif, met with Mir Shakil-ur-Rahman, publisher and editor in chief of the Jang Group of Newspapers, to demand the dismissal of a number of senior journalists who had written critically about the administration. Among those on the government's blacklist were: Lodhi, editor of *The News* (Rawalpindi); Haqqani, editor of *Jang* (Lahore); Khan, investigative editor of *The News* (Karachi); Marghob, editor of *Jang Sunday Magazine* (Lahore); Tahimi, feature editor of *Jang Magazine* (Lahore); Sham, editor of *Jang* (Karachi); Hyat, editor of *The News* (Lahore); Babar, a special correspondent for *The News* (Rawalpindi); Omar, a writer for *The News* (Karachi); Wariach, a senior assistant editor for *Jang* (Lahore); Sarwar, editor of *The News on Sunday* (Lahore); Chughtai, chief news editor of *Jang* (Karachi); Mirza, news editor of *Jang* (Karachi); Hashmi, chief news editor of *Jang* (Lahore); and Anwar, editor of *Jang Magazine* (Rawalpindi).

Sen. Rahman, head of the government's Ehtesab (Accountability) Bureau, established by the Sharif administration to investigate corruption charges against the previous government—warned Shakil-ur-Rahman that the Sharif administration was losing patience with the Jang Group, and would take action against the company if the demand to remove the journalists was not met.

The Jang Group is Pakistan's largest newspaper company, and publishes two of the country's most widely read papers: the daily Urdu-language *Jang* newspaper and *The News*, an English-language daily.

On August 27, Shakil-ur-Rahman held a press conference condemning the government's attempts to control his papers. He refused to make the staff changes, but by year's end several of the journalists targeted by the government were nevertheless silent on politically sensitive topics.

In October, the government served the Jang Group with tax notices totaling more than 720 million rupees (about US$13 million). Although the Income Tax Appellate Court stalled collection of these taxes pending a review of the claim's merits, employees of the Jang Group reported continued harassment by authorities.

On December 17, the income tax department filed a case against Shakil-ur-Rahman before a Karachi judge, charging the publisher with tax evasion for failing to properly declare an inheritance he had received more than six years ago. Journalists in Pakistan report that those in power have long used the country's tax code to punish those who oppose the government.

On December 14, the Jang Group published a story about a financial scandal involving the Sharif family's Ittefaq Group of Companies. Shakil-ur-Rahman said that the government applied intense pressure on him not to print the offending article, which ran prominently in both *Jang* and *The News*. The day the story was published, officers of Pakistan's Federal Investigation Agency (FIA) raided the Jang Group's Rawalpindi bureau. The FIA officers spent hours questioning newspaper staff, demanding to check *Jang*'s actual stock of newsprint against the company's records.

On December 15, CPJ sent a letter to Prime Minister Sharif, condemning the campaign against the Jang Group.

July 9
Dawn ATTACKED

Two bombs exploded within minutes of each other at the Karachi office of *Dawn*, the country's most widely circulated English-language daily. The first blast, at 12:40 p.m., came from a bomb that had been placed under a car parked outside the gates of *Dawn*'s headquarters. The second bomb went off at 1:05 p.m. in a restroom located on the first floor. Three passersby were injured by the car bomb, according to *Dawn*.

While police have said that there is no evidence linking the two attacks, Pakistan Herald Publications (Pvt) Ltd., publishers of the Dawn Group of Newspapers, issued a statement saying: "It is clear that the intention of the blasts was to send a direct warning from the political or terrorist forces to the journalists of *Dawn*, *Herald*, and *The Star* to desist from pursuance of independent editorial policies and from critical comment on the situation in the country."

According to *Dawn*, there have been 12 bombings in Karachi since February, all of which remain unsolved. In June alone, the Agence France-Presse reported more than 200 dead as a result of factional violence in the city.

On July 10, CPJ wrote a letter to Prime Minister Mohammad Nawaz Sharif, joining *Dawn*, the All Pakistan Newspaper Society, and the Pakistan Press Foundation in condemning the attack and calling for a thorough government investigation into the incident.

July 19
Ansar Naqvi, *The News* ATTACKED, HARASSED
M.H. Khan, *Dawn* ATTACKED, HARASSED

Assistant Sub-Inspector Saalim Rind stopped two journalists returning from the Phulleli police station, where they had gone to report on a story, and proceeded to attack them without apparent provocation.

The two journalists—Naqvi, Hyderabad bureau chief for *The News*, and Khan, a correspondent for the English-language daily *Dawn*—were asked to stop their motorcycle at Rind's checkpoint and ordered to produce identification. They were then beaten severely and thrown into a police vehicle. Rind reportedly instructed his subordinate at the checkpoint to deflate the tires of the journalists' motorbike and, when one of the reporters objected, said, "Don't teach me. I know how to deal with pressmen, and you can't hang me."

Police authorities have temporarily suspended Rind from the force, and Sub-Divisional Magistrate Suhail Rajput has ordered an inquiry into this attack. CPJ sources in Hyderabad report that Rind has a reputation for harassing journalists.

On July 20, CPJ sent a letter of inquiry to the chief minister of Sindh Province, urging him to ensure that an investigation is undertaken, and that Rind is punished if found guilty of the attack.

September 3
Zafaryab Ahmed, free-lancer HARASSED, LEGAL ACTION

The Lahore High Court ruled that it did not have the power to rule on a writ petition filed by Ahmed, a free-lance writer and human rights activist, in which he requested that his name be removed from Pakistan's Exit Control List. Inclusion on the list prevented Ahmed from traveling abroad. He was seeking permission to travel to the United States to accept a human rights fellowship at Colby College in Maine.

Ahmed had been barred from leaving Pakistan since June 1995, when he was arrested by the Federal Investigation Agency (FIA) on charges of sedition. The action came in response to his reporting. For years, Ahmed had written about child labor for such publications as the weekly magazine *Viewpoint*, and the newspapers *Frontier Post* and *The News*. The FIA accused him of collaborating with Indian intelligence agents to "exploit the murder of Iqbal Masih," a 12-year-old Pakistani boy who had received international recognition for speaking about inhumane conditions he suffered while working in a carpet factory.

The FIA's report on the charges against Ahmed states that his work to expose child labor abuses was divisive and paved the way for "economic warfare between India and Pakistan."

Ahmed was released on interim bail on health grounds on July 20, 1995, and ultimately secured permanent bail in November 1997. As of September 1998, the FIA had not presented its case against Ahmed in court, yet the sedition charges still made it impossible for him to leave the country.

On September 9, CPJ wrote to Prime Minister Mohammad Nawaz Sharif, requesting the dismissal of the charges against Ahmed, and asking that he be allowed to travel to the United States to accept the Colby College fellowship.

On December 2, the Interior Ministry issued a notice granting Ahmed the right to leave the country for 90 days, on the condition that he would then return to Pakistan. He arrived at Colby on December 15.

September 23
Saeed Iqbal Hashmi, *Mashriq* THREATENED
Ayaz Ali Shah, *Mashriq* THREATENED
Qaiser Butt, *Mashriq* THREATENED

Followers of the Jamiat Ulema-i-Islam (JUI) party, an organization that has called for an Islamic revolution in Pakistan, held a demonstration in Peshawar to denounce those responsible for publishing an article on the sexual harassment of minors that had appeared in the local Urdu-language daily *Mashriq*. Protesters displayed placards calling for the murder of Hashmi, the reporter who wrote the story, Shah, *Mashriq*'s chief editor, and Butt, an editor at the paper. After local ulema, or religious scholars, issued fatwas sentencing all three men to death, Hashmi went into hiding for two weeks.

Area religious leaders had been angered by Hashmi's feature on "Sexual Harassment of Children: A Serious Social Problem," which ran in *Mashriq*'s September 14 issue. The piece used statistics gathered from various NGOs to explain that sexual abuse of children commonly occurred in homes, schools, and even religious institutions. JUI leaders were outraged by this last charge, saying it was a blatant attempt to defame religious schools. (JUI runs several large madrassas, or religious schools, in the Northwest Frontier Province, which send many of their students to fight alongside the Taliban in neighboring Afghanistan.)

Journalists unions attempted to intervene with the JUI, but could not persuade the party to change its position. The week after the first

Attacks on the Press in 1998

demonstration, another protest was held, during which madrassa students burned copies of *Mashriq* and called for a boycott of the paper. Local clergy also led a drive to ban the paper in parts of the province.

Some local journalists believed that the JUI was exploiting the issue in retaliation for an earlier *Mashriq* story about the destruction of one of Peshawar's historic city walls to accommodate the construction of a new plaza owned by JUI leader Haji Ghulam Ali.

October 1
Newsline HARASSED

Plainclothes officers from Pakistan's Special Branch raided the Karachi office of the magazine *Newsline*, an English-language monthly run by a journalists' cooperative. The police officers pressed staff to reveal home telephone numbers and addresses of the magazine's editors, finally leaving after hours of fruitless interrogation.

According to Rehana Hakim, *Newsline*'s editor, the administration also ordered tax audits of the magazine and several staff members in apparent retaliation for a spate of recent articles exposing government corruption. Among the magazine's accusations were charges that Prime Minister Mohammad Nawaz Sharif had orchestrated tax deals for family members and friends, including his close aide Sen. Saifur Rahman.

After *Newsline* publicized the Special Branch's raid on their office, friends and family members of senior staff reported receiving intimidating phone calls asking them to disclose their home addresses.

CPJ sent a letter to Prime Minister Sharif on December 15, condemning the government's apparent efforts to intimidate the independent press.

November 26
Idrees Bakhtiar, *Herald*, BBC HARASSED

Police raided the home of Idrees Bakhtiar, chief reporter of the monthly *Herald* magazine and Karachi correspondent for the British Broadcasting Corporation (BBC), at around 1:45 a.m.

Officers from Karachi's Crime Investigation Agency (CIA), Saddar branch, forced open the door to Bakhtiar's home, and about a dozen armed police entered—some ransacking the house, others questioning the journalist and his family members at gunpoint. Police have said they were looking for a suspect in the October murder of Hakim Said, a prominent philanthropist and former governor of Sindh Province whose assassination became a flashpoint for those concerned about the ongoing political violence plaguing Karachi.

Police left the house after 45 minutes, but returned a short while later and took Bakhtiar's 28-year-old son, Moonis, to an armored personnel carrier parked outside. He was again interrogated, and only released at the threat of intervention by the deputy inspector general of police. The officers then left the residence.

The president of the Karachi Union of Journalists, Mazahar Abbas, told Agence France-Presse that the raid on Bakhtiar's home highlights the vulnerability of Karachi journalists to "threats from both police and terrorists." The BBC sent an official letter of complaint to the Interior Ministry on the day of the incident, pointing out that the attack inspires a "fear of further intimidation and harassment."

CPJ wrote to Prime Minister Mohammad Nawaz Sharif on November 30 condemning the police action.

November 28
Naseer Ahmad Saleemi, *Zindagi* HARASSED

Around 2:30 a.m., officers from the Saddar branch of Karachi's Crime Investigation Agency (CIA) forced their way into the home of Naseer Ahmad Saleemi, deputy editor of the Urdu-language weekly *Zindagi* magazine. The officers searched Saleemi's home, and questioned the journalist and his family members about the 1994 murder of a newspaper editor. They took

Saleemi's brother, Bashir Ahmad Saleemi, into custody and brought him to the CIA's Saddar headquarters, where he was detained until Karachi's deputy inspector general of police ordered his release.

This action against Saleemi was almost identical to the November 26 raid on the home of Idrees Bakhtiar, chief reporter of the monthly *Herald* magazine and Karachi correspondent for the British Broadcasting Corporation (BBC).

CPJ referred to the incident at Saleemi's home in a letter to the Pakistani government on November 30, expressing concern that two police raids on the homes of journalists within days of each other sent an alarming signal to the press in Sindh Province.

December 17
Saeed Iqbal Hashmi, *Mashriq*
THREATENED

Two men armed with pistols entered the home of Hashmi, a correspondent for the Urdu-language Peshawar daily *Mashriq*, around dawn. They fled when Hashmi's brother came upon them in the living room. Hashmi's father, returning from morning prayers, also saw the two men, who then fled. They took nothing from Hashmi's home.

Later that day, Hashmi received a telephone call from a person speaking Pashto, who told him that the intruders had left only because they did not want to kill innocent people. He warned Hashmi, "We have sworn on the Holy Koran to kill you. Whenever we get the chance, we will kill you for your enmity with the Islamic government of the Taliban."

Local religious leaders allied with the Taliban were angered by Hashmi's feature on "Sexual Harassment of Children: A Serious Social Problem," which ran in *Mashriq*'s September 14 issue and mentioned that sexual abuse of children commonly occurred in homes, schools, and religious institutions. The Jamiat Ulema-i-Islam (JUI), an Islamist political party that also runs a number of seminaries in and around Peshawar, was outraged by this last charge, saying it was a blatant attempt to defame Islamic schools. Meanwhile, area ulema (religious scholars) issued fatwas sentencing Hashmi and two of his colleagues to death. Following repeated death threats, as well as large-scale demonstrations calling for his assassination, Hashmi went into hiding for two weeks.

Feeling vulnerable after the attack on his home and badly shaken by the prolonged terrorist campaign against him, Hashmi again went into hiding just before the New Year, and planned to leave Pakistan.

Papua New Guinea

The worst drought in 50 years and a debilitating economic crisis combined to keep the pressure on Prime Minister Bill Skate's government. But he did not respond with the kind of punitive moves against the press used by some of his predecessors. Despite his general support for press freedom, Skate returned from visits to Malaysia and China impressed by the favorable treatment their governments receive from a censored press. He suggested establishing a journalists exchange program between China and Papua New Guinea so that local journalists could learn from their Chinese colleagues to be supportive of the government. Local journalists openly ridiculed the idea.

Reporters reacted angrily in August when a local police commander deployed armed police units around a courthouse to bar reporters from attending the trial of a woman accused of videotaping her sexual encounter with a government minister. After vigorous protests from several news

organizations, the trial was opened to the press and police authorities apologized for their action.

The country's two outspoken daily newspapers—the *National*, which is owned by a Malaysian company; and the *Post-Courier*, which is owned by Rupert Murdoch's News Corporation—were the targets of anti-foreign comments from conservative politicians, one of whom, Deputy Prime Minister Michael Nali, threatened to investigate the ownership status of the papers. Since there are no restrictions on foreign ownership of the media, Nali's threats amounted to nothing more than jingoistic bluster.

Philippines

Philippine politics took a comic-opera turn in May when action-movie star and avowed philanderer Joseph Estrada won the presidential election. Former First Lady Imelda Marcos emerged from political oblivion, claiming in December that far from being world-class kleptocrats, she and her late husband had legitimately amassed some $12 billion in assets during their 21 years in power. "We own practically everything in the country," she declared in an interview with *The Philippine Inquirer* newspaper. She has filed suit to try to recover the presumed assets.

In many other countries such shenanigans might be cause for political instability, but in the Philippines, with its rollicking democracy and perhaps the freest press in Asia, a skeptical public has access to dozens of news sources with little government interference. The open public discourse has strengthened the country's democratic institutions.

Since the overthrow of Ferdinand Marcos in 1986, the free press has become

Attacks on the Press in 1998

so well entrenched that many analysts credit it with shielding the country from the worst effects of the Asian economic crisis by making economic information widely available to investors. And despite the economic crisis and shrinking revenues, newspapers are expanding, with some 20 new tabloids opening in the last year and several mainstream dailies adding color pages and new editions in a bid to capture readers.

Along with a free press can come danger, however, and in 1998 outspoken radio commentator Rey Bancayrin was murdered in rural Zamboanga City while he was on the air at station DXLL. Thirty-three journalists have been murdered in the line of duty since the restoration of democracy in 1986. Almost all of the murders are unsolved.

Responding to the ethical challenges of a free press and the need to protect journalists from harm on both a national and a regional basis, Filipino journalists played a leading role in the founding of the Southeast Asian Press Alliance (SEAPA) in Bangkok in November. "We can learn from one another and draw strength from each other throughout Southeast Asia," said Melinda de Jesus, the executive director of the Center for Media Freedom and Responsibility, one of SEAPA's founding organizations. (See page 263 for a special report on SEAPA.)

March 30
Rey Bancayrin, DXLL KILLED

Two unidentified gunmen shot and killed Bancayrin, 34, a well-known commentator for radio station DXLL in the southern region of Mindanao. The assassins entered the DXLL broadcast booth in Zamboanga City and shot him three times at point-blank range, then calmly left the station and escaped, according to police reports.

Bancayrin was known for his outspoken

attacks on local corruption, illegal logging, and drug smugglers. His stinging critiques made him a popular radio personality and an influential voice in Zamboanga City. He was talking to a caller when he was killed.

CPJ believes that Bancayrin may have been targeted for assassination because of his work as a journalist. The Zamboanga press club called his death "a blow to press freedom."

Bancayrin is the 33rd journalist killed in the line of duty in the Philippines since the overthrow of Ferdinand Marcos in 1986. This record is among the worst in the world, despite the relative freedom of the press in the Philippines.

Samoa

In a move emblematic of the deteriorating climate for the press and following on the heels of a 1997 law compelling reporters charged with libel to reveal their sources, the Samoan government announced in May that officials could use public funds to pursue civil libel claims. Such suits, brought by officials vexed by news coverage of corruption and irregularities, have become drearily routine.

In September, the Supreme Court awarded Prime Minister Tofilau Eti Alesana a $40,000 judgment against Savea Sano Malifa, editor and publisher of the *Samoa Observer*—the latest blow to the nation's only daily newspaper. The prime minister had sued the paper for defamation over a 1997 story claiming that public funds were used to upgrade a hotel owned by Tofilau's children in preparation for a visit by Britain's Prince Edward.

After the ruling, Malifa said he may be forced to sell the paper because of mounting legal expenses. In 1994, the paper's printing press was burned down in a mysterious fire, and Malifa and his family have received death threats. Malifa's plight drew international attention in 1998 when he received the Commonwealth Press Union's Astor Award for press freedom.

Other journalists have also faced intimidation in their attempts to report on those in high office. The assistant editor of the weekly Samoan-language newspaper *Samoa Post*, Molesi Taumaoe, reported that Telecommunications Minister Leafa Vitale threatened him with death in May to prevent the newspaper from publishing a letter containing allegations of corruption against the minister.

The government continues to bar opposition politicians from appearing on the island's sole television station, which is state-run.

July 6
Samoa Observer LEGAL ACTION

On July 6, the Samoan Supreme Court found the *Samoa Observer* guilty of civil defamation against Prime Minister Tofilau Eti Alesana, assessing damages at 50,000 tala (approximately US$16,000). The *Observer*'s editor and publisher, Savea Sano Malifa, has told Agence France-Presse (AFP) that he may have to sell the newspaper in order to pay mounting legal debts. Malifa says that his legal fees already total nearly 230,000 tala (about US$76,000), and the paper still faces a separate charge of criminal defamation, which carries a sentence of six months in jail.

The *Samoa Observer*, the country's only independent daily newspaper, has faced a number of lawsuits over the years—many of them stemming from articles exposing government corruption.

On July 15, CPJ sent a letter to Prime Minister Alesana calling on him to end government harassment of the *Samoa Observer*.

In September, the judgment against the *Observer* was increased to US$40,000, including legal costs.

Singapore

Singapore's leaders are caught on the horns of a dilemma. They have acknowledged that the city-state's pliant, if prosperous, population needs to become more creative in order to cope with changes brought about by Singapore's declining manufacturing base. With the economy shrinking for the first time since 1985, the need for innovation is greater than ever. But harsh libel laws, official secrecy, de-facto censorship of the press, and decades of virtual one-party rule have made obedience, not creativity, the norm and authoritarianism a tough habit to break.

Singapore's leaders want their tiny nation to become the Silicon Valley of Southeast Asia. But they must first reconcile this desire with a staid and repressive media climate. The press remains among the most timid in Asia, especially in its coverage of domestic political affairs. Singapore has only three Internet services and one cable television service, all linked to the government. Singapore Press Holdings, a state-run company, controls all the newspapers. Singapore International Media PTE Ltd., another government-linked entity, holds a virtual monopoly on broadcasting.

In February, the government announced that its various censorship offices would be centralized in a new Films and Publications Department (FPD) under the Ministry of Information and the Arts (MITA). The new office was promoted as an efficient "one-stop center" for importers of everything from foreign newspapers and magazines to video tapes, films and computer graphics. The parliament also approved legislation this year amending censorship regulations to ban political parties from making videos or television advertisements and to expand censorship provisions to include new technologies such as compact discs, digital video discs, and electronic mail. Information Minister George Yeo offered cold comfort when he said it was not his intention to snoop into the private lives of people through their e-mail. "It is not our objective to increase the level of censorship in Singapore. Just maintaining the existing level of censorship is difficult enough," he said.

South Korea

Under the leadership of President Kim Dae Jung, the South Korean media are generally freer than at any time in the recent past. He has encouraged criticism of failed economic policies and spoken out forcefully in favor of democratic values. A former political prisoner who was once under a death sentence from a past military government, Kim was a hero to newspaper reporters and editors who frequently risked government sanctions and harassment to campaign for democracy in the late 1980s. In a dramatic demonstration of the turnaround in political fortunes, former dissident reporter Kim Chong-Chol was named president and publisher of Yonhap News, the official government news agency, in June. In 1976, the military government forced him out of his job at the newspaper *Dong-a Ilbo* for advocating press freedom.

Given President Kim's reputation as a champion of democracy, it is especially disturbing that he and his supporters have used existing criminal libel statutes, long a tool of authoritarian governments, against his right-wing opponents. Choi Jang-Jip of Korea University, a close adviser to the president, successfully sued *Monthly Chosun*, a right-wing magazine, for libel when it accused him of being pro-North Korea. A Seoul district court banned the sale and circulation of the magazine for the month of November.

And two conservative journalists were convicted and imprisoned on criminal libel charges brought by Kim's political party, the National Congress for New Politics. Ham Yun Shik, the publisher of *One Way* magazine, was sentenced to one year in prison in July. Son Chung Mu, the publisher of *Inside the World* magazine, was sentenced to two years in prison in October. Both men were accused of having defamed Kim during the election campaign with allegations that he was a communist sympathizer. CPJ appealed to Kim to drop the charges against the two publishers on the grounds that in a democracy libel should be treated as a civil matter and journalists should not be jailed for what they write or publish. The president's office failed to respond to CPJ's appeal.

As South Korea's economy foundered, the structure and performance of the news media have come under increasing scrutiny. Mainstream South Korean news outlets failed to apply a critical eye to economic reporting before the Asian slump, a fact that many analysts say contributed to the crash. "We journalists led them astray," veteran business reporter Sohn Byoung Soo said of his readers in an interview with the *Far Eastern Economic Review* in November. "We were guilty of printing government statements without checking the facts." Politically powerful families and massive conglomerates control the mainstream media, and some reporters say they have been discouraged from digging deeply into economic mismanagement issues which might displease their bosses. A nonprofit watchdog group, the Citizen's Coalition for Media Reform, headed by Kim Joong Bae, a well-known journalist, was established in September to monitor ethical practices and examine the structure of media ownership.

February 28
Ham Yun Shik, *One Way* IMPRISONED

Ham, publisher of *One Way* magazine, was charged with criminal defamation by President Kim Dae Jung's political party under Chapter 33, Article 309 of the South Korean criminal code ("Crimes Against Reputation"). The charges had been brought by the National Congress for New Politics (NCNP), as a result of highly critical articles regarding Kim's background and political ideology published in the magazine in 1997. If convicted, Ham faces severe monetary penalties and a prison term.

CPJ sent a letter of inquiry regarding this case to the Justice Ministry of Korea on April 2. The Prosecution Bureau of the ministry responded in a letter dated May 18, confirming the filing of the case. Upon his conviction, CPJ called for his release on the grounds that libel and defamation should be handled in civil court and that journalists should not be imprisoned for their work.

On July 2, a Seoul court sentenced Ham to one year in prison for criminal defamation.

April 27
Chon Bong Jae, *World Korea* LEGAL ACTION

Chon, the publisher of *World Korea* magazine, was charged with criminal defamation by President Kim Dae Jung's political party, the National Congress for a New Politics, under Chapter 33, Article 309, of the South Korean criminal code ("Crimes Against Reputation"). The charges stem from harshly critical stories about Kim published during the 1997 presidential campaign. If convicted, Chon faces severe monetary penalties and a prison term.

After the charges were filed, Chon went into hiding.

June 1
Son Chung Mu, *Inside the World* IMPRISONED

Son, the publisher of *Inside the World* magazine, was arrested by agents of the Seoul public prosecutor's office early on the morning of June 1 at his home in Seoul, according to family members. Prosecutors have charged Son with criminal defamation and of having accepted a bribe from former Agency for National Security Planning (NSP) chief Kwon Young Hae to slander then-presidential candidate Kim Dae Jung during the 1997 campaign. Son was also charged with related "crimes against reputation" in February by the public prosecutor's office but was not arrested at that time.

The charges stem from a series of complaints brought by the National Congress for a New Politics (NCNP), President Kim Dae Jung's political party, in the aftermath of his victory in the December 1997 presidential election. In addition to the charges against Son, similar cases have been filed against two other journalists, Chon Bong Jae, publisher of *World Korea* magazine; and Ham Yun Shik, publisher of *One Way* magazine.

CPJ had inquired of the Korean Justice Ministry on April 2 about the status of the cases against the three journalists. The Justice Ministry confirmed that the cases had been filed.

When Son was arrested, CPJ filed a formal protest with the government of Kim Dae Jung, encouraging him to release Son and to take steps to repeal Korea's harsh criminal defamation statutes. On July 17, CPJ again brought up the case of Son with Kim Dae Jung in a letter related to the criminal defamation charges filed against Ham Yun Shik. On September 23, Son was found guilty of criminal libel and sentenced to two years in prison. He had faced a maximum five-year term. The libel charges stemmed from articles in his magazine published in 1997 as well as a book he wrote during the 1997 election campaign, *Kim Dae-jung, X-File*, all of which were critical of Kim. Charges that he accepted a bribe from a top South Korean intelligence official to thwart Kim's election were dropped.

Attacks on the Press in 1998

Sri Lanka

Faced with an embarrassing and deadly stalemate in the 15-year war against Tamil separatists, President Chandrika Kumaratunga's government continued its retreat from the support for civil liberties that helped bring her to power in 1994.

In this climate, journalists who report on the military were particularly vulnerable. In February, armed men invaded the home of veteran military affairs reporter Iqbal Athas and threatened to kill him. A recipient of CPJ's 1994 International Press Freedom Award, Athas had recently written a series of articles on procurement irregularities in the Sri Lankan air force for his newspaper, *The Sunday Times*.

Kumaratunga imposed military censorship in June. The action stifled local and foreign reporters' attempts to investigate military policies and procurements. And it gave the aggressive propaganda department of the Liberation Tigers of Tamil Eelam (LTTE)—which provided figures on battlefield casualties to foreign news agencies more rapidly than the Sri Lankan military—an upper hand in shaping coverage of the war.

In August, the Defense Ministry expanded the scope of censored subjects to include a ban on news of the transfer of officers within the government security forces' high command. The ministry maintained that the LTTE could use this information in devising its military strategy.

Journalists' efforts to negotiate with the government on improving the climate for free expression mostly fell on deaf ears. In April, leaders of the Sri Lankan press and government officials held a conference in Colombo to promote mutual understanding. The journalists at the conference passed the "Colombo Declaration on Media Freedom and Social Responsibility," calling for a number of reforms, among them the replacement of the harsh Official Secrets Act with a Freedom of Information Act, and the passage of laws to protect journalistic sources from attack in the courts.

The conference initiated a brief period of cooperation between the media and the government, evidenced by the testimony of several journalists in parliament on a host of proposed reforms. But the rapprochement came to an end with the imposition of censorship less than two months after the gathering.

January 3
Nirupama Subramanian, *Indian Express*
HARASSED

About a dozen armed soldiers raided the home of Subramanian, a reporter for the Bombay-based daily newspaper *Indian Express*, and searched her office and bedroom. The soldiers searched the reporter's books and papers, including press statements from the Liberation Tigers of Tamil Eelam (LTTE). Local journalists believe that the soldiers wanted to know if Subramanian was in contact with the LTTE, who are fighting for a separate homeland for minority Tamils in the country's north and east.

The Indian government formally protested the raid to Sri Lankan authorities and asked them to ensure Indian journalists were not intimidated through military and police raids on their hotel rooms and homes.

Sri Lanka's Media Minister Mangala Samaraweera publicly apologized for the raid on Subramanian's home and told reporters that the government would take steps to ensure such incidents do not happen in the future.

February 12
Iqbal Athas, *The Sunday Times* ATTACKED, THREATENED, HARASSED

Armed men attacked the home of Iqbal Athas, an internationally respected journalist who is widely known for his column "Situation Report" in *The Sunday Times* of Colombo. In 1994, he was the recipient of CPJ's International Press Freedom Award for his courageous reporting in the face of grave dangers to himself and his family.

At approximately 9:00 p.m., Athas was in his room watching television with his wife and seven-year-old daughter on the second floor of his Colombo residence. Five armed men forced their way into the house at gunpoint and assaulted a guard and the family cook. Based on their appearance and the automatic pistols they were carrying, Athas believed the men were soldiers.

Before Athas could be led away, one of the five men in the house told the group to call off the attack, apparently out of concern that they might be caught.

Athas immediately filed a police complaint about the incident and informed Sri Lankan Defense Secretary Chandranda De Silva, who ordered that an armed guard be posted outside of the Athas home. Some three hours after the attack, however, Athas and some colleagues said that a vehicle that had earlier been seen carrying the attackers returned to the neighborhood and parked for a time outside the Athas home before leaving the vicinity.

Athas believes the attack came as a direct result of a series of exposés he has written for *The Sunday Times* on military corruption and irregularities in air force procurement practices. The incident follows an apparent attempt to discredit Athas in November when a former Tamil Tiger guerrilla was widely seen in a televised interview saying that Athas' reports in *The Sunday Times* were of great interest to the guerrilla movement fighting a secessionist war against the Sri Lankan army. In June of 1997, Athas reported that armed men had placed his home under surveillance. CPJ's records indicate that Athas has been the target of repeated attempts at harassment and intimidation which we believe are linked to his reporting on military affairs for *The Sunday Times*.

Attacks on the Press in 1998

On July 24, 1997, and again on December 4, 1997, CPJ wrote to President Chandrika Kumaratunga requesting that she investigate the harassment and threats against Athas.

CPJ sent a letter to President Kumaratunga on February 12, urging her to undertake an immediate and thorough investigation into this latest incident. CPJ asked that the results of any findings be made public and that her government demonstrate its commitment to a free press by finding the individuals responsible for this attack and guaranteeing the safety of Iqbal Athas and his family.

Two air force officers—Squadron Leader Rukmal Herath and Flight Lt. Prasanna Sujeeva Kannangara—were arrested by Sri Lankan authorities for involvement in the May 6 attack. Athas and his wife identified the two as having been among the intruders.

The suspects had been responsible for the security of the former commander of the air force, Oliver Ranasinghe, whom Athas has accused of being behind the attack.

Herath and Kannangara have yet to be formally charged and the case remains under investigation pending court action.

February 16
Pradeep Kumara Dharmaratne, *Dinamina*
ATTACKED, THREATENED, HARASSED

Armed policemen from Aranayake, in central Sri Lanka, broke into the home of Dharmaratne, a correspondent for the government-owned Sinhala-language newspaper *Dinamina* at around midnight. The attack was prompted by a story he had written, which was published on January 26, dealing with the region's booming kasippu (illegal liquor) trade.

The officers beat Dharmaratne before taking him to the police station, where he was tortured and threatened with death if he continued to file reports on the kasippu trade. Police also forced him to leave his fingerprints on several bottles of kasippu to substantiate their charges that he was involved in liquor trafficking.

Dharmaratne was released on February 19 on R15,000 bail (about US$250). He was hospitalized for more than a week with severe internal injuries.

February 19
All Media CENSORED

President Chandrika Bandaranaike Kumaratunga banned the publication of photographs of people killed or wounded in bomb blasts. The new policy states that "no person, except with the permission of competent authority may publish, or permit the publication, in any newspaper or in the electronic media, of any photograph depicting a person killed or injured as a result of a bomb explosion ... or any part of the body of any such person." President Kumaratunga justified the ban on the grounds that such imagery has negative effects on children.

The new restrictions came after several terrorist bombings. The government has blamed the bombings on the Liberation Tigers of Tamil Eelam (LTTE), who are fighting for an independent homeland for Tamil minorities.

February 27
Jin Hui, Xinhua IMPRISONED, LEGAL ACTION, EXPELLED

Jin Hui, the Colombo-based correspondent for Beijing's official Xinhua news agency, was threatened with expulsion when the secretary to the Ministry of Defense, Chandrananda De Silva, ordered his arrest on February 27. He was detained and interrogated overnight at the Police Criminal Investigations Department.

Bowing to international pressure, the authorities freed Jin without charge and withdrew the deportation order on February 28. Officials justified his arrest and detention, claiming that Jin refused to apologize for and correct a controversial Xinhua news story.

On February 23, Jin had filed a report about a recent Tamil rebel ambush on a naval convoy off the northern peninsula of Jaffna. He had reported that navy Vice Adm. Cecil Tissera was killed in the ambush. After the story ran, the Sri Lankan defense ministry demanded that Jin publish a correction to the story; however, Jin filed another story carrying the government's denial and added that his sources in the military were standing by their claims about Vice Adm. Tissera's death. When Xinhua refused Sri Lankan officials' demands for a public apology, DeSilva ordered Jin's arrest.

February 27
Pradeep Kumara Dharmaratne, *Dinamina* ATTACKED

Approximately eight armed men attempted to break down the door at the home of Dharmaratne, the Aranayake correspondent for the government-owned newspaper *Dinamina*, threatening to kill the journalist, his mother, and his sister if any of them gave evidence linking the police to illegal liquor trafficking. It was the second attack in less than 10 days on Dharmaratne in apparent retaliation for a story he published on January 26 about the region's booming kasippu (illegal liquor) trade. Although the gang did not enter Dharmaratne's home, they put a sword through his door, and left behind a poster warning "Danduwama Maranaya" (Punishment is Death).

March 4
Pradeep Kumara Dharmaratne, *Dinamina* ATTACKED

Arsonists burnt down the home of Dharmaratne, the Aranayake correspondent for the government-owned newspaper *Dinamina*.

The arson was the third attack in less than a month on the reporter in apparent retaliation for a story he had published on January 26 on the region's booming (illegal liquor) kasippu trade.

Following formal protests lodged against the police in the aftermath of the fire by press freedom groups, the officer-in-charge of the Aranayake police station and three of his deputies were suspended by the Police Inspector General. The Minister of Information announced in early March that all the station's officers were being transferred out of Aranayake. According to the Free Media Movement, the minister also pledged to rebuild Dharmaratne's house.

March 22
Joy Jeyakumar, *Thinakural* HARASSED
M.A.M. Nilam, *Thinakural* HARASSED

Jeyakumar, a photographer for the Tamil-language daily newspaper *Thinakural*, was intimidated and insulted by navy personnel while covering a joint action by the military and the police that resulted in mass arrests of more than 1,500 Tamils.

Jeyakumar was taking pictures of the dozens of Tamils detained outside the Foreshore police station in Colombo when navy personnel approached him in a van and questioned him. Although he showed them both his media accreditation card and his national identity card, the men demanded to see his residential declaration form—which he did not have, as he has been living and working in Colombo for many years. The navy personnel then seized his identity cards and camera and were hauling him off to the police station when he saw his colleague Nilam, a reporter for *Thinakural*, and asked him to intervene. Both journalists were then taken to the police station, where they were questioned and detained for nearly three hours before being released.

June 5
All Journalists CENSORED

On June 5, Secretary to the Ministry of Defense Chandrananda de Silva announced that President Chandrika Kumaratunga had ordered a ban on news about the Sri Lankan civil war

Attacks on the Press in 1998

through regulations "prohibiting the publication and transmission of sensitive military information." The regulations apply to both foreign and local news media.

The Defense Ministry statement said print and electronic media were prohibited from carrying news about military and police operations. They are also barred from making "any statement pertaining to the official conduct or the performance of the head or any member of any of the armed forces or the police force."

No reason was given for the regulations. On June 6, the ministry announced that all photographs, news reports, and television material on the war must be submitted to screening by the military. This is the first time that Sri Lanka has appointed a military censor; similar press restrictions on war coverage were administered by civilians for several months in 1996 before being lifted.

In an editorial, the *Sunday Times* of Sri Lanka said, "We hope this is not the first step towards martial law." In a protest against the censorship, Sri Lankan newspapers left columns blank over the weekend.

CPJ issued a statement denouncing the censorship and sent a letter to President Kumaratunga calling on her to rescind the censorship order.

June 17
Lasantha Wickrematunge, *Sunday Leader*
ATTACKED

At approximately 10:30 p.m., shortly after Wickrematunge, the editor of the *Sunday Leader* newspaper, and his family returned home from dinner, a Toyota Hi-Ace van pulled up outside the gates of their residence. A man emerged armed with a T-56 assault rifle and fired approximately 30 rounds into the house, causing extensive damage, according to witnesses. No one was injured in the attack.

The weekly *Sunday Leader* has been critical of the ruling People's Alliance government and had recently published articles questioning the integrity of Media Minister Mangala Samaraweera and other officials. "Someone is sending us a message," said Lal Wickrematunge, the managing director of the newspaper and the brother of Lasantha. Samaraweera quickly condemned the attack, and the police stationed armed guards outside the home of Wickrematunge announcing a full investigation into the incident.

This was the second attack on a prominent journalist in 1998. In February, armed men invaded the home of Iqbal Athas, the defense correspondent for the *Sunday Times* newspaper of Colombo.

Taiwan

Having abandoned authoritarian rule in the late 1980s, Taiwan's Nationalist Chinese government now presides over one of the freest presses in Asia. With a population of just under 22 million, Taiwan is home to more than 300 newspapers, four television networks, and 74 radio stations competing in a vibrant marketplace that stands in marked contrast to China's state-controlled media.

During freewheeling local elections at the end of the year, there was widespread coverage of alleged sex scandals involving several candidates, as the question of character came to the fore in a society largely free of rancorous ideological divisions.

Journalists still confront tough criminal libel statutes, however, but some legislators have called for statutory reforms to bring Taiwan in line with practices in other democracies in which libel is treated as a civil matter. Meanwhile, an appeal by the plaintiff seeking to overturn the 1997 acquittal of Ying Chan, a U.S. reporter, and Shieh Chung-liang, a Taiwanese reporter, both recipients of CPJ's 1997 International

Press Freedom Award, is still pending in the high-profile criminal libel case brought by the ruling Kuomintang party.

Press freedom remains one of the biggest issues to be reconciled if Taiwan and China are to reunite under the "One Country, Two Systems" formula being applied in Hong Kong. In a dramatic demonstration of Taiwan's commitment to democracy and its willingness to challenge Beijing on the issue, President Lee Teng-hui met in late December in Taipei with Wei Jingsheng, a writer and perhaps China's most famous exiled dissident. "Democracy is the trend of the times, freedom is what people hope," Lee told Wei, according to the president's office. "They are unstoppable. Democracy and freedom are the only opportunity for the long-term developments of any country and society."

Thailand

Thailand, one of the most open societies in Asia, is becoming a regional leader in press freedom. Its constitution, ratified at the end of 1997, has some of the strongest protections for the press in the developing world, and the country's leaders are using their influence in regional meetings of the Association of Southeast Asian Nations to urge neighboring countries to follow their lead on free expression issues. It is also one of the few developing countries to have a statutory guarantee of citizens' right to have access to government records.

In 1998, the Reporters Association of Thailand, together with CPJ, organized the founding conference of the Southeast Asian Press Alliance (SEAPA), in Bangkok in November. SEAPA, which brings together independent press organizations from the Philippines, Indonesia, and Thailand, is the first multilateral organization in Asia devoted primarily to promoting and protecting press freedom. SEAPA plans to establish a press freedom secretariat in Bangkok in 1999. (See page 263 for more information on SEAPA.)

Thai Foreign Minister Surin Pitsuwan, who spoke at SEAPA's founding conference, said that the best way to rebuild Asian economies in the aftermath of the economic crisis is by reforming press and information policies. "More open information policies will be the best guarantee of the sustainability of restored economies," he said at the meeting.

The next hurdle for the Thai press will be the privatization of the many radio and television frequencies still controlled by the military—a legacy of pre-1992 army-dominated governments. The constitution mandates that the military relinquish the frequencies, but implementing legislation that defines the terms of privatization has been slowed by the military's reluctance to part with lucrative advertising revenues.

January 10
Sayomchai Vijitwittayapong, *Matichon*
KILLED

Sayomchai, an investigative reporter with Bangkok's third-largest daily newspaper, *Matichon*, was found shot dead in the central city of Pichit on January 10. He was last seen leaving his Bangkok home on January 9 with a tape recorder and camera, on his way to meet a village headman.

Sayomchai's death may have been connected to his in-depth reporting on illegal logging, according to news reports in Thailand. His colleagues at *Matichon* issued a statement saying they believed he was killed because of his reporting on corruption in the construction industry. Earlier, he had received death threats and allegedly refused a bribe of US$6,000 to stop working on a corruption story about tenders for a construction project.

Sayomchai's murder was widely denounced by Thai newspapers and journalists associations.

Tonga

In the Pacific's last monarchy, King Taufa'ahau Tupou IV holds near-total power. The king rules with a 12-member cabinet he names and an 18-member legislature, half of which he also appoints. It is not a system that invites criticism.

The views of 'Akilisi Pohiva, a pro-democracy politician and the publisher of *The Kele'a* newspaper, have frequently provoked the government. In March, he was found guilty and fined several hundred dollars on two counts of defaming the minister of police through comments he made in his newspaper in 1997. Also in March, Pohiva was acquitted of criminal defamation stemming from a 1994 *Kele'a* article in which he called the king "a dictator" and accused him of "financial legerdemain" over a scheme to sell Tongan passports to foreigners.

In October, Tavake Fusimalohi, the general manager of government-owned Radio Tonga, was acquitted of charges of defamation brought by two senior government officials who alleged that an announcement broadcast by Radio Tonga in April had damaged their reputations. The station had accurately reported that the two men had been demoted and transferred to new jobs.

June 23, 1998
Michael J. Field, Agence France-Presse
CENSORED

Field, a correspondent with Agence France-Presse, was denied entry to Tonga for the second time in two years.

On June 19, Field requested permission to visit Tonga to report on King Taufa'ahau Tupou IV's upcoming 80th birthday. He received a letter on June 23 from Police Minister Clive Edwards, formally denying the application.

Although Tonga typically allows journalists free entry, Field, who is based in New Zealand and has covered the South Pacific for many years, has been barred from the country since 1993, after publishing several articles about Tonga's pro-democracy movement. The police minister at that time notified Field that he would thereafter be required to obtain advance approval before visiting the country. Field was then denied entry to Tonga in 1996 on the grounds that he had insulted the king. CPJ's own account of that incident indicates that Police Minister Edwards never substantiated that claim, but threatened to charge Field with criminal defamation if he attempted to visit Tonga.

CPJ sent a letter to the king on June 23, expressing concern over Field's exclusion from the country.

Vietnam

Communist Party directives set the tone for Vietnam's media, as political overseers micromanaged news coverage and maintained strict ideological controls on the press, all of which is state-owned.

Early in the year, Communist Party chief Lt. Gen. Le Kha Phieu told a gathering of journalists in Ho Chi Minh City to follow party directives in news coverage. Local branches of the party's Commission on Culture and Ideology meet weekly in every major city to issue instructions on coverage to editors, who pass the word along to their reporters. The party pays particularly close attention to limiting coverage of stories of official corruption that might implicate ranking officials.

"In the last year, things have tightened up. We feel less free now," said a

Vietnamese reporter, citing the case of Tamexco, an import-export company that became embroiled in a $40 million corruption scandal. Three top executives of the firm were executed by a firing squad in January, but the story stopped there and the Vietnamese press was told not to pursue the investigation beyond the executives, despite indications that the scandal may have reached deep into the political establishment.

In October, another corruption-related story led to the conviction of Nguyen Hoang Linh, the former editor in chief of the weekly newspaper *Doanh Nghiep* (Enterprise), on charges of "abusing democracy and damaging state interests." Linh was fired, arrested, and jailed in October 1997 after his newspaper published an unusually detailed series of articles that accused the customs department of corrupt practices in the purchase of second-hand patrol boats.

One happy moment occurred with the September release from prison of Doan Viet Hoat, who was imprisoned in November 1990 for his work as publisher of *Dien Dan Tu Do* (Freedom Forum), an underground pro-democracy magazine. Hoat, a 1993 recipient of CPJ's International Press Freedom Award, was exiled to the United States upon his release. Hoat had spent 19 of the past 22 years in jail for crimes related to free expression.

Perhaps in reaction to international condemnation of its dismal human rights record, Vietnamese sources report that the Communist Party is increasingly using orders of "administrative detention," a form of house arrest and police surveillance, against journalists and others. The orders are not subject to court review and receive little publicity.

Controls ban local reporters from "cooperating" or sharing information with foreign correspondents. Foreign news agencies are also required go through the Ministry of Foreign Affairs for any local hiring.

While Vietnam began allowing direct Internet access to the country in 1997, in December, party officials announced their intention to establish a committee in Ho Chi Minh City to monitor Internet use. It will be charged with "correcting mistakes and bias," according to a report in the influential daily newspaper *Liberated Saigon*. The report also said that the Commission on Culture and Ideology will draw up plans to stop "negative" information on the Internet, an apparent reference to dissident websites produced outside Vietnam.

September 1
Doan Viet Hoat, *Dien Dan Tu Do* (Freedom Forum) EXPELLED

Hoat was expelled from Vietnam midway through a 15-year sentence for publishing *Dien Dan Tu Do*, a pro-democracy newsletter. He was released from prison under an amnesty timed to coincide with Vietnam's national day.

After his release, Hoat was immediately flown to Thailand. He then left for the United States, where he was reunited with his wife and a number of family members. Hoat, who was kept in isolation throughout much of his imprisonment, is Vietnam's most prominent dissident.

A writer and academic, Hoat was arrested in 1990 for his role in producing *Dien Dan Tu Do*. He was sentenced to 20 years in prison in 1993—later reduced to 15 years—on charges of trying to overthrow the government. He had previously been detained without trial from 1976 to 1988, accused of being an "anti-communist reactionary." In 1993 he was awarded CPJ's International Press Freedom Award.

"Every one of us should be free to express his opinion, to speak up his mind on questions of culture and ideology openly and legally, and to have political rights ... if we are to have a country that is truly free," Hoat said when he was released.

Freedom Takes Hold:
ASEAN Journalism in Transition

by A. Lin Neumann

Since July 1997, the Asian economic crisis has dragged the countries of Southeast Asia through a nightmare of currency devaluation, shattered stock markets, rising unemployment, and political instability. But paradoxically, the crisis has also created opportunities for positive social and political change, including greater press freedom. Calls for greater openness and a freer press in the region vie with more closed and authoritarian responses to the extended economic downturn.

In recent years, the robust growth enjoyed by most of the nine members of the Association of Southeast Asian Nations (ASEAN) was frequently used to justify authoritarian governments and restrictive press laws. So-called "Asian values" were said to prize economic development and social harmony above individual freedom and civil liberties. The financial crisis may finally have revealed the fallacy of appealing to Asian values as a rationale for controlling the flow of information.

In Indonesia, for example, the nation hit hardest by the downturn, economic woes focused public attention on widespread corruption and a lack of government accountability. Anger over these abuses sparked massive protests and rioting, which in turn forced President Suharto to resign in May. Despite his ties to the old regime, Suharto's hand-picked successor Bacharudin Jusuf (B. J.) Habibie grasped that reform is the key to political survival. As part of that process, the government quickly lifted almost all restrictions on the press.

In contrast, as the economic crisis reached Malaysia, an internecine power struggle intensified and the government sought to muzzle dissent. Prime Minister Mahathir Mohamad, long an outspoken advocate of Asian values, invoked the country's draconian, colonial-era Internal Security Act to arrest his one-time protégé turned reformist political rival, former Deputy Prime Minister Anwar Ibrahim, for sodomy and corruption. The September 20 arrest prompted the largest public protests in

Malaysia in a generation. Mahathir, ASEAN's longest-serving leader, has used a timid, self-censoring press and a pliant legal system to mute dissent.

During the long period of turmoil that followed the ouster of Ferdinand Marcos in 1986, the Philippines was held in contempt by its authoritarian neighbors for its rowdy democracy and raucous free press. During the current crisis, however, the Philippines has held a peaceful election, withstood government transition, and weathered the economic meltdown with fewer negative effects than its ASEAN partners.

Although Thailand's monetary policies in July 1997 unwittingly triggered the regional financial upheaval, attempts to quell the crisis with authoritarian strategies failed. When Prime Minister Chavalit Yongchaiyudh blamed the media for the crisis, he was met with ridicule in the Thai press. In October 1997, Chavalit sought to impose a state of emergency, which would have included press censorship and a curfew. The military, reversing a history of intervention in civil affairs, refused to go along and in November 1997, Chavalit resigned. The new prime minister, Chuan Leekpai of the Democrat Party, presided over the implementation of a new constitution with the strongest press freedom protections in the region. A program of economic reforms and greater openness under Chuan has led Thailand to the forefront of the regional movement to encourage more transparency within ASEAN.

In his keynote speech at a CPJ-sponsored conference on regional press freedom in Bangkok in November, Thailand's foreign minister Surin Pitsuwan stated, "Freedom is indivisible. It is all or none. It is therefore the responsibility of each member of the society not only to safeguard the freedom of the press but also to ensure the safety of its practitioners."

The conference resulted in an unprecedented agreement among organizations advocating greater press freedom in Southeast Asia to cooperate across national boundaries. The Southeast Asian Press Alliance (SEAPA), made up of representatives from Thailand, the Philippines, and Indonesia, is planning to establish a working secretariat in Bangkok to monitor press freedom conditions throughout ASEAN.

Nowhere is the battle for openness more crucial than in Indonesia, where the press is suddenly free to report on corruption and investigate human rights abuses. The military so far has steered clear of taking power, authorities have given the green light to the formation of political parties, and the country appears to be on course for planned May 1999 elections.

Indonesia's liberated press, however, remains at risk; the Habibie government has yet to introduce a promised systematic reform of repressive media laws used by the Suharto government to close publications and imprison journalists. And the country's ongoing economic instability could still lead to a political backlash. But the Habibie government has surprised many analysts with its willingness to tolerate and even encourage far-reaching public debate in the press.

The May riots, ongoing student demonstrations, and ethnic violence have fueled fears that the country might spiral into widespread bloodletting of the sort that followed the 1965 overthrow of President Sukarno. Suharto frequently used the specter of social chaos to justify his New Order regime, and some analysts worry that reactionary forces may once again use the threat of instability as an excuse to derail reform. "Common sense is now being threatened in Indonesia," said Andreas Harsono, a journalist who works with the Institute for Studies in the Free Flow of Information. "In general, people do not feel secure these days."

But the socioeconomic particulars of Indonesian life are significantly different from those of a generation ago. Indonesia now has a substantial educated urban middle class with a stake in a stable democratic system. Today's vibrant, vigilant press can play a stabilizing role by airing the issues at the root of social strife.

As Southeast Asia's largest nation, Indonesia, with 200 million people, is the region's most important economy and a bellwether for its neighbors. Thus, if democracy takes root in Indonesia, it has the potential to change the political dynamic of the entire region. A free press in post-Suharto Indonesia can help open an ASEAN-wide dialogue on free expression, human rights, and other issues, such as the environment, that have long been kept under wraps.

"If Indonesia joins Thailand and the Philippines as a democratic state, it puts real pressure on the rest of ASEAN," said a Jakarta-based Western diplomat. "You can ignore everyone else in ASEAN, but you cannot ignore Indonesia. No one comes close to it in size and influence."

A History of Press Courage

ASEAN's "free press" nations—Indonesia, Thailand, and the Philippines—account for more than two-thirds of the total population of Southeast Asia's 483 million people. Their cumulative clout may provide an irresistible momentum toward press freedom in the rest of Southeast Asia. The authoritarian leaders of Malaysia, Vietnam, Burma, and elsewhere will no longer be able to pretend that a timid and cautious press is the regional norm.

"Look at Indonesia," said a senior Thai foreign ministry official. "It is moving along a process of reform that was not possible under the old regime or before the crisis. The crisis brought about a change, and that change has opened up opportunities. Habibie is committed to a process of reform and a schedule of elections that will lead to more changes. This wasn't possible without the crisis. The crisis itself has ushered in some dynamics [for change] in the domestic structure of every society here."

While ongoing economic upheaval has triggered the recent changes for the Indonesian press, courageous journalists throughout Southeast Asia have worked for years to open restrictive societies:

- During the Marcos dictatorship, a few journalists continued to test the regime's limits. When Marcos finally fled in 1986, it was in large part because the Philippine media had chipped away at his credibility.
- In May 1992, hundreds of thousands of people, including members of an emerging Thai middle class, took to the streets to protest a military-dominated government. When troops fired on the protesters, killing dozens, popular outrage against the killings led to the government's collapse, and a period of political liberalization began. It was newspaper reporting, in defiance of a ban on coverage of the protests, that galvanized the public against the bloodshed. Since 1992, Thai newspapers have grown increasingly bold. Thailand has become the de facto center for regional reporting, as well as a haven for human rights groups and regional non-governmental organizations, which operate in Thailand with little government interference.
- In the last years of the Suharto era, when the regime shut publications and sent some editors and reporters to prison,

a core of dedicated Indonesian journalists pushed the limits of free expression by publishing banned magazines on websites, and flouting government licensing requirements to print underground newspapers. The hard work has now begun to pay off.

A Challenge to ASEAN

Since its founding 31 years ago, ASEAN has been an economic alliance and a forum for the resolution of intraregional tensions. Most of its nine member states have had authoritarian governments. But the current crisis is changing the way ASEAN does business and exposing a dramatic contrast between the more democratic states and their repressive allies.

In July 1998, at the annual ASEAN foreign ministers' summit in Manila, Thailand's dynamic young foreign minister, Surin Pitsuwan, challenged the ASEAN orthodoxy by discussing what he called "flexible engagement," a policy initiative designed to supersede the alliance's core principle of "non-interference" in one another's domestic affairs and to encourage formal discussion of human rights and free expression within ASEAN.

Advisers close to Surin say that greater openness is necessary if the alliance is to maintain its relevance after the economic collapse. "Globalization, liberalization, accountability, transparency, and good governance—all these things are now being felt in every society and every government," said a senior official. "If you want to compete and you want to move along, you will have to make changes."

In human terms, non-interference also meant tolerance for even the worst human rights abuses. For example, Burma, despite being a virtual pariah state internationally, gained full ASEAN membership in 1997 with the tacit understanding that member states would turn a blind eye to its domestic policies.

Surin's proposal touched a raw nerve among most other ASEAN ministers, who recognized it as a far-reaching challenge to ASEAN's repressive history. In the end, after tense discussions, the Philippines was the only member state to openly support Thailand on the issue. The alliance watered down the idea, agreeing to encourage what is now termed "enhanced interaction." Whatever it is called, the message is clear: The reformist forces within ASEAN now feel free to criticize their neighbors.

The new dynamic has already had repercussions. The presidents of the Philippines and Indonesia both publicly criticized Anwar's arrest in Malaysia. Newspapers in Jakarta, Manila, and Bangkok editorialized against Mahathir's actions. The shock of this public rebuke prompted an angry reaction from the timid progovernment Malaysian press, which complained that other ASEAN countries were interfering in what was a purely internal matter.

The New Indonesia

For decades, the Indonesian state was virtually synonymous with one man, Suharto, whose hold on his nation was so strong that many observers could hardly conceive of life without him and even local journalists were unprepared for the rapid demise of his regime.

Habibie was thrust into office by Suharto's May 21 resignation, and he seemed to have inherited an impossible task. Demonstrators immediately called for his resignation, and many observers were convinced that he couldn't last in office for more than a few weeks. But a coterie of media-savvy advisers concluded that political reform and greater openness offered a way out of the maelstrom. Habibie's government acted quickly to allow the press to operate openly, and to encourage new political parties to function.

The changes caught journalists by surprise. "We were prepared for the long haul. We had safe houses, underground printing presses, and a network of discussion groups to prepare the ground gradually for the post-Suharto era," said Goenawan Mohamad, the founder and chief editor of *Tempo* magazine. "We are now dealing with a completely new and unforeseen situation. But of course we do not for a moment regret that Suharto is gone."

Tempo, once Indonesia's largest, most respected news magazine, is a prime example of the new openness. The information ministry revoked *Tempo*'s publishing license in 1994, following the publication of an article that exposed government infighting over the purchase of 39 East German patrol boats. Within days of Suharto's resignation, the new regime told Goenawan and others from *Tempo* that they would be free to reopen. Ironically, Habibie was the target of the article that offended the government four years earlier.

"Habibie is sophisticated enough to know that his situation was hopeless unless he allowed the reforms to go forward," said

Adam Schwarz, a former journalist who is now a consultant on Southeast Asian issues in Washington. "His advisors concluded that there was a lot of information out there already, and it was better for him to just open up the press."

The magazine's relaunch celebration on October 4 was a major event in Jakarta, drawing some 2,000 reporters, politicians, government ministers, and diplomats. *Tempo*'s newsstand sales have so far exceeded expectations, leading to talk within the company of expanding operations and a sense of buoyant optimism.

The reopening of *Tempo*, which was founded in 1971, marks the return of a magazine that is credited by many with nurturing a generation of journalists with standards of professionalism and courage that were new to Indonesian media. When it was closed, its 150 reporters and editors dispersed to other publications, sometimes working without bylines for fear of government reprisal. By all accounts, they have had a tremendous impact throughout the industry.

After the 1994 ban, *Tempo* veterans, led by Goenawan, organized the Alliance of Independent Journalists (AJI), which challenged the official Indonesian Journalists Association (PWI). Former Tempo reporter Ahmad Taufik, AJI's first president, and a 1995 recipient of CPJ's International Press Freedom Award, was sent to prison for three years in 1994, along with two other AJI staffers, for publishing articles critical of Suharto in *Suara Independen*, an unlicensed magazine. His case brought international condemnation to the Suharto government for its treatment of the press.

While independent journalists managed to keep the faith during the dark days of repression, support has recently come from an unexpected quarter: Lt. Gen. Mohamad Yunus, the active-duty officer who is Indonesia's minister of information and chief official champion of a free press.

Early in his career, Yunus gained a reputation as a tough combat officer during Indonesia's 1975 invasion of East Timor. His name has surfaced in official Australian government reports as the commander of troops accused in the 1975 murder of five Australia-based journalists in the town of Balibo, East Timor, a charge he denies. But he is also a well-traveled officer who received advance training in the United States and Great Britain.

During a stint at the U.S. Army's Command and General Staff College at Fort Leavenworth in 1979, he even wrote a thesis titled, "The Role of the Mass Media in Developing Countries." Under Suharto, he rose to become armed forces chief of social-political affairs, responsible for coordinating the army's significant role in Indonesian political life.

Yunus says that Habibie considered him for the post of military chief when Suharto stepped down, but instead named him to the information post on the day that the new president took office. Since then, Yunus has consistently espoused a belief that the road to stability in his country runs through a free press.

"I want to see more publications in Indonesia," he explained during a lengthy conversation in his office. "I really believe that such a thing will provide more competitive information for the people and it will enhance their views and build the creativity of the people."

It used to take as long as seven years—or the payment of hefty bribes—to open any kind of publication in Indonesia. Censors reviewed copies of all imported newspapers and magazines. Yunus has abolished the censor's office, effectively eliminating censorship. And Yunus advocates removing the remaining government controls on the media.

He has sought advice from Goenawan and other journalists on how to reform Indonesia's press laws, and he has eliminated the stranglehold of the PWI, allowing AJI and other journalistic associations to function freely. Yunus has even been a target of criticism from within his own ministry for being too liberal.

Under Yunus, approximately 350 new publication licenses were issued in 1998. New and old titles abound. Along with *Tempo*, other banned publications have been revived, such as the fiery magazine *Detik*, also shut by the government in 1994, which has reopened under a new name, *Detak*.

While repressive laws remain on the books, the nation's future is being openly debated, and Indonesia is no longer the exclusive province of one man's family and cronies. "The most likely thing the press could contribute in this new period is to develop a culture of transparency and accountability in the bureaucracy and the government," says Goenawan. "Tempo will hopefully become a place that will defend and expand our freedoms."

"This is a new experience for us. We are free now," adds Lukas Luwarso, the president of AJI.

Malaysia Holds Firm

Contrast the new freedom in Indonesia with Malaysia, where economic crisis and political opposition have been met with stiffer repression.

The first sign that Mahathir was going to move against Anwar Ibrahim, his erstwhile deputy, came in July, with the forced resignations of three prominent editors identified with Anwar's wing of the ruling United Malays National Organization (UMNO) party, which along with other pro-government political parties controls most of Malaysia's media. With a docile press now ensured, the charges of sodomy and corruption brought against Anwar went scarcely challenged in the media.

When foreign television reports documented the popular unrest and demonstrations that greeted Anwar's ouster, Malaysian authorities banned the use of domestic satellite facilities to transmit images of the demonstrations. A private doctor's report confirming that Anwar had been beaten made headlines abroad but wasn't reported by the Malaysian media.

Mahathir has frequently dismissed press freedom as a form of Western imperialism. In 1997, at the onset of the economic crisis, he said, "This is part of the freedom of the press—the freedom to influence adversely against other countries, the freedom to tell lies, which is part of the freedom as interpreted by them."

After Anwar's arrest, Malaysian officials predictably lashed out at the foreign press. Information Minister Mohamed Rahmat told local reporters, "I think the role of the local media is important in defending the country from its enemies…. Unfortunately, the Western media and certain foreign organizations are now working hand in hand with insiders to destroy all the good in this country."

As a result of the tight control exerted on the press, many Malaysian journalists say they live in a climate of fear and self-censorship, constantly worrying that their phones are tapped and that their jobs are at risk if they offend the powers that be. "The press is not only oppressed, it is totally shackled," said one veteran Malaysian reporter, who feared reprisals if his name was used. "They are trying to bury the press."

New Media, New Strategies

If the lessons of Indonesia, Thailand, and the Philippines are any guide, Malaysian officials can at best fight a rear-guard action against the public's right to know. "Information is just like water, in that when a rock impedes the flow, water still flows by the side of the rock, or through the crevices," wrote Goenawan in March, just as Suharto's crisis was deepening. "The more restrictions are imposed, the more new activity in the media will be generated."

The use of the Internet has had a profound effect in the region. In Indonesia, during the last days of Suharto, students went online to coordinate demonstrations and share information instantly in ways the government found impossible to control. Similarly, the Net has begun to play an effective role in disseminating news otherwise not easily available in Malaysia. Anxious to bill itself as a high-tech research and manufacturing center, Malaysia has allowed relatively easy Net access. Websites and discussion groups about Anwar's arrest have proliferated, carrying debate absent from the old-order press onto the World Wide Web.

No wonder the region's authoritarian leaders are afraid of the Internet. China, Burma, and Vietnam all restrict Internet access; Burma's generals have imposed prison terms of up to 15 years for possession of a modem. But time is on the side of those who believe in the free flow of information. Even Singapore, with its reputation for a timid press, has had to retreat from initial attempts to restrict political content on the Internet, because investors found the restriction onerous.

The Challenge

It has become axiomatic that the turmoil in the Asian economies was aggravated by the absence of a vibrant and vigilant press. After decades of cooperation with repressive governments and avoidance of sensitive media issues, the World Bank and the International Monetary Fund now see press freedom as an ally in global economic recovery. Addressing its recent annual meeting in Washington, World Bank president James Wolfensohn called the free flow of information necessary for good governance and sustained economic growth.

Unfortunately, it took an economic collapse to focus the attention of the world on the issue of the press in Southeast Asia. But it would be a mistake to believe that international financial institutions or Western pressure alone will force governments in the region to open their systems to greater freedom and accountability.

Free expression is the first right, and without it democracy and accountability are impossible. The big lie of Asian values as a justification for repression was the demeaning notion that freedom was somehow less valuable to an Asian than it was to anyone else. Fortunately, the new openness in Indonesia, the democratization of Thailand, and the tradition of freedom in the Philippines are creating a culture of free expression that is exemplified by the recent founding of the Southeast Asian Press Alliance (SEAPA) and the growing debate within ASEAN.

Through SEAPA, independent journalists in the region can band together to promote and protect one another. The press in Burma, Vietnam, Malaysia, Laos, Singapore, and Cambodia continue to operate under severe constraints. They are either directly controlled by their governments or forced to labor under a regime of threat and self-censorship. Instead of relying on protests lodged from outside the region, SEAPA will try to expand the scope of regional press freedom in a spirit of solidarity and respect for their colleagues and neighbors.

At stake is the future of free expression in Southeast Asia and the ability of the ASEAN nations to emerge into a stable and more open future. "Those of us in Indonesia know what it is like to lose our freedom," said Goenawan Mohamad. "But if we can right ourselves, maybe we can serve as something of an example for the rest of ASEAN. There are still so many problems in the rest of the region. We have to work together."

Attacks on the Press in 1998

OVERVIEW OF
Central Europe and the Republics of the Former Soviet Union

Measured by the yardstick of the Soviet era, media in the region now operate with considerable freedom. And measured against the dozens of journalists killed or kidnapped in the mid-1990s, this year's record is a significant improvement: two journalists killed in Russia, one in Georgia, and no new kidnappings in the secessionist region of Chechnya, where 21 journalists were captured in 1997.

But press freedom suffers when journalists are forced to avoid a story of the magnitude of the Russian-Chechen conflict because it is simply too dangerous to go to Chechnya anymore. And it is now apparent that gauging press freedom in the former Soviet republics' so-called "emerging democracies" by contrasting them to the totalitarian extreme produced some overly sanguine assessments of how much progress they had made.

By the standards of established democracies, only a handful of these countries, most notably the Czech Republic and Hungary, offer meaningful protection for their vibrant independent media. Elsewhere, journalists still face a variety of repressions. Some operate in countries that have not moved far from the old Soviet-era model. In Azerbaijan, for example, President Heydar Aliyev dropped formal censorship in August, but officials have increased the use of criminal libel statutes to suppress critical reporting about the president. The

---

Chrystyna Lapychak *is program coordinator for Central and Eastern Europe and the former Soviet republics.*
Paul LeGendre *is research assistant for the program. He did extensive research for this section and wrote the analyses of Azerbaijan, Croatia, the Czech Republic, Georgia, Kyrgyzstan, Poland, Tajikistan, and Turkmenistan.*
Irina Kuldjieva-Faion, *former research assistant for the program, did extensive research for this section and wrote the analyses of Albania, Bulgaria, Romania, and Slovakia.*
Ann Cooper, *CPJ's executive director, wrote the overview of the region, and the analyses of Belarus and Yugoslavia.*
Nicholas Daniloff, *director of the journalism program at Northeastern University, wrote the analyses of Kazakhstan and Uzbekistan.*
Anne Garrels, *special correspondent for National Public Radio, wrote the analysis of Russia.*
Elizabeth Gillette, *a communications consultant based in Munich, wrote the analysis of Bosnia-Herzegovina.*
Ronald Koven, *European representative of the World Press Freedom Committee, wrote the analysis of Armenia.*
James Ross, *associate professor of journalism at Northeastern University and the author of two non-fiction books,* Escape to Shanghai *and* Caught in a Tornado, *wrote the analysis of Ukraine.*
The John D. and Catherine T. MacArthur Foundation provided vital support for CPJ's efforts to foster press freedom in Russia.

government of Belarus President Aleksander Lukashenko banned distribution of official documents to independent media and forbade state agencies from advertising in non-state media. Tajikistan and the other former Soviet republics in central Asia are ruled by men who show little interest in democratic principles or free press guarantees. Even Kazakhstan's President Nursultan Nazarbayev—viewed by Western leaders as progressive in the Soviet era—has turned on the country's independent media, apparently fearing that vigorous public scrutiny would jeopardize his re-election.

In Russia, the regional giant, the early promise of democratic reform remains unfulfilled for the press as for other sectors of society. Though the press is diverse, irreverent, and lively, media are controlled by moguls who use these holdings to leverage political power. The result is a pattern of self-censorship among the editors of newspapers and broadcast outlets: Stories that might challenge the owner's goals often go unreported.

Scrutinizing the powerful remains a dangerous business in Russia: The two Russian journalists assassinated this year were both outspoken editors known for their investigative coverage of local officials. As with the other 14 murders of journalists in Russia documented by CPJ since 1994, no one has been convicted of these crimes.

Independent media throughout the region receive vital support from foreign donors, who consider a thriving, open press essential for strengthening fledgling democracies. Training programs, financial support, legal assistance and fellowships have helped independent publishers and broadcasters to survive in such hostile climates as Belarus, Croatia, and the Federal Republic of Yugoslavia.

But international support has not inoculated the region's independent media against the conditions that make their environment precarious. One of the most virulent threats this year came from Serb leader Slobodan Milosevic as he negotiated with the West to end his assault on the rebellious province of Kosovo. Milosevic had used the threat of NATO air strikes as a pretext to launch a crackdown on journalists who dared question his nationalist policies. But when the NATO threat was resolved, Milosevic's campaign of repression continued. By year's end, Yugoslav authorities had closed three newspapers and two radio stations, and the government threatened criminal charges against more media outlets. Serb journalists said they had learned a bitter lesson: Foreign aid would not ensure their survival unless Western donors were willing to make the safety of independent media a non-negotiable condition of peace in the region.

Albania

The financial and social chaos sparked by the collapse of nationwide pyramid schemes in 1997 contributed to the downfall of President Sali Berisha and the victory of the Socialist Party in June of that year. While the new government brought some political and social stability to the country, the relative calm ended in August 1998, when the crisis in the predominantly ethnic Albanian province of Kosovo in the neighboring Federal Republic of Yugoslavia spilled over into Albanian politics.

Berisha, whose Democratic Party (PD) has actively supported the rebel Albanian Kosovo Liberation Army (KLA), played on the Kosovo issue to undermine the government of Prime Minister Fatos Nano. On September 14, Berisha and his supporters attempted to stage a coup d'état, occupying the parliament and the state radio and television buildings. Unable to form a new cabinet, Nano resigned and was succeeded by the 31-year-old Socialist Party Secretary General Pandeli Majko.

The tumultuous environment has polarized Albania's print media, which has split along party lines. Those publications that remained independent, most notably the newspapers *Koha Jone* and *Gazeta Shqiptare*, saw their circulation dip by 33 percent. The independent newspaper *Dita Informacion* folded for financial reasons, while the PD papers *Rilindja Demokratike* and *Albania* slightly increased their circulation.

Violence against journalists has been part of the generally lawless environment that has prevailed since the pyramid scheme revelations. A bomb blast in May at the home of *Koha Jone*'s Vlora correspondent, Zenepe Luka, injured her two young sons. The attack came soon after a PD rally at which guards refused access to Luka—whose reporting has cast a negative light on Berisha's political maneuverings—and threatened her.

Several new private radio and television stations in the northern part of the country were unhampered by licensing requirements until October, when a new law on electronic media took effect, regulating the licensing of private media outlets and the transfer of state-owned Albanian television to public ownership. The private local television stations TV Teuta, TV Arberia, and TV Shijak, which had broadcast mostly entertainment programs, started producing their own news and public affairs programs. An independent, parliament-appointed National Council on Radio and Television decides on the eligibility of stations to receive licenses, while a telecommunications regulatory body grants broadcasting frequencies. In a climate of crime and corruption, the survival of private media outlets will most probably depend on their affiliation with those in power and with influential economic groups.

May 10
Zenepe Luka, *Koha Jone* ATTACKED

An explosion badly damaged the Vlora home of Luka, a correspondent for the daily *Koha Jone*. Approximately five kilograms of explosives tore up most of the first floor of her house. Luka's two children were hospitalized overnight with severe injures. The reporter and her husband suffered minor injuries. The Ministry of the Interior has launched an investigation, although so far there have been no arrests.

Luka had written extensively about the popular unrest in Vlora in 1997, when many Albanians lost their savings in the collapse of pyramid investment schemes, for which the then-ruling Democratic Party was blamed. Luka has remained critical of the party's role in the crisis and its lingering repercussions. In an article published just a few days before the bombing, she reported on local protests over a meeting organized by two representatives of the Democratic Party. Luka was barred from covering a party meeting held one day before the bombing of her home.

Armenia

Self-censorship pervaded the Armenian press throughout the year. In private, journalists seem eager to talk about the subjects they say are best not reported in the media, such as the numerous military executions of Azeri prisoners taken in fighting with Azerbaijan over Nagorno-Karabakh, an Armenian-majority enclave under Azerbaijani sovereignty, and the influence of Defense Minister Vazgen Sarkissian as the country's political kingmaker.

In March, Robert Kocharian, Armenia's prime minister and former president of the internationally unrecognized Republic of Nagorno-Karabakh, was elected president of Armenia. The voting took place after the forced resignation of President Levon Ter-Petrossian over his willingness to negotiate with Azerbaijan on Nagorno-Karabakh—the central issue in Armenian politics. Based on the reports of 180 foreign election observers, international organizations officially denounced ballot-box stuffing and other serious flaws in the presidential voting, but they concluded that Kocharian would have won anyway.

Despite continued tense governmental relations with the press, there were clear improvements over the year. The European Institute for the Media (EIM), a Düsseldorf-based communications research group which monitored press coverage of the presidential elections both in 1996 and in 1998, noted a marked reduction in the open slant of state television news—by far the leading source of political information for Armenians—toward the governmental candidate. But somewhat more subtle forms of bias continued, including frequent rebroadcasts of a tough satire of the leading opposition candidate, former Armenian Communist Party First Secretary Karen Demirchian, shown without disclosing that it was a paid political advertisement.

A1 Plus, a private television station, said one of its news teams was assaulted while filming fraudulent presidential vote-counting and that a camera was damaged. A1 Plus also reported an attempted break-in which station staffers said was intended to prevent the film from being broadcast.

Upon election, Kocharian moved to improve presidential relations with the press. He lifted a ban imposed in 1994 by his predecessor on the publications of the opposition Armenian Revolutionary Federation, the Dashnak Party. He instituted monthly off-the-record briefings with top editors—in sharp contrast with the almost inaccessible Ter-Petrossian. And he also abolished the value-added tax on press distribution, pledged to consider dropping it on newsprint, and reduced rent on news media premises to maintenance charges only.

Nevertheless, old habits died hard. Defense Minister Sarkissian—widely seen as the real power in Armenia—and his staff remained unreachable. An experienced journalist noted that the Defense Ministry's press center handles queries by simply never answering its official telephone number. During a public meeting President Kocharian held with Armenian writers, several participants objected because an interpreter was translating the president's words for a visiting U.S. journalist.

There has been a decline in defamation suits against journalists, but they report a steady stream of phone calls, official requests about what to cover, and warnings from officials and influential people. The occasional (often unreported) beating of an editor or reporter reinforces the tendency toward journalistic caution on sensitive subjects. Censorship is formally forbidden, but unofficial forms abound. These include government control over most of the classic choke points, such as printing, newsprint supply, distribution, allocation of broadcast frequencies, taxation, and assignment of premises.

Journalists say that Sarkissian has personally beat a chief editor whose paper's articles on Nagorno-Karabakh displeased him. When a foreign correspondent submitted a written question to President Kocharian asking whether he thinks the defense minister's comportment is good for Armenia's image abroad, a presidential spokesman declined to submit it, explaining that it was "not interesting."

Sarkissian is not the only official to show contempt for the press. For example, in July, the independent television station Ar was called to cover the police evicting a family from its apartment. At the scene, police beat the crew and broke two of its cameras. The Interior Minister said he would pay for the damaged equipment, but had not done so as of early 1999.

Because of poor economic conditions and low wages, most Armenians cannot afford to buy daily newspapers, and print press circulations are tiny. News kiosks rent copies of papers by the half hour. The state press distribution monopoly, Hay Mamoul, rarely provides next-day delivery of the national press to provincial newsstands. It pays publications for sales and subscriptions with enormous, crippling delays.

A press law passed by the Armenian Supreme Soviet in 1991 remains on the books. It bans the "abuse" of press freedom—making it illegal to publish state secrets, incitement to war or violence, hate speech, pornography, advocacy of drug use, erroneous or unverified information, or unauthorized information about a person's private life. Violations are punishable by a six-month suspension of the allegedly offending news media. (There were no suspensions during 1998.) Draft revisions of the law, even those proposed by groups of democratic journalists, have contained similarly restrictive clauses. For example, a draft freedom of information law, written in 1998 by a human rights group, would bar the publication of anything the government defines as a state secret.

There were 904 media outlets on the official register of the Armenian Justice Ministry in 1998, 141 of them added during the year. But very few—about 70 newspapers, 20 national and local television stations, and five FM radio stations—appeared regularly.

Azerbaijan

The end of official censorship was virtually the only positive development for the press this year. Unfortunately, this ostensible reform by the government of President Heydar Aliyev was overshadowed by the press freedom abuses that preceded and followed it.

After opposition parties threatened to withdraw from the October 11 presidential election if Aliyev failed to meet a variety of demands, including abolishing censorship, the president issued a decree on August 6 doing away with the General Directorate of State Secrets, known as GLAVLIT, its Soviet-era acronym. GLAVLIT had conducted business in violation of the 1992 Law on Mass Media as well as Articles 47 (freedom of opinions and convictions) and 50 (inadmissibility of censorship of the media) of the Azeri Constitution. Following GLAVLIT's abolition, government officials said that a new body would be created to monitor reporting on topics deemed to be state secrets, although the details of its structure and its effect on the media had not been spelled out at year's end.

From August through the October 11 presidential election, which Aliyev won easily amidst claims of electoral abuses, journalists experienced some freedom to cover political events. Few, however, believed that this slight opening was permanent—and it has not been. Although censorship is officially dead, authorities have found other ways to silence independent and opposition media.

Criminal and civil libel charges have become weapons of choice, leading to the proliferation of lawsuits against newspapers and journalists for "defaming the honor" of government officials. Although this is not a new form of harassment, there has been a noticeable rise in the number of libel suits filed since November 11, when the Milli Mejlis (Azerbaijan's parliament) issued a statement calling on the minister of information to take measures to prevent the media from publishing materials which insult the honor of President Aliyev. The opposition newspapers *Azadliq*, *Yeni Musavat*, *Mukhalifat*, and *Khurriyet*, among others, have been the defendants in civil law suits with fines collectively totaling millions of dollars, clearly intended to put them out of business. Editors of these and other newspapers also face criminal charges, most often under Article 121 of the penal code, which carries a sentence of up to three years for publishing false and dishonoring comments about public officials.

In addition to legal harassment, threats and violent assaults against editors and reporters continue to be common, as evidenced by the September 16 beating by police of 34 journalists who were covering an opposition rally in Baku.

The two state-owned television stations, AzTV-1 and AzTV-2, dominate the electronic media, and provide the population with most of its news. Several independent stations exist, although a tightening of private broadcasting regulations has forced them to narrow their coverage to a range of subjects acceptable to local authorities.

September 12
Azer Sariyev, *Express* ATTACKED, HARASSED
Tahir Mamedov, *Chag* ATTACKED, HARASSED
Rey Kerimoglu, *Sharq* ATTACKED, HARASSED
Azer Rashidoglu, *Ayna* ATTACKED, HARASSED
Faiq Qazanfaroglu, *Millet* ATTACKED, HARASSED
Elman Maliyev, *Khurriyet* ATTACKED, HARASSED
Mohammed Ersoy, *Yurd Yeri* ATTACKED, HARASSED
Ibrahim Niyazli, *Democratic Azerbaijan* ATTACKED, HARASSED
Anar Mammadli, *Azerbaijan Gencleri* ATTACKED, HARASSED
Movsun Mammadov, *Monitor* ATTACKED, HARASSED
Rasul Mursaqulov, *Chag* ATTACKED, HARASSED
Khalig Bahadur, *Azadliq* ATTACKED, HARASSED
Ajdar, *Azadliq* ATTACKED, HARASSED
Haji Zamin, *Azadliq* ATTACKED, HARASSED
Sarvan Rizvanov, *Azadliq* ATTACKED, HARASSED
Elmir Suleymanov, ANS TV ATTACKED, HARASSED
Ilqar Shakhmaroglu, *Qanun* ATTACKED, HARASSED
Nebi Rustamov, *Qanun* ATTACKED, HARASSED
Taghi Yusifov, *Qanun* ATTACKED, HARASSED
Shakhbaz Khuduoglu, *Qanun* ATTACKED, HARASSED

Attacks on the Press in 1998

Lachin Semra, *Mukhalifat* ATTACKED, HARASSED
Tahir Pasha, *Olaylar* ATTACKED, HARASSED
Natiq Javadli, *Olaylar* ATTACKED, HARASSED
Taptyg Farkhadoglu, Turan news agency ATTACKED, HARASSED
Movlud Javadov, *Yeni Musavat* ATTACKED, HARASSED
Kamil Taghisoy, *Yeni Musavat* ATTACKED, HARASSED
Shakhin Jafarli, *Yeni Musavat* ATTACKED, HARASSED
Sebukhi Mammadli, *Yeni Musavat* ATTACKED, HARASSED
Azer Qarachanli, *Yeni Musavat* ATTACKED, HARASSED
Zamina Aliqizi, *Yeni Musavat* ATTACKED, HARASSED
Eldaniz Badalov, *Bu Gun* ATTACKED, HARASSED
Allakhverdi Donmez, *Tezadlar* ATTACKED, HARASSED
Mekhseti Sherif, *Rezonans* ATTACKED, HARASSED
Tunzale Rafiqqizi, *Ana Veten* ATTACKED, HARASSED
Shahbaz Xuduoglu, *Qanun* HARASSED
Tahir Mamedov, *Chag* HARASSED

Police beat and harassed 34 journalists who were attempting to report on an opposition political rally in Baku. The officers were violently dispersing a crowd of several hundred opposition demonstrators who had gathered to demand the cancellation of the October 11 presidential elections. They assaulted the journalists and confiscated cameras, tape recorders, and press identification cards.

At least two journalists were detained for several hours. Khuduoglu, editor of *Qanun* magazine, was taken to the Baku City Police Station, then to the Sabayel District Police Station. He was released after nine hours. Mamedov, deputy editor of the newspaper *Chag*, was also detained.

Journalists reported that police also attempted to break into a building housing several opposition and independent news outlets, including *Azadliq* and *Chag* and the Turan news agency.

October 1
Yeni Musavat LEGAL ACTION

Just prior to the October 11 presidential elections, Ramiz Mehdiyev, chief of staff to President Heydar Aliyev, filed a civil libel suit against the daily *Yeni Musavat*. The complaint was in response to articles published on September 6 and 9, which cited opposition figure Nizami Suleymanov saying that Mehdiyev was Armenian.

On November 19, a court of first instance ruled in Mehdiyev's favor, but the paper appealed the decision. On December 15, an appeals court upheld the verdict and ordered *Yeni Musavat* to pay Mehdiyev 200 million manat (US$50,000).

November 9
Azadliq LEGAL ACTION
Yeni Musavat LEGAL ACTION
Sabina Avazqizi, *Yeni Musavat* LEGAL ACTION
Beyuqaga Agayev, *Azadliq* LEGAL ACTION

On November 9, the Ministry of Justice filed a civil libel suit against opposition newspapers *Yeni Musavat* and *Azadliq* for insulting the "honor and dignity" of President Heydar Aliyev. The charges stemmed from articles published on November 7 quoting former president Abulfaz Elchibey, now an opposition leader, saying that President Aliyev helped found the Kurdistan Workers' Party (PKK) during the 1970s.

On December 15, the Sabayel District Court, convicted the papers and fined each 150 million manat (about US$40,000) in moral damages. In addition, Avazqizi, a reporter for *Yeni Musavat*, and Agayev, a reporter for *Azadliq*, were fined 30 million manat (US$8,000) and 50 million manat (US$12,000), respectively. The court ordered each paper to publish a retraction of the stories and an apology.

November 13
Esmira Namiqqizi, *Yeni Musavat* ATTACKED
Ilhama Namiqqizi, *Yeni Musavat* ATTACKED
Zamina Aliqizi, *Yeni Musavat* ATTACKED
Aynur Eyvazli, *Yeni Musavat* ATTACKED

Police forcibly dispersed about 30 staff members of the opposition newspaper *Yeni Musavat* from outside the courthouse in Baku where the journalists were peacefully protesting a civil defamation trial against *Yeni Musavat* underway inside. They injured at least four of the protesters, Namiqqizi, Namiqqizi, Aliqizi, and Eyvazli.

December 5
Mahir Samedov, *Ulus*
LEGAL ACTION

The general prosecutor's office opened a criminal investigation of Samedov, editor of the independent pro-opposition newspaper *Ulus*, under Article 188-2 of the penal code, which outlaws the distribution of information dishonoring the president. The charge was in response to a November article, in which the newspaper reprinted a speech by Rasul Guliyev, former speaker of parliament and currently in exile, who said President Heydar Aliyev had sold some regions of the country to Armenia.

December 14
Azadliq LEGAL ACTION

A Baku city court ruled against the opposition newspaper *Azadliq*, requiring it to pay a fine of 500 million manat (US$130,000) under Article 7 of the civil code for insulting 14 public officials and relatives of the president. Judge Azer Huseinov heard the case and delivered his ruling even though no representative of *Azadliq* was present for the trial.

The suit was filed in early November after *Azadliq* published a series of articles titled "Great Owners of a Small Country," which reported that the officials owned valuable real estate in Great Britain and France.

Also on December 14, in connection with the same article, Judge Huseinov decided to open a criminal libel investigation against Gunduz Tairli, editor of *Azadliq*, under Article 121 of the penal code. If convicted, he faces up to three years imprisonment.

December 14
Gunduz Tairli, *Azadliq* LEGAL ACTION

In a Baku city court, Judge Azer Huseinov opened a seditious libel investigation of Tairli, editor of the opposition newspaper *Azadliq*, for allegedly violating Article 121 of the penal code by publishing "false and dishonoring" comments against public officials. The offense carries a prison sentence of up to three years.

The investigation stemmed from a series of articles published in the November 7-9 editions of the paper, titled "Great Owners of a Small Country," which claimed that valuable real estate in Great Britain and France was owned by 14 government officials and relatives of President Heydar Aliyev.

Also on December 14, and in connection with the same article, Judge Huseinov ruled against *Azadliq* in a civil libel suit. He fined the paper 500 million manat (US$130,000) under Article 7 of the civil code for publishing "false and dishonoring" comments against public officials.

December 15
Azer Guseinbala, *Khurriyet* LEGAL ACTION
Rauf Arifoglu, *Yeni Musavat* LEGAL ACTION
Gunduz Tairli, *Azadliq* LEGAL ACTION
Suleyman Osmanoglu, *Mukhalifat* LEGAL ACTION

A Baku city court opened an investigation into

criminal libel allegations against the editors of the four opposition newspapers under Article 121-2 of the penal code, which outlaws the publication of "false and dishonoring comments" about public officials. Aquil, Jalal, and Rafiq Aliyev, relatives of President Heydar Aliyev, filed the libel complaint against the four newspapers. They were among 15 papers that had run articles quoting political opposition figure Ashraf Mehdiyev, who claimed Aliyev was an ethnic Kurd.

December 15
Yeni Musavat LEGAL ACTION

In October, Nizami Gojayev, an official in the Minsitry of Internal Affairs, filed a libel suit for 20 million manat (US$5,000) against the opposition newspaper *Yeni Musavat* for articles published on October 7 and 8 which claimed that he was involved in plotting the assassination of Ziya Bundyadov, a member of parliament.

In November, a court of first instance ordered the newspaper to pay 20 million manat (US$5,000) to Gojayev. *Yeni Musavat* appealed the decision, but an appeals court upheld the verdict on December 15.

Belarus

With free enterprise stifled, opposition activists detained, and independent media restricted, the Soviet-style rule of President Aleksander Lukashenko continued to have disastrous effects on Belarus' economic and political life. The United States and other Western governments withdrew their ambassadors after Lukashenko locked diplomats out of their Minsk houses in June. And Belarussian citizens warned that their president's disdain for the West reflects his ultimate goal: to rule a Slavic union that includes Russia.

To combat his critics, Lukashenko increased the already onerous restrictions on the media. In April, the press in Minsk learned of an undated, secret government memorandum that directed state agencies not to give resolutions, orders, or other official documents to non-state media. The memorandum also barred state officials from commenting about official documents to independent journalists, and restricted state advertising to state-run media. The latter move was a severe financial threat to the emerging independent press, which mainly consists of small-circulation daily and weekly newspapers.

In May, CPJ named Lukashenko one of the world's 10 worst Enemies of the Press for the second year in a row (See page 62 for more on the Enemies of the Press.) When that news was reported by the Minsk-based independent weekly *Zdravy Smysl*, the State Committee on the Press issued a warning to the paper, charging it had provided "distorted information." The warning was based on the newspaper's use of the word "decree" to describe the secret memorandum forbidding distribution of government documents to non-state media.

In November, Lukashenko refused to allow Pavel Sheremet, Minsk bureau chief for Russian ORT television and editor of *Belorusskaya Delovaya Gazeta*, to travel to New York City to receive CPJ's 1998 International Press Freedom Award. (See page 66 for more about CPJ's International Press Freedom Awards.) Sheremet is a citizen of Belarus and ORT bureau chief in Minsk. The Belarus government has frequently targeted him for official harassment, including imprisonment, stripping him of his professional credentials, and barring him from traveling abroad. On November 26, two days after CPJ's awards ceremony, the government finally told Sheremet he was free to travel. Instead of going to New York City, Sheremet received the award from a

CPJ delegation that traveled to Minsk on December 8 to present the honor before dozens of independent journalists, diplomats, and Belarussian politicians.

January 28
Dmitri Zavadsky, ORT LEGAL ACTION
Pavel Sheremet, ORT, *Belorusskaya Delovaya Gazeta* HARASSED, LEGAL ACTION

The regional court in Oshmiani convicted Sheremet, Minsk bureau chief of ORT (Russian public television) and editor of *Belorusskaya Delovaya Gazeta*, and his cameraman Dmitri Zavadsky, of illegally crossing an unguarded section of Belarus' border with Lithuania (Article 80 of the penal code), as they were filming a documentary on border security and smuggling on July 22, 1997. The Oshmiani court also convicted them of exceeding their professional rights as journalists (Article 167 of the penal code), and of participating in a conspiracy (Article 17 of the penal code).

Sheremet and Zavadsky received suspended sentences of two years and 18 months, respectively, and Sheremet was barred from practicing journalism and from leaving the country until January 1999 as a reprisal for his investigative reporting. On October 30, CPJ wrote to President Aleksander Lukashenko asking him to temporarily lift Sheremet's travel restrictions so that he could travel to New York City to receive CPJ's 1998 International Press Freedom Award on November 24. On November 20, the government denied CPJ's request, but then lifted the travel ban on November 26, two days after the awards ceremony.

On December 8, CPJ representatives traveled to Belarus and presented the award to Sheremet.

March 26
All media CENSORED

The government issued a secret directive to state agencies to cease responding to inquiries from the independent media. According to the Belarusian Association of Journalists, the instructions were contained in a letter marked "for authorized use only" and signed by Alexey Bolozinski, a member of the State Committee on the Press and a senior adviser to the Department of Socio-Cultural Policy of the Council of Ministers.

The directive forbids state agencies from releasing to the independent media any information on official documents, such as laws, decrees, resolutions, or orders, and bars distribution of copies of official documents. It also prohibits government officials from commenting on official documents already in the public domain. And it bans state agencies from placing advertisements in the independent media.

Bosnia-Herzegovina

Three years after the Dayton peace accords ended the war in Bosnia and Herzegovina, physical dangers to journalists have abated, but nationalist political parties continue to control or influence most media, and to harass independent journalists.

During and immediately after parliamentary and presidential elections in September, police detained journalists in three separate incidents, but quickly released them when international agencies intervened.

Local officials are turning increasingly to criminal defamation law, which permits imprisonment for up to three years, as an instrument of intimidation. In a developing pattern, courts are handing down conditional jail sentences, suspended unless the journalist is found in violation of any law during the subsequent year. Both the Organization for Security and Cooperation in Europe (OSCE) and

the international community's new Independent Media Commission (IMC) in Bosnia—established in June to create an equitable broadcasting regulatory system and to promote media professionalism—have condemned the sentences and called for decriminalization of libel law in Bosnia.

With the economy still in deep recession, aid from Western governments and private donors remains crucial to the survival of Bosnia's independent media, as does the presence of the high representative, Carlos Westendorp, a special envoy with broad powers established by the Dayton Accords.

Under a supervisor appointed by Westendorp, public television and radio in the Muslim-Croat Federation (RTVBiH) acquired new management and a nonpartisan governing council. By year's end, programming showed significant improvement in balance and production quality. A second supervisor installed by Westendorp at the Serb entity's public television network SRT, made some progress in improving the balance of news coverage, but the SRT remains under the control of the nationalist but relatively moderate Republika Srpska (RS) government.

As the struggle between competing Serb political parties continued, the RS government attempted in July, seven weeks before national elections, to install its own management at 16 local radio and television stations controlled by hard-line nationalist Serb factions, but failed at all but six of the stations.

Since its inception, the IMC has promulgated a broadcasting code of ethics based in part on the Fairness Doctrine originated by the U.S. Federal Communications Commission. By year's end, it had begun licensing the approximately 290 radio and television stations in Bosnia.

Bulgaria

The pro-reform government of Prime Minister Ivan Kostov and his United Democratic Forces (UDF) coalition, elected in 1997 in the wake of nationwide political and economic upheaval, brought a degree of stability and recovery to the country after a year of crisis. The improved conditions have benefited the independent press, especially the national independent dailies *Trud* and *24 Chasa*, and the weeklies *Kapital* and *168 Chasa*. In some small towns, however, local authorities and prosecutors used their virtually unrestricted political power to intimidate the few critical voices of the independent press.

Widespread corruption and the influence of organized crime still plague the country. And for reporters who dig into these issues, Bulgaria is a dangerous place. Threats and violent attacks on news outlets, journalists, and their families occur with alarming frequency and virtual impunity.

In May, Anna Zarkova, a crime reporter and chief editor of the crime section of *Trud*, suffered severe burns and the loss of sight in her left eye when acid was thrown in her face in retaliation for her reporting, which has covered such explosive topics as corrupt prosecutors and government officials, police violence, and arms smuggling. Although her assailant has confessed, police have not identified those behind the attack. Zarkova met with CPJ staff, board, and supporters in New York City during her October visit to the United States to receive two international journalism awards and to seek medical assistance.

In another alarming trend, criminal libel prosecutions against independent journalists increased significantly. In May, CPJ joined local press freedom groups in petitioning the government to remove Articles 146, 147, and 148 of the penal code, which criminalize libel and defamation and carry prison sentences of up to three years for journalists convicted of violating these provisions. On July 17, the Constitutional Court ruled that the articles did not violate the constitution. Although authorities in September told a delegation from the International Press Institute that they planned to reassess the penal code in the near future, they continued to use the statutes to prosecute journalists throughout the year.

The results of this prosecutorial zeal are manifest in the plight of Yovka Atanassova, owner and editor of the independent daily *Starozagorsky Novini*. This year, appeals courts upheld two suspended criminal libel sentences she had received after being convicted of libeling local prosecutors and businessmen. (In 1997, Atanassova lost appeals of three other suspended sentences.) When the fifth five-month criminal libel sentence was upheld on appeal in December, the court ordered her to serve 16 months in prison. At press time, she remained free pending official notice of the start of her sentence.

In July, the parliament passed a draft law on radio and television. The draft legislation was intended to regulate the transition of state-run Bulgarsko Natsionalno Radio (Bulgarian National Radio, or BNR) and Bulgarska Natsionalna Televizia (Bulgarian National Television, or BNT) to public media. It stipulated that news and public affairs programs should be the exclusive province of BNT and BNR, while privately run stations should focus on music and entertainment programming. Journalists and press freedom advocates criticized the draft law for attempting to dictate the content of broadcast media. Because of these problems with the legislation, and its failure to guarantee the political independence of the members of the National Council on Radio and Television, which has the power to ban programs and suspend broadcasting

licenses, President Petar Stoyanov vetoed the draft bill in September. Parliament is likely to revise it in 1999.

Also in July, parliament passed a telecommunications law, which established financially and bureaucratically burdensome procedures for granting frequency licenses to independent broadcasters and created a telecommunications commission, tightly controlled by the cabinet, to oversee frequency distribution.

Most Bulgarians rely on state-run national television for their news. The government has delayed the promised privatization of the second national state-run television channel, Efir 2. The sole alternative station, Nova Televizia, is available only in the largest cities. Of the approximately 100 private radio stations, most operate without the required licenses and could be shut down at any time. For this reason and the weakness of their signals, they cannot compete with state-run radio's news coverage.

May 11
Anna Zarkova, *Trud* ATTACKED, THREATENED

An unidentified assailant threw acid in the face of Zarkova, a prominent crime reporter for the independent daily *Trud*, at a Sofia bus stop as she was on her way to work. She was hospitalized under guard with serious burns to her left eye, her left hand, and the left side of her face and neck. Doctors were uncertain at the time whether she would regain sight in her left eye. Zarkova learned several months later that she would never regain sight in that eye.

Zarkova has won several Bulgarian journalism prizes for her investigation of organized crime and corruption, ranging from street gangs to the highest levels of government. She and *Trud* deputy editor Nikolai Stefanov said they were convinced the attack stemmed from her work.

Stefanov said that nearly a year ago, Zarkova received several anonymous death threats by telephone at her office after publishing an exposé about a former deputy chief prosecutor. Zarkova also wrote a book examining high-profile murders in Bulgaria over the past several years.

In July, police questioned Emil Mariev, a 23-year-old former *Trud* staffer, who pleaded guilty to throwing the acid into Zarkova's face. Police are still trying to identify those who ordered the attack.

July 14
All media THREATENED

The Bulgarian Constitutional Court upheld Articles 146, 147, and 148 of the penal code, which make libel a criminal offense punishable by up to three years in prison. In so deciding, the court rejected a petition signed by 55 lawmakers and a number of independent journalists and human rights groups, who had requested the court rule those provisions unconstitutional.

The petitioners, led by Yovka Atanassova, owner and editor *of Starozagorsky Novini*, claimed the articles contradict the Bulgarian Constitution as well as international norms of press freedom. They argued that the statutes offer special protection for public officials by allowing public prosecutors to prosecute journalists on behalf of officials.

The Constitutional Court ruled that the statutes were not unconstitutional, arguing that many Western European countries have criminal and seditious libel statutes on the books, although they are rarely enforced.

In September, members of parliament assured an International Press Insititute delegation that the entire penal code, including the articles dealing with defamation, will be reappraised in 1999.

December 11
Yovka Atanassova, *Starozagorsky Novini*
LEGAL ACTION

The regional court in Nova Zagora convicted Atanassova, owner and editor of the daily *Starozagorsky Novini*, of defaming Dinko Bozajiev, a prosecutor from the regional court in Stara Zagora. She was sentenced to five months in prison and fined 700,000 leva (approximately US$450).

Atanassova had been charged under Articles 147 and 148 of the penal code for slander and defamation, stemming from a December 1995 article in *Starozagorsky Novini* which reported that Bozajiev was a Communist secret service agent.

According to Atanassova, the court ruled in the case when neither she nor her lawyer were present, and sent her the verdict a month later by mail. This prevented her from filing an appeal within the 10-day appeals period after the verdict was announced, as required by Bulgarian law. Because Atanassova has a number of other confirmed conditional imprisonment sentences pending, the Bulgarian criminal code requires that she serve an earlier five-month prison sentence and then file an appeal with the Supreme Court to overturn the December 11 conviction. She is expected to begin serving her sentence some time in January.

Croatia

The Croatian government stepped up its already vigorous use of criminal and civil libel suits to keep the independent press in check. By year's end, independent newspapers including *Globus, Feral Tribune, Nacional,* **and** *Novi List* **were facing more than 600 civil law suits. Individual claims generally range from about 100,000 kuna (US$15,000) to 4.6 million kuna (US$750,000), which 23 government ministers are demanding of** *Globus* **for an article reporting allegations of official corruption. Another 300 or so criminal libel cases have been lodged against individual journalists. The majority of plain-**

tiffs are government officials who claim to have suffered mental pain as a result of the articles in question.

Some good news can be derived from the fact that *Feral Tribune* journalists Viktor Ivancic and Marinko Culic were acquitted on December 21 of criminal libel charges in a long-standing criminal libel suit. Following an initial acquittal in September 1996, the state filed an appeal and new charges were brought against the two journalists in connection with the article "Jasenovac—The Largest Croatian Underground City." While this most recent acquittal could potentially serve as a precedent in future cases, it is unlikely to affect those in which newspapers have already been ordered by second instance courts to pay significant fines. This is the case with *Nacional*, which lost three cases this year for a total of 614,846 kuna (nearly US$100,000), and *The Feral Tribune*, which also lost three cases worth 160,000 kuna (US$27,000). Each of these verdicts has been appealed to the Supreme Court, although the newspapers could be forced to pay these fines until the decisions are overturned by a Supreme Court ruling.

The situation was only made worse by the frequent use of Article 25 of Croatia's Public Information Law, which stipulates that courts must hear these lawsuits within eight days of the initial filing. This leaves little time for the defendants to properly prepare a defense.

State-controlled distributors and printers exert financial pressure on the country's print media. Tisak, the country's largest distributor, allied with the ruling Democratic Party of Croatia (HDZ), controlled about 70 percent of all newspaper sales. They routinely withheld payments from independent newspapers and, to a lesser extent, state-owned newspapers. At one point toward the end of the year, the amount owed to *Nacional* exceeded 3 million kuna (approximately US$500,000). Other independent newspapers are equally dependent on Tisak for payments to employees and to printers, since the majority of their income comes from sales rather than advertising. On the other side of the squeeze is the largely state-owned printing house, Hrvatska Tiskara, which has threatened to stop printing independent newspapers if they fail to meet payments.

Amidst the legal and financial harassment, which showed no signs of abating during the year, independent journalists learned in November that the secret service had been keeping files on many of them. The security forces continued their more blatant forms of intimidation such as threats and physical attacks.

Croatia's privately owned electronic media struggle to compete with the state-controlled HTV Television and radio. HTV television, managed at nearly every level by HDZ operatives, remains the country's most influential station. But an association of prominent reporters from HTV known as Forum 21 has been vocal in calling for reforms within the television network, including greater editorial freedom and balance of political viewpoints.

November 27
Ivo Pukanic, *Nacional* THREATENED
Georgitsa Klancir, *Globus* THREATENED

Hrvoje Sarinic, former first secretary of the president's office, revealed that journalists from the independent media had been under surveillance by the state secret service for several years. Two journalists—Pukanic, the editor of *Nacional*, and Klancir, the editor of *Globus*—have already seen their dossiers, as well as those of other journalists, which contain very detailed information about their private lives. Klancir described the contents of the dossiers in a December 3 article published in *Globus*.

Attacks on the Press in 1998

Czech Republic

In an environment generally respectful of press freedom, the Czech media function with little government interference and play an increasingly important role in Czech society. The lively and in-depth coverage of candidates and issues in the run-up to June parliamentary elections was a positive departure from previous years, when the Czech media held back from criticizing leading political figures.

In January, the statute criminalizing defamation of the president was removed from the criminal code. Other criminal defamation provisions remain in place, although their removal may be a precondition of the Czech Republic's acceptance into the European Union.

While the ongoing prosecution of Zdenek Zukal, owner and director of the private ZZIP TV studio in Olomouc, is the exception rather than the rule in the Czech Republic, it demonstrates the insidious potential of criminal libel laws. CPJ wrote to President Vaclav Havel on January 8, arguing that the use of criminal libel statutes is antithetical to the country's democratization process.

January 5
Zdenek Zukal, TV Studio ZZIP HARASSED, LEGAL ACTION

Olomouc police detained Zukal, owner and director of TV Studio ZZIP, an independent television production company, on charges of criminal libel.

The police had summoned Zukal to headquarters to question him about a report produced by his studio that aired on TV Nova's November 19 evening news broadcast. Zukal refused to answer questions about his reporting for the broadcast, which attempted to prove that Vladimir Pryzna, a top police investigator, had accepted a bribe from a local businessman wanted on charges of fraud and counterfeiting. As a result, the police charged Zukal with making "biased and false accusations" against Pryzna under Article 174.1 of the Czech penal code. Zukal received the charges in the form of a document, which was backdated to December 22, 1997, without explanation.

Zukal was held for several hours at police headquarters before being taken in handcuffs to the local prosecutor's office. The prosecutor agreed to press charges and to detain Zukal for the duration of the criminal investigation.

On the same day, the journalist appeared before a local judge, who ruled that there was no reason to keep Zukal in detention and ordered him released, though the charges were not dropped.

After Zukal's release, police searched the facilities of TV Studio ZZIP, as well as the journalist's apartment, in an apparent attempt to find the materials on which Zukal's broadcast was based. His case had not yet gone to trial at the end of 1998.

Georgia

A number of politically destabilizing events rocked Georgia during the year. In February, President Eduard Shevardnadze narrowly escaped injury in an assassination attempt that left two of his bodyguards dead. A few weeks later, four members of a United Nations team sent to observe the peace agreement in the separatist region of Abkhazia were abducted. In May, hostilities, which had essentially ended since the 1993 cease-fire, were renewed in Abkhazia's Gali region. In October, supporters of Georgia's late President Zviad Gamsakhurdia attempted to oust Shevardnadze. As the government struggled to maintain political control and rein in the opposition, official harassment of journalists increased.

At least one journalist lost his life reporting on the fighting in Abkhazia, which flared again in May. Georgy Chanya, a reporter for the independent Tbilisi daily *Rezonants*, was killed on May 27 while covering the conflict between Abkhaz rebels and Georgian guerrillas near Gali. Chanya's death raises to four the number of journalists CPJ has documented as killed in the line of duty in Abkhazia since 1992, when fighting first broke out.

In June, the Ministry of Internal Affairs and the Ministry of State Security of the Autonomous Republic of Abkhazia in exile filed civil libel suits against the weekly independent newspaper *Kavkasioni* and against Sozar Subeliani, an editor from the newspaper. A decision in favor of the plaintiffs could set a dangerous precedent, especially since other independent newspapers, such as *Rezonants*, are also facing libel suits filed by government officials.

Independent journalists were targets of violent attacks. In September, armed assailants beat Lasha Nadareishvili and David Okropiridze, editor in chief and a reporter, respectively, for the independent weekly *Asaval-Dasavali*.

In an incident of harassment involving the military, Ministry of Defense officials called Amiran Meskheli, a correspondent for the newspaper *Orioni*, for military service on June 11 following the publication in May of an article that included Meskheli's interview with several soldiers. On August 20, a court ordered his temporary release, ruling that Meskheli had been "called up in violation of the law."

Journalists continued to face other obstacles to their work, such as the denial of access to public information by authorities. And local governments frequently pressured independent newspapers through overzealous tax inspections and other abuses of regulatory procedures.

May 27
Georgy Chanya, *Rezonants* KILLED

Chanya, a reporter for the independent Georgian daily *Rezonants*, was killed while reporting on fighting between Abkhaz rebels and Georgian guerrillas near Gali in the separatist region of Abkhazia, according to Amiran Dzotsenidze, deputy editor of *Rezonants*.

Chanya and two other Georgian journalists crossed into Abkhazia on May 20 to cover reports of ethnic cleansing of Georgians by Abkhaz rebels. The two reporters traveling with Chanya left Abkhazia as the violence escalated, but he stayed behind, choosing to follow a band of Georgian guerrillas to file reports from the front line. He was killed during a raid on a guerrilla camp. His mutilated body was returned to Georgia, together with the bodies of 10 guerrillas, in return for the release of two jailed Abkhaz rebels held by Georgian police. Chanya was identified by personal documents found on his body.

The 25-year-old Chanya was an ethnic Georgian who fled Gali with his family at the height of the civil war, which has raged on and off since 1992. He settled in the neighboring Zugdidi region and worked as a special correspondent covering Abkhazia for *Rezonants*. Chanya has been described by his colleagues as an able and prolific reporter, who had risked his life many times while on assignment in the secessionist region.

June 22
Sozar Subeliani, *Kavkasioni* LEGAL ACTION
Kavkasioni LEGAL ACTION

In the last week of June, the Ministry of Internal Affairs (MIA) of the Autonomous Republic of Abkhazia in exile in Tbilisi filed a civil libel suit against the weekly newspaper *Kavkasioni* and against Subeliani, the paper's editor, under Article 18 of the Georgian civil code for "damaging a reputation." The action came in response to an article by Subeliani in the May 25-31 issue, which described the activities of the MIA during the Abkhaz-Georgian war. The article, "Situation Not Controlled in Kodori Gorge," alleged that the MIA tried to buy information from the Abkhazian government in Sukhumi. The MIA sought 10,000 lari (then US$7,000) in damages, half to be paid by the paper and half by Subeliani.

On September 10, the lawyer representing both Subeliani and *Kavkasioni* filed a motion to dismiss the case. The lawyer stated that under Georgian law, a suit seeking compensation for material damages cannot be filed by a legal entity, only by a person. On this basis, Judge Gergenava of the Mtatsminda District Court in Tbilisi postponed the trial. On October 2, he agreed to pass the case to the Tbilisi city court, which was to decide whether the case would proceed or be dismissed. The case was still pending at the end of 1998.

The Ministry of State Security of the Autonomous Republic of Abkhazia in exile in Tbilisi also filed suit on June 22 against Subeliani and *Kavkasioni* over material in the same article.

June 22
Sozar Subeliani, *Kavkasioni* LEGAL ACTION
Kavkasioni LEGAL ACTION

In the last week of June, the Ministry of State Security (MSS) of the Autonomous Republic of Abkhazia in exile in Tbilisi filed a civil libel suit against the weekly newspaper *Kavkasioni* and against Subeliani, the paper's editor, under Article 18 of the Georgian Civil Code for "damaging a reputation." The action was in response to an article by Subeliani in the May 25-31 issue, which among other things described MSS activities during the Abkhaz-Georgian war. The article, "Situation Not Controlled in Kodori Gorge," alleged that at the last stage of the war, MSS officers selectively disarmed some Georgian troops and armed others, and provoked conflict between them.

Attacks on the Press in 1998

The MSS sought 15,000 lari (then US$12,000) in damages, half to be paid by the paper and half by Subeliani. The trial was scheduled to begin in early 1999.

The Ministry of Internal Affairs (MIA) of the Autonomous Republic of Abkhazia in exile in Tbilisi also filed suit on June 22 against Sukhumi and *Kakakasioni* over material in the same article.

September 12
Lasha Nadareishvili, *Asaval-Dasavali*
ATTACKED
David Okropiridze, *Asaval-Dasavali*
ATTACKED

A group of five or six unidentified armed men beat Nadareishvili, editor in chief of the popular independent weekly *Asaval-Dasavali*, and Okropiridze, a correspondent for the newspaper, at around 10 p.m.

The journalists were assaulted on a street corner in front of the newspaper's office in central Tbilisi. The attackers said nothing as they punched and kicked the editor and reporter, striking Okropidze in the head with a gun handle. Both were treated at a hospital for injuries. Neither of the journalists was robbed.

Nadareishvili and his staff believe the assault was in reprisal for their work, although they have no clues as to the identity of the assailants. The staff of *Asaval-Dasavali* has periodically received threatening phone calls after publishing exposés and articles critical of figures and forces across the political spectrum, from the government to the opposition.

Kazakhstan

Determined to prolong his hold on power, President Nursultan Nazarbayev manipulated Kazakhstan's electoral, legal, and media machinery. Engineering a special parliamentary vote whose constitutionality was

suspect, he moved the presidential elections from 2000 to January 10, 1999. And he used legal technicalities to bar his three political rivals, including his principal opponent, former Premier Akezhan Kazhegeldin, from the ballot. His machinations were so blatant that the U.S. State Department declined to send official monitors to observe the elections. The Organization for Security and Cooperation in Europe denounced the electoral fraud in advance of balloting.

In anticipation of this power grab, Nazarbayev started in 1997 to silence critics and rein in the press. His Justice Ministry continued throughout the year to threaten and harass the media for alleged violations of the press law, the Kazakh-language law requiring an equal volume of Kazakh-language broadcasts as those in other languages, and provisions banning insults aimed at the president. Apparently officially sanctioned violence against independent and dissident media also occurred. In this threatening environment, journalists increasingly resorted to self-censorship.

One of the clearest attempts at intimidation occurred on September 26, when unidentified assailants scaled a wall and hurled a Molotov cocktail into the offices of the opposition weekly *XXI Vek*, causing significant damage. Two days later, Almaty city authorities closed the newspaper without court order or explanation. This followed an earlier liquidation order by authorities against the newspaper *TOO Biik El*.

The regime also used legal methods to harass the independent press, especially privately owned newspapers with ties to former Premier Kazhegeldin. Exploiting the tax code, officials imposed large fines on broadcast outlets and newspapers considered to be too independent. State tax police repeatedly investigated such newspapers, including *Dat*, freezing bank accounts and confiscating office equipment, including computers. Customs officials seized print runs of newspapers which sought to avoid state interference by publishing in neighboring Kyrgyzstan. State security officials harassed the distributors of the newspaper *451 Gradusa po Farangeitu* (Fahrenheit 451). And the nominally private publishing house Franklin and the state-owned printing houses unilaterally broke publishing and distribution contracts with the newspapers *Tsentr* and *XXI Vek*.

The Kazakh government continued the process, begun at the end of 1996, to assert control over television and radio broadcasting, the major media of news throughout the country. The government rescinded the licenses of several independent broadcasters and made them available for tender offers before the expiration date of the original licenses. The Frequency Commission made sure that only investors favorably disposed to the government won the tenders. By this process, Nazarbayev's daughter, Dariga Nazarbayeva, gained control of the major television stations Khabar and NTK in 1997.

September 26
XXI Vek ATTACKED, HARASSED

Early in the morning, unidentified assailants tossed a Molotov cocktail through the third-floor office window of Bigeldin Gabdullin, editor in chief of the independent weekly *XXI Vek*. No one was injured in the attack. Paramedics, who arrived first at the scene, managed to extinguish the fire. The blaze destroyed office furniture, equipment, and an archive containing all 29 issues of the new weekly.

Prior to the attack, on September 10, a private press in Almaty stopped printing the paper, and the state-run distribution network refused to deliver it. The paper's management then began printing in Kyrgyzstan. Gabdullin said that the year-old publication was singled out for harassment in retaliation for its criticism of President Nursultan Nazarbayev's increasingly authoritarian regime, and its reporting on government corruption.

September 28
XXI Vek CENSORED
Big L Company CENSORED

Almaty Justice Ministry officials ordered the closure of the Big L Company, the founder and publisher of *XXI Vek*. The ruling contravenes Articles 49 and 50 of Kazakhstan's civil code, which stipulate that a legally incorporated entity can only be closed by court order or by the decision of its owners. Representatives of the Almaty city liquidation commission visited *XXI Vek*'s offices to enforce the Justice Ministry order to close the paper as part of the publisher's closure. They notified the editors and staff of their decision to close the weekly.

Bigeldin Gabdullin, *XXI Vek*'s editor in chief, appealed the ministry's decision, which came two days after unidentified assailants tossed a Molotov cocktail through the window of his third-floor office.

Kyrgyzstan

Under international pressure to maintain Kyrgyzstan's supposed commitment to a free press, President Askar Akayev battled unsuccessfully with the parliament over a draft amendment to the criminal code to remove criminal libel statutes, limiting punishment of this offense to the civil code. He also called for a referendum on a constitutional amendment to guarantee greater freedom of speech. On October 17, voters elected to amend the constitution to state that "the parliament shall pass no law that restricts freedom of speech or of the press." While such an amendment to the constitution—especially one supported by the population—is a positive sign, it alone cannot save Kyrgyzstan's waning reputation as "an island of democracy in a sea of authoritarian Central Asian states."

On January 8, the National Agency for Communications (NAC) announced that all of the country's television and radio stations would have to reapply for frequency licenses. Barely a month passed before accusations were flying regarding the NAC's alleged political biases. In one example, the agency ordered Radio Almaz to stop broadcasting for "technical reasons," although the director of the station believed the order was linked to the programming, which included broadcasts of Voice of America and Radio Liberty. The station was allowed to resume broadcasting on a temporary basis beginning in March. According to Article 8 of the Law on Media, a station can only be closed down by a decision of the founders or by a court decision.

Journalists who have taken a critical stance on government policies have been the target of legal action and physical violence.

The political pressure on journalists is compounded by the government's use of fees and taxation to squeeze the media. The long list of taxes on newspapers and broadcast outlets includes value-added tax, advertising tax, income tax, social fund tax, and import/export tax. In some cases, these onerous levies represent more than 50 percent of revenue for struggling newspapers, or radio and television stations.

Poland

Despite President Alexander Kwaniewski's assurances in 1996 that he would push for the abolishment of the country's criminal libel statutes, these disturbing laws remain in the penal code that took effect this year. Article 135 punishes defamation of the president with prison sentences of up to three years, while Article 226 covers defamation of other public officials. Although criminal libel prosecutions are rare, the existence of these provisions in the penal code continues to be a black spot on Poland's generally positive press freedom record.

Civil libel suits continue to be common. The president himself is pursuing a 2.5 million zloty (approximately US$800,000) suit filed in September 1997 against the editorial board of the newspaper *Zycie*. Kwaniewski alleges that the paper libeled him in an article which reported he had contacted a Russian spy during his 1994 vacation.

Other than the state-run television station, which observers say is highly politicized, there is a wide variety of independent media, including television and radio stations and newspapers. Privately owned distribution companies have emerged, but the country's largest distributor, Ruchs, remains state-owned. Print publications are licensed through the Communications Ministry.

Poland's laws governing electronic media are protectionist, and place a variety of restrictions on foreign media. These laws, at odds with European Union standards, will have to be reformed as a precondition of Poland's entry into the European community. The strict licensing process for electronic media has led some television stations to relocate outside Poland's borders.

Romania

Deep divisions in the governing coalition over policies and reforms stalled economic restructuring and led the government to the edge of crisis at year's end. Leftist-nationalist opposition parties boycotted Prime Minister Radu Vasile's cabinet, provoking calls for early elections. The political disunity was reflected in growing social unrest, unemployment, inflation, and crime.

In this environment, political and economic interests pervaded even the relatively independent private media. The lack of access to government documents and proceedings encouraged skewed coverage of events and reporting of unverified facts. On the other hand, well-documented investigative reporting on corruption and crime became the object of constant attacks. The penal code still contains articles punishing libel and defamation of public officials with up to three years' imprisonment.

The conviction and prison sentences of three journalists in criminal libel cases in May and July had a chilling effect on the country's press. In May, a city court in Bistritsa found Cornel Sabou, chief editor of the private news agency Trans Press, guilty of slander and sentenced him to 10 months in prison. The suit had been filed in 1996 by Mariana Iancu, a judge in Baia Mare, based on an article Sabou had published in the local daily *Ziua Nord-Vest*, reporting that Iancu had profited financially from some of her judicial rulings.

In July, a city court in Iasi sentenced Ovidiu Scutelnicu and Dragos Stingu, reporters for the independent daily *Monitorul*, to one-year prison terms each for defaming a local police official and his wife, a judge. In early January 1999, a Bucharest court reversed the decision, and suspended the reporters' sentences.

Numerous private radio and television stations provide an alternative to the heavily regulated Romanian National Radio and Television, offering independent coverage of news and public affairs.

July 23
Ovidiu Scutelnicu, *Monitorul* LEGAL ACTION
Dragos Stingu, *Monitorul* LEGAL ACTION

An Iasi city court sentenced Scutelnicu and Stingu, reporters for *Monitorul*, one of the most popular independent dailies in northeast Romania, to one year in prison each for criminal libel.

Petre Susanu, a local police colonel, and his wife, Otilia, a city court official, had brought libel charges against the journalists for a May 27 article, "Dismissal at the Top of the Iasi Police," which described Petre Susanu's dismissal from the police force. The article evaluated the grounds for Susanu's dismissal and questioned the sources of his wealth.

Scutelnicu and Stingu requested that their case be transferred to another venue because they believed they would not receive a fair trial in Iasi, where members of the Susanu family hold posts in the judiciary—the Susanus' daughter is a judge and their son-in-law is a prosecutor. But the Supreme Court rejected their request without explanation.

The reporters were convicted of libel under Article 206 of the penal code. In addition to the prison sentences, the court ordered the journalists to each pay a 1.5 billion lei fine (about US$170,000), stripped them of their civil rights, and barred them from practicing their profession for one year.

Scutelnicu and Stingu remain free, pending an appeal filed with the Iasi court on August 3. Under Romanian law, this is their only opportunity for appeal. But on August 5, Justice Minister Valeriu Stoica promised to file an extraordinary appeal with the Supreme Court on the journalists' behalf if the Iasi court rejects their appeal.

Upon a request by the justice minister, the venue for the appeal was moved to a Bucharest court. The hearing, which was originally slated for September 24, was delayed until January 11, 1999, because of a minor procedural error by the local court. On January 11, the Bucharest court modified the Iasi court's decision, handing Stingu and Scutelnicu suspended sentences of one year each.

Russia

The promise of press freedom, like that of other democratic ideals, remains unrealized seven years after the fall of the Soviet Union. Reflecting Russia's imperfect grasp of democratic principles, President Boris Yeltsin complained in a meeting with the directors of three national television channels, "We [the government] have the right to ask you to carry out state policy."

While the press is vibrant and diverse, reporters and editors nonetheless are buffeted by political and economic pressures, threats of physical violence, assaults, and even murder. The media moguls, interested in using their holdings as instruments of political and economic power, push employees directly and indirectly toward self-censorship and bias. As Alexei Pankin, editor of the trade magazine *Sreda*, noted, "The press can write the truth about anybody, but not its owner." Officials, meanwhile, use bribes as carrots, and libel suits and sometimes death threats as sticks to exact docility from journalists. The public's response to this well-known dynamic is skepticism about the reliability of the information it is receiving.

For those who dared to ignore the harassment and the threats, the murder of Larisa Yudina was a chilling reminder of the ongoing dangers faced by Russia's independent journalists. Despite repeated intimidation, the 53-year-old editor of the opposition *Sovietskaya Kalmykia Segodnya* continued to investigate corrupt business practices by regional officials in the autonomous republic of Kalmykia and Kirsan Ilyumzhinov, the republic's millionaire president. Yudina was murdered in June outside the Kalmyk capital of Elista, after leaving home to meet a source who promised to provide evidence for her reports.

And in August, Anatoly Levin-Utkin, deputy editor of the St. Petersburg weekly *Yuridichesky Peterburg Segodnya*, was fatally beaten while researching articles on local banks.

These assassinations highlight the pattern of killings that started with the October 1994 murder of Dmitry Kholodov, a reporter for the popular daily *Moskovsky Komsomolets*. Suspects were finally arrested this year in the Kholodov murder, but this case, like that of other murdered Russian journalists, has not been conclusively resolved.

Several journalists have survived brutal attacks. On May 27, Radio Titan, the only independent station in the Bashkir Republic, was violently shut down. Altaf Galeyev, the manager and news director, was jailed after police raided the station, beating employees and arresting Galeyev and several colleagues. The attack occurred after Radio Titan broadcast interviews with several opposition candidates who were barred from running against incumbent President Murtaza Rakhimov in the republic's June presidential elections.

At year's end, the trial of a journalist accused of espionage in connection with his work remained unresolved. Grigory Pasko, a naval officer and military reporter imprisoned in Vladivostok since 1997, faces charges of high treason stemming from his publication of a series of articles in Russian and Japanese media describing the environmental damage caused by nuclear waste from Russia's deteriorating submarine fleet in the Far East.

It is no exaggeration to say that there is no press freedom in the secessionist republic of Chechnya, whose status remains unclear despite its conflict with Russian forces from 1994 to 1996. Local authorities have closed down the region's television and radio stations, and newspapers still permitted to operate face severe penalties for publishing articles deemed by officials to be anti-government. Reporters from outside have stopped going into the republic, because kidnappers have targeted foreign correspondents, often holding them for ransom, and the Chechen government is either unable or unwilling to control the problem.

March 13
Timur Kukuyev, M-5 TV, ORT ATTACKED, THREATENED
Yuri Safronov, M-5 TV, ORT ATTACKED

Men in paramilitary uniforms beat Kukuyev and Safronov, members of an M-5 TV crew and stringers for ORT, as they tried to film at the Dagestani-Chechen border. The attackers destroyed the crew's video camera and confiscated videotapes. The crew members were not seriously injured. They reported that Dagestani border guards who witnessed the incident failed to intervene.

On the early evening of March 16, Kukuyev, the cameraman, was severely beaten in central Makhachkala by unidentified men who warned him against "filming anything else on a foreign territory in the future" as they assaulted him. He was admitted to a hospital with broken ribs, a concussion, and a disfigured face.

May 27
Altaf Galeyev, Radio Titan IMPRISONED, LEGAL ACTION
Lilia Ismagilova, Radio Titan HARASSED
Staff of Radio Titan ATTACKED, HARASSED, CENSORED

Bashkir police raided the Ufa offices of Radio Titan, the sole independent radio station in the Republic of Bashkortostan, beating and arresting staff members and supporters. Police seized radio equipment and detained the entire staff, including Galeyev, the manager and news director, and Ismagilova, the station's executive director.

The raid occurred came shortly after Radio Titan aired interviews with three opposition candidates who were barred from the June 14 presidential elections.

Ismagilova and the other staff members were released the next day, but Galeyev was held for firing several shots in the air when police stormed the office. On June 4, he was formally charged with "hooliganism" and the illegal use of firearms under Article 213(3) of the Bashkir penal code. If found guilty, he faces a possible prison sentence of four to seven years. Galeyev, who is in poor health, was allowed to see a lawyer, but no court hearing was held.

Radio Titan was closed following the attack. Ismagilova, the station's former executive director, left Ufa.

June 8
Larisa Yudina, *Sovietskaya Kalmykia Segodnya* KILLED

Yudina, a prominent journalist and political activist who edited *Sovietskaya Kalmykia Segodnya*, the only alternative news outlet in Kalmykia, was investigating reports of corrupt business practices by regional officials when she disappeared on June 7. The 53-year-old Yudina had gone to meet a source who promised to give her evidence of financial improprieties by local firms involved in an effort by Kalmyk President Kirsan Ilyumzhinov to set up an offshore zone in the republic.

She was found dead the next day in the outskirts of the Kalmyk capital, Elista, with multiple stab wounds and a fractured skull.

Yudina was frequently harassed and threatened for her exposés of local corruption and hard-line rule by the republic's millionaire president. For several years she was forced to publish *Sovietskaya Kalmykia Segodnya* in neighboring Volgograd after Ilyumzhinov ordered local printers to stop producing issues of the paper. Her troubles with Kalmyk authorities as a journalist and local leader of the liberal opposition Yabloko party were documented by foreign and Russian media, and by press freedom groups, but elicited no response from Russian leaders. Her death prompted public protests in Elista, demanding a federal investigation. Hundreds of residents gathered for her funeral on June 10.

Attacks on the Press in 1998

August 21
Anatoly Levin-Utkin, *Yuridichesky Peterburg Segodnya* KILLED

Levin-Utkin was deputy editor of the new St. Petersburg weekly *Yuridichesky Peterburg Segodnya*. He was beaten unconscious in the doorway of his St. Petersburg apartment and robbed of his briefcase, which contained materials he had gathered for the next installment of an investigative series on rivalries between local financial and political figures. Cash and personal valuables were stolen. The 41-year-old editor suffered numerous blows to his head, causing severe brain trauma. Despite two brain surgeries, he died on August 24 without regaining consciousness.

The newspaper's editor said in a news conference on August 25 that he believed the murder was connected to the series on the customs and secret services for which Levin-Utkin had done research and reporting, published in the first two issues of the then-three-week-old newspaper.

The editor said he had received phone calls demanding the names of those who worked on the series, but had refused to divulge the information. Levin-Utkin had just finished collecting documents and photos for the third installment of the series on the day he was attacked.

The local prosecutor's office is investigating the murder, but no arrests have been made.

Slovakia

In September, Prime Minister Vladimir Meciar and the ruling Movement for a Democratic Slovakia (HZDS) lost the general elections to a four-party coalition government headed by Mikulas Dzurinda of the center-right Slovak Democratic Coalition (SDK). Dzurinda's government, which has made admittance to NATO and the European Union a priority, faces a daunting list of tasks:

cleaning up the destructive effects of the Meciar-era kleptocracy while reforming the constitution and electoral laws, guaranteeing fuller independence of the judiciary, and pushing forward economic reform. The SDK government appointed a new director of Slovak State Television (STV), who replaced pro-Meciar editors and programs.

Before the elections, the HZDS government continued to keep a firm hold on the two channels of the national STV and to demonstrate openly, especially during the election period, its dislike for the independent media. Reporters from independent media outlets were denied access to government documents, briefings, and parliamentary discussions.

Threats and violence toward independent journalists increased with the approach of the September elections. During this time, Andrei Hric, director of the independent Bratislava-based Radio Twist, received anonymous death threats for his exposure of government corruption. And Karol Lovas, a reporter with the station, whose investigative coverage of the government led to the resignation of a Meciar spokesman, was the target of a smear campaign.

In May, Meciar's government passed amendments to the election law, which heavily restricted non-state media's campaign coverage. Article 23(1) allowed only state-funded media to broadcast reports of political activity during the 30-day official campaign period. Article 23(5) banned the publication of pre-election opinion polls for 14 days before the election.

During the run-up to the elections, the private HZDS-affiliated company Gamatex acquired the pro-opposition private television network Markiza TV. The new owners immediately fired the station's director and the news editor. This purge of pro-opposition journalists and the speed with which the sale moved through bureaucratic channels prompted opposition leaders and supporters to suspect that Meciar had engineered the acquisition to redirect Markiza TV's editorial policies. The station broadcast demonstrations protesting the change of ownership and the firings within the 30-day campaign period when independent media were banned from covering election-related activities. In response, the Council on Radio and Television fined the station 3.5 million Slovak crowns (US$120,000) and ordered it to announce three times a day that it had violated the law.

Investigative reporters writing on shady privatization deals and corrupt government officials continued to face intimidation and violence. In August, police stopped Vladimir Bacisin, an investigative reporter for the independent business daily *Narodna Obroda*, after he had jaywalked across a street in downtown Bratislava. After demanding Bacisin's identification, they beat him and subsequently detained him overnight. Bacisin believes the abuse was in reprisal for his investigation of illegal practices by VUB Investment Holding and Slovenska Poistovna, private companies with close links to the Meciar coalition.

August 19
Vladimir Bacisin, *Narodna Obroda*
ATTACKED, HARASSED, LEGAL ACTION

Four police officers violently assaulted Bacisin, a reporter for the newspaper *Narodna Obroda*, after he had jaywalked across a street in downtown Bratislava. He was taken into custody and held overnight at the police station on charges of physically and verbally attacking a public servant, under Articles 155 and 156 of the Slovak penal code.

Bacisin had just met with a source from the National Bank of Slovakia in the building housing Slovak Radio. When he crossed the street, two officers demanded he show his identification card and ordered him to pay a fine on the spot for the violation. Bacisin told the officers he did not have sufficient cash to pay the fine, but suggested they keep his I.D. card as collateral because he was in a hurry to get to another meeting.

One of the officers grabbed Bacisin, twisting his arms behind his back, while the other officer punched him in the face, knocking his glasses off. Bacisin, who has very poor eyesight, tried to pick up his glasses, but the officers pushed him to the ground, striking him several times against the pavement. Two more police officers arrived and the beating continued; two of the officers held Bacisin while the others hit him.

Bacisin was taken to a police station, where he was handcuffed to a bench for several hours and then locked in a holding cell. Police did not permit him to contact his lawyer and refused to return his glasses. Bacisin in turn refused to answer any questions in the absence of his lawyer and without his glasses. He was freed the next day.

Bacisin and his colleagues believe he was targeted in retaliation for his investigative reporting of illegal practices by VUB Investment Holding and Slovenska Poistovna, two private firms with close links to the ruling coalition. He believes he was followed and spied on by an Interior Ministry employee who he recognized in the Slovak Radio building just prior to the assault. Bacisin said he pleaded guilty to the jaywalking offense, but denied refusing to pay the fine and resisting arrest. He says he has also been pressured into leaving *Narodna Obroda* by the editor, Miroslav Tuleja, a government supporter.

Tajikistan

Although Tajikistan's four-year civil war came to an end in June 1997, the peace process has been constantly threatened by disputes between the government and the United Tajik Opposition (UTO), the two main parties to the peace agreement. Violence against peacekeepers has also been a serious deterrent to peace efforts. In July, four members of a U.N. observer mission were ambushed and killed, and on September 22, Otakhon Latifi, a leading opposition figure and former *Pravda* correspondent, was shot dead. Numerous rebel-led insurgencies in various parts of the country also dealt a blow to the peace process.

In this ongoing climate of violence and political factionalism, it has been difficult for an independent press—decimated during the civil war, when at least 29 journalists were murdered—to take root and thrive. And it is still dangerous for those reporters who try to cover political developments and conflicts. Sedzhar Khamidov, a Russian Television correspondent, was wounded in the head in November as he filmed government troops storming the regional airport at Chkalovsk, which had been seized by rebels.

Journalists have been targeted for abuse ranging from physical attacks to harassment. According to the Moscow-based Glasnost Defense Foundation, on October 1, two masked individuals burst into the apartment of Maksujon Guseinov, a correspondent of the independent newspaper *Charkhi Gardun*, severely beat his wife, and searched the apartment. Although Guseinov was not at home at the time of the assault, the assailants made clear the purpose of their visit by telling his wife that he should "stop writing."

Officials, opposition parties, and local warlords continued to show little tolerance for journalists who scrutinize the peace process and other domestic political issues. In July, Tajikistan's Minister of Foreign Affairs revoked the accreditation of Yelena Masyuk, a correspondent for the Russian television station NTV and a 1997 recipient of CPJ's International Press Freedom Award. The Tajik Interior Ministry issued a statement claiming that Masyuk's reports on Tajik politics "aim to discredit the Tajik government … and amount to interference in the sovereign affairs of a home state." The Foreign Ministry further threatened to suspend NTV's work in Tajikistan if the company made an issue out of Masyuk's expulsion.

The government actively sought to control the press in other ways. During the first half of the year, newspapers affiliated with opposition parties were harassed and pressured to close, and state-run printing presses, which monopolize the industry, stopped printing them. Under terms of the peace agreement, however, opposition political parties and their media outlets will be permitted to re-register following the demobilization of opposition military units, a process which is expected to come to a close in early 1999.

More subtle forms of harassment of the press were also common. Economic pressure on independent or opposition media, such as harassment by the tax police, compounded their chronic financial difficulties. The pressures are also political. In May, the Majlisi Oli (parliament) adopted a law "on the defense of the honor and dignity of the president" which, among other things, set out excessive fines and prison sentences for journalists or media outlets deemed to insult or slander the president. Fortunately, President Imomali Rakhmonov vetoed the legislation in response to international pressure.

There are approximately 10 independent newspapers, although most of them avoid politically sensitive topics, and journalists who do write about politics generally know where to draw the line of acceptability. This form of self-censorship seems to have taken the place of an official censorship policy. The government did, however, routinely attempt to influence the content of material on the more than a dozen independent television stations, using the regulatory mechanisms in its arsenal to pressure them to toe the official line. The State Committee of TV and Radio, which issues licenses, often delays or denies licenses for independent broadcasters.

Turkmenistan

Turkmenistan continued to be the most repressive post-Soviet republic in Central Asia. The government retained total control over the media and absolute intolerance for opposing viewpoints.

Authoritarian President Saparmurad Niyazov, who has dubbed himself "the father of all Turkmen people," has built a cult of personality; his image adorns everything from ubiquitous posters and statuary to the country's currency.

Niyazov's dictatorial regime has suffocated any dissident impulses in Turkmenistan and kept a lid on freedom of expression, earning him a place among CPJ's 10 worst Enemies of the Press in 1998. (See page 62 for more about CPJ's Enemies of the Press.) All media are state-run, and provide little information about the country's political and social issues; instead, they are in the service of the state, churning out devotional propaganda for Niyazov and his regime. Security personnel routinely confiscate foreign newspapers, tap foreign reporters' telephones, and harass those visiting reporters who stray from their official itinerary, which usually revolves around oil rather than politics.

Apart from the official media and sporadic Russian broadcasts, the only alternative source of information in the Turkmen language has been Radio Liberty, an international radio service, funded by the U.S. government, which broadcasts in Eastern Europe, the Caucasus, and Central Asia. According to Radio Liberty, Turkmen authorities continued to harass local journalists who worked for the service; some have been beaten, and even forced into exile.

Mesmerized by Turkmenistan's vast oil and gas reserves, Western business interests have largely closed their eyes to these egregious press freedom abuses. In April, Niyazov traveled to the United States. In addition to closing several deals with U.S. companies, he met with President Bill Clinton to discuss the development of a trans-Caucasian pipeline. CPJ and other international organizations wrote to President Clinton at the time, urging him to raise the issue of human rights and media conditions in Turkmenistan during his meeting with Niyazov.

Ukraine

Powerful politicians and businessmen continued to wield their influence to harass journalists and opposition newspapers, eroding press freedom and limiting the number and variety of voices available in the country. Officials have used tax and libel laws, as well as charges of illegally obtaining government documents, to close newspapers and silence journalists. Violence against the press persisted, including bombings of newspaper offices and assaults on reporters and editors, creating an atmosphere of fear and self-censorship.

Some of the hostilities were apparently timed to stifle opposition coverage of the March 29 parliamentary election. Similar activities are likely during the run-up to the October 1999 presidential election. President Leonid Kuchma, who is expected to seek re-election, has been critical of the press, particularly media with foreign ownership, such as the joint Ukrainian-Russian and Ukrainian-American television channels, which provide what little independent news coverage is available. Harsh tax laws and high production costs force most newspapers and broadcast outlets without foreign support to seek financial aid from businesses and politicians, who then demand favorable coverage.

The government used prosecutions and crushing fines to force three newspapers—the opposition papers *Pravda Ukrainy* and *Vseukrainskiye Vedomosti*, and the national weekly *Politika*—to close their doors. And other news outlets and journalists endured prosecution and fines for their critical reporting.

Violence against the press included a Molotov cocktail attack on the offices of *Vseukrainskiye Vedomosti* four days before it closed.

Amendments to broadcast regulations now exempt radio and television stations from libel charges for defamatory statements made on the air during political campaigns, but the new rules took effect only three days before the parliamentary election.

Attacks on the Press in 1998

January 22
Vseukrainskiye Vedomosti LEGAL ACTION, CENSORED

A Chernovtsi city court found the popular opposition daily, *Vseukrainskiye Vedomosti*, guilty of libeling Hryhoriy Surkis, president of the Kiev Dynamo soccer team and head of the national soccer federation. The court fined *Vseukrainskiye Vedomosti* 3.5 million hryvnyas (about US$1.8 million) in moral damages and ordered its bank account seized.

Surkis had filed suit against the paper on December 31, 1997, claiming it had defamed him in a September 17, 1997, article that cited him as the source of the rumor that an Italian team made a multimillion-dollar bid for Dynamo star player Andriy Shevchenko.

Volodymyr Ruban, the paper's editor in chief, said the team's press agents confirmed that Surkis had spread the rumor. Ruban claimed that the libel case was groundless

EUROPE

and illegal. He cited a number of improprieties, most notably the fact that it was filed with a regional arbitration court lacking jurisdiction in defamation cases. According to Ruban, the court's "arbitrary and harsh" decision showed its goal was to bankrupt and silence *Vseukrainskiye Vedomosti* before the March 29 parliamentary elections. Colleagues and legal experts, including former Justice Minister Serhiy Holovaty, protested the court's decision.

On February 23, a regional arbitration court in Kiev upheld the Chernovtsi court's ruling. The paper's lawyers filed an appeal, but the court enforced the ruling and seized the newspaper's bank account. *Vseukrainskiye Vedomosti* ran out of funds the week before the elections, and published its last issue on March 26.

January 28
Pravda Ukrainy LEGAL ACTION, CENSORED

Information Minister Zinoviy Kulyk effectively shut down the opposition newspaper *Pravda Ukrainy* three months before national parliamentary elections by ordering the state publishing house, Presa Ukrainy, to cease printing the paper. Shortly thereafter, *Pravda Ukrainy*'s bank accounts were frozen and the paper was threatened with eviction.

Kulyk gave the order after withdrawing *Pravda Ukrainy*'s registration because the percentage of shares listed in the paper's ownership documents added up to 110, rather than 100. The mathematical error actually occurred in September 1997, when Oleksander Horobets, the newspaper's editor in chief, attempted to reregister the paper and to register two new publications. The information ministry denied all three applications. *Pravda Ukrainy*'s original registration papers, valid since July 1994, contained no such error.

Volodymyr Malakhov, the paper's deputy editor, said the ministry's decision was most likely prompted by a series of articles about government corruption, particularly a story published on January 27 detailing how some top government officials improperly or illegally obtained apartments.

Horobets attributed what he called the "unprecedented move" against *Pravda Ukrainy* to its critical stance against the government, and its editorial support of the opposition political party Hromada. The newspaper's national circulation had grown from 70,000 to more than a half-million in the six months prior to the closure, adding to the government's perception that the newspaper threatened state domination of the media. In exchange for *Pravda Ukrainy*'s editorial support, Hromada gave pensioners gratis subscriptions to the paper, dramatically boosting its readership before the elections.

Following the ministry's order to Presa Ukrainy, the paper was printed for several weeks at a private printing house which publishes the popular opposition daily *Kievskie Vedomosti*. After producing several issues of *Pravda Ukrainy*, the private printer received an official warning from the ministry to terminate the relationship or be closed down. The newspaper stopped publishing in March.

March 22
Vseukrainskiye Vedomosti ATTACKED, HARASSED

Unknown assailants tossed Molotov cocktails at the daily *Vseukrainskiye Vedomosti*'s offices in Kiev. Several unlit, fuel-filled bottles broke through some windows and caused minor damage, while the flaming bottles broke against an outer wall. There were no injuries.

Volodymyr Ruban, the paper's editor, said police investigating the incident have accused *Vseukrainskiye Vedomosti* of staging the incident in an attempt to destroy financial records and cover up improprieties. The daily had been subjected to repeated random tax inspections in the previous six months, as have many other opposition and independent publications in Ukraine.

Attacks on the Press in 1998

Uzbekistan

April 29
Slovo HARASSED, LEGAL ACTION

The Mykolayiv regional arbitration court confirmed civil libel charges against the independent Odessa weekly *Slovo* and imposed a ruinous fine of 500,000 hryvnyas (about US$ 250,000). The suit, filed by the fishing company Antarktika in January, stemmed from a series of articles in *Slovo* on Antarktika's allegedly corrupt practices and its failure to repay debts, taxes, and workers' salaries in November 1996 and July 1997.

At the beginning of June, *Slovo* filed an appeal with the same court, but it was rejected. As the paper ran out of funds, the court ordered the confiscation of its equipment. The paper's editor in chief believed that these actions were in reprisal for *Slovo*'s support for Edward Gurvits, who was elected mayor of Odessa on March 29. *Slovo* could not pay its employees' salaries for several months, and at year's end was faced with the possibility of closing for lack of funds.

June 4
Kievskiye Vedomosti LEGAL ACTION

A district court in Kiev found the opposition daily *Kievskiye Vedomosti* guilty of libeling Interior Minister Yuri Kravchenko, and fined the tabloid a record 5 million hryvnia (then about US$2.5 million) in damages.

Yevhen Yakunov, the daily's editor, said the ruling was politically motivated, and aimed at bankrupting the newspaper. Kravchenko had sued the paper last year for a series of articles published in 1997 which attempted to prove he had purchased a Mercedes-Benz with money allegedly embezzled from a fund for families of slain police officers. *Kievskiye Vedomosti* appealed the decision in July.

Islam Karimov, Uzbekistan's autocratic president, has promoted a repressive campaign against both secular and religious media, making a mockery of laws guaranteeing freedom of expression and barring censorship. A new organization to monitor and control religious publications, the Qanoat Center, joined the secular press censorship inspectorate. And Karimov went on Uzbekistan's state television to denounce the Islamic fundamentalist Wahhabi sect as a major cause of instability in the republic. The 1992 constitution specifically allows freedom of speech and conscience and bans censorship as "impermissible." But two laws enacted in 1997—the law on the press and the law on protection of journalists—stress journalists' responsibility not to publish inaccurate information, disclose classified material, or violate provisions of the criminal code that forbid insults aimed at the president.

The state-run newspapers *Pravda Vostoka* and *Narodnoe Slovo*, the dominant national dailies, continued to act as official organs, promoting Karimov's personality cult. In this atmosphere, the small number of independent publications and local television stations feel pushed toward self-censorship. Journalists expressing critical or dissenting views received harsh treatment. In June, Shadi Mardiev, a veteran Samarkand radio journalist, was found guilty of criminal defamation and sentenced to 11 years in prison for a radio report on the corrupt activities of a high-ranking Tashkent official. CPJ appealed by letter to Karimov to use his influence to reverse the verdict and relax controls over freedom of expression. Two months later, on August 1, two Russian journalists were assaulted in Tashkent following a meeting with an Uzbek human rights activist. An official investigation failed to turn up the culprits.

Yugoslavia

War between the Serb-controlled Yugoslav government and the ethnic Albanian Kosovo Liberation Army (KLA) erupted in March in the province of Kosovo, with repressive repercussions for media throughout Yugoslavia.

Covering the Kosovo war has been an assignment fraught with danger and frustration. Foreign correspondents whose reports were deemed "anti-Serb" were denied reentry visas by the Serb government. Local journalists were blocked and harassed so routinely at military checkpoints that by summer most would not travel into conflict zones unless they were accompanying foreign news teams. But the presence of foreigners was no guarantee of protection; they, along with local journalists, encountered problems in the field that ranged from intimidation to violence to kidnapping.

The KLA was responsible for one of the most serious incidents—the October kidnapping of two journalists from the Yugoslav state news agency Tanjug who were later released. But the vast majority of incidents of harassment, intimidation, and physical assault documented by CPJ in Kosovo were carried out by the Serbian special police and military.

Elsewhere in Yugoslavia, the Kosovo war generated a fresh wave of Serbian government repression against independent media that dared challenge the hate speech and nationalist policies of President Slobodan Milosevic's regime.

Among the government's primary targets was the Association of Independent Electronic Media (ANEM), a network of 50 stations whose radio and television broadcasts reach 80 percent of Serbia's population. ANEM's flagship station, Radio B92, has long been a thorn in Milosevic's side, though in the government's May tender of broadcast licenses B92 was one of the few independent stations to be granted even a temporary right to broadcast. Dozens of unlicensed independent broadcasters stayed on the air even after the government shut down two ANEM radio stations in the summer for operating without licenses.

But in September, when NATO threatened air strikes against Belgrade to force Milosevic to withdraw his forces from Kosovo, the Serbian government used the West's threats to turn on independent journalists with a vengeance. A series of government statements in early October accused independent journalists of being spies, and on October 5 the Serb information minister ordered independent stations to stop rebroadcasting Serb-language programs from the Voice of America and other foreign services. The ban was formalized on October 8 in a temporary decree that also forbade articles or broadcasts deemed by the government to foment "fear, panic and defeatism" during the showdown with NATO.

One day after the decree took effect, a CPJ delegation met with then-U.S. Assistant Secretary of State John Shattuck to urge strong U.S. opposition to the crackdown. The State Department subsequently circulated a CPJ statement to U.S. ambassadors in Europe, urging them to work with their European counterparts to orchestrate diplomatic protests of the Serb government's actions.

Milosevic continued to lash out at the independent press after agreeing on October 13 to pull Serb forces out of Kosovo and allow international monitors into the region. By October 15, the government had shut down two ANEM radio stations and three independent Belgrade newspapers, *Danas*, *Dnevni Telegraf*, and *Nasa Borba*. On October 20, the Serbian government adopted a new Law on Public Information that codified much of the earli-

Attacks on the Press in 1998

er temporary decree, set crippling fines for violations, and eliminated basic judicial rights for those accused of violations.

Some independent Serb journalists said that the Western powers, led by the United States, were so eager for a diplomatic resolution of the Kosovo conflict that they had decided to look the other way while Milosevic decimated the independent media. Their sense of abandonment intensified as the new law led to more punitive action and crippling fines against the owner of *Dnevni Telegraf* and the weekly *Evroplijanin*.

On December 4 and 5, ANEM held a conference in Belgrade titled "Media for a Democratic Europe." Delegations from CPJ and other press freedom organizations met to assess the ongoing threat to the survival of Serbia's independent media. While journalists at the conference were buoyed by the support, most believed that the Serb government's persecution of the press would not ease as long as Milosevic remained in power.

March 2
Agron Bajrami, *Koha Ditore* ATTACKED
Veton Surroi, *Koha Ditore* ATTACKED

Serb police in Pristina beat Surroi, editor in chief of the Albanian-language daily *Koha Ditore*, and Bajrami, the paper's cultural editor, who were covering public protests during the crackdown against Albanian separatists in Kosovo.

Since the Kosovo armed conflict began in February, Yugoslavia's government has systematically infringed upon the ability of local and foreign journalists to work safely. Harassment, detentions, and assaults by police officers have been common.

March 2
Staff of *Koha Ditore* ATTACKED, THREATENED, HARASSED
Fatos Berisha, *Koha Ditore* ATTACKED

Police ransacked *Koha Ditore*'s Pristina offices and beat several staff members. They were searching the office for a videocamera and tapes of police brutality against demonstrators filmed by the paper's cameraman, Fatos Berisha, during that day's violent demonstrations.

During the raid, Berisha fell out the second-story window as he fled from the police. He was hospitalized with a broken leg.

Since then, reporters from *Koha Ditore* and other news media have been threatened and harassed while covering demonstrations. *Koha Ditore* has endured several random financial inspections by various government agencies since mid-April.

March 10
Gruica Spasovic, *Danas* HARASSED
Manjo Vucotic, *Blic* HARASSED
Slavko Curuvija, *Dnevni Telegraf* HARASSED
Lyubinka Milintic, *Demokratija* HARASSED
Ivan Mrcan, *Nasa Borba* HARASSED

The city prosecutor's office summoned the editors of five Belgrade independent dailies—*Danas, Blic, Dnevni Telegraf, Demokratija,* and *Nasa Borba*—for questioning on March 10 and 11 in apparent reprisal for the papers' coverage of the Serbian crackdown in Kosovo. Mjedrak Tmusic, the Belgrade city prosecutor, accused Spasovic of *Danas*, Vucotic of *Blic*, Curuvija of *Dnevni Telegraf*, Milintic of *Demokratija*, and Mrcan of *Nasa Borba* of encouraging terrorism in predominantly Albanian Kosovo by referring to the Albanians killed by police as "victims" or simply "Albanians" in their headlines, rather than as "terrorists."

Serbian authorities and government-controlled media openly called on the press in February to give only the official interpretation of events and use ethnic slurs against Albanians, reminiscent of the hate speech spread by the regime to foment the conflict in Bosnia.

EUROPE

March 19
Taras Protsyuk, Reuters TV ATTACKED
Michel Rouserez, RTBF, Belgian TV ATTACKED

Plainclothes policemen beat Rouserez, a cameraman for the French-language Belgian Radio-Television (RTBF), and Protsyuk, a Ukrainian cameraman working for Reuters TV, while they were attempting to film demonstrations in Pristina.

Protsyuk was attacked from behind as he shot footage of a weeping Albanian woman who said she was struck by police during a rally. He fell to the ground, and his video camera was smashed. The assailants repeatedly punched him in the face until his producer, Glen Felgate, managed to pull him away. Protsyuk suffered minor injuries. Rouserez was assaulted while covering a demonstration near the University of Pristina. He was hospitalized as a result of the incident.

April 21
TV Pirot CENSORED

Officials from the Yugoslav Telecommunications Ministry ordered the closure of TV Pirot and confiscated the station's equipment, citing the station's failure to comply with licensure procedures.

This action came shortly before the May 15 deadline for public disclosure of the ministry's decision on granting licenses to independent television and radio stations throughout the country.

Local journalists believe that authorities have targeted TV Pirot in retaliation for its independent news coverage. Legal experts at the Association of Independent Electronic Media (ANEM) told CPJ that TV Pirot's application met the legal requirements and was submitted on time. ANEM noted that dozens of new independent television and radio stations are unlicensed, yet authorities have allowed them to broadcast until their applications are approved.

May 16
All Serbian media HARASSED, CENSORED

The Yugoslav Federal Telecommunications Ministry announced that it had awarded broadcast frequencies to 247 television and radio stations out of 425 applicants. But only three independent stations from the Association of Independent Electronic Media (ANEM) received temporary frequencies: Radio B92 in Belgrade, RTV Pancevo, and F Kanal in Zajecar. The other 244 stations granted frequencies either support the government or broadcast only entertainment programs.

The ministry failed to explain why another 178 private stations, including 38 ANEM affiliates, were denied frequencies, a decision which effectively bans them from the air. All ANEM members submitted identical applications. Radio B92 alone submitted four applications—including two for radio frequencies, one for television, and one for a satellite uplink—yet it was awarded only one radio frequency. The ministry has announced it will charge monthly fees for the use of the frequencies, ranging from US$12,000 to US$15,000. Many station managers who won frequencies have said they may be forced to refuse them, because the exorbitant fees exceed their total monthly incomes.

June 22
Neils Brinch, TV2 Denmark ATTACKED
Heinrik Gram, TV2 Denmark ATTACKED
Unidentified Albanian interpreter, TV2 Denmark ATTACKED

Serbian soldiers opened fire on a Danish TV2 crew near the Glogovac mine in Kosovo. Brinch, a correspondent, Gram, a cameraman, and an Albanian interpreter who asked not to be identified were heading back to Pristina in a rented armored car after being turned away by guards at a Kosovo Liberation Army (KLA) checkpoint at Glogovac.

The white rented armored car was typical

of vehicles used by journalists to cover the conflict between Serbia and the KLA. The crew felt two shots hit their car, prompting Brinch, who was driving, to stop. A Serb soldier in uniform ran up to their car and pointed his gun at the crew. As Brinch lifted his arms to show he was unarmed, the soldier started shooting at the crew's car. Brinch sped away from the scene. No one was hurt, but the journalists found 21 bullet holes on the armored vehicle.

July 1
Radio Kontakt CENSORED

Serb police shut down Radio Kontakt, the first multi-ethnic broadcast outlet in Kosovo, only days after it started broadcasting in both Albanian and Serbian. Yugoslav authorities claimed it went on the air without a frequency license. The station's managers had applied for a license in the government's frequency tender in May, but received no reply.

July 6
Reuters TV cameraman HARASSED
Kurt Schork, Reuters ATTACKED
Anthony Lloyd, *The Times* ATTACKED
All journalists in Kosovo THREATENED

Serbian special police officers posing as journalists infiltrated an international press pool that was following a motorcade of diplomats in the Kosovo conflict zone and attacked Schork, a reporter with Reuters, and Lloyd, a correspondent with *The Times* of London. The officers were dressed as civilians and drove a red car with press markings.

As a pool video cameraman walked alongside the convoy filming its approach to Prekaz, the red car suddenly swerved toward him, nearly striking him.

When the convoy stopped near Prekaz, Schork and Lloyd approached the car's occupants to complain about the incident, then turned away and walked toward the town. One of the red car's occupants grabbed Schork by the shoulder and punched him in the face. Lloyd then struck the unidentified man, who retaliated with two karate kicks to Lloyd's chest. The incident took place in front of eight foreign envoys, who identified the occupants of the red car as Serbian special police.

August 18
City Radio CENSORED

Inspectors from the Yugoslav Telecommunication Ministry and two policemen entered the studios of City Radio in Nis, an affiliate of the independent ANEM broadcast network, and ordered the station to stop broadcasting immediately. Inspectors also seized the station's transmitter. City Radio had filed an application for a broadcast license in the May frequency tender, but had received no reply.

August 21
Djuro Slavuj, Radio Pristina MISSING
Ranko Perenic, Radio Pristina MISSING

Slavuj, a Radio Pristina reporter, and Perenic, his driver, disappeared while on assignment in Kosovo. They were last seen in the town of Orahovac, from which they left by car to travel to Malisevo to report on strife in the area.

Milivoje Mihajlovic, Slavuj's editor at the state-run radio station, expressed concern that the two may have been captured by armed Kosovo Liberation Army (KLA) fighters. If this theory is correct, it would be the first serious attack on ethnic Serb journalists by KLA members. Ethnic Albanian journalists have been frequent targets of attacks by Serb police since the conflict began in February. At press time, Slavuj and Perenic were still missing.

September 30
All independent media HARASSED

During a session of the Serbian parliament, top government officials and a leading pro-government legislator warned independent media and other critics of the regime that they would be targeted for reprisal in the event of a NATO air strike against Yugoslavia.

"The Americans found their fifth column here," charged Serbian Deputy Prime Minister Vojislav Seselj. "It is composed of politically irrelevant parties and independent media. We can't shoot down every NATO plane, but we can grab those agents who are at hand," he said.

Serbia's prime minister, Mirko Marjanovic, accused the independent media of spreading lies and fear, while lawmaker Zeljko Simic charged the journalists with "high treason" for aiding Albanian separatists by reporting on the war in Kosovo.

October 6
All independent media HARASSED, CENSORED

Serbian Deputy Prime Minister Milovan Bojic and Information Minister Aleksandar Vucic met with editors and managers of independent media. During the 15-minute meeting, the officials accused the independent media of treason and spreading propaganda on behalf of the West concerning the Kosovo conflict. They also announced a ban on rebroadcasts of Serbian-language programs by foreign broadcast media, including the Voice of America, Radio Free Europe, the British Broadcasting Corporation, Deutsche Welle, and Radio France International, and promised that the Serbian government would soon issue a formal decree to that effect.

October 7
Dejan Anastasijevic, *Vreme* HARASSED

During a session of the Yugoslav Federal Assembly, Serbian Information Minister Aleksandar Vucic threatened Anastasijevic, a reporter with the independent weekly *Vreme*, with criminal prosecution for his coverage of war crimes in Gornje Obrinje, Kosovo.

At the beginning of October, a Serbian Interior Ministry officer telephoned *Vreme*'s offices demanding information about Anastasijevic, including details of his whereabouts. The officer said the public prosecutor had ordered him to make the inquiries. Anastasijevic was never charged.

October 8
All media CENSORED

The Serb Ministry of Information issued a decree on "Special Measures in Circumstances of NATO's Threats With Military Attacks Against Our Country." It banned any coverage deemed "unpatriotic" and forbade reporting that, in the government's view, foments "defeatism, panic and fear" among citizens in the face of possible Western military intervention over Kosovo.

The new restrictions were issued in the form of a "temporary decree" authorizing the ministry to close news media after a single warning. The edict also banned the rebroadcast of programs from foreign news media, including the British Broadcasting Corporation, Deutsche Welle, Radio France International, Radio Free Europe, and the Voice of America.

The decree targeted the Association of Independent Electronic Media (ANEM), the 50-station network of radio and television outlets headed by Radio B92. On October 15, Aleksandar Vucic, the Minister of Information, declared that "the decree will remain in power until the government decides so." Serbia's Deputy Prime Minister Vojislav Seselj stated that "even after we lift the decree we will continue to ban broadcasting of foreign spy programs."

October 9
Radio Senta CENSORED

The Yugoslav Telecommunications Ministry closed the independent Radio Senta, a bilingual station in Vojvodina, and seized its transmission equipment. According to the ministry, the reasons for the closure were "exclusively technical," although the station had received a document from the same ministry stating that the "broadcasts caused no diffusion problems," and expected to have its license application approved.

After the closure, Radio Senta continued to broadcast by sending its signal to another transmitter.

October 13
Dnevni Telegraf HARASSED
Danas HARASSED
Nasa Borba HARASSED

The Serbian Information Ministry issued warnings to the three independent Belgrade dailies—*Dnevni Telegraf*, *Danas*, and *Nasa Borba*—for allegedly breaking a new temporary decree prohibiting news media from "fomenting defeatism, panic and fear" in their coverage of the regime's standoff with the West over Kosovo. The decree called for the closure of any news outlet that continued to violate its provisions after a single warning from the ministry.

The ministry's warning to the newspaper said publication of the warning itself was also forbidden.

October 13
Danas CENSORED
Dnevni Telegraf CENSORED

The Serb Information Ministry ordered the temporary closure of the independent Belgrade daily newspapers *Danas* and *Dnevni Telegraf* for violating an October 8 decree on "Special Measures in Circumstances of NATO's Threats With Military Attacks Against Our Country."

The two papers received warning notices from the ministry on October 12. On October 13, police enforced the decision to ban the stations by sealing their newsrooms and seizing their equipment. They also confiscated the entire print run of *Danas*' October 14 edition. The ministry said the ban on the papers would remain in effect for the life of the decree.

Dnevni Telegraf and *Danas* resumed publishing the week after the ban was imposed by registering and printing in Montenegro, where the decree did not apply.

October 15
Nasa Borba CENSORED

The Yugoslav Ministry of Information ordered the temporary shutdown of the independent Belgrade daily newspaper *Nasa Borba* for violating a government decree banning texts "spreading fear, panic and defeatism" through coverage of the Serbian offensive in Kosovo. The shutdown followed the closure of two other dailies, *Dnevni Telegraf* and *Danas*.

The ministry's decision was based on two articles allegedly violating the recent decree. One of the articles contained a statement from the Serb Movement for the Defense of Human Rights, condemning "state terrorism." The other article, by Adem Demaci, the political representative of the Kosovo Liberation Army (KLA), welcomed NATO's ultimatum to Serb President Slobodan Milosevic, threatening air strikes unless he ceased his military campaign against the ethnic Albanians of Kosovo.

After the temporary ban, the editors of *Nasa Borba* refused to continue publishing under the new restrictive media conditions.

October 18
Nebojsa Radosevic, Tanjug IMPRISONED
Vladimir Dobricic, Tanjug IMPRISONED

Radosevic and Dobricic, a reporter and photographer, respectively, with the Yugoslav state news agency Tanjug, disappeared on the road to Magura, in the Kosovo region, where two Serb police officers had been killed on the previous day.

According to a statement by the Kosovo Liberation Army (KLA) released on November 1, Radosevic, 32, and Dobricic, 50, were convicted by a KLA military tribunal of violating the group's code of military and civilian conduct. They were sentenced to 60 days' imprisonment. The communique provided no further details.

They were freed on November 27 into the custody of William Walker, a U.S. diplomat and head of the Organization of Security and Cooperation in Europe's (OSCE) Kosovo Verification Mission, who negotiated their release. Radosevic and Dobricic were reunited with their families the same day.

October 20
All media CENSORED

The Serbian parliament approved a draconian law on public information, incorporating and strengthening most of the restrictions in a temporary decree cracking down on independent media coverage of the Kosovo crisis. The new law gives Serbian authorities greater freedom to interfere with and control the media.

The law introduces stiff fines, speeds up the judicial process for misdemeanor violations of the law, and allows court decisions to be enforced before appeals are filed. It also mandates close government monitoring of media content, giving government officials authority to determine what is considered "unpatriotic" and hence subject to prosecution. It also bans the rebroadcast in any local language of foreign programming which the government finds to contain "political propaganda."

November 17
Monitor HARASSED, LEGAL ACTION

A Belgrade court found the independent weekly *Monitor* of Podgorica, Montenegro, guilty of "calling for the violent overthrow of the constitutional order" under Article 67 of Serbia's law on public information. Earlier in November, the paper published an announcement for the student organization Otpor (Resistance Movement), in which members of the organization expressed their opposition to the imprisonment of four of the group's members.

Although *Monitor* is published in another republic, the court justified the application of Serbian law because one-third of the weekly's circulation is within Serbia. The paper was fined 2.8 million dinars (US$280,000).

Inspectors from the Serb Ministry of Information subsequently seized deliveries of *Monitor*'s November 20 and 27 issues en route from Montenegro to Serbia.

December 4
Nikola Djuric, City Radio LEGAL ACTION

The Municipal Court in Nis charged Djuric, manager of the City Radio station, which was closed by the government, with illegal possession and operation of a radio station under Article 218 of the Serbian penal code. This is the first criminal lawsuit against the manager of a banned radio station. City Radio was shut down in August for operating without a frequency license, and remained off the air at the end of the year. Djuric had applied for a license in the government's frequency tender in May, but had not received a response. His trial is scheduled for January 18, 1999. If convicted, Djuric faces up to one year in prison.

On August 19, City Radio filed a complaint with the Yugoslav Telecommunications Ministry. When the ministry failed to respond to these complaints, City Radio filed an administrative suit against the ministry with the Yugoslav Federal Court.

OVERVIEW OF
The Middle East and North Africa
by Joel Campagna

The authoritarian regimes, quasi-police states, and military-backed governments that dominate the political landscape of the Middle East and North Africa persisted in their efforts to keep independent journalism in check throughout 1998. As in previous years, states attempted to muzzle dissent and critical reporting in the press through state control, censorship, intimidation, criminal prosecutions, and imprisonment.

In the region's most repressive states—Iraq, Syria, Saudi Arabia, Libya, and Tunisia—independent or critical journalism remains nonexistent; the print and broadcast media are harnessed in the service of the state.

In countries where the press enjoys a greater degree of freedom, governments nevertheless use press laws and criminal defamation statutes to deter outspoken journalists. In Jordan, a harsh new press law bans news coverage on a wide array of topics, legalizes censorship, and mandates stiff penalties for offending journalists. Throughout the year, criminal libel and other statutes were employed against journalists in Algeria, Egypt, Iran, Jordan, Kuwait, Lebanon, Turkey, and Yemen in response to news coverage or commentary.

Forty-five journalists were in prison at the end of 1998—more than half (27) were imprisoned in Turkey, where journalists affiliated with far-left or pro-Kurdish publications are the primary targets. In Egypt, there was a significant contraction of press freedom; for the first time, CPJ documented cases of journalists imprisoned for criminal defamation. Dozens more faced similar punishment in cases pending before the courts or under investigation. At the end of the year, Syrian journalist and human rights activist Nizar Nayyouf was believed to be precariously close to death in his Damascus prison cell, where authorities have denied him medical treatment for Hodgkins disease.

Heightened tension between authorities and the press in Iran accompanied

---

Joel Campagna *is program coordinator for the Middle East and North Africa.*
Karam Tannous, *research assistant for the Middle East and North Africa, contributed valuable research to this report.*
Nilay Karaelmas, *a consultant to CPJ, provided important research on Turkey for this report.*
The Freedom Forum contributed significantly to CPJ's work in Egypt, Israel, and Algeria.

the notable increase in press freedoms under reformist President Muhammad Khatami. Caught in the middle of the deepening power struggle between reformers and conservatives, journalists were the targets of concerted state efforts to silence them. Throughout the year, newspapers were suspended and journalists arrested, prosecuted, and, even violently attacked for provocative reporting on social and political issues.

Critical reporting on international affairs can be a pretext for reprisals in many countries. On two occasions during the year, Yasser Arafat shut down private radio and television stations to silence reporting of pro-Iraqi sentiments during Saddam Hussein's standoff with U.N. weapons inspectors and the U.S.-led military strikes against Iraq. Criticism of the peace treaty with Israel or of fellow Arab states can land a Jordanian journalist in court, while in Lebanon, the press shied away from criticism of Syria and its ongoing military presence in Lebanon.

Saudi Arabia exerts such tremendous leverage over the regional and Pan Arab press that criticism of the kingdom is scant. Scrutiny of Saudi officials or policies often draws swift official responses in such countries as Egypt, Jordan, and Lebanon.

Self-censorship continues to be a regionwide phenomenon, reinforced by the fear of arrest or legal action. Following the enactment of Jordan's press law, self-censorship on political issues has increased markedly as journalists steer clear of issues that might result in fines or the possible closure of their papers. In Algeria, fear of state reprisal has kept journalists from shedding light on many facets of the seven year conflict, including state human rights abuses. Similarly, in Turkey, where Kurdish insurgents are still locked in armed conflict with the state, details of the counter insurgency war and alternative viewpoints about the conflict remain scarce in the mainstream press.

Throughout the region, however, journalists exhibited tremendous courage and determination in their efforts to report the news. Palestinian reporters and photographers regularly ran the gantlet of rubber bullets and other physical attacks from Israeli soldiers and right-wing Jewish settlers to bring images of the West Bank and Gaza to the world. And in Algeria, journalists were dogged in their attempts to report from the field about civilian massacres despite lingering fears of assassination.

Satellite dishes increasingly provided people in the region with access to alternative sources of information, such as the Pan-Arab broadcast media and television stations from countries such as Egypt, Lebanon, Jordan, and Yemen. Although the regional broadcast media were generally cautious in their coverage of regional political issues, one exception was the Qatar-based station

Al-Jazeerah, which often enraged intolerant leaders through its provocative news coverage and political debates.

Although Internet access is increasing in some countries, it is still commercially unavailable in Saudi Arabia, Iraq, Libya, Syria or, as in Algeria, it is limited by poor infrastructure. For most people in the region, the cost remained prohibitive, but for those who can afford it, the Internet served as a medium for otherwise unavailable regional and international news. Newspapers from Algeria to Yemen joined the growing number of on-line publications from the region.

The editor of the London-based *Al-Quds al-Arabi*—temporarily banned in Jordan but available to Jordanians through its on-line edition—summed up the importance of the medium in an editorial: "[The Internet] has penetrated all borders and made press censorship the joke of the century."

Algeria

The bloody civil war between the military-backed regime and militant Islamist groups, now into its seventh year, has made Algeria one of the most isolated and difficult environments for journalists. In October, CPJ representatives conducted the organization's first fact-finding mission to the country, meeting with dozens of journalists, editors, lawyers, and government officials in Algiers. The mission's findings and CPJ's recommendations to the Algerian government appear in a special report on page 352.

After years of working under constant threat of death, the targeting of journalists for assassination has apparently ceased—for the second year, no journalists were murdered. Some members of the press exhibited more daring, tackling such previously taboo subjects as atrocities committed by state-backed militias, the issue of "disappeared" persons, and allegations of high-level government corruption. And despite some recurrent difficulties reporting from the scenes of political violence that continue to punctuate the conflict, journalists are generally able to report from the field on massacres and bombings, for example. The government's decision in December 1997 to abolish the notorious "reading committees" it had set up at printing houses in 1996 to enforce pre-publication censorship on accounts of the war has enhanced newspapers' ability to publish independent news about the strife.

Nevertheless, many details about the civil war remain out of the public eye. Self-censorship, problems obtaining information, and residual fear among reporters for their safety continue to keep news about crucial issues such as government rights abuses and the counterinsurgency war out of the newspapers.

Authorities maintain their policy of providing mandatory escorts for foreign reporters, severely curtailing the ability to conduct serious investigative journalism. Journalists also have trouble obtaining visas to enter the country; some of those denied access complained that authorities had singled them out for what they perceived as unfavorable reporting on the political situation. The lack of foreign news outlets in the country—only Agence France-Presse maintains a bureau in Algiers—has led to reliance on the local media for information.

Privately owned publications remained subject to the often arbitrary practices of the country's state-owned printing facilities. State printers forced the month-long closure of two leading dailies, *El-Watan* and *Le Matin*, in October on the pretext of outstanding debts, after they published articles critical of both a former adviser to President Liamine Zeroual and the former Minister of Justice.

Criminal defamation statutes continued to pose a threat to journalists. Although new criminal prosecutions of editors and reporters for their coverage of the conflict now appear to be a thing of the past, journalists were implicated in suits brought by public officials or with apparent political motivations.

At year's end, a newly drafted information code stood before parliament, set to replace the 1990 law. The draft offered several reforms, including abolishing the penalty of imprisonment for journalists convicted of publications offenses and permitting the privatization of broadcast media. The bill, however, grants authorities considerable latitude to punish independent reporting through exorbitant fines for offenses such as defamation. Critics have expressed their concern that authorities will use the law to economically cripple outspoken newspapers.

Journalists felt more secure perhaps than at any time since suspected armed militants launched a vicious assassination campaign in 1993, claiming the lives of 58 journalists between 1993 and 1996. "Now it's all over," said one reporter from the state-owned television station ENTV. "I go shopping where I live. I feel secure. The pressure and terrorism has really subsided." Still, journalists remain cautious in their daily routine, fearful of a possible resumption of attacks. Hundreds remain housed in cramped, government-run hotels under armed guard. Indicative of their safety concerns were the vehement protests of a government attempt in July to relocate some 70 journalists from the government-run Mazafran Hotel in the town of Zaralda. Journalists argued that the proposed location, the Matares Hotel in Tipaza, would jeopardize their security because of its considerable distance from the capital, where most regularly commute to work. Four journalists went on a hunger strike that lasted more than three weeks, while privately run newspapers observed a one-day strike in a show of solidarity with their colleagues. The government eventually acquiesced to the pressure, accommodating the journalists at the Al-Manar Hotel in Sidi Faraj.

CPJ continued to press the Algerian government for information about "disappeared" journalists Djamel Eddine Fahassi and Aziz Bouabdallah, who were apprehended by men presumed to be security agents on May 6, 1995, and April 12, 1997, respectively. In a meeting with Communications Minister Habib Chawki Hamraoui on October 27, 1998, a CPJ delegation led by board member Peter Arnett urged the government to locate and ensure the safety of the missing journalists.

June 16
Touhami Madjouri, *Al-Alam al-Siyassi*
HARASSED

Police detained Madjouri, a reporter for the Arabic-language daily *Al-Alam al-Siyassi*, at the Dar El Beida airport in Algiers and held him for about 20 hours. He had gone to the airport customs office to pick up books sent to him from Jordan, where he had recently traveled.

Madjouri was questioned about a book titled *The Military Authority in Algeria Continues to Plan for the Assassination of the Islamic Will*. He told police that it was his right as a journalist to bring books into the country.

Police, who had confiscated his books, returned them to Madjouri when they released him.

July 1
El-Borhane CENSORED

In July 1998 El Moudjahid, a state-owned printer, refused services to the newly established weekly *El-Borhane*, a bilingual French and Arabic weekly representing the Islamist perspective. After waiting nearly two years for its license, the paper was granted permission to publish in 1998.

The paper was able to print four issues in June and July after it secured the services of SIA, another state-owned printer. Prior to the publication of the fifth issue, however, SIA informed the editors of *El-Borhane* on July 12 that it could no longer print the paper, which would have to return to El Moudjahid. El Moudjahid, in turn, again refused to print the paper.

El-Borhane believes that it has been kept off the market because it is an Islamist paper which supports the concept of dialogue and reconciliation between the combatants of Algeria's civil war.

September 22
Shafiq Abdi, *Le Jeune Indepéndent*
LEGAL ACTION
Said Tissegioune, *Le Jeune Indepéndent*
LEGAL ACTION

Judicial authorities informed Abdi, director of the daily *Le Jeune Indepéndent*, that he and

Tissegioune, a reporter for the paper, were under investigation for allegedly "humiliating organized institutions." The allegations stemmed from an August interview published in *Le Jeune Indepéndent* with Fatma Merzouk, head of a women's organization affiliated with the Socialist Forces Front (FFS). In the interview, conducted by Tissegioune, Merzouk criticized the Algerian army for failing to come to the aid of civilians during a recent massacre near the town of Relizane and charged the military with financial corruption. Both journalists face possible imprisonment if convicted of the charge.

October 17
El-Watan CENSORED
Le Matin CENSORED
Le Soir d'Algérie HARASSED
La Tribune HARASSED

State-owned printers forced the month-long closure of two leading dailies, the French-language *El-Watan* and *Le Matin*, citing outstanding debts.

On October 14, the printers faxed a letter to four daily papers—*El-Watan*, *Le Matin*, *La Tribune*, and *Le Soir d'Algérie*—demanding payment of all outstanding debts in full within 48 hours. Three days later, the printers refused printing services to *El-Watan* and *Le Matin*, leading to their closure for nearly a month.

The printers' action came as a surprise to both papers and, according to their publishers, violated verbal agreements they had reached with the printers. Both were engaged in negotiations with the printers at the time, and had discussed reaching an agreement to reconcile their debts by January 1999.

Local observers believe that the sudden closure of *El-Watan* and *Le Matin* came in response to their sustained and often zealous criticism of Gen. Muhammad Betchine, the former adviser to President Liamine Zeroual, and former Minister of Justice Muhammad Adami, whom they had accused of massive corruption and abuse of power. Both Betchine and Adami eventually resigned in October in the wake of the press's relentless criticism in what local journalists claimed as a victory for press freedom.

Five other newspapers ceased publishing to protest what they described as a politically motivated action by the printers, leaving the country's newsstands bare of the leading newspapers until the dispute was resolved in early November. *El-Watan* resumed publishing on November 11. *Le Matin* was able to resume publishing through the temporary services of a private printer on November 14. On December 22 it was able to return to its original printer, after making arrangements to repay its debt.

Egypt

The imprisonment of journalists and the censorship and closure of newspapers punctuated a dark year for press freedom in Egypt. On February 24, an appellate court upheld a libel conviction against Magdy Hussein and Muhammad Hilal, the editor in chief and reporter, respectively, of the biweekly *Al-Sha'b*, sentencing each to one year in prison for publishing a story that said that the son of a former minister had used his father's position in government to profit from business deals. Their conviction and subsequent imprisonment were the first cases documented by CPJ of journalists imprisoned in Egypt for libel. Over the next three months, two other journalists were imprisoned for libel; by April, another 72 faced possible imprisonment for alleged libel charges that were either pending in court or under investigation.

Egyptian journalists expressed increasingly vocal opposition to the threats they faced from a variety of criminal statutes in the penal code. Highly interpretive charges such as "inciting hatred," "violating public

morality," "harming the national economy," and offending a foreign head of state carry prison sentences of one to two years. Those charged with defamation face a maximum prison sentence of one year, and in cases where public officials are involved, they are subject to up to two years in prison. Fines reach as high as 20,000LE (US$5,900) for each offense.

Offering a ray of hope to journalists, a misdemeanor court in November gave the green light to the Cairo-based Center for Human Rights Legal Aid (CHRLA) to file a suit with the Supreme Constitutional Court to challenge the constitutionality of the country's criminal defamation statutes. A favorable ruling could abolish the imprisonment penalty against journalists convicted of publications offenses.

Along with the jailing of journalists, authorities stepped up harassment and censorship of private newspapers. On February 26, the Ministry of Information revoked the publishing license of the popular weekly *Al-Dustur*.

Censorship of so-called "off-shore" publications—publications that register abroad in order to circumvent government restrictions on publishing licenses—intensified throughout the year. Because they register in foreign countries, these publications are subject to pre-censorship by the Ministry of Information. The fortnightly magazine *Cairo Times* was targeted on numerous occasions throughout the year.

Intensifying its assault, the General Authority for Free Zones and Investment issued a decree ordering the suspension of all printing services for magazines and newspapers which publish in the free investment zone established in Nasser City where most off-shore publications print. More than 30 publications were forced to secure expensive alternative printing services abroad until the decree was reversed. The government defended the move as an effort to crack down on tabloid journalism. "Any newspaper published from outside Egypt can be banned if it does not abide by Egyptian social values and seeks to stir up sectarian rift," President Hosni Mubarak said.

Authorities also stepped up censorship of foreign publications such as the London-based *Al-Quds al-Arabi*, whose editors estimated that an average of 10 issues a month were banned for covering politically sensitive issues that included the November U.S./British military attack on Iraq.

February 24
Magdy Hussein, *Al-Sha'b*
IMPRISONED, LEGAL ACTION
Muhammad Hilal, *Al-Sha'b*
IMPRISONED, LEGAL ACTION

The Bulaq Misdemeanor Appeals Court upheld a libel conviction against Magdy Hussein, editor in chief of the biweekly Islamist-oriented *Al-Sha'b*, and Muhammad Hilal, head of the Governorates Department for the newspaper. The appellate court confirmed one-year prison sentences against Hussein and Hilal and fined the journalists 7,500LE each (US$2,200) for libeling Alaa' al-Alfi, the son of former Interior Minister Hassan al-Alfi. The libel charges stemmed from a series of articles and cartoons published in *Al-Sha'b* in 1996, alleging that Alaa' al-Alfi had used his father's government position to profit from business deals. Hussein and Hilal were taken into custody on March 8 and March 11, respectively, and imprisoned in Torah Mazraa Prison.

In a letter sent to President Hosni Mubarak on February 25, CPJ condemned the court's decision and urged the government to end its use of criminal defamation statutes against the press.

On July 2, the Court of Cassation overturned the convictions against the journalists and ordered their release. Both were freed from Torah Mazraa Prison on July 3 after serving four months of their sentence.

February 26
Al-Dustur CENSORED

Staff of the weekly *Al-Dustur* were informed by Al-Ahram Printing House, the paper's printer, that the Ministry of Information had revoked its publishing license. The move came as a result of an article published in the February 25 edition of the newspaper, which reported on a communiqué allegedly issued by the militant Islamic Group threatening to kill three prominent Coptic businessmen it accused of being agents for the United States.

Since its inception in December 1995, *Al-Dustur* has developed a wide readership and high circulation. It has been the target of repeated state harassment stemming from its coverage of sensitive political issues in Egypt.

March 4
Ahmed Ezzedine Suleiman, *Misr al-Fatah*
LEGAL ACTION
Taher Mahmoud Taher, *Misr al-Fatah*
LEGAL ACTION
Mukhtar Mahmoud Abdel Al, *Misr al-Fatah*
LEGAL ACTION

A state prosecutor charged Suleiman, chairman of the Misr al-Fatah Party organ weekly *Misr al-Fatah*; Taher, its director; and Abdel Al, the editor in chief, with libeling Finance Minister Mohieddin al-Gharib. The charge stemmed from a February 19 article which accused the minister of "wasting public funds and corruption." If convicted, the journalists face the possibility of imprisonment under Egypt's harsh press laws.

March 21
Gamal Fahmy, *Al-Arabi*, *Al-Dustur*
IMPRISONED

Fahmy, managing editor of the now-defunct weekly *Al-Dustur* and a writer for the weekly *Al-Arabi*, was taken into custody by police at his Cairo home and brought to Torah Mazraa Prison to begin a six-month prison sentence for libel.

On March 16, an appellate court upheld a criminal conviction against Fahmy for allegedly libeling Egyptian writer Tharwat Abaza. The charge stemmed from a 1995 column in *Al-Arabi* in which Fahmy criticized Abaza's views about the 1956 Suez crisis and labeled Abaza's father a British sympathizer.

Fahmy was the third Egyptian journalist jailed for libel in 1998. CPJ protested his imprisonment in a letter to President Hosni Mubarak on April 2, citing the case as part of a disturbing pattern of the Egyptian government's use of criminal libel prosecutions against journalists for their work and asking Mubarak to initiate reforms of the statutes used for this purpose.

Egypt's Court of Cassation on August 30 overturned the lower court's conviction, citing procedural errors in Fahmy's trial and ordering the journalist's immediate release, but ruled that Fahmy be retried.

March 21
Cairo Times CENSORED

Censors at the Ministry of Information banned distribution of the March 19 issue of the fortnightly magazine *Cairo Times* after Hisham Kassem, the magazine's publisher, refused to comply with the censor's demand that he remove several articles from the magazine. The articles included an interview with Islamic writer Khalil Abdel Karim, and five opinion pieces by Egyptian writers commenting on recent government restrictions on the press. (In January, two of Karim's books were seized from the printer by order of the state security prosecutor.) The censor also objected to a review of an English translation of *Al-Balad Okhra*, a book about life in Saudi Arabia.

Previously, on March 3, censors at the Ministry of Information had threatened to ban the magazine's March 5 edition because of an article describing the authorities' February 17 detention of Andrew Hammond, the paper's deputy editor, and a free-lance photographer working with the magazine. Both were held for nearly six hours in the Ezbekia police station and State Security Investigation (SSI) headquarters.

In an April 2 letter sent to President Hosni Mubarak, CPJ protested the censorship of *Cairo Times* and urged that authorities cease their harassment of the magazine.

March 31
Print Media CENSORED

The General Authority for Free Zones and Investment issued a decree ordering the suspension of all printing services for magazines and newspapers which publish in the free investment zone established in Nasser City. Some 36 publications can print only in the free investment zone because they are licensed abroad—a tactic they adopted in order to circumvent government restrictions on printing licenses.

The suspension forced the newspapers and magazines to suspend publication or to secure more expensive printing services abroad.

Prime Minister Kamal Ganzouri reversed the decree on May 21. "Prime Minister Kamal Ganzouri decided that books, reviews or periodicals can again be printed in the free zones," Cabinet Affairs Minister Talaat Hammad said in a statement.

May 20
Amer Nassef, *Al-Ousbou', Al-Ahrar*
IMPRISONED, LEGAL ACTION

Nassef, a journalist who writes frequently for the weekly *Al-Ousbou'*, was convicted on appeal of libeling Egyptian writer Tharwat Abaza in an article published in the daily newspaper *Al-Ahrar*, organ of the Liberal Party, in 1996. He was sentenced to three months in prison. Nassef turned himself in to police on May 25 and began serving his sentence in Torah Mazraa Prison.

Attacks on the Press in 1998

In a letter to President Hosni Mubarak on July 9, CPJ called on the president to examine legal options to secure the release of Nassef and end the use of criminal defamation statutes against journalists.

Nassef was released from prison on August 30 after completing his term.

May 30
Cairo Times CENSORED

Cairo Times publisher Hisham Kassem was informed by his printer, Sahara Printing House, that it would no longer print his magazine in Egypt by order of the General Authority for Free Zones and Investment (GAFI). Like several other publications, *Cairo Times* had been printing in the free investment zone established in Nasser City. It is the only place they may print in Egypt, because they are licensed abroad—a tactic they adopted to circumvent government restrictions on printing licenses.

The justification for the printing ban on *Cairo Times* was that authorities consider the magazine a political publication, and hence not able to publish in the zone according to current regulations. The ban on *Cairo Times* came just weeks after Prime Minister Kamal Ganzouri reversed a GAFI decree issued in late March, which had ordered the suspension of all printing services for magazines and newspapers publishing in the free investment zone.

The magazine estimated that it had lost US$30,000-$50,000 since March as a result of government censorship because of lost sales and advertising revenue on the banned issues, and the increased costs of having to print in Cyprus after the GAFI decree went into effect.

In a June 4 letter to President Hosni Mubarak, CPJ condemned the move as an example of government harassment of the magazine.

August 12
Alf Lela CENSORED

Ministry of Information censors confiscated the inaugural August 12 issue of the new cultural weekly *Alf Lela*, saying that the newspaper contained articles of a "political nature" although it was licensed as a cultural publication. Staffers from *Alf Lela* suspect that one of the articles in question was a piece that discussed a recently released movie about the late Egyptian President Gamal Abdel Nasser.

One week later, authorities banned the August 19 issue of *Alf Lela* without giving a reason.

Alf Lela, which is published in Cyprus, was founded by former staff members of the now-defunct weekly *Al-Dustur*. The Ministry of Information revoked the license of *Al-Dustur* on February 26 after it had published a report on death threats allegedly made by the militant Islamic Group against prominent Coptic businessmen.

September 16
Middle East Times CENSORED

Censors at the Ministry of Information ordered editors to excise two articles from the September 19 edition of the English-language weekly *Middle East Times*. One of the censored articles discussed the campaign by Coptic Christian organizations outside Egypt against alleged government persecution of Egypt's Christian minority. The second article discussed a recently released report by the Egyptian Organization for Human Rights on social violence in Egypt.

One week later, on September 23, censors forced *Middle East Times* editors to remove another article about military service from the forthcoming issue. In the article, Egyptian men were asked their opinions on compulsory military service. According to the *Middle East Times*, the censor explained that military service is a "matter of national security and is not allowed to be written about in the press."

October 22
Mustafa Bakry, *Al-Ousbou'* LEGAL ACTION
Mahmoud Bakry, *Al-Ousbou'* LEGAL ACTION

The Helwan misdemeanors court ruled that Mustafa and Mahmoud Bakry—editor in chief and managing editor, respectively, of the weekly *Al-Ousbou'*—were guilty of libeling former Justice Party President Muhammad Abdel Aal. The charges stemmed from a series of articles they wrote for the daily *Al-Ahrar* in 1996, which included an accusation that Aal had illegally seized property in Cairo.

The Bakry brothers each received a one-year prison sentence, but they struck an agreement with the prosecutor general and were allowed to remain free until the Court of Cassation rules on the case.

Iran

Since President Muhammad Khatemi took office in August 1997, Iran's press has benefited from his agenda of social and political reforms. Newspapers are now tackling political subjects that would have been unthinkable only a year earlier. But almost as quickly as journalists realized their new freedoms, the press found itself the target of a relentless attacks from hard-line supporters of Iran's spiritual guide Ayatollah Ali Khamenei.

In what proved to be a year of dramatic developments, several newspapers were suspended or permanently closed, while journalists were arrested and prosecuted for their reporting on a variety of sensitive political topics. To most observers, the clampdown against the more vocal press was part of the power struggle being waged between supporters of Khatemi's reformist program and Khamenei loyalists. For much of the year, Khamenei exerted

Attacks on the Press in 1998

his control over the judiciary to harass or close outspoken newspapers for their reporting on such subjects as criticism of the Islamic Republic and its philosophical foundations.

The pro-Khatemi daily *Jameah*, which in a short span of time had made a name for itself through its bold coverage of social and political issues, was closed in July after a court found it guilty of publishing insults and false information in its criticisms of public officials. *Jameah*'s successor, the daily *Tous*, was closed in September for "publication of articles against national security and general interests." Several members of the newspaper's staff were arrested and held without charge for several days.

One day before *Tous's* closure, Khamenei publicly accused certain newspapers of succumbing to Western attitudes about Islam and the revolution. He said, "I am giving final notice to officials to act and see which newspapers violate the limits of freedom."

By year's end, nine newspapers—*Rah-e-Noh, Tavana, Jameah Salem, Khaneh, Jameah, Tous, Asre-e-Ma, Sobh*, and *Gozaresh-e-Ruz*—were either permanently closed or suspended for long periods. And journalists—including some from the official Islamic Republic News Agency (IRNA)—were arrested or indicted for publications offenses for their reporting on controversial subjects. Several were fined or handed suspended prison sentences and fines. Explaining the crackdown, Khamenei said, "Critique and criticism of the government's policies are not bad, but when someone attempts to undermine the foundations of the government, it is a treason and not freedom of expression."

In the face of mounting government pressure, journalists remained defiant toward official attempts to limit their freedom. And they enjoyed support from students, who in December demonstrated in Tehran against the state's repressive measures against the press.

The disappearances and suspicious deaths of several writers and free expression advocates in the last months of the year sent a chilling message to independent-minded writers and journalists alike.

June 10
Hamid Reza Jalaipour, *Jameah*
LEGAL ACTION
Jameah LEGAL ACTION

In a one-day trial, a Tehran court ordered the closure of the liberal daily *Jameah* and banned its managing editor, Hamid Reza Jalaipour, from heading a newspaper for one year for publishing insults and false information.

The charges stemmed from several articles published in *Jameah* which were critical of Iranian public figures, including Revolutionary Guards commander Brig. Gen. Yahya Rahim Safavi, whom the paper quoted as making threatening statements against "liberals" and "antirevolutionaries."

Since its founding in early 1998, *Jameah* had earned a reputation for its daring coverage of political and social issues in Iran. Following the June 10 ruling, the paper was allowed to continue publishing until an appellate court ruled on the case on July 23, revoking *Jameah*'s publishing license effective July 25. The court reduced the ban against Jalaipour to two months.

CPJ protested the July 23 ruling in a July 24 letter to Ayatollah Muhammad Yazdi, the head of Iran's judiciary. To circumvent the closure order, *Jameah* resumed publishing on June 25 under a different title, *Tous*.

July 13
Ali Mohammad Mahdavi-Khorrami,
Gozaresh-e-Ruz LEGAL ACTION

A court banned Mahdavi-Khorrami, managing

MIDDLE EAST

editor of the daily *Gozaresh-e-Ruz*, from owning or managing a newspaper in Iran for three years and fined him US$4,000 for publishing lies and violating press ethics.

Gozaresh-e-Ruz closed voluntarily on June 10—just a few weeks after it was launched—after the legal action was initiated against Mahdavi-Khorrami. He had been detained for six days beginning on June 9 in connection with the charges.

The charges stem from an article and a cartoon published in *Gozaresh-e-Ruz*. The offending cartoon, which appeared on the front page of *Gozaresh-e-Ruz* in late May, depicted a teenage boy and girl with the caption "Friendship Under Fear." The article, which appeared in June, reported that Iranian leaders had transferred large sums of money to bank accounts outside the country. The story reportedly had been published in the Paris-based Arabic newspaper *Al-Watan al-Arabi*.

CPJ protested the court's ruling in a July 23 letter to Ayatollah Muhammad Yazdi, the head of Iran's judiciary.

August 1
Mashallah Shamsolvaezin, *Tous* ATTACKED

A mob of demonstrators attacked Shamsolvaezin, editor in chief of the reformist daily *Tous*, outside the newspaper's office in Tehran. He was pushed and punched by the demonstrators, who had assembled outside the newspaper's office and shouted slogans against the reformist publication.

Shamsolvaezin was not seriously injured in the attack.

August 1
Tous HARASSED, CENSORED

A Tehran court ordered the closure of the reformist daily *Tous* for allegedly violating Iran's press law. A Justice Department official said the paper had violated the law by using the same layout, content, and staff as a banned publication—the daily *Jameah*, which was *Tous'* predecessor.

Despite the ruling, *Tous* resumed publication on August 2 under a different name, *Aftab-e-Ruz*. On the same day, a Tehran public court lifted the original ban, provided that the newspaper abide by regulations pertaining to layout.

August 3
Khaneh CENSORED
Muhammad Reza Za'eri, *Khaneh* LEGAL ACTION

An Iranian court handed down a six-month suspended sentence and a fine of 3 million rials (US$1,000) against Muhammad Reza Za'eri, managing director of the conservative weekly *Khaneh*.

Za'eri was first summoned by the court in late July, and charged with insulting Islamic principles, the Iranian nation, and the values of the Islamic revolution by publishing a letter from a reader in the July 15 edition which criticized the late Ayatollah Ruhollah Khomeini. The anonymous letter commented on the Iran-Iraq war and said, "When I think of Khomeini, all that comes to mind are the horrifying sounds of the midnight bombs that used to fall on Tehran, and the blood of thousands of innocent young Iranians who died in that war."

The letter also criticized Khomeini's fatwa against British author Salman Rushdie, saying, "Do you call me to follow someone who has transformed Iran into an international terrorist state with his order to murder Salman Rushdie?"

On July 28, *Khaneh*'s office was damaged in a petrol bomb attack believed to have been carried out by militants in retaliation for the letter. Za'eri was arrested on July 29. He was released on bail following his conviction on August 3. On August 5, the same court permanently revoked *Khaneh*'s license on the same charges leveled against Za'eri.

Attacks on the Press in 1998

September 15
Tous CENSORED
Hamid Reza Jalaipour, *Tous* IMPRISONED
Mashallah Shamsolvaezin, *Tous* MPRISONED
Muhammad Sadeq Javadi-Hessar, *Tous* IMPRISONED
Ibrahim Nabavi, *Tous* IMPRISONED

Judicial authorities ordered the closure of the reformist daily *Tous*, effective September 16, for its "publication of articles against national security and general interests." Muhammad Sadeq Javadi-Hessar, the publisher, received a letter on September 15 which stated that *Tous* would remain closed until further notice, pending an investigation. Authorities sealed the *Tous* offices on the evening of September 15 and prevented distribution of the following day's edition. The paper's license was revoked on September 28.

Jalaipour, the chairman of the paper's publishing company, Jameah-e-Ruz; Shamsolvaezin, its editor in chief; Javadi-Hessar; and Nabavi, a reporter, were detained by police between September 16 and 20 for questioning in front of a revolutionary court. Jalaipour was finally released on bail on October 13, while the remaining three were freed on bail on October 21. The four are awaiting trial.

The actions against *Tous* came one day after Iran's spiritual leader, Ayatollah Ali Khamenei, accused "certain newspapers" of succumbing to a "Western cultural onslaught ... targeting people's faith, Islam, and the revolution," and adding that "I am giving final notice to officials to act and see which newspapers violate the limits of freedom." Although authorities offered no official explanation for their actions, some observers believe that it was because the paper had recently criticized Iran's military build-up on the Afghan border during tensions between the two countries. Others suspect that the closure order may have been in response to a published story citing the views of the late Ayatollah Abol Qasem Khoei, who had challenged the concept of Veliyat-e-Faqih (rule by a supreme religious legal scholar).

Both *Tous* and its predecessor—the daily *Jameah*—earned reputations for daring coverage of political and social issues in Iran, and both have been targets of concerted state reprisal.

In a September 18 letter to Khamenei, CPJ condemned the closure of *Tous* and the arrest of its staff.

September 22
Muhammad Reza Sadeq, IRNA HARASSED
Ali Reza Khosravi, IRNA HARASSED

Police arrested Sadeq, deputy managing director of the Islamic Republic News Agency (IRNA), and Khosravi, editor of IRNA's social news desk, after the two were summoned to a Tehran public court and questioned for five hours. The summons and arrest followed a complaint made by Mohsen Rafiqdoust, head of the Foundation for the Oppressed and (War) Disabled—a government-sponsored charitable organization—in relation to a September 13 IRNA news report about an assassination attempt on his life that day.

The journalists were released on September 23, and Rafiqdoust withdrew his complaint.

September 29
Jameah Salem LEGAL ACTION
Siovash Guran, *Jameah Salem* LEGAL ACTION

A Tehran press court revoked the license of the monthly *Jameah Salem* for allegedly insulting the late Ayatollah Ruhollah Khomeini. Although the court did not cite specific news articles that constituted the offense, some local and foreign journalists speculate that the court acted in response to a story published earlier that month describing the sentiment among young Iranians that the country has made little progress under the Islamic Republic. Guran, the paper's director, received a one-year suspended sentence for the offense and was fined 3 million riyals (about US$1,000).

MIDDLE EAST

Iraq

Press freedom remains nonexistent in Saddam Hussein's notorious police state. The media function as outlets for propaganda extolling the Iraqi strongman's virtues. Hussein's son Uday exerts considerable influence over the media as head of the Iraqi Journalists Union and owner of the newspaper *Babil*.

Information continued to be a precious commodity for most Iraqis. The government has banned satellite dishes, and a seven-year-old United Nations embargo keeps foreign publications from entering the country. Radio offers the main source of alternative information for the population, although the government in the past has reportedly attempted to jam foreign radio broadcasts.

July 1
Dawoud al-Farhan, *Al-Iraq*, *Al-Musawwar al-Arabi*, Middle East News Agency
IMPRISONED

Al-Farhan, a veteran writer working with the daily *Al-Iraq*, the weekly *Al-Musawwar al-Arabi* and Egypt's Middle East News Agency (MENA), was arrested at his office in the Ministry of Information building in Baghdad by Iraqi authorities in July. His fellow journalists believe that he was detained as a result of a series of columns he had written about alleged government corruption in Iraq.

In a September 2 letter to President Saddam Hussein, CPJ urged that the government make public the reason for al-Farhan's arrest. In October, CPJ confirmed the journalist's release.

Israel and the Occupied Territories

Physical assaults and shootings by Israeli Defense Forces (IDF) and police against journalists continue to occur with shocking regularity. Throughout the year, numerous reporters—mostly Palestinians covering political violence in the West Bank—were beaten and subjected to other forms of physical harassment. Israeli soldiers shot several reporters, some of whom had been wounded before by IDF gunfire. The circumstances of the attacks, including the distance of journalists from the political unrest and their conspicuous camera equipment, led many to believe that the IDF singled them out.

In one shocking incident, soldiers using rubber-coated metal bullets shot nine Palestinian journalists who were covering clashes in Hebron between Jewish settlers and Palestinian protesters on March 13. Video footage of the incident showed two bullets hitting one of the wounded journalists, Nael Shiyoukhi of Reuters, as he lay on the ground, bleeding profusely from his head.

As disturbing as the attacks themselves was the seeming impunity enjoyed by the soldiers involved. To date, CPJ is unaware of a single case in which members of the IDF or police have been prosecuted or severely disciplined for attacks against members of the press.

Israeli journalists were not immune to IDF reprisals. Avichai Nudel, an Israeli reporter with the daily *Maariv*, was wounded by IDF gunfire in May in Hebron. Yaacov Erez, *Maariv*'s editor, said, "This is not the first time IDF soldiers have hurt journalists. Until now, these were Palestinian journalists, and the official word was that they mingled with the rioters and could not be singled out from among them."

When not contending with IDF or police, journalists were often fending off attacks by militant Jewish settlers in the West Bank. In some instances, journalists complained about physical assaults occurring in the presence of Israeli police who made no effort to intervene.

Restrictions on their freedom of movement continued to hamper Palestinian journalists. Citing security concerns, Israeli authorities tightly control most West Bank Palestinian journalists' access to East Jerusalem and Israel. Those wishing to travel to these destinations must obtain Israeli press cards and official permission, both of which are distributed arbitrarily and sparingly to the Palestinian press. As a result, most West Bank journalists are forced to avoid military checkpoints, and many enter Jerusalem illegally. Even with the proper certification, journalists are denied entry into Israel during the closures of the territories in the aftermath of suicide bombings or other violent incidents. For Palestinian journalists in Gaza, access to Jerusalem and the West Bank is almost impossible, except for a handful of reporters who possess the required paperwork. According to journalists, it is slightly easier to obtain permission to go to Gaza than to East or West Jerusalem.

In a case emblematic of these arbitrary strictures, authorities continued to prohibit Taher Shriteh, a Palestinian journalist from the Gaza Strip, from entering Jerusalem and the West Bank. Shriteh, a free-lance reporter who works for *The New York Times*, CBS, Reuters, and the British Broadcasting Corporation, has been denied permission to enter Jerusalem without explanation since March 1995. The apparent justification for the ban is his reporting about the activities of the Islamic Resistance Movement (Hamas) in Gaza.

Print and broadcast media operating in Israel remain subject to military censorship, which requires editors to submit news on topics related to national security for review. In one notable instance in February, censors banned reporting of the details of a failed operation in Switzerland by the Israeli spy agency Mossad, in which the Swiss arrested a Mossad agent for espionage. Most news outlets are able to circumvent the restrictions by attributing sensitive reports to foreign media.

Authorities continued their harassment of former navy captain, author, and freelance journalist Michael Eldar, whose book *Dakar*—about an Israeli submarine that disappeared in the Mediterranean Sea in 1968—was banned last year by court order. Eldar was arrested on July 21 after he set up a website dedicated to his banned works which featured a secret document relating to his research of the Dakar case. During his detention, which lasted for several hours, police confiscated documents and computer disks from his home and instructed him to shut down the site or face imprisonment. He was released after he agreed to take down the website and posted 60,000 NIS (US$15,000) bail.

March 13
Nael Shiyoukhi, Reuters ATTACKED
Mazen Dana, Reuters ATTACKED
Bilal al-Joneidi, Reuters ATTACKED
Majdi al-Tamimi, ABC ATTACKED
Amer Jabari, ABC ATTACKED
Hazem Bader, Associated Press ATTACKED
Imad al-Said, Associated Press ATTACKED
Wael Shiyoukhi, Amal TV ATTACKED
Ayman al-Kurd, Amal TV ATTACKED

Israeli soldiers in Hebron opened fire with rubber-coated metal bullets on a group of reporters covering clashes between Palestinian protesters and Israeli troops. Those wounded included: Nael Shiyoukhi, Mazen Dana, and Bilal al-Joneidi of Reuters; Majdi al-Tamimi and Amer Jabari of ABC News; Hazem Bader and Imad al-Said of the Associated Press; and Wael Shiyoukhi and Ayman al-Kurd of Amal TV.

Witnesses characterized the incident as the Israel Defense Forces' intentional targeting of the journalists, who were in the vicinity of the clashes. Three of the wounded journalists told CPJ that they were at least 200 meters from Palestinian protesters when they were fired upon. These journalists also maintain that soldiers continued shooting at them despite their attempts to identify themselves as members of the press and entreaties to the soldiers to halt their fire.

Bullets hit Nael Shiyoukhi in the head, back, and leg. Video footage of the incident revealed that he was shot twice as he lay on the ground with blood flowing from his head. Mazen Dana was shot in the shoulder while going to Shiyoukhi's aid. According to Dana, soldiers continued to fire at the reporters as they attempted to carry Shiyoukhi to a nearby automobile.

CPJ protested the attack in a letter to Prime Minister Benjamin Netanyahu on March 16.

May 14
Eddo Rosenthal, NOS ATTACKED

Rosenthal, a veteran correspondent for the Dutch National Public Broadcasting Service (NOS), was wounded in the chin by what he described as indiscriminate Israeli police gunfire while he was covering protests in East Jerusalem on the 50th anniversary of al-Nakba—the day Palestinians commemorate the events of 1948 that led to the creation of the State of Israel.

Rosenthal was shot as he was leaving a group of between 25 and 30 journalists and bystanders at an intersection near the National Palace Hotel. At the time, police were attempting to enter the hotel while stone-throwers pelted the intersection.

"As I started walking away, I heard a shot," said Rosenthal. "Automatically, I turned and saw a lone policeman ... He had a gun at his shoulder pointing in the direction of the journalists and bystanders on the pavement, among whom I had just been standing." A few moments later, Rosenthal "heard a second shot and simultaneously felt a punch on my chin."

Rosenthal noted that police did not order bystanders to leave the area, nor did the officer who fired at him appear to be in a "life-threatening situation." He added that, "It must have been clear to the policeman that there were many journalists among the civilians standing on the sidewalk, as several of them were carrying equipment."

On May 17, Rosenthal filed a complaint with the Israeli police and is currently awaiting the outcome of their investigation.

May 15
Avichai Nudel, *Maariv* ATTACKED

Nudel, a photographer for the Israeli daily *Maariv*, was wounded in the stomach by a rubber bullet fired by Israeli Defense Forces (IDF) soldiers while he was covering clashes between Israelis and Palestinians in the West Bank city of Hebron.

Nudel was far from the disturbances, with other journalists, when he was shot. He was sent to the hospital for treatment and is recovering from his injuries.

"Avichai was shot from a 40-meter range," wrote *Maariv* editor Yaacov Erez. "It was not accidentally discharged or a stray bullet. It's possible that the soldier who shot him had intended to shoot at the journalists who were covering the unrest, or that he acted in haste and was criminally negligent."

August 7
Joseph al-Ghazi, *Ha'aretz* ATTACKED

Arab demonstrators attacked al-Ghazi, a reporter for the Israeli daily *Ha'aretz*, in the city of Jaffa while he was attempting to cover a

Attacks on the Press in 1998

protest calling for the opening of the al-Taybeh mosque. The mosque had been closed since the creation of the State of Israel in 1948. Police intervened to halt the attack.

August 24
Amer Jabari, ABC ATTACKED
Tareq al-Kayal, ARD ATTACKED
Muwafaq al-Kayal, ARD ATTACKED

Israeli soldiers and police assaulted Jabari, a cameraman for ABC television, in the West Bank city of Hebron while he was attempting to film two other Palestinian journalists being beaten by Israeli forces.

Police officers approached Jabari and asked him for his identification, and then one of the officers struck him in the groin with his rifle butt. Several other officers joined in the beating.

Jabari had been attempting to film Tareq and Muwafaq al-Kayal of Germany's ARD television, who had been stopped and beaten by Israeli forces. The soldiers destroyed Tareq al-Kayal's camera and microphone.

The journalists were detained at the scene for three hours after the incident.

September 28
Imad al-Said, Associated Press ATTACKED

Israeli police beat al-Said, a cameraman for the Associated Press, while he was attempting to cover a clash between Palestinians and Jewish settlers in the West Bank city of Hebron. Al-Said was on his way to the Tal al-Remaideh neighborhood in Hebron when two police officers from the Anti-Terrorism Unit approached him and told him that the area was closed by military order. After al-Said requested to see the written order, one of the officers threatened him, saying, "If you don't go away you will see what will happen to you." The officer then grabbed al-Said by the neck and kicked him in the back. The officer also began to choke him and kicked him in the groin. Footage of the incident, filmed by al-Said's colleagues, was broadcast later that evening on Israeli television's Channel One.

Israeli police quickly responded to the incident, dismissing the officer in question from his unit. But CPJ later learned that he remains on active duty in another unit.

In an October 2 letter to Prime Minister Benjamin Netanyahu, CPJ condemned the attack and called on authorities to ensure that the officer responsible be prosecuted to the fullest extent of the law.

September 30
Nasser Shiyoukhi, Associated Press ATTACKED
Imad al-Said, Associated Press ATTACKED
Mazen Dana, Reuters ATTACKED
Nayef Hashlaman, Reuters ATTACKED
Nael Shiyoukhi, Reuters ATTACKED

Israeli police assaulted a group of Palestinian reporters and cameramen who were attempting to film clashes between Palestinians and Jewish settlers in Hebron. Among those attacked were Nasser Shiyoukhi, a photographer; Imad al-Said, a cameraman for the Associated Press; and three Reuters journalists—Mazen Dana, a reporter and cameraman, Nayef Hashlaman, a technician, and Nael Shiyoukhi, a cameraman and sound technician.

According to the journalists, Israeli police punched and kicked them after telling them that the area was closed to the press. Israeli and foreign reporters were allowed access to report the conflict. Jewish settlers who were in the vicinity of the attack joined the fray; one of them kicked Dana in the face. The journalists said that police also hit them with their rifles and eventually forced them to evacuate the Israeli-controlled section of Hebron.

CPJ protested the attack in a letter to Prime Minister Benjamin Netanyahu on October 2, urging him to conduct an immediate and vigorous investigation into the incident and make its findings public. CPJ also

MIDDLE EAST

urged the Israeli government to ensure that those implicated be swiftly brought to justice.

October 24
Muhammad Abdel Nabi al-Lahham, Al-Roa' TV ATTACKED
Shadi Ubeid, Al-Roa' TV ATTACKED

Al-Lahham, a reporter with the Bethlehem-based Al-Roa' TV (Shepherds TV), and Ubeid, a cameraman for the same station, were attacked by five Jewish settlers in the West Bank city of Hebron while working on a story about tensions between Palestinians and Israelis in Hebron. The settlers assaulted the journalists and threw hot tea at them. They also seized Ubeid's camera, removed the film, and smashed it. According to the journalists, the settlers threatened them, saying, "Wait, we will kill each one of you in Hebron."

Israeli soldiers arrived at the scene and detained the journalists, taking them to a police station near the Jewish settlement of Kiryat Arba, where they were held for three hours. Police accused al-Lahham and Ubeid of attempting to enter the home of Anan Cohen, one of the five assailants, and of entering Israeli-controlled areas without permission. Police refused to accept a complaint which the journalists attempted to file against the settlers.

Jordan

Ignoring vocal international protests, the cabinet, parliament, and King Hussein pushed forward a repressive press law in a year that saw a continued deterioration of press freedoms. Its ratification by royal decree on September 1 marked the culmination of a year-long battle between journalists and the government of Prime Minister Abdel Salam al-Majali, which had introduced similarly draconian amendments to the press and publications law in May 1997. In January, the High Court of Justice overturned the amendments because they had not gone through the parliamentary process, prompting the government to submit a similar law to parliament in June.

Several provisions of the new law legalize censorship and provide authorities with a variety of methods to sanction independent or critical journalism. Article 37 bans coverage on a wide array of topics, including any news or information deemed to "infringe on the independence of the judiciary"; "defame the heads of Arab, Islamic, or friendly states"; or harm "national unity." Violators of these prohibitions are subject to fines as high as 10,000JD (US$14,090), while repeat offenders are subject to penalties of up to 20,000JD (US$28,180). There has been a marked increase in self-censorship among the press, which the ambiguously worded restrictions appear designed to promote.

Article 31 empowers the Press and Publications Department (PPD) to censor foreign publications deemed to violate the law's numerous prohibitions, while Article 35 allows for censorship of books published in the kingdom. The former provision directly contradicted a pledge made by King Hussein in June, when he directed then-Prime Minister al-Majali to "put an end to every form of censorship and restrictions on the Arab and foreign press."

Other censorship provisions include Article 39, which grants the judiciary sweeping powers to censor news coverage on criminal investigations or trials. And perhaps most disturbing of all is Article 50, which allows the judiciary to indefinitely close down publications that are the subject of litigation for matters of "public interest" or "national security."

Authorities continued to gag the press in a variety of other ways. On three occasions, there were media blackouts on coverage of major events, such as the trial of leading

Attacks on the Press in 1998

political opposition figure Leith Shubeilat; a triple homicide in Amman; and a water pollution crisis. Foreign newspapers were banned by the PPD for their coverage of domestic political issues. Journalists continued to be arrested in connection with their published criticisms, further enhancing an atmosphere of intimidation, while criminal defamation statutes were employed against outspoken members of the press.

In August, Prime Minister al-Majali resigned under pressure and was succeeded by Fayez Tarawneh. Since taking office, Tarawneh has attempted to portray a more congenial image in the government's relations with the press. One of his first official acts was to replace PPD Director Bilal al-Tal, who was notorious for his heavy-handed treatment of journalists. Foreign newspapers reported that bans on their distribution had all but stopped by the end of the year. PPD Director Iyyad Qattan announced that the government had instructed the attorney general to cancel all prosecutions of journalists initiated by the PPD during the year, and Minister of Information Nasser Judeh publicly declared that the government was committed to a "soft implementation" of the new press law. But self-censorship remained widespread.

At year's end, it appeared the government was intent on passing the responsibility of reining in journalists to the pro-government Jordan Press Association and its disciplinary council, which has the power to sanction journalists accused of ethics violations and strip them of their accreditation. It remains to be seen to what extent the association was prepared to implement this plan.

March 2
Omar Qoulab, *Al-Bilad* IMPRISONED
Sami Zubaidi, *Al-Bilad* IMPRISONED

Security agents took Qoulab and Zubaidi, editors for the weekly *Al-Bilad*, into custody at the paper's Amman office. The detention stemmed from an article published in the newspaper discussing former Prime Minister Abdel Karim Kabariti's alleged links to a Jordanian bank.

Both men were held without charge at General Intelligence headquarters in Amman for five days and then released. It is unclear whether formal charges were brought against them.

March 2
Abdel Hadi Raji al-Majalli, *Abed Rabbo* IMPRISONED

Security agents detained al-Majalli, editor in chief of the satirical weekly *Abed Rabbo*, at his home in response to a front-page photograph published in the newspaper satirizing Prime Minister Abdel Salam al-Majali.

The photograph depicted the prime minister holding a microscope under a person's belt and calling to Interior Minister Nathir Rashid: "Come on Nathir, I found an infiltrator and a Kalashnikov." The image lampooned the government's response to pro-Iraq riots that broke out in the southern town of Ma'an in February.

Majalli was held for questioning at General Intelligence headquarters in Amman until his release on March 7. It is unclear whether he has been formally charged with an offense.

March 7
Bassam Badareen, *Al-Quds al-Arabi* LEGAL ACTION

Badareen, Amman correspondent for the London-based daily *Al-Quds al-Arabi*, was formally charged with "distorting Jordan's image abroad," harming state relations with a friendly country, and offending the state, all of which are criminal offenses.

The case against Badareen stems from a series of articles he wrote for *Al-Quds al-Arabi* in late 1997, dealing with such topics as tensions between the government and the Islamist opposition following its boycott of the

November 1997 parliamentary elections, and criticism of the Arab-Israeli peace process. Badareen faces up to three years in prison if convicted of the charges.

March 16
Raja Talab, *Shihan* LEGAL ACTION
Riad Hroub, *Shihan* LEGAL ACTION
Riham Farra, *Shihan* LEGAL ACTION
Abdel Hadi Raji al-Majalli, *Shihan* LEGAL ACTION

The Court of First Instance convicted Talab, editor in chief of the weekly *Shihan*; Hroub, the paper's publisher; Farra, a columnist; and al-Majalli, a former editor, of defaming parliamentary deputy Muhammad Ra'fat. The four were each sentenced to six months in prison and a fine of 1,000 JD (US$1,400).

The charge stemmed from an article and a cartoon published in *Shihan* in late 1997, which criticized Ra'fat for a visit he made to the Israeli Knesset. The four journalists appealed the court's decision during the week following the verdict.

CPJ protested the convictions in a March 18 letter to King Hussein, sent during his meeting in March with U.S. President Bill Clinton.

March 19
All journalists CENSORED

Jordanian authorities imposed a media ban on coverage of the case of Leith Shubeilat, a leading political opposition figure and former member of parliament, who was standing trial in the state security court.

In a March 19 letter to the Jordanian press, Press and Publications Director Bilal al-Tal informed newspapers that they could not publish any information about the case of Shubeilat, who had been charged with inciting an illegal demonstration in the southern town of Ma'an in late February. Al-Tal's letter was accompanied by a separate letter from state security court prosecutor Mamoun Khaswaneh requesting that the media refrain from publishing any "news or commentary" about the case.

Khaswaneh cited Article 42 of the Press and Publications Law (1993) as the basis for the ban. Article 42 states: "The publication of proceedings of any case pending before the Courts prior to the pronouncement of a final ruling shall be prohibited, unless the court sanctions publication."

Authorities issued further warnings after several newspapers ignored the media blackout and published criticisms of the ban. On March 26, al-Tal sent a second letter to newspapers, accompanied by a letter from Khaswaneh, reiterating the ban and threatening that violators would be subject to prosecution. He sent a third letter on March 30, along with a letter from Yousef al-Fa'oury, a military judge at the state security court, again warning publications against violating the ban.

CPJ wrote to Prime Minister Abdel Salam al-Majali on April 9, protesting the ban as evidence of increasing state interference with the print media in Jordan.

April 10
Al-Arab al-Yawm HARASSED, CENSORED

Police surrounded the Amman office of the independent daily *Al-Arab al-Yawm* and informed the staff that the Ministry of Information had imposed a news blackout on coverage of the April 8 triple homicide in Amman of Hannah Naddeh, a prominent lawyer; his son, Suhail; and Awni Saad, a psychiatrist. Police delayed the paper's distribution until senior officers were able to screen an article about the homicide slated for publication on April 10.

According to newspaper staffers, the April 16 and 17 issues of *Al-Arab al-Yawm* were also delayed to allow authorities to pre-censor them.

April 11
Yousef Gheishan, *Al-Arab al-Yawm*
IMPRISONED

Security agents arrested Gheishan, a satirical columnist with the independent daily *Al Arab al-Yawm* and a contributor to the weeklies *Al-Bilad* and *Abed Rabbo*, at his home in Amman. They searched his house and confiscated copies of documents and articles he had written.

Gheishan, a vocal critic of the Jordanian government, was held for seven days at General Intelligence headquarters in Amman. He was accused of lèse-majesté (insulting the dignity of the king) and distributing anti-government leaflets—charges which he denied. He was released on April 18 and the charges against him were dropped.

Gheishan believes that the arrest was intended to discourage him from writing columns critical of the government.

May 12
Al-Quds al-Arabi CENSORED

Jordan's Press and Publications Department (PPD) banned the distribution of the London-based daily *Al-Quds al-Arabi*. Agence France-Presse quoted PPD Director Bilal al-Tal as saying that the move came in response to the paper's "published reports and analysis which violate the most basic rules of professionalism and objectivity."

Al-Quds al-Arabi has been the target of repeated government harassment. Dozens of issues of the newspaper have been confiscated by the PPD in response to what authorities have deemed unfavorable coverage of political affairs in Jordan.

CPJ wrote to Prime Minister Abdel Salam al-Majali on May 13, protesting the ban, which was lifted on May 18.

June 2
Nidal Mansour, *Al-Hadath*
LEGAL ACTION

The Amman Court of First Instance sentenced Mansour, editor in chief of the weekly *Al-Hadath*, to six months in prison.

Mansour was charged in 1994 under Jordan's penal code with harming the country's relations with a friendly state in connection with a 1994 article published in the weekly *Al-Bilad*, of which Mansour was then editor in chief. The article reported on allegations that Lebanese parliamentarians and the son of Lebanon's President Elias Hrawi were involved in narcotics trafficking. The story was widely reported in both the Lebanese and international media. Mansour is free pending the outcome of his appeal.

June 28
Al-Hadath THREATENED

Over the course of three days beginning on June 28, the office of the independent weekly newspaper *Al-Hadath* received approximately 20 threatening telephone calls after the paper ran a front-page story about Ahmed Awaidi al-Abadi, a controversial nationalist member of parliament.

The story reported that a number of members of parliament, lawyers, and politicians had requested that Abadi's parliamentary immunity be lifted in order to press charges against him for statements he had made to the Qatar-based television station Al-Jazeerah about divisions in Jordan between Palestinians and Jordanians.

According to Nidal Mansour, *Al-Hadath*'s editor, one of the anonymous callers said that he "would see to it that the paper would not continue." Mansour alerted local authorities, who stationed an armed police guard at the newspaper's office.

June 29
Mansour Shamout, *Al-Arab al-Yawn*
LEGAL ACTION

The Amman Court of First Instance sentenced writer Mansour Shamout to four months in prison for allegedly defaming judicial authority in Jordan.

The conviction stemmed from an article Shamout wrote in the March 4 edition of the independent daily *Al-Arab al-Yawm* titled "The Judiciary, al-Kilani, and the Minister of Justice." The article discussed the case of Judge Farouq al-Kilani, head of the Judicial Council (JC) and the Court of Cassation, who was voted into early retirement in February by council members. Shamout strongly criticized Minister of Justice Riad al-Shakaa, who had recommended that the JC take this action.

Al-Kilani's dismissal was widely believed to have been triggered by his efforts to effect comprehensive judicial reform in Jordan, and his support of a ruling in January by the Court of Cassation that struck down draconian temporary amendments to the Press and Publications Law. Shamout is currently free pending the outcome of his appeal.

June 30
Nidal Mansour, *Al-Hadath* LEGAL ACTION

The Amman Court of First Instance fined Mansour, editor in chief of the weekly *Al-Hadath*, 100 dinars (US$140) for allegedly libeling the director of the Ministry of Public Works in the town of Ma'an. The case stemmed from a 1994 news article published in the weekly *Al-Bilad*, of which Mansour was then editor in chief, accusing Nayef al-Nuwaisi of misappropriating ministry funds for his personal use.

July 2
Hussein al-Umush, *Abed Rabbo* IMPRISONED

Police apprehended al-Umush, editor of the satirical weekly *Abed Rabbo*, at his newspaper's Amman office, took him into custody, and held him for nine days, first at the Qasr al-Adl police station and then at Juwaydah Prison in Amman. The action followed the weekly's publication of several articles and photographs lampooning public officials.

During al-Umush's detention, a judge charged him with defamation in relation to five articles published in *Abed Rabbo* between May and June—one of them a photo depicting government officials as members of the British band the Spice Girls.

Al-Umush had previously been held by Jordanian intelligence agents from June 2 to June 7 and accused of lesè-majesté (insulting the dignity of the king) for published articles in *Abed Rabbo* which were critical of the Jordanian government. No formal charges were brought against him in response to these complaints.

August 8
Nahed Hattar, *Al-Mithaq* ATTACKED

In the late evening, Hattar, editor in chief of the weekly *Al-Mithaq*, was violently assaulted by four unidentified men wielding clubs as he exited his car with his wife and child in front of his home in Jabal Hussein. The assailants beat him until he lost consciousness. Hattar was taken to the hospital for treatment and released on August 10.

The precise motive for the attack was unclear, but *Al-Mithaq* has earned a reputation for its provocative coverage of news and politics in Jordan. Hattar had accused former Prime Minister Abdel Karim Kabariti, the Israeli embassy in Amman, and the Palestine Liberation Organization of being behind the incident. Some Jordanian observers suspect that the attack may have come in response to a story which was published in *Al-Mithaq* on the sensitive issue of succession in Jordan after King Hussein.

In an August 12 letter to Prime Minister Abdel Salam al-Majali, CPJ called for an immediate and thorough investigation of the incident and urged that those responsible be brought to justice.

August 10
Hussein al-Umush, *Abed Rabbo* IMPRISONED

Ten policemen went to the home of al-Umush, editor of the satirical weekly *Abed Rabbo*, in Zarqa and arrested him after he had published a photo of Minister of Urban and Rural Affairs and the Environment Tawfiq Kreishan. Kreishan alleged that the photo, which lampooned him for a recent trip to Italy, constituted defamation.

Al-Umush remained in police custody for 10 days before his release. It is unclear whether he was formally charged.

August 25
All journalists CENSORED

Prosecutor General Muhammad Kharabsheh imposed a media blackout on news coverage of a water pollution crisis which struck Amman in July.

Kharabsheh instructed Press and Publications Director Bilal al-Tal to inform newspapers that they could not publish "any news item involving the water pollution case until the prosecution concluded its investigation."

The ban was the third news blackout imposed by Jordanian authorities in 1998.

Lebanon

One year after imposing prior censorship on news and political programming broadcast abroad by private television stations, the cabinet of Prime Minister Rafiq Hariri went a step further by banning the practice of broadcasting political programming abroad in January. The move immediately followed a live television interview with Najah Wakim, an opposition member of parliament, broadcast on the private station LBCI in which Wakim excoriated Hariri and the government on a wide range of topics.

A variety of laws and decrees continued to threaten journalists in both the print and broadcast media. Decree 7997 (enacted in 1996) bans stations from broadcasting news that seeks to "inflame or incite sectarian or religious chauvinism," or which contains "slander, disparagement, disgrace, [or] defamation," while the Audiovisual Law (1994) empowers the Ministry of Information to close television and radio stations that violate these and other equally ambiguous statutes. Authorities continued to use criminal defamation statutes against outspoken journalists, and reined in undesirable criticism by banning foreign publications.

In November, parliament elected Gen. Emile Lahoud as the country's 11th president since independence, replacing Elias Hrawi. Lahoud's election was a cause for optimism among journalists as the new president pledged his commitment to the protection of press freedom. In late December, Lahoud publicly promised that he would not invoke criminal libel statutes against critical journalists as his predecessor had done. "Whatever is published against me, the final judge will be my actions," he said in a newspaper interview, "and if I'm able to prove that what is being published or said is wrong with actions, why should I care about what is said, especially if it is criticism on a personal level?"

Regardless of Lahoud's policies, Lebanon's journalists will have to contend with Syria's ongoing military presence, which continues to interfere with independent reporting. Since Syrian troops entered the country in 1976, the heavy-handed and arbitrary practices of Syrian security forces have instilled fear among the press, and journalists largely avoid any meaningful criticism of Syrian President Hafez al-Assad and Syria's controversial presence in Lebanon.

January 7
Broadcast media CENSORED

The government of Prime Minister Rafiq Hariri issued a decree banning private television stations from broadcasting political news and programming by satellite.

According to Information Minister Basem Sabaa, the move came as a result of recent broadcasts which "posed problems by tarnishing the image of Lebanon abroad and harming its economic interests." The minister was apparently referring to a January 4 interview with Najah Wakim, an opposition member of parliament, which was broadcast live on Lebanese Broadcasting Corporation International (LBCI), in which Wakim sharply criticized Hariri's government and its policies.

The channels affected by the ban were Future TV and LBCI—the two private stations with a license to broadcast via satellite. The state-owned Tele-Liban was appointed as the sole provider of political news for transmission abroad.

February 23
Charles Ayyoub, *Al-Diyar* LEGAL ACTION
Yousef Howayyek, *Al-Diyar* LEGAL ACTION
Elie Saliba, *Al-Diyar* LEGAL ACTION

A Lebanese court charged Ayyoub, owner of the daily *Al-Diyar*, and Howayyek, the paper's director, with allegedly defaming President Elias Hrawi.

The charge, filed under Decree 104 (1977) and several provisions of the penal code, stemmed from a column published in the October 15, 1997, edition of *Al-Diyar* titled "Farm of the Troika." Among the aspects of the column deemed offensive by Judge Mirzaa were Ayyoub's assertion that violation of the constitution has become normal government practice, "tolerated by President Hrawi." If convicted, Ayyoub and Howayyek face up to two years in prison and fines ranging from 50 million to 100 million Lebanese pounds (US$33,000-$66,000).

Saliba, a cartoonist for *Al-Diyar*, was also charged with defamation in the same indictment for a cartoon published in *Al-Diyar* on September 30, 1997, which challenged the independence of the judiciary in Lebanon. Like Ayyoub and Howayyek, Saliba was charged under Decree 104 and faces up to two years in prison in addition to fines amounting to 100 million Lebanese pounds.

CPJ protested these indictments in a March 13 letter to Prime Minister Rafiq Hariri, saying that members of the press should never face criminal prosecution because of material they publish.

June 27
Hassan Sabra, *Al-Shira'* ATTACKED

Sabra, owner and editor in chief of the weekly magazine *Al-Shira'*, was slapped in the face by Lebanese President Elias Hrawi at the home of Interior Minister Michel al-Murr. Sabra had gone to al-Murr's home to express condolences to the minister over the death of his mother.

The incident occurred as Sabra approached the president, who was quoted in the *Daily Star* as telling the journalist, "Get out of here. Get out of my face," before striking him.

Hrawi's fury was widely believed to stem from Sabra's relentless criticism in *Al-Shira'* of the president's policies, particularly Hrawi's support for optional civil marriage in Lebanon.

Mauritania

Government censorship continued to plague Mauritania's independent press. Regulations require newspapers to submit six copies of each edition to Ministry of Interior censors, who frequently delay distribution of newspaper runs without explanation or under Article 11 of Mauritania's 1991 press ordinance. The ordinance empowers authorities to ban the distribution and sale of any newspaper or periodical deemed detrimental to Islam or state authority, threatening to public order, or defamatory to heads of foreign states. In recent years, Article 11 has been used to

punish news reporting on such sensitive topics as slavery in Mauritania, alleged government improprieties, or internal power struggles within the regime.

Journalists resort to self-censorship on political topics, since the loss of revenue resulting from a ban would have serious economic consequences for Mauritania's financially shaky independent papers. In January, authorities placed a three-month ban on the weekly *Mauritanie Nouvelles*, leading to what one journalist termed its "slow death." The paper had been repeatedly censored in 1997.

January 17
Sheikh Saad Bou Kamara IMPRISONED
Brahim Ould Ebety IMPRISONED
Boubacar Ould Messaoud IMPRISONED

Kamara, Ebety, and Messaoud—prominent Mauritanian human rights activists—were arrested following the airing of a television documentary about slavery in Mauritania, which had aired on France's TF1. Messaoud had been featured in the documentary, while the others were implicated as a result of their assistance in making the film.

The three were charged with discrediting the government through disseminating information on slavery in Mauritania abroad and with membership in an unauthorized association.

On February 4, the activists' lawyer, Fatimata Mbaye, was also arrested and similarly charged.

The four were tried and convicted on February 12 and sentenced to 13 months in prison with a fine of 30,000 ougiya (US$190) each. They were convicted of spreading false information, illegally disseminating information for a documentary on slavery, and belonging to an unauthorized association.

On March 24, President Maaouya Ould Sid Ahmed Taya pardoned the four.

June 10
La Tribune CENSORED
The Mauritanian Interior Ministry banned the June 10 edition of the weekly paper *La Tribune* without explanation, citing Article 11 of the press law, which empowers the ministry to censor any publication. According to Muhammad Fall Oumere, the paper's editor in chief, this was the fifth time in less than a month that an issue of the paper was banned from circulation.

Morocco

As in other monarchies in the Middle East, Morocco's King Hassan II sets the tone for permissible journalism in the kingdom. Although the country's private newspapers sometimes offer critiques of government policies, there is widespread self-censorship on political issues. Journalists shy away from critical news coverage of the monarchy and expressions of skepticism about the country's territorial sovereignty over Western Sahara, because they are guaranteed to provoke authorities' ire.

The government has a variety of tools at its disposal to pressure outspoken newspapers. The press code prescribes stiff penalties for journalists who publish news that offends the king or other members of the royal family, or defames public officials. Under the press and penal codes, authorities have the power to confiscate or suspend publications that, among other things, are deemed a "threat to public order." And foreign publications that report unfavorably about the king and government officials risk confiscation or outright ban.

Palestinian National Authority

Five years after Yasser Arafat's Palestinian National Authority (PNA) assumed control of areas of the West Bank and Gaza, fear and self-censorship continue to hamper the Palestinian press. The PNA's authoritarian-style tactics against independent-minded journalists have forced most to steer clear of sensitive topics such as corruption, mismanagement, or any news that would cast Arafat or his authority in a negative light.

To some journalists, the daily press functions more as a mouthpiece for the PNA than as an independent institution. Two of the three private Palestinian dailies have direct financial or political links to the PNA. The third—the private-owned, Jerusalem-based *Al-Quds*—stays well within the boundaries of what Arafat's coterie considers acceptable journalism. "They [the editors] censor about 40 percent of my articles concerning Palestinian policies, corruption, and mismanagement," said one columnist. "I don't send them sensitive stories because I know what they will and will not publish." Although the weekly newspapers *Al-Istiqlal* and *Al-Risala*—publications linked to the militant organization Islamic Jihad and the Khalas party (made up of former Hamas members), respectively—were allowed to resume publishing this year after lengthy closures, both continued to face pressure in the form of arrests of journalists or threats of arrest. For example, one of the editors of *Al-Risala* was on the run for several weeks after he learned that authorities were trying to arrest him for his criticisms of Arafat's leadership.

The nascent private broadcast media were targets of repeated harassment and censorship. In an attempt to silence coverage of pro-Iraqi sentiment during the February standoff between United Nations weapons inspectors and Saddam Hussein, the Ministry of Information banned all broadcasting of opinion and analysis about the crisis. Soon afterward, more than 100 police surrounded the offices of the Bethlehem-based Al-Roa' TV and forced the station to suspend broadcasting after it had aired news about pro-Iraqi demonstrations in the West Bank and other programming about the standoff. The station remained closed without official explanation for five months. In a scene reminiscent of the February crackdown, police in December ordered six private television and radio stations in the West Bank cities of Ramallah and Bethlehem to suspend broadcasting until further notice. The move was widely seen as an attempt by authorities to silence news coverage pertaining to the U.S.-led military attack on Iraq, specifically coverage of anti-U.S. sentiment and expressions of sympathy with Iraq from Palestinians.

Police and security forces continued to operate outside the law, arbitrarily intimidating and arresting reporters. One of the year's most disturbing incidents occurred in May when security forces detained Reuters freelance journalist Abbas Moumani, holding him incommunicado for nine days.

Following the October signing of the Wye River peace accord between the PNA and Israel, Palestinian authorities moved to muzzle criticism of the deal. The day after the signing, 10 journalists were detained while attempting to interview Sheikh Ahmed Yassin, a Hamas leader, about the Wye agreement. Palestinian authorities subsequently ordered that foreign journalists would have to obtain official permission before entering areas under PNA control, and that Palestinian journalists would

Attacks on the Press in 1998

need approval before covering political or security issues. At year's end, it was unclear how rigorously authorities intended to implement these restrictions.

Journalists and human rights activists expressed further dismay over the PNA's November promulgation of an anti-incitement decree, which fulfilled a requirement of the Wye agreement. The decree contained a host of vague proscriptions such as "incitement to racist discrimination," "offending religious sensitivities," and "incitement to ... breaching the agreements that have been signed with brotherly and foreign states." Journalists said that the decree leaves authorities considerable room to punish future criticism of the peace process or other policies.

January 5
"60 Minutes" THREATENED

In a two-page letter, Bassam Abu Sharif, advisor to Palestinian National Authority (PNA) President Yasser Arafat, informed Don Hewitt, producer of the U.S. television newsmagazine program "60 Minutes," that journalists associated with the show would "no longer be given unrestricted access to either our officials of government or the territories under [the PNA's] control."

The threat came in response to a "60 Minutes" segment that aired on December 7, 1997, titled "Brother vs. Brother." The broadcast focused on human rights abuses committed by the PNA, as well as allegations of corruption among Palestinian officials. In his letter, Sharif complained that "60 Minutes" failed to follow up on information the PNA provided about the alleged involvement of Israeli officials in monopolies of the sale of certain goods in the West Bank and Gaza.

According to CBS, the network that airs "60 Minutes," the PNA later disavowed the letter after it had became public in early January. The Palestinian Information Ministry said that Sharif was only expressing his opinion on the matter and that the PNA had taken no formal action against the station.

February 15
All broadcast media CENSORED

The Palestinian Ministry of Information issued a written order to Palestinian broadcast media banning commentary or analysis about the February standoff between Iraq and U.N. weapons inspectors. Journalists and observers in the West Bank interpreted the move as an attempt by the Palestinian National Authority (PNA) to curtail media coverage of pro-Iraqi sentiment among Palestinians in the West Bank and Gaza.

The ban stated that in order "to protect national interest and Palestinian security," private television and radio stations under PNA control are prohibited from broadcasting "any Palestinian commentary or declarations of any kind that concern the special development of the Iraq crisis."

In a February 19 letter to President Yasser Arafat, CPJ protested the ban and urged authorities to rescind it immediately.

February 16
Al-Roa' TV CENSORED

An estimated 100 police officers surrounded the offices of Al-Roa' TV (Shepherds TV), a private television station in Bethlehem, and forced the station to suspend broadcasting. The verbal order came one day after the Palestinian Ministry of Information banned all broadcasting of opinion and analysis about February's standoff between U.N. weapons inspectors and Iraq.

Although police gave no reason for the closure of Al-Roa' TV, it was widely believed that the closure was in reaction to the station's programming about pro-Iraqi demonstrations in the West Bank. Specifically, Al-Roa' TV had aired a nightly program on which viewers

MIDDLE EAST

phoned in to express solidarity with Iraq on a variety of social and political issues.

In a February 19 letter to President Yasser Arafat, CPJ protested the closure of Al-Roa' TV. The station was allowed to resume broadcasting on July 2.

April 10
Reuters CENSORED

Palestinian police temporarily closed the Gaza office of the Reuters news agency in response to a videotape the news agency distributed to the media containing a statement by an alleged member of the Islamic Resistance Movement (Hamas).

On April 8, Reuters broadcast and distributed a videotape of a man identifying himself as Adel Awadallah, who accused Palestinian security officials—including Preventive Security chief Jibril Rajoub—of complicity in the killing of suspected Hamas bomb-maker Muhyideen al-Sharif. Al-Sharif was found dead on March 29 in the West Bank city of Ramallah, next to a car that had exploded.

"It is a temporary closure until the issues are verified and clarified by the senior officials in Reuters and after they take all the measures against whoever of their representatives is biased," Palestinian Authority police chief Ghazi Jebali said at the time.

Jebali said that the Palestinian Authority closed the office because Reuters had "issued news that provoked sedition in the Palestinian state."

The office was permitted to reopen after five days.

April 12
Abbas Moumani, Reuters HARASSED
Majed Arouri, Associated Press HARASSED

Palestinian security forces summoned Moumani, a Palestinian free-lance photojournalist working with the Reuters news agency, and Arouri, a reporter with the Associated Press, and questioned them for nearly two hours about a videotape broadcast that was distributed by Reuters earlier in the month.

The tape contained footage of a masked man claiming to be Adel Awadallah, a leading Hamas figure. In the video, the man accused Palestinian security officials of involvement in the assassination of Hamas figure Muhyideen al-Sharif, who was found dead in Ramallah on March 29 next to a car which had been destroyed by a bomb.

May 5
Abbas Moumani, Reuters IMPRISONED

Palestinian General Intelligence (GI) agents detained Moumani, a Palestinian free-lance photojournalist from the West Bank city of Ramallah, who was working with the Reuters news agency. He was taken to GI headquarters in Ramallah for questioning about an April Reuters broadcast of video footage of a masked man claiming to be Adel Awadallah, a leading Hamas activist. In the video, the man accused Palestinian security officials of involvement in the assassination of Hamas figure Muhyideen al-Sharif, who was found dead in Ramallah on March 29 next to a car which had been destroyed by a bomb.

On May 10, Moumani escaped from the GI facility by jumping from a third-floor window after being severely beaten. He was apprehended later the same day and returned to detention.

In a May 8 letter to President Yasser Arafat, CPJ protested Moumani's incommunicado detention and called for his immediate release.

Moumani was released on the evening of May 14.

August 18
Abdullah al-Shami, *Al-Istiqlal* IMPRISONED

Officers of the Palestinian National Authority's (PNA) Criminal Investigation Unit detained al-Shami, a teacher from the Gaza Strip and an alleged leader of the Islamic Jihad organization, a militant Islamist movement which opposes peace with Israel.

Al-Shami was taken into custody without warrant at his home in the town of al-Shujaeyyah. The action followed the publication of an article which appeared in the August 14, 1998, edition of the pro-Islamic Jihad paper *Al-Istiqlal* titled "Change of Ministers or Persistence of Sin." In the article, al-Shami described what he called "the growing resentment in the street toward those ministers portrayed as the symbols of financial and administrative corruption in the newly formed cabinet of ministers."

Al-Shami was held at the Gaza Criminal Department and interrogated about the article, which he was told attacked PNA President Yasser Arafat and provoked the PNA.

In a letter to Arafat on September 10, CPJ urged al-Shami's immediate and unconditional release.

Al-Shami spent 41 days in solitary confinement. He was released on September 27 after signing a statement promising that he would no longer provoke the PNA.

August 29
Munir Abu Rizq, *Al-Hayat al-Jadida*
ATTACKED

Palestinian police assaulted Abu Rizq, the Gaza correspondent for the Palestinian daily newspaper *Al-Hayat al-Jadida*, as he attempted to enter the Al-Jawazat police building at the Madinat Arafat Police Station, where a military court hearing was taking place.

When Abu Rizq drove up to the compound's gate, a group of police officers refused him entry. The journalist then attempted to enter the compound on foot after parking his car and was told by an officer that he could not enter.

According to Abu Rizq, when he told the officers he was a journalist, one of the officers began to curse him, saying, "A journalist like you wants to teach me manners? I thought for a second that you were an official." The officer then slapped Abu Rizq in the face while other policemen began beating and kicking him, some striking him with their rifle butts.

A ranking officer eventually intervened to stop the assault and allowed Abu Rizq to enter the compound.

December 18
Nasser Shiyoukhi, Associated Press
HARASSED

Palestinian security officers briefly detained Shiyoukhi, a reporter for the Associated Press, while he was photographing Palestinian demonstrators burning a U.S. flag in the city of Bethlehem in the West Bank. The demonstrations took place two days after the United States and Britain launched military strikes against Iraq. Shiyoukhi was released after two hours on the condition that he not photograph any anti-U.S. actions.

December 18
Al-Roa' TV CENSORED
Mahid TV CENSORED
Bethlehem TV CENSORED
Al Watan TV CENSORED
Nasr TV CENSORED
Voice of Love and Peace CENSORED

Police verbally informed three Bethlehem-based television stations—Al-Roa' TV, Al-Mahid TV, and Bethlehem TV—that they must immediately suspend all broadcasts. According to journalists, police failed to provide a written order or reason for the suspensions. Three stations in Ramallah—Al-Watan TV, Nasr TV, and the radio station Voice of Love and Peace—were also forced off the air in the same manner.

Broadcasters believe that the closures were in direct response to the stations' coverage of the December U.S. and British military strikes against Iraq, including their coverage of anti-U.S. sentiment and expressions of sympathy with Iraq from Palestinians. According to the Associated Press, "Al-Watan TV had broadcast pro-Iraqi interviews; Al-Nasr TV had broadcast nationalist music; and the Voice of Love and Peace had devoted its broadcasts on Thursday to a popular nationalist Iraqi singer." Al-Roa' TV on December 17 aired a live panel discussion which heavily criticized U.S. President Bill Clinton for the military strikes.

In a December 18 letter to President Yasser Arafat, CPJ condemned the closures and urged the Palestinian leader to ensure that they be allowed to resume broadcasting immediately. The six stations were permitted to re-open on December 19.

December 18
Associated Press CENSORED

Authorities from the Palestinian National Authority's (PNA) Anti-Crime Unit ordered the closure of the Associated Press (AP) Gaza bureau after informing local staffers of the decision. According to AP, no explanation was given other than that authorities were trying to protect "national interests."

CPJ protested the closure in a December 18 letter to President Yasser Arafat.

The office was allowed to re-open on December 19.

Saudi Arabia and Other Members of the Gulf Cooperation Council

The member states of the Gulf Cooperation Council (GCC) include Saudi Arabia, Bahrain, Kuwait, Oman, Qatar, and the United Arab Emirates (UAE). Although the press in these countries is largely in private hands and among the most technologically advanced in the Arab world, independent reporting on local affairs remains hindered by state controls and self-censorship. Saudi Arabia, the largest and most influential member of the GCC, tolerates no dissent from journalists. The Ministry of Information approves the hiring of editors and can dismiss them at will. Criticism of the royal family and reporting on sensitive political topics are taboo. Fear of reprisal from authorities—notorious for having one of the region's worst records on human rights—helps to keep journalists in line. The state closely monitors foreign publications entering the kingdom, censoring news deemed to cast the kingdom in a negative light or offend Islam. Foreign journalists continue to face impediments in gaining entry to the country.

In April, the London newspaper *The Independent* reported that Saudi writer and journalist Zuheir Kutbi had been arrested, beaten, and imprisoned for several weeks by the country's religious police, because of a recently published book in which he criticized their arbitrary and often brutal treatment of civilians. According to the report, news of his arrest was quashed in the Saudi media, and Kutbi was permanently banned from writing books or for the press.

Saudi Arabia also exerts considerable influence over the Pan-Arab media, which over the last eight years have come under the control of Saudi businessmen with links to the royal family. Saudi-owned publications include the influential Arabic daily newspaper *Al-Hayat* and the weekly magazine *Al-Wasat*, both based in London and owned by Prince Khaled Bin Sultan, a nephew of King Fahd. Another influential Pan-Arab paper, the London-based daily *Al-Sharq al-Awsat*, is owned by Prince Ahmad

Attacks on the Press in 1998

Bin Salman. And the popular Middle East Broadcasting Corporation (MBC), with a regionwide viewership in the tens of millions, is owned by prominent Saudi businessman Sheikh Walid al-Ibrahim, a brother-in-law of King Fahd. The other main broadcasting networks that service the region, such as Arab Radio and Television (ART) and Orbit, are also Saudi-owned. News and programming from these sources rarely, if ever, disseminate criticism of the Saudi regime or report on issues regarded as sensitive in the kingdom. While such media outlets are ostensibly independent, the fear of alienating Saudi advertisers and the threat of being banned in the country typically prove sufficient disincentives to unfavorable coverage.

Throughout the Middle East and North Africa, criticism of Saudi Arabia often triggers swift official responses—a result, some journalists say, of informal agreements between Saudi Arabia and the other Arab states.

In Kuwait—where the press has gained a reputation for being among the freest and most lively in the Arab world—journalists increasingly have come under attack. In the year's most prominent case, a Kuwaiti criminal court in June handed down a six-month prison sentence against Muhammad Jasim al-Saqr, editor in chief of the daily *Al-Qabas*, and Ibrahim Marzouk, a free-lance journalist based in Egypt, for writing a four-line joke about Adam and Eve. Al-Saqr, a 1992 recipient of CPJ's International Press Freedom Award, and Marzouk were charged with "insulting the essence of the Divine Being." Al-Saqr remained free pending the outcome of his appeal.

In a separate threat to free expression, a government committee in September drafted a law proposal to censor satellite television programming that is deemed offensive to Islamic norms. At year's end, no action had been taken to enact the law.

CPJ continued to press the Kuwaiti government for the release of five journalists who remain in prison for their work with the Iraqi occupation newspaper *Al-Nida*. CPJ learned in November that one of the journalists, Jordanian national and former KUNA editor Abdel Rahman al-Husseini, was suffering from several ailments including heart disease and was at risk of a heart attack. In a December 14 letter to Kuwait's Crown Prince and Prime Minister Sheikh Saad al-Abdullah al-Sabah, CPJ urged for the release of al-Husseini and the other four imprisoned journalists—Usamah Suhail Abdallah Hussein, Fawwaz Muhammad al-Awadi Bessisso, Ahmad Abed Mustafa, and Ibtisam Berto Sulaiman al-Dakhil.

In Bahrain, the local press remained submissive—voluntarily censoring news of the country's ongoing political unrest, details of which remained largely off the pages of newspapers. Journalists who exhibited more independence provoked authorities' anger. The Ministry of Information banned Hafedh al-Sheikh, a columnist for the daily *Akhbar al-Khaleej*, from writing for local or international papers throughout much of the year. The ban stemmed from an article al-Sheikh submitted for publication in April titled, "When the Universities Fall in the Hands of the Tribal Militarist Mind," which indirectly criticized the state's meddling in universities.

June 24
Muhammad Jasim al-Saqr, *Al-Qabas*
LEGAL ACTION
Ibrahim Marzouk, *Al-Qabas*
LEGAL ACTION
Al-Qabas LEGAL ACTION

In a suit filed in February by Kuwait's Ministry of Information, a criminal court convicted al-Saqr, editor in chief of the leading daily newspaper *Al-Qabas*, and Marzouk, a free-lance journalist based in Egypt, of "insulting the essence of the Divine Being" (misas bilzat al-ilahiyya). Al-Saqr and Marzouk were tried in absentia and each sentenced to six months in prison in connection with a joke published in *Al-Qabas* on January 5. In the four-line item, a teacher asks a student, "Why did God expel Adam and Eve from Paradise?" and the student responds, "Because they did not pay the rent."

In addition to the prison sentence, the court ordered *Al-Qabas* to close for one week. The court's ruling was effective immediately. The paper appealed the verdict, but the sentence was to be enforced in the interim.

In a June 25 letter to Kuwait's Crown Prince and Prime Minister Sheikh Saad al-Abdullah al-Sabah, CPJ strongly protested the court's decision and called for an end to the use of criminal statutes to prosecute journalists for their work.

On June 28, a Kuwaiti court suspended the enforcement of the sentences until an appellate court rules on the case.

June 27
Al-Ahram al-Arabi CENSORED

Kuwaiti authorities confiscated copies of the June 27 issue of the Cairo-based weekly *Al-Ahram al-Arabi*, apparently in response to an article titled "Kuwait Anticipates Wide-Reaching Political Reforms." The article discussed the political crisis in Kuwait between the prime minister and parliament, and predicted future changes in government which could limit the authority of the ruling al-Sabah family.

Syria

Syria's press languishes in the iron grip of the state, as it has for much of President Hafez al-Assad's 28-year authoritarian rule. Independent journalism has been virtually nonexistent since the regime's eradication of political opposition in the early 1980s.

Authorities maintain tight control over the dissemination of news and information through the media. The Ministry of Information closely supervises the country's state-run dailies and broadcast media, and provides strict content guidelines for editors and journalists. State controls also extend to foreign newspapers, as authorities continued to censor the few foreign publications allowed into the country. The London-based daily *Al-Quds al-Arabi*, which began distribution in Syria in 1997, was barred from distributing issues in the country on several occasions for what its editor described as its coverage of Syrian affairs. Because of the state's monopoly over domestic media, increasing numbers of Syrians rely on satellite dishes to access foreign news programming.

The year's most ominous development involved Nizar Nayyouf, a leading member of the independent Committees for the Defense of Democratic Freedoms and Human Rights in Syria (CDF) and editor in chief of its monthly newsletter *Sawt al-Democratiyya*. Nayyouf, who is serving a 10-year sentence in solitary confinement in Mezze military prison, is gravely ill and may die unless he receives immediate treatment for Hodgkins disease. Syrian authorities have refused him treatment unless he pledges to refrain from political activity and renounces alleged "false statements" he made about the human rights situation in Syria.

In a September 24 letter hand-delivered to Syria's Foreign Minister Farouq al-Sharaa at the United Nations, CPJ's Vice Chairman Terry Anderson urged Nayyouf's immediate release on humanitarian grounds.
(To join the campaign for the release of Nizar Nayyouf, visit CPJ's website at <www.cpj.org>.)

Attacks on the Press in 1998

Tunisia

During little more than a decade in power, President Zine Abdine Ben Ali has reduced Tunisia's once-respectable press to one of the most restricted in the Arab world. On World Press Freedom Day, May 3, CPJ named Ben Ali as one of the world's 10 worst Enemies of the Press. (See page 62 for more on the Enemies of the Press.) Tunisian journalists continue to operate in a climate of fear, practicing near-total self-censorship on a host of political and social issues. Indeed, independent-minded journalists over the years have experienced swift government reprisal for their reporting. Attempts to cover such sensitive topics as human rights and the activities or viewpoints of the political opposition have resulted in intimidation, prosecution, and imprisonment of offending journalists. Others have been dismissed from their jobs, denied accreditation, and barred from leaving the country for what authorities perceived as critical coverage. As a result, journalists today avoid criticism of even the most benign political topics, leading to a banal press largely devoid of substantive news coverage.

Since self-censorship has become virtually universal, the government has little cause to actively harass journalists. But when journalists do cross the boundaries of accepted journalism, authorities are quick to respond. On June 18, the Ministry of Interior summoned Taoufik Ben Brik, a correspondent for the Paris-based daily *La Croix*, following the publication of an article about police harassment. An official accused Ben Brik of writing "subversive" material and urged him to stop working as a journalist.

The local press has not been the only target of state reprisal. This year, authorities maintained their hold on the flow of information, once again banning foreign publications entering the county. The London-based daily *Al-Quds al-Arabi*, for example, estimates that the paper was banned an average of three to five times a month. Issues of the French-language *Le Monde* were also confiscated during the year.

Along with its muzzling of the press, the government oversees one of the more sophisticated public relations programs, extolling Ben Ali for his purported human rights achievements. A government-run website, <www.amnesty-tunisia.org>, proclaims that Tunisia has "distinguish[ed] itself in a striking way by its exemplary work in the domains of Human Rights, freedom of expression and public liberties." Authorities have gone to even greater lengths to protect their image by banning Internet access to websites that contain information critical of the regime, like that of Amnesty International.

At year's end, Hamadi Jebali and Abdellah Zouari, journalists with the now-defunct weekly *Al-Fajr* who have been imprisoned since 1991, remained behind bars.

June 18
Taoufik Ben Brik, *La Croix-L'Envenement*
HARASSED

Two plainclothes police officers took Ben Brik, a correspondent for the Paris-based daily *La Croix-L'Evenement*, to the Ministry of Interior headquarters in Tunis, where he was brought before Mohammad Ali Ganzoui, assistant to the Minister of Interior. Ganzoui accused Ben Brik of writing "subversive" material—a reference to a June 12 article carrying the double byline of Ben Brik and Julia Ficatier, a senior reporter for *La Croix*.

The article discussed police harassment in Tunisia, among other things, and told of arbitrary raids and searches of people's homes. Ganzoui subsequently suggested that Ben Brik should think about leaving journalism and looking for another profession.

In a June 23 letter to President Zine El-Abidine Ben Ali, CPJ condemned the incident and urged the Tunisian government to allow journalists to express a diversity of opinion, including criticism of official policy, without fear of reprisal.

Turkey

Although Turkey's mainstream press enjoys considerable freedom, authorities continue to punish independent reporting on sensitive political topics such as the government's 14-year-old conflict with Kurdish insurgents in the country's southeast region. Pro-Kurdish, far-left, and Islamist publications were the main targets of this state harassment that included censorship, the prosecution and imprisonment of journalists, and the suspension of newspapers. But mainstream journalists were also subjected to official reprisal for their independent views on sensitive political subjects. At year's end, 27 journalists were imprisoned because of their published work or their affiliation with far-left or pro-Kurdish publications.

In a year that saw the collapse of the government of Prime Minister Mesut Yilmaz, hopes of improved press conditions appeared decidedly remote. A year and a half after the Yilmaz government made a firm commitment to press freedom during meetings with a CPJ delegation in Ankara, meaningful reform has failed to materialize.

A proposed reform package, aiming to amend some of the laws used most often to criminalize journalism, appeared to be on indefinite hold. Although amendments to Articles 17, 159, and 312 of the Penal Code and Article 8 of the Anti-Terror Law were approved by the council of ministers, the parliament has taken no action on the measures. The proposed amendments fall far short of comprehensive reform, and would leave journalists as vulnerable as ever to the penalty of imprisonment for "separatist propaganda" or "inciting racial hatred." "It's not possible to change existing legislation on separatist propaganda, because this is a sensitive topic in Turkey," State Minister for Human Rights Hikmet Sami Turk told a CPJ delegation in Washington, D.C., in June. "There are many people who have lost lives in the war on terrorism."

New prosecutions and jailings of journalists continued while repressive laws such as the Anti-Terror Law and statutes of the Penal Code remained on the books, representing a threat to dissident or critical journalists. Ragip Duran, the Istanbul correspondent for the French-language daily *Libération*, began serving a 10-month prison sentence in June.

Hundreds of issues of publications—mainly far-left and pro-Kurdish papers—were confiscated or suspended by court order. Most notably, a State Security Court in October banned the pro-Kurdish daily *Ülkede Gündem* for 30 days for allegedly inciting hatred in a published column—demonstrating the pattern of harassment of the paper that has persisted for years, beginning with its predecessor publications including the now-defunct *Özgür Gündem*.

Censorship of the broadcast media has become common. Authorities issued closure orders against numerous radio and television stations throughout the year for broadcasting deemed separatist or morally offensive. The Supreme Radio and Television Board (RTUK), formed in April 1994 to regulate and monitor the broadcast media, wields broad powers to sanction stations that run afoul of the many sweeping provisions of Turkey's laws that punish expression. In May, for example, RTUK handed out one-day bans to prominent sta-

Attacks on the Press in 1998

tions such as Channel D, ATV, and Interstar for morally offensive and violent programming. Pro-Kurdish stations appeared to suffer the most severe punishments. The Diyarbakir-based Metro FM was shut down in July for a year for "undermining the unity of the state" in apparent retaliation for broadcasting Kurdish-language music. Radyo Karacadag in Sanliurfa, which has been a repeated target of official harassment, was also closed for a year for allegedly inciting hatred through its political programming. By August, RTUK had imposed sanctions against television and radio stations that totaled 420 days over a four-year period.

Incidents of police violence against journalists occur with disturbing frequency. In March, the long-awaited court decision in the trial of police officers accused of the fatal beating of *Evrensel* journalist Metin Goktepe came to a discouraging end. Five of the 11 defendants were convicted and sentenced to a mere seven and a half years in prison, with the likelihood of an early release on parole. An appeals court later ruled that the case would be re-tried, and by December, a judge had ordered the release of the five convicted officers.

Self-censorship, editorial censorship, and partisanship in the mainstream press often compromised coverage of sensitive topics such as the Kurdish question or Islamist politics. And journalists' self-restraint was often reinforced by routine harassment and intimidation by military and government officials. Some journalists contend that the military keeps files on journalists and exerts pressure through routine harassment of editors when their reporting is viewed as unfavorable. Editors complained about harassment in the form of telephone calls from military figures. "It's unbelievable how many calls we get from the leaders," remarked the editor of a leading daily in August when describing pressure he experienced from military authorities over coverage.

In a flagrant display of the military's meddling with the press, liberal columnists Cengiz Candar and Mehmet Ali Birand were suspended and fired respectively from the daily *Sabah* after the military had leaked that the two had allegedly been on the payroll of the outlawed Kurdistan Workers' Party (PKK). The information was reportedly part of the confession of captured PKK military commander Semdin Sakik. Journalists viewed the actions as reprisals because both columnists had been critical of state policies. Candar was soon able to resume his work with the paper, but was reportedly warned not to provoke authorities in his column. Birand, meanwhile, was dismissed for what the paper says were professional reasons.

January 26
Haluk Gerger, *Özgür Gündem* IMPRISONED

Gerger, a political essayist and contributor to the now-defunct pro-Kurdish daily *Özgür Gündem*, was jailed in Güdül Prison following the Court of Cassation's ratification of a one-year sentence handed down by the Court of Appeals in December 1997. He was also fined 208 million Turkish Lira (US$676).

Gerger had been convicted under Article 7 of the Anti-Terror Law (engaging in propaganda on behalf of an outlawed organization) in connection with an article he wrote for the December 15, 1993, edition of *Özgür Gündem* titled "Gündem ve PKK" ("Agenda and PKK"). In the article, Gerger urged the government to negotiate with the outlawed Kurdistan Workers' Party, or PKK.

Gerger was released on September 18 prior to the expiration of his term sentence.

February 22
Mert Ilkutlug, *Milliyet* ATTACKED
Hakan Gulce, ATV ATTACKED

Celal Baslangic, *Radikal* ATTACKED
Selma Yildiz, *Radikal* ATTACKED
Ahmet Sik, *Radikal* ATTACKED

Turkish police forced a large group of Turkish journalists from a courtroom in the town of Aydin, where they were attempting to cover the trial of a police officer for the 1993 murder of a Turkish student.

After pushing the journalists outside the court house, police beat at least five of them: Ilkutlug of the daily *Milliyet*; Gulce, from the television station ATV; and Baslangic, Yildiz, and Sik from the daily *Radikal*. Some of the five were taken to the hospital for treatment of their injuries.

March 2
Koray Duzgoren, *Radikal* CENSORED

Duzgoren, a columnist for the daily *Radikal*, was dismissed from his post, apparently as a result of pressure from the Turkish military. The paper's editor in chief, Mehmet Yilmaz, told Duzgoren that Turkish military officials had forced *Radikal*'s publisher, Aydin Dogan, to fire him.

Duzgoren believes his sustained coverage of the infamous Susurluk scandal, which unveiled the state's links with armed criminal gangs in Turkey, prompted the dismissal.

March 5
Aydin Koral, *Selam* LEGAL ACTION

An Istanbul State Security Court convicted Koral, editor of the Islamist weekly newspaper *Selam*, of violating Article 312/2 of the Penal Code ("inciting hatred through religious discrimination"). He was sentenced to 20 months in prison.

Koral had been tried in connection with a column he wrote for the May 16, 1997, edition of the newspaper titled "Secular-Militarist Oligarchy and Zionist Occupier of Jerusalem."

The column criticized the Turkish military and its relations with the State of Israel. Koral wrote, "Now in Turkey the foreign enemy has been replaced by the internal enemy which has been declared as Islam and Sharia."

On May 28, the Court of Cassation approved Koral's prison sentence. He was scheduled to begin serving his sentence on November 26, but his whereabouts are unknown. It is believed that he may have fled the country or gone into hiding.

March 7
Yasar Kaplan, *Akit* IMPRISONED, LEGAL ACTION

Kaplan, a reporter with the Islamist daily *Akit*, was arrested on a warrant and subsequently charged by a military court for violating Article 95/4 of the military penal code by allegedly insulting the military and harming the military hierarchy. The charge was based on three articles he wrote for *Akit* between February 18-20 which discussed sectarian divisions in the Turkish military. The trial began on April 22, after which Kaplan was released pending its outcome. On July 14, the court convicted and sentenced him to 14 months in prison. His lawyer appealed the decision to the Military High Court on July 21. Kaplan remains free pending the outcome of his appeal.

March 20
Mehmet Ali Birand, *Sabah* HARASSED
Yalcin Dogan, *Milliyet* HARASSED
Muharrem Sarikaya, *Hurriyet* HARASSED

The office of the chief of staff of the armed forces issued a statement banning Birand; a columnist for the daily Sabah; Dogan, a columnist for the daily *Milliyet*,; and Muharrem, a reporter for the daily *Hurriyet*, from covering events organized by the army. The ban specified that the three journalists would not be permitted to attend press conferences, interview members of the armed forces, or visit military sites. The ban followed what

Attacks on the Press in 1998

military authorities called the journalists' publication of "false information" that threatened "territorial integrity." The ban was lifted on March 25.

June 16
Ragip Duran, *Özgür Gündem* IMPRISONED

Duran, Istanbul correspondent for the French-language daily *Libération* and a veteran reporter who has worked for the Agence France-Presse news agency, the British Broadcasting Corporation, the now-defunct pro-Kurdish daily *Özgür Gündem*, and other Turkish daily newspapers, began serving a 10-month jail term in Saray Prison for violating provisions of Turkey's Anti-Terror Law.

Duran was tried and convicted in December 1994 of propagandizing on behalf of an outlawed organization under Article 7 of the Anti-Terror Law, and his sentence was ratified by the Court of Cassation in October 1997. The charge stemmed from an article he wrote about his interview with Abdullah Ocalan, leader of the outlawed Kurdistan Workers' Party, which appeared in *Özgür Gündem* on April 12, 1994.

June 21
Ülkede Gündem ATTACKED

A bomb exploded outside a building housing the Batman bureau of the pro-Kurdish daily *Ülkede Gündem*. No one was injured, but the early morning blast caused considerable damage to the office, which is located on the third floor, according to journalists at *Ülkede Gündem*.

On July 2, CPJ sent a letter to Turkey's Prime Minister Mesut Yilmaz expressing grave concern over the bombing, and urging authorities to conduct a thorough investigation and bring those responsible to justice.

July 21
Oral Calislar, *Cumhurriyet* LEGAL ACTION

The trial of Calislar, a prominent journalist with the daily *Cumhurriyet*, began in an Istanbul State Security Court on the charge of disseminating "separatist propaganda" (Article 8 of the Anti-Terror Law) in his 1993 book entitled *The Kurdish Problem with Ocalan and Burkay*. The trial is expected to resume in February 1999.

Calislar had initially been charged after the book—composed of interviews with Abdullah Ocalan, leader of the outlawed Kurdistan Workers' Party, and Kurdish leader Kemal Burkay originally published in *Cumhurriyet* in June and July 1993—was published in November 1993. He was convicted of the charge in 1995 and sentenced to two years in prison and fined 250 million Turkish Lira (then about US$6,270). While the case was under appeal, however, the Turkish Parliament approved amendments to Article 8, resulting in the nullification of his conviction.

In 1996, the State Security Court arraigned Calislar on charges of violating Article 6 of the Anti-Terror Law (publishing the statements of a terrorist organization), again citing *The Kurdish Problem with Ocalan and Burkay* as the principal evidence. He was convicted of this charge, and fined 5 million Turkish Lira (then about US$85). All copies of the book were confiscated.

On March 5, the Court of Cassation quashed the 1996 ruling, stating that Calislar's book constituted "separatist propaganda," and ordered a retrial under Article 8. Calislar faces up to three years in prison if convicted.

October 24
Ülkede Gündem CENSORED

A State Security Court ordered the closure of the pro-Kurdish daily *Ülkede Gündem* for 30 days for allegedly "inciting racial hatred" and publishing "separatist propaganda." The action stems from an August 1997 editorial titled "Once Again the Peace Train," which criticized the military's ongoing conflict with Kurdish insurgents in southeastern Turkey.

November 18
Hayrettin Demircioglu, *Ülkede Gündem*
IMPRISONED
Yurdusev Özsökmenler, *Ülkede Gündem*
IMPRISONED
Filiz Duman, *Ülkede Gündem*
IMPRISONED
Yasemin Öztürk, *Ülkede Gündem*
IMPRISONED
Tülay Kilinç, *Ülkede Gündem*
IMPRISONED
Tülin Bozkurt, *Ülkede Gündem*
IMPRISONED
Kahraman Yapicilar, *Ülkede Gündem*
IMPRISONED
Salih Erol, *Ülkede Gündem*
IMPRISONED
Narin Adsan, *Ülkede Gündem*
IMPRISONED
Filiz Yürek, *Ülkede Gündem*
IMPRISONED
Ersin Öngel, *Ülkede Gündem*
IMPRISONED
Habip Çelik, *Ülkede Gündem*
IMPRISONED
Seyda Basmaci, *Ülkede Gündem*
IMPRISONED
Adil Harmanci, *Ülkede Gündem*
IMPRISONED
Ali Kemal Sel, *Ülkede Gündem*
IMPRISONED
Eylem Kaplan, *Ülkede Gündem*
IMPRISONED
Ayse Onan, *Ülkede Gündem*
IMPRISONED

Over the course of two days, Turkish police raided 10 offices of the pro-Kurdish daily *Ülkede Gündem* throughout the country, arresting 17 journalists. The paper's bureaus in Istanbul, Ankara, Adana, Izmir, Mersin, Diyarbakir, Urfa, Malatya, Batman, and Van were targeted. Police confiscated computer diskettes, photographs, magazines, books, and telephone directories.

The roundup was viewed by some Turkish journalists as part of a wider clampdown on pro-Kurdish sympathizers, following the November arrest in Rome of Abdullah Ocalan, leader of the outlawed Kurdistan Workers' Party (PKK).

All but three of the journalists were released in the next few days. Sel, *Ülkede Gündem*'s Malatya bureau chief and one of those kept in custody, was charged with aiding an outlawed organization under Article 169 of the Penal Code.

According to official court documents, Sel was accused of using two reporters from the paper to collect political and military information "in the name of news" in the towns of Elazig, Tunceli, and Bingol and passing it on to the PKK. The state's charge read: "In the so-called newspaper, he used Eylem Kaplan and Ayse Onan to collect political and military information" such as "the starting hours of the soldiers and their routes; the lists of the material the soldiers were going to pass from the check-points; the pressure put on the people of the region; information about village evacuations. This information, which was against the state and in accordance with the PKK's views, was sent to the so-called newspaper *Ülkede Gündem* in the name of news."

Prosecutors said that during a search of Sel's office and home they found "documents that were pro-PKK." His trial is currently underway in the Malatya State Security Court, and he is confined to Malatya Prison.

Kaplan and Onan were also charged under Article 169 and remain in custody.

Ülkede Gündem was suspended by a State Security Court on October 24 for 30 days for allegedly disseminating "racial hatred" by publishing articles about the military's ongoing conflict with Kurdish insurgents in southeastern Turkey.

Yemen

Despite enjoying perhaps the freest press on the Arabian Peninsula, Yemeni journalists have noticed a narrowing of their freedoms

in the last four years. Since the country's 1994 civil war, authorities have increased their harassment of independent journalists through the censorship of newspapers and the intimidation and harassment of reporters.

Journalists continued to face the threat of Political Security forces and other state agents who arrested and detained reporters as they attempted to carry out their work. Others complained of constant monitoring by security forces, creating an atmosphere of fear. Authorities resorted to censorship, most notably in July when a prosecutor banned coverage of a trail involving alleged bombing suspects in the southern town of Aden. And in late December, an edition of the weekly *Al-Rai al-Aam* was banned without explanation in apparent retaliation for its recent criticism of government officials.

The press law criminalizes journalism through such highly interpretative charges as the publication of "false information" or news that threatens "public order." In March, the Ministry of Information issued a decree imposing a series of financial regulations on newspapers, including capital requirements that range from 3 million rials (US$22,727) for daily papers to 700,000 rials (US$5,303) for weeklies. The new regulations also called for the annual renewal of newspaper licenses, which journalists say gives the Ministry of Information considerable discretion over publications. The moves were decried by journalists as an attack on press freedom. By year's end, the government had not enforced the regulations, but future enforcement could put newspapers out of business and hinder the emergence of new publications.

While the press remained robust in its reporting and commentary, the broadcast media—under state control—continued their uncritical support of the government. Radio and television are particularly influential in Yemen, because of the country's relatively high illiteracy rate. In a May interview with the *Yemen Times*, Minister of Information Abdel Rahman al-Akwa'a stated that the government was "formulating the legal bases to regulate" the licensing of private radio and television.

April 27
Arafat Mudabish, *Al-Thawri* HARASSED

Agents from Military Intelligence (MI) detained Mudabish, a veteran reporter for *Al-Thawri*, the weekly newspaper of the Yemeni Socialist Party (YSP), at YSP headquarters in the town of al-Mukallah in Hadrahmawt Province during a raid on the office. Mudabish had traveled to al-Mukallah to cover an opposition demonstration.

Mudabish was taken to MI headquarters and interrogated for 30 minutes before being transferred to a detention facility in al-Mukallah. Agents confiscated his camera and film. He was held incommunicado for nearly three days before his release on the evening of April 29. Intelligence officers warned him not to return to Hadrahmawt Province.

May 26
Raggeh Omaar, BBC
IMPRISONED, LEGAL ACTION
Robin Barnwell, BBC
IMPRISONED, LEGAL ACTION
Frank Smith, BBC
IMPRISONED, LEGAL ACTION

Ministry of Interior forces detained Omaar, a British Broadcasting Corporation (BBC) regional correspondent; Barnwell, a BBC producer; and Smith, a BBC cameraman, upon their return from filming a story in an isolated area in northern Yemen, where a British national had recently been held hostage by Bani Dhabyan tribesmen.

On June 4, the journalists were charged with "contravening the provisions of the press law" and "noncompliance with regulations and laws in press coverage in the areas controlled by the Bani Dhabyan."

The charges stem from a three-day visit the journalists made to the Khawlan region in northern Yemen, where they were filming a story about the Bani Dhabyan. Authorities confiscated their passports, preventing them from leaving the country.

The government contended that Smith, Barnwell, and Omaar ignored government warnings not to travel to Khawlan and violated regulations for foreign journalists by failing to inform authorities of their travel outside of Sanaa. According to the journalists, however, Yemeni authorities did not clearly communicate the ban on travel to Khawlan or other regulations governing the foreign press in Yemen. According to the BBC, the journalists "were in the country with full accreditation and made clear what it was they wanted to film."

On June 4, CPJ wrote to President Ali Abdullah Saleh, urging him to see to it that the charges against the three be dropped. On June 7, the three journalists were tried, acquitted, and allowed to leave the country.

June 10
Mohammad Ben Mohammad Saleh al-Dakim IMPRISONED

Police in the town of al-Dalea' detained al-Dakim, a 19-year-old high school student who sold copies of the biweekly *Al-Ayyam*, as he was distributing the newspaper.

Al-Dakim was held for several hours at a police detention center. He was severely beaten by police before being released the same day. The attack was viewed as part of a pattern of harassment against the independent paper. Reporters have been detained, copies of the paper have been seized, and reporters threatened by security forces.

June 22
All journalists CENSORED

Judge Faheem Abdullah Mohsen, acting on a request from the state prosecutor, banned news coverage of court proceedings in the trial of several suspects accused of bombings in the southern city of Aden in 1997. Mohsen, who was overseeing the trial, invoked Article 103 of the Yemeni press law in ordering a halt of coverage until the end of the trial. According to local journalists, the ruling followed testimony by some of the defendants, who said that they had been tortured.

August 8
Awad Kashmeem, *Al-Tariq* IMPRISONED

Security forces arrested Kashmeem, the Hadrahmawt correspondent for the daily *Al-Tariq*, in the town of Dawaan. He was held in police custody for 28 hours. The arrest stemmed from articles he published in *Al-Tariq* in late July about alleged government corruption and embezzlement in Yemen's telecommunications industry. Kashmeem was released without charge on August 9.

October 21
Anwar al-Ansi, Al-Jazeerah TV HARASSED, CENSORED

Yemeni soldiers arrested al-Ansi, a correspondent for the Qatar-based Al-Jazeerah satellite television, in the southern city of Aden after he filmed the trial of bombing suspects accused of carrying out attacks there.

According to al-Ansi's account, published in the *Yemen Times* on November 2, "About 30 soldiers swarmed into the Seera Court entrance and arrested me. They took me to Brig. Gen. Mohammed Turaiq, Aden's Director General of Security. I was forced to spend the afternoon in his custody."

Al-Ansi, friend of President Ali Abdullah Saleh, then telephoned the Yemeni leader, who asked the journalist to censor certain aspects of his report. Al-Ansi complied.

As a result of al-Ansi's detention, the story was not broadcast until the following day.

Attacks on the Press in 1998

December 24
Al-Rai al-Aam CENSORED

The Ministry of Information telephoned state printers, ordering them not to print the December 25 issue of the weekly *Al-Rai al-Aam*. According to staff at the newspaper, the move came in retaliation for several articles it published in previous weeks that were critical of Saudi Arabia and of Yemeni officials.

Two days later, *Al-Rai al-Aam* printed the edition through the services of a private printer, Al-Mufaddal. Al-Mufaddal, however, was instructed in another telephone call from the ministry not to distribute the paper.

The edition was eventually released on December 29, after a judge ruled that the ministry's actions were illegal.

Siege Mentality:
Press Freedom and the Algerian Conflict

by Joel Campagna

Introduction

Since the Algerian army canceled legislative elections in January 1992, to prevent victory by the Islamic Salvation Front (Front Islamique du Salut, or FIS), Algeria has been embroiled in a brutal civil conflict. An estimated 75,000 people have been killed in the violence, now in its seventh year.

The country's emergent private press has faced tremendous hardship as a victim of both sides of the conflict between the state and armed Islamist groups. A three-year assassination campaign by suspected religious extremists beginning in May 1993 claimed the lives of 58* journalists and forced most of those choosing to remain in the country to operate under siege-like conditions. And the state has vigorously controlled press coverage of the violence through blanket censorship, the suspension of newspapers, and the arrest and criminal prosecution of journalists who attempt independent reporting.

While Islamist extremists, who are believed responsible for most of the killings, no longer target journalists for death—there have been no murders of journalists since August 1996—the legacy of that nightmare period is a press decimated in number and tethered to the state for protection and even shelter. Those journalists who seek to take a more independent path have incurred the government's wrath and endured a variety of judicial and extra-judicial retaliatory strikes.

In recent months, the state has eased some of the more obviously draconian restrictions on the press that were common in the early years of political strife—a result of international pressure and perhaps of the regime's increasing confidence in its battle against extremists. In December 1997, the government abolished the notorious "reading committees" it had established at printing houses the previous year to ensure that newspapers conform to the official line on the conflict. Reporters say they now have greater opportunity to gather information on political violence in the field and publish it than at any time in the last six years. While criminal defamation prosecutions of reporters continue, authorities have refrained from using the courts against newspapers and journalists who report on political violence as in years past. Algeria's press is able to criticize government policies and offer dissent on many issues.

In October, the Algerian government invited CPJ to visit the country for a first-hand view of conditions for the press—part of an apparent campaign to deflect international criticism on the issue of human rights. CPJ has monitored Algeria's isolated and besieged press throughout the conflict, and viewed this as an opportunity to show solidarity with Algerian journalists and raise our concerns about freedom of expression in the country with its leaders. I traveled to Algiers accompanied by Kamel Eddine Labidi, a consultant to CPJ who also works as a free-lance journalist based in Arlington, Virginia, to meet with reporters, editors, lawyers, and officials. Despite the mandatory presence of armed escorts when traveling about the city, we conducted dozens of interviews with journalists representing a variety of private and state-owned newspapers during a two-week period. On October 27, CPJ board member and CNN correspondent Peter Arnett joined us for a meeting with Minister of Communications and Culture Habib Chawki Hamraoui. The delegation presented the minister with the preliminary findings of its research.

Out of these interviews and meetings emerged a picture of the Algerian press today. Despite the recent favorable changes, the print media remain subject to a variety of constraints which hamper independent reporting. The state continues to use subtle tactics to discourage reporting on sensitive political issues, such as the country's security concerns and alleged government improprieties. It controls the printing presses and the distribution of public-sector advertising, using both to exert economic pressure on dissenting publications. Officials use criminal defamation and other statutes to silence or sway editors and reporters, while other repressive laws and decrees remain on the books as a sword over journalists' heads.

The press is also hindered by less conspicuous obstacles. The practice of self-censorship on issues central to the conflict—such as state human rights abuses, the counter-insurgency war, government corruption, and the viewpoints and activities of the FIS—is widespread. "You can't talk about freedom of the press and freedom of expression in a country run by security services and the army," said one Algerian political observer, noting the level of fear confronting the press.

Restrictions on the foreign media, the sheer difficulty of obtaining sources of information, and an overall lack of media pluralism further contribute to keeping many details about Algeria's bloody war beyond the reach of the public. And perhaps equally significant, many Algerian journalists continue to operate under a siege mentality. Despite what many have described as an overall feeling of greater safety in Algiers, their dependence on the government—for information, even for shelter—persists.

In 1998, as international scrutiny of the violence intensified—specifically with regard to a wave of massacres of civilians in the Algerian countryside—the question of the press's ability to fulfill its role in documenting one of the region's most lethal conflicts has become more urgent than ever.

Based upon our investigations in Algeria, CPJ recommends that the Algerian government:

- Guarantee the right of journalists to "seek, receive, and impart information and ideas through any media and regardless of frontiers," as stipulated in Article 19 of the Universal Declaration of Human Rights;
- Initiate efforts to locate and bring to safety "disappeared" journalists Djamel Eddine Fahassi and Aziz Bouabdallah, who were apprehended by men presumed to be security agents on May 6, 1995, and April 12, 1997, respectively. Launch an investigation to determine the whereabouts of missing journalists Muhammad Hassaine* and Kaddour Bouselham;
- Conduct a thorough and transparent independent investigation into the assassinations of journalists since 1993 and ensure that those responsible are swiftly brought to justice;
- Encourage and facilitate the creation of private printing services for newspapers, and in the interim, establish clear guidelines governing all facets of the business relationship

between newspapers and state-owned printers;
- End the state monopoly of the distribution of advertising by state agencies to newspapers, and ensure that any future privatization of advertising distribution is free of government influence;
- End the legal harassment of journalists and newspapers through the use of criminal defamation or other statutes to prosecute newspapers for their publication of news and opinion;
- Abolish provisions of the draft information code, now before parliament, which directly threaten the right of journalists to free expression. These include Articles 4, 12, 21, 50, 51, 75, 81, and 82;
- State publicly that the Algerian government recognizes its duty under internationally recognized norms of free expression to ensure media pluralism, including the dissemination of a diversity of views, even if these views are opposed to or critical of prevailing policies;
- Permit newspapers banned by decree or under emergency law to resume publication; and
- End restrictions on foreign journalists working in Algeria, including the use of mandatory escorts, and facilitate the process of obtaining visas for journalists wishing to work in Algeria.

Historical Overview

Following bread riots and political unrest that swept the country in October 1988, the government initiated a process of wide-reaching political reform, opening the door for the emergence of private newspapers. In 1989, President Chadli Benjedid championed a new constitution—adopted by national referendum in February—legalizing political parties and ending 27 years of one-party rule by the National Liberation Front (FLN). In line with the political opening, the state ended its monopoly over the media by authorizing and assisting in the creation of private print media and ending government censorship.

In 1990, the first private newspapers appeared, and over the next two years, dozens of daily and weekly publications in both French and Arabic appeared, representing a wide array of political and social trends. Specialized publications dealing with cultural issues and science emerged, while party newspapers provided a platform for the country's nascent multi-party system. Between 1990-1992, the Algerian media enjoyed a freedom and vibrancy unparalleled in the Arab world, with newspapers providing caustic criticism of public officials and government policy while offering a diversity of opinion and analysis on a broad spectrum of political, economic, and social issues. Although the state remained in firm control of the broadcast media, radio and television expanded their coverage, providing opportunities for the political opposition to voice its criticisms, and spotlighting the social hardships faced by ordinary Algerians.

The political turmoil and the outbreak of violence across the country in 1992 signaled the decline of press freedom. As the social divide between secular and Islamist widened, the press, too, became increasingly polarized, openly taking sides on the army's move to deprive the FIS of its almost certain electoral victory. Newspapers and journalists soon came under attack from the state. Initially, the clampdown focused on FIS organs such as the weeklies *El-Mounqidh* and *El-Forqane*, which were permanently closed in March 1992. Other Islamist publications like the weekly *Al-Balagh*, which was sympathetic to the FIS and had criticized the coup, met similar fates. Along with the closure of publications, journalists were arrested and charged with a host of offenses ranging from "spreading false information" to "endangering state security" for their published calls to the army not to shoot at demonstrators and their condemnation of the military's intervention in the elections.

The clampdown on news coverage gradually extended to independent Arabic publications which had been critical of the state, as well as to the largely Francophone secular press which had predominantly supported the suppression of the Islamists. Newspapers were suspended and reporters endured similar repression for attempting to report on political unrest. After the assassination of President Muhammad Boudiaf in June 1992, state repression of the press intensified. A new state of emergency decree was brought into force on August 11, allowing authorities to suspend or close any institution—including the media—whose "activities endanger public order and security."

In the ensuing years, the state continued its clampdown on news coverage of the conflict. In June 1994, an inter-ministerial decree banned all reporting on political violence except for information provided by the official Algerian Press Service (APS). Violators of the decree were subject to prosecution under a variety of provisions of the information code and the penal code. The decree was accompanied by "recommendations" to newspapers for the presentation and layout of security-related information with the aim of downplaying violence and portraying the Islamist opposition in a negative light. In February 1996, authorities established "reading committees" at the state-run printing houses to ensure that newspapers' coverage of the conflict conformed to state accounts.

As the state tightened its grip on independent reporting, another, more sinister threat emerged. On May 26, 1993, Tahar Djaout, editor of the cultural weekly *Ruptures*, was shot outside his home near Algiers and died several days later. The attack marked the beginning of a three-year assassination campaign. So-called "black lists" with the names of journalists singled out for death were reportedly circulated in Algiers.

Journalists and other observers believe that many if not most of the assassinations were the work of the extremist Armed Islamic Group (Groupe Islamique Arme, or GIA), in apparent response to what it viewed as the press's complicity with the state in the war against Islamists. Others, however, suspect the state's involvement in some of the murders, although no concrete evidence has yet emerged to support this claim. "Some journalists believe that the political and financial Mafia killed a number of journalists and not the terrorists," said the editor of a leading daily newspaper. "[*Le Matin* columnist] Said Mekbel for example wrote daily on corruption and the Mafia. You can't underestimate the role of terrorists but many are convinced." Further arousing suspicions, authorities to date have failed to bring any of those responsible for the murders to justice and have refused any independent inquiry into the killings. As the murders mounted, dozens of journalists fled the country, while those remaining took refuge in state-run hotels under armed guard, living and working in constant fear.

While the violence against journalists has subsided considerably, hundreds still live under armed guard in state-run facilities like the Al-Manar—an outdated and dreary hotel in the Algiers suburb of Sidi Faraj. The tiny, sparsely furnished rooms are crowded, often accommodating several journalists or family members. The daily threat of assassination led some journalists to drug or alcohol addiction. One journalist working in the state broadcast media told CPJ, "Journalists would take pills and get drunk to cope. Some of my friends have become addicted to alcohol and sleeping pills."

While many journalists admit that the security situation in the capital has improved, few have the means to relocate to flats in safe neighborhoods. "Now there is a social aspect," said a journalist living with his wife and child at the Al-Manar. "Those who have flats can go back. But we don't have an apartment."

Over the past six years—due in considerable measure to a concerted effort by the authorities to eradicate newspapers critical of the abrogation of the 1992 election and other human rights abuses—the private press has become increasingly accommodationist, supporting the state in the battle against Islamism. Most newspapers reject the idea of dialogue between the combatants, and exclude the viewpoints and concerns of the Arabo-Islamist trend in society. Independent Arabic-language papers such as *Al-Wajh al-Akhar*, *Essah-Afa*, *Ennour*, *Al-Djazair al-Youm*, and *Hiwar*—with an estimated combined circulation in the hundreds of thousands—were closed by decree between 1992 and 1995. "All of the journalists who were opposing the regime were eliminated," commented one columnist.

Government Restrictions

Since the emergence of private newspapers, the state has controlled printing and the supply of paper through its ownership of the country's four printing houses. Authorities have used this leverage to suspend outspoken newspapers and place economic pressure on publications that have reported on sensitive political topics, or have adopted editorial lines that are critical of the state. Since 1993, state printers have arbitrarily refused services to newspapers without explanation or by invoking the contentious issue of debt.

Most recently, in October 1998, state printers forced the month-long closure of two leading dailies, the French-language *El-Watan* and *Le Matin*, citing outstanding debts. (See case summary, page 316.) Five other newspapers ceased publication to protest what they described as a politically motivated attack by the printers, leaving the country's newsstands without the leading newspapers until the dispute was resolved in early November. (*Le Matin* was able to resume publishing through the temporary services of a private printer on November 14. Eventually, on December 22, it was able to return to its original printer after reaching an arrangement to repay its debt.)

The printers' move followed the papers' sustained criticism of two government officials—Gen. Muhammad Betchine, a former adviser to President Liamine Zeroual, and former Minister of Justice Muhammad Adami. Both papers had reported that Betchine and Adami were involved in massive corruption and abuse of power. The two officials resigned in October in what journalists claimed as a victory for press freedom.

To some journalists, the closure of *El-Watan* and *Le Matin* demonstrated the state's adoption of new, subtler approaches to censoring newspapers, replacing harsher tactics used in the early years of the conflict. "The government can no longer afford to carry out heavy administrative censorship on the newspapers because of strong international pressure against that," says Omar Belhouchet, *El-Watan*'s director.

In fact, the suspensions are only the most recent examples of the practice of closure over the issue of debt, now aggressively targeting leading publications as well as opposition papers. Between 1993-1996, similar actions forced several papers off newsstands; most of them had advocated reconciliation to end the civil conflict or had reported on government human rights abuses. Publishers and lawyers say that while debts are a fact of life for newspapers, the printers are selective in demanding payment, and usually exact impossible terms.

The state printers also have adopted more arbitrary measures. In another recent case, a state printer, in July 1998, refused to provide services to the newly established weekly *El-Borhane*, a bilingual French and Arabic weekly described by one of its founders as representing the Islamist viewpoint. After waiting nearly two years for its license, *El-Borhane* received permission to publish in 1998. But the paper's assigned printer, El Moudjahid, refused to produce it. *El-Borhane* printed four issues in June and

July after some bureaucratic maneuvering in which it was able to make arrangements with another state printer. But before the publication of the fifth issue, the printer, Société d'Impression d'Alger (SIA), informed the paper's management that it could no longer service the paper and that it would have to return to El Moudjahid. Since then, El Moudjahid has refused to print the paper. *El-Borhane*'s editors believe that it has been kept off the market because of its Islamist perspective and support for dialogue and reconciliation between the combatants in Algeria's civil war.

Efforts by publishers to set up private printing facilities have been met with official opposition. In 1992, the dailies *El-Watan* and *Le Soir d'Algérie* failed in their bid to establish a printing facility when authorities refused to register a plot of land on which the facility would be built. They also were denied a bank loan for the project in what they described as direct pressure from the government of then-Prime Minister Belaid Abdel Salam. Again, in 1996, the Algerian government rejected a funding proposal by UNESCO for a private printing press on the grounds that the move infringed on the country's sovereignty.

Meeting with CPJ representatives on October 27, Communications and Culture Minister Hamraoui reaffirmed his government's stated commitment, made in March to the World Association of Newspapers (WAN) in Algiers, to allow the establishment of private printing presses. Despite these verbal assurances, owners and publishers remain wary of embarking on such a venture, citing financial risk and the lack of specific guarantees from the state.

The state also uses its control over the distribution of public-sector advertising—a main source of revenue for the press in Algeria's largely state-owned economy—to exert economic pressure on outspoken newspapers. The monopoly—reinstated by the government in September 1992—is exercised through L'Agence Nationale d'Edition et de Publicité (ANEP), a state body responsible for overseeing the purchase of newspaper advertising. ANEP has pursued a systematic policy of discrimination against several private papers. Newspapers that are both beneficiaries and victims of ANEP agree that its current practices are unfair and arbitrary. In 1998, the government had submitted a bill to parliament that would allow for the privatization of advertising distribution. At year's end, however, no action had been taken.

Like its control of advertising and its monopoly on printing, the state's hold on the supply and price of paper has proved economically detrimental to publications. Printing houses have forced both private and state-owned newspapers to pay high prices for newsprint and hold publications hostage to paper shortages. *El-Watan* has asked the printing house for permission to import its own paper, but the request was turned down.

Legal Restrictions

Algerian authorities use a variety of legal weapons against journalists. The Information Code of April 1990, which journalists dubbed the "second penal code," prescribes harsh penalties for vaguely defined offenses. Under Article 86, for example, journalists face five to 10 years in prison for the deliberate publication of "false or misleading information capable of harming national order or state security." Over the years, authorities have invoked these and other provisions of the penal code and other statutes to punish independent journalists in the courts.

Omar Belhouchet estimates that between 1993 and 1997 authorities initiated 30 prosecutions against him for publishing security-related information or articles implicating government officials in alleged corruption. Several of the pending cases force him to appear in court two or three times a week. Another editor, *Le Matin*'s Muhammad Benchicou, estimates that more than two dozen prosecutions have been brought against him for the paper's published work.

Although new prosecutions against journalists for their coverage of security matters have nearly come to a halt, old cases continue to work their way through the courts. And despite Hamraoui's promises in March 1998 to the World Association of Newspapers that journalists would no longer be arrested or prosecuted for their work, there have been at least two criminal prosecutions since then.

On September 30, Muhammad Benchicou was convicted of criminal defamation in a suit initiated by *L'Authentique*—a paper with financial links to former presidential adviser Muhammad Betchine. The suit stemmed from a column he wrote in August titled "Call Back Your Dogs, Mr. Betchine," in which Benchicou had referred to journalists at *L'Authentique* as "harem girls." The remark culminated several weeks of harsh exchanges between the two papers over the case of Ali Ben Saad, an Algerian student leader who was sentenced to death in absentia for alleged terrorism. The student's only real offense appeared to have been articles critical of Betchine which he had previously published in Algerian newspapers. On October 3, Benchicou was given a four-month suspended prison sentence and assessed 18,000,000 dinars (US$300,000) in damages in a trial that moved through the courts with remarkable speed. The fine was reportedly the highest ever levied against an Algerian journalist. Although Benchicou has appealed the decision, forced payment of the fine could potentially put the paper *Le Matin* out of business.

In September, authorities launched a defamation investigation of the daily *Le Jeune Indépendent* for allegedly "humiliating organized institutions." In an August interview with Fatma Merzouk, head of a women's organization affiliated with the Socialist Forces Front (FFS), Merzouk had criticized the Algerian army for failing to come to the aid of civilians during a recent massacre near the town of Relizane, and also charged it with "economic crimes," or corruption. Shafiq Abdi, the paper's director, and Said Tissegouine, its reporter in the city of Tizi Ouzou who conducted the interview, face imprisonment if tried and convicted of the charge. Abdi complained that he was only informed of the case after he appeared in court on September 22 in connection with another case against his paper.

At this writing, Algeria's parliament has a new draft information code and is expected to review it in the coming months. The draft bill contains several reforms, such as the abolition of imprisonment as a penalty for journalists who commit publications offenses (criminal statutes, however, still exist under the penal code), and provisions for the privatization of the broadcast media. But several provisions empower authorities to stifle independent journalism. For example, journalists convicted of defamation or libel face fines up to 500,000 dinars (US$8,200) for each offense, while those who publish information that breaches "national security," "national unity," or "the constitutional rights and freedoms of the citizen" are subject to the same fines. "We oppose the substitution of penalizing press violations with monetary fines," says Khaled Bourayou, a lawyer who represents several journalists. "This is very dangerous and can have damaging effects on newspapers. For example, Omar Belhouchet, who is charged in a number of cases, would be forced to pay thousands of dollars."

Covering the Conflict
Despite some notable examples of greater boldness in recent reporting on certain human rights and corruption stories, critics point to the conspicuous absence of reporting about issues of central importance to the civil conflict, specifically, the activities of the Islamist opposition; attempts at dialogue between the government and Islamists; corruption in the military; criticism of the 1992 coup; and state human rights violations.

Fear, self-censorship, ideological prejudices, and the lack of sources contribute to the absence of coverage on sensitive topics related to the political strife. "The reading committees took responsibility for not reporting news; now the journalists are responsible," a journalist working for an Arabic language daily told CPJ in October. "Now censorship is greater. Journalists are afraid of everything."

Stories questioning the status of imprisoned FIS leaders, such as Ali Bel Hadj, who has been in secret detention for three years, are taboo. Efforts at dialogue between the state and the FIS, meanwhile, have also been the subject of sporadic self-censorship in recent years—a result, say some, of shifting support in military circles for the idea. According to some journalists, newsroom censorship on the issue at certain papers increased markedly after 1996.

Journalists complain of the dearth of information about the Islamist opposition, which stems in part from the fact that most Islamist leaders are imprisoned or under house arrest. "It's nearly impossible to get good information with regard to the FIS," observed a journalist with the daily *Quotidien d'Oran*. In fact, while some information is available, "journalists don't want information from that side," he adds. The limited contacts of journalists among the Islamists also play a role in the lack of coverage.

Self-censorship, whether out of fear or political motivation, is pervasive and makes for an often one-sided depiction of events. A former journalist at the daily *La Tribune* told CPJ how the paper increasingly resorted to internal censorship after it resumed publication in February 1997 following a six-month suspension for publication of a political cartoon depicting the Algerian flag. In early 1997, the paper's director censored an article by the journalist on the trial of men accused of assassinating a government official. "In my article I said that not all of those being tried were terrorists—only two or three were actually responsible," she said, noting that many of the defendants were teenagers arrested in a police dragnet. "But the director of the paper refused to publish this viewpoint." Another journalist who left the paper in August 1998 noted that "journalists are often reminded not to write pieces which could provoke the authorities' anger and the suspension of the newspaper."

Editors avoid or censor coverage of human rights abuses such as torture, abductions, problems with the justice system, and abuses by state-supported self-defense militias. While newspapers often report on the findings of international human rights organizations, independent investigative reporting on these subjects rarely makes it into print. "I think the biggest difficulty is not getting information but it's publishing it," said a journalist formerly with *La Tribune* and *Le Matin*.

Some editors blame their papers' lack of coverage of human rights abuses on the dearth of sources. According to the editor of a leading daily paper, authorities continue to refuse journalists access to prisons, and information on one of the country's biggest tragedies—the "disappeared"—is scant. Lawyers for the "disappeared" disagree; according to one, since 1991 newspapers have refused to publish information he provided them on human rights cases, particularly those of the "disappeared." He noted that coverage of the issue during the visit in July by a high-profile United Nations panel, which was sent to gather information on political violence, characterized him as a lawyer for "terrorists."

Many editors in the mainstream press echo the regime's dismissive stance on state human rights abuses. "Most [international and human rights organizations] support terrorists," said the editor in chief of a leading daily newspaper. "Why do these organizations talk more about human rights than the papers? It's because their information comes from terrorists."

In April, May, and June, Algerian newspapers wrote about the mayor of the Western town of Relizane and another local official from the nearby town of Jdiouia who were implicated along with militiamen in summary executions of civilians and other abuses against citizens. The coverage marked the first time that the media reported on the involvement of the controversial state-supported militias in atrocities.

But many journalists and observers are skeptical that the press's treatment of the incident represents a barometer for press freedom. "I have a file on the victims of Relizane here in the office—about 20 [individual] files on the victims of violence, yet the press has not [previously] reported on it," says a lawyer who has documented the cases of many of the Relizane victims. Similarly, in the summer and fall of 1998, there was considerable coverage of the plight of families of the "disappeared" after they organized public demonstrations that attracted thousands of Algerians. Several journalists believe that editors got an official green light on the stories because the Algerian government felt immense pressure from the United Nations and international NGOs on its human rights record. "This is a development of the last six months," said a reporter with a French-language daily. "First the families of the disappeared held demonstrations … and the issue became prominent and impossible to ignore."

Information and the Ability to Report

The state's clampdown on reporting developed gradually after 1992 and was a prelude to more overt censorship measures. According to journalists, censorship increased in 1995 and 1996 in the run-up to the presidential elections, when the state's aim was to reinforce its claim that terrorism in Algeria had abated.

But in late 1996 and 1997, when large-scale massacres of civilians were being committed in the Algerian countryside, it became increasingly difficult for the state to censor the news coverage. The press began covering the violence with greater regularity, while avoiding the sensitive issue of army or security forces' casualties. "The publishers didn't comply with the instructions given by the Minister of Interior," says Belhouchet, referring to the June 1994 inter-ministerial decree that banned all independent reporting on political violence. "If we implement these instructions we cease to be newspapers. This cannot be done. As a result some newspapers were suspended."

Today, estimates Belhouchet, his newspaper relies on the official Algerian Press Service (APS) for about 5 percent of its published news on the security situation. According to another editor, reporting on security matters in 1998 has become routine. "Journalists now go to sites of bombings, for example, and bring back the information and publish. Before they would be closed for publishing it," observed a correspondent for *El-Watan*.

But fear continues to deter investigative reporting in the field. "We still sign our articles with pseudonyms and do not publish our own photographs in the newspapers," one reporter told CPJ in late 1997. "There are no guarantees that the assassinations will not resume in the future."

Although authorities have abolished formal censorship and the suspension of papers has slowed, the experience of state reprisal has had a lasting effect on journalists. Several reporters described examples of security-related information they had obtained but were fearful of submitting to their editors. One reporter who covers security affairs for a daily newspaper told of information he had obtained in October 1998 about the security forces' apparent extra-judicial execution of suspected Islamists in Tipaza, 45 miles west of Algiers. The official news agency APS had reported that security forces killed a group of armed Islamists after they had feigned surrender and opened fire on the security forces. Eyewitnesses, however, told the journalist a different story—that security forces opened fire on the building, killing the men inside without resistance. "I censored myself," he said, explaining his decision not to submit the story to his editor. "Anyone who attempts to publish this sort of information could be in danger. You could be kidnapped or 'disappeared.' There are many examples like this where a journalist gets information but knows that he can't publish it."

Journalists tend to rely heavily on security forces as sources for information in the field, although authorities are often reluctant to divulge information. "Journalists covering security issues are always the last to arrive on the scene. They often share the same official pieces of information," said one reporter for a daily. "Relations with the security forces are based on a give-and-take formula. You need to socialize with security guys and buy them drinks if you want to get bits of information from them." Other journalists simply feel more comfortable dealing directly with authorities. A leading security reporter for a French-language daily admitted, "While doing my job, it is easier for me to get on with and communicate with the security forces than ordinary citizens."

But journalists complain that authorities keep them in the dark. Security forces or the army regularly provide false information on the number of victims at massacres and other scenes of violence. Journalists are often forced to seek alternative sources to confirm death tolls. "I am a former student at a medical school and I know people working at hospitals," said a security reporter. "For instance, a friend of mine working at an emergency service told me that 26 people died at Bab al-Oued following a bomb explosion. The official news agency reported that only 17 people died and that was not true."

Some information, such as the result of counter-insurgency operations and the identities of rebel casualties, is impossible to obtain without the help of authorities. Given the danger and inaccessibility of most operations which take place outside the capital, journalists are forced to rely almost exclusively on the army for details of fatalities. And it is virtually impossible to independently confirm the identities of the thousands who have been killed by security forces.

Massacres
From August 1997 throughout 1998, a series of large-scale massacres were committed in several villages and hamlets outside of Algiers. Hundreds of men, women, and children were decapitated or had their throats slit. Others were hacked to death with axes. Authorities blamed armed Islamist groups. While such groups almost certainly committed much of the carnage, observers speculate that the state may have been involved in some of the atrocities. Official silence on the details of the violence and the state's refusal to allow an international investigation into the matter has further raised suspicions.

Despite formidable obstacles, Algerian journalists have actively covered massacres, traveling to the countryside at great risk to interview survivors and make first-hand assessments. While suggesting official involvement in the atrocities is taboo, newspapers have criticized the authorities for their failure to protect civilians and intervene in some attacks.

Reporters have described harassment by security forces in their attempts to view massacre sites. In other cases, reporters have recounted how security forces monitored their activities and spoke of incidents in which authorities produced impostors as witnesses for them to interview.

Some Algerian journalists who cover security issues said that following mounting international pressure on the Algerian government, authorities eased restrictions on journalists' access to massacre sites. But harassment by police and security forces persists. "When you go to the scene of a massacre, access is very difficult, and when the authorities realize you are a journalist they make you feel unwelcome," said one reporter. Another reporter said that after massacres, security forces generally "don't want you to have first-hand statements from witnesses."

Ultimately, however, the answers to questions concerning possible state complicity or involvement of government-backed militias in massacres remain in the hands of the state. "Official information on the atrocities remains scarce," writes Lahouari Addi. "The perpetrators are never taken alive before the courts. Since there is no freedom of the press, the media confirm the version put forward by the authorities. The army has no intention of letting an international inquest try to uncover the truth."

Despite the doggedness of some reporters, detailed information from massacre cites remains scarce. Reporting often focuses on the trauma experienced by survivors and lacks depth and probing detail as to who may be responsible. Fear among survivors is often cited as a reason for sketchy reporting. "You have a situation where 90 percent of it is fear. They have no faith in the media. They are scared. The people are hostages to this violence and as a journalist you think you are a target," said one Algerian political observer who has closely monitored the violence.

Some journalists assert that the only way to conclusively determine who is behind the massacres is through serious investigative journalism—which, under present conditions, is virtually impossible. Said one editor: "If you want to find out what's happening in Bentalha, you must send a journalist for a month and that's not technically possible. It's an area that's controlled by the militias and the army. You cannot access information. We have testimony that people who were brought [before journalists] weren't living there before ... A journalist would have to go in anonymously. It's nearly impossible."

According to another editor, "It is technically impossible to do our jobs. So we try to compare information maybe two to three weeks after the incident, but we really can't do investigations in the field." The same journalist cites a report that appeared in the French press in early 1998 alleging that authorities had executed Islamist prisoners in a village. "If I try to investigate this, it will take four to six months and I will need to get special permission from the authorities and find [witnesses]. You can't investigate this matter."

Limitations on the foreign media deepen the murkiness of coverage from Algeria. To date, only one Western news agency— Agence France-Presse (AFP)—maintains an Algeria bureau. As a result, foreign media rely heavily on local accounts. According to a BBC correspondent, "this has made it increasingly difficult to know what is going on inside Algeria. News organizations are forced to take unconfirmed reports from Algerian newspapers at face value, even if they do it with a touch of skepticism." Even AFP's staff in Algeria attributes much of its news to local papers.

Foreign journalists who visit Algeria encounter government prohibitions on travel around the country without escorts, which severely inhibits investigative reporting. Although authorities have at times described these escorts as optional, they ignore journalists' requests to go it alone. In 1997, security agents detained *Newsweek* reporter Mark Dennis overnight after he ditched his escort to interview Islamic Salvation Army commander Ahmed Benaicha in the field. Dennis was subsequently expelled from the country for evading his escort.

When foreign reporters travel to massacre sites, they do so under military convoy and in the presence of security forces. One American journalist described the procedure as "preposterous in terms of reporting." In further restricting access for the foreign media, Algerian authorities have denied visas to reporters in apparent response to what they have deemed their unfavorable coverage of events. Several European correspondents, such as *Libération*'s José Garçon, have failed to secure visas despite repeated requests over the years. Since 1993, authorities have ignored numerous visa requests by Garçon, who has covered Algeria for more than 10 years for her paper. The journalist says that she simply stopped requesting permission for the last two years; however, in 1997, she was formally denied a visa without explanation when requesting to travel to Algiers with a French politician. Requests for visas from other journalists, who have no reason to suspect official anger, have gone unanswered. During his meeting with CPJ representatives, Communications and Culture Minister Hamraoui stated that "only four or five [foreign] journalists" who he declined to name were banned from traveling to Algeria because "they don't come to Algeria for professional reasons."

The press holds a crucial position for an understanding of the Algerian conflict, in which information has proven to be a precious commodity. Beyond overt government constraints, the press is hostage to fear, which leads to such pernicious restrictions as self-censorship. The prevailing state of fear among journalists will dissipate only when respect for human rights and the rule of law take hold in Algerian society. The development of democratic institutions is the critical component to greater freedom for the press, since it is the state itself that holds the key to unraveling the many mysteries of Algeria's agony.

CPJ previously reported that our research had confirmed 59 journalists killed for their work in Algeria since May 1993. The change to 58 is the result of new information received during our fact-finding mission about the disappearance of Mohamed Hassaine, a reporter with the daily Alger Républicain. *Hassaine was kidnapped by unknown assailants on March 1, 1994. Our original determination that Hassaine had been murdered was based on his newspaper colleagues' reports of the discovery of Hassaine's decapitated body. During interviews in Algiers in October, however, we learned that Hassaine's body was in fact never found, and that since his disappearance there has been no circumstantial or material evidence confirming his death. We therefore have reclassified Mohamed Hassaine as missing.*

Also, it should be noted that CPJ's figure of 58 killed does not include the several other non-journalists working in the media sector who have been killed since 1993.

Look for this report and other news of the press in Algeria on CPJ's website at <http://www.cpj.org>.

CPJ AT A GLANCE

Facts About the Organization and Its Activities

The Committee to Protect Journalists is a nonpartisan, nonprofit organization founded in 1981 to monitor abuses against the press and promote press freedom around the world.

How did CPJ get started?
A group of U.S. foreign correspondents created CPJ in response to the often brutal treatment of their foreign colleagues by authoritarian governments and other enemies of independent journalism.

Who runs CPJ?
CPJ has a full-time staff of 14 and five part-time research staffers at its New York headquarters, including an area specialist for each major world region. The committee also has a part-time representative in Washington, D.C. CPJ's activities are directed by a 32-member board of prominent U.S. journalists.

How is CPJ funded?
CPJ is funded by contributions from individuals, corporations, and foundations. CPJ does not accept government funding.

The press is powerful; why does it need protection?
The press in the United States does have great power and enjoys legal protection. But that is not the case in most countries. Scores of journalists are imprisoned every year because of what they have reported. Hundreds more are routinely subjected to physical attack, illegal detention, spurious legal action, and threats against themselves or their families. In 1998, CPJ documented 24 journalists killed in the line of duty. Even in the United States, journalists have been murdered—in New York; California; Florida; Virginia; Washington, D.C.; Colorado; and Arizona.

How does CPJ protect journalists?
By publicly revealing abuses against the press and by acting on behalf of imprisoned and threatened journalists, CPJ effectively warns journalists and news organizations where attacks on press freedom are likely to occur. CPJ organizes vigorous protest at all levels—ranging from local governments to the United Nations—and, when necessary, works behind the scenes through other diplomatic channels to effect change. CPJ also publishes articles and news releases, special reports, a quarterly newsletter and the most comprehensive annual report on attacks against the press around the world.

Where does CPJ get its information?
Through its own reporting. CPJ has full-time program coordinators monitoring the press in the Americas, Asia, the Middle East, Africa, and Europe. They track developments through their own independent research, fact-finding missions and firsthand contacts in the field, including reports from other journalists. CPJ shares information on breaking cases with other press freedom organizations worldwide through the International Freedom of Expression Exchange (IFEX), a global e-mail network.

When would a journalist call upon CPJ?

- In an emergency. Using local contacts, CPJ can intervene whenever foreign correspondents are in trouble. CPJ is also prepared to immediately notify news organizations, government officials, and human rights organizations of press freedom violations.
- When traveling on assignment. CPJ maintains a database of local journalist contacts around the world. CPJ also publishes practical "safety guides" that offer advice to journalists covering dangerous assignments.
- When covering the news. Attacks against the press are news, and they often serve as the first signal of a crackdown on all freedoms. CPJ is uniquely situated to provide journalists with information and insight into press conditions around the world.
- When becoming a member. A basic membership costs only US$45, and each donation helps assure that CPJ will be there to defend you or a colleague if the need arises. Members receive CPJ's quarterly newsletter, *Dangerous Assignments*, and a discount on other publications.

CPJ Publications

To order the publications listed below, please call (212) 465-9344, ext. 113. Members receive a 50-percent discount on the cost of publications. We accept Visa, MasterCard, American Express, checks, or money orders. Please make checks and money orders payable to CPJ in U.S. currency drawn on a U.S. bank or U.S. resident branch. Several of the publications can only be found online at CPJ's website <http://www.cpj.org>.

Attacks on the Press $30
A comprehensive annual survey of attacks against journalists and news organizations around the world.

Dangerous Assignments Quarterly $45/year
CPJ's newsletter reports on international press conditions and attacks on the press. Free to members.

Paradoxes in the Caucasus: A Report on Freedom of the Media in Azerbaijan and Armenia $10
Veteran journalist Nicholas Daniloff explores the maze of contradictions faced by independent journalists in Armenia and Azerbaijan—two Caucasian republics which must shed the legacy of Soviet-era attitudes and institutions to reach their goal of democratization. January 1998

The Anatolian Archipelago: CPJ's Campaign to Free Turkey's Imprisoned Journalists $10
After an intensive media campaign to raise international awareness of Turkey's woeful press freedom record, CPJ sent a mission to Turkey to meet with the new prime minister and push for reforms. This report chronicles CPJ's campaign, the meetings in Turkey, and the aftermath of the mission: Six freed editors and promises of far-reaching reforms. Includes CPJ's documentation of Turkey's record number of imprisoned journalists. October 1997

Freedom Under the Dragon: Can Hong Kong's Press Still Breathe Fire? (see CPJ's website)
Asia program coordinator A. Lin Neumann and a variety of Hong Kong watchers explore press freedom in Hong Kong 100 days after the handover. September 1997

Clampdown in Addis: Ethiopia's Journalists at Risk $10
Based on a fact-finding mission to Ethiopia, this comprehensive report by Africa program coordinator Kakuna Kerina documents how the Ethiopian government uses provisions of a restrictive press law to limit the news the independent press may report and to silence opposing viewpoints. Introduction by Josh Friedman. October 1996

Briefing on Press Freedom in Bosnia and Herzegovina Before the September 14 Elections $10
A comprehensive review of press freedom violations in Bosnia and Herzegovina in the run-up to the September 14, 1996, national elections. The report also cites all clauses in the 1995 Dayton peace accords that specifically seek to protect the freedom of the press. September 1996

Briefing on Press Freedom in Russia Before the Presidential Elections $10
This report details the numerous murders, attacks, and other difficulties Russian journalists have endured under President Boris Yeltsin's rule; highlights potential threats to a free press; and offers background on the economic hardships of the Russian media that foster a continued dependence on the government. June 1996

On a Razor's Edge: Local Journalists Targeted by Warring Parties in Kashmir $10
Based on a fact-finding mission to Kashmir, this report documents how local journalists are attacked by Indian armed forces and militant separatists for their reporting on the battle for control of the Indian-held state. July 1995

Double Jeopardy: Homophobic Attacks on the Press, 1990-1995 $10
A sampling of 21 cases from 14 countries, this report demonstrates that in nations as politically and culturally disparate as Canada, Russia, and Zimbabwe, censorship is imposed selectively against gay journalists and news outlets covering gay issues. October 1995

Journalists' Survival Guide: The Former Yugoslavia $10
This essential booklet provides advice from journalists for journalists on everything from where to get flak jackets, insurance, and rental cars to tips on avoiding sniper fire in Sarajevo. It includes a list of phone numbers for U.N. and other relief agencies in the area, as well as organizations to call when making travel plans or in case of emergency. November 1994

Don't Force Us to Lie: The Struggle of Chinese Journalists in the Reform Era $20
A detailed study of the determined efforts of Chinese journalists to speak and write freely throughout the 1980s and early 1990s, this book is one of the most comprehensive accounts available of how journalism works in the world's most populous country. With a foreword by Dan Rather and contributions by China scholar Anne Thurston. January 1993

In the Censor's Shadow: Journalism in Suharto's Indonesia $10
A comprehensive account of media repression in Indonesia, this report includes eyewitness accounts by two American reporters of the army massacre in Dili, East Timor. November 1991

The Soviet Media's Year of Decision $10
Pulitzer Prize-winning journalist Hedrick Smith analyzes the press in Gorbachev's Soviet Union and events leading up to the attempted coup of August 1991. September 1991

Attacks on the Press in 1998

How to Report an Attack on the Press

CPJ needs accurate, detailed information in order to document abuses of press freedom and help journalists in trouble. CPJ corroborates the information and takes appropriate action on behalf of the journalists and news organizations involved.

What to report:

Journalists who are:
- Missing
- Killed
- Arrested or kidnapped
- Wounded
- Assaulted
- Threatened
- Harassed
- Wrongfully expelled
- Wrongfully sued for libel or defamation
- Denied credentials
- Censored

News organizations:
- Attacked, raided, or illegally searched
- Closed by force
- Wrongfully sued for libel or defamation
- Censored
- Materials confiscated or damaged
- Editions confiscated or transmissions jammed

Information Needed:
- Journalists and news organizations involved
- Date and circumstances of incident
- Background information

Anyone with information about an attack on the press should call CPJ.
Call collect if necessary: (212) 465-1004

Or send us a fax at (212) 465-9568

Contact information for regional programs:
Africa:
(212) 465-9344, x103
E-mail: africa@cpj.org
Americas:
(212) 465-9344, x108
E-mail: americas@cpj.org
Asia:
(212) 465-9344, x140
E-mail: asia@cpj.org
Central Europe and the republics of the former Soviet Union:
(212) 465-9344, x101
E-mail: europe@cpj.org
Middle East and North Africa:
(212) 465-9344, x120
E-mail: mideast@cpj.org

What happens next:
Depending on the case, CPJ will:
- Confirm the report
- Pressure authorities to respond
- Notify human rights groups and press organizations around the world, including IFEX, Article 19, Amnesty International, Reporters Sans Frontières, PEN, International Federation of Journalists, and Human Rights Watch
- Increase public awareness through the press
- Publish advisories to warn other journalists about potential dangers
- Send a fact-finding mission to investigate

Ways to Participate in CPJ

Become a Member (see membership form, p. 379)
CPJ welcomes the participation of **individual members** interested in supporting press freedom and staying informed about press conditions around the world. Gift memberships are also available. All memberships include a subscription to CPJ's quarterly newsletter, *Dangerous Assignments*. Contributions of $100 and higher also include a complimentary copy of *Attacks on the Press*. A membership form can also be found at CPJ's website at <www.cpj.org> and join on-line.

CPJ works on behalf of journalists everywhere. If you represent a **news organization**, your membership commitment will send a powerful message that journalists throughout the globe are looking out for the rights of their colleagues. Demonstrate your organization's commitment to the profession and to your colleagues' safety by joining CPJ. For corporations, the free flow of information is vitally important to business in the global marketplace. Private-sector institutions in the legal, financial services, and communications industries have become increasingly involved in supporting the freedom of the press to report on political and economic conditions. Show your company's support for CPJ's critical analyses and actions by becoming a **corporate member**.

Support our Membership and Fundraising Campaigns
Encourage your colleagues to become members of CPJ by distributing our membership materials at your office. Contact your public/corporate affairs office and find out if your company will match your contribution to CPJ. In-kind donations and services can also make a significant difference to CPJ. Consider donating a broad range of products and services, including research; technology; advertising; publicity; printing; graphic design; photography; video; computer equipment; and even office space.

Contribute to CPJ's Emergency Response Fund
In the fall of 1996, the John S. and James L. Knight Foundation awarded CPJ a three-year grant of $100,000 per annum—predicated on a one-to-one match from new or increased funding sources. CPJ is proud to have successfully completed the Challenge within a record one and a half years. The challenge grant was geared to the establishment and maintenance of the CPJ Emergency Response Fund, which allows the organization to respond swiftly and effectively to press freedom crises in Africa, Asia, Central Europe and the former Soviet Republics, Latin America, and the Middle East.

Your ongoing support of the Emergency Response Fund will significantly advance the cause of global press freedom.

Support the Ninth Annual International Press Freedom Awards Dinner, Fall 1999, New York City
The International Press Freedom Awards Dinner honors the efforts of journalists who risk their lives to report the news. The annual gala is a major industry gathering of journalists, publishers, and communications professionals, as well as leaders in the entertainment, finance and legal spheres. A highlight of New York's fall benefit season, the gala historically has raised more than half of CPJ's annual operating funds. Please show your support for freedom of the press by attending this event, and by contributing direct gifts to CPJ in honor of the press freedom awardees. Corporations can

demonstrate their commitment to CPJ's work by becoming corporate sponsors of the gala program and of the awardees' tour of major U.S. cities.

Purchase CPJ's Publications (Members receive a 50-percent discount)
For **journalists and media executives**, CPJ's safety manuals and press freedom reports are invaluable tools. Buy them for your newsroom and help us defray the costs of this important service. The general public also can follow emerging developments through CPJ's reports on press conditions around the world. They are essential reading for anyone interested in freedom of expression or human rights. International businesses can benefit as well from CPJ's publications, which shed light on political and economic developments.

Provide Information on Cases and Support CPJ's Efforts on Behalf of Endangered Journalists
CPJ should be contacted at once whenever a colleague or news organization is threatened, harassed, or attacked. **Journalists**, **media executives** and **concerned individuals** should provide CPJ with accurate and reliable information immediately. Letters, petitions, and communiqués from journalists in support of colleagues under attack or in prison do make a difference. Stay on top of late-breaking developments by visiting CPJ's website at <http://www.cpj.org>.

Becoming a Member of CPJ

I wish to join as an individual member:
- [ ] Participant $45
- [ ] Contributor $100
- [ ] Supporter $500
- [ ] Benefactor .... $1,000 and above
- [ ] Student $20
   (student identification required)

My company is subscribing to a corporate membership:
- [ ] Activist $1,000
- [ ] Champion $2,500
- [ ] Advocate $5,000
- [ ] Catalyst $10,000
- [ ] Corporate Supporter $15,000
- [ ] Corporate Leader $20,000

Contingent on the level of support, CPJ offers a range of services to our corporate members. Among these are an annual by-invitation-only forum with key CPJ board members; availability of select news reports; special consultation with CPJ staff about specific areas; as well as advertising opportunities in the CPJ newsletter, *Dangerous Assignments*.

Member Name Mr./Miss/Mrs./Ms. (as you wish to be listed for acknowledgement)

Corporation
(Please indicate preferred mailing address)   [ ] Home   [ ] Business

---

Title

Company

Street

City   State   Zip

Home Phone   Business Phone

Fax   E-Mail

PAYMENT INFORMATION

My corporation will match my gift to CPJ: [ ] Yes [ ] No (Enclosed is the relevant matching gift form.)

Enclosed please find my tax-deductible contribution of $_____, or charge my gift of $_____.

[ ] Visa   [ ] MasterCard   [ ] American Express   [ ] Check Enclosed

---

Card Number   Expiration Date

Name on Card   Signature

Please make checks or money orders payable to Committee to Protect Journalists (funds must be drawn on a U.S. bank or U.S. resident branch), or indicate charge information, and send to:

Director of Development • CPJ • 330 Seventh Avenue, 12th Floor, New York, NY 10001, USA
(212) 465-9344, ext. 113 • Fax: (212) 465-9568 • E-Mail: lharrop@cpj.org

Contributions in Support of the Challenge Grant from the John S. and James L. Knight Foundation

CPJ extends its deepest gratitude to the John S. and James L. Knight Foundation, which recently completed its $300,000 challenge grant with a final payment of $100,000. We are profoundly thankful to the individuals and institutions listed below whose response to the challenge has helped establish CPJ's Emergency Response Fund.

Leader
$50,000 and above
Tom Brokaw
The Times Mirror Foundation

Philanthropist
$25,000 and above
The New York Times Company Foundation
Gene Roberts

Guardian
$10,000 and above
James S. Copley Foundation
Kati Marton

Grantor
$5,000 and above
Franz and Marcia Allina
Mr. and Mrs. James E. Burke
James C. and Toni K. Goodale
Mr. and Mrs. Henry Grunwald
Drue Heinz
Ted and Grace Anne Koppel
Dan and Sylvia Lufkin
The McClatchy Company
National Broadcasting Company, Inc.

PaineWebber
Peter G. Peterson
Dan Rather
Mr. and Mrs. W.J. Ruane
Howard Stringer
Universal Studios, Inc.
Ted Waitt
John C. Whitehead

Provider
$1,000 and above
Peter Arnett
Cheryl Gould
Isobel and Ron Konecky
Judith and Harry Moses
Victor Navasky
Frank del Olmo
The Phillips-Green Foundation
Walter Haskell Pincus and Ann Terry Pincus
Erwin Potts
Joyce Purnick and Max Frankel
The Steven H. and Alida Brill Scheuer
  Foundation
The Ruth and Frank Stanton Fund
Star Tribune/Cowles Media Company
Thomas Winship

(To contribute to the Emergency Response Fund, please fill out and return the form on the next page.)

CPJ Emergency Response Fund

All donors contributing to CPJ's Emergency Response Fund at these levels will be given permanent recognition on a plaque at CPJ headquarters, and will also be listed in the annual report, *Attacks on the Press*, as well as in other CPJ literature.

[ ] Sponsor ....$100,000 and above
[ ] Leader ....$50,000 and above
[ ] Philanthropist ....$25,000 and above
[ ] Guarantor ....$20,000 and above
[ ] Guardian ....$10,000 and above
[ ] Grantor ....$5,000 and above
[ ] Provider ....$1,000 and above

Donor Name Mr./Miss/Mrs./Ms. or Institution/Organization
(as you wish to be listed for acknowledgement)

(Please indicate preferred mailing address)   [ ] Home   [ ] Business

Title

Company

Street

City   State   Zip

Home Phone   Business Phone

Fax   E-Mail

PAYMENT INFORMATION

My corporation will match my gift to CPJ: [ ] Yes [ ] No (Enclosed is the relevant matching gift form.)

Enclosed please find my tax-deductible contribution of $_____, or charge my gift of $_____.

[ ] Visa   [ ] MasterCard   [ ] American Express   [ ] Check Enclosed

Card Number   Expiration Date

Name On Card   Signature

Please make checks or money orders payable to Committee to Protect Journalists (funds must be drawn on a U.S. bank or U.S. resident branch), or indicate charge information, and send to:

Director of Development • CPJ • 330 Seventh Avenue, 12th Floor, New York, NY 10001, USA
(212) 465-9344, ext. 113 • Fax: (212) 465-9568 • E-Mail: lharrop@cpj.org

Contributors

The Committee to Protect Journalists is extremely grateful to the following foundations, corporations, and individuals for their invaluable support of our annual fund during 1998:

Executive Leadership—$100,000 and above
The Ford Foundation
The Freedom Forum
John S. and James L. Knight Foundation
Robert R. McCormick Tribune Foundation
Open Society Institute

Leadership—$50,000 to $99,999
A. H. Belo Corporation Foundation
The Tinker Foundation

Underwriters—$25,000 to $49,999
Bloomberg News
C-SPAN
Phil Donahue and Marlo Thomas
Katharine Graham
The Hearst Corporation
John D. and Catherine T. MacArthur Foundation
Merrill Lynch & Co., Inc.
Joyce Mertz-Gilmore Foundation
The New York Times Company
Samuel I. Newhouse Foundation Inc.
Dan Rather
St. Petersburg Times
The Star-Ledger
Time Inc.
Times Mirror Newspapers
U.S. News & World Report/Daily News/ The Atlantic Monthly/Fast Company

Sponsors—$15,000 to $24,999
ABC News
Agence France-Presse
CBS News/CBS Corporation
Fox News
James C. and Toni K. Goodale
Harper's Magazine
NBC
Gene Roberts
The Scherman Foundation
The Washington Post Company
World Press Freedom Committee
Mortimer B. Zuckerman

Patrons—$10,000 to $14,999
Adelphia
Franz and Marcia Allina
Business Executives for National Security (BENS)
The Coca-Cola Company
Dow Jones & Company
Institute for International Education
Kati Marton
The McGraw-Hill Companies
The New Yorker
Reuters America Inc.
Courtney Sale Ross
Sony Corporation of America
Katrina vanden Heuvel
Viacom Inc.

Donors—$5,000 to $9,999
Abernathy MacGregor Frank
American Lawyer Media
Anonymous
Automatic Data Processing, Inc.
Baker & Hostetler LLP
Bell Atlantic
The Blackstone Group
Brill's Content
James E. Burke
BusinessWeek
CBS Foundation
CNN
Joan and Joseph F. Cullman 3rd
Debevoise & Plimpton
Dow Jones Foundation
Geraldine Fabrikant
Ford Motor Company
Nicholas C. Forstmann
The Freedom Forum First Amendment Center

Hachette Filipacchi Magazines
Johnson & Johnson
John R. MacArthur
Lockheed Martin
The Markle Foundation
The McClatchy Company
Miramax
The New York Times
Newsday
Newsweek
PaineWebber Group Inc.
Prudential Securities Incorporated/Prudential Insurance Company of North America
Reader's Digest magazine
The Reebok Human Rights Foundation
Richard and Edna Salomon Foundation
Salomon Smith Barney
Starr & Company, LLC
The Sun
A. Robert and Jacqueline Towbin
Weil, Gotshal & Manges LLP
Thomas Winship

Benefactors—$1,000 to $4,999
American Institute of Certified Public Accountants
Deborah Amos and Rick Davis
Ken Auletta and Amanda Urban
Marie Brenner and Ernie Pomerantz
Liane Beebe Brent and Christopher Brent
David Brock
Phil Bronstein
José Carreño
The Chase Manhattan Corporation
Communications Workers of America
Condé Nast Publications, Inc.
Joan Ganz Cooney and Peter G. Peterson
Helen K. Copley
Walter Cronkite
Stanley Eisenberg Charitable Gift Fund
Mr. and Mrs. Milton Esterow
Fascitelli Foundation
Fortune
The Gottesman Fund
Drue Heinz
Don and Marilyn Berger Hewitt Fund

James F. Hoge
Peter Jennings Foundation Inc.
Mr. and Mrs. George M. Keller
Khizer Foundation International
Calvin Klein
LIFE magazine
Jerome & Kenneth Lipper Foundation
Harry Macklowe
Douglas S. Makepeace
David and Kerry Smith Marash
Gilbert G. Menna
The Miami Herald
Andrea Mitchell
Judith and Harry Moses
Anne and Victor Navasky
Steven Newhouse and Gina Sanders
Bill Orme and Debbie Sontag
PR 21, A Daniel J. Edelman Company
Hannah Pakula
Pearson plc
The Playboy Foundation
Steven Rattner & P. Maureen White Foundation
Liz Robbins and Doug Johnson
David Rockefeller
Rogers & Wells
Andrew A. Rooney
Robert M. Rosencrans
Daryl and Steven Roth Foundation
The Rudin Foundation, Inc.
Charles R. Schwab
John Seigenthaler
Neal Shapiro
Ron Silver
Skidmore, Owings & Merrill
Chung Mu Son and Suzy Lee
Dorothy Teitelbaum
Mr. and Mrs. Seymour Topping
Garry and Jane Trudeau
Universal Press Syndicate
USA TODAY
The Washington Spectator
Allen Weinstein
Lilyan Wilder and Sophie Stenbeck
Young & Rubicam Foundation

List complete as of February 8, 1999.

Attacks on the Press in 1998

We also extend our deepest gratitude to the many individuals and organizations who support the Committee to Protect Journalists with gifts below $1,000 and cannot be recognized in this list because of space limitations.

We thank the following for their in-kind services and contributions during the past year—vital resources that help make possible the work of CPJ.

ABC News	Dow Jones Interactive
Agence France-Presse	IDT
Associated Press	Dan Rather
CBS News	Reuters America Inc.
Columbia Journalism Review	

The Committee to Protect Journalists is proud to work in partnership with LEXIS•NEXIS, whose continued in-kind donation of information technology services is critical to the implementation of our mission.

Staff

EXECUTIVE DIRECTOR
Ann K. Cooper
(212) 465-9344, ext. 102
acooper@cpj.org

EDITORIAL DIRECTOR
Alice Chasan
(212) 465-9344, ext. 110
achasan@cpj.org

DIRECTOR OF DEVELOPMENT
Lucy Mayer Harrop
(212) 465-9344, ext. 113
lharrop@cpj.org

DIRECTOR OF MEDIA RELATIONS
Judith Leynse
(212) 465-9344, ext. 105
jleynse@cpj.org

DIRECTOR OF FINANCE AND ADMINISTRATION
Lanny Mitchell
(212) 465-9344, ext. 116
lmitchell@cpj.org

WASHINGTON, D. C. REPRESENTATIVE
Murray Seeger
(301) 949-9051
mseeger@cpj.org

REGIONAL PROGRAMS
Africa
Kakuna Kerina
Program Coordinator
(212) 465-9344, ext. 103
africa@cpj.org

Matt Leone
Research Assistant
(212) 465-9344, ext. 118
mleone@cpj.org

The Americas
Joel Simon
Program Coordinator
(212) 465-9344, ext. 108
americas@cpj.org

Marylene Smeets
Research Assistant
(212) 465-9344, ext. 107
msmeets@cpj.org

Asia
A. Lin Neumann
Program Coordinator
(212) 465-9344, ext. 140
asia@cpj.org

Kavita Menon
Research Assistant
(212) 465-9344, ext. 115
kmenon@cpj.org

Central Europe and the Republics of the Former Soviet Union
Chrystyna Lapychak
Program Coordinator
(212) 465-9344, ext. 101
europe@cpj.org

Paul R. LeGendre
Research Assistant
(212) 465-9344, ext. 115
plegendre@cpj.org

Middle East and North Africa
Joel Campagna
Program Coordinator
(212) 465-9344, ext. 120
mideast@cpj.org

Karam Tannous
Research Assistant
(212) 465-9344, ext. 104
ktannous@cpj.org

DEVELOPMENT DEPARTMENT
Amy Bodow
Development Associate
(212) 465-9344, ext. 109
abodow@cpj.org

Karen Chesnut
Development Assistant
(212) 465-9344, ext. 142
kchesnut@cpj.org

Trenton B. Daniel
Development and Special Projects Assistant
(212) 465-9344, ext. 117
tdaniel@cpj.org

EDITORIAL DEPARTMENT
Jesse T. Stone
Associate Editor
(212) 465-9344, ext. 112
jstone@cpj.org

Joseph Topornycky
Website Assistant

Jennifer Dunham
Intern

ADMINISTRATION
Shermaine Craigwell
Office Manager
(212) 465-1004
scraigwell@cpj.org

Save on *Attacks on the Press in 1998*

Libraries • Schools • Teachers
Save 50% on orders of five copies or more
US$15.00 per copy (cover price: US$30.00)

Please send me _____ copies of *ATTACKS ON THE PRESS IN 1998* at _____ US$15.00 each (discount)

Name: _____

Title: _____

Institution/Affiliation: _____

Street Address: _____

_____

City: _____ State: _____ Zip Code: _____

Telephone number:
(home) _____

(office) _____

E-mail: _____

Payment Information
Enclosed is a (check) (money order) in the amount of US$_____

or

Charge my credit card:
[ ] Visa   [ ] MasterCard   [ ] American Express

Card number: _____

Expiration date: _____

Please make checks or money orders payable to:
Committee to Protect Journalists (funds must be drawn on a U.S. bank or U.S. resident branch).

Mail this order to:
Committee to Protect Journalists
330 7th Avenue, 12th Floor, New York, NY 10001 USA

Index of Countries

Country	Page	Country	Page
Afghanistan	212	Liberia	107
Albania	277	Macau	239
Algeria	314	Madagascar	108
Angola	77	Malawi	109
Antigua and Barbuda	162	Malaysia	240
Argentina	162	Mauritania	334
Armenia	278	Mexico	183
Azerbaijan	279	Morocco	335
Bangladesh	213	Namibia	110
Belarus	283	Nepal	243
Bolivia	165	Nicaragua	187
Bosnia and Herzegovina	284	Niger	112
Brazil	166	Nigeria	114
Bulgaria	285	North Korea	245
Burkina Faso	78	Pakistan	245
Burma	220	Palestinian National Authority	336
Burundi	79	Panama	188
Cambodia	221	Papua New Guinea	250
Cameroon	80	Paraguay	189
Cape Verde	82	Peru	190
Chad	82	Philippines	251
Chile	167	Poland	293
China, People's Republic of	223	Romania	294
Colombia	168	Russia	295
Congo	83	Rwanda	120
Costa Rica	171	Samoa	252
Croatia	287	Saudi Arabia and Members of the Gulf Cooperation Council	340
Cuba	172		
Czech Republic	289	Sierra Leone	121
Democratic Republic of Congo (Zaire)	84	Singapore	253
Djibouti	92	Slovakia	297
Dominican Republic	178	Somalia	126
Ecuador	178	South Africa	127
Egypt	316	South Korea	253
El Salvador	180	Sri Lanka	255
Equatorial Guinea	93	Sudan	129
Eritrea	93	Suriname	195
Ethiopia	94	Syria	342
Fiji	228	Taiwan	259
Gabon	98	Tajikistan	299
The Gambia	100	Tanzania	129
Georgia	289	Thailand	260
Ghana	101	Togo	131
Guatemala	180	Tonga	161
Guinea	103	Trinidad and Tobago	196
Haiti	181	Tunisia	343
Honduras	182	Turkey	344
Hong Kong	229	Turkmenistan	300
India	230	Uganda	132
Indonesia	233	Ukraine	301
Iran	320	United States	196
Iraq	324	Uruguay	197
Israel and the Occupied Territories	324	Uzbekistan	303
Jamaica	183	Venezuela	197
Jordan	328	Vietnam	261
Kazakhstan	291	Yemen	348
Kenya	104	Yugoslavia	304
Kyrgyzstan	293	Zambia	133
Lebanon	333	Zimbabwe	136
Lesotho	106		